DEDICATE TEACHER AWARDS

Teachers play an important part in shaping futures. Our Dedicated Teacher Awards recognise the hard work that teachers put in every day.

Thank you to everyone who nominated this year; we have been inspired and moved by all of your stories. Well done to all of our nominees for your dedication to learning and for inspiring the next generation of thinkers, leaders and innovators.

Congratulations to our incredible winners!

WINNER					
Regional Winner Middle East & North Africa	**Regional Winner** Europe	**Regional Winner** North & South America	**Regional Winner** Central & Southern Africa	**Regional Winner** Australia, New Zealand & South-East Asia	**Regional Winner** East & South Asia
Annamma Lucy GEMS Our Own English High School, Sharjah – Boys' Branch, UAE	Anna Murray British Council, France	Melissa Crosby Frankfort High School, USA	Nonhlanhla Masina African School for Excellence, South Africa	Peggy Pesik Sekolah Buin Batu, Indonesia	Raminder Kaur Mac Choithram School, India

For more information about our dedicated teachers and their stories, go to
dedicatedteacher.cambridge.org

CAMBRIDGE
UNIVERSITY PRESS

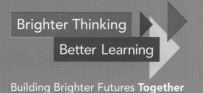
Brighter Thinking
Better Learning

Building Brighter Futures **Together**

> Contents

> Introduction

Welcome to the new edition of our Cambridge International AS & A Level Psychology coursebook, which has been developed to support you with the Cambridge International AS & A Level Psychology syllabus (9990) for examination from 2024. The syllabus covers a range of approaches to the study of psychology including biological, cognitive, learning and social. You are encouraged to think like a psychologist and explore key concepts and debates in psychology including the nature versus nurture debate and cultural differences.

You will also develop skills of analysis, application and evaluation. At A Level you will apply knowledge and understanding to important real-world issues in two of the four options: clinical, consumer, health and organisational psychology. Research Methods are an essential part of psychology and underpin both AS and A Level Psychology. You need to apply a scientific approach and consider the benefits and limitations of different methodologies.

This coursebook is designed to provide a comprehensive and engaging course that fully supports the syllabus. The various features that you will find in these chapters are explained in the How to use this book section.

The information in this section is taken from the Cambridge International 9990 syllabus for examination from 2024. You should always refer to the appropriate syllabus document for the year of your examination to confirm the details and for more information. The syllabus document is available on the Cambridge International website at www.cambridgeinternational.org

> How to use this series

We offer a comprehensive suite of resources for the Cambridge International AS & A Level Psychology syllabus (9990). All of the books in the series work together to help students develop the necessary knowledge and skills required for this subject.

This coursebook provides full coverage of the Cambridge International AS & A Level Psychology syllabus (9990). Each chapter contains in-depth explanations of psychological concepts with a variety of activities, classroom discussions and projects to keep students engaged. The application of research methods and issues and debates are highlighted in every topic through features. Each chapter ends with exam-style questions to help learners consolidate their understanding. Discussion points and activities promote active learning and assessment for learning.

This digital teacher's resource provides detailed guidance for teaching all of the topics of the syllabus. Common misconceptions are identified, which indicate the areas where students may need extra support, also included is an engaging bank of lesson ideas for each syllabus topic. Differentiation is emphasised with advice on the identification of different learner needs and suggestions for appropriate interventions to support and stretch learners.

This workbook contains a wide range of exercises, carefully constructed to help learners to develop the skills that they need to progress through their Psychology course, providing further practice for all of the topics in the coursebook. Learners encounter a variety of research methods throughout the course, and questions about these research methods appear at the end of each chapter for learners to practise applying their knowledge and understanding.

> How to use this book

Throughout this book, you will notice lots of different features that will help your learning. These are explained below.

LEARNING INTENTIONS

These set the scene for each chapter, help with navigation through the coursebook and indicate the important concepts in each topic.

GETTING STARTED

This contains questions and activities on subject knowledge you may already have that is relevant to the topic.

MAIN ASSUMPTIONS IN CONTEXT

This AS Level-only feature presents real-world examples and applications of the content in a chapter, encouraging you to look further into topics. There are discussion questions at the end which look at some of the benefits and problems of these applications.

Questions

Appearing throughout the text, questions give you a chance to check that you have understood the topic you have just read about. You can find the answers to these questions in the digital edition of the coursebook. The answers to these questions are accessible to teachers for free on the Cambridge GO site.

RESEARCH METHODS

Specific aspects of research methods that relate to content are included in all chapters after chapter 1.

ISSUES AND DEBATES

Areas of each topic that relate to current issues and debates in psychology are highlighted through each chapter, providing extra opportunities for discussion in class.

KEY WORDS

Key vocabulary is highlighted in the text when it is first introduced. Meanings of these words and phrases are given in the feature boxes close to where the word is highlighted. You will also find definitions of these words in the Glossary at the back of this book.

COMMAND WORDS

Command words that appear in the syllabus are highlighted in the exam-style questions when they are first introduced. In the margin, you will find the Cambridge International definition. You will also find these definitions in the Glossary at the back of the book with some further explanation on the meaning of these words.

ACTIVITIES

Activities give you an opportunity to check and develop your understanding throughout the text in a more active way, for example by creating presentations, posters or role plays.

Peer/Self assessment

At the end of some activities you will find opportunities to help you assess your own work, or that of your classmates, and consider how you can improve the way that you learn.

REFLECTION

These activities ask you to look back on the topics covered in the chapter and test how well you understand these topics and encourage you to reflect on your learning.

SUMMARY

There is a summary of key points at the end of each section.

SELF-EVALUATION

The summary is followed by self-evaluation checklists with 'I can' statements which correspond to the Learning intentions at the beginning of the chapter. You might find it helpful to rate how confident you are for each of these statements when you are revising. You should revisit any coursebook or workbook topics that you rated "Needs more work" or "Almost there".

I can	Needs more work	Almost there	ready to move on	Coursebook	Workbook

PROJECT

Projects allow you to apply your learning from the whole chapter to group activities such as making posters or presentations, or taking part in debates. They may give you the opportunity to extend your learning beyond the syllabus if you want to.

EXAM-STYLE QUESTIONS

Questions at the end of each chapter provide more demanding exam-style questions, some of which may require use of knowledge from previous chapters. Answers to these questions can be found in the Digital edition of the coursebook. The answers to these questions are accessible to teachers for free on the Cambridge GO site.

> Key concepts in psychology

One of the most significant key concepts in contemporary psychology is the relative contributions of nature and nurture to human and animal thinking and behaviour. The influence of innate, genetic factors (nature) and the environmental influences that shape us from conception (nurture) and discussed throughout this book in the Issues and Debates section. Nature versus nurture is an important consideration as we plan studies and evaluate theory and research.

In addition, ethical considerations are an essential part of designing and carrying out research in psychology. Psychologists must gather data without harming participants mentally or physically. The role of ethics in research has increased in importance over time; some early psychological research you may learn about would no longer be considered acceptable or carried out today. There are specific guidelines that support an ethical approach to conducting research with both human and animal participants, so psychologists must continually evaluate the ethical and moral implications of psychological research.

Psychologists have a range of research methods they can use to test their explanations or theories and these also have strengths and weaknesses. The alternative methods can therefore be considered in terms of their relative usefulness and limitations. For all psychological investigations, both those you learn about and those you design yourself, it is important to consider how well the research could be or has been done. Two important considerations for any psychological research are validity (whether the research is really testing what it claims to) and reliability (the consistency of the measures used).

Psychology can be defined as 'the science of mind and behaviour'. The topics explored in psychology include ways to understand, explain and predict the behaviour, thinking and emotions of humans and animals. Most topics in psychology can be explored from a number of different approaches (e.g. biological, cognitive, learning and social). This means that explanations or theories used to understand a topic could be based on one of several different perspectives. The range of core studies explored in this book illustrates a variety of approaches, and each approach has its own assumptions, strengths and weaknesses. There are therefore debates both within and between approaches meaning no one view in psychology is definitive. Instead, the approaches are alternative ways of thinking about and explaining topics, ideas or observations.

Psychological research and explanations aim to improve our understanding and the way we live: therefore this book aims to show the relevance of psychology to contemporary society. Research that helps us to understand psychological phenomena may or may not have practical applications to everyday life, which often depends on the way in which it was carried out. The findings of useful research or psychological theories can be applied to explain or help solve day-to-day problems in our lives and in wider society.

> Issues and debates at AS Level

At AS level we will consider a number of issues and debates including how they relate to each core study. One debate is the nature versus nurture argument. This is about whether behaviour, feelings or thinking processes could result from nature (innate, genetic factors) or from nurture (can be explained in terms of the environmental influences). These two sides of the debate are not necessarily in opposition. For example, an adult who is academically successful may have high levels of intelligence which could be attributed to genetics (nature); but may also have been encouraged to study hard and given the resources to do so (nurture). Contemporary psychology considers the relative contributions of each influence, and how nature and nurture interact to explain human thinking and behaviour. So in this example observable behaviour like academic success has been shown to be a combination of genetic predisposition and socio-economic advantages.

The second debate is about the relative importance of individual versus situational influences in explanations. This refers to the role played by factors such as the person's personality or physiology that are unique to them (individual influence).The debate also considers the situational factors within the setting, for example the presence of others and the setting in which the behaviour being studied takes place. To give an example, you could think about watching a film with a friend. Afterwards perhaps you noticed small details your friend did not. Is this because you have a more attentive personality (individual explanation) or because you had a better view in the cinema, or whilst yuor friend left for ten minutes to get a drink (situational)? Again, such factors may be present simultaneously and may interact, rather than being the influences working in isolation in a way which would be 'one or the other'.

Another issue to consider is the application of psychology to everyday life. As mentioned in the Key Concepts section, all psychological research is planned with a specific purpose which intends to address an aspect of everyday life. Examples of this might be trying to improve how people treat one another or ways in which we can improve mental health. As you progress through the course you will consider how the findings of studies can be applied in a range of ways to the real-world. However, there may be some cases where the way in which the research was conducted (e.g. in a lab or with a very limited, unrepresentative sample) may mean that the findings cannot easily be applied to the real-world.

Psychologists wishing to find out about the thinking and behaviour of children must adhere to specific guidelines in order to protect children's well-being. There are additional considerations when working with children as opposed to adults, because children generally may not understand, communicate or behave in the same way as adults.

Consider the additional safeguards that might need to be in place for working with children. Will they understand the task or a new situation, or could this be confusing or distressing? Children under 16 years of age cannot give informed consent to participate in psychological research, partly because it is uncertain whether they can understand the implications of taking part. Psychologists must also consider the methodological issues of working with children, as children are often expected to be compliant and respectful towards adults. When asked to give their thoughts and opinions, younger participants could be more likely to give socially desirable responses, for example.

Likewise, there is debate about the ethics of conducting research with animals, which is sometimes considered more practical and/or ethical than research with human participants. Psychologists currently working in this area also have a particular set of rules to which they must adhere. These guidelines inform what psychologists can and cannot do when working with animals; and the methodological and ethical implications of these are discussed in detail in Chapter 1. Additionally, psychologists must consider carefully whether the findings of their research with animals can be applied to other species. For example, this book will explore ways in which animals and humans learn by observing others. Because of differences in the complexity and types of thinking and behaviour between different species, we must be cautious about generalising from animal research.

› Acknowledgements

The authors and publisher acknowledge the following sources of copyright material and are grateful for the permissions granted. While every effort has been made, it has not always been possible to identify the sources of all the material used, or to trace all copyright holders. If any omissions are brought to our notice, we will be happy to include the appropriate acknowledgements on reprinting.

Table 2.4 from 'Sex differences in rhesus monkey toy preferences parallel those of children' Hormones and Behaviour Vol 54, (3) Hassett, Janice M and Siebert, Erin R and Wallen, Kim, Pages No.359–364, © 2008, with permission from Elsevier; **3.1 Core Study 1** Extract from 'What does doodling do?' from Applied Cognitive Psychology: The Official Journal of the Society for Applied Research in Memory and Cognition, Volume, 24 (1), 2010 Reproduced with permission from Wiley Online Library; **Fig 4.5 & Table 4.3** Data extract from 'Positive reinforcement training for a trunk wash in Nepal's working elephants: Demonstrating alternatives to traditional elephant training techniques' by Fagen, Ariel and Acharya, Narayan and Kaufman, Gretchen E, from Journal of Applied Animal Welfare Science, 2014, and Taylor & Francis, reprinted by permission of the publisher (Taylor & Francis Ltd, www.tandfonline. com); **Table 4.5** Reprinted from Journal of the American Academy of Child & Adolescent Psychiatry, Vol 41 (11), Saavedra, Lissette M and Silverman, Wendy K 'Case study: Disgust and a specific phobia of buttons', Pages No.1376– 1379, © 2002, with permission from Elsevier; **Table 5.1** from 'Behavioral Study of obedience' by by Milgram, S. (1963) from The Journal of Abnormal and Social Psychology 67(4), 371–378; **Figures 5.6, 5.7 & Tables 5.2–5.5** use data from Social Cognitive and Affective Neuroscience, 'OT promotes closer interpersonal distance among highly empathic individuals', 2014, Volume 10, Issue 1, January 2015, Pages 3–9, by Anat Perry, David Mankuta, Simone G. Shamay-Tsoory, reproduced with permission of Oxford University Press; **Table 5.6** Extract from 'Good samaritanism: an underground phenomenon?' by IM Piliavin, J Rodin, JA Piliavin Reproduced with permission. Copyright © 1969 by American Psychological Association; **Fig 6.3 & Table 6.1** from 'Can Virtual Reality be Used to Investigate Persecutory Ideation?'in The Journal of Nervous and Mental Disease: August 2003, Volume 191, Issue 8, p 509–514 by Freeman, Daniel BA, PhD, DClinPsy; Slater, Mel MSc, DSc; Bebbington, Paul E. MA, PhD, FRCP, FRCPsych; Garety, Philippa A. MA, MPhil, PhD; Kuipers, Elizabeth BSc, MSc, PhD; Fowler, David BSc, MSc Copyright © 2003 by Lippincott Williams & Wilkins; **Fig. 6.23** Lovell et al. (2006) figure 2 Research from 'Telephone administered cognitive behaviour therapy for treatment of obsessive compulsive disorder: randomised controlled non-inferiority trial' BMJ 2006; 333 doi: https://doi.org/10.1136/bmj.38940.355602.80; **Fig. 7.2** redrawn from Fohlio.com Blog by Darren Gilbert; **Fig. 7.6** Gil et al 4 patterns of movement; **Fig. 7.8** Pavesic, Dave, 'The Psychology of Menu Design: Reinvent Your 'Silent Salesperson' to Increase Check Averages and Guest Loyalty' (2005). Hospitality Faculty Publications. 5. https://scholarworks.gsu.edu/hospitality_facpub/5; **Fig. 7.15** del Campo, C., Pauser, S., Steiner, E. et al. 'Decision making styles and the use of heuristics in decision making'. J Bus Econ 86, 389–412 (2016). https://doi.org/10.1007/s11573-016-0811-y; **Fig. 7.17** 'Competitive Interference and Consumer Memory for Advertising', Raymond R. Burke ,Thomas K. Srull; **Fig. 7.19** Figure from Liza Becker, Thomas J.L. van Rompay, Hendrik N.J. Schifferstein, Mirjam Galetzka, 'Tough package, strong taste: The influence of packaging design on taste impressions and product evaluations', Food Quality and Preference, Volume 22, Issue 1, 2011, Pages 17-23, ISSN 0950-3293,; **Fig. 8.1 & Table 8.1** photo and Table 3 from p277 of McKinstry, B., and Wang, J. X. (1991), 'Putting on the style: what patients think of the way their doctor dresses', in British Journal of General Practice, vol. 41, no. 348, [online], pp. 270, 275–278.; **Table 8.3** from Savage, R and Armstrong, D, 1990, 'Effect of a general practitioner's consulting style on patients' satisfaction: a controlled study', in BMJ: British Medical Journal, p968 Table 1, vol.301, no.6758, pp.968–70.; **Fig. 8.23** 'Perfusion functional MRI reveals cerebral blood flow pattern under psychological stress', © 2009, National Academy of Sciences, U.S.A.; **Fig 8.25** Figure 2 from 'An instrument for producing deep muscle relaxation by means of analog information feedback 1' Thomas H. Budzynski and Johann M. Stoyva; **Fig 8.27 & Table 9.6** from 'The Long-term Effects of a Token Economy in Safety Performance in Open Pit Mining', in Journal of Applied Behavior Analysis, vol. 20, no. 3, [online], pp. 215 – 224 by Authors Fox, D. K., Hopkins, B. L., and Anger, W. K. (1987) Reproduced with permission of John Wiley and Sons; **Table 9.1** Table from 'The Work of Leadership' by Ronald A. Heifetz and Donald L. Laurie in the December 2001 issue Reproduced with the permission of Harvard Business School; **Table**

9.2 Academy of Management PerspectivesVol. 1, No. 4 Articles 'The Case for Directive Leadership' Authors Jan P. Muczyk and Bernard C. Reimann by Academy of Management; **Table 9.3** From Kouzes and Posner (1987); **Table 9.5** Extract from 'The Psychology of Social Impact', American Psychologist, 36(4), 343. by B Latané Reproduced with permission. Copyright © 1969 by American Psychological Association; **Table 9.7** Table from Job Descriptive Index (Smith et al., 1969). **Fig 9.10** Dimensional representation of followers Figure 'In Praise of Followers' by Robert Kelley Harvard Business Review (November 1988). Reproduced with the permission of Harvard Business Publishing

Thanks to the following for permission to reproduce images:

Cover Hiroshi Watanabe/GI; *Inside* Chapter 1 Westend61/GI; Fig. 1.1 Kues/Shutterstock; Fig. 1.2 Compassionate Eye Foundation/Robert Daly/OJO Image/GI; Fig. 1.3 Electravk/GI; Fig. 1.4 Carol Yepes/GI; Fig. 1.5 Quizlet; Fig. 1.8 Luis Alvarez/GI; Fig. 1.9 Maskot/GI; Fig. 1.1 Juanmonino/GI; Fig. 1.11 Music Division/New York Public Library/Science Photo Library; Fig. 1.12 Tom Merton/GI; Fig. 1.14 Granger Historical Picture Archive/Alamy Stock Photo; Fig. 1.2 Ezra Bailey/GI; Chapter 2 SCIEPRO/GI; Fig. 2.6 Jose Luis Pelaez Inc/GI; Fig. 2.6 © Peter Lourenco/GI; Fig. 2.7 By Jon Climpson/GI; Fig. 2.10 Portra/GI; Fig. 2.11 Hans Bjurling/GI; Chapter 3 SEAN GLADWELL/GI; Fig. 3.5 kupicoo/GI; Fig. 3.7 eyes from the Reading the Mind in the Eyes test, reproduced with permission of Autism Research Centre; Fig. 3.11 Jason_V/GI; Fig. 3.12 AF archive/Alamy Stock Photo; Fig. 3.12 ArcadeImages/Alamy Stock Photo; Chapter 4 MoMo Productions/GI; Fig. 4.1 Caia Image/GI; Fig. 4.2 Stills from the Bandura study, reproduced with permission of Trustee of The Albert Bandura Trust; Fig. 4.3 Chaideer Mahyuddin/GI; Fig. 4.9 Anurak Pongpatimet/Shutterstock; Fig. 4.1 Advertising Archives; Chapter 5 AzmanJaka/GI; Fig. 5.1 Bruno de Hogues/GI; Fig. 5.3 Atlaspix/Alamy; Fig. 5.4 Marius Mangevicius/GI; Fig. 5.8 New York Daily News/GI; Chapter 6 D3sign/GI; Fig. 6.2 Just_Super/GI; Fig. 6.7 Raleigh News & Observer/GI; Fig. 6.1 Fertnig/GI; Fig. 6.11 Azat Anbekov/GI; Fig. 6.12 Nes/GI; Fig. 6.15 Mangpor_2004/GI; Fig. 6.17 ljubaphoto/GI; Fig. 6.18 PeopleImages/GI; Fig. 6.19 The Drs. Nicholas and Dorothy Cummings Center for the History of Psychology, The University of Akron.; Fig. 6.2 Erik Von Weber/GI; Fig. 6.21 D3sign/GI; Fig. 6.22 Sean Justice/GI; Chapter 7 Noel Hendrickson/GI; Fig. 7.1 Flavia Morlachetti/GI; Fig. 7.3 IndiaPix/GI; Fig. 7.4 Philip Fong/GI; Fig. 7.5 muratart/Shutterstock; Fig. 7.7 Martin-Dm/GI; Fig. 7.9 Creative Crop/GI; Fig. 7.11 Tetra Images/GI; Fig. 7.12 Matthew Horwood/GI; Fig 7.13 ElenaBs/Alamy Stock Vector; Fig. 7.14 AlpamayoPhoto/GI; Fig. 7.16 PamelaJoeMcFarlane/GI; Fig. 7.18 Tortoon/GI; Fig. 7.20 Noel Hendrickson/GI; Fig. 7.21 UrbanImages/Alamy Stock Photo; Fig. 7.22 SOPA Images/GI; Fig. 7.23 Sergei Supinsky/GI; Fig. 7.24 Justin Tallis/GI; Fig. 7.25 Anders Blomqvist/GI; Fig. 7.26 Helen Sessions/Alamy Stock Photo; Fig. 7.28 Retro AdArchives/Alamy Stock Photo; Fig. 7.29 Popartic/GI; Fig. 7.3 Anadolu Agency/GI; Fig. 7.31 Justin Sullivan/GI; Chapter 8 andresr/GI; Fig. 8.2 SDI Productions/GI; Fig. 8.4 Tom Merton/GI; Fig. 8.5 Douglas Sacha/GI; Fig. 8.6 SCIENCE PHOTO LIBRARY/GI; Fig. 8.7 FunHaler - figure 1 Chaney et al; Fig. 8.9 Defense Department photo/Donna Miles; Fig. 8.14 SasinParaksa/GI; Fig. 8.15 Ac Productions/GI; Fig. 8.16 javi_indy/GI; Fig. 8.18 Diagram adapted from How Stress Affects the Body - Doctor Wilson's Original Formulations; Fig. 8.19 Peter Dazeley/GI; Fig. 8.20 Martin-Dm/GI; Fig. 8.21 FS Productions/GI; Fig. 8.22 Peter Dazeley/GI; Fig. 8.24 Ftwitty/GI; Fig 8.26 The Food Dudes Healthy Eating Programme was first developed by the Food Activity Research Unit, School of Psychology at Bangor University, Wales. Copyright © 2004 © 2009 © 2013 Bangor University; Chapter 9 Hispanolistic/GI; Fig. 9.2 Science History Images/Alamy Stock Photo; Fig. 9.3 Fizkes/GI; Fig. 9.4 Jon Feingersh Photography Inc/GI; Fig. 9.5 Michael Ochs Archives/GI; Fig. 9.6 Silver Screen Collection/GI; Fig. 9.9 Changyu Lu/GI; Fig. 9.12 Ryan McVay/GI; Fig. 9.13 Vm/GI; Fig. 9.15 Reading Room 2020/Alamy Stock Photo; Fig. 9.16 Monkeybusinessimages/GI; Fig. 9.17 Dean Mitchell/GI; Fig. 9.18 George D. Lepp/GI; Fig. 9.19 Mikulas1/GI; Fig. 9.20 Skaman306/GI; Fig. 9.22 IndiaPix/GI; Fig. 9.23 Peter Dazeley/GI

GI = Getty Images

Dedications from the authors:

Julia Russell: To Rory, with love and hope, Great-aunt Julia

Lizzie Gauntlett: To Nathan and Alex, love Mum

Amy Papaconstantinou: To Noah and Max, with all my love, Mummy

> Chapter 1
Research methods

LEARNING INTENTIONS

In this chapter, you will learn how to:

- describe and use the concepts and terminology relating to research methods

- describe, evaluate and apply the six main research methods

- explain and use other concepts relevant to planning and conducting studies and analysing their results

- apply the concepts of research methods to novel situations

- consider the debate surrounding ethics in psychology.

Introduction

Psychological phenomena are explored using a 'research process' and the methods used to investigate questions in psychology are called 'research methods'. This chapter will help you to understand how those methods are used by psychologists to find out about human (and animal) cognition, emotions and behaviour.

The chapter is divided into several sections, covering the basic research methods that you need to understand: experiments, self-reports, case studies, observations, correlations and longitudinal studies. Once you have studied these sections, you should be able to apply your knowledge of research methods to novel research situations.

In addition, you will learn about the other features of the research process or 'research methodology'. These features are the steps a psychologist takes in developing and conducting studies to investigate a question or problem. This research process can be thought of as having several stages, the first of which is to develop an aim. Although developing an aim is one of many steps, it is useful to consider it here before moving on to the main part of the chapter.

The aim is the intention of the study, the idea it is trying to test, problem it is intended to solve or the question it is attempting to answer. Consider the idea of different ways to help students to study, perhaps using mind maps or revision apps. Imagine that a psychologist, Dr Huang,

asks a few of her psychology students which method they prefer, and finds that both are quite popular. Dr Huang wants to know which is most effective. This is Dr Huang's aim: *to investigate whether mind maps or revision apps are more effective at helping students to learn*. So, the *aim* tells you the purpose of the investigation: in this case, an experiment. It is generally expressed in terms of what the study intends to show. An aim can also express the intention to investigate a link or relationship between two variables, such as between the number of computer games a student plays and their final A Level grade: in this case, the study would be a correlation.

This chapter therefore covers the whole of this research process:

- development of an aim

- selection of a research method and the designs, formats or techniques to be used within that research method

- definition, manipulation, measurement, control of variables and variables in hypotheses

- selection of participants

- ethical considerations

- analysis of data, including the drawing of conclusions

- evaluation of research.

GETTING STARTED

Why do psychologists do research?

As students, you may be bombarded with 'facts' about how to improve your learning. Perhaps you have heard of different learning styles, or the benefits of repetition or mind maps to help you to revise. Each of these ideas should have been tested to see if they actually work (although many haven't!). The process of research allows scientists such as psychologists to test ideas to discover whether there is evidence to support them. This is how we decide which drugs or therapies work best for mental illnesses, whether different displays or music help to sell products, and how we should organise factories to help workers to be efficient and healthy.

To be trustworthy, research needs to be planned well and conducted effectively. Imagine an investigation comparing a new classroom technique to an old one. If the researcher didn't know how hard the students worked and used the new technique on a lazy class, and the old one on a highly motivated class, this would produce false results. Consider a study into consumer psychology that compared how many goods were sold with and without music playing in the store. If the researcher only played music at the weekends and played no music on weekdays, would you believe the findings of the study?

CONTINUED

Figure 1.1: Where do we focus when we concentrate on a problem?

Watch or imagine someone thinking really hard, perhaps trying to remember a name or work out the answer to a question, where do they focus their eyes? It has been suggested that in such situations, we look upwards and to the left (Figure 1.1). Consider how you might test whether this is true. Would you wait for people to get confused and then look at what they do, or would you give them a puzzle to make them think? How would you decide where they are looking? What would you do to be sure that they aren't just looking around the room for clues? Being able to decide on the answers to questions such as these is the basis of designing experiments in psychology.

1.1 Experiments

An **experiment** is an investigation that allows researchers to look for a cause-and-effect relationship. The researcher investigates the way one variable, called the **independent variable**, is responsible for the effect on another, the **dependent variable**. To test this, the researcher manipulates the independent variable (IV) to produce two or more 'levels' or conditions, such as creating 'bright' or 'dull' lighting or selecting 'early' and 'late' in the day. The effect of these conditions on the dependent variable (DV) is measured. For example, an IV of the brightness of lighting might affect attention, with people being better at paying attention when the light is bright. How well people pay attention would be the DV. If there is a big difference in the DV between the conditions, the researcher would conclude that the IV has caused the difference in the DV, i.e. that the brightness of light affects attention (Figure 1.2).

KEY WORDS

experiment: an investigation that allows researchers to look for a causal relationship; an independent variable is manipulated and is expected to be responsible for changes in the dependent variable

independent variable (IV): the factor under investigation in an experiment that is manipulated to create two or more conditions (levels) and is expected to be responsible for changes in the dependent variable

KEY WORD

dependent variable (DV): the factor in an experiment that is measured and is expected to change under the influence of the independent variable

Figure 1.2: An experiment can investigate whether the brightness of lighting affects how well we concentrate

To be more certain that the difference between the conditions is caused by the IV, the researcher needs to control any other variables that might affect the DV. For example, people might find it harder to be attentive if they have recently eaten, exercised or sat through a very dull class.

The effect of such uncontrolled variables should therefore be minimised, e.g. by keeping all factors except the IV the same in each condition (or 'level of the IV').

The levels of the IV being compared may be two or more experimental conditions (such as bright and dull artificial lights) or there may be one or more experimental conditions that are compared to a control condition (e.g. artificial light compared to daylight). The control condition is simply the absence of the experimental variable. For example, in a comparison of the effect of eating chocolate on paying attention, we might compare either the effect of eating one bar or two bars (two experimental conditions) or the effect of eating one bar to no chocolate at all (one experimental and one control condition).

KEY WORDS

uncontrolled variable: a variable that either acts randomly, affecting the DV in all levels of the IV, or systematically, i.e. on one level of the IV (called a confounding variable) so can obscure the effect of the IV, making the results difficult to interpret, the effects of which have not or cannot be limited or eliminated

experimental condition: one or more of the situations in an experiment that represent different levels of the IV and are compared (or compared to a control condition)

control condition: a level of the IV in an experiment from which the IV itself is absent. It is compared to one or more experimental conditions

RESEARCH METHODS IN PRACTICE

A researcher might conduct an *experiment* to test the effect of the *independent variable* of time of day on the *dependent variable* of happiness of students. They might always use lessons immediately after a break or lunch so the students had always eaten recently since this might affect happiness and act as an *uncontrolled variable*. This would be a comparison between two *experimental conditions*.

ACTIVITY 1.1

Look at the Research methods in practice box. Can you suggest:

- two different times of day to use as the levels of the *independent variable*

- how the *dependent variable* might be measured

- one other *uncontrolled variable* that it would be important to control?

Experimental design

The way that participants are allocated to different levels of the IV is called the experimental design. They may participate in all, or only one, of the levels of the IV.

The three experimental designs are:

- independent measures design

- repeated measures design

- matched pairs design.

KEY WORDS

experimental design: the way in which participants are allocated to levels of the IV

independent measures design: an experimental design in which a different group of participants is used for each level of the IV (condition)

Independent measures design

In an independent measures design, a separate group of participants is used for each experimental condition or level of the IV. This means that the data for each level of the IV is 'independent' because it is not related to any other data: it has come from different people. Note that this is a different use of the word 'independent' from that in the 'independent variable'.

If we wanted to know whether seeing people behaving aggressively on television had long-term effects, we could (rather unethically) expose a group of young people to aggressive television and then wait for them to grow older. However, it would much quicker to compare two groups of adults, one group who had been allowed to watch aggressive TV as children and one group who had not been allowed to. This second example uses an independent measures design.

An independent measures design is good because the participants only encounter the experimental setting once. They are therefore unlikely to notice or respond to clues that might tell them the aims of the experiment (demand characteristics). One problem is that there might be individual differences between participants in the groups for each level of the IV that could influence the findings. For example, in a study on the effect of noise on dreams, more people who normally remember their dreams well might end up in the 'no noise' group. If so, it could look as though noise prevented dream recall when in fact it had little effect. This risk can be reduced by the random allocation of participants to different conditions. This spreads possible differences between individuals across the levels of the IV. To randomly allocate participants, each person is given a number, and the numbers are then randomly divided into two groups. This can be done by giving each participant a number, putting numbers into a hat and drawing out two sets, or by using a random number generator (e.g. on a computer) to do the same thing. This and other strengths and weaknesses of independent measures designs are presented in Table 1.1.

KEY WORDS

demand characteristics: features of the experimental situation which give away the aims. They can cause participants to try to change their behaviour, for example to match their beliefs about what is supposed to happen, which reduces the validity of the study

random allocation: a way to reduce the effect of confounding variables such as individual differences. Participants are put in each level of the IV such that each person has an equal chance of being in any condition

Repeated measures design

In a repeated measures design, the same group of people participate in every level of the IV. To help you to remember, think of the participants 'repeating' their performance under different conditions. For example,

in a study looking at the effects of doodling on learning, we could count the number of words recalled in the same group of people when they did doodle and when they did not.

The main advantage of a repeated measures design is that each person acts as their own baseline. Any differences between participants that could influence their performance and therefore the DV will affect both levels of the IV in the same way. Individual differences are therefore unlikely to bias the findings. Imagine that in our experiment on doodling, one person was generally very quick to learn and another quite slow. In an independent measures design this might cause a problem if they were in different groups, but using a repeated measures design makes the differences between them less important, as both could show an improvement with doodling. Individual differences between participants that could affect the DV are called participant variables. These variables, such as age, gender, personality or intelligence, could hide or exaggerate differences between levels of the IV, i.e. confound or confuse the results. Such variables can be referred to as 'confounding variables'. It is therefore important to limit the possible effects of these variables in order to be sure that any change in the DV is due to the IV. A repeated measures design does so by comparing the same people in each condition of the IV. This and other strengths and weaknesses of repeated measures designs are presented in Table 1.1.

KEY WORDS

repeated measures design: an experimental design in which each participant performs in every level of the IV

participant variables: individual differences between participants (such as age, personality and intelligence) that could affect their behaviour in a study that would hide or exaggerate differences between levels of the IV

confounding variable: an uncontrolled variable that acts systematically on one level of the IV so could hide or exaggerate differences between levels and therefore 'confound' or confuse the results making it difficult to understand the effect of the IV on the DV

As each individual participates in every level of the IV, they will perform the same or similar tasks two or more times. This can lead to a problem called an **order effect**. Repeated performance can cause two different kinds of order effects. When participants' performance improves because they have encountered the task before this is a **practice effect**. This matters because participants who were tested on a condition second would perform better than those who did it first. Alternatively, repetition might make performance worse, perhaps if they were bored or tired: a **fatigue effect**. In addition, the participants see both levels of the IV and have more opportunity to work out what is being tested, so are more likely to respond to demand characteristics.

Order effects can be solved in two ways: by randomisation or counterbalancing. Imagine an experiment with two conditions: learning while listening to music (M) and learning with no music (N). In **randomisation**, participants are randomly allocated to do either condition M followed by N, or vice versa. As some will do each order, any advantage of doing one of the conditions first will probably be evened out in the results. To be more certain that possible effects are evened out, **counterbalancing** can be used. Here, the group of participants is divided into two, so one half will do M followed by N and the other half N followed by M. If on the second test there was a risk of participants accidentally including items learned in the first test, this would be a problem for exactly half the participants in the 'music' condition, and exactly half in the 'no music' condition. Alternatively, a different design could be used.

KEY WORDS

order effects: practice and fatigue effects are the consequences of participating in a study more than once, for example in a repeated measures design. They cause changes in performance between conditions that are not due to the IV, so can obscure the effect on the DV

practice effect: a situation where participants' performance improves because they experience the experimental task more than once, for example due to familiarity or learning the task

fatigue effect: a situation where participants' performance declines because they experience the experimental task more than once, e.g. due to physical tiredness or boredom with the task

KEY WORDS

randomisation: a way to overcome order effects in a repeated measures design. Each participant is allocated to perform in the different levels of the IV in a way that ensures they have an equal chance of participating in the different levels in any order

counterbalancing: a way to overcome order effects in a repeated measures design. Each possible order of levels of the IV is performed by a different sub-group of participants. This can be described as an ABBA design, as half the participants do condition A then B, and half do B then A

matched pairs design: an experimental design in which participants are arranged into pairs. Each pair is similar in ways that are important to the study and one member of each pair performs in a different level of the IV

Matched pairs design

The problems associated with both independent measures and repeated measures designs are overcome in a **matched pairs design**. For each participant, another person is found who is similar in ways that are important to the experiment, such as age, gender, intelligence or personality, to make a pair. This matching is done on variables relevant to the study, so in a study on the effects of playing a violent computer game, participants might be matched on their existing level of aggression. Identical twins make ideal matched pairs as they are both genetically the same and are likely to have had very similar experiences (Figure 1.3).

Figure 1.3: Identical twins are perfect participants for a matched pairs design

Experimental design		
	Independent measures	Repeated measures	Matched pairs
Strengths	Different participants are used in each level of the IV so there are no order effects. Participants see only one level of the IV, reducing the effect of demand characteristics. Random allocation to levels of the IV can reduce the effects of individual differences.	Participant variables are unlikely to distort the effect of the IV, as each participant does all levels. Counterbalancing reduces order effects. Uses fewer participants than independent measures or matched pairs so this is good when participants are hard to find or if participants are at risk.	Participants see only one level of the IV, reducing the effect of demand characteristics. Participant variables are less likely to distort the effect of the IV than in an independent measures design as individual differences are matched. Different participants are used in each level of the IV so there are no order effects.
Weaknesses	Participant variables can distort results if there are important individual differences between participants in different levels of the IV. More participants are needed than in a repeated measures design so the study may be less ethical if participants are harmed and less effective if there is a small sample because participants are hard to find.	Order effects could distort the results. As participants see the experimental task more than once, they have greater exposure to demand characteristics.	The similarity between pairs is limited by the matching process, so the right matching criteria must be chosen in advance for this to be effective. Availability of matching pairs may be limited, making the sample size small (although some studies conducted on twins use very large numbers of pairs).

Table 1.1: Strengths and weaknesses of experimental designs

Different groups of participants are then used for each level of the IV, with one participant from each pair being in each level of the IV. By using different participants in each group order effects are avoided and the matching of participants minimises the influence of individual differences. This and other strengths and weaknesses of matched pair designs are presented in Table 1.1.

RESEARCH METHODS IN PRACTICE

A child psychologist conducted an experiment to look at the effect of violent computer games (Figure 1.4). There were two experimental conditions (violent and non-violent). The *dependent variable* was the children's subsequent violent behaviour. The *experimental design* chosen was an *independent measures design*, with different children in each of the experimental conditions. If a *repeated measures design* had been used, in which the same children played each type of game, there could be *order effects*. For example, aggression caused by playing the violent game could still affect children in the non-violent game condition if they did this second. If this were the case, the problem could be reduced by using *counterbalancing*.

However, the use of an independent measures design risks *participant variables*, such as the original level of violence of each child, affecting the results. This could be reduced by either using *random allocation* of participants to each condition or by using a *matched pairs design*. In this case, children with similar aggression levels would be put in the different conditions. To avoid *demand characteristics*, the children would ideally be unaware that they are in an experiment, perhaps by telling them that they are in a computer games competition.

Figure 1.4: Are children more violent after they have played a violent computer game than before?

ACTIVITY 1.2

Look at the Research methods in practice box. Think about the following:

- The study could have had another level of the IV that did not use a computer game but did use a computer, such as looking at non-violent pictures. Would this have been a control condition or another experimental condition?

- An order effect that could arise if a repeated measures design was used for this study is that the children might get fed up with playing computer games by the second condition. Is this a practice effect or a fatigue effect?

- Suggest a participant variable, other than initial level of violence, that could affect the results of this study.

Types of experiment

Laboratory experiments

Many experiments in psychology are conducted in artificial surroundings. Experiments conducted in this way are called **laboratory experiments**; the participants are not in their usual environment for the behaviour they are performing. The artificial situation means that the researcher can try to limit the effect of variables that might affect the DV. For example, a laboratory experiment on the attention of schoolchildren in high and low light levels could be conducted. It might be investigated by testing the children on a computerised attention task conducted in a psychology room in a university. In this situation, the researcher could choose to control variables such as noise, that could also affect the children's concentration.

KEY WORD

laboratory experiment: a research method in which there is an IV, a DV and strict controls. It looks for a causal relationship and is conducted in a setting that is not in the usual environment for the participants with regard to the behaviour they are performing

Evaluating laboratory experiments

Laboratory experiments have a range of strengths and weaknesses, these are summarised in Table 1.2. Experiments in general, and laboratory experiments in particular, use many controls. In addition, researchers in laboratory experiments can use standardisation, which means that the procedure for each participant can be kept exactly the same. Both controls and standardisation help to make the findings of the experiment reliable, that is, the researchers would be more certain that the procedures and measures they are using are consistent. Controlling variables also improves validity, that is how certain the researcher can be that they are testing what they claim to be testing. By keeping the situation the same, the researcher can be more certain that any differences in the DV really are due to the differences between levels of the IV rather than due to any uncontrolled variables.

One way to identify uncontrolled variables is by conducting a pilot study. This is a preliminary test of the procedure and can lead to changes in the procedure or materials to improve the validity and reliability. In the example of the experiment testing children's attention, it might be found that hunger also affects attention.

A control could then be introduced to give all the children a snack before the study begins. A pilot study should not be used to test whether a study is ethical; this is the responsibility of the researcher and ethical committees.

Another strength of laboratory experiments is that they are relatively easy for a researcher to repeat using exactly the same procedure and materials. This is called replication. The level of standardisation and controls in laboratory experiments help with replicability, as does the operationalisation of the independent and dependent variables, that is the clear and precise way that they are defined. It is important to be able to replicate studies so that they can be checked by other researchers and so that other comparisons can be made. For example, if a study shows that a new drug is better than no drug for treating a mental health condition, other researchers might want to verify this, to check it against a placebo – a pill or procedure that appears to a treatment but in fact has no active 'ingredient' – or against other drugs.

As participants are usually aware that they are involved in a laboratory experiment they can be told what to expect to happen and can be given a choice about whether to participate. They can also be given a full explanation at the end of the study. This may be necessary as experimenters sometimes need to actively lie to or mislead participants to reduce the risk of demand characteristics affecting participants.

KEY WORDS

controls: ways to keep potential confounding variables constant, for example between levels of the IV, to ensure measured differences in the DV are likely to be due to the IV, raising validity

standardisation: keeping the procedure for each participant in a study (e.g. an experiment or interview) exactly the same to ensure that any differences between participants or conditions are due to the variables under investigation rather than differences in the way they were treated

reliability: the extent to which a procedure, task or measure is consistent, for example, that it would produce the same results with the same people on each occasion

validity: the extent to which the researcher is testing what they claim to be testing

pilot study: a small-scale test of the procedure of a study before the main study is conducted. It aims to ensure that the procedure and materials are valid and reliable, so that they can be adapted if not

KEY WORDS

replication: keeping the procedure and materials exactly the same between studies when attempting, for example, to verify results or to enable other studies to use exactly the same techniques to answer related questions

operational definition: the clear description of a variable such that it can be accurately manipulated, measured or quantified, and the study can be replicated. This includes the way that the IV and DV in experiments, and the co-variables in correlations, are described

placebo: a pill or procedure given to a patient who believes it to be a real treatment which in fact has no active 'ingredient', i.e. no active drug in the case of a pill or no therapeutic value in the case of an intervention

RESEARCH METHODS IN PRACTICE

Dr Singh is conducting a laboratory experiment to test whether older adults detect emotions as quickly as younger people. He has two groups of participants, older and younger ones. This is his IV. He tests them by comparing how quickly they press a button to say that they have recognised the emotion on a face of a screen. This is the DV. Each participant sits at the same distance from the screen. This is one aspect of the *standardisation* of the procedure. In a *pilot study*, Dr Singh had shown the participants pictures and used a stopwatch to time their reactions himself, but he found he was not very consistent in his ability to stop timing exactly when the participant responded. He therefore changed to the computerised system to improve *reliability*. The pictures of faces included both younger and older people to ensure it was a *valid* test. The controls and standardisation mean that it would be possible for Dr Singh's colleague, Dr McArthur, to *replicate* the study exactly.

ACTIVITY 1.3

Look at the Research methods in practice box.

- Write an operational definition for the independent variable.

- Write an operational definition for the dependent variable.

- Name and explain the experimental design being used in this study.

- Suggest why the use of faces of a range of ages would have improved validity.

Field experiments

Returning to the idea at the beginning of this section, about the effect of light levels on attention, the school children could alternatively be tested by altering the number of lights turned on in their normal classroom. Light level would still be the IV and the levels of the IV could be 'all the lights on' and 'half the lights on'. The DV of attention could then be measured by looking at the children's scores on a topic test they were due to take that day. This is still an experiment because it has an IV and a DV (and there will still be some controls, such as the amount of time they spend studying for the test). However,

it would be a **field experiment** because the children are being tested on a usual behaviour (performance in a topic test) in their normal environment (the classroom).

Evaluating field experiments

Field experiments, like laboratory experiments, have a range of strengths and weaknesses, these are summarised in Table 1.2. It is a little harder to control variables and standardise procedures in a field experiment than a laboratory experiment, although some controls can still be used. Reliability and validity may therefore be lower. However, validity may benefit as the participants are performing a task that seems normal, in a familiar environment. School students taken into a university laboratory might concentrate really hard because they are nervous or interested, which might cover up any differences between the different light level conditions. This means the findings from the laboratory would not **generalise** to other settings as well as findings from the classroom. This is a problem of **ecological validity**, and field experiments often have better ecological validity than laboratory experiments (but not always).

Another advantage arises if the participants are unaware that they are in an experiment. If so, there may be fewer demand characteristics than there would be in a laboratory experiment. These are any features of the experiment that give away the aims and cause participants' behaviour to change, for example to try to 'make the experiment work'. However, if participants are unaware that they have been in a study they have not been given a choice about participating and may not have wanted to.

KEY WORDS

field experiment: an investigation looking for a causal relationship in which an independent variable is manipulated and is expected to be responsible for changes in the dependent variable. It is conducted in the normal environment for the participants for the behaviour being investigated and some control of variables is possible

generalise: to apply the findings of a study more widely, e.g. to other settings and populations

ecological validity: the extent to which the findings of research conducted in one situation would generalise to other situations. This is influenced by whether the situation (e.g. a laboratory) represents the real world effectively and whether the task is relevant to real life (has mundane realism)

	Type of experiment	
	Laboratory experiment	Field experiment
Strengths	Good control of variables, raising validity. Causal relationships can be determined as only the IV should be affecting the DV. Standardised procedures raise reliability and allow replication.	As participants are in their normal situation for the activity being studied, they are likely to behave naturally, making the results representative. If participants are unaware that they are in a study, the problem of demand characteristics is less than in laboratory experiments.
Weaknesses	The artificial situation could make participants' behaviour unrepresentative, lowering ecological validity. Participants could respond to demand characteristics and alter their behaviour.	Control of variables is harder than in laboratory experiments, lowering reliability and making replication difficult. The researcher will be less sure that changes in the DV have been caused by changes in the IV than in a laboratory experiment. Participants may be unaware that they are in a study, raising ethical issues.

Table 1.2: Strengths and weaknesses of experimental methods

RESEARCH METHODS IN PRACTICE

A research team is deciding how to test the effect of watching television on children's pro-social behaviour, that is, how kind children are to others. They will measure pro-social behaviour by observing how often the children help a doll that cries. They are considering two experimental methods, both using an independent measures design. One is a *laboratory experiment*, in which each child is either shown a cartoon in which the characters are very helpful or a cartoon with characters who behave in a neutral way. Each child is then given a doll for 10 minutes and observed to count how many times they help the crying doll. Alternatively, the children could be observed in a *field experiment*. In this study, half of the children's parents would show their child the pro-social cartoon on the family television. The other half would show their child the neutral cartoon. Each child would be videoed with doll for 10 minutes and the researchers would view the video to count how many times the child helped the crying doll. The field experiment would have more *ecological validity* than the laboratory experiment because the children would be in a familiar environment, in which they would normally play, so would be less likely to be nervous than if they were in a laboratory. For this reason, the results of this study may *generalise* to other situations, such as performing pro-social behaviours in school or at the park. However, a disadvantage of the field experiment, is that there may be distractions in the home that prevent them from paying attention to the cartoon.

ACTIVITY 1.4

Look at the Research methods in practice box. Which of the following can you identify?

- Independent variable
- Dependent variable.

Does the field experiment have a *control condition*?

Can you suggest a *variable* that it would be important to *control*?

What effect might *demand characteristics* have in this study?

What other details would you need to be able to *replicate* the laboratory experiment?

Hypotheses in experimental studies

At the very beginning of this chapter, we considered a study that Dr Huang was conducting, with the aim to investigate whether mind maps or revision apps are more effective at helping students to learn (Figure 1.5). Dr Huang would also need to write a hypothesis based on this aim. A **hypothesis** is as a testable statement. It provides a little more detail about the variables being investigated than the aim.

Importantly, a hypothesis should be *falsifiable*, that is it should be possible for it to be shown to be wrong. This is essential, otherwise an alternative hypothesis would always be accepted! At A2 you may learn about the psychodynamic approach and the work of Sigmund Freud, a famous early psychologist. Aspects of his work were contentious, partly because some of his ideas were non-falsifiable, such as his ideas about our behaviour being the consequence of unconscious motives. It has been argued that one problem with unconscious motives is that they are impossible to test in an objective way. Here is a basic example: a young woman is slightly rude to a young man. Freud could use two different explanations. One is that the young woman unconsciously hates the young man, and she is avoiding being as rude as she unconsciously wants to be. The other is that the young woman unconsciously loves the young man, and she is avoiding showing her unconscious desire so is behaving in a contrary way. The problem here is that Freud cannot be wrong–either

she feels unconsciously positive or negative–both would fit with his explanations.

The main hypothesis in a study (sometimes called the **alternative hypothesis**) can be written in several different ways. They differ in terms of the nature of the prediction they make about the results of an investigation.

KEY WORDS

hypothesis (plural hypotheses): a testable statement based on the aims of an investigation

alternative hypothesis: the testable statement predicting a difference in the DV between levels of the independent variable in an experiment (or a relationship between variables in a correlation)

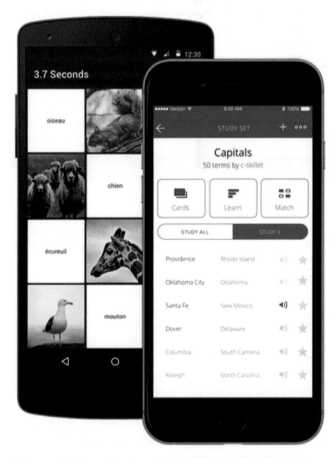

Figure 1.5: Revision apps such as Quizlet and Gojimo may, or may not, help students to learn

Hypotheses should have operationalised variables. For example, in the hypothesis 'Students using revision apps will learn better than students using mind maps', we do not know how 'better learning' will be measured, or which apps are being used because the variables are not operationalised. To be complete, the hypothesis needs more detail, such as 'Students using the Gojimo revision app will gain better test marks than students using mind maps.'

Non-directional hypotheses

A **non-directional (two-tailed) hypothesis** predicts that there will be an effect, but not the direction of that effect (Figure 1.6). In an experiment, this means that the hypothesis suggests that the IV will change the DV but not whether the effect will be an increase or a decrease. This type of hypothesis is chosen if the effect of the variable is being tested for the first time, so there are no previous results to suggest what the results might be. For example, Dr Huang's hypothesis could be: *There is a difference between the effectiveness of mind maps and revision apps in helping students to learn.* Note that it is predicting a difference, but not which condition will be better at helping with learning.

Figure 1.6: Unlike with a one-tailed hypothofish, you can't see which way a two-tailed hypothofish will swim

Directional hypotheses

When most previous research or other evidence suggests the nature or 'direction' of an effect we can use a **directional (one-tailed) hypothesis**. In an experiment, this means saying which condition will be 'best', i.e. produce the 'highest' scores (and in a correlational study, whether there will be a positive or negative correlation).

Returning to Dr Huang's study, there might be evidence that revision apps are better than mind maps, perhaps because they are more 'active' and being actively engaged helps memory. This is a directional prediction so the hypothesis might be: *Students using revision apps will learn better than students using mind maps.* Note that the opposite prediction could also be expressed as a directional hypothesis. This would be: *Students using mind maps will learn better than students using revision apps.* We might make this prediction if we believed that writing a mind map yourself was more effective than just re-using ready-made materials on revision apps.

Null hypotheses

The alternative hypothesis is an alternative to the **null hypothesis**. In an experiment, the null hypothesis states that any difference in the DV between levels of the IV is so small that it is likely to have arisen by chance. The concept of chance becomes important in 'inferential statistics'. These are mathematical processes used to find out how likely it is that the pattern of results (a difference or a correlation) found from the sample of participants could have arisen by chance. This information helps us to *infer* whether the findings would apply to the wider population. When you read about the core studies, the most important results are the 'significant' ones. This word has a particular meaning, that there is a mathematically significant probability that the pattern in the results could not have arisen by chance. So, when inferential statistics are used, a 'significant' pattern enables the researchers to reject their null hypothesis and accept their alternative hypothesis. If, on the other hand, the pattern in the results is non-significant, the researchers must accept their null hypothesis: that the difference or correlation could have arisen by chance.

There are two ways to write a null hypothesis for an experiment. In the case of Dr Huang's study, the null hypothesis could be written either as: *There will be no difference between the effectiveness of mind maps and revision apps in helping students to learn* or *Any difference in effectiveness of mind maps and revision apps in helping students to learn is due to chance.*

KEY WORDS

non-directional (two-tailed) hypothesis: a statement predicting only that one variable will be related to another, for example that there will be a difference in the DV between levels of the IV in an experiment (or that there will be a relationship between the measured variables in a correlation)

directional (one-tailed) hypothesis: a statement predicting the direction of a relationship between variables, for example in an experiment whether the levels of the IV will produce an increase or a decrease in the DV (or in a correlation whether an increase in one variable will be linked to an increase or a decrease in another variable)

null hypothesis: a testable statement saying that any difference or correlation in the results is due to chance, that is, that no pattern in the results has arisen because of the variables being studied

Ethics in experiments

The role of ethics in psychology is discussed in Section 1.10. Here we will briefly consider ethics in experiments (Figure 1.7). A participant in a laboratory experiment is likely to know that they are participating in a study and can readily be asked for their **informed consent**. However, for the sake of validity, it may be necessary to deceive them to avoid them working out the aim of the study and altering their behaviour, i.e. to reduce demand characteristics. There is therefore a need to balance good ethics and good science, such as high validity. In field experiments, in contrast, it may not be possible to gain consent as the participants may be unaware that they are even in a study. This is an ethical problem because participants should have the right to know what they are entering into and to agree to participate or not. They should also have the **right to withdraw**, which they cannot do if they do not even know that they are in a study. In order to achieve a balance between good science and good ethics, it is therefore very important that participants in a field experiment are effectively **protected from harm**.

In experiments, whether they are in a laboratory or the field, experimenters may sometimes need to actively lie to or mislead participants. This is called **deception** and may be necessary to reduce the risk of demand characteristics affecting participants. Deception should be avoided and, where possible, the reality of the study should be explained to the participants afterwards in a debrief. This is often much harder to do in a field experiment than a laboratory experiment and it may even be impossible. The use of deception should, however, be avoided if possible.

Figure 1.7: Researchers must achieve a balance between good ethics and good science

In all experiments, privacy and confidentiality are important. **Privacy** can be respected in laboratory experiments because the tests or questions used are pre-planned. In the natural settings of a field experiment, however, there is a risk of invading a participant's personal space, or perhaps discovering something that they wouldn't want the researcher to know so researchers must be careful of this. **Confidentiality** can be respected in all experiments by keeping the participants' data secure and anonymous, although if the participants are unaware that data has been collected, as in a field experiment, it is important to ensure that they cannot be individually identified, for example by their place of work.

> KEY WORDS
>
> **informed consent:** knowing enough about a study to decide whether you want to agree to participate
>
> **right to withdraw:** a participant should know they can remove themselves, and their data, from a study at any time
>
> **protection from harm:** participants should not be exposed to any greater physical or psychological risk than they would expect in their day-to-day life

> KEY WORDS
>
> **deception:** participants should not be deliberately misinformed (lied to) about the aim or procedure of the study. If this is unavoidable, the study should be planned to minimise the risk of distress, and participants should be thoroughly debriefed. It may be done to reduce the effects of demand characteristics but should be avoided
>
> **privacy:** participants' emotions and physical space should not be invaded, for example they should not be observed in situations or places where they would not expect to be seen
>
> **confidentiality:** participants' results and personal information should be kept safely and not released to anyone outside the study

RESEARCH METHODS IN PRACTICE

A psychology department ethical committee is looking at a research proposal for a study about the effect of cognitions on a therapy designed to help people to relax. The researchers only plan to ask for *consent* about part of procedure they will use – listening to an imagery-based relaxation recording – and not their full aim. Although they intend to tell all the participants they will have pulse monitors and be in darkened rooms, they also intend to use deception. They will *deceive* the participants about which level of the independent variable they will be allocated to. Rather than telling them what will really happen – their pulse rate should fall – the researchers will give them false information by telling them that some people see disturbing flashing lights. When the participants are given the limited information at the start of the study they will also be told that they can leave at any time, thus giving them the *right to withdraw*. The instructions on the recording tell the participants to imagine relaxing, intimate thoughts. The participants will also be reassured that they will not be asked about these thoughts, which ensures their *privacy* is protected. When the participants join the study, each will be given a number, which will be used to identify their data so that their names do not have to be used, ensuring their *confidentiality*.

ACTIVITY 1.5

Look at the Research methods in practice box. Which of the following can you identify?

- The type of *experiment* being planned
- The experimental condition of the independent variable
- The dependent variable
- The experimental design

Can you suggest one way in which participants would not be *protected from harm* in this study?

Suggest why participants may want to withdraw.

Why might it be necessary for the researchers to *deceive* the participants?

What is wrong with the hypothesis 'an imagery-based recording will help people to relax'?

Applying your knowledge of experiments to novel research situations

You should be able to recognise experiments (including the IV and DV, and be able to operationalise them, i.e. define them in detail), to decide whether an experiment is a laboratory or field experiment and to evaluate them, e.g. in terms of controls, standardisation, ethics, and reliability and validity.

In addition, you should be able to plan an experiment; choosing the type of experiment (laboratory or field), deciding on and operationalising an IV and a DV, choosing an experimental design and implementing suitable controls.

Questions

Barry and Anouk are deciding how to test whether gender affects artistic ability. Barry suggests doing a study in the psychology department where they ask students to come in for a study about memory in which they must redraw a complicated image. Barry and Anouk can then see how well they do it. Anouk thinks it would be better to persuade the art teacher to use an art class and set a lesson where students have to copy the same complicated image.

1   Explain the type of experiment that is being suggested:
    a   by Barry
    b   by Anouk.
2   The independent variable is the same in Barry's and Anouk's studies, as is the dependent variable.
    a   Describe the independent variable (IV).
    b   Describe the dependent variable (DV).
3   Explain **one** ethical issue that is clear from the procedure that Barry suggested.
4   Suggest **one other** ethical issue and how they could avoid problems with this issue.

1.2 Self-reports

In a **self-report**, the participant gives the researcher information about themselves directly. This is different from experimental tests or observations where the researcher finds the data out from the participant. There are two main ways to conduct a self-report: using a questionnaire or an interview. Both types of self-report allow the researcher to ask the participant questions.

Questionnaires

In a **questionnaire**, the questions are presented to the participant in written form. The two techniques for doing this are as a 'paper and pencil' exercise or online. There are several different types of question. The two most important question formats are **closed questions**, which have a fixed set of possible responses, and **open questions**, which ask for descriptive answers in the participant's own words.

Closed questions can take the form of simple choices, such as those asking for yes/no answers or items from a list. Other forms of closed questions include rating scales (where a number is chosen, e.g. between 0 and 5) and Likert scales, which ask the respondent to say how much they agree with a statement such as 'Obesity is not important' or 'Exercise is a necessity' using the choices 'strongly agree / agree / neither agree nor disagree / disagree / strongly disagree'. Some examples of closed questions are as follows:

- What is your gender: boy or girl?
- How do you travel to school? walk / bicycle / bus / train / car
- Indicate which animal(s) scare you: dog, spider, cat, rat, fish, rabbit, bird. [You may tick as many as you like]
- How much do you like psychology on a scale of 0–4? (0 = not at all, 4 = very much)

> ## KEY WORDS
>
> **self-report:** a research method, such as a questionnaire or interview, which obtains data by asking participants to provide information about themselves
>
> **questionnaire:** a self-report research method that uses written questions through a 'paper and pencil' or online technique

> ## KEY WORDS
>
> **closed questions:** a question format in questionnaires, interviews or test items that produces quantitative data. They have only a few, stated alternative responses and no opportunity to expand on answers
>
> **open questions:** a question format in questionnaires, interviews or test items that produces qualitative data. Participants give full and detailed answers in their own words, that is, no categories or choices are given

Open questions prompt the respondent to give detailed answers, which may be quite long. They contain more depth than the answers to closed questions and are more likely to be able to explore the reasons behind behaviours, emotions or reasoning. They typically ask 'Why…?' or simply 'Describe…'. Some examples of open questions are as follows:

- Why do you believe it is important to help people who suffer from phobias?
- Describe your views on the use of social media sites with regard to encouraging helping behaviour.
- Explain how you would respond if you were told to hurt another person.

Evaluating questionnaires

Questionnaires, which often use mainly closed questions, are fairly easy to analyse as they produce a total of each category of answers making it simple to summarise the findings. It is also possible to work out averages, which can help to describe the patterns in the results. Where qualitative data is gathered from questionnaires, it produces more detailed, in-depth information. This is an advantage, although it also leads to a problem. Answers to open questions have to be interpreted, and this can lead to a lack of reliability as the researcher may not be consistent in their interpretation. If more than one researcher is involved, there may also be differences between them. This would be a lack of **inter-rater reliability**.

> ## KEY WORD
>
> **inter-rater reliability:** the extent to which two researchers interpreting qualitative responses in a questionnaire (or interview) will produce the same records from the same raw data

Another problem with questionnaires is that it is easy for participants to ignore them, which means the return rate may be very low. Importantly, the people who do reply to a questionnaire may all be quite similar, for example have time to spend because they are unemployed or retired. This would mean all the people who filled out the questionnaire would have shared characteristics making applying the findings to other people less appropriate, i.e. could result in poor **generalisability**.

Another problem with questionnaires is that participants may lie. They may do this because they want to look more acceptable; this is called a **social desirability bias** (Figure 1.8). Participants may also lie if they believe they have worked out the aim of the study. To avoid this, researchers sometimes include **filler questions** among the real questions. The answers to filler questions are not analysed in the research since they serve only to hide the real purpose of the study.

Figure 1.8: People may lie in questionnaires, lowering validity, for example giving socially desirable responses to questionnaires about eating habits

KEY WORDS

generalisability: how widely findings apply, e.g. to other settings and populations

social desirability bias: trying to present oneself in the best light by determining how to respond to the task in a way that would be most acceptable to other people, rather than to the researcher

filler questions: items put into a questionnaire, interview or test to disguise the aim of the study by hiding the important questions among irrelevant ones so that participants are less likely to work out the aims and then alter their behaviour

RESEARCH METHODS IN PRACTICE

Dr Huang is a psychology teacher. She wanted to know how her students were progressing on the course. She decided to use the *self-report* method and used an online *questionnaire* that the students did in their free time to collect data. This included several *closed questions* (see questions 1–4 which follow), which collected quantitative data, and some *open questions* (questions 5 and 6), which collected qualitative data. She asked her colleague to help her to interpret the responses to the open questions and to help to ensure that they had good *inter-rater reliability*, she devised a list to help them to interpret questions 5 and 6. For question 5, it included looking for comments about:

* reading up notes
* copying out notes

* reading the textbook
* looking things up online
* asking friends
* checking with the teacher.

For question 6, it included looking for comments about:

* copying out notes
* making summary notes
* making mind maps
* using past paper questions
* making test cards.

CONTINUED

Some of the questions on the questionnaire were:

1   How often do you do the homework set?

    always ☐ *sometimes* ☐ *never* ☐

2   Have you written yourself a research methods glossary?

    yes ☐ *no* ☐

3   'Psychology is a difficult subject.' Do you:

    strongly agree ☐ *agree* ☐ *neither agree nor disagree* ☐ *disagree* ☐ *strongly disagree* ☐

4   Rate from 0 to 6 how well you understand the topic we have just completed:

    0 = don't understand at all ☐

    6 = completely understand ☐

5   Explain what you do after each lesson to help you to remember what you have learned.

6   Describe how you will plan your revision for the next test.

ACTIVITY 1.6

Look at the Research methods in practice box.

- Explain the difference between the *open* and *closed questions*.

- Suggest *one* more open question.

- Suggest one more closed question.

- Suggest why Dr Huang may have chosen to use an *online* questionnaire rather than one the students did on paper in the classroom.

- Explain why it was important that Dr Huang took steps to raise *inter-rater reliability*.

Interviews

An **interview** is a research method in which the researcher can use two alternative techniques. Typically they are face-to-face with the participant but the interview can also happen via the telephone. Interviews can, however, be conducted in other ways that allow real-time interaction, such as through a chat facility. The same formats of questions can be asked in interviews as in questionnaires, although often interviews use more open questions than closed questions.

The schedule of questions, that is the range of questions that are asked and the order of them, differs between different interview formats. In a **structured interview**, the questions asked are the same for every participant and the order is fixed. There may even be instructions for the interviewer about their tone of voice, how to sit or how to dress so that the procedure is standardised each time

data is collected. In an **unstructured interview**, in contrast, the questions asked depend on what the participant says, so the questions may be different for each participant. This is a very flexible format but it may be hard to compare data collected from different participants or by different researchers. A compromise is a **semi-structured interview**. Here, there are some fixed questions, which make sure that there is some similar information from every participant. This means that comparisons can be made between them, and averages can be calculated if this is appropriate. In addition, it is possible to ask some questions that are specific to individual participants. This allows the researcher to develop ideas and explore issues that are particular to that person.

KEY WORDS

interview: a research method using verbal questions asked directly, using techniques such as face to face or telephone

structured interview: an interview format using questions in a fixed order that may be scripted. Consistency might also be required for the interviewer's posture, voice, etc. so they are standardised

unstructured interview: an interview format in which most questions (after the first one) depend on the respondent's answers. A list of topics may be given to the interviewer

semi-structured interview: an interview format using a fixed list of open and closed questions. The interviewer can add more questions if necessary

Evaluating interviews

As with questionnaires, interviewees may lie either because they want to seem more acceptable (a social desirability bias) or because they think they know the aim of the study and are either trying to help the researcher by giving the answers they need, or to disrupt the research by doing the opposite. Interviewing is often time consuming and this can be a problem if it restricts the types of participant who volunteer for the research because it would give a narrow representation of feelings, beliefs or experiences.

When interpreting participants' responses to questions in an interview, researchers must be careful not to be subjective, that is, to produce findings which are based on their personal perspective. Instead, they should aim for objectivity, i.e. taking a view that is not led by their own feelings or beliefs. To achieve this, the interviewer may ask other researchers, who are experienced but unaware of the aims of their research, to interpret the findings.

how the method used affects the availability of different types of participant and their honesty, as this affects the validity of the findings.

You should also think about the kinds of data that are produced, and the way the data will be used. Although numerical data from closed questions can be analysed mathematically, data from open questions provides more in-depth information that may be more valid. For example, a closed question might not have a response close to a person's view, whereas an open question would allow that person to express views that they could not do in the choices available in the closed question.

The reliability of self-report data is also important. Questionnaires and structured interviews may be higher in reliability because they are likely to be administered in a consistent way and because they generate numerical results that do not need interpretation. Responses to open questions, in contrast, have to be interpreted by the researcher and since the researchers may differ in their opinions there is the possibility that they will be subjective.

Finally, you should be able to plan a study using a self-report and be able to write questions in different formats (open or closed) for either research method (a questionnaire or an interview). For a questionnaire, you should be able to describe how to plan a questionnaire with a pencil and paper or online format. For an interview, you need to be able to describe how to conduct an interview using each of the formats (structured, semi-structured and unstructured) and either of the techniques (telephone or face to face).

KEY WORDS

subjectivity: the effect of an individual's personal viewpoint on, for example, how they interpret data. Interpretation can differ between individual researchers as a viewpoint may be biased by one's feelings, beliefs or experiences, so is not independent of the situation

objectivity: the impact of an unbiased external viewpoint on, for example, how data is interpreted. Interpretation is not affected by an individual's feelings, beliefs or experiences, so should be consistent between different researchers

---

Applying your knowledge of self-reports to novel research situations

You should be able to recognise self-report studies and decide whether they use questionnaires or interviews as a method. You should also be able to choose which of these to use in a new situation. In addition, you should be able to recognise questions using different formats (open and closed) and to identify and evaluate different interview formats (structured, semi-structured and unstructured) and techniques (telephone or face to face). When doing this, it is important to consider

---

RESEARCH METHODS IN PRACTICE

Dr Singh is planning an *interview*-based study because he wants to confirm that a new shopping centre layout is making people more helpful to each other. He wants to collect objective data about the number of times people are helpful so has devised a *structured interview* with a list of specific questions such as 'How many times has someone held a door open for you? once, twice, three times or more.' 'Have you helped anyone carry their shopping? yes / no.' and 'Have you seen anyone assisting a parent with a buggy? yes / no.' However, he is worried that this may produce very limited data so has an alternative plan to use an *unstructured interview*. This would begin with the question 'Please can you describe how friendly or helpful you have found people to be at the new shopping centre', after which he would base his

CONTINUED

questions on what they said. A colleague, Dr McArthur suggests that both methods have limitations. Interpreting the responses to the unstructured interview might lead to very *subjective* data, especially as Dr Singh already believes the finding that the new shopping centre layout encourages helpfulness. Although the data from the closed questions in the structured interview might produce more objective measures, this would limit opportunities for asking participants to expand on their answers. The colleague suggests that a *semi-structured interview* might be better.

ACTIVITY 1.7

Look at the previous Research methods in practice box.

- Why is the first of Dr Singh's suggestions a *structured interview*?

- Why would the data from these questions be more *objective*?

- Why is the second plan an *unstructured interview*?

- What is the problem with *subjective* interpretations of the participants' responses in the unstructured interview?

- Suggest why a *semi-structured interview* would be better in this case.

Questions

5   Shareen and Judith are investigating people's phobias. They have decided to use self-reports. Shareen is suggesting using a questionnaire and Judith wants to interview people instead.

   a   Suggest **one** closed question and **one** open question that Shareen could use.

   b   Suggest **one** reason why Judith might want to conduct an unstructured interview.

   c   Describe **one** ethical problem that might arise in **either** Shareen's **or** Judith's version of the study.

1.3 Case studies

A **case study** is a detailed investigation of a single instance, usually just one person, although it could be a single family or institution. The data collected is detailed and in-depth, and may be obtained using a variety of different techniques. For example, in one case study, a participant may be interviewed, observed, given tests and asked to fill in questionnaires. Case studies are particularly useful for looking at rare cases where a detailed description is useful, and for following developmental changes where the progress of a child, or a person with a disorder, can be tracked through their improvement or decline. Case studies are therefore sometimes linked to therapy but it is important to remember that when the case study as a research method is being discussed, the therapeutic purpose is not the main aim.

In addition to using different methods or techniques within a case study, different sources of evidence may be used. These could include interviewing the participant themselves, their relatives or other people such as colleagues to obtain a wide range of information about the individual's history, as well as accessing pre-existing information such as medical or school records.

Evaluating case studies

In some ways, the findings from case studies are highly valid, as the individual is explored in great depth and within a genuine context such as their work or family. Validity may be improved further using **triangulation**, where the use of different techniques should produce similar findings, for example observations and interviews with the participant and questionnaires for their family should all lead to similar conclusions.

KEY WORDS

case study: a research method in which a single instance, e.g. one person, family or institution, is studied in detail

triangulation: is when different techniques, e.g. observations, interviews and tests, are used to study the same phenomenon. If they produce similar results, this suggests the findings are valid

The research includes details such as the participant's past as well as their present situation, their social interactions, their thinking and their emotions as well as their behaviours. Such detail, however, carries risks. One potential problem is the development of a close relationship with the researcher. This may make the researcher subjective in their outlook, which would reduce the validity of the study. The level of detail can also be an ethical threat, as the questions asked may intrude into the participant's private life and they may feel unable to refuse to answer them. The detail about the individual may make it hard to disguise their identity, even if they are not referred to by name, which would risk breaking the guideline of confidentiality.

Reliability is also an issue, as there is a single participant and perhaps one or only a few researchers. This, and their involvement with the case, means that they may find it hard to be objective, that is to take an external, unbiased view of the findings, for example when they interpret what the participant has said. So, a different researcher, with a truly external viewpoint, might interpret the findings differently. In addition, the findings are specific to the individual being studied so may only apply to very few other instances, or to none at all, i.e. the generalisability of findings from a case study is very limited.

Applying your knowledge of case studies to novel research situations

You should be able to recognise case studies, and when it is appropriate to use one. You should also be able to suggest possible techniques that could be used in a case study. When making these decisions, it is important to consider the validity and reliability of the findings. One way that the validity can be improved is through triangulation, where different methods are used within the case study to obtain the same information: for example, finding out about the participant's behaviour by observing them, interviewing them and asking their relatives to fill out a questionnaire. If the same results are obtained by all the methods, this suggests that the results are valid. Another consideration in planning case studies is an ethical one. Participants should be aware of their commitment so that they can give their informed consent, and particular attention should be paid to ensuring their privacy is not invaded and that confidentiality is maintained.

In addition to being able to evaluate the case study method, you should be able to plan a case study. This could involve giving details about the participant (or instance such as a family or institution) you would choose, and describing a range of methods and techniques you would use in your study to enable triangulation. You would also need to be able to explain how you would plan the analysis and interpretation of the results.

RESEARCH METHODS IN PRACTICE

A psychologist in a sleep clinic has been conducting a *case study* on a patient, PMA, who has had very bad dreams for several years. The clinic has a sleep laboratory where sleeping patients can be videoed to record behaviours such as sleep-talking and sleep-walking. The psychologist uses an EEG (electroencephalograph – a machine that records brain waves) to follow PMA's sleep cycles and to detect when the patient is dreaming. The patient is then woken up and asked about their emotional state and what the dream is about. A test is also conducted when the patient is not dreaming, they are again woken up and asked about their emotional state. PMA has been asked to keep a dream diary to record when the bad dreams occur. Members of PMA's family have been interviewed to find out when the problems with nightmares started and how often they occur.

ACTIVITY 1.8

If you can, work in a pair. Individually, look at the Research methods in practice box and answer the following questions or share the questions between you with one person doing the even-numbered questions and one person doing the odd-numbered questions.

1   How many different methods and techniques can you identify?

2   Give **two** reasons why this is a case study.

3   The psychologist is concerned that if the patient PMA wanted to *withdraw* from the study, this might be quite difficult. Explain why this might be so.

4   Explain the *ethical* reason for the researcher referring to the patient as PMA.

5   Suggest one **other** ethical issue that might be a problem in this study.

6   Suggest **one** methodological issue that might be a problem in this study.

Peer assessment

In your pairs, look at the answers given by your partner. Consider the following points for each question:

1   Is each of the ideas given a research method or a technique? Are there any others?

2   There are only two features that make a study a case study. Do they have them both? Are other features, which are not strictly necessary for a case study, also included?

3   Is the explanation complete?

4   Check the reason given. It should be 'confidentiality' not 'privacy'. Why would 'privacy' be incorrect?

5   Is the ethical issue suggested relevant to this study? If so, why? If not, why not?

6   Is the methodological issue suggested relevant to this study? If so, why? If not, why not?

Questions

6   Damon and Inka are planning a case study of a person living with a disability, to investigate responses to situations involving help.

   a   Suggest **three** techniques that Damon and Inka might use in their case study.

   b   i   Describe **two** ethical problems that might arise in the study that Damon and Inka are planning.

      ii   For **one** of these problems, suggest a possible solution.

   c   Explain whether the results from Damon and Inka's study would be typical of the way everyone would respond to such situations.

1.4 Observations

Observations involve watching human or animal participants. There are many different choices in the way that observations are conducted and we will consider each in turn. An awareness of these choices is important both for understanding and planning observational studies. The setting in which the observation takes place is one such choice. A **naturalistic observation** is conducted in the participants' normal environment, without interference from the researchers in either the social or physical environment. A **controlled observation** is conducted in a situation that has been manipulated by the researchers. This may be in terms of the social environment, such as varying group sizes or adding a model, or in terms of the physical environment, such as providing objects for play, different foods or new locations. Controlled observations can be done in either the participants' normal environment or in an artificial situation such as a laboratory.

KEY WORDS

naturalistic observation: a study conducted by watching the participants' behaviour in their normal environment without interference from the researchers in either the social or physical environment

controlled observation: a study conducted by watching the participants' behaviour in a situation in which the social or physical environment has been manipulated by the researchers. It can be conducted in either the participants' normal environment or in an artificial situation

KEY WORDS

KEY WORDS

unstructured observation: a study in which the observer records the whole range of possible behaviours, which is usually confined to a pilot stage at the beginning of a study to refine the behavioural categories to be observed

structured observation: a study in which the observer records only a limited range of behaviours

behavioural categories: the activities recorded in an observation. They should be operationalised (clearly defined) and should break a continuous stream of activity into discrete recordable events. They must be observable actions rather than inferred states

At the beginning of a study, observations may be non-focused, that is, the whole range of possible behaviours is considered. If this continues throughout the study, it is called an **unstructured observation**. More often, the range being studied is narrowed to a fixed set of behaviours, a technique is called a **structured observation**. The specific activities to be recorded are clearly defined in **behavioural categories**. This helps the observers to be consistent, i.e. it improves **inter-observer reliability**.

Another decision to be made is the role of the observer in the social setting. This may be participant or non-participant. A **participant observer** is part of the social setting so may, for example, engage in conversation with adults or play with children. A **non-participant observer** does not become involved in the situation being studied. This can be achieved by watching through one-way glass or by keeping apart from the social group of the participants, for example by sitting in a separate place such as a bench in a park.

KEY WORDS

inter-observer reliability: the consistency between two researchers watching the same event, i.e. whether they will produce the same records

participant observer: a researcher who watches from the perspective of being part of the social setting

non-participant observer: a researcher who does not become involved in the situation being studied

The role played by the observer may be either **overt** (it is obvious that they are an observer) or **covert** (they are hidden or disguised so the participants do not know the individual is an observer). A participant observer would be overt, if they were holding a clipboard. When a participant observer is disguised as a member of the social group (Figure 1.9), or when a non-participant observer is physically hidden (e.g. by using CCTV), they are covert.

Participants cannot be aware that they are being watched if the observer is covert. This increases validity as it is unlikely that participants would be affected by being observed, so demand characteristics and the effects of social desirability are reduced. However, covert observations raise practical issues, as the observer must be either hidden, far away or disguised in their role. This may make data collection more difficult, potentially reducing validity and reliability. Furthermore, covert observation raises ethical issues as the participants cannot give informed consent, and if they work out a participant observer's role this can cause distress.

KEY WORDS

overt observer: the role of the observer is obvious to the participants

covert observer: the role of the observer is not obvious, e.g. because they are hidden or disguised

Figure 1.9: A covert participant observer is disguised by being part of the social group

Evaluating observations

Naturalistic observations have the advantage that the behaviours seen are true to life. They are more likely to reflect the way the individuals really behave than if there is interference in the situation from researchers, as is the case in controlled observations. However, there is no guarantee that the behaviours being studied will actually occur in a naturalistic situation, so it may be necessary to use a controlled observation.

Using an unstructured observation ensures that any important behaviours that happen are recognised and recorded. However, it may be very difficult to collect data on all the activities accurately and many behaviours may be irrelevant to the aims of the study. It is therefore likely, especially when only specific activities are of interest, that a structured observation will produce more reliable data as the observer will only need to focus on a small number of categories.

The role played by the observer, and the participants' awareness of this, affect validity. If participants are unaware of the observer, or can ignore them, their activities are more likely to reflect their normal behaviour. This means that covert observers would produce more valid results than overt ones. However, in the case of covert participant observers there is an ethical issue of deception. The participants may interact with the observer in ways that they might have chosen not to if they had been aware that the individual was a researcher. This could invade their privacy and cause harm by distressing them. However, an overt observer may alter the behaviour of the participants as they are aware that they are being watched. This would reduce the validity of the findings as the activities being recorded are less likely to reflect real-world behaviour.

Applying your knowledge of observations to novel research situations

Observations can be used either as a research method or as a means to collect data in other research methods such as case studies, experiments or correlations. You should be able to distinguish between these two situations. Observation is being used as a research method in itself when the study consists solely of a means to collect data by watching participants and recording their behaviour directly to provide data. Observations are used as a technique to collect data about variables in other research methods when they are used to measure the dependent variable in an experiment or one or both variables in a correlation. In a case study, observations can be used alongside other techniques to explore a single instance in detail.

You will need to be able to decide when it is appropriate to use observations as a method, or as a technique within other methods. You should be able to recognise and justify choices about naturalistic versus controlled, structured versus unstructured, participant versus non-participant and covert versus overt observations. You will also need to be able to suggest ways of achieving these, such as how to make an observer participant, or covert.

In addition to being able to select and evaluate the observational method and the different techniques, you should be able to plan studies using any of the techniques in a way that is appropriate to a given aim. All of the 'technique' decisions (e.g. naturalistic, structured, participant, overt) need to be made for every observation. So, you may need to choose and describe the location for a naturalistic observation or how the environment will be controlled; the behavioural categories to be recorded in a structured observation; how observers would aim to be included in the social setting (participant observation) or avoid the social setting (non-participant) and how an observer could be made covert.

RESEARCH METHODS IN PRACTICE

Dr Huang is interested in whether her students detect each other's emotions and plans a *controlled observation*. She asks three students to act as confederates. They are told to take it in turns to appear quite sad in the common room at lunchtime. Dr Huang is on lunch duty with a colleague so they can act as *non-participant*, *overt* observers as they walk through the common room. The students will take no notice of them as they are used to them being there. Dr Huang suggests that she and her colleague use a list of specific behaviours to record, so they are doing a *structured observation*. This will also help to raise *inter-observer reliability* as they will be working from the same definitions, such as recording 'shows concern without action' if people look at the confederate without moving towards them, 'verbalises concern' if someone goes up to the confederate and asks them if they are OK and 'takes action' if they engage in a behaviour such as putting their arm round the confederate or buying them a drink.

ACTIVITY 1.9

Look at the Research methods in practice box.

- Suggest **one** other *behavioural category* that might have been included in the structured observation and define it.

- If Dr Huang had conducted an *unstructured observation*, how would the method have differed?

- An alternative plan would have been to have conducted a *naturalistic observation* and watched to see if any students appeared to be sad and how others responded. Outline **one** way it would have been ethically more acceptable and **one** way in which it would have been ethically less acceptable.

- Suggest how Dr Huang could have used a *participant, covert observer* rather than being an overt observer.

Questions

7 Debra and Jin want to use observations to find out about the behaviour of animals. Debra wants to go to the park and hide in a tree to observe the animals that live there. Jin thinks it would be better to set up an artificial situation and watch laboratory rats interacting with objects they would put in a special box.

    a Who is suggesting a naturalistic observation and who is suggesting a controlled observation?

    b Explain whether the observers in Debra's study would be overt or covert.

    c For either Debra's or Jin's suggestion, decide whether it should be conducted as an unstructured or a structured observation and justify your choice.

1.5 Correlations

A correlational analysis is a technique used to investigate a link between two **co-variables** (measured variables). **Correlations** are useful when it is possible only to measure variables, rather than manipulate them, i.e. when an experiment cannot be conducted. This may be because changing the variables would not be practical or would be unethical. For example, it would

not be practical or ethical to conduct an experiment which controlled children's long-term exposure to television and it would not be ethical to increase real-life exposure to violent television programmes. Both of these could, however, be investigated using correlations. Real-life exposure of a group of children to violent television could be measured and correlated with another measured variable, such as how aggressive their behaviour was in school.

KEY WORDS

co-variables: the two measured variables in a correlation

correlation: a research method that looks for a relationship between two measured variables. A change in one variable is related to a change in the other (although these changes cannot be assumed to be causal)

causal relationship: a link between two variables such that a change in one variable is responsible for (i.e. causes) the change in the other variable, such as in an experiment

To look for a correlation between two variables, each variable must exist over a range, sometimes called 'continuous data', and it must be possible to measure them numerically. Suitable variables would include durations of time, totals of tallies, numbers from a rating scale or test scores. Several techniques can be used to collect data for correlations, such as self-reports, observations and different kinds of tests and tasks.

It is important to recognise that any link found between two variables in a correlation cannot be assumed to be a **causal relationship**, that is, we cannot know whether the change in one variable is *responsible* for the change in the other variable (Figure 1.10). This is possible in the case of an experiment, as we can know that there is a causal relationship between the IV and the DV because changes in the IV are shown to be the cause of changes in the DV.

However, we cannot say from one correlation that an increase in one variable has caused an increase (or decrease) in the other because it is possible that the changes in both variables could be the result of another factor. Imagine that two variables are being measured: attention in class and score on a test. If these co-variables correlate it would be tempting to say that paying attention in class is responsible for good test

Figure 1.10: A bizarre positive correlation has been reported between ice cream consumption and murder rates. This relationship is a correlation, however, so we cannot conclude that eating ice cream causes people to commit murder

results but we cannot be sure of this. It could be that both of these factors depend on a third variable, such how hard-working the individual student is. The sort of student who pays more attention in class might also study much harder for the test. All we can conclude is that the two factors we have measured vary together, not that there is a cause-and-effect or causal relationship between them. As a consequence, it is important that you refer to 'co-variables' or 'measured variables' in a correlation and not independent and dependent variables. To make judgements about causality, an experiment must be used, so that we can be more certain that it is the manipulation of one variable that is responsible for the change in the other. If, on the other hand, we conduct a correlational study and find that there is *no* link between two variables, then we can conclude that there is no causal relationship.

The nature of the relationship between the two variables in a correlation can be described in terms of its *direction*. In a positive correlation, the two variables increase together. The change is in the same direction, so higher scores on one variable correspond with higher scores on the other. For example, in a positive correlation between exposure to aggressive models and violent behaviour, greater exposure to models would be linked to higher levels of violence. When two variables are negatively correlated, higher scores on one variable correspond with lower scores on the other. For example, a negative correlation might exist between number of years in education and level of obedience: people with fewer years of education are more obedient

(see also Section 1.9 on how to draw a scatter graph and a discussion of the *strength* of a correlation).

KEY WORDS

positive correlation: a relationship between two variables in which an increase in one accompanies an increase in the other, i.e. the two variables increase together

negative correlation: a relationship between two variables in which an increase in one accompanies a decrease in the other, i.e. higher scores on one variable correspond with lower scores on the other

Hypotheses in correlational studies

As with hypotheses in experimental studies, a hypothesis in a correlational study needs to operationalise the co-variables as it predicts that there will be a relationship between them. The hypothesis 'There will be a correlation between amount of sleep and emotional reactivity' does not operationalise either variable. This could be improved by saying 'There will be a correlation between the number of hours a person sleeps for and their emotional reactivity indicated by how loudly they cry during a sad film.'

At the beginning of this chapter, we considered Dr Huang's idea that there could be a link between computer-game playing and A Level performance. A non-directional hypothesis in a correlational study testing this idea could predict that *There will be a correlation between the number of computer games a student plays and their final A Level grade*. Both of the co-variables are operationalised here.

A directional hypothesis for this study could say: *There will be a negative correlation between the number of computer games a student plays and their final A Level grade*. We may make this prediction if we believed that the time spent playing games might stop students working. However, a different directional hypothesis could be: *As the number of computer games a student plays increases, their A Level grade increases*. We might make this prediction if we believed that students who engaged more with technology, even through games, were also more likely to benefit from technology-based learning aids. Remember that hypotheses in correlational studies should not say that one factor *causes* the change in the other.

Evaluating correlations

A correlational study can only be valid if the measures of both variables test real phenomena in effective ways. To achieve this, the variables must be clearly defined and relate directly to the relationship being investigated, making them valid. The reliability of a correlation depends on the measures of both variables being consistent. So, for some correlations, such as those using scientific scales, such as volume in cm³ or time in seconds, the measures will be highly reliable. In other cases, such as studies correlating variables measured using self-reports or observations, there is a risk that reliability will be lower. This is because results from these measures may be less objective than from scientific measurements. The main issue with correlations, however, is to remember that the conclusions do *not* necessarily reflect a causal relationship.

Applying your knowledge of correlations to novel research situations

Correlations provide a good starting point for research. They can indicate whether a relationship exists that might be worth pursuing with other research methods, such as experiments. Correlations are also useful because they enable researchers to explore problems when it is not practically or ethically possible to conduct experiments. You should be able to distinguish between correlations (with *two* co-variables which are both measured) and experiments (where there is one variable–the IV–that is manipulated by the researcher and only *one* that is measured: the DV). You should also be able to recognise the difference between positive and negative correlations.

You will need to be able to decide when it is appropriate to use a correlation rather than any other method, for example when it is impossible to manipulate variables for practical or ethical reasons. You should also be able to justify choices about ways to measure the variables in a correlation and to suggest whether you would expect a positive or a negative correlation in a study. Finally, you will need to understand how to display the results of a

correlational study on a scatter graph. This is discussed in Section 1.9.

In addition to being able to select and evaluate the correlational method, you should be able to plan studies using a correlation in a way that is appropriate to a given aim. Remember that you must create two co-variables that can each be measured on a scale. So, you may need to choose a technique for measuring these, which could be different for each variable, for example by using a test or a questionnaire, interview or observation that produces quantitative data.

RESEARCH METHODS IN PRACTICE

Professor Chao is studying phobias. She thinks that there may be a *correlation* between how long a phobia has lasted and how severe it is. She is asking her sample of participants with phobias to record how many years they have suffered with their fear and rate how much the phobia interferes with their life on a scale of 1 (hardly at all) to 10 (almost constantly and prevents me from functioning normally). When looking for a link between the co-variables, there are several possible outcomes. One is that there may be a *positive correlation*: phobias that have lasted longer may be more severe. Another is that there is no relationship between the two variables. If so, when she plotted the results on a *scatter graph*, the points would appear randomly placed, rather than lying on a line.

ACTIVITY 1.10

Look at the Research methods in practice box.

- An alternative outcome might have been that phobias that have lasted longer are less severe. Explain why this is a negative correlation.

- If Professor Chao had written a hypothesis for a negative correlation saying *Phobias that last longer will be less severe* what would it need to make it complete?

- If Professor Chao found a positive correlation, it would be tempting, but incorrect, to say that the passage of time makes phobias worse. Why would this conclusion be incorrect?

Questions

8 Ekua and Takis are going to find out if there is a correlation between the amount of coffee people drink and the number of dreams they recall.

   a   Explain why this is a correlational study and not an experiment.

   b   Suggest whether the results will show a positive correlation or a negative correlation.

   c   i   Suggest **one** way to measure the amount of coffee that people drink.

       ii Explain either **one** strength or **one** weakness of the way you have suggested measuring this variable.

1.6 Longitudinal studies

A **longitudinal study** is one that follows a single group of participants over time, studying one or more variables at intervals. By measuring variables over weeks, months, years or even decades, a longitudinal study can detect changes in individuals. People change over time, not just as they age but as they accumulate life experiences. In addition, longitudinal studies can explore the effect of specific 'experiences' such as interventions or events on development.

The use of longitudinal studies is an alternative to cross-sectional studies as a way to look at effects over time. In a **cross-sectional study**, differences between people of differing ages, or at different stages (such as different periods after an intervention) are explored by comparing different groups at one point in time. For example, to explore changes in mindfulness with age, a cross-sectional study could look at 10-, 20-, 30-, 40- and 50-year-olds. Although a cross-sectional study allows researchers to investigate long-term influences, it is difficult to separate changes over time from differences due to the individuals growing up at different times. For example, if a cross-sectional study looking at helpfulness in people of different ages found a pattern in the results, this could be due to differences in upbringing at the time when they were children or the changing expectations of society rather than their age. Such problems are avoided in a longitudinal study as a single **cohort**, a group of participants all selected at the same age or stage, are chosen and tested at different time points. A cohort might be individuals born in a certain year, people about

to embark on a course of treatment, such as a new drug regime or people experiencing a life change, such as at the beginning of a pregnancy.

Longitudinal studies may have different intentions or designs. Some studies track patterns of change in variables to investigate them, such as changing emotions or beliefs as we get older. Other studies record longitudinal changes in two or more variables to investigate possible correlations between them, such as exposure to a multicultural society and prejudice. Yet others use an experimental design where one or more variables, measured over an extended period of time, are expected to change as a consequence of a deliberate manipulation. In the last case, the variables being measured are dependent variables and the testing at different time points in relation to the deliberate manipulation is an independent variable. To provide a baseline for tracking long-term change, the variable is usually measured at the outset of the study, and again after one or more periods of time. This procedure can be thought of as a very long-term repeated measures design, so is sometimes referred to as a 'quasi-experimental' design. This procedure can be used, for example, to measure the consequences of interventions such as educational, health, mental health or occupational ones that aim to improve outcomes. One level of the independent variable is the baseline test or 'pre-intervention' time point and one or more repeat testing sessions occur, providing a 'post-intervention' level of the independent variable and possibly more time points during or long after the intervention as a follow-up.

KEY WORDS

longitudinal study: a research method that follows a group of participants over time, weeks to decades, looking at changes in variables to explore development or changes due to experiences, such as interventions, drugs or therapies

cross-sectional study: compares people at different ages or stages by comparing different groups of participants at one point in time

cohort: a group of participants selected at the same age or stage

Evaluating longitudinal studies

A longitudinal study has the clear advantage over a cross-sectional study in that researches can be confident any changes they detect are due to the passage of time and not the effect of differences between the cohorts of participants representing each age or stage. This has two benefits. **Longitudinal designs**, like repeated measures designs, retest the same individuals. This means that the researchers can be confident that differences are not due to participant variables. A second consequence is that it also overcomes potential confounding variables. For example, in the Terman study of highly intelligent children (see Figure 1.11), differences in educational methods, career opportunities and other societal factors that could have been problematic in a cross-sectional study would not influence this longitudinal study. Confounding variables such as this, which are aspects of the environment, are called **situational variables**. This method is therefore the most valid test of developmental changes.

Figure 1.11: Lewis Terman, who began a long-running longitudinal study in 1922

A very long-running longitudinal study is the Terman Life Cycle Study of Children with High Ability, which began in 1922. Although the study eventually debunked the myth that a high **intelligence quotient (IQ)** inevitably leads to success, some of its participants did become famous, such as the psychologist Lee Cronbach, who specialised in psychological testing and measurement, became president of the American PsychologicalAssociation.

However, precisely because longitudinal studies last for a long time, the sample size is likely to fall; this is called **sample attrition**. Terman's initial sample, in 1922, was 1528 children. In a comparison between data collected in 1996 and 1999, although 162 questionnaires were returned in 1999 just 119 participants provided data on both occasions (Holahan & Velasquez, 2011). Where did they go? Participants may leave studies for many reasons, but these tend to be more apparent in a longitudinal study. They include: growing older and deciding to withdraw consent (e.g. when consent was originally given by a parent), boredom (from being repeatedly tested), moving home and becoming uncontactable, life events that prevent participation (poor physical or mental health, lack of time, becoming homeless or going to prison) and, ultimately, dying.

A smaller sample is likely to be less representative, but especially so in this case. Sample attrition means that generalisability is progressively threatened as the sample becomes concentrated on willing, motivated, people who live stable, healthy, law-abiding lives. These people may not be the most psychologically interesting! The people who stay in a longitudinal study may even do so because they feel 'special' by participating, creating an issue for validity. For example, Terman's participants knew they had high IQs and the sense of being important was reinforced by having a name: they were referred to as Terman's 'Termites'. Participation could, for example, have given them a motive to compete or succeed, or a sense of community i.e. the very act of participation will had made these individuals different from non-participants, even ones of similarly high intelligence.

Another problem caused by the duration of longitudinal studies relates to reliability. To ensure that data collection at each time point is consistent, the measures used need to be standardised. However, over time, ways to measure variables may be improved, potentially leading to the need to introduce different, better measures. In addition, researchers working on the study may move on so, for example, the individuals administering interviews may not remain constant. Conversely, if researchers continue working on a study for a long period of time, they are likely to get to know the participants if they have direct contact with them. The changing development of these relationships can also be confounding variables.

Finally, longitudinal studies can present particular ethical issues. For studies starting with children, obtaining consent in a way that the children understand is desirable, as well as gaining consent from their parents or guardians. Furthermore, it is harder to decide whether a child wants to withdraw from a study than it is with adults, who are more likely to speak up for themselves. Participants must also be repeatedly asked for consent (and reminded of their right to withdraw) and must be recontacted at each time point. This requires the maintenance of an extensive bank of contact details, which presents an issue for confidentiality.

Applying your knowledge of longitudinal studies to novel research situations

Longitudinal studies provide information about long-term changes. They are therefore suitable for investigating aims that relate to development and ageing, but also to any other life changes. Such changes include both those that are the result of a life event, such as recovery from an illness or the effects of a marriage or divorce, and those that are the consequence of a manipulation, such as attending a course or planned exposure to social groups. You should be able to identify the variables being measured and whether these are simply being tracked over regular time points to monitor possible changes, or whether there is a manipulation or influence which is actively intended to cause change. In the latter case, time points could be 'before, during, after and follow-up' in relation to the manipulation. This situation would be a longitudinal study with an experimental design.

You will need to be able to decide when to use a longitudinal study rather than any other method, and which type of longitudinal study is appropriate in a given situation. You should also be able suggest variables to study and ways to measure them, e.g. using a test, questionnaire, interview or observation, and how the results could be analysed and used.

In addition to being able to select and evaluate the longitudinal method, you should be able to plan a longitudinal study in a way that is appropriate to a given aim, such as whether or not there is a manipulated independent variable. Remember that you need to identify one or more variables to investigate, consider how they will be measured, and decide on the intervals between the testing time points and how you will standardise procedures to ensure consistency over time, as well as planning how to re-contact participants to retest them.

Questions

9   Hanif is planning a longitudinal study to measure changes in professional ability as adults progress through their careers. He has a sample of participants from different types of employment and has various measures of career progression such as how much they earn, the seniority of their position in their organisation and how many staff in the organisation are above and below them.

   a   Suggest how often Hanif should contact his participants to track their progress.

   b   Hanif wants to measure how happy they are in their career. Suggest how Hanif could measure this.

   c   The participants will need to be recontacted each time Hanif wants to test them. Suggest how Hanif could do this.

1.7 The definition, manipulation, measurement and control of variables

Variables are factors that change or can be changed. In experiments, these are the independent and dependent variables as well as variables that are or are not controlled. In correlations, there are two measured variables called co-variables.

Experiments look for changes or differences in the dependent variable (DV) between two or more levels of the independent variable (IV), which are set up by the experimenter. It is important that the IV is operationalised, so that the manipulation of the conditions represents the intended differences. At the beginning of this chapter, we discussed the idea of the **aim** of a study, that is, what the researcher is trying to find out. The aim refers to the variables but not necessarily very clearly. Operational definitions of variables help to add clarity to the intention expressed in the aim.

Consider a study testing the effect of age on susceptibility to false memories. The IV would be age, with, for example, 'young', 'middle-aged' and 'old' groups. It is important to know *how* old the people in the groups are; this is operationalisation. You might operationalise 'young' as under 20 years old, 'middle-aged' as 40–50 years old and 'old' as over 70. The DV must also be operationalised, so it can be measured effectively. We could operationalise the DV by counting the number of details 'remembered' about the false memory or how convinced the participants were that it was true.

RESEARCH METHODS IN PRACTICE

Dr Huang is thinking about buying new chairs for her classroom. Her *aim* is to explore whether hard or soft chairs help her students to work better (Figure 1.12). She wonders whether to predict a *non-directional (two-tailed) hypothesis: There is a difference in work rate of students sitting on comfortable and uncomfortable chairs.* Another psychology teacher says that students respond well to other comforts like access to a drinks machine or snack bar, and the soft chairs might make them happier, so they work harder. Dr Huang rewrites her prediction as a *directional (one-tailed) hypothesis*, saying: *Students on comfortable chairs will have a higher work rate than ones sitting on uncomfortable chairs.* A third teacher is not convinced and suggests that if the students are too comfortable, they will become sleepy and lazy, so work less. The hypothesis would then be: *Students on comfortable chairs will have a lower work rate than ones sitting on uncomfortable chairs.* This is also a directional (one-tailed) hypothesis. Her *null hypothesis* (in all cases) would be: *Any difference in work rate of students sitting on comfortable and uncomfortable chairs is due to chance.*

Now imagine a study that aims to look for a link between sleep and emotions. A non-directional hypothesis might be: *There will be a correlation between amount of sleep and emotional reactivity.* A possible directional hypothesis could say: *There will be a positive correlation between amount of sleep and how emotional someone is.* Note that the hypothesis does *not* say that one factor *causes* the other to change. The null hypothesis here would be: *Any correlation between amount of sleep and emotional reactivity is due to chance.*

Figure 1.12: Would you work harder in lessons if you had more comfortable classroom chairs?

Controlling variables and standardising procedures

Controlling of variables

Psychologists need to control variables in their studies to be more certain about their findings, i.e. to improve validity. In particular, in experiments, it is important to control confounding variables, that is, ones that have a consistent effect so they confound, i.e. confuse, the results. Confounding variables act on the DV selectively in one level of the IV so can interfere with the results in one of two ways. One possibility is that they can work against the effect of the IV, counteracting its effect on the DV, so preventing a real effect from being identified. Alternatively, they can increase the apparent effect of the IV and so suggest that there is an effect that doesn't really exist. These variables are the most important to control.

Other uncontrolled variables, which have a random effect on the DV across all levels of the IV, are not so problematic. The difficulty is to identify which variables will be important to control before the experiment starts. This is one function of a pilot study, a preliminary test of the procedures of a study. The intention is to identify potentially problematic uncontrolled variables and control them. This prevents or limits their effect to avoid making the results difficult to interpret if it is hard to separate their effects from those of the IV.

Consider Dr Huang's study of students and chairs. Perhaps Dr Huang compares one class in a room with the new (soft) chairs and another class in a different room with the old (hard) chairs. If the room containing the new chairs happens to have better lighting, Dr Huang may find that the students in the 'soft chairs' condition perform better. However, this may be due to the confounding variable of brighter lighting rather than the comfort level of the chairs. This is an example of a situational variable, because lighting is an aspect of the environment. Another possible confounding variable is how hard-working the individual students are. We might expect normally hard-working students to be randomly distributed among the different classes, in which case this variable is not a problem. However, suppose that all the students in the 'soft chairs' class do arts and humanities subjects and all the students in the 'hard chairs' class do maths and sciences. If Dr Huang happens to use a test of data analysis as her measure of the DV, she might find that the students in the 'hard chairs' level of the IV perform better. This would suggest that the soft chairs make students perform worse but could in fact be due to the uncontrolled variable of subject groups. This is an example of a participant variable, because the difference has been caused by a feature of the individuals, i.e. their ability in maths.

Standardisation

Controls make sure that the levels of the IV represent what they are supposed to, i.e. that the differences between them are going to create the intended situations to test the hypothesis. This helps to ensure validity. It is also important that every participant is treated in the same way. This is the process of standardisation. One way that this is achieved is by having **standardised instructions** that give the same advice to every person in the study. Imagine a questionnaire testing attitudes to helping behaviour. All participants would need to have the same advice about how to fill it in, so that any effects of social desirability–the influence of needing to give answers that were acceptable to society–were equally likely.

KEY WORD

standardised instructions: the written or verbal information given to participants at the beginning and sometimes during a study that ensure the experience of all participants, regardless of level of the IV, is as similar as possible

---

The procedure itself also needs to be standardised. This involves having equipment or tests that are consistent, i.e. that measure the same variable every time and always do so in the same way. Consider the questionnaire about attitudes to helping again. All the questions should focus on the same aspect of behaviour, i.e. helping, rather than some looking at a different but possibly related factor, such as being friendly or happy. In laboratory experiments, standardisation is easier than in other studies, as equipment is likely to be consistent, for example stopwatches or brain scans. However, some of these measures, such as brain scans, may need to be interpreted and this must also be done in a standardised way (Figure 1.13).

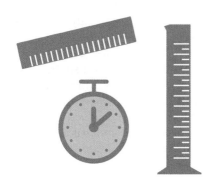

Figure 1.13: Scientific instruments are likely to produce objective, reliable data

Applying your knowledge of variables and controls to novel research situations

In experiments it is important to be able to decide how to operationalise the IV to produce the different conditions (to achieve validity) and to measure the DV in a consistent (reliable) way, and to be able to justify these choices. You will also need to be able to decide what controls it is appropriate to use and to suggest how these can be implemented.

RESEARCH METHODS IN PRACTICE

In Dr Huang's experiment about classroom chairs, the IV of hard and soft chairs must be operationalised. The text also referred to them as 'comfortable' and 'uncomfortable' chairs, but this still does not make clear what is meant by 'hard' and 'soft'. This could be done by saying 'chairs with wooden/plastic seats' *and* 'chairs with padded seats'. *Operationalisation* of the DV is also needed. The text referred to working 'better' and 'harder' but this is also incomplete. We need to expand on the idea of *work rate*, which was also used. This might be measured by counting the number of pieces of homework handed in late, or the time spent doing extra work. Either of these would indicate the amount of work being done. There are many *confounding variables* that could be important in this study, for example, some of

CONTINUED

the students might work harder anyway or the rate of work might vary with the weather. If students worked harder on sunny days, this would be a *situational variable*. The important variables to control are those that could confound the results. For example, if there was a choice of chairs, the students who chose to sit on comfy ones might be the laziest. If left as an *uncontrolled variable*, this could alter the results by making it look as if soft chairs made students work less.

In the description of the correlation on sleep and emotions, the co-variables were the 'amount of sleep' and 'how emotional someone is' or their 'emotional reactivity'. It is important to operationalise variables in correlations too. An operational definition of 'amount of sleep' could be the hours and minutes spent unreactive, or could be identified with an EEG indicating rapid eye movement (REM) and non-rapid eye movement (nREM) sleep. A questionnaire could be used to measure their emotions, with an operational definition of 'emotional reactivity' as how likely a person is to respond negatively to innocent comments, or how often they argue.

ACTIVITY 1.11

Look at the Research methods in practice box.

For the experiment:

- Suggest **one** other way the IV could be operationalised.

- Suggest **one** other way the DV could be operationalised.

- Would a possible difference between how lazy students were be a *situational variable* or a *participant variable*?

- Suggest **one** other possible *uncontrolled variable*.

For the correlation:

- Suggest **one** other way the variable of 'emotions' could be operationalised.

Questions

Umar and Saira are conducting an experiment on revision strategies. They are comparing students who revise alone and students who revise with other people. They are testing the hypothesis 'Revising alone is more effective than revising with other people.' Their teacher has told them that they are unlikely to find out anything useful as there will be too many uncontrolled variables to produce useful results.

10 a Identify the IV and the DV in Umar and Saira's experiment.

 b Explain whether Umar and Saira's hypothesis is directional (one-tailed) or non-directional (two-tailed).

11 a Umar suggests that one confounding variable could be that students who work with other people find the company motivating, so are able to work for longer.

 i Explain how this confounding variable could affect the results of their experiment.

 ii Suggest how this variable could be controlled.

 b Saira suggests that another confounding variable could be that students who work with other people find them distracting, so work less effectively.

 i Explain how this confounding variable could affect the results of their experiment.

 ii Suggest how this variable could be controlled.

 c A friend says that student ability could be an uncontrolled variable. Umar and Saira hope that this will have a random effect on their results.

 Explain whether this would be more or less important than the uncontrolled variables that Umar and Saira identified.

1.8 Sampling of participants

A **population** is a group of people (or animals) with one or more characteristics in common. For example, the population of a country is all the people who live there, the population of internet users is everyone who can access the internet. A population could also be people who share a particular interest, such as 'all football supporters' or who have a particular feature, for example 'all left-handed people'. The **sample** is the group of people who participate in a study. They are taken from a population and should ideally be representative of that group so that the findings will be generalisable. Details about the sample, such as age, ethnicity and gender are often important in investigations, so are commonly reported in the core studies. This is because these features may have an influence on psychological differences. Other characteristics of the sample, such as socio-economic status, education, employment, geographical location or occupation, may also be relevant.

The size of the sample also matters. Small samples are less reliable and are likely to be less representative. This is because a smaller group of people is unlikely to contain all the differences or variations that exist with the populations and some of those will be important to any study.

The different **sampling techniques** described next produce samples that differ in terms of how well they represent the population. The extent to which they are representative of the population determines how effectively generalisations can be made.

Opportunity sampling

Studies are often conducted with the people who are around at the time. Selecting participants in this way is called **opportunity sampling**. An opportunity sample is unlikely to represent the population fairly because readily available people will tend to be alike so will probably not include the variety that exists.

KEY WORDS

population: the group, sharing one or more characteristics, from which a sample is drawn

sample: the group of people selected to represent the population in a study

sampling technique: the method used to obtain the participants for a study from the population

opportunity sample: participants are chosen because they are available, for example university students are selected because they are present at the university where the research is taking place

---

For example, many studies are conducted using university students as they are convenient for the researchers. However, this means that the sample will be predominantly young, with a better than average education. The results may not, therefore, reflect the scores that people of different ages or educational opportunities might produce. Despite this potential problem, opportunity sampling is a very commonly used method, even by professional psychologists, because, for many investigations the results are unlikely to be affected by age or education.

Volunteer (self-selected) sampling

Rather than the researcher choosing individuals to ask, they may invite people to take part in their study. They might put up an advertisement, make an announcement or post a request on the internet. In this way, the people who respond and become participants choose to do so, i.e. are volunteers, so are described as a **volunteer (self-selected) sample** (Figure 1.14). As the individuals are self-selected, that is they choose whether to join in, this sampling technique is unlikely to be representative of the population. Volunteers may have more free time than average and, apart from being willing, often have other characteristics in common such as being better educated. Nevertheless, it is a useful technique when looking for participants who are unusual in some way, for example in Baron-Cohen et al.'s study (see Chapter 3), where people with autism spectrum disorder were needed.

KEY WORDS

volunteer (self-selected) sample: participants are invited to participate, for example through advertisements via email or notices. Those who reply become the sample

random sample: sampling all members of the population (i.e. possible participants) are allocated numbers and a fixed amount of these are selected in an unbiased way, for example by taking numbers from a hat

> ### Public Announcement
>
> **WE WILL PAY YOU $4.00 FOR ONE HOUR OF YOUR TIME**
>
> **Persons Needed for a Study of Memory**
>
> • We will pay five hundred New Haven men to help us complete a scientific study of memory and learning. The study is being done at Yale University.
> • Each person who participates will be paid $4.00 (plus 50c carfare) for approximately 1 hour's time. We need you for only one hour: there are no further obligations. You may choose the time you would to come (evenings, weekdays, or weekends).
>
> • No special training, education or experience is needed. We want:
>
> | Factory workers | Businessmen | Construction workers |
> | City employees | Clerks | Salespeople |
> | Laborers | Professional people | White-collar workers |
> | Barbers | Telephone workers | Others |
>
> All persons must be between the ages of 20 and 50. High school and college students cannot be used.
> • If you meet these qualifications, fill out the coupon below and mail it now to Professor Stanley Milgram, Department of Psychology, Yale University, New Haven. You will be notified later of the specific time and place of the study. We reserve the right to decline any application.
> • You will be paid $4.00 (plus 50c carfare) as soon as you arrive at the laboratory.
>
> -
>
> TO:
> PROF. STANLEY MILGRAM, DEPARTMENT OF PSYCHOLOGY, YALE UNIVERSITY, NEW HAVEN, CONN. I want to take part in this study of memory and learning. I am between the ages of 20 and 50. I will be paid $4.00 (plus 50c carfare) if I participate.
>
> NAME (Please Print)..
>
> ADDRESS...
>
> TELEPHONE NO.......................Best time to call you............................
>
> AGE.................OCCUPATION..SEX...................
> CAN YOU COME:
>
> WEEKDAYS.....................EVENINGS.............................WEEKENDS.........

Figure 1.14: Would you respond to this advert?

Random sampling

Opportunity and volunteer samples may be biased – they will probably contain very similar people so are unlikely to include the spread of characteristics in the population. In **random sampling** each person in the population has an equal chance of being chosen so the sample is much more likely to be representative. Imagine a researcher is looking for a sample of students at a school and puts an advert for volunteers on the library notice board. Students who never go to the library cannot be included so the sample might be biased towards those who work the hardest. Similarly, if they took an opportunity sample from the common room, it would only include students who are relaxing. Now their sample might be biased towards the *least* hard-working. To obtain a representative sample the researcher could instead use a numbered list of all students and use a random number generator to choose the participants. This would be a random sample as any individual is equally likely to be chosen. If the population is small, such as all the members of one class, the researcher can simply give each person a number, put pieces of paper with each number on in a hat, and draw out numbers until there are enough for the sample.

Applying your knowledge of sampling techniques to novel research situations

An early step in any research is to obtain an appropriate sample. The extent to which generalisations can be made from research depends in part on how representative the sample is. It is therefore important to get the best possible sample. However, practical constraints prevent researchers from using random samples most of the time and, for many psychological phenomena, it is reasonable to believe that processes happen in a fairly universal way so some sample bias is unproblematic. However, to assume there are no differences in emotional responses, cognitive processing or behaviour between populations would be misleading. Indeed, cross-cultural research, the

psychology of individual differences and developmental psychology are three areas specifically devoted to the study of such differences. It is therefore important that you can recognise limitations in the sampling technique used. This means that you should be able to identify possible differences between individuals or groups that might matter for the particular phenomena being explored in a study. Imagine two researchers at different universities are both studying obedience and both want samples from people nearby but not their own students. One university is near a police college and the other is next to a hospital and the researchers both obtain opportunity samples with the same age and gender spreads from these workplaces. Even though the samples are similar in age and gender, the difference in occupations could mean that the results of their studies may be different, for example if police officers were more obedient than nurses.

You will need to be able to explain how you would use each sampling technique and to explain reasons for choosing each technique. For example, why it might be difficult to use a technique in practice or why generalisations could or could not be made from the sample obtained. Table 1.3 will help to remind you of the key advantages and disadvantages of one sampling technique compared to another.

Sampling technique			
	Opportunity sampling	Volunteer (self-selected) sampling	Random sampling
Strengths	Quicker and easier than other methods as the participants are available, therefore a larger sample can be readily obtained.	Relatively easy because the participants come to the researcher. They are also likely to be committed, e.g. willing to return for repeat testing.	Likely to be representative as all types of people in the population are equally likely to be chosen.
Weaknesses	Likely to be non-representative as the variety of people available is likely to be limited, so they will tend to be similar and the sample could therefore be biased.	Likely to be non-representative as people who respond to requests may be similar, e.g. all have free time.	In reality everyone may not be equally likely to be chosen, e.g. if they cannot be accessed (if the original list is incomplete) or if mainly one type of participant, e.g. girls, happen to be selected. This is particularly important if the sample is small.

Table 1.3: Strengths and weaknesses of sampling techniques

RESEARCH METHODS IN PRACTICE

Your teacher has asked you to do a cognitive psychology investigation. You want it to work well so you want a *sample* of 30 people from which you can generalise. You think it would be easiest to take an *opportunity sample* from your classes at your college but you realise this might produce a biased sample as all your subjects are sciences. This might matter as the investigation is about using logic to solve problems and you think that science students might be especially good at the task. If so, their results might not be representative of the college *population* as a whole. A friend suggests making an announcement in the canteen asking for students studying all different subjects. This *volunteer sampling* technique might be better but there would be no guarantee of getting a range of people. You decide that the best sampling technique would be to choose individuals at random from a list of all the students in the college. You hope that this would mean you would be equally likely to get students taking each subject. You decide to use this *random sampling* technique based on the students' examination candidate numbers. You enter the candidate numbers into a random number generator and use the first 30 numbers that are generated.

ACTIVITY 1.12

Look at the Research methods in practice box. What problems would the following situations lead to?

* You revert to your idea of an *opportunity sample* but use your neighbours, who are mainly retired people.

* You followed your friend's advice about *volunteer sampling* but lots of the younger students were in detention at lunchtime that day.

Read the examples which follow. Which *sampling technique* is being used in each situation?

* Professor Chao is doing some internet research and is recruiting participants by posting on social media asking for people to help with her study.

CONTINUED

* Dr Singh is investigating the effects of ageing and is asking all the residents at two local care homes for their help.

* Dr Huang pulls student numbers on the college register from a hat to select a sample for a new study on homework and part-time jobs.

Questions

12   Ichiro is planning a study about the benefits that students gain from doing non-academic work, such as clubs, music, art, sports or part-time jobs. He is asking his friends for advice on how to obtain his sample.

    a   Kiaria says he should use an opportunity sample.

        Explain a disadvantage of using an opportunity sample in Ichiro's study.

    b   Haniya says he should use a volunteer sample.

        Explain a disadvantage of using a volunteer sample in Ichiro's study.

    c   Habib says he should use a random sample.

        Explain a disadvantage of using a random sample in Ichiro's study.

1.9 Data and data analysis

Psychologists, like all scientists, often produce numerical results from their investigations. These results are called the 'raw data'. As it is difficult to gain an understanding from large amounts of figures, the results are often simplified mathematically so they can be represented visually on graphs. This makes the meaning of the results easier to interpret. We will discuss a range of analytical techniques in this section. It is important that you are confident that you can count up scores, find the mode or the range of a data set, make simple comparisons and interpret data from tables or graphs.

Types of data

As you may know from the core studies or from earlier parts of this chapter, psychologists use a variety of different research methods. These methods can produce a range of different types of data. The main types are quantitative and qualitative data. When psychologists collect data, they can collect either numerical results, called **quantitative data**, or they can collect **qualitative data**, which is detailed and descriptive.

> ### KEY WORDS
>
> **quantitative data:** numerical results about the amount or *quantity* of a psychological measure, such as pulse rate or a score on an intelligence test
>
> **qualitative data:** descriptive, in-depth results indicating the *quality* of a psychological characteristic, such as responses to open questions in self-reports or case studies and detailed observations

Quantitative data

Quantitative data indicates the *quantity* of a psychological measure, such as a total or frequency. Many psychological variables are measured as the strength of a response and tend to be measured on scales, such as time or ratings. Alternatively, quantitative data can be a numerical score on a test such as for IQ or personality. Quantitative data is associated with experiments and correlations which use numerical scales but it is also possible to obtain quantitative data from observations, questionnaires or interviews. For example, a record of the number of times a behaviour is seen or the total number of different responses to a closed question in an interview would be quantitative data. The sources of quantitative data are typically highly objective, as the scales or questions used need little if any interpretation making them high in validity. In addition, the sources are highly reliable, as the measures are fixed quantities.

Qualitative data

Qualitative data indicates the *quality* of a psychological characteristic. Such data is more in-depth than quantitative data and includes detailed observer accounts and responses to open questions in questionnaires, interviews or case studies. Although there is a risk of subjectivity in the interpretation of such data by the researcher, qualitative data may be more representative as the participant can express themselves fully, so in some senses qualitative data can also be valid. Table 1.4 will help to remind you of the key advantages and disadvantages of quantitative compared to qualitative data.

Data type		
	Quantitative	**Qualitative**
Strengths	Typically uses objective measures. Scales or questions often very reliable. Data can be analysed using measures of central tendency and spread making it easy to compare.	Data is often valid as participants can express themselves exactly rather than being limited by fixed choices. Important but unusual responses are less likely to be ignored because of averaging.
Weaknesses	Data collection method often limits responses so the data are less valid, e.g. if the participant wants to give a response that is not available.	The data is often relatively subjective so findings may be invalid as data recording or interpretation may be biased by the researcher's opinions or feelings. If detailed data can only be gathered from one or a few individuals it may not generalise to the majority.

Table 1.4: Quantitative versus qualitative data

RESEARCH METHODS IN PRACTICE

Dr Singh and Professor Chao disagree over the best way to collect data about people's emotions when their personal space is invaded. Dr Singh wants to collect *quantitative data* by measuring their pulse rate and give them scales of *very — quite — not at all* to rate how stressed they feel. Professor Chao thinks it would be better to collect *qualitative data* by interviewing each participant and getting them to describe their feelings. She plans to ask questions such as 'How do you feel if you think someone is standing too close to you?' and 'Describe how you felt the last time you had a professional very close to you such as a doctor, dentist or optician.'

ACTIVITY 1.13

Look at the Research methods in practice box. What are the strengths and weaknesses of each suggested data collection method?

1   Are the questions suggested by Professor Chao open or closed questions?

2   Using ethical ideas only, suggest two more questions that could be used in the *interview*, **one** open question and **one** closed question. State which question format would be used to collect *qualitative data* and which would collect *quantitative data*.

Descriptive statistics

This section explores different ways that mathematics can be used to simplify and understand the data produced by studies in psychology. Studies produce 'raw data', the original information from the participants, which may be quantitative or qualitative. This section discusses how quantitative data is analysed. Studies often produce a great deal of raw data, and it is important to summarise it, simplify it and interpret it. There are several ways to do this, some of which–such as inferential statistics–are beyond the scope of this book. Here, we will focus on 'descriptive statistics', that is, ways to simplify and describe the data so that it is easier to summarise, compare and understand what the data shows.

The first step in this process is often to produce a summary table. This might be the totals from a tally chart in an observation, percentages from a questionnaire or summary information about averages and the spread of data, such as described next. Whenever a table is produced it should have a title, and the rows (going across) and the columns (going down) should always have headings that indicate what the figures are about. For an experiment, these are likely to be the measure(s) of the DV and the levels of the IV. If figures, such as scores on the DV, are measured in units (seconds, volts, etc.) the units should appear just once, in the heading. They should not be repeated in each 'cell' ('square' in the table).

This advice will help you to draw tables correctly but will also help you to interpret the data they contain. You can, for example, compare data between columns, or between rows. Imagine a study that compared A Level students and degree level students on several measures, such as the time they spent studying or socialising and how stressed they felt. The information in Table 1.5 would enable you to make different comparisons. You could compare across columns, e.g. to see which group of students spent the most time working, or were most stressed or compare the rows, e.g. to see that A Level students spend more time working than socialising.

Student group		
	A Level	Degree level
Average time spent working per week (hours)	6	14
Average time spent socialising per week (hours)	4	20
Average stress level	10	11

Table 1.5: A summary data table for a study about student time use and stress

Measures of central tendency

A set of quantitative results can be summarised to one number that represents a 'middle' or typical score, called a **measure of central tendency** or 'average'. There are three different measures of central tendency: the **mode**, **median** and **mean**.

KEY WORDS

measure of central tendency: a mathematical way to find the typical or average score from a data set, using the mode, median or mean

mode: the measure of central tendency that identifies the most frequent score(s) in a data set

median: the measure of central tendency that identifies the middle score of a data set, which is in rank order (smallest to largest). If there are two numbers in the middle, they are added together and divided by two

mean: the measure of central tendency calculated by adding up the values of all the scores and dividing by the number of scores in the data set

---

The mode

The mode is the most frequent score in a data set. It can be used with numerical data, such as scores on a test, and also with data sets that are choices that can be counted. Data that can be counted to produce a frequency also includes results in separate (discrete), named categories, such as in response to a question 'What is your favourite subject: maths, English or psychology?' Importantly, the mode is the *only* measure of central tendency that can be used on data in discrete categories. However, although the mode considers all the scores in a data set, it doesn't consider their values, so it is less informative than the median or mode.

If two (or more) responses are equally common there will be two (or more) modes. For example, the faces in Figure 1.15 could be used in a test to compare people with a diagnosis of autism spectrum disorder with a control group. The participants could be asked 'Which face looks the happiest?' The face that was chosen most frequently as the happiest in each group would be the mode for that group.

Figure 1.15: A facial expression test

A self-report in a school produced the data set in Table 1.6. The mode for subject choice is 'Psychology', because more people said this subject was their favourite: ten compared to four and six for the other subjects.

	Subject		
	Maths	English	Psychology
Number of people	4	6	10

Table 1.6: Number of people choosing each subject as their favourite

	Night of the week						
	Monday	Tuesday	Wednesday	Thursday	Friday	Saturday	Sunday
Number of boys	0	1	2	3	3	0	11
Number of girls	1	1	2	4	6	0	6

Table 1.7: Main homework night

Another question asked 'On which day of the week do you do most homework?' (see Table 1.7). The responses from girls and boys were compared.

In Table 1.7 more boys have 'Sunday' as their main homework night, so this is the mode for boys. Girls have said that 'Friday' and 'Sunday' are their main homework nights, but these two categories are the same, so there are two modes, each containing six girls. We could also combine the totals to work out an overall mode. Adding together the totals for each day shows that for all students Sunday is the most popular homework night, with 17 students in total.

The median

Unlike the mode, the median cannot be used with data in separate (discrete) categories, it is only used with numerical data on a linear scale (i.e. points in a sequence). To find the median, all the scores in the data set are put in a list from smallest to largest (ranked). The middle one in the list is the median. If there is an even number of scores, so there are two numbers in the middle, these are added together and divided by two to find the median. The median is more informative than the mode because it considers the rank order of the values of scores in a data set rather than just how many there are. It also is uninfluenced by a small number of outlying scores. This can be a benefit, in that it is less swayed by a small number of extreme scores, but, on the other hand, it does not take these values into account so is less representative than the mean.

Another question in the school survey asked participants to rate how hard they thought they worked, from 1 to 10. Students in their AS and A Level years were asked.

AS student data:

8, 6, 9, 1, 5, 6, 2, 7, 3, 6, 9, 8, 5, 6, 3, 8, 5, 10, 2, 3

A Level student data:

7, 9, 6, 7, 9, 7, 10, 10, 7, 10, 9, 4, 9, 6, 10, 10, 7, 9, 7, 7

Putting these data into order for the two groups separately:

AS students:

1, 2, 2, 3, 3, 3, 5, 5, 5, 6, 6, 6, 6, 7, 8, 8, 8, 9, 9, 10

There are two numbers in the middle: 6 + 6 = 12, 12/2 = 6 so the median = 6

A Level students:

4, 6, 6, 7, 7, 7, 7, 7, 7, 7, 9, 9, 9, 9, 9, 10, 10, 10, 10, 10

There are two numbers in the middle: 7 + 9 = 16, 16/2 = 8 so the median = 8

The median for the A Level group, 8, is higher than the median for AS students, which is 6. This suggests that A Level students believe they are working harder than AS students do.

The mean

The mean is the measure of central tendency that we usually call the 'average'. It can only be used with numerical data from linear scales. The mean is worked out by adding up the values of all the scores in the data set and dividing by the total number of scores (including any that were zeros). The mean is the most informative measure of central tendency because it considers the values of each of the scores in a data set (rather than just the rank order of those values, as the median does), so can be influenced by outlying scores. This can be a problem, as the mean can be swayed by a small number of extreme scores but, on the other hand, by taking these values into account the mean is more representative than the median or mode.

Looking back at the data used in the section on the median, a mean could be calculated instead. There were 20 students in each group. For the AS students, the calculation is therefore all the scores added together, then divided by 20, i.e. 112/20 = 5.6, so the mean is 5.6. For the A Level students, the calculation is again all the scores added together, and divided by 20, i.e. 160/20 = 8, so the mean is 8. Like the median, this too shows that the A Level students believe they are working harder than the AS students do.

Measures of spread

A measure of spread is an indicator of how varied the results are within a data set: are they clustered together or widely dispersed? If two data sets are the same size, with the same average, they could still vary in terms of how close most data points were to that average. Differences such as this are described by measures of spread: the range and the standard deviation.

KEY WORDS

measure of spread: a mathematical way to describe the variation or dispersion within a data set

range: the difference between the biggest and smallest values in the data set plus one (a measure of spread)

standard deviation: a calculation of the average difference between each score in the data set and the mean. Bigger values indicate greater variation (a measure of spread)

The range

The range is the simplest measure of spread and is calculated in the following way:

1 Find the largest and smallest value in the data set.

2 Subtract the smallest value from the largest value, then add 1.

You may have learned to calculate the range without adding 1. In psychology we do this because the scales we use measure the gaps between points, not the points themselves. Consider a scale of student happiness from 1 (sad) to 8 (very happy). This can be represented on a line (see Figure 1.16):

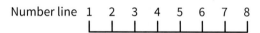

Figure 1.16: Happiness scale

If we say someone's happiness is at level of 3, they could be anywhere between 2.5 and 3.5, and someone scoring 6 has a happiness level somewhere between 5.5 and 6.5. So, if 3 and 6 were the lowest and highest scores, the real spread extends to those limits, i.e. from 2.5 to 6.5, so this spread works out as 6.5 − 2.5 = 4. This figure is one bigger than the largest score (6) minus the smallest score (3) = 3.

The range for the two sets of data given in the section on the median would be calculated in the following way:

AS students:

> 1, 2, 2, 3, 3, 3, 5, 5, 5, 6, 6, 6, 6, 7, 8, 8, 8, 9, 9, 10
>
> 10 − 1 = 9, 9 + 1 = 10 so the range = 10

A Level students:

> 4, 6, 6, 7, 7, 7, 7, 7, 7, 7, 9, 9, 9, 9, 9, 10, 10, 10, 10, 10
>
> 10 − 4 = 6, 6 + 1 = 7 so the range = 7

So, not only are the medians and means for these two data sets slightly different, but the ranges are also different. This tells us that the diversity of opinion about how hard they are working is greater for AS students than A Level students. We could also say that although most A Level students think they are working very hard, AS student opinion varies from 'not working hard' to 'working very hard'.

One problem with the range is that it does not accurately reflect outliers. That is, it would not be clear from the range whether the most extreme scores, e.g. very large scores, were single odd scores or typical of the data set. Imagine that the least hard-working student in the A Level set had rated themselves as working at level 1 rather than 4. This would make very little difference to the mean (it would be 7.85 instead of 8), but would change the range from 7 to 10 (the same as the range for the AS group).

The standard deviation

In the same way that the mean can tell us more than the mode, a measure of spread called the standard deviation can tell us more than the range. Rather than looking only at the extremes of the data set, the standard deviation (given the name s, SD or σ) considers the difference between each data point and the mean. This is called the *deviation*.

As the standard deviation tells us the spread of values of scores in a data set, sets with scores that are more spread out have larger standard deviations, while sets with closely clustered scores have smaller standard deviations. When the standard deviations of two groups of participants' scores are similar, this means that they have a similar variation around the mean.

Returning to the data about how hard students believe they are working (from the section on the median) the standard deviations for the two sets of data would be:

AS students: SD = 2.62

A Level students: SD = 1.72

These figures show, as the range did, that there is greater variation in the opinions of the AS students as the figure of 2.62 for the standard deviation for this group is larger than 1.72, the figure for the A Level group. Note that if the standard deviation is calculated for the A Level group with the opinion score of 4 for one student being replaced with a 1, the standard deviation increases, as this makes the group more varied. However, it still does not become as large as the figure for the AS group. This is different from the effect of this same change in one participant's score on the range. The range of the two year groups become the same (they would both be 10), whereas in fact *within* the groups, the AS students are more varied. This is reflected in the standard deviation however, which changes from 1.72 when the student has a score of 4 to 2.16 if they have a score of 1. So, the main advantage of the standard deviation over the range is that it takes every score into account and therefore provides a representation of variation *within* the data set. As it is not just considering the extremes is not distorted by outliers like the range would be.

RESEARCH METHODS IN PRACTICE

A new psychology teacher, Jamal, has tested a group of ten of his students on their recall of the aims, methods, results and conclusions of one of the core studies. The test was marked out of 15. Two students scored 0, and one student scored each of the marks 3–10. Jamal works out the *mode* and is horrified to find that the modal score is zero! Jamal's colleague Nurul recommends he works out the *median* instead, so he finds the two middle scores in the group (5 and 6), adds them together and divides by 2. This is 5.5, so Jamal feels much better. He wonders if calculating the *mean* will make him feel better still, but it doesn't. When Jamal adds up all the scores and divides by 10 (because he had ten students), the mean is only 5.2. This is because the median does not consider the absolute value of all the scores, only their relative values. So the two zero scores do not affect the median because they are simply 'lower than the central values in the rank order'. However, for the mean, the absolute values of the zeros, being the smallest values possible, do affect the mean. These three figures are different *measures of central tendency*. Jamal wants to compare this group to his colleague Nurul's students, who scored 0, 1, 1, 2, 2, 2, 3, 4, 4, 5. He calculates two different *measures of spread*. The biggest and smallest values in her set are 0 and 5, so he subtracts 0 from 5 and adds 1, giving a *range* of 6. The *standard deviation* for her group is 1.58.

ACTIVITY 1.14

1 Look back at Figure 1.15. For the data set in the table shown, which is the modal response?

	Face A	Face B	Face C	Face D
Number of participants selecting each face as the happiest	0	3	7	1

2 Look back at the data for AS and A Level students in the section on the median. What is the mode for each group?

3 Using the information about Jamal and Nurul's students in the Research methods in practice box, answer the following questions:

   a What is the mode for Nurul's group?

   b Which group does this suggest performed better on the test?

   c What is the median for Nurul's group?

   d Which group does this suggest performed better on the test?

   e The mean for Nurul's group was 2.4. Which group does this suggest performed better on the test?

   f What is the range for Jamal's own group?

   g When compared to the range for Nurul's group, what does this tell you?

   h The standard deviation for Jamal's group was 3.49. Does this tell you that his group was more varied or less varied than Nurul's?

Graphs

A graph is a visual illustration of data. There are many different types of graph and in this section we will consider only bar charts, histograms and scatter graphs, each of which you should understand well enough to be able to name, recognise, draw and use to interpret data.

Bar charts

A **bar chart** is used when the data is in separate categories rather than on a continuous scale. Bar charts are therefore used for the totals of data collected in named categories and for all measures of central tendency (modes, medians or means). To construct a bar chart, the bars must be separate, with each bar representing a total or average of a category of data. This is because the *x*-axis represents the distinct groups and not a linear scale. For a bar chart of the results of an experiment, the levels of the IV go along the bottom (on the *x*-axis) and the DV goes on the *y*-axis. To help you to remember which is the *x*-axis and which is the *y*-axis, think 'X is a-*cross*' (Figure 1.17).

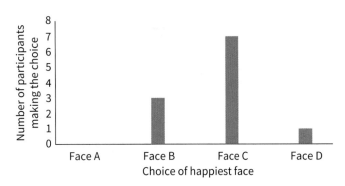

Figure 1.17: A bar chart showing the number of participants selecting each face as the happiest

Histograms

Histograms can be used to show the pattern in a whole data set, where this is continuous data, i.e. data measured on a scale rather than in separate categories. A histogram may be used to illustrate the distribution of a set of scores. In this case, the DV is plotted on the *x*-axis (across) and the frequency of each score plotted on the *y*-axis (up the side). The scores along the *x*-axis may be grouped into categories (e.g. if the DV is age, the data may be grouped into 0–5 years, 6–10 years, 11–15 years, etc.). To construct a histogram, each bar, e.g. representing a value on the scale of the DV, is plotted at the height representing the frequency of that value. As the scale represented on the *x*-axis is continuous the bars

are drawn next to each other, unlike in a bar chart. This means that if there are no scores in a category, a gap must be left to show that the category is empty (see Figure 1.18, which shows 'empty' categories on the *x*-axis).

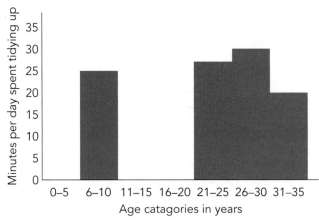

Figure 1.18: A histogram of the time spent tidying by people of different ages

Scatter graphs

The results from a correlational study are displayed on a scatter graph. To construct a **scatter graph**, a dot is marked at the point where an individual's scores on each variable cross. Sometimes you will see a 'line of best fit' drawn on a scatter graph. The position of this line is calculated and its line is drawn so that it comes close to as many points as possible (see Figure 1.19a–d). In a strong correlation all the data points lie close to the line, but in a weak correlation they are more spread out. Note that you will often see the strength of a correlation described as a number (an 'r' value) from +1 to −1. Values close to +1 are strong positive correlations and values close to −1 are strong negative correlations. Lower or 'smaller' values (closer to 0) are weaker correlations. Where there is no significant correlation, the points do not form a clear line (and this has a 'r' value of 0 or very close to zero).

It is important to remember that you *cannot* draw a causal conclusion from a correlational study. Therefore, scatter graphs such as the ones in Figure 1.19 only tell you that there is a relationship between the co-variables but not which (if either) of them, is the cause of this link. An experiment could help to find this out.

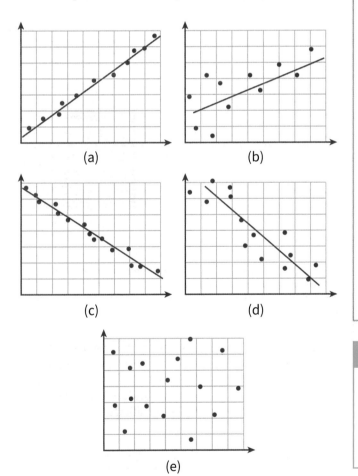

Figure 1.19: Scatter graphs showing (a) strong positive correlation, (b) weak positive correlation, (c) strong negative correlation, (d) weak negative correlation and (e) no correlation

Groups of students in Dr Huang's class are doing different psychological investigations into altruism. Group A is counting the number of times boys and girls in the class say 'thank you'. They find that on average the boys said thank you six times and the girls said thank you seven times. They are going to plot a *bar chart* of these averages.

Group B is asking everyone the question, 'Which of these situations have you ever helped in: a parent with a pram / an elderly person with their shopping / a child crossing the road / an injured person?' The totals for each group are 14, 7, 16 and 3, respectively. They are also going to plot a bar chart.

Group C is using an online computer game to test how many seconds it takes each student to respond to another player's request for help. They work out the percentage of students who took 0–5, 6–10, 11–15, 16–20 and 21–25 seconds. The results are 0%, 15%, 45%, 20% and 5%. They plot a *histogram* of their results.

Group D asks every person to answer two questions 'How many times have you lent your notes to someone else?' and 'How likely on a scale of 1–10 are you to give away your lunch to somebody who is hungry?' Their results were:

Lend notes	5	3	9	4	2	6	9	7	3	4
Give lunch	7	2	7	10	1	8	8	7	4	5

They are correlating the two sets of scores and will draw a scatter graph.

ACTIVITY 1.15

Look at the Research methods in practice box. If you can work in a pair, each plot one bar chart (from either Group A's or Group B's results). In addition, plot one other graph from the results of Groups C and D.

CONTINUED

Peer assessment

In your pairs, look at the two graphs plotted by your partner. Consider the following points:

- Has the correct type of graph been chosen?
- Does the graph have a title?
- Is the x-axis labelled?
- Are there units or categories marked on the x-axis?
- Is the y-axis labelled?
- Are there units or categories marked on the y-axis?
- Are all the bars or points correctly plotted?

If you think any of these points are missing or could be better, suggest to your partner how their graph could be improved.

Questions

13 Read the data from the histogram in Figure 1.18. Draw a suitable table into which you can put this data.

14 Look back at Table 1.5. Plot a bar chart for the data about 'average time spent working per week' for A Level and degree level students.

15 Dorothy has conducted a study looking at the development of language in a sample of ten infants. She has worked out the average number of different words the infants could say each month from the age of 1 year to 2 years old. The number of words varies from 0 to 60. At 18 months the ten infants could say 3, 45, 32, 14, 21, 18, 38, 29, 14 and 39 words.

    a Work out the modal number of words the babies could say at 18 months.

    b Work out the range of the number of words the babies could say at 18 months.

    c Describe how the median number of words the babies could say at 18 months would be calculated.

    d Describe how the mean number of words the babies could say at 18 months would be calculated.

    e Draw and label the axes for a histogram for Dorothy's data.

16 Ethelred has collected data by measuring two variables: hours of sleep and happiness. He has drawn a scatter graph of his data and found a negative correlation. Sketch a graph to illustrate the pattern of Ethelred's data.

1.10 Ethical considerations

As you will see from the discussion of the core studies, psychologists need to consider **ethical issues** when they conduct research. It is important that they take steps to make sure that their research follows ethical guidelines. In this section, we will look at some of these ethical issues and consider the ethical guidelines that help psychologists to deal with these issues effectively.

Ethical issues

As you will have seen from examples of psychological research, investigations using humans or animals have the potential to cause concerns about the welfare of the participants. Such concerns are called ethical issues. Problems may arise through the nature of the study, such as the potential for psychological discomfort caused by a study about stress, or from aspects of the procedure, such as the need to hide the real aim of the study. Ethical issues may also arise from the implications of the research, for example the possibility for results having a negative impact on part of society.

> **KEY WORD**
>
> **ethical issues:** problems in research that raise concerns about the welfare of participants (or have the potential for a wider negative impact on society)

To help psychologists to cope with potential ethical issues that could arise in their research, many countries have an organisation that produces a code of conduct. In addition, research that is being conducted at a university is likely to require approval from the institution's ethical committee. An ethical code provides advice, for example as a set of **ethical guidelines**, that helps psychologists to work in a way that satisfies the primary concern of the welfare of individuals involved in the research as well as the perception of psychology in society. Participants who are deceived or distressed may not want to participate again, may view psychology badly and pass this message on to others, and are less likely to trust the findings of psychological research. These are all outcomes that should be avoided.

KEY WORD

ethical guidelines: pieces of advice that guide psychologists to consider the welfare of participants and wider society

---

Ethical guidelines relating to human participants

The discussion that follows is based on the British Psychological Society Code of Ethics and Conduct (2018), although there are many other similar ethical codes in use throughout the world. All of these guidelines help to contribute to the objective of minimising harm and maximising benefit, which is one of the key principles of the Code of Ethics and Conduct.

Protection from harm

Sometimes research carries risks for participants. Although this should be minimised in the planning of the study, some level of risk may be inevitable. A study may have the potential to cause participants psychological harm (e.g. embarrassment, self-doubt or stress) or physical harm (e.g. engaging in risky behaviours or receiving injections). Participants in such studies have the right to be protected and should not be exposed to any greater risk than they would be in their normal life. Care should be taken to eliminate such risks (e.g. by screening participants), experienced researchers should be used and studies should be stopped if unexpected risks arise.

Valid consent

Sometimes it is important in experiments to hide the aims from participants to reduce demand characteristics. However, participants have the right to know what will happen in a study so they can give their informed consent. The researcher's need to hide the aim makes it hard to get genuine consent. Ideally, valid consent should be obtained from participants before the study starts. To do this, the researcher must get agreement or permission from potential participants by giving them sufficient information about the procedure for them to decide whether they want to participate, so that their decision is *informed*. This is often possible without needing to misinform i.e. lie to or otherwise mislead participants. Participants can be told what will happen to them in the study and any possible risks so that they can consent to the procedure without the researchers telling them the full aim. This can satisfy to needs of ethical requirements without leading to demand characteristics causing a change in the participants' behaviour.

For consent to be valid it must not only be informed but must also be freely given by a competent individual. The researcher must be sure that the participant understands what is being asked of them and feels that they have a choice about participating. This may be difficult for some groups of potential participants, such as people with mental health problems, learning difficulties or a low level of literacy, people who are working in an additional language or have amnesia, and for children. Furthermore, researchers should ensure that participants do not feel pressured to participate, such as prisoners may under some circumstances, or if the process of recruitment of participants is inappropriately persuasive.

When working with child participants, it may be difficult to obtain valid consent in the same way as with adults. It is therefore important to ask their parents or guardians for consent, but also the children themselves where possible. In this case, consent should be requested in a 'child friendly' way that is suitable for the level of understanding the child has.

In some situations, it is not even possible to ask for consent. This is often the case in naturalistic observations and field experiments. In such situations, a researcher may ask a group of people similar to those who will become participants whether they would find the study acceptable if they were involved.

This is called **presumptive consent** because it allows the researcher to presume that the actual participants would also have agreed to participate if asked. Especially when participants have not been fully informed, it is important to **debrief** them at the end of the study.

> ### KEY WORDS
>
> **presumptive consent:** this can be obtained when informed consent cannot be obtained from actual participants. A similar group of people to the anticipated sample are given full details of the proposed study and asked if they would find the study acceptable or not. If they would be happy to be involved, the study can continue
>
> **debriefing:** giving participants a full explanation of the aims and potential consequences of the study at the end of a study so that they leave in at least as positive a condition as they arrived

Right to withdraw

Participants should be able to leave a study whenever they wish. This is their right to withdraw and it must be made clear to participants at the start of the study. Although participants can be offered incentives to join a study, these cannot be taken away if they leave. This prevents participants thinking that they have to continue. Researchers should not use their position of authority to encourage participants to remain in a study if they want to stop. So in practice, participants may need to be reminded of this right and researchers should follow this guideline even if data will be lost.

Lack of deception

Participants should not be deliberately misinformed, i.e. deception should be avoided. When it is essential to deceive participants, e.g. to avoid the effects of demand characteristics, they should be told the real aim as soon as possible and be allowed to remove their results if they want to. When participants have been deceived and they know they have been in a study, a debrief should follow (see later section on debriefing).

Confidentiality

All data should be stored separately from the participants' names and personal information held, and names should never be published unless the individuals have specifically agreed to this. Such information should be stored securely and should not be shared with anyone outside the study. These measures ensure confidentiality. The identity of participants should be protected by destroying personal information. However, where it is needed to re-contact participants or to pair up an individual's scores in each condition in a repeated measures design, each participant can be allocated a number that can be used to identify them.

When conducting a case study or field experiment with institutions, confidentiality is still important and identities must be hidden. For example, the names of schools or hospitals should be concealed. One common way to anonymise individuals in to use their initials. However, where an individual is well known, this may not be sufficient to conceal their identity. For example, one participant in the study about sleep and dreams by William Dement and Nathanial Kleitman had the initials WD.

Figure 1.20: Privacy should still be maintained even if consent cannot be given by participants

The only exception to this is that personally identifiable information can be communicated or published when the participant gives their informed consent for this or in exceptional circumstances when the safety or interests of the individual or others may be at risk.

Privacy

Observations, self-reports that ask personal questions, and any study that uses personal information all risk invading privacy. This means that the researcher may enter physical space or emotional territory that the individual would want to keep to themselves. In a questionnaire, interview or case study, participants should be aware of their right to ignore questions they do not want to answer. When completing a questionnaire in a laboratory situation, participants should be given an individual space. In observations, people should only be watched in situations where they would expect to be on public display, see Figure 1.20.

Debriefing

All participants who are aware that they have been in a study should be thanked and given the chance to ask questions. Debriefing participants provides them with an explanation at the end of the study that explains fully the aims of the study and ensures that they do not want to withdraw their data. If participants have been negatively affected by a study the researcher must return them to their previous condition. However, debriefing is not an alternative to designing an ethical study, so it is important to consider all the ways in which a study could cause distress and to minimise them.

Ethical guidelines relating to the use of animals

Animals are used in psychological research for a number of different reasons. Driscoll and Bateson (1988) suggested animals may be: convenient models (e.g. for processes such as learning), a way to carry out procedures that could not be done ethically on humans (e.g. isolation or brain surgery) or be good or interesting examples in their own right (e.g. communication in birds, bats or whales). As a consequence, much psychological research is conducted on animals and therefore their welfare needs protecting.

The discussion that follows is based on the British Psychological Society Guidelines for Psychologists Working with Animals (2020), although there are many other similar ethical codes in use throughout the world. Animals are also often protected by law. These guidelines encompass appropriate legal requirements and specifically consider the effects of psychological research in which animals may be confined, harmed, stressed or in pain, so suffering should be minimised. Veterinary advice should be sought in any case of doubt.

Researchers must aim to ensure that in any research, the means justify the ends, i.e. that the animal suffering caused by the planned experiment is outweighed by the benefits. One way to consider this question is to use Bateson's (1986) cube (see Figure 1.21). When the certainty of benefit (e.g. to humans) is high, the research is good and the suffering is low, the research can be argued to be worthwhile. The following guidelines help to contribute to the objective of minimising harm and maximising benefit.

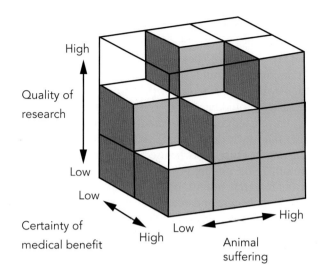

Figure 1.21: Bateson's cube (1986). According to Bateson, research should only be conducted if it falls within the clear part of the cube

Replacement

Researchers should consider replacing animal experiments with alternatives, such as videos from previous studies or computer simulations.

Species

The chosen species should be the one least likely to suffer pain or distress. Other relevant factors include whether the animals were bred in captivity, their previous experience of experimentation and the sentience of the species (its ability to think and feel).

Number of animals

Only the minimum number of animals needed to produce valid and reliable results should be used. To minimise the number, pilot studies, reliable measures of the dependent variable, good experimental design and appropriate data analysis should all be used.

Procedures

Research on animals is controlled by legal requirements and/or guidelines from relevant organisations because studies will, necessarily, affect the animals in some way. However, for research on animals to be effective the animals' experience should, as far as possible within the constraints of the research being conducted, be a normal and positive one. There are therefore guidelines to help psychologists to care for their research animals well.

Pain, suffering and distress

Research causing death, or suffering, such as disease, pain, injury, physiological or psychological distress and discomfort should be avoided. Where possible, designs which improve rather than worsen the animals' experience should be used (e.g. studying the effect of early enrichment on development compared to normal rather than early deprivation). Alternatively, naturally occurring instances may be used (e.g. where stress arises naturally in the animal's environment or lifetime). During research, attention should be paid to the animals' daily care and veterinary needs and any costs to the animals should be justified by the scientific benefit of the work (see Bateson's cube).

Housing

Isolation and crowding can cause animals distress. Caging conditions should depend on the social behaviour of the species (e.g. isolation will be more distressing for social animals than solitary ones). Overcrowding can cause distress and aggression (therefore also physical harm). The level of stress experienced by individuals should also be considered (e.g. the animal's age and gender). Between testing, animals should be housed with enough space to move freely and with sufficient food and water for their health and well-being, both in terms of their biological and ecological needs. However, the artificial environment only needs to recreate the aspects of the natural environment that are important to welfare and survival, e.g. warmth, space for exercise or somewhere to hide. Environments that are 'visually appealing' to people may not be those that are best for an individual species. Cage cleaning should balance cleanliness against avoiding stress, e.g. caused by unfamiliar smells or disturbance by humans.

Reward, deprivation and aversive stimuli

Deprivation is the removal of resources that are important to an animal. In planning studies using deprivation the normal feeding or drinking patterns of the animals should be considered so that their needs can be satisfied (e.g. carnivores eat less frequently than herbivores, young animals need greater access to food and water). The use of preferred food should be considered as an alternative to deprivation (e.g. for rewards in learning studies) and alternatives to aversive (unpleasant) stimuli and deprivation should be used where possible.

Ethical guidelines and their evaluation and application to research

All research with human participants should be ethical. Researchers should, for example, always follow the guideline of confidentiality. Although ethical guidelines should always be followed, sometimes it is necessary to accept some risks to participants in order for a study to achieve its objectives. When this is the case, the researchers must consider whether the risks can be justified and, if so, how they can be minimised. Ethical issues may arise because of the nature of the topic being studied, such as phobias, as this threatens participants' psychological well-being, or they may be at risk of physical harm. Alternatively, ethical issues may arise from the need to use controls which limit participants' knowledge or choices so threaten their privacy, informed consent or right to withdraw. This, in turn, has the potential to cause psychological harm. Although debriefing can help to reduce any harm that has been done, it is not a substitute for designing a more ethical study. Researchers must therefore consider all appropriate guidelines when planning a study, if necessary consulting with colleagues and following the advice of an ethical committee.

You will need to be able to make decisions based on ethical guidelines, and these can be applied to a study you already know about, a novel example that is presented to you or a study that you are asked to plan. So, in relation to informed consent, protection (physical and psychological), right to withdraw, deception, confidentiality, privacy and debriefing, you will need to be able to explain why issues have arisen and how and why each guideline has been broken or has been followed.

All research with animals should be ethical. However, for any good research to be conducted a compromise must be reached between animal suffering and the good that will come out of the research. In evaluating studies, it is important to remember that when the research is planned, decisions must be based on *expected* outcomes, i.e. the potential gains of the study. This is governed by the importance of the work, how certain it is that there will be a valuable benefit and this, in turn, is in part determined by the effectiveness of the research itself. So, in deciding whether a piece of research is ethical, we must think about:

- how much the animals suffer (e.g. in terms of pain, deprivation, distress)

- what the positive outcomes might be (e.g. the benefits for people and whether these are worthwhile)

- whether the research is sufficiently well planned to achieve these possible benefits.

You can consider these three elements in terms of Bateson's cube, illustrating each one with examples relating to the particular study. The same ideas can be used whether you are considering a study you already know about, a novel example that is presented to you or a study that you are asked to plan. So, in relation to the three points, you will need to be able to explain or justify:

- choices about the animals and their care, such as the species and how they are housed, and the procedures chosen, e.g. the number of animals used and the design of the study in terms of the aspects of feeding, access to companions or pain and distress that arise as a consequence of the study

- why the study is being done, for example in terms of the need for new research or the ways in which humans (or animals) could benefit from the findings

- the strengths of the design of the study, e.g. in terms of controls and ways that good objectivity, validity and reliability have been achieved.

RESEARCH METHODS IN PRACTICE

Professor Chao is planning an *experiment* on emotions in animals. She wants to see if, like us, non-human animals tend to approach things they like and avoid things they don't like. She considered *replacing* the use of animals with videos of animals in the wild responding to different stimuli but decided that she would not know for certain what they were reacting to so the findings might not be valid. She chose to use rats as the *species* is bred for laboratory use and rats can be *housed* alone without distressing them. She decided to use a *repeated measures design* as it would limit the *number of animals* used compared to an *independent measures design*. To reduce *pain and distress*, she used food they liked a lot (peanuts) in the 'approach' condition and food they did not like a lot (lettuce) in the 'avoidance' condition. Although the rats were tested before they were given fresh food in their cages, they were not *deprived* of food.

ACTIVITY 1.16

Look at the Research methods in practice box.

- Professor Chao considered using *aversive stimuli* such as loud noises or electric shocks in the 'avoid' condition but decided this was unethical. Why?

- Suggest one problem with Professor Chao's decision to use a repeated measures design, and explain how this problem might be solved.

Questions

17 Rashid is conducting a study to investigate people's helpfulness when they see someone who needs help to cross the road. Rashid is going to ask his friend Kinza to act as a stooge (confederate) and pretend to need help so that he can observe people's actions.

    a Why could Rashid's study raise ethical issues?

    b What could Rashid do to follow ethical guidelines and minimise these issues?

18 Dr Hadid is planning a study using laboratory mice to test their ability to learn to jump over a small wall.

    a What could Dr Hadid do to ensure he follows animal guidelines relevant to his laboratory mice?

    b What should Dr Hadid *not* do to ensure he follows animal guidelines relevant to his laboratory mice?

1.11 Evaluating research: methodological issues

As well as evaluating research in terms of ethics, it can also be considered in terms of whether it is 'good science', i.e. by looking at methodological issues. There are several key methodological issues that you have encountered elsewhere in the chapter, such as reliability, validity and generalisability.

We will now explore these again in a little more depth and see why they, and **replicability**, are important in the evaluation of research.

Reliability

Whenever research is conducted data is obtained, researchers must attempt to ensure that the way in which these results are collected is the same each time, otherwise differences could occur (between participants, between conditions in an experiment or between the data obtained by different researchers). Such inconsistencies would be problems of reliability.

The reliability of the measures used to collect data depends on the 'tool' used. A researcher collecting reaction times or pulse rates as data will probably have reliability as the machines used are likely to produce very consistent measures of time or rates. One way to check reliability is to use the **test–retest** procedure. This involves using a measure once, and then using it again in the same situation. If the reliability is high, the same results will be obtained on both occasions, i.e. there will be a high correlation between the two sets of scores. Imagine an experiment on emotions in which a researcher is not sure whether their questionnaire is a reliable measure of 'happiness'. They use a group of participants and give them the questionnaire on two separate occasions. All the participants would need to be tested at the same time of day and the same day of the week to ensure that their happiness levels were indeed the same. If the 'happiness scale' was reliable, this test–retest procedure would produce a high correlation between the scores on the first and second tests. If the reliability was low, the test would need to be redesigned.

KEY WORDS

replicability: the extent to which the procedure of a study can be kept the same whenever the research is repeated. This is especially important when a study is repeated, either by the same or different researchers to verify results. It also enables researchers conducting other studies to follow exactly the same procedure to test different aspects of a problem, different participant groups, etc

test–retest: a way to measure the consistency of a test or task. The test is used twice and if the participants' two sets of scores are similar, i.e. correlate well, it has good reliability

---

Another reliability problem relates to subjective interpretations of data. For example, a researcher who is using a questionnaire or interview with open questions may find that the same answers could be interpreted in different ways, producing low reliability. If these differences arose between different researchers, this would be an *inter-rater reliability* problem. Similarly, if in an observation researchers gave different interpretations of the same actions, this would be low *inter-observer reliability*. If the reliability was low, the researchers in either case would need to discuss why the differences arose and find ways to make their interpretations or observations more similar. This can be done by agreeing on operational definitions of the variables being measured and by looking at examples together. These steps would help to make the researchers more objective.

To minimise differences in the way research is conducted that could reduce reliability, standardisation can be used, that is, the procedure is kept the same. This could include instructions, materials and apparatus, although remember that there would be no reason to change many of these. Important aspects of standardisation are those factors which might differ, such as an experimenter's manner towards participants in different levels of the IV, an interviewer's posture or tone in asking questions or an observer's success at concealing their presence.

Replicability

When a researcher conducts a useful study, they often publish their results and conclusions, along with clear details of how the study was conducted. The core studies are examples of such publications. One reason for the level of detail in these published studies is to allow other psychologists to repeat the research, i.e. to replicate it. This helps to ensure that researchers are honest about their work as it must be possible for others to reproduce their findings otherwise the research loses credibility. Furthermore, if this were not possible–and achieved–the impact on psychology in general would be to lower confidence in research as a whole, damaging the potential for a positive impact on society. It is therefore essential that details about how the study will be conducted are considered at the planning stage so that they can be rigorously followed by the researchers themselves, and by others. Such details include many of the key points in this chapter, such as the variables that were measured and manipulated and how they were operationalised; features of the sample and how this was obtained; the procedure that was followed including, for example, controls, counterbalancing and allocation to groups; and the materials used.

Validity

Many factors affect validity, including reliability: a test or task cannot measure what it intends to measure unless it is consistent. Objectivity also affects validity: if a researcher is subjective in their interpretation of data, their findings will not properly reflect the intended measure.

To have face validity, a test or task must seem to test what it is supposed to. Imagine a test of helping behaviour that involved offering to assist people who were stuck in a bath full of spiders or worms. It might not be a valid test of helping because people who were frightened of spiders or worms would not help, even though they might otherwise be very altruistic. This would be a lack of face validity.

If participants think that they understand the aim of a study, their behaviour or responses are likely to be affected. This would also lower validity. In the design of a study, the researcher should aim to minimise demand characteristics, that is, those features which could indicate to the participants what is expected. For example, in a study about false memories, the researcher needs to hide the aim from the participants otherwise they will try to spot which memory is false. They might then try to remember this information particularly well, or might not report it at all if that is what they think the researcher expects.

Another problem for validity is whether the results obtained in one situation will apply to other situations. If not, then the test or task is too specific to be measuring the general phenomenon it was intended for. This is the problem of ecological validity, which applies more widely than considering just whether findings from the laboratory apply to the 'real world'. For example, a test of stress conducted in a laboratory may indeed not reflect the stress experienced in day-to-day life. But equally, a test of stress conducted at home might not reflect the stressful experiences people endure at work or during healthcare procedures. If so, the results may not generalise beyond the situation tested.

The task itself matters too. If the task participants are asked to do is similar to tasks in day-to-day life,

it has mundane realism. This is important as the findings are more likely to have high ecological validity if the task is realistic. For example, in an experiment on emotions, responses to dangerous polar bears or dangerous insects could be used. As fewer people would encounter polar bears, responses to insects are likely to have higher mundane realism and therefore higher ecological validity.

Generalisability

Ecological validity contributes to the generalisability of the results. Another factor that affects the ability to generalise is the sample. If the sample is very small, or does not contain a wide range of the different types of people in the population, it is unlikely to be representative. Restricted samples like this are more likely to occur with opportunity or volunteer samples than with a random sample.

Evaluating and applying concepts relating to methodological issues

You will need to be able to make evaluative decisions about methodology in relation to studies you already know about or a novel example of research or a study that you are asked to design yourself. In all of these cases, you need to ask yourself the following questions:

- Are the measures *reliable*? The study will collect data. Does the tool used to collect that data work consistently? Are the researchers using that tool in a consistent way? Is it *objective* or could they be *subjective* in their interpretation of the data?

- Is the study *valid*: Does it test what it is supposed to? This may depend on the reality of the task and the relevance of setting (*ecological validity*). Might the participants have been affected by *demand characteristics*?

- Are the findings *generalisable*: if not, why not? If so, how widely? This may depend on *ecological validity* or on the types and size of the sample.

- Could the research be *replicated*? What details would you need to know? Why might it be important to be able to do so?

You will also need to be able to suggest ways to improve the methodology used. You can consider improving the:

- *method* (e.g. a field versus a laboratory experiment or a questionnaire versus an interview)

- *design* (independent measures will have fewer problems with order effects but repeated measures could overcome issues with individual differences)

- *sample* (using opportunity sampling might allow a larger sample to be collected, volunteer sampling could help to find particular types of participant and random sampling would give better generalisability)

- *tool* (measuring the inter-rater reliability or test–retest reliability and changing procedures to make improvements)

- *procedure* (to raise validity by reducing demand characteristics, making the task more realistic, etc.).

RESEARCH METHODS IN PRACTICE

Dr Singh is planning an experiment on obedience. He wants to test whether drivers are more obedient to traffic wardens wearing white clothing or black clothing. He wants the test to be *valid*, so he uses the same male traffic warden wearing different clothing in each condition. He has four observers, one watching cars approaching a junction in his town from each direction. It is important that they are *reliable*, so he gives them operational definitions for the behavioural categories they are to observe:

- *Obedient behaviours*

  - slowing down: visibly reducing speed

  - stopping: coming to a halt before the line on the road.

- *Disobedient behaviours*

  - stopping late: coming to a halt past the line on the road

  - driving on: failing to stop when instructed to do so by the traffic warden.

CONTINUED

He aimed for these categories to be very *objective*. He believes that it is unlikely that the participants (the drivers) will respond to *demand characteristics* as they would not know that they were in an experiment. The drivers who stop past the line are given a note by a confederate while they are stationary. This *debriefs* them and asks if they would be happy to answer questions by telephone. Dr Singh's office number is given for them to call.

ACTIVITY 1.17

Look at the Research methods in practice box.

- Dr Singh is concerned about the *generalisability* of his findings. He has two ideas for changes to the procedure: conducting the same test in a village as well as his town and repeating the procedure using a female traffic warden in both conditions. Explain how each idea would improve generalisability.

- The proposed study has high *ecological validity*. Explain why.

- Dr Singh thinks that the observations in one of the behavioural categories, visibly reducing speed, could be subjective. Explain why this is likely.

- Dr Singh wants to measure the *inter-observer reliability* of his four observers. Explain why this is important.

- In the final part of the study, some participants find out that they have been in a study. Suggest one ethical problem that could arise from this.

- By giving the drivers a number to call, rather than taking their number and calling them, Dr Singh is giving the participants their *right to withdraw*. Why is this important?

CONTINUED

- Dr Singh asks the participants who do call him why they stopped and why they stopped over the line. He asks two of his colleagues to interpret the reasons they give but wants to ensure that they have high inter-rater reliability. He gives them a list of possible interpretations including a numerical scale to indicate how strongly the participant felt they may be punished. As both colleagues interpreted the responses from all the available drivers, Dr Singh can *correlate* the score given to each driver by the two colleagues to see if they are similar. What can he conclude if this produces a strong positive correlation?

- What other details would you need to know about this study to be able to *replicate* it in a town near you?

Questions

19 A teacher, Mr Nguyen, is planning to conduct an experiment using his students as participants. He is aiming to investigate whether more frequent or less frequent testing of the students during his course produces better results at the end of the course.

He is teaching the same course to two different groups. He gives the 'more frequent test' group a mini test every week and the 'less frequent test' group a test every two months.

a At the end of the course, Mr Nguyen assesses all the students with the same essay-based exam. His school expects pairs of teachers to 'double mark' all exams, so Mr Nguyen and his colleague both mark the exams from Mr Nguyen's classes using a detailed mark scheme. They mark one student's exam together to make sure that they are marking in the same way.

Explain whether this procedure will improve reliability or validity.

b After his study is complete, Mr Nguyen discovers that the students in the 'more frequent test' group have been sharing their mini tests with the students in the 'less frequent test' group each week.

Explain whether this will have been a threat to reliability or validity.

c Mr Nguyen hopes the study can be conducted again, the following year, asking students not to share the tests. However, he is also concerned about the generalisability of his findings.

Suggest what changes could be made to improve generalisability.

SUMMARY

Psychologists can use several different research methods; experiments (laboratory and field), self-reports (questionnaires and interviews), case studies (detailed investigations of a single instance, e.g. one person), observations, correlations and longitudinal studies.

In experiments, there is an independent variable (IV), which is manipulated, changed or used to create different conditions and a measured dependent variable (DV). By imposing controls, the experimenter can be more certain that changes in the IV are the cause of changes in the DV. There are three experimental designs. In an independent measures design there are different participants in each level of the IV, in a repeated measures design the same

participants are used in all levels of the IV and in a matched pairs design the participants are paired up with one member of each pair in each level of the IV. In a repeated measures design counterbalancing helps to overcome order effects (fatigue and practice effects) and in an independent measures design random allocation helps to overcome the effects of individual differences. In experiments it is important to control variables to raise validity. The most important are confounding variables. If these are left as uncontrolled variables, they can alter the apparent effect of the IV on the DV. Uncontrolled variables can be described as participant variables (due to differences between individuals or between the same individual at different times) or situational variables (due to differences in physical setting or the social situation).

CONTINUED

In self-reports, different question formats can be used, including open questions (producing qualitative data) and closed questions (producing quantitative data). An interview can have different formats: structured, unstructured or semi-structured. Different techniques can also be used. 'Paper and pencil' or online for questionnaires and telephone or face-to-face for interviews. Observations have many different features, for example structured (observing known categories) or unstructured (recording any events) and naturalistic (observing whatever is happening) or controlled (constructing events to observe). The role of the observer may be obvious to the participants (overt) or hidden (covert) and the observer themselves may be part of the social situations (participant) or not (non-participant).

Correlations are used to look for relationships between two co-variables that are measured. The findings of correlational studies can produce a positive correlation (the two variables increase together) or a negative correlation (as one variable increases the other decreases) but conclusions cannot be drawn about causal relationships between the variables. All variables, e.g. those in correlations, the IV and DV in experiments and behavioural categories in observations should all be operationalised.

Any research begins with an aim, which is developed into a testable hypothesis. This can be directional (one-tailed) or non-directional (two-tailed). This is compared to a null hypothesis, which proposes that there is no difference or relationship (or that any pattern in the results has arisen due to chance). To test the hypothesis, a group of participants (the sample) is selected from the population. This can be done by opportunity sampling (choosing people who are available), random sampling (selecting participants so that each individual has an equal chance of being chosen) or volunteer (self-selecting) sampling (inviting participants, e.g. by advertising).

Studies can collect different types of data. Quantitative data is numerical and qualitative data is descriptive. Data analysis of quantitative data includes using various measures of central tendency (the mean, median and mode) and measures of spread (the range and standard deviation). Data can be displayed graphically using bar charts, histograms or scatter graphs.

Research in psychology raises ethical issues. Some important issues relate to informed consent (knowing about the study and agreeing to do it), protection of participants (physically and psychologically), the right to withdraw (being able to leave a study), deception (being misled), confidentiality (keeping participants' data anonymous), privacy (not invading physical or mental space) and debriefing (explaining the study to participants afterwards and returning them to their previous state). There are also ethical guidelines relating to the use of animals, including issues relating to the species used, number of animals, the pain and distress they experience, the way they are housed and rewarded or deprived and their suffering.

Two very important methodological issues are validity and reliability. Ecological validity relates to how well the findings from one situation, e.g. a laboratory, represent what would happen in other situations. Subjectivity threatens validity because it causes researchers to interpret findings from their personal viewpoint, whereas objectivity allows researchers to measure variables in ways that are independent of their own perspective. Demand characteristics also threaten validity because they inform participants about the aim of the study which can alter their behaviour. Results of studies should be generalisable, that is they should apply to other people, situations and times. Reliability refers to the consistency of measures. In an experiment it is important to use standardisation of procedures to ensure that all participants are treated in the same way. This raises reliability. When researchers interpreting data are consistent, they have good inter-rater reliability (e.g. due to practice or operational definitions). Inter-observer reliability is the consistency in the records made by observers who are watching the same events. The reliability of a test, e.g. a questionnaire or a task in an experiment can be evaluated using a procedure to measure test–retest reliability, by conducting the test twice and correlating the two sets of data.

SELF-EVALUATION CHECKLIST

After studying this chapter, copy and complete a table like this:

I can	Needs more work	Almost there	Ready to move on	Coursebook	Workbook
describe and use the general concepts and terminology relating to research methods, including applying these to novel scenarios					
describe, evaluate and apply experiments (laboratory and field)					
describe, evaluate and apply self-reports (questionnaires and interviews)					
describe, evaluate and apply case studies					
describe, evaluate and apply observations					
describe, evaluate and apply correlations					
describe, evaluate and apply longitudinal studies					
explain and use aims and hypotheses					
explain and use variables, including operational definitions, uncontrolled variables, participant and situational variables and controls					
explain and use types of data including qualitative and quantitative					
explain and use samples, populations and sampling techniques					
explain and use ethical issues and guidelines for humans and animals in psychological research					
explain and use the concept of reliability					

CONTINUED

I can	Needs more work	Almost there	Ready to move on	Coursebook	Workbook
explain and use the concept of validity					
explain and use the concept of generalisability					
explain and use descriptive statistics including measures of central tendency and spread, tables and graphs.					

PROJECT

Plan a laboratory experiment and produce a written document containing:

- Your aim.

- Your IV and an operational definition for each level of the IV.

- Your DV with an operational definition and full details of how it will be measured.

- A statement of which experimental design you would use, and a justification of why you would choose this design.

- Details of controls you would impose, with a justification of why they are necessary.

- How you could, if you were to conduct the study, obtain a sample, including details of the sampling technique, the sample size and any special features of the sample.

- The materials that would be needed, such as any stimulus materials (such as word lists or images), questions that would be asked in a questionnaire or interview and a description of the format if appropriate as well as a scoring system for questions producing quantitative data.

- A description of any ethical issues that could arise and the steps that would be taken to follow all relevant ethical guidelines.

- A table that could be used to collect the raw data.

- A table that could be used for descriptive statistics and an indication of what these would be, including the measure of central tendency you would use.

- The axes for a graph, with a title, axis labels and units that could be used to display the data.

Note that, unless you have explicit approval from your teacher, you must **NOT** conduct this experiment.

REFLECTION

Think back to how you planned your study. This is the same process that psychologists use in research. They work from an aim, to devising a study that tests their aim in an ethical way that will produce valid, reliable and generalisable results. Can you identify any steps you included in your plan that contributed to reliability? To validity? Or to generalisability? If not, think about ways that you could change your study to improve it.

EXAM-STYLE QUESTIONS

1   A hypothesis in a study says 'Greater mindfulness will be achieved after a period in mindfulness training than after a period of waiting.'

   a   Is this an alternative hypothesis or a null hypothesis? Explain your answer. **[1]**

   b   Is this a directional (one-tailed) hypothesis or a non-directional (two-tailed) hypothesis? Include a reason for your answer. **[1]**

2   Jun is conducting a self-report study about attitudes to people with phobias. He cannot decide whether to use a questionnaire or an interview.

   a   **Suggest one** strength and **one** weakness of using a questionnaire for Jun's study. **[4]**

   b   Write **one** closed and **one** open question that Jun could ask. **[2]**

   c   Jun is concerned that his interpretation of the responses to questions might not be consistent. Is this mainly a reliability or a validity issue? **Explain** your answer. **[2]**

3   Priya is planning an experiment to find out whether boys or girls in her school doodle more.

   a   **Describe** how Priya could conduct her experiment. **[10]**

   b   Identify **one** possible weakness / limitation with the procedure you have described in your answer to part **a** and suggest how your study might be done differently to overcome the problem. **[4]**

4   A student is designing an experiment that aims to test whether parrots are more intelligent than cats. He has three parrots and two cats, which he plans to use as his sample. To find out which is most intelligent, he is going to hide their food bowl inside a box and time how long it takes the animal to get to the food.

   a   **Identify** and operationalise the independent variable in this experiment. **[1]**

   b   Identify and operationalise the dependent variable in this experiment. **[1]**

   c   Identify and outline the sampling technique used in this study. **[2]**

   d   Which measure of central tendency would be best to find out the average time taken to find the food? **[1]**

   e   A friend suggests that this is not a very valid test of intelligence because it might depend on how well the animal can smell the food. Explain this criticism. **[2]**

COMMAND WORDS

suggest: apply knowledge and understanding to situations where there are a range of valid responses in order to make proposals / put forward considerations

explain: set out purposes or reasons / make the relationships between things clear / say why and/or how and support with relevant evidence

describe: state the points of a topic / give characteristics and main features

identify: name / select / recognise

CONTINUED

5   A study into sleep obtained participants by placing advertisements in
    shops near to the university. The participants who responded were a
    sample of nine females and one male and were mainly retired people.
    The study was testing a new way to help people to fall asleep, using
    a recording of a bubbling stream. Half the participants were told it
    would help them to sleep, the others were told it would keep them awake.

    a   Identify and outline the sampling technique used in this study.   [2]

    b   Explain **one** possible problem with generalisability in this study.   [2]

    c   Describe **one** ethical issue that would arise in this study.   [2]

    d   How well the participants slept was measured in two ways, by
        self-report and by how many minutes they stayed asleep for.
        Which of these measures is more reliable and why?   [2]

                                                                    [Total: 39]

Additional references

Bateson, P. (1986). When to experiment on animals. *New Scientist, 1496*, 30–32.

Holahan, C. K., & Velasquez, K. S. (2011). Perceived strategies and activities for
successful later aging. *The international journal of aging and human development*, *72*(4),
343–359. doi:10.2190/AG.72.4.d.

Chapter 2

Biological approach

LEARNING INTENTIONS

In this chapter, you will learn how to:

* describe and apply the concepts and terminology of the biological approach and its main assumptions

* explain and apply the psychology being investigated in the biological approach

* describe, evaluate and apply the three core studies from the biological approach

* apply relevant research methods to the biological approach

* consider issues and debates that are relevant to the biological approach.

Introduction

The aim of this chapter is to introduce you to the biological approach to psychology and to explore three core studies that illustrate this approach:

- **Dement and Kleitman (1957)** is a study using experimental and correlational methods to investigate the relationship between dream content and eye movements during sleep. It uses EEGs and interview techniques to collect data. The main psychology being investigated was sleep, dreaming and ultradian rhythms.

- **Hassett et al. (2008)** is an experiment exploring toy preferences in monkeys by observing and coding the reactions of the monkeys to 'boy toys' and 'girl toys'. The researchers compare data from the monkeys to reactions of children to similar toys which had been collected in a different study. The main psychology being investigated was sex differences, socialisation, play and the role of hormones.

- **Hölzel et al. (2011)** uses brain scans and questionnaires in a longitudinal study to investigate how training in mindfulness changes brain structure. The main psychology being investigated was mindfulness and localisation of function.

GETTING STARTED

Biological psychology is about the way the physical systems of our bodies, including the brain, the nervous system and hormones, influence the way we act, think and feel. It is also about the way that we are shaped by our genes and evolution.

What have you been thinking, doing and feeling today? Your answer could range from 'nothing at all' to 'I've run a marathon', 'I've sat an exam' or 'I've cried because I couldn't do my homework.' All of those things are in some way controlled by your biology. Even if you were 'doing nothing' your brain was active, that is, a biological process of electrical and chemical signals along and between nerve cells (neurons) was happening. The movements when you run are controlled by your brain, and messages are sent along the neurons inside your arms and legs. The decisions you make answering exam questions are controlled by your brain too. Emotional responses like crying, even though we may not be able to control them, are governed by the brain, and hormones are important in the control of emotions too. A hormone called adrenalin would be released during the excitement of a marathon and would help you to run.

Hormones are released in particular situations. For example, adrenalin would be released if you were running away because you were scared. Adrenalin has effects that would help you to run faster, such as providing extra blood to the muscles. Biological responses like this have evolved because they help us to survive – by running faster we can stay safe. In order to be affected by evolution, aspects of a response, or the physiology that controls it, must be genetically controlled. Imagine a situation in which you were sleeping, and dreaming about jumping out of a window. If you actually did this in your sleep, it would be very risky. However, a system has evolved to protect us. When we are dreaming almost all of the muscles we use for movement (except the ones surrounding our eyes) are paralysed.

Think of a behaviour or an emotional response that could have been useful to survival during the early evolution of humans. Do you think it could be (partly) controlled biologically, by genes and hormones or the nervous system?

MAIN ASSUMPTIONS IN CONTEXT

Biological systems and processes

The main assumptions of the biological approach to psychology are that:

- behaviour, cognitions and emotions can be explained in terms of the working of the brain and the effect of hormones, genetics and evolution

- similarities and differences between people can be understood in terms of biological factors and their interaction with other factors.

Brain, hormones, genetics and evolution

Cognitive psychology compares our minds to computers. In biological terms, the brain (the structural element of the 'mind') is not like a computer. It is a living organ, made of cells. The cells in the brain (**neurons**) and **nervous system** are specialised for communication. Neurons send electrical signals along their length and interact using chemicals at **synapses**, where branchlike projections from different neurons are very close (see Figure 2.1). In the brain, neurons form areas with specific jobs, such as vision or hearing.

Hormones are also used to communicate within the body. These chemicals are released into the bloodstream from glands, such as the adrenal glands

that produce adrenalin in response to fear. Other glands include the testes (releasing **testosterone**) and the ovaries (releasing **oestrogen**). The nervous system sends very rapid but short-lived messages, whereas the messages sent to target organs using hormones are slower and longer lasting.

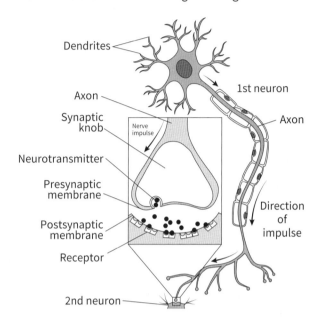

Figure 2.1: The structure of a neuron and a synapse

KEY WORDS

neurons: cells of the nervous system that are specialised for communication. They have a cell body, dendrites and an axon

nervous system: the brain, spinal cord and 'body' neurons, which detect and process incoming sensory messages, make decisions, and send messages out to organs and tissues, such as glands and muscles, to coordinate the body

synapse: the region of communication between neurons that is specialised to send and receive chemical messages

hormones: chemicals that are released from glands and travel around the body in the blood to communicate between organs

testosterone: a hormone released mainly by the testes, so is considered to be a 'male' hormone. It is therefore an example of an androgen

oestrogen: a hormone released mainly by the ovaries, so is considered to be a 'female' hormone

CONTINUED

A **gene** is a hereditary unit; an instruction that is passed from parent to child. Everyone's genes are individual, except for identical twins. Our genes determine our biological structure and function, including that of the brain and nervous system so underpin many functions. Biological systems are also affected by the environment so biological psychologists also study how genes and the environment interact to produce our behaviour, cognitions and emotions.

Genes are also fundamental to **evolution**. When genes pass from one generation to the next, changes called mutations can occur. Mutations produce variations between individuals which may be advantageous when the environment is challenging. When early humans faced threats from wild animals, starvation, etc, any mutation which aided survival would be likely to be transferred to future generations because those individuals were more likely to reach reproductive age and have children they could feed and care for. This is the process of 'natural selection' that drives evolution.

Biological factors, interactions and influences on individual differences

Identical twins have the same genes but are not entirely the same. Twins may have different interests, likes and dislikes, or abilities. This is because our psychological makeup is governed by the interaction of our genes and our environment. By 'environment', psychologists mean our physical situation plus the people around us, our opportunities and our experiences. You have probably been influenced by your family, school life, resources you can access such as books, events such as holidays and even injuries. These cultural, social and personal experiences work with our biology to create 'individual differences' between us. Individual differences encompass all the ways that people can vary from one another, for example in terms of intelligence, emotions and personality.

Looking back through your life, can you remember any specific experiences or social influences that have shaped you into who you are? Now think of some ways that you are like a relative, such as your parents or siblings. Could these similarities be due to genes or experiences?

KEY WORDS

genes: units of heredity, which carry instructions coded in deoxyribonucleic acid (DNA) from one generation to the next to control development and influence, for example personality and intelligence

evolution: the consequence of the process of natural selection, such that offspring that have inherited beneficial characteristics are more likely to survive

ACTIVITY 2.1

When learners discuss evolution, they usually imagine physical examples, such as giraffes with slightly longer necks being able to feed better than ones with shorter necks, or humans who could run faster being better able to survive attack than slower ones.

CONTINUED

However, psychological advantages matter too. For example:

- quick thinking can aid survival

- having the emotional skills for good social co-operation can help people to obtain food

- being able to communicate could offer protection.

For each of these examples, think of a specific way that early humans could have been different from one another in a way that would have given them a better chance of staying alive or having children and looking after them.

2.1 Core study 1: Dement and Kleitman (sleep and dreams)

Dement, W., & Kleitman, N. (1957). The relation of eye movements during sleep to dream activity: an objective method for the study of dreaming. *Journal of experimental psychology, 53, 339–346.*

The psychology being investigated

Sleep is an altered state of consciousness. We are less aware of our surroundings than when awake and move very little. In spite of the risk this would have presented in our evolutionary history, by making us vulnerable, we sleep every day. Our pattern of sleeping and waking on a 24–hour cycle is called a **circadian rhythm**; it occurs approximately daily. Within each 24 hours there are more frequent cycles, called **ultradian rhythms**. The basic rest–activity cycle (BRAC) occurs approximately every 90 minutes throughout the day and night. During sleep, this rhythm controls the stages of sleep that we experience (see Figure 2.2).

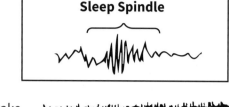

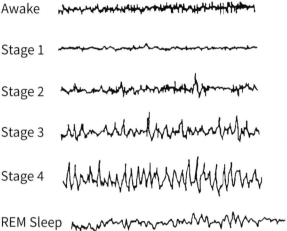

Figure 2.2: EEG recordings: the different stages of sleep

ACTIVITY 2.2

When you are working over several hours, note down the time you start working and any times when you feel tired or find your mind is wandering. Try to do this several times, perhaps over several days. At the end, look at the times when you felt less wake or motivated. Are they happening at intervals, perhaps close to regular number of minutes? If so, you may be looking at your own waking BRAC.

Work out a way to present this data visually. You will need a time scale and a way to differentiate between 'tired' and 'not tired'.

KEY WORDS

sleep: a state of reduced conscious awareness and reduced movement, which occurs on a daily cycle

circadian rhythm: a cycle that repeats daily, i.e. approximately every 24 hours, such as the sleep/wake cycle

ultradian rhythm: a cycle hat repeats more often than daily, e.g. the occurrence of periods of dreaming every 90 minutes during sleep

electroencephalograph (EEG): a machine used to detect and record electrical activity in nerve and muscle cells when many are active at the same time. It uses macroelectrodes, which are large electrodes stuck to the skin or scalp

Sleep is difficult to study as the participant is not responsive so cannot communicate their experience. To overcome this problem, a machine called an **electroencephalograph (EEG)** is used. This records changes in brain activity using electrodes stuck to the surface of the participant's head that, because they are recording electrodes, cannot give the participant an electric shock! An EEG produces a chart (an electroencephalogram) showing how electrical activity in the brain or 'brain waves' varies. The brain waves change in terms of their **frequency** (how rapidly they occur) and **amplitude** (height). These two features of the electrical activity change in a patterned way over time. The chart records changes which indicate the sleep stage the participant is in. Figure 2.3 shows the pattern of a typical night's sleep: we enter sleep in stage 1, then work through stages 2, 3 and 4 with our sleep becoming deeper so that we are harder to wake. From here, we re-enter stages 3, then 2 but instead of re-entering stage 1, we go into 'dream sleep' before repeating this cycle several times each night. During the night, the length of time we spend in dream sleep increases and the depth of each cycle reduces. The total length of each cycle therefore stays about the same, i.e. the ultradian rhythm is maintained.

Dreams are vivid, generally visual sequences of imagery that occur during sleep. Like sleep in general, dreams are difficult to study. Although the EEG can detect when we are dreaming, there is no machine that can 'read' our dreams. The sleeper must be woken to give a description of their dream. It is possible, however, to detect eye movements that occur during sleep. An EEG can be used to detect activity in the muscles moving the eyes, so can be used to measure the frequency and direction of these eye movements. The recording this produces is called an electrooculogram (EOG). During dream sleep,

these eye movements are faster than in any other stage of sleep, hence this is called **rapid eye movement** or **REM sleep**. The other stages of sleep are referred to as **non-rapid eye movement** or **nREM sleep**.

KEY WORDS

frequency: the number of events per fixed period of time, e.g. the number of eye movements per minute (approximately 60 per minute in REM sleep) or the number of brain waves (cycles) per second, or Hertz (Hz), e.g. 13–30 Hz for beta waves

amplitude: the 'height' of waves, e.g. on an EEG (indicating voltage)

dream: a vivid, visual sequence of imagery that occurs at regular intervals during sleep and is associated with rapid eye movements

rapid eye movement (REM) sleep: a stage of sleep in which our eyes move rapidly under the lids, which is associated with vivid, visual dreams

non-rapid eye movement (nREM) sleep: the stages of sleep (1–4) in which our eyes are still. It is also called quiescent (quiet) sleep. It is not associated with dreaming

---

RESEARCH METHODS

Measures of *frequency* and *amplitude* produce quantitative data. Data such as this tends to be highly *reliable*, as the machines used to produce it, such as the *EEG*, do not vary in the way that they measure the variables. In general, would you expect *qualitative data* to be more or less reliable? Why?

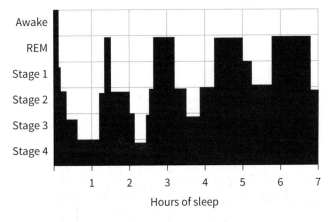

Figure 2.3: This chart illustrates the cyclical nature of sleep stages through the night, showing four phases of REM sleep and nREM stages (1–4)

Background

Aserinsky and Kleitman (1955) began the objective, physiological measurement of sleep using an EEG to explore the relationship between sleep and dreaming. They showed that participants woken from REM sleep were more likely to report a vivid, visual dream than when woken in other stages. They also found a characteristic brain wave pattern during REM sleep, called alpha waves, which is similar to brain activity when we are awake. However, unlike wakefulness, during these periods of rapid eye movement other muscles in the body were completely inactive.

From the EOG, Aserinsky and Kleitman could determine the frequency of the eye movements. Furthermore, they demonstrated that with recordings from electrodes in different locations, the difference between horizontal and vertical eye movements could be detected. They checked their ability to accurately record eye movements by looking at similar, deliberate movements in waking participants, and by watching, and filming, movements of the eyes during sleep and comparing these with the EOG records. Aserinsky and Kleitman also demonstrated that the rapid eye movements happened simultaneously in both eyes and that these movements happened on a 90-minute cycle.

In addition to the changes in brain waves and reduction in body muscle activity that Aserinsky and Kleitman linked to dream sleep, they also identified increases in breathing and heart rates during REM sleep. Together, this led them to suggest that this pattern of changes represented a particular level of activity in the brain. Aserinsky and Kleitman suggested that rapid eye movements were likely to be associated with the experience of dreaming, and specifically that the strikingly vivid visual reports of dreams that some participants reported when woken from REM sleep indicated that the eye movements were likely to be associated with the visual imagery of dreams. However, they also recognised that this would be difficult to test. The study by Dement and Kleitman aimed to explore this exact problem.

Aim

The aim of this study was to find out more about dreaming, specifically to answer three questions:

1   Does dream recall differ between rapid eye movement (REM) and quiescent (nREM) stages of sleep?

2   Is there a positive correlation between **subjective** estimates of dream duration and the length of the REM period before waking?

3   Are eye-movement patterns related to dream content?

KEY WORD

eye-movement patterns: the pattern that most people tend to follow when looking at, for example, a menu. This can be helpful in designing menus

---

Method
Research method and design

This study was conducted in a laboratory but several methods were used. To answer question 1 in the Aim section, about the difference in dream recall between REM and nREM sleep, an experiment with a *repeated measures design* was used. The independent variable was whether the participant was woken from REM or nREM sleep. The dependent variable was whether they recalled a dream or not. The test of question 2, about the relationship between dream duration and the length of the REM period, was a correlation. A further comparison of participants' estimates of whether they had been dreaming for 5 or 15 minutes was another repeated measures design experiment. To find out about question 3, the relationship between eye-movement patterns and dream content, *self-reports* were compared to the direction of eye movements observed.

Sample

Seven male and two female adults took part in the study. Of these, five participants were studied in detail. Results from the remaining four participants were used to confirm the results of the first five.

Procedure

On each day of the study a participant ate normally, excluding caffeine-containing drinks (such as coffee) and alcohol. The participant arrived at the laboratory just before their normal bedtime. The participant went to sleep in a dark, quiet room with electrodes attached beside the eyes and on the scalp (the EEG), which fed into the experimenter's room. The wires were gathered together into a single cord from the participant's head (like a pony-tail) so they could move easily in bed (see Figure 2.4).

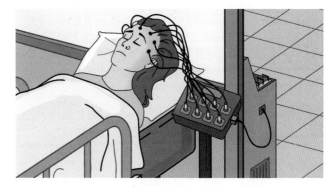

Figure 2.4: The participant slept in a bed with wires from the EEG electrodes leading into the room where the experimenter sat

Participants were woken (by a doorbell) at various times during the night, asked to describe their dream if they were having one, then returned to sleep. They were not told about their EEG pattern or whether their eyes were moving.

The procedure for the three questions differed:

Question 1

Participants were woken either from REM or nREM sleep but were not told which. The choice of REM or nREM waking was decided in different ways for different participants:

- using a random number table (participants PM and KC)

- in groups of three REM then three nREM (participant DN)

- by telling the participant that they would only be woken in REM but actually waking them in REM or nREM randomly (participant WD)

- in no specific order, the experimenter just chose (participant IR).

Immediately after being woken, the participant stated whether they were having a dream or not and then, if appropriate, described the content of the dream into a recorder. When the participant had finished, the experimenter occasionally entered the room to ask further questions about the dream (they were given a brief *interview*). There was no other communication between the experimenter and the participant.

Question 2

Initially, participants were woken after a variety of REM durations and asked to estimate the time they had been dreaming. Although roughly accurate, this was too difficult for participants. Subsequently, they were woken after either 5 or 15 minutes in REM sleep. The participant guessed which duration they had been dreaming for. Longer REM periods were also used. The number of words in the dream narrative after each duration, if given, was counted.

Question 3

The direction of eye movements was detected using EEG electrodes around the eyes. Participants were woken after a single eye-movement pattern had lasted for more than 1 minute and asked to report their dream. The eye-movement patterns detected were:

'mainly vertical', 'mainly horizontal', 'both vertical and horizontal' and 'very little or no movement'. Comparison EEG records were taken from awake participants, 20 naive ones and five of the experimental sample, who were asked to watch distant and close-up activity.

The environment was highly controlled, for example the doorbell used to wake participants was sufficiently loud to rouse them immediately from any sleep stage. If the experimenter asked any questions, this was not done until the participant had definitely completed their recording. Also, reports were not counted as 'dreams' if the participant could only recall having dreamed, rather than any specific content, or had only a vague, fragmented impression of the dream.

Results

Dement and Kleitman reported some general findings, such as that all participants dreamed every night, as well as those relating to their three questions. They found that uninterrupted dream stages:

- lasted 3–50 minutes (with a mean of approximately 20 minutes)

- were typically longer later in the night

- showed intermittent bursts of around 2–100 rapid eye movements.

In addition, they observed that:

- no rapid eye movements were seen during the onset of sleep even though the EEG passed through a stage of brain waves similar to those produced during REM sleep

- the cycle length (from one REM stage to the next) varied between participants from 70 to 104 minutes (with a mean of 92 minutes for all participants), but was consistent within individuals

- when woken from nREM sleep participants returned to nREM but when woken from REM sleep they typically did not dream again until the next REM phase (except sometimes in the final REM phase of the night). As a consequence, the pattern of REM and nREM periods was very similar in experimental participants whose sleep was disturbed to those who had an uninterrupted night's sleep.

The *mean* sleep cycle length was calculated for each individual. This would have been worked out by adding together the cycle lengths in minutes for every complete cycle a participant had slept through. This would then have been divided by the number of complete sleep cycles that had been observed for that participant.

Can you work out how variable the average cycle length was?

In relation to their three questions, Dement and Kleitman's results were as follows.

Question 1: Does dream recall differ between REM and nREM stages of sleep?

Participants frequently described dreams when woken from REM but rarely did when woken from nREM sleep although there were some individual differences (see Table 2.1). Participants were able to recall a dream from 152 of 191 awakenings from REM (79.6%) whereas for 93.1% (149/160) of awakenings from nREM they did *not* recall a dream. This difference was most noticeable at the end of the nREM period. In 17 nREM awakenings soon after the end of a REM stage (within 8 minutes), five dreams were recalled (29% of occasions). However, from 132 awakenings following periods longer than 8 minutes after a REM stage, only six dreams were recalled (less than 5% of occasions). In nREM awakenings, participants tended to describe feelings but not specific dream content. They were least likely to remember a dream if they were woken at the stage of sleep in which the EEG has 'spindles' (i.e. stage 2, see Figure 2.2). They tended to be bewildered and report feelings as such as anxiety, pleasantness or detachment.

It is important to note that participant DN was no more or less likely to report or not report dreams in REM or nREM than other participants even though he could have learned the pattern of awakenings. Also, participants did not become any more accurate over time, i.e. they did not improve with practice.

RESEARCH METHODS

The *practice effect* is when an individual's response improves due to familiarity with a task. It is possible that this could have happened for participant DN but not for other participants.

Can you explain why is it unlikely that other participants would have been affected?

Participant	Rapid eye movements		No rapid eye movements	
	Dream recall	No recall	Dream recall	No recall
DN	17	9	3	21
IR	26	8	2	29
KC	36	4	3	31
WD	37	5	1	34
PM	24	6	2	23
KK	4	1	0	5
SM	2	2	0	2
DM	2	1	0	1
MG	4	3	0	3
Totals	152	39	11	149

Table 2.1: Dream recall following awakenings from REM or nREM sleep

Awakenings from REM sleep did not always produce dream recall; absence of dreaming in REM was more common early in the night. Of 39 REM awakenings when dreams were not reported, 19 occurred in the first 2 hours of sleep, 11 from the second 2 hours, 5 from the third 2 hours and 4 from the last 2 hours. In contrast, awakenings from nREM always produced a low incidence of dream recall.

Question 2: Is there a positive correlation between subjective estimates of dream duration and the length of the REM period before waking?

The results of two tests help to answer this question. Firstly, the experiment to determine whether participants' subjective experience of dream duration matched the measured REM duration. Second, the correlation between the measured REM duration and the estimate of duration based on the participants' dream narrative length. When participants were offered a choice of estimating that they had been dreaming for 5 or 15 minutes, the accuracy of estimation was very high (88% and 78% respectively). Table 2.2 shows the results of this experimental comparison.

The r values for the correlation of duration of REM period (in minutes) and number of words in the dream narrative for each participant varied from $r = 0.4$ to $r = 0.71$; all were significant positive correlations.

Narratives from dreams recalled after 30–50 minutes of REM were not much longer than those after 15 minutes even though the participants felt they had been dreaming for a long time. This is probably because they could not remember all the details from very long dreams.

Question 3: Are eye-movement patterns related to dream content?

Eye-movement patterns were found to be related to dream content. This part of the study was based on 35 awakenings from nine participants. Periods of only vertical or only horizontal movements were very rare. There were three dreams with mainly vertical eye movements. In one dream, the participant was standing at the bottom of a tall cliff operating a hoist (a lifting machine) and looking up at climbers at various levels then down at the machine. In another dream, a man was climbing up a series of ladders looking up and down as he climbed. In the third dream, the participant was throwing basketballs at a net, shooting, looking up at the net, and then looking down to pick up another ball from the floor (Figure 2.5). There was one instance of a dream with horizontal movement, in which the dreamer was watching two people throwing tomatoes at each other.

Participant	Number of occasions when participants' judgement of 5 or 15 minutes was correct or not			
	5 minutes		15 minutes	
	correct	incorrect	correct	incorrect
DN	8	2	5	5
IR	11	1	7	3
KC	7	0	12	1
WD	13	1	15	1
MP	6	2	8	3
Total	45	6	47	13

Table 2.2: Results of the comparison of dream duration estimates after 5 or 15 minutes of REM sleep

Figure 2.5: Dreams of climbing ladders and throwing basketballs produced vertical eye movements

Ten dreams had little or no eye movement and the dreamer reported watching something in the distance or staring at an object. Two of these awakenings also had several large eye movements to the left just a second or two before the awakening. In one, the participant had been driving a car and staring at the road ahead. He approached a road junction and was startled by a speeding car suddenly appearing to his left (as the bell rang). The other dreamer also reported driving a car and staring at the road ahead. Immediately before being woken, he saw a man standing to the left of the road and acknowledged him as he drove by.

Twenty-one of the awakenings had mixed eye movements. These participants reported looking at objects or people close to them, for example talking to a group of people, looking for something and fighting with someone. There was no recall of distant or vertical activity in these cases.

The eye-movement patterns recorded from the awake (control) participants were similar in amplitude and pattern to those occurring in dreams. Similarly, there was virtually no eye movement when watching distant activity and much more when watching close-up activity. Vertical eye movements were rare in awake participants,

except during blinking, and when the experimenter threw a ball in the air.

Conclusion

The results indicate that dreaming is experienced in REM but not nREM sleep, participants can judge the length of their dream duration and REM patterns relate to dream content. Dreaming is more likely at the end of the night, as the REM stages are longer. These latter two observations fit with those reported by other researchers. The occasional recall of dreams from nREM is likely to happen because dreams are being remembered from the previous REM phase, and this is more likely closely following REM sleep. The finding that REM sleep occurs in phases during the night helps to explain why participants in other studies who were awoken randomly may not have reported dreaming. They may have been woken in nREM stages, or were dreaming about distant objects so had few REMs, making accurate detection difficult. Measurements using the EEG to record eye movements and brain waves show that differing stages of brain activity and the presence or absence of dreams provides objective evidence supporting the idea that dreams progress in 'real time'. This provides a more valid way to study dreaming than using dream recall alone, which is subjective and can be affected by forgetting.

Strengths and weaknesses

One method used was the *laboratory experiment*. It was therefore possible to limit the effect of some *uncontrolled variables*. If some individuals, or participants in different stages of sleep, had woken more slowly they may have forgotten more of their dream. This was avoided by using a loud doorbell that woke them instantly from any sleep stage. The participants were not told about their EEG pattern or whether their eyes were moving, or were given false information about this. Both of these procedures help to eliminate potential demand characteristics. For example, if the participant expected to remember more detailed dreams in REM sleep, they may have made greater effort to do so.

Another method used was a correlation. This demonstrated a positive correlation between REM duration and the number of words in the dream narrative. As with any correlation, this could only demonstrate whether there was a link between variables, not a *causal relationship*. Furthermore, although participants' estimates were roughly (and occasionally exactly) accurate, the task of unstructured time estimation was too difficult, so the method was changed to explore the link in a more controlled way. The task was limited to a choice between 5 and 15 minutes. This experimental study helped to raise validity as it reduced participant variables such as differences in the ability to recall dreams.

The definition of a 'dream' was clearly operationalised, as a recollection that included content, rather than just having the impression that they had been dreaming. This helped to raise validity, as Dement and Kleitman could be sure that the details being recorded were of dreams.

An EEG is an objective way to investigate dreaming as it is a biological measure. Differences in narrative length, however, depended not only on the length of the REM phase but also how expressive the participant was, making these reports more subjective. Nevertheless, this means that the study collected both quantitative data, from the brain waves, eye-movement patterns and REM sleep duration, and qualitative data, which helped to provide an insight into the reason for the eye movements detected. The EEG also provides a very reliable measure because it is unaffected by the experimenter's personal view. The consistent placing of the electrodes ensured that recordings taken from each participant would provide the same information. The *reliability* of the findings is supported by the similarity of the results to those of previous studies.

As there may be differences in the dreaming of men and women, or between the way they report their dreams, it was useful in terms of *generalisability* that there were both genders in the sample. However, as there were only nine participants in total, the small size of the sample limits generalisability. As these individuals had chosen to participate in a study on dreaming, they may have dreamed more frequently than the population in general, remembered their dreams better, or had more visual dreams for example.

Several aspects of the procedure potentially reduced the ecological validity of the findings. People who were used to drinking coffee or alcohol could have experienced sleep or dreams that were not typical for them as they had been asked to refrain from those drinks. Also, all participants would have found sleeping in a laboratory, connected to machines and under observation, quite different from sleeping in their normal bed. This could also have made their sleeping behaviour less typical.

Ethical issues

One aspect of the method that raised an ethical issue was the *deception* of participant WD who was misled about the stage of sleep he was being woken in. Researchers should avoid using deception as it can cause distress and means they cannot give their *informed consent*. However, in some cases the aim cannot be achieved without doing so and, in this case, it provided a way to test whether expectation of being woken in REM (at least sometimes) would affect a participant's dream reports.

Summary

Dement and Kleitman's study explored the relationship between eye movements during sleep and dream recall. An EEG provided information about participants' sleep stages, such as REM sleep, and about eye movements. Dream recall was measured by self-report. The correlational results showed that estimates of dream duration based on the number of words in the dream narrative correlated positively with REM duration. Results from the laboratory experiments showed that dreams occurred in REM rather than nREM sleep and confirmed that participants had a sense of the duration of a dream as they could accurately estimate whether they had been dreaming for 5 or 15 minutes. Furthermore, the content of the dream narratives related to EOG records of the direction and amount of eye movements during dream sleep showing that this is related to dream content, e.g. that vertical movements of the eyes occur when there are vertical events in a dream. Many variables, such as food and drink that could affect sleep, were controlled and demand characteristics were reduced where possible. However, the laboratory, and equipment, meant that the situation was unusual for sleeping. Nevertheless, objective, quantitative data was obtained from the EEG, eye movements and timing, allowing for valid and reliable comparisons to be made.

Questions

1   Eye-movement patterns were found to be related to dream content. What type of eye movements were observed in the dream about a man who was climbing up a series of ladders looking up and down as he climbed, and why?

2 What could a person be dreaming about if they have few eye movements during REM sleep?

3 Why was it necessary for Dement and Kleitman to change the way they tested whether there was a positive correlation between estimates of dream duration and the length of the REM period?

2.2 Core study 2: Hassett et al. (monkey toy preferences)

Hassett, J. M., Siebert, E. R., & Wallen, K. (2008). Sex differences in rhesus monkey toy preferences parallel those of children. *Hormones and behaviour*, 54(3), 359–364.

The psychology being investigated

Sex differences are the ways that males and females differ that are caused directly by sex, and include both physical and behavioural differences. There are differences in male and female brains, and in their hormones, that impact on human behaviour. For example, in our discussion of the brain for the key study by Hölzel et al., we will describe how language functions are localised to areas in the left hemisphere. This is the case for men and women, although in women language functions are relatively more bilateral, i.e. spread over both sides of the brain. This is one of several known biological differences between male and female brains. There are several differences in hormones too. The most obvious is that, post puberty, males have about ten times more testosterone than females, and females have much more oestrogen than males.

However, it is difficult to determine the extent to which some behavioural differences between males and females are the product of biological differences due to their sex, or social differences in their experiences due the different ways in which society treats males and females. Many factors are involved in the way a child experiences the social world and these add together to create the process of socialisation, that is, the way we are moulded by society into adults who 'fit in'. Differences in behaviours between men and women are traditionally believed to be rooted in socialisation. Boys watch, copy and are rewarded for behaving like men: being tough, active and oriented towards doing things. Girls, in contrast, are rewarded for watching and copying the behaviour of women, so tend to become more passive and caring. So, the socialisation process is, at least partly, determined by gender. This cultural bias, or gender stereotype, is based on a culturally determined, oversimplified belief that all members of one gender share the same characteristics and that these are different from the other gender. Toys can therefore be described as 'masculine' or 'feminine' according to gender stereotypes.

> **KEY WORDS**
>
> **socialisation:** the process of learning to behave in socially acceptable ways. This may differ somewhat for the two genders and in different cultures
>
> **gender stereotype:** a bias exhibited in society, which may be held by people and represented, for example, in books or toys that assign particular traits, behaviours, emotions, occupations, etc. to males and females
>
> **play:** behaviour typical of childhood, that appears to be done for fun rather than any useful purpose. It may be solitary or social and may or may not involve interaction with an object. Objects designed for the purpose of play are called 'toys'

One behaviour in which differences can be seen between males and females is in play. We often see boys engaging in active, sometimes aggressive, play with guns, toy tractors and building sets. Girls, however, are more usually seen engaging in nurturing play with dolls, playhouses and kitchen sets, i.e. being more passive and caring. In terms of socialisation, this isn't surprising, as girls and boys are encouraged to play with gender-stereotyped toys, that is, toys that fit society's view of gender-appropriate behaviour (Figure 2.6). This influence has long been assumed to be the primary cause of gender differences in play.

Figure 2.6: Children playing with stereotypically 'girl toys' and 'boy toys'

Background

Humans are complicated. Our brains are highly complex in structure and function and our behaviour is affected by our social and physical environments as well as our biology. This complexity makes humans difficult to study, as so many factors could be affecting any one outcome. In some research, the complexity of the human experience can be simplified by excluding many variables, for example in a laboratory experiment where the effect of a single independent variable can be studied by controlling other, potentially confounding, variables and by having a control condition from which the independent variable is absent. It is nevertheless sometimes impossible to conduct such studies because isolation of variables cannot ethically, or practically, be done. One such instance is in the case of children's development.

Hassett et al. described an important finding that prenatal hormonal exposure of human infants (the hormones they are exposed to during gestation) affects toy preferences in children. Some girls have a genetic condition that causes increased androgens (male hormones) during foetal development. Such girls preferred to play with traditionally 'boys' toys than their unaffected sisters or control females. This was the case even when they receive increased socialisation to encourage 'female-appropriate' activities. Opportunities to study these hormonal differences in children are rare and the validity of the findings will be limited by uncontrolled variables such as the exact amount of hormonal exposure and the extent of gender-related socialisation.

It would be unethical to deliberately expose developing human foetuses or children to hormones, or to remove key factors from a child's environment to control their experience. However, a model for such research exists. A model is nothing more than a representation of a phenomenon, often on a smaller or simpler scale. In the case of human development, a simpler model is needed, and one that offers the opportunity to control experiences. Higher primates, closely related to humans genetically, and with some very similar behaviours, can provide such a model.

Social activities such as 'rough-and-tumble', peer preferences and interest in infants differ between the genders. These activities are seen not only in children but also in other primates, who show genders differences which match those of children with, for example, males engaging in more rough-and-tumble play and less interest in infants than females. By looking at primate models of human behaviour it may be possible to see whether gender differences in behaviour could be caused by biological rather than social differences. Young primates, like young humans, have different levels of hormones according to their sex. Prepubescent males have more testosterone, a hormone associated not only with strength and aggressive behaviour but also, at least in humans, being associated with spatial skills for example. Young females have more oestrogen than males, and this hormone is associated in adult females with nurturing behaviours such as caring for offspring.

Aim

The aim of the study was to investigate whether toy preferences in monkeys resemble those in children, in order to test whether sex differences in toy choice is biologically determined by sex.

Method

Research method and design

This was a *field experiment* as the environment in which the participants were tested was their normal, outdoor housing area and they were free to interact with the toys or not. Although the toys were new to them, they would not have been unfamiliar with objects being placed in their enclosures. The *experimental design* was independent measures as the independent variable was gender; each animal being recorded was either male or female. *Observations* were used as a technique to measure the dependent variable of activities with the toys. As well as looking for differences between the genders, a correlation was also conducted on the results, to look for a relationship between individual monkeys' ranks within the social hierarchy and the frequency or duration of activities with each toy type. Finally, data from the monkeys was compared to similar data relating to children obtained from a different study. This was an independent measures comparison.

Sample

The participants were 21 male and 61 female rhesus monkeys (Figure 2.7) living in natal (birth) groups as part of a wider group of 135 animals at the Yerkes primate research station in the USA. Of these 135 animals, 14 adults were not studied as they had received hormone treatments and 39 young infants were excluded as they could not be reliably identified. Each natal group was housed in a 25 × 25 metre outdoor area with access to a temperature-controlled indoor environment. They had water available, were given a standard monkey feed twice a day and additional fruit and vegetables once daily.

Figure 2.7: Young rhesus monkeys

Procedure

To reflect differences in activity preferences in sexually differentiated behaviours the toys chosen were divided into two categories by their properties as objects rather than gender-typing, although the outcome of this categorisation was comparable to the traditional 'boys' toys', 'girls' toys' divide. The category of 'wheeled toys' matched vehicle toys, typically for boys, and 'plush toys' matched typical girls' toys. 'Plush' toys are soft, cuddly ones. There were six wheeled toys ranging in length from 16 to 46 cm (wagon, truck, car, construction vehicle, shopping cart, dump truck) and seven plush toys ranging in length from 14 to 73 cm (Winnie-the-Pooh™, Raggedy-Ann™, koala hand puppet, armadillo, teddy bear, Scooby-Doo™, turtle). Apart from size, the toys also varied in terms of shape and colour.

For each social group, seven trials, each lasting 25 minutes, were observed using two video cameras. Each trial began with all the monkeys in the group indoors while one plush toy and one wheeled toy were placed 10 metres apart in the outdoor enclosure. One video recorder was directed towards each toy and the plush and wheeled toys were *counterbalanced* between left and right locations on each trial. After each trial the toys were removed and the video tape was analysed by two observers working together to achieve a consensus. They identified each animal interacting with a toy and coded specific activities directed towards the toys using a behavioural checklist (see Table 2.3). The exact time at which each activity occurred was also recorded so, in addition to the frequency of each behaviour, a record of the duration of continuous activities was kept.

ISSUES AND DEBATES

The use of animals in psychological research: rhesus monkeys are a highly intelligent, social species, so their needs in terms of housing and protection from pain and distress are great. However, those same characteristics, of intelligence and sociability, make them excellent models for human behaviour. There is therefore a balance between the potential benefits of conducting valid research on a species closely related to ourselves and the costs to the individual animals involved in the research.

Monkey behaviour	Description of behaviour
Extended touch	Placing a hand or foot on toy
Hold	Stationary support with one or more limbs
Sit on	Seated on the toy or a part of the toy
Carry in hand	Moving with the toy in hand and off the ground
Carry in arm	Moving with the toy in arm and off the ground
Carry in mouth	Moving with the toy in mouth and off the ground
Drag	Moving the toy along the ground behind the animal
Manipulate part	Moving, twisting or turning a part
Turn entire toy	Shifting 3-D orientation of toy
Touch	Brief contact using hands or fingers
Sniff	Coming very close to the toy with the nose
Mouth	Brief oral contact – no biting or pulling
Destroy	Using mouth or hands to bite or tear toy
Jump away	Approach, then back away from toy with a jumping motion
Throw	Project into air with hands

Table 2.3: Specific activities coded in interactions with the wheeled and plush toys

To analyse the data, the records for each behaviour for each animal were converted into an overall average frequency and duration for that individual. This was because each animal could have participated in a different number of activities in different trials. Not all individuals interacted with the toys and those with fewer than five total recorded behaviours were not used in the analysis (14 males and 3 females). The final number of individuals used in the analysis was 11 males and 23 females.

RESEARCH METHODS

The descriptions of behaviours in Table 2.3 are examples of *operational definitions*. They enabled the observers who were coding the video tapes to work together to achieve inter-coder reliability and would allow other researchers to *replicate* the study.

Results

Comparisons were made between males and females and between each gender's preference for wheeled or plush toys. It was possible to make such comparisons on the basis of number of interactions (frequency) and how long was spent interacting with the toy type (duration). The data in Table 2.4 is a summary of the results used in these comparisons.

Statistical analyses comparing toy preferences *within* each sex, using frequency data, found that males preferred wheeled compared to plush toys but that females did not show a preference for plush toys over wheeled toys. A comparison *between* the sexes, again using frequency data, also found that females interacted

Toy type	Sex of monkey	Frequency		Duration (minutes)	
		Mean	Standard deviation	Mean	Standard deviation
Wheeled	Male	9.77	8.86	4.76	7.59
('masculine' toy)	Female	6.96	4.92	1.27	2.2
Plush	Male	2.06	9.21	0.53	1.41
('feminine' toy)	Female	7.97	10.48	1.49	3.81

Table 2.4: The mean frequency and duration of interactions with the wheeled and plush toys for males and females

with plush toys more than males, but there was no sex difference for wheeled toys. In comparisons of the duration data, males interacted for a longer time in total with wheeled toys than with plush toys. However, the duration of time spent interacting with the different toy types did not differ for females, who played for a similar total length of time with wheeled and plush toys. Even though the difference in play durations for the male monkeys was big enough to show a significant difference between time spent playing with wheeled and plush toys, no significant difference was found in a between-sex comparison. This means that there was no overall difference between the time that males and females spent with playing with the wheeled and plush toys.

Further comparisons were made to calculate 'magnitude of preference', that is, how much males preferred the 'masculine' (wheeled) toy and how much females preferred the 'feminine' (plush) toy. For males, this was calculated by taking the difference 'total frequency of wheeled toy interaction − total frequency of plush toy interaction'. For females, the equation 'total frequency of plush toy interaction − total frequency of wheeled toy interaction' was used. The same type of comparison was also performed on the duration scores. Statistical analysis of these differences confirmed that male monkeys had a higher preference for 'masculine' (wheeled) toys than female monkeys had for the 'feminine' (plush) toys. The results of a comparison of toy preferences of individual male and female animals are shown in Table 2.5.

	Percentage of individuals preferring each toy type	
	Males	Females
Preference for wheeled toys	73	39
Preference for plush	9	30
No significant preference	18	30

Table 2.5: Preferences of individual monkeys for different toy types

Differences between the sexes were still evident when the data was re-examined taking into account the social ranks of the individuals. Furthermore, correlations were also conducted on the results to look for relationships between individual monkeys' ranks within the social hierarchy and the frequency or duration of activities with each toy type.

For males and females combined, rank and total frequency of interactions were positively correlated for the wheeled toy and for the plush toy. Using just the data for males, neither frequencies nor durations correlated with rank. For females, however, rank was positively correlated with frequency of interactions for the wheeled toy and for the plush toy, although rank only correlated with duration for the plush toy, not the wheeled toy. As this shows that rank may be related to toy interactions in females but not in males, it is unlikely that social rank is responsible for the sex differences in toy preference overall. Furthermore, although the sample size was too small for a detailed analysis of the results by age, comparisons were possible between wider groups. A comparison between juvenile, subadult, adult and old animals did not differ in terms of frequency or duration for either toy type.

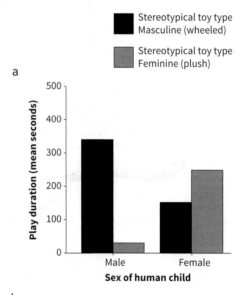
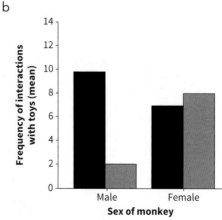

Figure 2.8: Sex differences in children's and rhesus monkeys' play with stereotypically masculine and feminine toys

Hassett et al. compared the data for the frequencies of interactions by the monkeys with different toy types to data for the durations of similar behaviours in children. The data for children was taken from another study (Berenbaum and Hines, 1992). The comparison is shown in Figure 2.8, which illustrates that the patterns are very similar. Both the rhesus monkeys and the human children showed gender differences, with males preferring masculine toys and females preferring feminine toys. In addition, for human children, as with rhesus monkeys, the preference was much more marked for males than for females.

Conclusion

The results show that, like boys, male monkeys have a strong preference for masculine-type toys, in this case ones with wheels. Female monkeys, like young girls, are more variable in their toy preferences. In addition, the extent to which individuals preferred masculine or feminine (in this case plush) toys differed between males and females, with male monkeys showing much stronger preferences for wheeled toys than female monkeys did for plush toys.

Hassett et al. argue that their findings support a biological explanation for toy preferences. Specifically, they concluded that these preferences develop in the absence of socialisation. This is because in monkeys, unlike in humans, only hormonal differences not social ones can be responsible for the differences in development of males and females. Importantly, such biologically driven differences could interact with social pressures on children. Boys choosing girls' toys tend to receive more negative responses than girls choosing boys' toys. This would reinforce a pre-existing biological tendency for boys to be more masculine in their toy choices and for girls to remain more variable in their choices.

Strengths and weaknesses

A key strength of this study was the use of animals to eliminate the effect of socialisation. This was taken further, to exclude *confounding variables* that could affect social interactions, such as age and social rank. The age of individuals was known as the monkey group had been established for over 25 years. Social rank had been assessed though behavioural observations of who groomed whom, dominance behaviours and submissive behaviours. Analysis demonstrated that these social factors had little effect on the sex differences in toy preference.

The observation process was highly *standardised*, for example with clear operational definitions of behaviours to improve reliability. The trials were of a standard length of 25 minutes, however, one had to finish 7 minutes early as the plush toy was torn into pieces.

A weakness of the study was that were some differences in the way that the monkeys and the children were compared. For example, the masculine and feminine toys offered to the monkeys were chosen for their object properties rather than because they were gender-stereotyped toys for children. The measures of 'masculine' and 'feminine' play were also different for the monkeys and the children. The children were assessed in a different study using different toys and only measuring duration of play not frequency. Furthermore, the most significant comparison was between frequency for the monkeys and duration for the children, rather than duration for both.

The study used to provide data about children tested each participant individually. In contrast, this study observed the monkeys in groups. This methodological difference may have been important. Alexander and Hines (2002) studied the interactions of vervet monkeys with toys and found the same pattern of gender difference in that a greater proportion of males' toy interactions were with masculine toys and a greater proportion of females' toy interactions were with feminine toys. However, in contrast to both children and Hassett et al.'s rhesus monkeys, the vervet males interacted for a similar amount of time with masculine and feminine toys, unlike females, who were more gender-specific in their duration of play, spending more time with feminine toys. Rather than being a genuine species difference, this pattern could have been explained by the way toys were presented to the vervet monkeys — one at a time rather than together–thus, they were not given a genuine 'choice'. Similarly, testing monkeys in groups and children alone could have influenced the findings in Hassett et al.'s study.

ISSUES AND DEBATES

Nature versus nurture: Has the study by Hassett et al. overlooked the possibility that early socialisation in primates may influence the gendered development of play behaviours? This would suggest there may be a 'nurture' explanation, even in animals. However, Hassett et al. report a study by Alexander and Hines (2002) on vervet monkeys, which found that unlike human boys, male vervets

---

play as much with masculine as with feminine toys. In contrast to human girls, who spend very similar amounts of time with 'masculine' and 'feminine' toys, the female vervets played for significantly longer with feminine than with masculine toys. Although this may superficially look as though it supports a nature view, it would require that female vervet monkeys are more strongly socialised to prefer female toys than human girls are. This seems unlikely, so overall findings from animal studies support the idea that gender differences in toys preferences are the result of nature.

Ethical issues

Research with non-human animals is typically controlled by laws, and psychological institutions offer guidelines for their use. This study was conducted following appropriate *ethical guidelines* for the care of animals in the USA and was approved by Emory University Ethical committee on animal care and use. In terms of feeding, the animals received regular and appropriate food (twice daily monkey feed plus daily fruit and vegetables) and had constant access to water. They were ethically housed in family groups, in large enclosures, with access to both a temperature-controlled indoor area and an outdoor area. The observation using cameras would not have been distressing and the level of interactions with the toys suggests that their novelty was not in general a source of psychological distress or physical pain. However, one toy was destroyed but it is unknown whether this was a playful act or a reflection of distress.

Summary

Hassett et al.'s study investigated whether rhesus monkeys show a similar pattern of sex differences in toy preferences to children. In studies where the participants are children, it is difficult to separate any biological causation from social effects. In monkeys, however, the role of hormonal influences on toy preferences, without the effect of socialisation, would be clear. Videoed observations of groups of monkeys given a masculine (wheeled) toy and a feminine (plush) toy were analysed using a behavioural checklist of interactions. They found that male monkeys, like boys, prefer masculine toys and female monkeys, like girls, have less fixed preferences in their toy choices. This evidence supports a biological

explanation for toy preference because the monkeys' preferences must have developed without the effect of socialisation to which children are normally exposed.

Questions

4 Hassett et al. used two types of toy, 'masculine toys' and 'feminine toys'. How were these two types of toy different?

5 Why did Hassett et al. exclude some of the monkeys from this study?

6 How was the data about children obtained?

7 Why was a correlation of social rank and total frequency of interactions conducted?

2.3 Core study 3: Hölzel et al. (mindfulness and brain scans)

Hölzel, B., Carmody, J., Vangel, M., Congleton, C., Yerramsetti, S., Gard, T., & Lazar, S. (2011). Mindfulness practice leads to increases in regional brain gray matter density. *Psychiatry research*, *919*(1), 36–43.

The psychology being investigated

Very early in the study of psychology, researchers thought that there might be meaning behind the shape of a person's skull. Nowadays, psychologists focus on the role of areas within the head, i.e. brain regions. Many parts of the brain are associated with particular types of information processing or with specific activities. This is called 'localisation of function'. For example, Figure 2.9 shows areas responsible for deliberate movements (the motor cortex), skin and muscle sensation (the somatosensory cortex), language functions (Broca's and

KEY WORD

localisation of function: refers to the way that particular brain areas are responsible for different activities

Wernicke's areas) and sleep (part of the brain stem). Much of our brain structure is symmetrical down the centre line (from the nose to the back of the head). As a consequence, many brain areas are 'bilateral', that is they are found in both the left and right sides or 'hemispheres'. The motor and somatosensory cortex are present on both sides of the brain (although the left side of the body is represented on the right side of the brain and vice versa). Broca's and Wernicke's areas, in contrast, are usually found only in the left hemisphere.

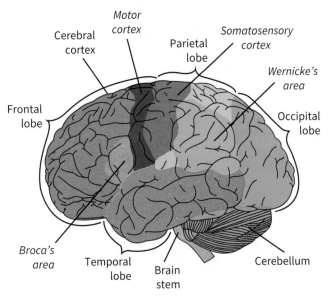

Figure 2.9: Localisation of the brain

Localisation can be investigated in various ways, historically by studying dead bodies or using surgery, on both animals and humans. Brain scanning techniques are a huge advance in biological psychology. Psychologists can now study the brains of living people and draw conclusions about the relationship between behaviours, cognition and the structure or function of the brain. There are two basic types of brain scan: functional and structural. Structural scans take detailed pictures of the shape of brain areas whereas functional scans show activity levels in different areas of the brain. Using modern structural magnetic resonance imaging (MRI) allows detailed images of living brains to be made. During an MRI scan, the participant is placed in a scanner which produces a strong magnetic field around their head. Protons in the brain line up with the magnetic field, and when the magnets are turned off, the scanner detects the energy released as the protons return to their original positions. As the proton concentration varies in different kinds of brain matter,

the scanner is able to create a very detailed picture of the brain. During an MRI scan, the participant lies on a bed that enters the narrow tube of the scanner. During the scanning process, there is a loud noise inside the scanner and some people find the narrow tube confining, although it remains open by their feet (see Figure 2.10). Although the scanning process is not painful and is harmless, it is unsuitable for people who have some metals in their bodies, such as pacemakers, metal plates or shrapnel because these would be attracted to the magnet.

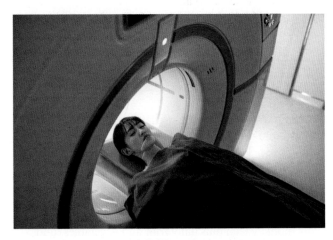

Figure 2.10: To study the brain in an MRI scanner, the participant enters the tunnel head first

One of the regions being investigated in this study is the hippocampus. This brain area has many roles, such as in memory and navigation. It is also believed to be involved in controlling emotion and the arousal and responsiveness of the cortex. The hippocampus can therefore determine which of many sources of incoming we find stimulating. These are ways in which the hippocampus could be involved in the effects of mindfulness mediation. Furthermore, the hippocampus is a brain area which is known to show plasticity, that is, to be capable of creating new neurons and many new synapses between neurons. Examples of this plasticity include negative emotional experiences such as stress reducing hippocampal volume and treatment with antidepressant drugs increasing hippocampal volume.

Some brain areas have, for a long time, been known to play particular roles for instance the pons (in the brain stem), is involved in the control of sleep and dreams and the cerebellum controls 'automatic' or well-learned movements. For other activities of interest to psychologists, the importance of particular brain regions is still being discovered. One such activity – for which localisation is still being investigated – is **mindfulness**. Through mindfulness, a person becomes more aware of their current experience, their physical sensations as well as their thoughts and feelings. This helps them to enjoy life more by seeing themselves in a kinder, more accepting way. This can help us, for example, to appreciate simple positive experiences such as smells, sounds or sights and to notice signs that we are becoming anxious, stressed or depressed. This self-awareness enables us to act earlier and more effectively to reduce these problems. Mindfulness mediation is a formalised way to raise mindfulness. It typically involves being silent and directing attention to oneself, for example focusing on our own thoughts, sensations and sounds such as the regular rhythm of breathing.

KEY WORD

mindfulness: is a state achieved through meditation that aims to increase awareness of the present-moment experience and enable a person to look at themselves in a compassionate, non-judgemental way

Background

Mindfulness involves thinking and sensations, and this information is processed by the brain. It could therefore be possible to study what part or parts of the brain are involved in the changes in attention and thinking associated with mindfulness. Early studies of mindfulness and the brain used the EEG (as used by Dement and Kleitman in Core study 1) but it is now possible to use the more detailed process of MRI. This neuroimaging procedure enables precise measurement to be taken of the brain. For example, the size of different structures can be calculated and the amount of grey matter (the cell bodies of neurons) compared to white matter (the axons of neurons). MRI is able to detect small structural changes in the concentration of grey matter over time, and such changes are apparent in different kinds of training, including the learning of physical skills, and cognitive skills such as juggling (Figure 2.11), medical students revising for their exams and mirror reading.

Figure 2.11: Training in juggling produces changes in brain structure that can be detected by an MRI

Studies have compared individuals who engage in different kinds of meditation, including mindfulness mediation, and those who do not and have found differences in grey matter in various brain areas that appear to be associated with meditation. However, these studies have been *cross-sectional*, that is, they compared different groups of people: those who meditated and those who did not. It is therefore possible that brain differences found between the groups were caused by pre-existing differences between the participants rather than by the meditation itself. For example, if people who choose to meditate have more grey matter to start with, the results would appear to show that meditation increased grey matter, but this would be a misleading conclusion.

ACTIVITY 2.3

If you had the use of a brain scanner and could localise a function, what function would you want to locate? Explain why you would want to study this function to a partner or write an email to a psychologist to justify why they should conduct this research.

Peer assessment

Present your argument to one of your peers, by email or face to face. Let them judge how convincing your argument is.

Discuss with a partner whether it is an advantage for the human brain to have specialised locations for some tasks or whether there is a benefit to having tasks distributed across the brain. If you can, try taking opposing viewpoints.

Aim

Hölzel et al. planned their study to overcome the potential problem experienced in earlier cross-sectional studies by using a *longitudinal design*. The *aim* was to identify changes in specific brain regions, and the whole brain, by comparing grey matter concentration before and after a mindfulness course.

Method

Research method and design

This was an *experiment* using a longitudinal design, as a group of participants was tested before (pre) and after (post) an intervention. They were also compared to a control group. The *independent variable* was exposure to an eight-week mindfulness-based intervention, the Mindfulness-Based Stress Reduction (MBSR) course. Participants were tested pre- and post-attendance on a course consisting of a two-and-a-half-hour session each week for eight weeks, and a full day session in the sixth week. They were trained in mindfulness exercises intended to develop awareness of present-moment experiences and a compassionate non-judgemental view. The exercises included:

- 'body scan', where attention is guided in a sequence through the whole body, which ends with a perception of the body 'as a complete whole'

- 'mindful yoga', which includes gentle stretching and slow movements, and breathing exercises, which aim to raise awareness of the moment-to-moment experience

- sitting meditation, which focuses on the sensation of breathing, and progresses to sounds, sights, tastes, other body sensations, as well as thoughts and emotion.

A 45-minute recording of these guided mindfulness exercises was given to each participant with the instruction to practise them daily at home (their 'homework'). In the sessions participants attended, guidance was given for how to engage in mindfulness in everyday life, such as such as while eating, walking, washing the dishes or taking a shower. Instruction was also given on how to use mindfulness to cope with stress in daily life.

In addition, a comparison of the MRI results from part of the study was made between the experimental (MBSR) group and a control group of participants who had not experienced the mindfulness intervention. This part of the experiment used an *independent measures design*.

The main *dependent variable* was the change in grey matter assessed using MRI scans. In addition, participants completed *questionnaires* to measure five mindfulness scales (both before and after the intervention).

Sample

Participants were recruited from people already enrolled on MBSR courses at the University of Massachusetts. They enrolled to help with stress reduction either because they had chosen to attend the course or had been referred by their doctor. All participants described themselves as physically and psychologically healthy and not taking medication. In addition, they had limited experience of meditation classes (none in the last six months and a maximum of four in the last 5 years, or ten in their lifetime), were aged 25–55 years, were safe to have an MRI scan (e.g. no metal in their bodies and not claustrophobic) and committed to attend all sessions and complete the homework exercises.

The initial experimental *sample* of eight males and ten females fell to 16 as two males left after the first MRI session due to discomfort. The remaining sample had a *mean age* of 38 years (*standard deviation* 4.1 years) and included 13 Caucasian, one Asian, one African American and one multi-ethnic participant.

The control sample consisted of seven males and ten females with a mean age of 39 years (standard deviation 9.2 years) and included 13 Caucasian, two Asian, two African American and one Hispanic participant. These two groups did not differ in terms of their educational level. Importantly, these control participants had the same eligibility criteria as the experimental participants for admission to the mindfulness course, hence they are described as a 'wait-list' control group.

The study was approved by the University of Massachusetts Institutional Review Board (ethical committee) and all participants gave written consent and received a discounted MBSR course fee.

Procedure

The experimental and control groups both completed the Five Facet Mindfulness Questionnaire (FFMQ), which has 39 items that measure:

- Observing: attending to/noticing internal and external stimuli, such as thoughts, feelings and sensations, including sights, sounds and smells

- Describing: mentally labelling these observations with words

- Acting with awareness: being attentive to current actions rather than responding automatically or absentmindedly

- Non-judging (of inner experience): not evaluating sensations, cognitions or emotions

- Non-reactivity (to inner experience): allowing thoughts and feelings to drift in and out.

Each item on the FFMQ is a statement and is responded to on a five-point Likert-type scale (see Figure 2.12). For items with standard scoring, such as 'I'm good at finding words to describe my feelings' a mindful participant might choose the response 'Very often or always true', scoring 5, or 'Often true', scoring 4, whereas a less mindful participant might choose 'Rarely true' (2) or 'Never or very rarely true' (1). Other items are 'reversed scored', such as 'I am easily distracted'. For these, a mindful participant might choose to respond with 'Rarely true' (scoring 4) or 'Never or very rarely true' (scoring 5). The total score for each of the five subscales is added up (there are seven or eight items for each subscale) and these totals are added together for a total FFMQ score. The questionnaire was completed by the experimental group before and after the MBSR course. The control group also completed the questionnaire twice. In each group, 14 participants provided useable data at both time points.

RESEARCH METHODS

Reverse scoring is often used in questionnaires as it helps to improve the *validity* of the data. In this case, the 'most mindful' responses were not always on the left-hand side of the questionnaire sheet. Why would this be important to validity?

Please rate each of the following statements with the number that best describes *your own opinion* of what is *generally true for you*.		Never or very rarely true	Rarely true	Sometimes true	Often true	Very often or always true
1	When I'm walking, I deliberately notice the sensations of my body moving.	☐ 1	☐ 2	☐ 3	☐ 4	☐ 5
3	I criticize myself for having irrational or inappropriate emotions.	☐ 5	☐ 4	☐ 3	☐ 2	☐ 1
4	I perceive my feelings and emotions without having to react to them.	☐ 1	☐ 2	☐ 3	☐ 4	☐ 5
5	When I do things, my mind wanders off and I'm easily distracted.	☐ 5	☐ 4	☐ 3	☐ 2	☐ 1

Figure 2.12: Extract from the Five Facet Mindfulness Questionnaire (Baer et al., 2006), items 1, 3, 4 and 5

Participants in both the experimental and control groups had MRI scans of their brains on two occasions. For the experimental group, these were during the two weeks before and two weeks after the eight-week MBSR intervention (an average gap of approximately 56 days). These are called the 'pre' and 'post' tests. Participants in the control group had an average gap of approximately 66 days between their two scans.

The data from the MRI scans was used in two ways: to produce a 'regions of interest' (RoI) analysis, of particular brain areas, and to provide a 'whole-brain analysis'. Two regions of interest were the hippocampus on both sides of the brain (bilateral hippocampi) and bilateral insulae (see Figure 2.13). The whole-brain analysis was used to explore other regions potentially affected by the mindfulness intervention.

ACTIVITY 2.4

You can obtain a copy of the FFMQ online. Type in the whole name or just FFMQ and you should be able to find free pdfs of the whole questionnaire and shortened versions of it. Have a look at the questions and their scoring system.

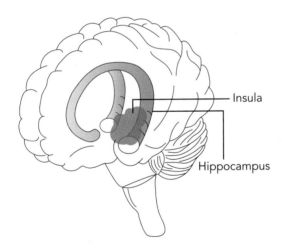

Figure 2.13: The location of the hippocampus and insula in the left hemisphere

Finally, participants reported the time they spent on formal homework exercises over the eight weeks, and

the amount of time spent on each of the three exercises (body scan, yoga and sitting meditation).

Results

The experimental (MBSR) participants spent an average of 22.6 hours on mindfulness homework during the course, or approximately 27 minutes per day. Table 2.6 gives detailed data for the different exercises. None of the three measures were significantly *correlated*. For example, the **correlation coefficient** between body scan and sitting meditation was $r = -0.26$ and between yoga and sitting meditation was $r = 0.49$.

KEY WORD

correlation coefficient: a number between −1 and 1 that shows the strength of a relationship between two variables with a coefficient of −1 meaning there is a perfect negative correlation and a coefficient of 1 meaning there is a perfect positive correlation

MBSR exercise	Minutes			
	Minimum	Maximum	Mean	Standard deviation
Body scan	335	1002	699	217
Yoga	103	775	327	194
Sitting meditation	0	755	332	211

Table 2.6: Time spent by MBSR participants on homework exercises

Useable FFMQ data from both time points was obtained from 14 MBSR and 14 control participants. Participants in the MBSR group significantly increased their mindfulness scores on three of the subscales between the pre and post questionnaires (acting with awareness, observing and non-judging). Furthermore, when this change was compared to that of the control group – which was not expected to change at all – the changes in mindfulness scores of the MBSR group were significantly greater on all three subscales.

In the test of grey matter concentration in the left hippocampus, no differences were detected between the MBSR and control groups at the start of the study (i.e. at the pre-test stage). Nor were there any changes in grey matter concentrations in the control group between the two test points. Importantly, changes in this region of interest were detected in the MBSR group between the pre- and post-tests, based on a group size of 16 (see Table 2.7). This change did not, however, correlate with either the amount of homework completed by the participant or changes in their FFMQ scores. The grey matter concentration in other regions of interest did not show significant changes between the pre- and post-intervention tests.

The results from the whole-brain analysis also revealed changes. Four clusters in the brains of participants in the MBSR group were found to have significantly increased in grey matter concentration between the pre- and post-tests. These clusters were in the posterior cingulate cortex, the left temporo-parietal junction and in two parts of the cerebellum (the lateral cerebellum and the cerebellar vermis/brainstem) as shown in Table 2.7. These differences were also significantly greater than changes in corresponding areas of the brains of participants in the control group. As with the regions of interest findings, there were no correlations between the changes in these four areas and the amount of homework completed by the participant or changes in their FFMQ scores. In the MBSR group, no parts of the brain were found to have significant decreases in grey matter concentration after the MBSR intervention although there were some small reductions in grey matter concentration in the control group over the study period.

RESEARCH METHODS

'Grey matter concentration' is the proportion of grey matter compared to other tissues in an area. When changes are expressed as a positive number, they represent increases. When they are negative numbers, this means that the change is a decrease. As the measures are relative changes rather than absolute volumes, the figures can be converted to percentages, for example the change of +0.01 for the left hippocampus in the MBSR group means that the volume of grey matter in the left hippocampus increased by 1% between the pre- and post-test.

Conclusion

The results from the regions of interest findings show that structural changes in the left hippocampus arise within an eight-week period of participation in a mindfulness course. This finding suggests that localised increases or decreases in hippocampal volume that have been demonstrated in other situations may happen in response to mindfulness meditation. Since the hippocampus plays a role in learning and memory, this suggests that during the MBSR course participants had learning experiences that changed the hippocampal grey matter.

Furthermore, increases in grey matter concentration in the left temporo-parietal junction (TJP), posterior cingulate cortex (PCC), and cerebellum of the MBSR

	Approximate changes in grey matter concentration				
	Region of interest	Whole-brain analysis			
	Left hippocampus	Posterior cingulate cortex	Left temporo-parietal junction	Lateral cerebellum	Cerebellar vermis/ brainstem
MBSR group	+ 0.01	+ 0.01	+ 0.007	+ 0.015	+ 0.014
Control group	+ 0.001	− 0.005	− 0.002	+ 0.001	− 0.001

Table 2.7: Changes in grey matter concentration in the brains of MBSR and control participants

group but not the control group also suggest that participation in an eight-week mindfulness course causes structural changes in these brain regions. Although not specifically predicted, these findings reflect other research that has shown the involvement of these areas in responses linked to mindfulness.

The TJP is important in the way we see ourselves or 'self-referential processing', for example the unity of our sense of self and our physical body. When processing in the TJP is impaired, this self-referential system can become faulty and can lead to out-of-body experiences. This links to the role of mindfulness training in learning to perceive the body as a 'complete whole'. Similarly, the PCC has a role in the way we judge the relevance of stimuli to ourselves, for example assessing how important an experience is to our emotional or autobiographical context. These functions arise in mindfulness too, for example in noticing internal and external stimuli and being attentive to moment-to-moment experiences of such stimuli.

In addition, one of the key areas of the cerebellum identified as changing due to the mindfulness practice has a role in regulating emotions and cognition for healthy psychological functioning. That areas of the hippocampus, TPJ and PCC were found to change in response to the mindfulness intervention is interesting as they, together with parts of the prefrontal cortex, form a brain network with many related functions, such as recalling the past, thinking about the future, and considering others' viewpoints such as in turn-taking. Together, these areas contribute to the way that autobiographical information enables the individual to consider alternative perspectives. This is a crucial step in achieving a mindful state.

ISSUES AND DEBATES

The application of psychology to everyday life: mindfulness is encouraged for not just stress reduction but potentially for helping people to sleep and improving physical health. By understanding the brain changes associated with mindfulness, combined with knowledge of the roles of the areas of the brain affected, mindfulness techniques, and their benefits, can be improved.

Strengths and weaknesses

The main method was a *longitudinal study* as a group of participants was tested before and after a lengthy

intervention, in contrast to previous cross-sectional studies in which *participant variables* may have confounded results. This is a strength because, by allowing time for the intervention to have an effect, the researchers were able to wait for the experiences of the intervention to affect brain plasticity in a measurable way. The addition of a control group allowed a comparison to ensure that such changes were not simply attributable to the passage of time.

The use of an MRI scanner to measure the dependent variables was a strength because it provided the researchers with *quantitative data*, enabling them to carry out statistical analyses such as comparisons between pre- and post-test levels of grey matter volume and between the MBSR and control groups. The experience in an MRI scanner is hardly *ecologically valid* as it is noisy and confining, features which are potentially emotional and therefore relevant. However, it would not be possible for the participants to alter their grey matter volume in response to *demand characteristics*, which increases the validity of the data collected.

Using MRI scanners to measure brain structure gives *objective* data as the recorded volumes themselves do not need the researcher to interpret any results, which is also a strength. However, we need to be careful that we do not infer too much from MRI results as there are still many unknowns about the localisation of specific behaviours in the brain and the meaning of changes in volume. Although MRI is a widespread technique, the interpretation of data with respect to neural changes and how this maps onto changes in thoughts and emotions is much less objective, which is a potential weakness.

Another weakness is the absence of correlations between increases in grey matter in any brain area examined and either the amount of mindfulness homework completed or changes in FFMQ scores. This is important because it suggests that the number of minutes spent in mindfulness practice is not the direct cause of brain changes. Instead, the researchers propose that the effect is mediated by the MBSR programme as a whole. If so, further research would be needed including a control group given only the non-mindfulness-specific parts of the course to isolate the effects of mindfulness meditation itself. For example, the control group would need to attend seven weekly sessions plus a full day experience of social contact, which they believed would reduce stress, as well as committing ongoing time to their wellness.

Ethical issues

This study raised few *ethical issues*. To ensure the participants were protected during scanning, none accepted for the study had any metal implants, which could present a risk of physical harm, or claustrophobia, which could present a risk of psychological harm. Also, following their *right to withdraw*, two participants left the study after the first MRI scan as they found the procedure uncomfortable. All of the participants were experiencing stress, identified through doctor- or self-referral. The participants allocated to the control group had to wait for at least eight weeks before they could receive assistance. This delay in help again risks a failure to *protect participants from harm*. However, it is unknown whether there was capacity for people to begin the course in advance of this time, so this may have been an issue beyond the researchers' control.

Summary

Hölzel et al.'s study was an experiment using a longitudinal design. This tested exposure to an eight-week Mindfulness-Based Stress Reduction (MBSR) intervention, in comparison to a wait-list *control condition*. Participants in the intervention group kept a record of their mindfulness activities. All participants were given two tests at the start and end of the time period: an MRI scan to measure grey matter concentration in the brain and a questionnaire testing mindfulness. Brain areas found to increase in the MBSR participants compared to the controls were the left hippocampus, PCC, TJP and cerebellum. The mindfulness scores of the MBSR group but not the controls increased, however, this increase did not correlate with brain changes. The findings suggest that an MBSR intervention can cause changes in grey matter concentration in brain areas that play roles in learning, memory, self-referential processing, emotions and considering the viewpoints of others.

Questions

8   Controls are ways that the levels of the independent variable are kept the same. What controls did Hölzel et al. use in their experiment?

9   Why was Hölzel et al.'s longitudinal study more valid that the earlier cross-sectional studies?

10   a   What 'homework' did Hölzel et al.'s experimental participants do?

   b   How sure were Hölzel et al. that it was this homework that produced the brain changes they found?

Issues, debates and approaches

The application of psychology to everyday life

The EEG, as used by Dement and Kleitman, allows psychologists to accurately detect dreaming. This has useful applications for assessing people with sleep and dream disorders, for example people with insomnia, nightmares or people who sleep walk.

The study by Hassett et al. supported a biological explanation for toy preferences. This shows that socialisation is not the only important factor in the development of gender-specific behaviours. One possible outcome from this could be to suggest that some gender differences in children are inevitable. Such an interpretation could maintain the disadvantage already experienced by individuals wanting to succeed in careers typically associated with the opposite sex. However, it could alternatively – and more beneficially – help to stress the need for gender neutral socialisation to enable all individuals to access all possible opportunities. This would recognise that gender-typed socialisation threatens to widen the divide between males and females early in childhood.

The study by Hölzel et al. found that an MBSR intervention significantly increased mindfulness. As mindfulness is important to 'self-referential processing', for example the unity of our sense of self and our physical body, this could offer a way to help people with temporo-parietal junction (TJP) impairments in which this system can become faulty. For such individuals, learning to perceive the body as a 'complete whole' may help to reduce their out-of-body experiences. Similarly, the areas of the cerebellum in which Hölzel et al. identified changes caused by the intervention are important in regulating emotions and cognition for healthy psychological functioning, thus identifying another possible beneficial role for mindfulness.

Individual and situational explanations

The study by Hassett et al., although demonstrating a clear role for biology, also recognises that this interacts with the situational effects of exposure to gender stereotyping within society. Both through cultural expectations and the direct reinforcement and punishment of 'gender-appropriate' or 'inappropriate' behaviours, and through sheer exposure to gender stereotypes.

Nature versus nurture

The biological approach focuses mainly on the nature side of this debate, which is why it is possible to obtain evidence through procedures like the EEG, which was used in the Dement and Kleitman study to measure brain waves and eye movements. It is useful to be able to collect physiological evidence about brain activity as it provides direct evidence for the underlying biological processes, such as the link between dream content and eye movements.

Dream content relates to our experiences, so is a product of nurture. This, at least partly, explains the differences in dreams between individuals. Nurture influences will vary; thus, the content of people's dreams will differ. However, as even a foetus in the uterus experiences REM sleep, the capacity to dream appears to be a product of nature. Similarly, the biological processes underlying emotions are the product of the brain and of hormones.

Hölzel et al.'s study also has a clearly 'biological' focus on brain structure. This is determined largely by processes of nature, hence the similarities between individuals and even between humans and animals. However, Hölzel et al. demonstrated that the experience of the MBSR programme changed brain structure. This is an effect of nurture and shows that even those structures and processes that seem highly constrained by biology can be influenced by experience.

The study by Hassett et al., in contrast, demonstrated biological effects that were likely to be the result of differences in sex hormones, to show an enduring influence of nature. This illustrated that sex differences in the human play of boys and girls, often assumed to be a product of socialisation, may not, after all, be entirely caused by nurture.

The use of children and animals in psychological research

The study by Hassett et al. demonstrated a common technique, the use of comparative psychology.

This is a process of finding evidence that helps to explain human behaviour by comparison to animal models. As non-human animals are less complex than humans, and their environment and experiences can be controlled, they provide a way to investigate the origins of human behaviours. This study was able to isolate the effect of biology (hormones) and experience (socialisation) to help to explore the causes of gender differences in children. Apart from the practical benefits, the use of animals both solves and raises ethical issues. It could be argued that it is or that it is not ethically acceptable to manipulate the environments of rhesus monkeys, whereas it would certainly be ethically unacceptable to manipulate the experiences of children such that they were not exposed to culturally driven socialisation.

In addition, it is useful to consider whether the other studies in this section could have used animals and what the findings might have shown. If you have a mammal for pet, you may have seen it apparently dreaming about running as it moves its legs, making quiet sounds or twitching its nose. Non-human animals such as mammals do demonstrate REM sleep, and this has been studied extensively. It is very difficult, however, to determine the content of their dreams. This has been done indirectly, by using brain-cell recording techniques to explore repeated waking behaviours (such as bird song and rats running mazes). It has been found that the patterns of brain activity during sleep closely resemble those of the waking behaviours, indicating what the animals are dreaming about.

ACTIVITY 2.5

It is possible to use EEGs on the brains and eyes of babies. Plan a study to investigate the dream content of babies. This could include whether they are dreaming about objects that are still/distant or moving, and in which direction moving objects are travelling.

REFLECTION

Consider what steps you took in your planned study to ensure that it was ethical, and how these steps differed for a baby compared to an adult. If you found that you were unable to plan an ethical study, explain why this was so.

SELF-EVALUATION CHECKLIST

After studying this chapter, copy and complete a table like this:

I can	Needs more work	Almost there	Ready to move on	Coursebook	Workbook
state what is meant by the biological approach					
explain the psychology being investigated in the biological approach					
describe the main assumptions of the biological approach and link them to the studies					
use terminology relevant to the biological approach					
describe and evaluate the study by Dement and Kleitman (sleep and dreams)					
describe and evaluate the study by Hassett et al. (monkey toy preferences)					
describe and evaluate the study by Hölzel et al. (mindfulness and brain scans)					
apply relevant research methods to the biological approach					
consider issues and debates that are relevant to the biological approach.					

PROJECT

If you remember your dreams, keep a dream diary for a week. When you wake up and remember a dream, guess how long it lasted, write this down, then turn the page or cover up your estimate. Try to write down a description of the dream you can remember. Finally, think about whether each dream would have had few or many eye movements and whether these would have been vertical or horizontal.

At the end of the week, look at how many dream records you have. If it isn't very many, you may want to continue with your dream diary for longer. If you ever woke up in the night, decide whether you were more or less likely to remember a dream than when you woke up in the morning. Can you explain your answer?

CONTINUED

When your dream diary is complete, count the number of words in each dream narrative and convert your time estimate into whole numbers (e.g. whole seconds or whole minutes). Record your data in a table with a row for each day that you dreamed and two columns, one for the time estimate and another for the number of words. Finally, draw a *scatter graph* of your data. Does it look as though you have a positive correlation? If so, why? If not, suggest what you could do to improve the likelihood of finding one.

Your final piece of work should include:

- an example of a dream narrative that you are willing for other people to read
- the raw data table of duration estimates and word counts
- a scatter graph
- answers to the questions.

EXAM-STYLE QUESTIONS

1 Biyu is planning a study on dreams and is concerned about a problem: if her participants know the aim, they might make dreams up to please her.

   a i   **State** the type of problem that Biyu is concerned about. [1]

      ii   Explain why this would be a problem. [1]

   b   Biyu had decided to solve this problem by telling her participants the study was about insomnia, but her teacher says she cannot do this. Explain why Biyu's teacher has said this. [3]

2 Karl is aiming to find out whether people sleep for longer because they have eaten more. He plans to do a correlation, asking people how much they have eaten during the day and how long they sleep for that night. Karl's teacher says this will not work.

   a   Suggest why Karl will not be able to use the information he obtains from his study to come to a conclusion about his aim. [2]

   b   Karl decides to do the study anyway. Explain how he could operationalise the variables of sleeping and eating. [4]

3 There are some ethical problems with the study by Hassett et al. and also some ethical strengths. **Outline one** ethical strength of this study. [2]

4 **Compare** the biological approach and the learning approach to show two ways in which they are different. Use the study by Hassett et al. as an example of the biological approach. [4]

5 Simi is using a brain scan to investigate localisation of autobiographical memories. These are the memories we have of our own lives.

   a   Explain how Simi could decide which brain areas to study. [2]

   b   Suggest why it would be important for Simi to use participants who had clear autobiographical memories. [2]

6 From the study by Hölzel et al., explain whether the sample of participants used was representative or non-representative. [2]

7 **Evaluate** the study by Dement and Kleitman, including two strengths and two weaknesses. [10]

[Total: 33]

COMMAND WORDS

outline: set out main points

compare: identify/comment on similarities and/or differences

evaluate: judge or calculate the quality, importance, amount, or value of something

> Chapter 3
Cognitive approach

LEARNING INTENTIONS

In this chapter, you will learn how to:

- describe and apply the concepts and terminology of the cognitive approach and its main assumptions

- explain and apply the psychology being investigated in the cognitive approach

- describe, evaluate and apply the three core studies from the cognitive approach

- apply relevant research methods to the cognitive approach

- consider issues and debates that are relevant to the cognitive approach.

Introduction

The aim of this chapter is to introduce you to the cognitive approach to psychology and to explore three core studies that illustrate this approach:

- **Andrade (doodling)** suggests that doodling can improve concentration on, and memory for, a conversation. The main psychology being investigated was attention and memory.

- **Baron-Cohen et al. (Eyes test)** investigates how a test for 'theory of mind' has been improved, to better identify differences in the way that adults with Asperger syndrome or autism recognise emotions. The main psychology being investigated was theory of mind and social sensitivity.

- **Pozzolu et al. (line-ups)** explores child eyewitnesses' ability to identify the perpetrator of a crime and factors that affect their accuracy. The main psychology being investigated was false positive responses and eyewitness testimony.

GETTING STARTED

Cognitive psychology is all about what we do with information: how it gets inside our heads, what we do with it once it's there and how we get that information back out again. Think about the information that you have dealt with in the last 10 minutes. By 'information' you can include things you have heard, seen or become aware of through other senses, as well as your own thoughts. You probably know about the five senses already and what information they each process. Now consider the information you have encountered in the last few hours.

Cognitive psychology is not just about how information gets into the system, but how we keep it in our heads and take it out again. These are the processes of storage and retrieval: memory processes. Storage is about keeping hold of memories. How much of the information from the last few hours can you remember, and how clearly? How certain are you that what you can remember is correct? Look back at the last week. What did you eat each day? Even though you saw, smelled and tasted the food you ate, and formed an opinion about it, you probably can't recall every meal. Was it because you weren't concentrating? Were you doing something else at the same time as eating? Have those memories gone forever?

Once memories have been stored, we then need to retrieve them. Talk with someone else about what they ate. Can you tell from their facial expressions how much they enjoyed each meal? Have their descriptions reminded you of any more of your meals? What else could help you to recall your experiences from last week? Are there any factors you think could have made your memory less clear than it was at first?

MAIN ASSUMPTIONS IN CONTEXT

The main assumptions of the cognitive approach to psychology are that there are:

- similarities between the way people and computers process information

- individual differences in cognitive processes such as attention, language, thinking and memory, which can help to explain our differing behaviours and emotions.

Cognitive psychologists study concepts such as attention, memory, decision-making and language development. They also apply their knowledge, for example to how cognition affects behaviour and the accuracy of memories such as when giving evidence about a crime.

Similarities between human and computer information processing

Memory is a cognitive process of encoding, storing and retrieving information.

CONTINUED

When we experience an event, we 'encode' (convert) the sensory information so that it can be stored. 'Storage' is the brain's record of the event. Finally, to use that information, it must be 'retrieved', through recognition or recall (Figure 3.1).

Figure 3.1: Memory and information processing

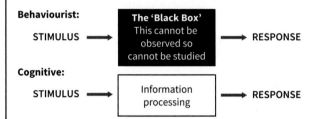

Figure 3.2: The behaviourist 'stimulus-response' model and the cognitive information processing model

Cognitive psychologists study 'information processing'. This contrasts with behaviourist (learning) psychologists, who believe that only activities that can be seen can be studied. Behaviourists therefore only explore situations by observing the 'stimulus' and the 'response', for example, how changing a stimulus changes behaviour. Cognitive psychologists are interested in the events *between* detecting a stimulus and making a response (see Figure 3.2). The sequence they study can be compared to the working of a computer, as input ➡ processing ➡ output (see Table 3.1). The similarities between computers and human minds can help us to understand human cognition (see Figure 3.3). Like computers, we take information in (encode) in different ways, we have more than one memory store, and produce outputs from this processing of information, such as movements and sounds (see Table 3.1). There are also differences: computers are less likely to forget but are less good at guessing.

	People	Computers
INPUT	Eyes (detecting light, colour and movement)	Camera, scanner
	Ears (detecting sound)	Microphone
	Skin (detecting pressure)	Touch pad, keyboard, mouse
PROCESSING	Thinking and decision-making in the brain	Central processing unit (CPU), the control centre of the computer
	Brain functions such as short-term memory	Random access memory (RAM), the computer's fast, temporary memory – which you lose if the computer crashes
	Brain functions such as long-term memory	Hard drive, a computer's 'permanent' memory
OUTPUT	Voice	Speakers
	Body, e.g. hands for writing, drawing, moving	Screen, printer

Table 3.1: Similarities between computer and human information processing

CONTINUED

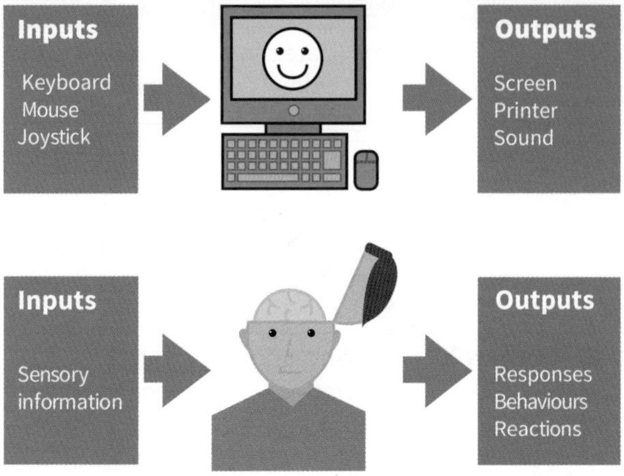

Figure 3.3: Cognitive psychologists often compare the way the brain processes information to a computer

Individual differences in cognitive processes

Psychologists aim to make generalisations about people but are also interested in **individual differences**. These are the ways that people are dissimilar from one another. Individual differences in cognitive processes can help to explain our differing behaviours and emotions, for example, making some of us happier or better at sport. Computers vary too, in terms of processing capacity, memory size, interactive screens or 'skill learning'.

Some cognitive differences are direct, for example human information processing speeds differ, leading to quicker reading or arithmetic. The effects of cognitive differences affect behaviour, so some people speak faster than others and keen sportsmen and women react faster than less sporty people. Individual differences in cognition also help to explain differences in emotions. For example, stimuli such as noises make some people grumpy.

KEY WORDS

input: how we take incoming information in, for example eyes (detecting light, colour and movement), ears (detecting sound), skin (detecting pressure)

processing: how information is dealt with, for example thinking and decision-making in the brain and brain functions such as short-term and long-term memory

output: how we send information out, for example voice and body (such as hands for writing, drawing, moving)

individual differences: stable and enduring ways in which people vary in terms of emotion behaviour or cognition. These can result in differences such as in personality, abilities or mental health. They may be the consequence of the environment or genetics (or both)

3.1 Core study 1: Andrade (doodling)

Andrade, J. (2010). What does doodling do?, *Applied cognitive psychology,* **24(1), 100–106.**

The psychology being investigated

Sometimes when our minds wander, we scribble absent-mindedly. We might draw a picture or sketch a pattern, perhaps shading in the shapes while we are thinking about something else, this is called 'doodling' (see Figure 3.4). Teachers often tell learners off for doodling. 'I didn't even know I was doing it', you think to yourself in self-defence. Perhaps your teacher's complaint is justified: research has shown that we perform less well when our attention is divided between tasks.

Figure 3.4: Doodling: does it help or hinder concentration?

It makes sense to assume that if we are engaged in sketching irrelevant patterns and figures, we cannot be attending as well to any other (primary) task, so would be worse at the **primary task** than if we were not doodling. However, in your defence, doodling might be useful (see Figure 3.5).

Figure 3.5: You're on the phone and think you're listening properly, but you've doodled an enormous, elaborate leaf pattern during the call. Do you think this doodling is helping you to concentrate or making it more difficult?

Doodling, even though we feel it is 'unconscious', takes up some of our information processing capacity, but how could this affect task performance? It is possible that doodling could take cognitive resources away from the intended (primary) task if it placed simultaneous demand on cognition by dividing **attention**. By making our information processing system perform a **divided attention** task, doodling would therefore *worsen* performance.

> **KEY WORDS**
>
> **primary task:** the activity we are supposed to be concentrating on, even though we may be doing something else as well, such as doodling
>
> **attention:** the concentration of mental effort on a particular stimulus. It may be focused or divided
>
> **divided attention:** the ability to split mental effort between two or more simultaneous tasks (called 'dual tasks'), for example driving a car and talking to a passenger

Whether or not we attend to a stimulus determines whether we remember it. In other words, attention is required for the encoding stage of the memory process. Recall can therefore be used as a measure of attention: if you do not attend to something, you will be unable to transfer it to long-term memory.

Divided attention is easier when the tasks involved are simple, well practised and automatic. If you have travelled with an inexperienced driver, you may have noticed that they found conversing difficult; indeed, any driver may stop mid-sentence if the road conditions become difficult. The primary task in this case, is driving, and the additional task (talking) is called the **concurrent task** because it is happening at the same time. So, although the concept of divided attention suggests doodling would worsen performance, if both tasks are highly practised and 'automatic', it may not.

An alternative explanation for the effect of doodling is that it could *improve* performance by raising arousal and enhancing **focused attention** on the primary task. Doodling might aid concentration (Do & Schallert, 2004), for example by reducing *daydreaming* so that you stay *focused*. This idea is based on the working memory model. This model of short-term memory suggests that two different types of current or 'working' memory can be used at the same time, one is visuo-spatial and the other auditory. These are governed by an overall 'central executive'. A primary 'listening' task would use the auditory memory and a concurrent 'visual' task (doodling) would use the visuo-spatial memory.

> **KEY WORDS**
>
> **concurrent task:** an additional activity with a cognitive demand that we can perform at the same time as a main (primary) task
>
> **focused attention:** the picking out of a particular input from a mass of information, such as many items presented together, or a rapid succession of individual items, for example concentrating on your teacher's voice even when there is building work outside and the learner next to you is whispering

Daydreaming is also linked to **arousal**. When we are bored and daydreaming, this uses important cognitive processing resources (the 'central executive') so inhibits performance on tasks that use this resource, including attention and memory. Alternatively, doodling may help to maintain arousal (Wilson and Korn, 2007), for example by giving you something physical to do while you think. It could raise arousal to help to keep you awake if you are sleepy or reduce arousal if you are agitated because you are bored. These effects would also enhance performance on the primary task.

> **KEY WORDS**
>
> **daydreaming:** a mildly altered state of consciousness in which we experience a sense of being 'lost in our thoughts', typically positive ones, and a detachment from our environment
>
> **arousal:** the extent to which we are alert, for example responsive to external sensory stimuli. It has physiological and psychological components and is mediated by the nervous system and hormones

Background

Andrade defines doodling as the sketching of patterns and figures that are unrelated to the primary task.

She used several strategies to increase boredom in her participants. These increased the possibility of boredom affecting the participants' attention, therefore creating a situation in which there would be a potential for doodling to affect their attention, for better or worse. Her expectation was that the concurrent task of doodling would interfere less with overall processing than devoting a greater amount of central executive function to daydreaming: doodling should, therefore, improve attention and thus recall should increase.

In Andrade's study, the primary task of listening to a message was an auditory task, whereas doodling is a visuo-spatial task. This ensured that the two tasks would not be in direct competition for one memory resource, as the working memory model suggests that the visuo-spatial and the auditory modules can be used at the same time.

Aim

Doodling, such as shading in all the Os in 'psychology' on a worksheet, is a common activity. Andrade was interested to know whether this activity assisted information processing. This could happen because doodling enables people to attend more effectively, or it could enhance their memory.

Method

Research method and design

This was a laboratory experiment; the environment was not the normal place in which people would respond to telephone messages and the situation was controlled. The design was independent measures as participants were either in the **control group** or in the doodling group.

> **KEY WORD**
>
> **control group:** a group of participants often used in an experiment, who do not receive the manipulation of the independent variable and can be used for comparison with the experimental group or groups

Sample

The participants were 40 members of a participant panel at the UK's Medical Research Council unit for cognitive research. The panel was made up of members of the general population aged 18–55 years and they were paid a small sum for participation. There were 20 participants in each group, mainly females, with two males in the control group and three in the doodling group (one participant in this condition did not doodle and was replaced). They were asked to join the study immediately after participating in an unrelated experiment for a different researcher. This was intended to enhance boredom.

Procedure

All participants were given a piece of paper to use as a response sheet. For the control group this was a sheet of lined paper so they could have doodled if they wanted to. However, they were given no specific instructions about doodling. Participants in the doodling group had a sheet of A4 with printed shapes and with a wide margin in which to write their responses. They were asked to shade in the shapes with a pencil, without worrying about the speed and the neatness of their shading, with the task being described to them as 'just something to relieve the boredom'. All participants listened to a monotonous mock telephone call about a party.

> 'Hi! Are you doing anything on Saturday? I'm having a birthday party and was hoping you could come. It's not actually my birthday, it's my sister **Jane's**. She'll be 21. She's coming up from *London* for the weekend and I thought it would be a nice surprise for her. I've also invited her boyfriend **William** and one of her old school friends, **Claire**, but she doesn't know that yet. Claire's husband Nigel was going to join us but he has just found out that he has to go to a meeting in *Penzance* that day and won't be back in time. I thought we could have a barbecue if the weather is nice, although the way it has been so far this week, that doesn't look likely. I can't believe it has got so cold already. And the evenings are really drawing in aren't they? Anyway, there is plenty of space indoors if it rains. Did I tell you that I have redecorated the kitchen? It is mainly yellow—the wallpaper is yellow and so is the woodwork, although I thought it would be better to leave the ceiling white to make it look lighter. I've still got the old blue fittings—they are pretty battered now but I can't afford to replace them at the moment. Do you remember **Craig**? I used to share a flat with him when we were both working for that bank in *Gloucester*. He has bought a house in *Colchester* now but he promises to take time off from gardening to come to Jane's party. **Suzie** is going to be there too. She's the person I met at the pottery class in *Harlow* last year. Apparently, she has got really good at it and may even be having an exhibition of her work soon. Will you be able to bring some food? Maybe crisps or peanuts, something along those lines. **Jenny** from next door is going to bring a quiche and I'll do some garlic bread. I found a good recipe for punch—you warm up some red wine with gin and orange juice plus cloves and cardamom and cinnamon. Add some brown sugar if it's not sweet enough. The boys from the house down the road have promised to bring some of their homebrew. There are three of them sharing that house now—John, Tony and Phil. I think they were all at college together. Phil teaches at a primary school in *Ely* now and the other two commute to *Peterborough* each day. I think they both work in the hospital there— I know Tony was training to be a nurse at one point so maybe he is qualified now. John can't come on Saturday because his parents are coming to stay for the weekend but **Phil** and **Tony** should be there. Tony has to pick their cat Ben up from the vet so he may be a bit late.

By the way, did I tell you about our holiday in *Edinburgh*? It was a complete disaster. We were camping and it rained constantly. We spent most of the time in museums, trying to keep dry and then, to make matters worse, Nicky got her handbag stolen. I was quite glad to get back to work after that. Anyway, hope you can make it on Saturday—let me know if you want to stay over. Bye!' (pages 105–106).

During this task they were expected to either doodle (the experimental group) or not doodle (the control group). This was the independent variable. They were told beforehand they would be tested on the names of people who were attending the party (and not the ones who were not going to be there). This was the 'monitoring' task. They also had an unexpected test, on the names of places mentioned. This was the 'recall' task. The order of these tests was *counterbalanced*, i.e. half the participants in each condition were asked to recall the names of party-goers then the places mentioned. The other half recalled the places first, then the names. These two tasks were the measures of the dependent variable (DV) of recall. To *operationalise* the DVs, plausible mishearings, such as 'Greg' for 'Craig', were counted as correct. Other names that were on the tape but were not party-goers (e.g. John) were scored as false alarms, as were completely new names generated by the participants. Other words relating to people, such as 'sister', were ignored. The final memory score for monitored information (names) and for incidental information (places) was the number of correct names/places minus false alarms.

The mock telephone message lasted 2.5 minutes and was recorded in a monotonous voice at an average speed of 227 words per minute. It had eight names of people attending a party, and the names of three people and one cat who could not attend. Eight place names were mentioned, as well as irrelevant details.

The participants were given the standardised instructions: 'I am going to play you a tape. I want you to pretend that the speaker is a friend who has telephoned you to invite you to a party. The tape is rather dull but that's okay because I don't want you to remember any of it. Just write down the names of people who will definitely or probably be coming to the party (excluding yourself). Ignore the names of those who can't come. Do not write anything else' (pages 101–102).

An A4 sheet with alternating rows of squares and circles, ten per row, was given to the participants in the doodling condition. There was also a wide margin on the left for recording the target information. These participants were also given a pencil and asked to shade in the squares and circles while listening to the tape. They were told 'It doesn't matter how neatly or how quickly you do this – it is just something to help relieve the boredom' (page 102). The control participants were given a sheet of lined paper to write their answers on (which could have been used for doodling).

Each participant listened to the tape at a comfortable volume, and wrote down the names as instructed. The experimenter collected the response sheets, then talked to the participants for 1 minute, including an apology for misleading them about the memory test. They then completed the surprise test of recalling names of places then people or vice versa. Finally, the participants were debriefed and asked if they suspected they would be given a memory test.

RESEARCH METHODS

When you are asked to think about parts of the procedure of a study, it is helpful to consider reliability and validity. Is the procedure likely to produce similar results each time with similar participants? This is a question of reliability. Is the procedure really resulting in the manipulation of the intended *independent variable* and is the way that the *dependent variable* is being assessed really measuring that variable or something different? These are questions of validity. Ask yourself these questions about Andrade's study: you will be helping yourself to 'think like a psychologist'.

Counterbalancing is often used as a control procedure against order effects. It is mainly used in repeated measures designs, when participants encounter both levels of the IV. In Andrade's study it is used to control for potential order effects caused by the two different measures of recall, the DV.

Results

In the doodling condition, the mean number of shaded shapes on the printed sheet was 36.3, with a range of 3–110 and no participants in the control condition doodled spontaneously.

Task type	Measure	Mean results for each group	
		Control	Doodling
Names (monitored information)	correct	4.3	5.3
	false alarms	0.4	0.3
	memory score	4.0	5.1
Places (incidental information)	correct	2.1	2.6
	false alarms	0.3	0.3
	memory score	1.8	2.4

Table 3.2: Mean recall for doodling and non-doodling groups

RESEARCH METHODS

Three doodlers and four controls suspected a memory test. This suggests that there were *demand characteristics* that made the aim apparent to the participants. However, none said they actively tried to remember information.

Participants in the control group correctly recalled a mean of 7.1 (SD 1.1) of the eight party-goers' names and five people made a false alarm (see Table 3.2). Participants in the doodling group correctly recalled a mean of 7.8 (SD 0.4) party-goers' names and one person made one false alarm. Overall, the doodling participants recalled a mean of 7.5 names and places, 29% more than the mean of 5.8 for the control group. Recall for both monitored and incidental information was better for doodlers than controls, even when the participants who suspected a test were excluded (to eliminate effects due to demand characteristics).

Conclusion

Andrade concluded that doodling helps concentration on a primary task. This was because the experimental participants, for whom doodling acted as a concurrent task, performed better than control participants who were just listening to the primary task with no concurrent task. However, because the doodling group were better on both the monitored and incidental information there are two possible explanations. One is that the doodlers noticed more of the target words, an effect on attention. This would be explained by doodling increasing arousal and therefore reducing daydreaming, so maintaining attention on the primary task. The other is that doodling improved memory directly, for example by encouraging deeper information processing. However, without any measure of daydreaming (which could have blocked attention) it is difficult to distinguish between these two explanations. This could have been done by asking participants about daydreaming retrospectively by self-report. Alternatively, a simultaneous brain scan could have indicated whether doodling reduced activation of the cortex, which is associated with daydreaming.

ISSUES AND DEBATES

Doodling could be a useful strategy when we have to concentrate and don't want to, for example in an important but boring lecture or when you are waiting to hear the faint sound of a friend's car arriving. By stopping our minds from straying we should be better able to focus on the primary task (see Figure 3.6). This would be an *application to everyday life*.

ACTIVITY 3.1

Self-reports are a useful way to find out more about participants' thoughts or feelings when they have participated in an experiment but can also be used as the main method for a study. Conduct a pilot study using an interview or a questionnaire to collect self-report data about the types of doodle that people do and the situations in which they doodle.

Figure 3.6: Although doodles have some shape and form, they are relatively unplanned so require little processing themselves but may be sufficient to prevent us from daydreaming

Strengths and weaknesses

The main method was a laboratory experiment using an independent measures design. This means that it was possible to limit *uncontrolled variables,* for example ensuring the participants were listening at a volume comfortable for them and using a recorded telephone message so that the important words were said in the same way in each condition. It was also *standardised* so that the participants were all equally likely to be bored and therefore to daydream. This was achieved by the monotony of the recording, using a dull, quiet room and asking them to do the experiment when they were expecting to go home. This means the research was more *valid*–they could be sure that the differences in results between conditions were due to whether or not the participants were doodling–and more *reliable*, because all participants were similarly bored. The *operationalisation* of doodling was also standardised, using the doodling sheets, otherwise there may have been individual differences in doodling between participants and some more may not have doodled at all. This also increased *validity*. Validity was further increased by the

attempt to encourage the experimental participants to doodle in a relatively naturalistic way. Nevertheless, there is a risk of *participant variables* confounding the results, as the number of shapes the individuals shaded differed. However, it was an effective strategy as no participants in the non-doodling condition did doodle (this was discouraged by giving them lined paper) and only one in the doodling condition did not (and they were replaced).

The participants were varied in age (18–55 years), so were representative in terms of adult ages. However, they were all members of a recruitment panel and the kinds of people who volunteer for such panels may all be very similar, for example having time to spare or an interest in psychology. This could bias the sample, lowering validity. There was a risk of demand characteristics because some of the participants suspected a memory test, but they were roughly equal in each condition and did not actively try to remember, so this is unlikely to have reduced validity. Furthermore, removing their data from the analysis did not alter the conclusion. The study collected quantitative data, the number of names and places recalled, which is an objective record of memory. However, it would also have been useful to have asked the participants for self-reports of any daydreaming. This would have helped to explore whether the advantage for the doodlers over the non-doodlers on both monitored and incidental information was due to attention or memory. It would be important only to ask participants whether they daydreamed, not what they were daydreaming about, as this would be an invasion of their privacy.

Ethical issues

This study raised some ethical issues. The participants were unable to give *fully informed consent* as they were given an unexpected test on place names. This had the potential to make them distressed if they were unable to remember the names, so could breach the ethical guideline of protection from harm. Although a debrief is not a substitute for good ethical procedures, the experimenters debriefed the participants and apologised for misleading them about the unexpected recall test.

Summary

Andrade's study tested whether doodling could improve concentration on and memory of a conversation. Participants in the doodling condition *remembered* more of the people's names they had been asked to recall and *attended to* the message better, as they recalled more in a surprise test of the place names mentioned. This laboratory experiment was well controlled with a recorded stimulus message and specific shapes to colour in for the doodlers. The data from the words recalled was quantitative and objective. However, it would also have been useful to have had qualitative data about whether the participants daydreamed as this would have helped to distinguish between two possible reasons for the improved memory: deeper processing or better attention.

ACTIVITY 3.2

Cognitive psychology often uses a rigorous scientific approach in its studies.

- Working with another person, each think separately about whether this approach can really tell us about:
  - how we feel?
  - how we behave?
  - how we think?

  These three questions are central to many aspects of psychology, and it may be useful to remember them as the 'A, B, C' of psychology. 'A' stands for 'affect', a psychological term for feelings or emotions, 'B' stands for behaviour and 'C' stands for cognition.

- Compare your answers. You may find that you disagree – so do psychologists!

- Together, try to come up with reasons for why it might be difficult to measure processes we cannot see.

RESEARCH METHODS

There were *individual differences* between the participants in Andrade's study. As it was an independent measures design, such differences were a bigger problem than they would have been had Andrade been able to use a repeated measures design. This was not possible, however, as the participants would have known they would be tested on the place names in their second condition. As a consequence, individual differences in attention or memory between the participants in the two groups could have been responsible for differences in recall.

Questions

1 What were the two conditions in Andrade's study?
2 How did Andrade measure the effect of the IV in this study?
3 Andrade used many ways to control variables. Choose one and explain why it was important to the success of the study.
4 Andrade found that the doodling group were better at recalling both the monitored and incidental information. Why did this make it difficult to draw a conclusion?

3.2 Core study 2: Baron-Cohen et al. (Eyes test)

Baron-Cohen, S., Wheelwright, S., Hill, J., Raste, Y., & Plumb, I. (2001). The 'Reading the Mind in the Eyes' test revised version: a study with normal adults, and adults with Asperger syndrome or high-functioning autism. *Journal of child psychology and psychiatry, 42*(2), 241–251.

The psychology being investigated

A person with an **autism spectrum disorder (ASD)** does not fully develop cognitive processes linked to social interaction. ASD occurs in approximately 1% of the population. Individuals with ASD share difficulties in social functioning, such as limited social sensitivity, communication and ability to cope with change, and may have narrow interests. The term ASD is now used to refer to both high-functioning autism (HFA) and Asperger syndrome (AS), however the terms HFA and AS were used at the time that the Baron-Cohen et al. study was published.

Baron-Cohen et al. suggest that people with ASD lack or have an underdeveloped cognitive process called a **theory of mind**. A theory of mind is a cognitive ability enabling people to realise that others have different feelings, beliefs, knowledge and desires from their own. Individuals with ASD find it difficult to understand that other people have their own plans, thoughts or

---

KEY WORDS

autism spectrum disorder (ASD): a diagnostic category (previously including autism and Asperger syndrome). Symptoms, appearing in childhood, present a range of difficulties with social interaction and communication and restricted, repetitive, or inflexible behaviours or interests

theory of mind: a cognitive ability that enables one person to comprehend that other people have separate feelings, beliefs, knowledge and desires that can be different from their own. It enables one person to detect the emotional state of another person

---

points of view. A theory of mind is often linked to empathy. Empathy is the ability to understand the world as another person does; to appreciate their feelings or emotional state separate from our own.

There are several different tests available to measure a person's theory of mind but most of these are designed for children. Baron-Cohen et al. (1997) developed a test called the 'Reading the Mind in the Eyes' task to use with adults to test their ability to identify the emotional state that other people are in. They suggest that this task tests the first stage of theory of mind: assigning an appropriate mental state to another person, and argues that this task is a good measure of social cognition. If this ability is limited, the individual's social sensitivity is reduced.

Background

Using their first version of the 'Reading the Mind in the Eyes' task, Baron-Cohen et al. (1997) investigated whether adults with ASD had problems with theory of mind. They compared a group of individuals with ASD to individuals who did not have a diagnosis of ASD. The participants were shown photographs of eyes and asked to identify the emotion that was being shown from two options (see Figure 3.7).

Figure 3.7: A pair of eyes from the Reading the Mind in the Eyes test

The 'Reading the Mind in the Eyes' task (Eyes test) was believed to use the cognitive processes associated with a theory of mind as participants needed to empathise with the person in the photograph to work out their emotional state.

The results of this study (using the first version of the task) by Baron-Cohen et al. (1997) showed that ASD participants correctly identified fewer emotions than participants in the non-ASD group. However, the researchers identified several practical issues with the original task, which were solved in the revised version (see Table 3.3).

Problems with the original Eyes test	Solutions in the revised Eyes test
The questions were forced choice, with only two options which were always opposite in meaning (semantic opposites), e.g. Sympathetic or Unsympathetic, so the task was too easy	The number of options choices for responding was increased to four, and they were not opposites
Only 25 sets of eyes were used in the test (so many in the ASD group scored 24 or 25, causing a **ceiling effect**)	36 sets of eyes were used in the final analysis of the revised Eyes test results
The eyes illustrated both **basic emotions** and **complex emotions** and the former were too easy	Only eyes expressing complex emotions were used
The emotion in some photos could be solved by checking the direction in which the eyes were gazing, e.g. ignoring	These sets of eyes were deleted from the test
Imbalance of male and female faces	Equal number of male and female faces
Participants might not have understood the words in the task	Participants were given a glossary

Table 3.3: Differences between the original 'Reading the Mind in the Eyes' task and the revised version of the test

> ## KEY WORD
>
> **ceiling effect:** this occurs when a test is too easy and all participants in a condition achieve a very high score. This is problematic as it does not allow the researcher to differentiate between results

> ## KEY WORDS
>
> **basic emotions:** feelings such as happy, sad, angry, afraid and disgust. They are understood worldwide, and by very young children, and can be recognised without the need to attribute a belief to the person
>
> **complex emotions:** require an understanding of someone else's cognitive state, that is the attribution of a belief or intention to the person. They are therefore harder to identify

Aim

The main aim of this research was to investigate whether an improved 'revised' version of the Eyes test would show a clear impairment in a group of adults with ASD to assess its effectiveness.

The researchers also wanted to test whether there was an association between performance on the revised Eyes test and measures of traits of ASD, and to investigate whether there were sex differences in those without ASD on this task.

They were testing five hypotheses:

- Participants with ASD will score significantly lower scores on the revised Eyes test than the control group.

- Participants with ASD will score significantly higher on the **Autism Spectrum Quotient Test (AQ)** measure than the control group.

- Females in the 'normal' groups (Groups 2 and 3) will score higher on the Eyes test than males in those groups.

- Males in the 'normal' group (Group 3) would score higher on the AQ measure than females.

- Scores on the AQ and the Eyes test would be negatively correlated.

> ## KEY WORD
>
> **Autism Spectrum Quotient Test (AQ):** a self-report questionnaire with scores ranging from 0 to 50. A higher score suggests that the person completing it has more autistic traits

Method

Research method and design

This was a laboratory experiment as the environment in which the participants were tested was not comparable to everyday situations in which we detect the emotions of others.

This is an example of a **quasi-experiment**. In a true experiment, participants can be randomly assigned to any of the experimental conditions. This is not the case in a quasi-experiment, where participants are usually assigned to a condition based on a given characteristic (e.g. whether they have ASD).

The independent variable was the type of participant in each condition. There were three control or comparison groups in this study (Groups 2–4) and the experimental group containing participants with AS or HFA (Group 1). The experimental design was an independent groups design because comparisons were made between different groups of participants; Group 1, consisting of participants with ASD were compared to the control groups 2, 3 and 4 (see Table 3.4).

There were two key measures of the dependent variable. The first was a score on the revised Eyes test. For those participants in the AS/HFA and the **IQ** (Intelligence Quotient)-matched control condition, IQ was also measured. IQ was assessed using the short WAIS-R, which measures four aspects of intelligence using tests of: block design, vocabulary, similarities and picture completion.

Sample

The study used four groups of participants. These differed in several ways (see Table 3.4). Group 1 consisted of all males and groups 2 and 3 included both males and females.

Group	Number	Average
Group 1: AS/HFA	15	Age 29.7; IQ 115
Group 2: Adult comparison group	122	Age 46.5
Group 3: Student comparison group	103	Age 20.8
Group 4: IQ matched group	14	Age 28; IQ 116

Table 3.4: The number of participants in separate conditions along with average group characteristics. Groups 2, 3 and 4 are control groups

Group 1: AS/HFA

The group comprised 15 adult males with AS or HFA with a mean IQ score of 115 and mean age of 29.7 years. The sample was self-selecting through adverts in the Autistic Society magazine and support groups and all had been diagnosed in specialist centres using the **Diagnostic and Statistical Manual (DSM)** or **International Classification of Disorders (ICD)** criteria.

Group 2: Adult comparison group

The group comprised 'normal' adults, who did not have a diagnosis of AS/HFA. They were selected from adult community and education classes in Exeter (UK) and public library users in Cambridge (UK) with a mean age of 46.5 years.

Group 3: Student comparison group

The group comprised 'normal' students, who did not have a diagnosis of AS/HFA, from the University of

Cambridge with a mean age of 20.8 years. Cambridge is a highly selective university so these students are not representative of the general population.

Group 4: IQ Matched group

The group comprised 14 IQ matched participants with those in the AS/HFA group with a mean age of 28 years and mean IQ score of 116. These participants were randomly selected from the general population.

Procedure

Following the changes that Baron-Cohen et al. made to the original Eyes test, the revised Eyes test was used in this experiment as a measure of theory of mind. They started with 40 sets of eyes, target words and **foil** words chosen by the first two authors, Simon Baron-Cohen and Sally Wheelwright. The one target word and three foil (alternative) words for each set of eyes were developed using groups of eight judges. At least five of the judges had to agree that the target word was the most appropriate for the eyes. If more than two of the judges selected a foil word instead of the target word, a new target word, new foils, or both, were generated and the item was retested until it met the criterion. In addition, when the results of Groups 2 and 3 were combined after testing, four of the items produced inconsistent results, that is, these control participants often chose foil words. These four items were removed from the analysis so the final results were based on 36 sets of eyes (18 male, 18 female), each with four choices of emotion for the face of the target (e.g. reflective, aghast, irritated, impatient).

To begin the Eyes test, each participant read through a glossary of words used in the experiment to describe the emotions to ensure they knew the meaning of each word (Figure 3.8) and were told they could refer back to the glossary whenever they needed to. Each participant was then shown a practice item followed by the sets of eyes. For each set of eyes, they had to pick the correct word for the emotion in the photograph from a set of four possibilities.

The Eyes test for all participants, and a gender recognition test for Group 1 given as a control task, were completed with a researcher in a quiet room in Exeter or Cambridge. A pilot study had shown that 'normal' adults usually achieved 100 % on gender recognition, so the control groups were not tested on this. The purpose of this control test was to show that participants in Group 1 were able to identify characteristics of the eyes used in the test that were not dependent on having a theory of mind. Participants in all conditions except the 'normal' adult comparison (Group 2) were also asked to complete the AQ test (a questionnaire) at home and returned it by post.

All participants consented to take part in the study and were aware of the nature of the research. The data was also made anonymous so that it was not possible to identify any individual from their scores.

FLUSTERED
confused, nervous and upset
Sarah felt a bit *flustered* when she realised how late she was for the meeting and that she had forgotten an important document.

RELAXED
taking it easy, calm, carefree
On holiday, Pam felt happy and *relaxed*.

Figure 3.8: Two items from the glossary used in the study by Baron-Cohen et al.

KEY WORDS

foil: a 'foil' is something that is used as a contrast to something else. In Baron-Cohen et al.'s study the 'foil words' were the (incorrect) alternative words participants could choose to describe the eyes

RESEARCH METHODS

A *pilot study* is used to check the validity and reliability of the procedures. It is not a check of whether the study is going to 'work' or whether it is ethical, although they can be conducted to find out whether a question is worth investigating. When you have finished reading the procedure for this study, decide why the pilot study was important.

Experimental comparisons were used to test each of the first four hypotheses. In addition, the results were used in two tests of correlational relationships. One was between AQ and Eyes test scores and the other between the IQ and Eyes test scores. These scores were the 'measured variables' or 'co-variables'.

ACTIVITY 3.3

Find two photographs of unknown people, i.e. not people who are friends, live locally or are famous. Choose two that have different facial expressions and cut the image down so that it just shows the eyes. For each of your two photographs choose four different words that could be used, one for the correct description of the expression and three foil words.

Why did you choose the words you did? Are you certain they are not semantic opposites? Do you think any of the words you have chosen as foils are too close to the real expression, meaning they could also be a plausible answer?

If you can discuss these questions and your answers with someone else, do so. However, remember that these are just your images of eyes and sets of words, they are not from the Eyes test and do not indicate any ability or otherwise in anybody that responds to them. This is a very important ethical consideration.

Results

On the Eyes test, participants with AS/HFA (Group 1) correctly identified significantly fewer target words than participants in the three comparison groups (Table 3.5, Figure 3.9). No participant in

any of the conditions checked the glossary for more than two definitions during the experiment. In the Adult comparison and Student comparison groups (Groups 2 and 3), sex differences were apparent between males and females on the Eyes test but this was not significant. All participants in the AS/HFA condition scored 33 or above out of 36 on the gender recognition task.

On the AQ task, participants with AS/HFA scored significantly higher than the Student comparison and IQ matched comparison groups (see Figure 3.10). There was also a smaller, but significant difference between male and female AQ scores in the Student comparison group.

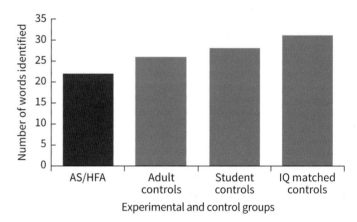

Figure 3.9: Average number of words correctly identified on the Eyes test

Group	Number of participants	Mean scores (standard deviations)	
		Eyes test	AQ test*
Group 1: Asperger syndrome / High-functioning autism (AS/HFA)	15	21.9 (6.6)	34.4 [N = 14] (6.0)
Group 2: Adult comparison group	122	26.2 (3.6)	–
Group 3: Student comparison group	103	28.0 (3.5)	18.3 [N =79] (6.6)
Group 4: IQ matched group	14	30.9 (3.0)	18.9 (2.9)

* Not all participants returned the AQ test. The number in square brackets is the number of participants who did return it.

Table 3.5: Mean Eyes test and AQ scores

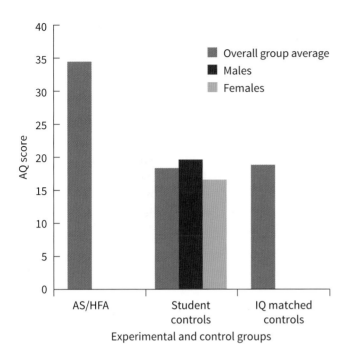

Figure 3.10: Average AQ scores

There was a significant *negative correlation* between the AQ and Eyes test scores (–0.53) but no correlation between the IQ and Eyes test scores. This suggests that as the AQ score increases (illustrating greater levels of autistic traits) the ability to identify the correct target word on the Eyes test decreases and that this is independent of the individual's intelligence.

RESEARCH METHODS

The *measure of central tendency* used to calculate the averages used for Figures 3.9 and 3.10 was the *mean*. A *median* could have been used as an alternative measure of central tendency, although the mean would be more representative as it uses the absolute value of each score, whereas the median only considers rank positions. The *mode* would have been an unsuitable measure of tendency for this data as the possible range of scores was wide so it is unlikely that the most frequent score would be representative.

Conclusion

The results indicate that the participants in the AS/HFA group had a specific deficit in a cognitive process that should help them to identify emotions in other individuals, i.e. that contribute to a theory of mind. This conclusion is validated by the AS/HFA group being able to identify the gender of the eyes accurately. This shows that the Eyes test was able to detect a subtle and specific impairment in the otherwise intelligent participants in the HFA/AS group.

There was evidence of a sex difference between males and females in the comparison groups; although less marked, the pattern of results for males was similar to the participants with ASD. Males had lower scores on the Eyes test, and showed greater levels of autistic traits on the AQ test, than females. However, some of these differences were not significant so further research is needed to clarify whether there are differences between the sexes in terms of their AQ or ability to attribute emotions to others.

This study showed that the revised Eyes test is a more sensitive measure of adult social intelligence than that used in previous studies, so will allow future research to discriminate individual differences in a more meaningful way.

Strengths and weaknesses

The main method was a laboratory experiment as all participants completed the task in a standardised way, through administration of the Eyes test by a researcher. This allowed *confounding variables* to be controlled, for example reducing the risk of distractions by being in a quiet room and ensuring all participants had read the glossary before starting. This improves the internal validity of the experiment and allows the research to be repeated to check the reliability of the results. The validity of the Eyes test has improved compared to previous versions due to the changes made which have led to normal performance being below the ceiling of the test.

As this is a quasi-experiment, it was not possible for Baron-Cohen et al. to *randomly allocate* participants to the conditions. This could introduce a confounding variable, as there could be a factor other than ASD, which happens to be different between the ASD and control groups, which is causing the difference in the scores between the conditions. This study partly resolved this issue by having two different control groups so that some participants were matched on IQ to make the groups as similar as possible.

Although the Eyes test was vastly improved for this research, there are still several issues that affect the *ecological validity* of the task. In an everyday situation, a person's eyes would not be static or be shown in isolation from the rest of their face. Consequently, any attempt to apply the results from this research to an everyday situation will be flawed. Future research might choose to use videos of eyes rather than images, and whole faces rather than just eyes, to improve the validity of any conclusions.

The experimental sample in this research (the AS/HFA participants) was only 15 participants so they may not be representative of all individuals with a diagnosis of AS/HFA. Caution is therefore needed if generalisations are made from the findings.

Ethical issues

As all participants were able to give informed consent and their data was kept confidential, few ethical issues were raised within the study itself. However, ethical issues could arise from the findings. Evidence such as this, which identifies 'normal' performance of control groups and 'impaired' performance of the AS/HFA group could be seen as representing neurodiverse groups in a negative way. Alternatively, by identifying such differences, this research has the capacity to provide both an understanding of the nature of the experience of people with ASD and, therefore, the potential for greater understanding in society and potentially in situations such as school or the workplace. This would be an ethical strength.

ACTIVITY 3.4

Can we be sure it is really all in the eyes? What else could be important when we are interpreting emotions? To answer this question, think about whether there are any issues with using photographs of eyes rather than a real person in this study. How could this experiment be conducted in a more ecologically valid way? What impact would it have?

Summary

Baron-Cohen et al.'s study investigated how a lack of a 'theory of mind' in adults with autism spectrum disorder (ASD) relates to problems with recognising emotions. The ASD group's scores on the Eyes test were lower than those of the control group even though their IQ was no different. There was also a negative correlation between the Eyes test score and Autistic Spectrum Quotient. The test itself was valid because the still images of the eyes were standardised in terms of size and colour (all black and white) although this could also be a weakness as emotions are usually detected on live faces, which move. The findings suggest that the revised Eyes test is better at detecting individual differences in social sensitivity than the previous version, i.e. it is more valid.

Questions

5   Choose one possible emotion that Baron-Cohen et al. could have used.

    a   State the emotion you have chosen.

    b   Write a glossary entry for this emotion.

    c   List some possible foils that could be used with this emotion and justify why they are suitable.

6   If Baron-Cohen et al. had found that there was still a ceiling effect, what could have been done to solve this problem?

3.3 Core study 3: Pozzulo et al. (line-ups)

Pozzulo, J., Dempsey, J., Bruer, K. C., & Sheahan C. (2011). The culprit in target-absent lineups: understanding young children's false positive responding. *Journal of police and criminal psychology, 27(1), 55–62.*

The psychology being investigated

Our memory works like a computer's in some ways (see Main Assumptions in Context) but differs with respect to the way that stored data can be accidentally changed or damaged. Excluding events such as crashing, or getting a software virus, computers reproduce an error-free copy of a 'memory'. If information has not been deliberately processed, it comes out of storage identical to when it went in. This is not the case for human memory. We may feel as though our recall is perfectly accurate, but cognitive psychologists have shown that memories can be distorted, for example by other information that we are exposed to during and after encoding. Sometimes these changes don't matter, but when a human memory is a key source of evidence in a criminal trial, they are vitally important.

Additional information given after the event seen by an eyewitness, called post-event information, can produce **'false memories'**. The witness confidently believes these false memories to be true. For example, even asking the witness a question that contains extra information can distort their recall. A classic experiment by Loftus and Palmer (1974) used a video of a vehicle that had an accident. The results showed that the words used in a question affected participants' speed estimates for the vehicle. The adult participants estimated faster speeds when asked 'How fast were the cars going when they smashed into each other?' than when they were asked 'How fast were the cars going when they hit each other?'

Children, as well as adults, can be witnesses to crimes. Sometimes a child may be the only person to see a crime, so the legal system must rely on their **eyewitness testimony**. For such evidence to be useful, children need to be reliable witnesses, but are they?

> **KEY WORDS**
>
> **false memory:** a piece of stored information an individual believes to be an accurate memory but which is the consequence of later additional and untrue information, such as in a question about an event seen by an eyewitness
>
> **eyewitness testimony:** evidence provided by an individual who has seen (or heard) a crime being committed. This information is used by the legal system

Background

Pozzulo et al. studied child witnesses and recognised that cognitive effects, such as those caused by post-event information, including the way questions are asked, can be responsible for errors in decision-making by children. Some of their earlier research (Pozzulo & Lindsay, 1997) showed that children were less likely than adults to say 'I don't know' in response to a question even when they knew this response was possible.

One way that witness information is used by the police is in a **line-up**, where the witness is asked to identify the perpetrator of the crime from a selection of individuals presented to them (whether or not the perpetrator is actually present), see Figure 3.11. However, this system can create mistakes and therefore miscarriages of justice. A witness may be more likely to make errors if they are asked to make a decision from a line-up and are then presented with another line-up containing the same suspect. Pozzulo and Lindsay (1998) found that when the culprit is not among the people in a line-up, children are more likely than adults to identify an innocent person, this is called a **false positive response**.

> **KEY WORDS**
>
> **line-up:** a source of evidence used by the legal system. A witness is shown a line of people or array of photographs of faces and is asked to attempt to identify the perpetrator of the crime (although they may not be present)
>
> **false positive response:** giving an affirmative (positive) but incorrect answer to a question. For example, mistakenly picking out a person in a line-up when the real culprit is not there

This study focused on social effects on child witnesses. Pozzulo et al. suggested that children may be more likely to make incorrect decisions in a line-up as a result of several different social factors, such as:

- If a child is asked to select which of the people in the line-up is the culprit, they may think that they need to choose one of the people. Not making a choice, i.e. saying the culprit is not there, could be seen as a 'non-response' from the child's perspective. They may think 'If I am given a selection I must make a choice.'

- A child is likely to view the adult who asks them the question as an authority figure, especially if it is a police officer. This would make them more likely to comply with the request.

- Children may feel more pressured to make a choice than adults. They will want to comply with the request and may even fear getting into trouble if they do not choose somebody.

Figure 3.11: A police line-up

Aim

Social factors may have a greater effect on child witnesses than adults. One eyewitness test is 'identification' of a suspect, that is, picking them out from a 'target-present' line-up where the culprit is among the faces presented. Another eyewitness test is the ability to correctly *reject* faces when the culprit is not presented, i.e. in a 'target-absent' line-up. To explore the effect of social versus cognitive factors on children's performance as eyewitnesses Pozzulo et al. needed to minimise any cognitive effects that could impair the children's decision-making. They did this by comparing

identification and rejection of a cartoon character. As cartoon characters are familiar, a child should identify them with the same accuracy as adults, approximately 100%. This is because it is a cognitively easy task; it only requires matching an existing memory to the faces they can see in the line-up. However, in a target-absent task, matching is not possible so a selection must be made. Faced with a harder task, children should rely more heavily on social factors, and make more errors than adults.

The aims were to test the following four predictions:

- Children will be as good as adults at identifying cartoon faces in a target-present line-up

- Children will be worse than adults at identifying human faces in a target-present line-up

- Children will be worse than adults at rejecting cartoon faces in a target-absent line-up

- Children will be worse than adults at rejecting human faces in a target-absent line-up

Method

Research method and design

This study was a *laboratory experiment*. Participants were in a laboratory whereas real line-ups would take place somewhere official, such as at a police station.

There were three *independent variables*:

- Age: young children versus adults

- Line-up type: identification (target-present) versus rejection (target-absent line-up)

- Level of cognitive demand (familiarity of target): cartoon (familiar, low cognitive demand, so differences due to social demand) versus human (unfamiliar therefore higher cognitive demand)

For the comparison between children and adults, the experimental design was *independent measures*. For the comparisons of line-up type (target-present versus target-absent) and familiarity of target (cartoon versus human), the experimental design was *repeated measures*.

To test identification/recognition, participants were presented with a photoarray of black and white photographs of close-cropped faces for the cartoons and head-and-shoulder images for the humans. The *dependent variable* was whether the participant identified the correct face if present or the empty silhouette if not. The children's response, given by pointing, was recorded by the experimenter and adult participants recorded their responses on a sheet.

RESEARCH METHODS

Line-ups are commonly used in legal cases worldwide. The procedure tends to be highly controlled to minimise errors, for example ensuring photographs of faces are the same size and either all in colour or all in black and white. Nevertheless, there is a problem that cannot be easily resolved. People are less able to accurately identify a person of a different ethnic group from themselves. When setting up studies in psychology to test line-up procedures, it is therefore important to consider the ethnic groups of the participants and of the individuals in the line-up as potential confounding variables.

Sample

There were 59 child participants aged 4–7 years with a mean age of 4.98 years, 21 females and 38 males. They were recruited from pre-kindergarten/kindergarten classes in three private schools in Eastern Ontario, Canada. There were 53 adult participants aged 17–30 years with a mean age of 20.54 years, 36 females and 17 males. They were recruited from the Introductory Psychology Participant Pool at Eastern Ontario University.

Information was provided by the adults, and by children's parents/guardians, to ensure that all participants were familiar with the two target cartoons in the study (Dora the Explorer and Go, Diego, Go!, see Figure 3.12).

Procedure

To conduct the experiment, the researchers prepared video clips and line-up photograph arrays.

- Human face targets were two Caucasian students. They were used to make two types of stimulus material:

  - For the videos, a 6-second clip was filmed of an everyday task: a female brushing her hair and male putting his coat on. Each video was in colour with no sound and showed 2 to 3 seconds of the individual's face.

  - For the photoarrays, the two human 'targets', the students, were photographed wearing different clothes than in the video. For each target, four 'foil' photographs were chosen by three raters to look similar to the targets in terms of facial features, hair length and colour. All photographs were cropped to include only the face, neck and the top of the shoulders.

- Cartoon face targets were two cartoon characters. The two types of stimulus were:

  - For the videos, the two 6-second clips were Dora the Explorer talking to the audience and Go, Diego, Go! putting on a pair of gloves for safety. Each video was in colour with no sound or other characters and showed 2 to 3 seconds of the target cartoon character's face.

  - For the photoarrays, still images of the two cartoon 'targets' were used in addition to four 'foils' selected from cartoon images from the internet. Three raters judged the similarity of approximately ten cartoons for each target. The four most similar ones in terms of facial

Figure 3.12: Dora the Explorer and Go, Diego, Go!

features, hair length and colour were chosen. All photographs were cropped to include only the character's face, as they tended to wear similar clothing in all episodes so this could not affect the familiarity of the appearance of the character.

Target-present line-ups contained the target and three foils; target-absent line-ups contained four foils. Every line-up contained a blank silhouette to enable a choice to be made even if the participant judged that the target was not present. The line-up was shown to participants as a simultaneous array, which means that the target (if present), all the foils and the blank silhouette were all shown at once. The position of each target in the line-up was *randomised* but for the equivalent 'target-absent' line-up, the fourth foil was located in the same position as the original target. All photographs were in black and white, which was important as the bright colours of the cartoon characters could have become the focus of recognition rather than the identity of the character. Each participant watched four videos, one each for the conditions of cartoon target-present, human target-present, cartoon target-absent and human target-absent. These videos were presented in a random order, each being followed by a line-up task. In each of the four line-up tasks, the position of the target or its matching foil was *counterbalanced*. Videos and photoarrays were presented on 13-inch laptop screens.

Each child participant's parents/guardians, and the adult participants, were given a written consent form to complete. The adult participants attended the laboratory and were given a brief saying that it was a study about memory. To test the children, three female experimenters went to the children's school. They briefed the children saying that they were researchers from the university doing a project on TV shows and computer games. It was also made clear to the children that they could change their minds about whether they wanted to join in and would not get into trouble. To help to make the children comfortable, the experimenters did some craft work with them prior to starting the experiment.

For each participant, the following sequence was used:

- The three female experimenters were neatly dressed, wearing professional-casual clothing, for example a sweater or blouse and smart trousers (dress-pants). This was not overly formal because this could influence the children's responses to the line-ups through social pressure, for example by suggesting authority.

- Child and adult participants were tested individually and were asked to pay attention because they would be asked some questions and shown some pictures after watching the video.

- Following each video, participants were asked a free recall *filler question* ('What did the cartoon character/person look like?') For child participants, a non-specific probing question ('Do you remember anything else?') was then asked. If the child did not respond to the initial question, the experimenter asked 'Do you remember anything from the video?' The children's replies were recorded by the researchers. For adults, the initial question was followed by, 'Do you remember anything else about the cartoon character/person?' The adults recorded their own responses by writing them down.

- After each filler task, child participants were told, 'Please look at the photos. The person/cartoon may or may not be here. If you see the person/cartoon, please point to the photo. If you do not see the person/cartoon, please point to this box' (indicating the blank silhouette). Similar instructions were given to the adults, but they indicated their response on a matching sheet.

- This procedure was repeated so that all four videos had been seen and responded to with the line-up task. The dependent variable was whether the participant identified the correct face if present or the empty silhouette if not.

ACTIVITY 3.5

Controls and standardisation help to improve the validity of studies. Working with a partner, list the ways the experimenters standardise the procedure. List as many as you can. For each one, explain why that part of the procedure was important for validity.

Peer assessment

Swap your lists with another pair and look carefully at their list of ways to standardise the procedure. Do you agree with them?

Then look at the explanations of why each way is important for validity. Do you agree with those? Finally, discuss your comments on each other's lists and explanations, and try to produce one final list that you feel is complete.

Results

The researchers wanted to investigate two key differences. The first was the difference between children's and adults' identification and rejection accuracy. The second was the difference in children's identification and rejection accuracy between cartoon characters and humans. Table 3.6 shows the rates for accurate and inaccurate responses in all conditions and Figure 3.13 shows the average (mean) identification and rejection rates for cartoon and human targets. Here you can see that adults were better than children at most tasks and that responses to cartoons were generally more accurate than responses to human targets. However, there was little difference between the responses of children and adults in the target-present test for cartoons.

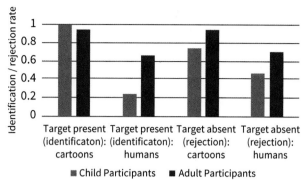

Figure 3.13: Mean identification and rejection rates for cartoon and human targets

Participant group	Target type	Specific target	Identification		Rejection	
			Identification response (target/foil/false rejection)	Correct identification rate	Rejection response (target/false identification)	Correct rejection rate
Children	Cartoon	Dora	Target (Dora)	1	Target correctly rejected (Dora)	0.8
			Foil	0		
			False rejection	0	False identification	0.2
		Diego	Target (Diego)	0.97	Target correctly rejected (Diego)	0.67
			Foil	0		
			False rejection	0.03	False identification	0.33
	Human	Female	Target (Female)	0.24	Target correctly rejected (Female)	0.47
			Foil	0.38		
			False rejection	0.38	False identification	0.53
		Male	Target (Male)	0.21	Target correctly rejected (Male)	0.43
			Foil	0.45		
			False rejection	0.34	False identification	0.57
Adults	Cartoon	Dora	Target (Dora)	1	Target correctly rejected (Dora)	0.96
			Foil	0		
			False rejection	0	False identification	0.04
		Diego	Target (Diego)	0.89	Target correctly rejected (Diego)	0.92
			Foil	0		
			False rejection	0.11	False identification	0.08
	Human	Female	Target (Female)	0.46	Target correctly rejected (Female)	0.72
			Foil	0		
			False rejection	0.54	False identification	0.28
		Male	Target (Male)	0.85	Target correctly rejected (Male)	0.67
			Foil	0.15		
			False rejection	0	False identification	0.33

Table 3.6: Responses of children and adults in target-present and target-absent line-ups

ACTIVITY 3.6

Based on the data in Table 3.6, choose a suitable graph to display the results. You may want to select just some of the data from this table, such as only the two different cartoon characters, or only the data about humans. Plot the results carefully on a graph, and make sure that you label both axes, put scales on the axes where relevant and give the graph a title.

Line-up type	Participant group	comparison	Conclusion from statistical testing	As predicted
Target-present Identification	Children	Cartoons versus humans	Children significantly more accurate at identifying cartoon faces than human faces	
	Adults	Cartoons versus humans	Adults significantly more accurate at identifying cartoon faces than human faces	
	Children versus adults	Cartoons	Children have similar accuracy as adults for identifying cartoon faces	yes
	Children versus adults	Humans	Children significantly less accurate than adults when identifying human faces	yes
Target-absent Rejection	Children	Cartoons versus humans	Children significantly more accurate at rejecting cartoon faces than human faces	
	Adults	Cartoons versus humans	Adults significantly more accurate at rejecting cartoon faces than human faces	
	Children versus adults	Cartoons	Children significantly less accurate than adults when rejecting cartoon faces	yes
	Children versus adults	Humans	Children significantly less accurate than adults when rejecting human faces	yes

Table 3.7: Results and conclusions for Pozzulo et al.'s four predictions

The results in Table 3.7 show that each of the four predictions made by Pozzulo et al. (see 'Aims' in Section 3.3) were supported by the findings.

Conclusion

As predicted, the children could easily find the correct face in the target-present line-up with cartoons, identifying with almost 100% accuracy (a ceiling effect)

in this task. Pozzulo et al. concluded, therefore, that any error in the target-absent line-up for cartoons must be a result of social factors rather than cognitive factors. This is because it cannot be explained by a faulty memory for the faces of the cartoon characters. The most likely social factor affecting a low correct rejection rate by children is the child's expectation that they should make a selection, rather than a 'non-selection', i.e. to correctly say that the target character is absent from the line-up. Furthermore, this suggests that the difference seen between children and adults in their rejection rates for human faces, which resembles that for the cartoon faces, can also be explained by the effects of social demands. Finally, these effects of cognitive versus social demands are relative not absolute: both tasks, identification and rejection, will be affected to an extent by both cognitive and social factors. The suggestion from the results is only that for children, social factors play a larger part in decision-making in target-absent line-ups than in target-present ones.

ISSUES AND DEBATES

This study has the potential for *application to everyday life*. The findings suggest that strategies should be devised to minimise social demands that could influence children's responses to line-ups. This is important as it could improve the reliability of child witness information. This could raise the quality of decisions based on children's evidence and thus the effectiveness of court proceedings against perpetrators whose crimes are either only witnessed by children or are against child victims. However, the evidence only contributes to identifying the problem, and not offering solutions. Further investigation is needed to find out how improvements could be made to the line-up procedure.

Strengths and weaknesses

The main method was a laboratory experiment, so all of the participants were tested in a *standardised environment*. The experience of the adults and children was as identical as possible, although there were some differences, such as the children responding to the line-ups by pointing, which is a simpler response that writing. It is possible that seeing the alternatives to choose from on paper affected the adult participants differently. Nevertheless, such differences were necessary to make the task equally accessible to the children. The differences also ensured that the dependent variable, of choice of individual in the line-up, was a clearly operationalised measure of line-up accuracy. The data produced by accurate identification or rejection was *quantitative*, enabling Pozzulo et al. to use statistics such as means to compare the conditions so that they could look for differences caused by the IVs of age and target type (human or cartoon).

One significant weakness of using a laboratory study in this research was that the 'line-up' was not real. Therefore, the situation would not have felt as important to the participants as it would have done in a real criminal case. The emotional experience, for both the children and the adults, would therefore have been different from being faced with a genuine line-up. This, in turn, could lower the *ecological validity* of the research as it was specifically looking at social effects, which could be influenced by emotions. Further research, in more realistic environments, is needed to see whether the differences found extend to actual experiences in the judicial system.

In order to reduce the likelihood of participants working out the aim of the experiment, potential demand characteristics were controlled, for example by giving minimal information about the purpose of the study. The adult participants were told it was a study about memory and the children were told it was about TV shows and computer games. This avoided explaining the true aim, increasing *internal validity*, as the researchers could be more confident that the independent variable (of age) was the only variable having an impact on the dependent variable of line-up accuracy. However, believing you are participating in a memory study may have different effects on recall than believing you ae involved in a study about television and games.

Ethical issues

Ethical issues are not only about the implications for the participants of research but also for wider society. Clearly, the findings of this study make a valuable contribution to the use of children as witnesses and therefore help to improve lives. However, any potential benefits must be measured against potential damage to the participants. If the children in this research had been victims of real crimes, this would have risked considerable potential for harm. However, the experimental situation was not crime-related and the children were not at risk. Furthermore, consent was gained from the parents/guardians of each child, as well as informed consent being gained from the children themselves in a child-friendly way. Finally, the children's comfort and their right to withdraw were ensured as well as ongoing monitoring of their fatigue, anxiety and stress to protect them from harm.

Summary

Pozzulo et al.'s study explored factors affecting children's accuracy as eyewitnesses when presented with a line-up. Adult and child participants were tested using a line-up photoarray that tested cognition: remembering and identifying the culprit when they are present. This was compared to a task that could be readily influenced by social factors: a target-absent line-up where the task was rejection rather than identification. In this situation it is possible for the child to give a false positive response by incorrectly identifying an innocent individual as the perpetrator. To be certain that the tasks were as familiar as possible, Pozzulo et al. used images of cartoon characters as targets and foils, as well as humans. The results showed that children were as good as adults at identifying cartoon characters, but less able to correctly identify humans and less able to correctly reject either type of target. The tendency of children to choose an incorrect face (cartoon or human) in a target-absent line-up suggests that these errors are due to social effects. They cannot be cognitive errors as the children's memory for the faces was excellent, as their identification was accurate. Therefore, the social demand of choosing a face when the target was not there must have been the cause of the rejection errors.

Questions

7   Jaina is planning a study about false memories. She wants to compare false memories about emotional events and false memories about non-emotional events.

    a   Suggest how Jaina could operationally define the IV in her study.

    b   Suggest one possible ethical problem with Jaina's study.

8   Shaun is piloting a photoarray line-up procedure which uses six faces.

    a   Suggest one advantage of this line-up array compared to Pozzulo et al.'s array.

    b   Suggest one disadvantage of this line-up array compared to Pozzulo et al's array.

Issues, debates and approaches

The application of psychology to everyday life

When we are trying to focus, such as when listening to a lecture, allowing ourselves to doodle might be advantageous. However, this doodling must be undemanding. In Andrade's study, the doodling was just shading, a simple process that would not interfere with the primary task. However, this implies that any attempt to deliberately 'draw' something specific could be counterproductive. The drawing itself might become the primary task, distracting us from the lecture rather than allowing us to concentrate better. This knowledge is useful to enable students to use doodling in an effective way.

The eyes provide a lot of information when we are attributing an emotion to an individual. On the basis of the findings from the study by Baron-Cohen et al., it might be possible to develop a programme to help teach individuals diagnosed with ASD to help them develop skills of interpreting emotions. The Eyes test could also be developed further to help aid initial diagnosis of individuals who could be signposted to appropriate clinical staff to investigate if there is an underlying autism spectrum disorder.

Pozzulo et al. demonstrate that children would not be as reliable witnesses as adults in everyday life. In a police line-up it is unknown whether the actual perpetrator of the crime is present and children are more likely to make errors when the real target is absent, that is, to produce false positive responses. However, this difference is more likely to be because of social reasons than cognitive ones. In other words, it is due to the social situation rather than because children have worse memories. This finding is important as it could be used to improve the reliability of child witness information. This means that the next step is to investigate ways to combat the social factors that reduce the accuracy of witness identifications by children.

Individual and situational explanations

As doodling affected recall, this means it has a situational effect on information processing. Furthermore, as Andrade deliberately ensured that her participants would be bored so that they were more likely to doodle, this implies that there are situational causes for doodling itself. However, there were very large differences between the doodles of participants initially allocated to the doodling group (from 0 to 110 shaded shapes) and we know that people who doodle do not all doodle in the same way. This means that there are also individual causes behind doodling behaviour.

Individuals who had a diagnosis of AS/HFA performed significantly worse on the Eyes test than 'normal' individuals, suggesting that the ability to read emotions in the eyes is an individual skill that is developed, rather than being the result of the external environment. The environment was standardised across those participants in both the AS/HFA and 'normal' conditions, providing further support for the individual explanation.

The effect Pozzulo et al. found was a social one: the relatively poor performance of child witnesses in target-absent line-ups was due to social demands, such as feeling pressured. Although it may appear that the difference in accuracy between children and adults should have an individual explanation, such as poorer cognitive abilities of children, the evidence from Pozzulo et al. shows that this is unlikely.

Nature versus nurture

The *nature versus nurture debate* is a long-running debate, which considers whether we have the characteristics we do because of nature (genetics) or nurture (experiences and influences after conception). There is no known single cause for autism spectrum disorder (ASD) and there are both generic and environmental arguments. Evidence is, however, emerging that is identifying genes that are involved specifically with theory of mind problems. Researchers are also investigating the role environmental factors on theory of mind, such as the effects of maternal speech, and early interactions with siblings and peers.

Children as participants

Baron-Cohen et al.'s research does not focus on children as participants, so it might be useful to consider how similar research could be conducted on younger individuals. Baron-Cohen et al.'s research was conducted on adult male participants using pictures of adult eyes and relatively sophisticated words to describe the emotion displayed. This would not be appropriate for children and alternative methods should be considered to investigate similar aims in children. Baron-Cohen has devised a 'Theory of Mind' test for children called the 'Sally and Anne' test that involves asking children questions following a short scene that is acted out with dolls.

The study by Pozzulo et al. demonstrates effective ways to successfully conduct research using children. Practical changes were made to the procedure to ensure the children could access the tasks and respond easily, such as a researcher recording the open filler task and the use of pointing to record the children's line-up responses. The ethical procedures also differed for the child participants, such as the right to withdraw being given and consent being gained by explaining to them in a child-friendly way, settling them down and monitoring their fatigue, anxiety and stress.

SELF-EVALUATION CHECKLIST

After studying this chapter, copy and complete a table like this:

I can	Needs more work	Almost there	Ready to move on	Coursebook	Workbook
state what is meant by the cognitive approach					
explain the psychology being investigated in the cognitive approach					
describe the main assumptions of the cognitive approach and link them to the studies					
use terminology relevant to the cognitive approach					
describe and evaluate the study by Andrade (doodling)					
describe and evaluate the study by Baron-Cohen et al. (Eyes test)					
describe and evaluate the study by Pozzulo et al. (line-ups)					
apply relevant research methods to the cognitive approach					
consider issues and debates that are relevant to the cognitive approach.					

PROJECT

Working as a pair, find as many examples of doodling as you can. You could search for images on the internet, or ask your friends and family to look for examples of their own. Use only doodles that are 'spontaneous', do not use any that are 'colouring in' of drawings designed for that purpose, such as colouring books. Look for common patterns in the doodles. For example, are they mainly angular or flowing, are they nonsense patterns or do they include images of 'things', such as flowers? Are they always completed in the same pen/pencil or do people swap pens to elaborate their doodles? Try to find as much as you can about the doodles.

From your findings, suggest at least two different experiments you could conduct to explore more about different types of doodle or doodling. Are different types of doodle drawn at different times of day? Are they drawn by different people, or when we are in different moods? These are just a few of the many ideas that could form the basis for your project.

Your final piece of work should include:

- some examples of doodles, which must be anonymous

CONTINUED

- an explanation of how you have described or classified the types(s) of doodles each one contains, and anything else you have noticed about each doodle

- at least two ideas for experiments which provide the aim and how you would test the idea (e.g. the IV and DV of your experiment and a basic procedure). You do not need to give details of the sample unless this is relevant to the IV.

REFLECTION

After you have completed your project, reflect on some of your key decisions. You might want to talk to your project partner about this, if you had one. Consider these questions when thinking about your project:

- How did people respond when you asked about their doodles?

  - If they were cautious, what problems could this lead to in the experiments you have designed?

- If they were very interested in what you were doing, what problems could this lead to in the experiments you have designed?

- When you classified the types of doodle, how did you do it? Why would definitions of the types of doodle be important if you conducted the experiments you have designed?

EXAM-STYLE QUESTIONS

1 Danvir is planning a laboratory experiment about doodling. He decides to score the doodles for how colourful they are. **Suggest one** problem with the way Danvir plans to score his participants' doodling. [2]

2 Professor Patel notices that many of his students write poetry on their examination papers. He wonders if this has a beneficial effect like doodling.

   a If Professor Patel's expectation is correct, **explain** how writing poetry could help the students in their exams. [3]

   b Professor Patel intends to correlate poetry writing and student exam success. Explain the correlation he would find if his expectation is correct. [2]

   c Suggest how Professor Patel could operationalise and measure 'writing poetry' when he studies his students' exam papers. [2]

3 The study by Baron-Cohen et al. investigated the Eyes test.

   a In the original Eyes test used by Baron-Cohen et al., there was an imbalance of male and female faces. Explain why this could have been a problem. [2]

   b Explain how the Eyes test could be further improved. [2]

CONTINUED

4   In the study by Baron-Cohen et al., different types of intelligence were measured.

   a   **Identify** the different types of intelligence measured in this study.   **[2]**

   b   Explain what the results of the study show about different types of intelligence in people with autism spectrum disorder.   **[2]**

5   **Give one** weakness of the study by Pozzulo et al.   **[2]**

6   Apply individual explanations and situational explanations to the conclusions of the study by Pozzulo et al.   **[4]**

7   **Evaluate** the strengths and weaknesses of the study by Andrade et al.   **[8]**

   [Total: 31]

COMMAND WORD

give: produce an answer from a given source or recall / memory

Additional reference

Baer, R. A., Smith, G. T., Hopkins, J., Krietemeyer, J., & Toney, L. (2006). Using self-report assessment methods to explore facets of mindfulness. *Assessment*, *13*(1), 27–45.

Wilson, K., & Korn, J. H. (2007). Attention during lectures: beyond ten minutes. *Teaching of psychology*, *34*(2), 85–89.

> # Chapter 4
Learning approach

LEARNING INTENTIONS

In this chapter, you will learn how to:

- describe and apply the concepts and terminology of the learning approach and its main assumptions

- explain and apply the psychology being investigated in the learning approach

- describe, evaluate and apply the three core studies from the learning approach

- apply relevant research methods to the learning approach

- consider issues and debates that are relevant to the learning approach.

Introduction

The aim of this chapter is to introduce you to the learning approach to psychology and to explore three studies that illustrate this approach.

- **Bandura et al. (aggression)** is based on social learning theory and looks at the effect on children's behaviour of seeing an adult behaving aggressively. The main psychology being investigated was social learning theory and aggression.

- **Fagen et al. (elephant learning)** explores the use of positive reinforcement training for a trunk wash in elephants to improve their welfare. The main psychology being investigated was operant conditioning, reinforcement (positive, negative, primary and secondary), shaping and behavioural chaining.

- **Saavedra and Silverman (button phobia)** is a case study of a young boy with a phobia of buttons and the use of classical conditioning to help reduce his fear and disgust. The main psychology being investigated was evaluative learning, operant conditioning, classical conditioning and phobias.

GETTING STARTED

The learning approach to psychology is concerned with how humans and animals acquire or change their behaviour, including learning from others, learning by association, and learning from rewards and punishments. Think about what you have done so far today. Apart from basic biological activities, such as breathing or blinking, almost everything you have done you will have learned. You are reading this, so you have learned to read, maybe in more than one language. Hopefully you've eaten a meal and maybe travelled to class. How did you learn how to eat or how to get to your classroom?

We can learn through different mechanisms and most of these mechanisms can also be seen in animals. In some respects, however, our learning is different. Learning means new, permanent changes in behaviour following experience. If you have a pet, or regularly see wild animals, how do you think your learning is similar to and different from theirs? You might have thought of two different kinds of answers. The *way* we learn might differ and *what* we can learn might differ. Both of these are good answers.

MAIN ASSUMPTIONS IN CONTEXT

Live to learn or learn to live?

When you think about 'learning' the first thing that probably occurs to you is trying to learn a task like multiplication tables. However, this is in fact a memory task. In psychology we use 'learning' to refer to the acquisition of new behaviours. The main assumptions of the learning approach to psychology are:

- Each life begins as a 'blank slate': observable changes to our behaviour can result from interactions with our environment.

- The processes of social learning, operant conditioning and classical conditioning are the ways in which humans and animals learn. These processes involve stimulus-response i.e. experiences within our environment (stimuli) shape our behaviour (response).

KEY WORDS

blank slate: the idea that all individuals are born without any mental content, and that all knowledge must come from experience

stimulus: an event or object which leads to a behavioural response

Kimble (1961) defined learning as 'a relatively permanent change in behavioural potential which accompanies experience'.

Looking carefully at this statement, we can see that it has three parts:

- learning results in the acquisition of new responses (the relatively permanent change)

- learning may occur without new behaviours necessarily being demonstrated (the behavioural *potential*)

- the environment influences and provides opportunities for learning (by providing experiences).

In this chapter, we will be looking at the changes that occur in learning, how we can measure changes in behavioural potential and how the environment contributes to learning. We will consider repeated exposure to stimuli, rewards and role models, each of which is a feature of the environment.

Looking back over your childhood, think about three different behaviours that you can definitely say you learned, rather than things you were just able to do once you got older. Consider how you might have

learned them. Did you discover them for yourself or did something or someone in the environment help you? If something or someone was involved, think about what it was that enabled you to learn. Now think about someone much older than yourself. What has this person learned recently? Maybe they are developing the ability to use a new piece of technology, or are being told about new music by younger family members. We continue to learn throughout our lifetimes.

Finally, think critically about yourself. Is everything you have learned positive? Have you acquired any bad habits? The answer to this is likely to be 'yes', even though you probably made no effort to learn these things. This suggests that although some learning involves effort, sometimes we can learn simply by being in a certain environment – and that not all learning is a good thing.

4.1 Core study 1: Bandura et al. (aggression)

Bandura, A., Ross, D., & Ross, S. A. (1961). Transmission of aggression through imitation of aggressive models. *Journal of abnormal and social psychology, 63*(3), 575–582.

The psychology being investigated

Children copy adults. One reason for this is because the immediate social setting encourages the child to imitate what he or she is watching (Figure 4.1). This helps influences their behaviour, making it more likely that the child will do what others are doing around them. Alternatively, the observation of a behaviour can lead a child to acquire a new response that he or she could reproduce independently. If this is the case, the new behaviour should generalise to new settings and so would be produced in the absence of an adult **model**.

Albert Bandura had previously conducted experiments on **social learning** and was interested in studying social learning in the context of **aggression**. To learn from others, the observer (e.g. a child) must be paying attention to behaviour of a model. They must retain (remember) the behaviour they have observed, in order to reproduce it. When social learning occurs, it could potentially lead to either aggressive or non-aggressive behaviour. Bandura expected then that watching an aggressive model should lead to more aggressive behaviours being demonstrated, and that observing a non-aggressive model should lead to more non-aggressive behaviour being produced, i.e. even less aggressive behaviour than normal.

KEY WORDS

model: a person who inspires or encourages others to imitate positive or negative behaviours

social learning: the learning of a new behaviour that is observed in a role model and imitated later in the absence of that model

aggression: behaviour that is aimed at harming others either physically or psychologically

Figure 4.1: A child imitates seen behaviour

Background

Previous research had shown that children imitated behaviour of a model when in the presence of the model. Bandura et al. wanted to investigate whether social learning theory could be used to explain aggression, specifically when the child was no longer in the presence of an aggressive model.

Children are rewarded in different ways for imitating adults. In general (at least, in the USA in the 1960s when this study took place), boys were rewarded for behaviours considered to be sex-appropriate and punished for inappropriate ones, such as cooking or 'playing mother'. Similarly for girls, rewards and punishments would be applied to discourage what was considered sex-inappropriate behaviours. This, Bandura et al. suggested, would lead to two kinds of differences.

First, boys and girls should be more likely to imitate same-sex models and, second, they should differ in the readiness with which they imitate aggression, with boys doing so more readily as this was seen as a more masculine-type behaviour.

Aim

The aim was to investigate whether a child would learn aggression by observing a model and would reproduce this behaviour in the absence of the model, and whether the sex of the role model was important. Specifically, there were four hypotheses:

1   Observed aggressive behaviour will be imitated, so children who see an aggressive model will be more aggressive than those seeing a non-aggressive model or no model.

2   Observed non-aggressive behaviour will be imitated, so children seeing non-aggressive models will be less aggressive than those seeing no model.

3   Children are more likely to copy a same-sex model.

4   Boys will be more likely to copy aggression than girls.

ISSUES AND DEBATES

Nature versus **nurture** describes the importance of the environment, or nurture, can be seen in the role adults take as models for children, as well as in the rewards and punishments adults give to children.

KEY WORDS

nature: innate, genetic factors which influence behaviour

nurture: environmental influences on behaviour

Method

Research method and design

This was a laboratory experiment; the environment was not the normal place where the children played and the situation was controlled. The design of the experiment was that of independent measures as different children were used in each of the levels of the independent variables (IVs) (although these children were *matched* for aggression in threes; see the Research Methods box). There were three IVs:

- *model type*: whether the child saw an aggressive model, non-aggressive model or no model

- *model sex*: same sex as child (boys watching a male model and girls watching a female model) or different sex (boys watching a female model and girls watching a male model)

- *learner sex*: whether the child was a boy or a girl.

The dependent variable (DV) was the behaviour the child displayed. This was measured through a *controlled observation* of the children and measures of aggressive behaviour were recorded.

> ## RESEARCH METHODS
>
> In the *matched participants design* described here, the participants were divided into threes, all with very similar initial aggression levels. One of each of these individuals was placed into each of the three different conditions of model type (aggressive model, non-aggressive model and control).

Sample

Seventy-two children aged 3–6 years (36 boys and 36 girls) were recruited from Stanford University nursery school.

Procedure

Prior to the experimental part of the study, the children were observed in their nursery school by the experimenter and a teacher who knew them well. They were rated on four different measures of physical aggression, verbal aggression, aggression to inanimate objects and aggression inhibition (anxiety) each on a five-point scale. They were then assigned to three groups, ensuring that the aggression levels of the children in each group were matched. Of the 51 children rated by both observers (the rest were rated by only one observer), similar ratings were generally produced. Their ratings were compared as a measure of *inter-rater reliability*, which showed a high correlation between the observers, of $r = 0.89$.

> ## RESEARCH METHODS
>
> *Inter-rater reliability* is the extent to which two researchers rate the same activity that they have observed, heard in an interview, etc., in the same way. This is judged using a correlation (an 'r' value) between the two ratings, which will be high (close to 1) if they are reliable.

Twelve boys and 12 girls were allocated to control groups who saw no model. The remaining children were divided equally by sex between aggressive and non-aggressive model groups and, within those, between same and opposite-sex models.

The experimenter and child entered the observation room, where the experimenter showed the child to a table and chair in their 'play area', where they were shown how to make potato prints and sticker pictures: activities previously identified as interesting for children. The opposite corner of the room also contained a table and chair, a Tinkertoy set (a wooden building kit), a mallet and a five foot (152 cm) Bobo doll: an inflatable clown-like doll that bounced back when hit (Figure 4.2). This is where the model sat, in those conditions where there was one. The experimenter remained in the room so that the child would not refuse to be alone or try to leave early but they appeared to be working quietly at their desk.

Figure 4.2: Observing and imitating aggressive behaviours with a Bobo doll

The three groups were then treated differently. In the non-aggressive condition, the model assembled the Tinkertoys for 10 minutes. In the aggressive condition, this lasted only 1 minute after which the model attacked the Bobo doll. The doll was laid on its side, sat on and punched in the nose, picked up and hit on the head with a mallet, tossed up in the air and kicked. This sequence was performed three times over 9 minutes accompanied by aggressive comments such as 'Kick him' and two non-aggressive comments such as 'He sure is a tough fella'. Of children in the model groups, half saw a same-sex model, the others saw a model of the opposite sex. A *control group* did not see any model, and therefore saw no aggression.

The experimental procedure continued with a stage in which all participants were deliberately mildly annoyed. This was done for two reasons:

- because watching aggression may reduce the production of aggression by the observer (even if it has been learned) and it was necessary to see evidence of learning

- to ensure that even the non-aggressive condition and control participants would be likely to express aggression, so that any reduction in that tendency could be measured.

RESEARCH METHODS

The non-aggressive model group might appear to be a *control group* because the key factor of 'aggression' is missing. However, the important aspect is the presence of a model – and in the non-aggressive group a model was still present. This means the real control group is where the IV is absent: the group where there is no model at all.

A test of the child's aggression then followed in which the child was observed for 20 minutes using a one-way mirror. The mirror appeared transparent on the researcher's side (so they could observe behaviour) but appeared as a normal mirror on the child's side (so they could not see that they were being observed from another room). For the aggressive model group, this was a test of delayed imitation. The experimental room contained a three-foot (92 cm) Bobo doll, a mallet and peg board, two dart guns and a tether ball with a face painted on it which hung from the ceiling. It also contained some non-aggressive toys, including a tea set, crayons and colouring paper, a ball, two dolls, three bears, cars and trucks, and plastic farm animals. These toys were always presented in the same order.

The children's behaviours were observed in 5-second intervals (240 response units per child). There were three 'response measures' of the children's *imitation*, with a range of possible activities in each:

- *Imitative physical aggression:* striking the Bobo doll with the mallet, sitting on the doll and punching it in the nose, kicking the doll, and tossing it in the air.

- *Imitative verbal aggression:* repetition of the phrases, 'Sock him', 'Hit him down', 'Kick him', 'Throw him in the air' or 'Pow'.

- *Imitative non-aggressive verbal responses:* repetition of 'He keeps coming back for more' or 'He sure is a tough fella'.

Partially imitative aggression was scored if the child imitated these behaviours incompletely. The two behaviours here were:

- *mallet aggression:* striking objects other than the Bobo doll aggressively with the mallet

- *sits on Bobo doll:* laying the Bobo doll on its side and sitting on it, without attacking it.

Two further categories were:

- *aggressive gun play:* shooting darts or aiming a gun and firing imaginary shots at objects in the room

- *non-imitative physical and verbal aggression:* physically aggressive acts directed toward objects other than the Bobo doll and any hostile remarks except for those in the verbal imitation category (e.g. 'Shoot the Bobo', 'Cut him', 'Stupid ball', 'Horses fighting, biting' 'Knock over people').

Finally, behaviour units were also counted for *non-aggressive play* and sitting quietly *not playing* at all, and records were kept of the children's remarks about the situation.

The male model scored all the children's behaviours. Except for those conditions in which the male was the model, he was unaware of which condition the child had been in. However, the condition in which the child had been was usually obvious, as in the case of the aggressive model children as they performed the specific behaviours exhibited by the model. To test the reliability of the scorer, a second scorer independently rated the behaviour of half of the children. The reliability score was high at approximately $r = 0.9$ for different categories of behaviour.

Results

Children exposed to aggressive models imitated their exact behaviours and were significantly more aggressive, both physically and verbally, than those children in the non-aggressive model or control groups. One-third of the children in the aggressive condition also copied the model's non-aggressive verbal responses, but none of the children in either the non-aggressive or control groups made such remarks. The mean aggression scores can be seen in Table 4.1.

The mean for imitative physical aggression for boys with a male model (25.8) was much higher than that for girls (7.2). This indicates that the boys imitated the physical aggression of a male model more than the girls did. However, with a female model, girls imitated less (5.5) than with the male model. Girls imitated more verbal aggression of the same-sex model than boys (although not significantly so). Children were also more likely to imitate a same-sex model than an

opposite-sex model; this effect was stronger for boys than for girls.

Children seeing a non-aggressive model were much less likely than either the aggressive model group or controls to exhibit mallet aggression, and this pattern was especially apparent for girls. Although the aggressive model did not appear to affect levels of gun play or punching the Bobo doll, non-imitative physical and verbal aggression other than these activities were higher following exposure to an aggressive model compared to the other two conditions.

There were also differences in non-aggressive play. Girls played more with dolls, tea sets and colouring, and boys engaged in more exploratory play and gun play. There were no sex differences in play with farm animals, cars or the tether ball. Both boys and girls seeing the non-aggressive model engaged in more non-aggressive play with dolls than either of the other groups, and spent more than twice as much time sitting quietly, not playing.

Response category	Experimental groups				Control groups
	Aggressive		Non-aggressive		
	Female model	Male model	Female model	Male model	
Imitative physical aggression					
Female participants	5.5	7.2	2.5	0.0	1.2
Male participants	12.4	25.8	0.2	1.5	2.0
Imitative verbal aggression					
Female participants	13.7	2.0	0.3	0.0	0.7
Male participants	4.3	12.7	1.1	0.0	1.7
Mallet aggression					
Female participants	17.2	18.7	0.5	0.5	13.1
Male participants	15.5	28.8	18.7	6.7	13.5

Response category	Experimental groups				Control groups
	Aggressive		Non-aggressive		
	Female model	Male model	Female model	Male model	
Punches Bobo doll					
Female participants	6.3	16.5	5.8	4.3	11.7
Male participants	18.9	11.9	15.6	14.8	15.7
Non-imitative aggression					
Female participants	21.3	8.4	7.2	1.4	6.1
Male participants	16.2	36.7	26.1	22.3	24.6
Aggressive gun play					
Female participants	1.8	4.5	2.6	2.5	3.7
Male participants	7.3	15.9	8.9	16.7	14.3

Table 4.1: Mean aggression scores from Bandura et al.'s study

ACTIVITY 4.1

Consider the data for the mean aggressive behaviours and the non-imitative verbal responses.

1   Which data is qualitative and which is quantitative?

2   Draw a bar chart showing the results for imitative physical aggression. Include the mean scores for the experimental groups and control group. Make sure you give the chart labels and an appropriate title.

ISSUES AND DEBATES

In the nature versus nurture debate, we can consider why the boys and girls showed different responses. This could be because they are genetically different; a nature explanation. Boys might be biologically predisposed to be aggressive, so more likely to copy aggressive models. Alternatively, boys might be more likely to copy aggressive models because they have been rewarded for aggressive behaviours more than girls have. This would be a nurture argument.

In addition to the observations, records of the remarks about the aggressive models revealed differences, both between reactions to the actions of the male and female models and between boys and girls. Some comments appeared to be based on previous knowledge of sex-typed behaviour, such as 'Who is that lady? That's not the way for a lady to behave. Ladies are supposed to act like ladies . . .' and 'You should have seen what that girl did in there. She was just acting like a man. I never saw a girl act like that before. She was punching and fighting but no swearing.' Whereas comments about the female model's behaviour were disapproving, those about the male model were not. This was more likely to be seen as appropriate and approved by both boys and girls, for example in comments such as 'Al's a good socker, he beat up Bobo. I want to sock like Al' and 'That man is a strong fighter, he punched and punched and he could hit Bobo right down to the floor and if Bobo got up he said, 'Punch your nose.' He's a good fighter like Daddy.'

> **KEY WORD**
>
> **sex-typed behaviour:** actions that are typically performed by one particular sex and are seen in society as more appropriate for that sex. For example, aggression is seen as masculine-type behaviour and was more commonly imitated by boys in the study

Conclusion

The results strongly suggest that observation and imitation can account for the learning of specific acts without reinforcement of either the model or observer. All four hypotheses were supported:

- Observed aggressive behaviours are imitated: children who see aggressive models are likely to be more aggressive than those seeing a non-aggressive model or no model.

- Observed non-aggressive behaviours are imitated: children seeing non-aggressive models will be less aggressive than those seeing no model.

- Children are more likely to copy a same-sex model, although this may depend on the extent to which this behaviour is sex-typed.

- Boys are more likely to copy aggression than girls.

Strengths and weaknesses

The main method was a laboratory experiment. This means that it was possible to control extraneous variables such as ensuring there was a possibility that the children in any condition would show aggressive

> **KEY WORD**
>
> **extraneous variable:** this either acts randomly, affecting the DV in all levels of the IV or systematically, i.e. on one level of the IV (called a confounding variable) so can obscure the effect of the IV, making the results difficult to interpret

behaviour. This was done by showing them nice toys but then taking them to another room. Also, all children in both experimental groups saw a model for the same length of time, and in each condition their behaviours were standardised. This means the research was more *valid* – the researchers could be sure that the differences in results between conditions were due to the differences between the models – and more *reliable*, because each child within a condition experienced exactly the same exposure. *Inter-observer reliability* was also checked for both the initial observations of aggressiveness and for the data recording, and was very high. The pre-testing of the children's aggressiveness as part of the matched pairs design was another factor that increased validity, because it ensured that differences between conditions were due to the models and not to individual differences between the children who happened to be in each group.

The main measure of the DV was through observation. As the observers were behind a one-way mirror, the children were unaware that they were being watched. This increases validity as they were likely to behave naturally rather than responding to *demand characteristics* as they might have done had they known they were being observed. The observation period was divided into time intervals (of 5 seconds) and the categories were clearly defined (e.g. imitative and non-imitative behaviours), which also helped to improve both validity and reliability.

Among the weaknesses of the study is that only six children were used in each experimental condition and, although they were matched to reduce the risk of *participant variables* confounding the results, it is still a small sample. Furthermore, it is possible that the children were quite similar, as they all attended the same nursery based at a university, suggesting that they all had academically able parents. This could bias the *sample*, lowering validity.

The study collected both quantitative data and qualitative data. The quantitative data provided an *objective* record of the number of imitative actions in each category. The qualitative data, although more *subjective*, provided some explanation of the reasons behind the tendency of the children to copy some behaviours and not others. It could have been useful to have asked the children for self-reports of their emotions when they were observing the model or reacting towards the Bobo doll. This may have helped to further explain differences such as the influence of sex-typing on imitation. It would also have been useful to have followed the children up to see how long the children's acquired behaviours lasted. If imitation leads to learning, the change in behaviour should be relatively permanent.

Ethical issues

One ethical issue with the study was some of the children might have been harmed by becoming more aggressive during the research. For example, they could have physically injured themselves with the toys they were given to play with after watching an aggressive model. Even if this were not the case, the children were still deliberately annoyed in the procedure of the study. This could have been psychologically distressing for the children. These aspects of the study go against the ethical guideline of protecting participants from physical and psychological harm.

Summary

Bandura et al.'s study used adults being aggressive to a Bobo doll to show that children's behaviour can be affected by the behaviour of a model. Exact aggressive behaviours were imitated although the study showed that non-aggressive modelling was also effective. Children were more likely to copy a same-sex model. Additionally, boys engaged in more aggressive imitation than girls. This was a well-controlled laboratory experiment measuring the dependent variable through objective observations that were reliable. Qualitative data suggested that the children recognised sex-typing and were surprised by behaviour that did not fit the pattern. The findings suggest practical applications for protecting children, e.g. through film certification and the use of parental controls on media devices.

Questions

1 Why might Bandura et al. have chosen to record the children's behaviour in 5-second intervals, rather than 1-second or 1-minute intervals?

2 Consider the data for the mean aggressive behaviours and the non-imitative verbal responses.

   a Which are qualitative data?

   b Which are quantitative data?

3 The procedure was standardised in many ways.

   a Identify the ways in which the procedure was standardised.

   b Explain why standardisation was necessary – what might have happened if each participant had not been treated in the same way?

4.2 Core study 2: Fagen et al. (elephant learning)

Fagen, A., Acharya, N., & Kaufman, G. E. (2014). Positive reinforcement training for a trunk wash in Nepal's working elephants: demonstrating alternatives to traditional elephant training techniques. *Journal of applied animal welfare science, 17(2): 83–97.*

The psychology being investigated

The term **operant conditioning** is used simply to mean learning from the outcome of our behaviour. For example, when we perform a behaviour that has a good consequence, we are more likely to repeat it. Psychologists would state that this behaviour has been reinforced. **Positive reinforcers** might include food or praise. Another type of reinforcement is negative reinforcement; when

---

KEY WORDS

operant conditioning: learning through the consequences of our actions

positive reinforcer: a reward for behaviour that fulfils a biological need is known as a primary positive reinforcer. A stimulus that is associated with primary reinforcers can also be learned and is known as a *secondary reinforcer*

something unpleasant is removed or avoided in response to a stimulus. One example of this could be going outside and feeling unpleasantly cold (stimulus) and then putting on a coat (response). We quickly learn that putting on more clothes keeps us warm (reinforcement).

Some reinforcers occur naturally. These include things which help us to survive such as water, food, shelter or sleep. Alternatively, secondary reinforcers have to be learned, and are associated with primary reinforcers. Money is one example as it can help us to acquire food, water, shelter and so on.

The theory of operant conditioning can explain how humans and animals develop complex behaviours. The behaviour of humans and animals can be shaped gradually. A good example of this is how children are rewarded with praise as they learn to speak. At first a child's vocalisations might sound only slightly like real words, but with encouragement these words become more accurate and the child's speech is very clear. Also simple, individual actions can be combined in sequences or 'behaviour chains'. Like riding a bicycle, the rider must first learn to pedal, then steer, then balance on two wheels.

However, the theory does not try to explain underlying, unseen reasons for behaviour, such as thoughts or feelings. According to operant conditioning theorists, the majority of behaviours are learned through trial and error.

ACTIVITY 4.2

Sometimes humans try to train animals to behave in certain ways.

Think of at least two different training methods that are used for pets and/or domestic animals.

Copy and complete Table 4.2 to explain how each method might work, how the trainer would know if it had worked, and which method you think is more effective.

Description of training technique	How it works/ how we can see if it works	Which method is likely to be more effective

Table 4.2: Example table for training techniques

Traditionally, captive elephants are given 'free' (unlimited) contact with their handlers (known as mahouts) and elephant behaviour is managed using punishment (Figure 4.3). This form of operant conditioning relies on unpleasant stimulus such as pain or fear to shape behaviour. One type of punishment used to shape elephant behaviour is the pain inflicted by a bamboo stick. However, because of concerns for **captive animal welfare** and keeper safety, there is increased interest in reward-based training (**positive reinforcement**) using 'protected' contact (a barrier between elephant and handler). In particular, positive reinforcement methods have been shown to improve the psychological well-being of elephants (Desmond & Laule, 1991).

Figure 4.3: Elephants are trained by mahouts who use sticks as punishment

KEY WORDS

captive animal welfare: psychologists working with animals that are confined or outside of their normal environment must ensure the health and well-being of the animals. As part of this captive management, an animal's natural needs for accommodation, environment, freedom of movement, food, water and care should be appropriately met

positive reinforcement: a form of operant conditioning. It involves rewarding desirable behaviour to encourage it to be repeated. For example, praising a child for saying 'please' and 'thank you' positively reinforces good manners

One type of positive reinforcement training is **secondary positive reinforcement (SPR) training**. This method teaches animals to associate specific sounds with food; specific noises like these are called 'markers' or 'sound-markers'. Once the animal is conditioned to the sound-marker relationships, the marker can be used to reward wanted behaviours. Using a sound marker is better than rewarding with food on its own as the marker can precisely indicate to the animal when it has correctly performed the desired behaviour, whereas there is a delay for preparing and delivering food. To maintain the association between secondary and primary reinforcer, food rewards are still given at intervals.

KEY WORD

secondary positive reinforcement (SPR) training: training in which a secondary reinforcer such as a sound marker is used and then followed with administration of a primary positive reinforcer (typically food)

Background

Diagnosing and treating illness in elephants is an important part of captive animal welfare. In order to avoid using traditional methods such as punishment, Fagen et al. investigated the use of SPR training to teach elephants to reliably and voluntarily engage in a trunk washing procedure designed to maintain their well-being.

SPR has been used successfully with several animal species, including pandas, primates and antelope. One advantage the method offers is the ability to shape captive animals' behaviour to help improve their health and well-being. In this study the focus of using SPR was as a method for detecting tuberculosis in elephants. Tuberculosis is a serious respiratory disease which is a significant concern in the captive elephant population, and can be passed between animal and human. The disease is best detected through taking a sample from the elephant's trunk through a 'trunk wash' method. However, getting elephants to trunk wash correctly can be challenging, with many samples being insufficient for testing.

Aim

The aim of this study was to see whether free-contact, traditionally trained elephants can be trained to participate in a trunk wash by using positive reinforcement.

Method

Research method and design

This was a *controlled observation* involving a small group of elephants living in captivity who were trained over a period of weeks. The researchers watched the elephants' behaviour in response to a specific stimulus, and used a behavioural checklist to record the elephants' responses as a percentage pass. This means the study can also be described as a *structured observation*.

Sample

This study included five female elephants: four juveniles and one adult, all housed at the same elephant stable in Nepal. The juveniles were between 5 and 7 years old and had been born at the stable. The adult elephant was estimated to have been in her 50s. The elephants were chosen from others at the stable as they were docile, not currently pregnant or looking after a calf and their mahouts were willing to take part in the study. The elephants were all traditionally trained and in free contact with their mahouts. None of the elephants had previous experience of SPR.

The elephants spent most of the day grazing in the jungle under the control of their mahouts. They spent the rest of the day leg-chained in a stable with the freedom to move 6–8 feet (1.83–2.4 m) around the stake. The elephants' diet was fresh grasses, grain and nutritional supplements and they were given access to water at a river during grazing hours.

ACTIVITY 4.3

Humans share a number of cognitive and behavioural traits with animals.

1   Explain the reasons why psychologists might use animals instead of human beings in their research.

2   As discussed in Chapter 1, the British Psychological Society (BPS) Guidelines for Psychologists Working with Animals (2020) include a number of ethical guidelines on the topics of:

*   replacement

*   species

*   number

*   procedures

CONTINUED

- pain and distress
- housing
- reward
- deprivation and aversive stimuli.

Design an advertisement that could be sent to organisations who look after captive elephants, in order to recruit animal participants for the study by Fagen et al. The advertisement should focus on how the well-being of the animals will be maintained throughout the research. Choose at least **two** appropriate ethical guidelines from those listed above in your advertisement.

Procedure

The method of training used in this study was SPR, with chopped banana as the primary reinforcer and a short whistle blow as the secondary reinforcer. Training was conducted during the indoor sessions (7:30 a.m. to 10:00 a.m. and 4:00 p.m. to 7:00 p.m.) by a trainer, with the mahout present for safety. The mahouts stood to the side and did not speak to or signal to the elephants. No elephant went longer than two days without a training session. Elephants could choose not to engage with a session by turning or walking away from the trainer.

The purpose of training was to teach the elephants to perform a voluntary trunk wash in several behavioural steps, actively moving their trunks in response to a cue. After establishing the marker-reward relationships (banana-whistle), elephants were taught using the following three methods:

- Capture: waiting for animal to perform a behaviour naturally then 'capturing' it by marking it with a reward
- Lure: for non-natural behaviours, an animals is 'lured' into a certain body position by placing a reward in a certain place
- Shaping: after starting either capture or lure, rewards are then only given for the behaviours that are 'best', i.e. incrementally closer to the goal behaviour

Task

Using these training methods, elephants were trained to do the following behavioural tasks separately (see Table 4.3 and Figure 4.4).

Behavioural task	Role in the trunk wash	Description	Method
Trunk here	To allow for saline or water to be instilled into trunk	Elephant places end of trunk in trainer's hand	Lure (chopped banana placed in trainer's hand)
Trunk up	To allow saline or water to run to the base of the trunk	Elephant lifts trunk upwards	Lure and Shaping (trainer lifts chopped banana above head so elephant reaches trunk upwards)
Bucket	To allow placement of trunk into bucket ready to exhale	Elephant places end of trunk in bucket	Lure (chopped banana placed at bottom of bucket)
Blow	To exhale the sample for collection	Elephant exhales through trunk into bucket	Capture and Shaping (wait for natural exhale and reward, then shape with further reward for more forceful exhales)
Steady	To allow the elephant to hold any position for the required amount of time	Elephants hold the position they have previously been asked to do	Shaping (extending the period of time the position or behaviour was held for with reward)

Table 4.3: Behavioural tasks and methods taught to the elephants

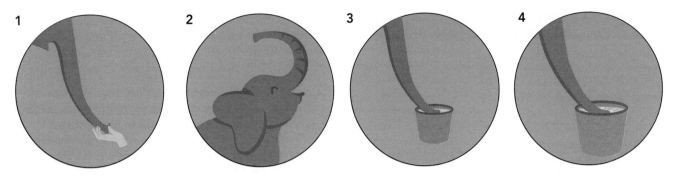

Figure 4.4: The trunk wash consisted of (1) trunk here, (2) trunk up, (3) bucket, (4) blow and (5) steady (not pictured)

There were three other tasks (targeting, trunk down, trunk out) that were introduced, but partway through the training were discarded as they are not essential for the performance of a trunk wash. After the elephant performed the individual behavioural tasks, each task was then paired with a verbal cue. The verbal cue was a one-syllable word with no meaning in English or Nepali to avoid having any meaning to the elephants or mahouts.

Once all the behavioural tasks were established, the trainers put the behaviours together in small sequences in a process known as behaviour chaining. This technique meant that performing the first behaviour in a sequence correctly earned the animal the chance to perform the second behaviour correctly and gain a reward. Separate behavioural tasks were at first paired (starting with bucket and blow), then put together in longer sequences until they formed the entire trunk wash procedure.

In addition, the trainer also introduced the use of a syringe to the trunk-here position. This was done incrementally using a desensitisation method. Over a series of repetitions of the whole trunk wash sequence, the syringe was gradually brought closer to the elephant's trunk, then touching the trunk, then inserted, then inserted with increasing amounts of fluid until the elephant tolerated the full 60ml required for sample collection.

To avoid the elephants drinking the saline or water, they were offered drinks before each training session. One elephant preferred drinking saline and would drink the saline solution after rejecting the drinking water, so was switched to a water solution for the behavioural task.

There was no time limit put on each stage of the training process; it was determined by the success of the individual elephant meaning that the training plans varied according to the individual elephant's needs.

An assistant recorded the length of each training session in minutes. The assistant recorded the total number of times the elephant was given a cue or 'offer' for behaviour. After Session 10, elephants were tested approximately every five sessions on previously taught behaviours. A passing score was 80% (i.e. eight or more correct out of ten offers/cues). Once the 80% or higher score had been achieved on a sequence this was considered a 'pass'. Once the whole behavioural sequence was 'passed' at a rate of 80% or higher, the training was considered complete.

Results

It was found that the four juvenile elephants successfully learned the trunk wash, however, the adult elephant did not (see Table 4.4). Elephants 2 and 4 never passed

Elephant	Number of sessions	Mean duration of sessions (mins)	Total training time (mins)
1 (juvenile)	30	12.42	373
2 (juvenile)	25	10.29	257
3 (juvenile)	35	13.27	389
4 (juvenile)	35	11.11	451
5 (adult)	n/a	n/a	424

Table 4.4: The results of training sessions for the trunk wash

their steady test, but were able to pass their full trunk wash tests. Elephant 5 did not pass her blow-into-bucket, desensitisation to syringe or steady test. There are a number of factors which may have influenced the behaviour of elephant 5. She was older and likely had both some visual impairment and trunk weakness. The elephant was reported as being distracted and inpatient during the last week of the study and had a foot abscess during this period. Also, a calf from an adjacent stall interrupted some of her sessions by entering the training area.

Another result was that some behavioural tasks were more difficult than others. For example, the trunk-here task required more offers/cues than the bucket or blow-into-bucket tasks.

The elephants gradually improved their performance over time (see Figure 4.5). The mean success rate went from 39% after 10 sessions of training to 89.3% after 35 sessions of training (mean percentage score never reach 100% as 90% was given as default to individual behaviours within a sequence, once the sequence was 'passed').

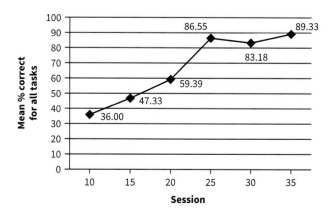

Figure 4.5: Mean percentage correct among all elephants for all tasks during each test

Conclusion

The researchers concluded from this study that juvenile, free-contact, traditionally trained elephants can be trained to participate in a trunk wash using only SPR training techniques. Moreover, this training can be carried out with the voluntary participation of the elephants, avoiding punishment, to produce reliable results.

Strengths and weaknesses

This study involved a small group of female elephants. Using a small sample in a psychological study can make it difficult to *generalise* the results to a larger population. As the elephants were captive animals from one elephant stable, it would be hard to say that they are *representative* of the general population.

The researchers mention that elephants were chosen for their temperament (docile). Because of their large size, elephants can pose a risk to themselves and humans, which is a major challenge for those conducting research with them. Other practical challenges included trying to control for distractions to the elephants. The presence of tourists and other elephants during the training sessions might have affected the elephants' concentration or willingness to participate.

Controlled observations such as this can be easily replicated, using the same observation schedule. This means the study can be tested for *reliability*. However, the researchers state that the training sessions were flexible to suit the mood and ability of each animal. If this study was repeated with other elephants, it is likely that the experience of the trainer and personalities/conditions in which elephants were kept (e.g. their stress levels, previous experience of SPR training) could affect the results. This creates an issue for reliability.

There were attempts to maintain the *validity* of the research; for example, the mahouts were asked to not speak to or give signals to the elephants. The verbal cues given had no meaning in Nepali or English. Both of these controls limited the influence of *demand characteristics* on the elephants' responses to the tests.

As a structured observation, the study collected *quantitative data* in the form of correct behavioural responses to the verbal cues/offers. This allows us to make an objective analysis of whether or not the SPR was a successful method for learning the trunk wash. Quantitative data is also easier to analyse, compared with unstructured observations.

Ethical issues

When using animals as participants, different sorts of ethical issues must be considered. In this instance, the elephants were reported to be well treated and did not appear to have been physically harmed as a result of the research. The elephants were able to graze freely for a large portion of the day, were fed adequately and were able to socialise with the other elephants in the jungle. Investigating the effectiveness of positive reinforcement training in elephants that are already captive rather than capturing and using wild animals is a more ethical approach.

The study was carried out with the intention of developing a method for producing useable trunk wash samples. The purpose of this was to help with captive management of elephants and to enable tuberculosis to be quickly diagnosed and treated, which is highly beneficial to the elephants. The researchers actively avoided using punishment and instead focused on a training method which minimised harm to the animals.

Summary

Fagen et al.'s study used a small group of five female elephants to show that trunk washing can be learned through positive reinforcement. Through a lengthy process of training and testing, researchers were able to establish that most of the animals could perform a series of actions designed to act as a health check. This was a controlled observation with a small sample meaning it had limited generalisability and could be difficult to replicate. Using objective, quantitative measures of correct responses, however, did show that juvenile elephants can learn trunk washing using SPR training.

Questions

4   What was the purpose of teaching elephants the trunk washing task?

5   The elephants' mahouts were present in each session. However, they didn't look at the elephants or speak to them. Can you explain why the mahouts were asked to behave this way?

6   What influence do you think individual differences between the elephants had on the results of this study?

4.3 Core study 3: Saavedra and Silverman (button phobia)

Saavedra, L. M., & Silverman, W. K. (2002). Case study: disgust and a specific phobia of buttons. *Journal of the American Academy of Child and Adolescent Psychiatry, 41*(11), 1376–1379.

The psychology being investigated

Classical conditioning is a form of learning in which an unconditioned response becomes linked to a previously neutral stimulus to create a learned association. It was investigated by Ivan Pavlov (1927), who observed dogs salivating in a laboratory as part of a totally different experiment. Salivation is an unconditioned (i.e., uncontrolled) response to being presented with food (unconditioned stimulus). Pavlov noticed that the dogs began to anticipate the food when they saw researchers in the lab, before feeding times. Pavlov presented the food alongside a range of neutral stimuli, such as bells, which created a learned association. Over the course of several trials, when the dogs heard the bell (conditioned stimulus) they began to salivate (conditioned response).

This learning process can be applied to any new stimulus, which initially has no effect (the neutral stimulus, NS) when it becomes associated with another stimulus (the unconditioned stimulus, UCS). The UCS already produces a response (the unconditioned response, UCR), which is often an innate (instinctive) reaction. Following pairing of the UCS and NS, sometimes only once but more often repeatedly, the NS will produce a response similar to the existing UCR, so the NS becomes known as the conditioned stimulus (CS) and the newly learned response, the conditioned response (CR). A famous example of this process can be seen in Figure 4.6, in which we can see the following stages of classical conditioning:

1 Before conditioning: unconditioned stimulus (food) → unconditioned response (salivation)

2 Before conditioning: neutral stimulus (bell ringing) → no response

3 During conditioning: unconditioned stimulus (food) + neutral stimulus (bell ringing) → unconditioned response (salivation)

4 After conditioning: conditioned stimulus (bell ringing) → conditioned response (salivation).

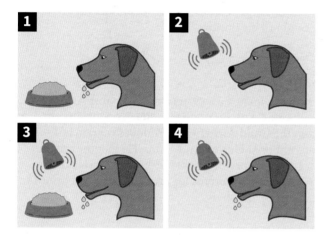

Figure 4.6: Pavlov's dog and bell

Some psychologists believe that behaviour such as phobias can also be both learned (and unlearned) in the same way as any other type of behaviour. There are several subtypes of classical conditioning, including expectancy learning, in which a previously neutral or non-threatening object or event becomes associated with a potentially threatening outcome. The consequence is that the individual *expects* the negative outcome, so experiences fear in the presence of the previously non-threatening situation.

Phobias may be caused by evaluative learning, that is, another type of classical conditioning in which the individual forms an association between a previously neutral stimulus and a negative emotion, but this is a negative *evaluation*, for example disgust, rather than fear. This suggests that disgust, as well as fear, may be an appropriate target emotion for the treatment of phobias, as well as the primary emotion of fear. In the case of phobias, an emotional response such as fear or anxiety becomes associated with a particular neutral stimulus, such as buttons.

A strictly behaviourist approach to classical conditioning would suggest that there is little role for thinking and feeling in this learning process. However, the case study we will look at now involves a deeper exploration of the role of cognition and emotion in changing phobic behaviour, known as evaluative learning.

> ## KEY WORDS
>
> **classical conditioning:** learning through association, studied in both humans and animals
>
> **phobia:** the irrational, persistent fear of an object or event (stimulus) that poses little real danger but creates anxiety and avoidance in the sufferer
>
> **evaluative learning:** a form of classical conditioning wherein attitudes towards stimuli are considered to be the product of complex thought processes and emotions, which lead an individual to perceive or evaluate a previously neutral stimulus negatively. Attitudes acquired through evaluative learning may be harder to change than more superficial associations

Another form of conditioning is known as operant conditioning. When a person or animal performs a new behaviour, this can become associated with a consequence. For example, receiving a sticker as a reward for allowing a dentist to perform a check-up makes it more likely a child might be happy to return for future check-ups. In other words, rewards reinforce behaviour and make the behaviour more likely to occur. Operant conditioning can also be used as an explanation for how people acquire phobias. When people avoid the object of their phobia this can reinforce future avoidance behaviours, because their anxiety is reduced when they don't have to encounter the thing they are afraid of. This reinforces or helps to maintain phobias once they have been learned. Psychologists can use the reinforcement principle of operant conditioning to treat phobias as well. Praising or giving other rewards for remaining calm when approaching a phobic stimulus can reinforce more positive behaviours towards such stimuli. Such treatment might mean that the person can better tolerate the phobic stimulus.

Background

The study by Saavedra and Silverman focused on how phobias can be treated using the application of different theories of learning. These included operant conditioning to reinforce desirable behaviour. The researchers compared this treatment to evaluative learning as a form of classical conditioning to reduce feelings of disgust.

From their study of adults with a blood phobia, Hepburn and Page (1999) suggested that treating patients' disgust, as well as their fear, would helped them to make progress. De Jong et al. (1997) worked with children who had a spider phobia. Although no attempt was made to manipulate feelings of disgust, their feelings of disgust declined alongside their reduction in fear.

ISSUES AND DEBATES

In classical conditioning, the environment is considered the main influence on behaviour. Individuals are considered to be 'blank slates' when they are born, and are shaped purely by nurture.

Aim

The aim was to examine the role of classical conditioning in relation to fear and avoidance of a particular stimulus. In the context of the case study participant's specific phobia of buttons, researchers wanted to see if using a type of exposure therapy could reduce the disgust and distress associated with buttons.

Method

Research method and design

This was a clinical *case study* as it involved just one participant whose life history and treatment were studied in depth. Data was collected using self-report measures. Both the boy and his mother were interviewed by the researchers about the onset of his phobia and his subsequent behaviour. The boy was observed throughout the treatment sessions to see if his phobic behaviour showed any improvement. The results of the treatment were measured using a nine-point scale of distress known as the 'Feelings Thermometer'.

RESEARCH METHODS

A case study involves studying one or a very small number of participants (such as a family unit) in great depth. It is particularly suitable in researching phenomena that are unusual or rare. Case studies often collect a large amount of qualitative data; this is often the main reason they are chosen as a method. In this study, interviews produced a history of the boy's experience with buttons and helped researchers understand the origin of his phobia.

Sample

The participant was a 9-year-old Hispanic American boy. Along with his mother, he had sought support from the Child Anxiety and Phobia Program at Florida International University, Miami. He met the criteria for having a specific phobia of buttons and had been experiencing symptoms for around four years prior to the start of the study.

Procedure

The boy and his mother both provided informed consent to participate in the study. They were interviewed in order to determine whether any trauma or abuse could explain the boy's phobia. The phobia had begun at age five, when the boy had knocked over a bowl of buttons in front of his class and teacher. He found the incident distressing, and from that time onwards his aversion to buttons steadily increased. When he was interviewed the phobia was interfering significantly with his normal functioning; he could no longer dress himself and had become preoccupied with avoiding touching buttons or clothing that could have touched buttons.

It was necessary for the researchers to understand the boy's specific feelings towards buttons prior to starting treatment. Through discussion with the participant, they created a hierarchy of feared stimuli, with each item on the list provoking increasing fear (see Table 4.5). The most difficult items for the child were small, clear plastic buttons. These were rated at an '8' on the nine-point Feelings Thermometer. Handling these or touching someone wearing them was the most unpleasant task for the boy.

Stimuli	Distress rating (0-8)
1. Large denim jean buttons	2
2. Small denim jean buttons	3
3. Clip-on denim jean buttons	3
4. Large plastic buttons (coloured)	4
5. Large plastic buttons (clear)	4
6. Hugging Mom when she wears large plastic buttons	5
7. Medium plastic buttons (coloured)	5
8. Medium plastic buttons (clear)	6
9. Hugging Mom when she wears regular medium plastic buttons	7
10. Small plastic buttons (coloured)	8
11. Small plastic buttons (clear)	8

Table 4.5: The participant's hierarchy of fear/disgust

The boy was treated with two interventions, one after the other. The first was contingency management, a form of positive reinforcement therapy. This was a behaviour-focused approach which meant the boy was rewarded for showing less fear and for actually handling the buttons. The positive reinforcement was given to the boy by his mother only after he had completed a gradual exposure to buttons. These treatment sessions lasted between 20 and 30 minutes. Researchers observed how the boy approached the buttons (e.g. whether the numbers of buttons he handled increased). They also measured his subjective rating of distress (on a 9-point scale) using the Feelings Thermometer.

The second form of therapy, and the main focus of the study, was known imagery exposure therapy. Interviews with the boy had revealed that he found buttons touching his body disgusting, and he also believed that buttons smelled unpleasant. These ideas formed the basis for disgust imagery exercises. Unlike *in vivo* exposure, where the individual actually physically handles or is exposed to fearful stimuli, imagery exposure therapy uses visualisation techniques.

Disgust-related imagery exposures were incorporated with cognitive self-control strategies. The boy was asked to imagine buttons falling on him, and to consider how they looked, felt and smelled. He was also asked to talk about how these imagery exposures made him feel. The exposures progressed from images of larger to smaller buttons, in line with the boy's fear hierarchy. At each session, self-report measures were taken of the boy's subjective ratings of distress using the Feelings Thermometer.

> ## KEY WORD
>
> **imagery exposure therapy:** therapy in which the person is asked to vividly imagine their feared object, situation or activity
>
> **self-control:** a form of cognitive-behaviour therapy. It involves using 'self-talk'; the individual is taught to recognise difficult situations, acknowledge troubling thoughts and consider alternative, positive thoughts

Results

Positive reinforcement therapy

The outcome of the first intervention, positive reinforcement therapy, was a successful completion of all the exposure tasks listed in the hierarchy of fear. The boy was also observed approaching the buttons more positively. One example of this was that he started handling larger numbers of buttons during later sessions.

However, his subjective ratings of distress increased significantly between sessions two and three, and continued to rise (see Figure 4.7). By session four, a number of items on the hierarchy such as hugging his mother while she was wearing buttons had increased in dislike from the original scores. So, despite his behaviour towards the fearful stimuli improving, his feelings of disgust, fear and anxiety actually increased as a result of the positive reinforcement therapy. This finding is consistent with previous research into evaluative learning; despite repeated exposure to the phobic object evaluative reactions (i.e. disgust) remain unchanged or even increase. So, while the participant was showing improved behaviour, the level of fear and disgust he was experiencing from this intervention worsened.

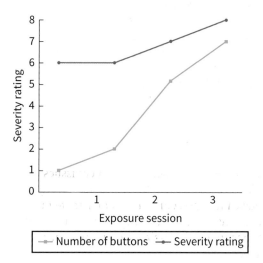

Figure 4.7: Ratings of distress: positive reinforcement therapy

Imagery exposure therapy

The second intervention, imagery exposure therapy, appeared to be successful in reducing the boy's rating of distress. One example of this is shown in Figure 4.8, relating to imagery of 'hundreds of buttons falling all over his body'. Before imagery therapy, the boy rated this experience the most fearful and disgusting (score of 8 on the Feelings Thermometer). This reduced to 5 midway through the exposure, and just 3 after the exposure was complete.

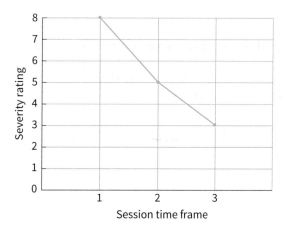

Figure 4.8: Ratings of distress: imagery exposure therapy: (1) before, (2) midway and (3) after imagery exposure

Following his treatment, six-month and 12-month follow-ups were conducted. At these assessment sessions, the boy reported feeling minimal distress about buttons. He also no longer met the diagnostic criteria for a specific phobia of buttons. His feelings towards buttons no longer affected his normal functioning; he was also able to wear small, clear plastic buttons on his school uniform on a daily basis.

Conclusion

The researchers concluded that the positive reinforcement therapy was successful in changing observable behaviour, and the imagery exposure therapy was successful in reducing feelings of fear and disgust. In particular they argue that:

- emotions and cognitions relating to disgust are important when learning new responses to phobic stimuli

- imagery exposure can have a long-term effect on reducing the distress associated with specific phobias as it tackles negative evaluations.

ACTIVITY 4.4

This study found that phobias can be both learned and treated through processes of classical conditioning.

Create a poster that illustrates the learning process involved in this study. This can be created using a computer, hand-drawn or a combination of both.

You will need to focus on the steps which make up the classical conditioning process. Refer to the information in the Background section to remind yourself of the stages.

Ensure you include the following terminology on your poster:

- unconditioned stimulus
- unconditioned response
- neutral stimulus
- no response
- conditioned stimulus
- conditioned response.

Select images that will support your explanation at each stage.

Strengths and weaknesses

This piece of research involved a case study. This means that the sample is small (in this case, one person). Like the piece of research by Fagen et al. discussed in Section 4.2, using a small sample in a psychological study can make it difficult to *generalise* the results to a larger population. As the participant was diagnosed with a specific phobia of buttons, it makes the case even less likely to be representative of the general population. However, the case study is highly *valid*; the participant was studied over a period of time using several different methods of data collection. The researchers used *standardised* measures such as the Feelings Thermometer before, during and after therapy. Collecting and analysing *quantitative data* means the researchers could compare the phobic reactions of the boy at the start and end of his treatment to assess any improvement.

A substantial amount of *qualitative data* was also gathered about the boy. An example of this was the background information obtained by interviewing the boy and his mother about the button incident at his school. This type of data is useful because it can help us to understand the reasons underlying psychological disorders.

In many ways, this study could be considered to be *subjective*. The participant created his own hierarchy of fear and disgust relating to his button phobia. He also gave personal ratings which were highly individual to his own thoughts and feelings. However, as the aim of this study was to understand the experience of evaluative learning in an individual with specific phobia, these measures were appropriate. A scale created by the researchers for use with all phobic patients would not have been as relevant or informative about personal progress.

Working on a case study involves building rapport with the participant. There is less room for anonymity

or objectivity. This means there is a higher risk of *bias*, which may compromise the *validity* of the study. There may be researcher bias as the researchers select and report on a particular participant (who may be more likely to have a positive outcome). *Demand characteristics* may be more obvious also. For example, the boy was fully aware he was undergoing therapy with the intention of improving his phobic symptoms. This might have affected the ratings he gave to the different levels of exposure therapy.

Ethical issues

When using children as participants, ethical issues can be a major concern. In this instance, the boy and his mother gave informed consent to participate in the study. This was important as the therapy involved deliberate exposure to distressing stimuli, whether real or imagined. Overall, the aim of the study was to improve the boy's quality of life and minimise psychological distress, which is more ethical than trying to create phobias in participants and then attempting to treat them. In addition, the boy's anonymity was preserved, which allowed him to maintain his privacy.

Summary

The study by **Saavedra and Silverman** aimed to investigate the role of evaluative learning in treating a specific phobia of buttons. They used a case study of a young boy to explore the origin of his phobia, and treated him using both reinforcement and imagery exposure therapies. He responded best to the imagery exposure technique which relates closely to the thoughts and feelings associated with learned responses. This was a unique piece of research which gained both qualitative and quantitative data about the participant's progress through therapy. It has practical applications for the treatment of specific phobias, e.g. through imagery exposure relating to disgust.

Questions

7 Imagine a phobia of something different from buttons, for example of spiders or heights.

   a Define what is meant by a 'phobia'.

   b Suggest eight scenarios that could be imagined by a person receiving similar treatment to that described in the study by Saavedra and Silverman.

8 This study used only one participant, a nine-year-old boy.

   a Can you explain the limitations of the results of the study, based on using only one participant?

   b Why are the results still useful?

Issues, debates and approaches

The application of psychology to everyday life

There are clear implications from Bandura et al.'s work on the application of psychology to everyday life. Children all over the world are exposed to aggression. This aggression can be either real, such as domestic violence in the home or violence on the news, or fictional, such as in cartoons, films and computer games. This study shows how such models can influence the behaviour of children, especially of boys. One consequence of the recognition of such potential effects

is that many countries have restrictions on viewing television programmes, films and computer games. For example, there may be a certain time in the evening before which you cannot show television programmes with content that is inappropriate for children (this is called the 9:00 p.m. 'watershed' in the UK) and certifications for films and games which indicate that they are only suitable for children over a certain age.

The research by Fagen et al. into elephant learning raises interesting possibilities. It shows how elephants can learn to engage in behaviours that help ensure their well-being (trunk wash testing for tuberculosis) using positive reinforcers rather than physical punishment or intimidation. Using these learning techniques can enhance captive animal welfare and help increase the safety and well-being of those working with animals. The SPR training for truck wash technique encourages the use of safety barriers in protected contact and helps identify a disease that is transmissible between humans and animals.

The study by Saavedra and Silverman shows how therapy based on the principles of classical conditioning can be used to treat specific phobias. A phobia is a distressing mental health condition that can negatively affect people's quality of life. Methods such as disgust imagery exposure are used in clinical practice to challenge the fearful associations with phobic stimuli. This piece of research demonstrates the potential long-term improvement that can result from exposure therapies.

Nature versus nurture

In the study by Bandura, the situational influence of models on the acquisition of aggressive behaviours (and the suppression of them by the non-aggressive model) are examples of nurture. However, the differences between the responses of boys and girls to the same models could be explained by either nature or nurture. Boys were more likely to imitate aggressive behaviour than girls, possibly because of nature factors which include the influence of hormones on brain development. Alternatively (or additionally), boys may be more likely to imitate aggression because they have already acquired stereotypes about what is acceptable behaviour for males or have been rewarded for masculine-type behaviours. These would be examples of nurture.

The theory of operant conditioning demonstrated in Fagen et al. relies on a nurture-based approach to learning. As human training shaped the elephants' behaviour through rewards, they were able to demonstrate trunk washing as a learned behaviour. However, the findings of the adult elephant showed that positive reinforcement did not successfully shape her behaviour. This could have been due to a decline in her natural ability to learn as she aged, or a natural (or acquired) personality difference, trunk weakness or vision problems.

The theory underlying the acquisition and treatment of phobias in the study by Saavedra and Silverman is classical conditioning. Classical conditioning relies solely on a nurture-based explanation of learning. Phobias are not considered innate or genetically inherited. Instead, they are considered to be products of negative experiences with previously neutral stimuli. Treatment is based on the same principles; that subsequent neutral or positive experiences with the phobic stimuli (along with cognitive therapy) can reduce fearful responses.

Individual and situational explanations

The individual and situational explanations debate is relevant to the study by Bandura. Imitation clearly suggests that situational factors matter in that the model is an aspect of the situation, as are differences between male and female models. However, individual factors could also explain some differences in imitation. Individual factors in operant conditioning can explain why, even when girls and boys are exposed to the same models, their acquisition of behaviours differs because boys and girls may be differently rewarded for sex-typed behaviours. For example, a daughter may be praised for *not* fighting but a son praised for 'sticking up for himself'.

Individual and situational explanations can also be considered in the context of the study by Fagen et al. For example, most of the elephants in the study successfully had their behaviour changed by situational changes; the SPR technique used by their mahouts. However, this finding was not consistently true of whole group. This suggests that individual differences (namely the age and personality of an elephant) may affect an animal's ability to learn new behaviours such as trunk washing.

The use of children in psychological research

The children used in Bandura et al.'s study did not appear to have been given the opportunity to consent to the study, or to withdraw. Since children are particularly vulnerable, the study had the potential to cause distress, which is an ethical concern. Although the head teacher at the nursery school is thanked in the study, so she was clearly aware of the procedure, there is no indication of whether the parents' consent was obtained. When children are used in studies, ethical guidelines typically suggest that parents' or guardians' consent should be obtained in addition to the child's own.

On a practical level, the use of children rather than adults in Bandura's study was ideal. Children have been exposed to much less violence than adults and there are likely to be fewer extraneous factors affecting their aggression levels (such as a bad day at work). In general, children are more naive than adults, so the participants would have been less likely to suspect that they were being shown aggressive models to investigate the effects of these on their own behaviour. These considerations all lead to the greater potential for representative effects of the procedure on children than if the same study were conducted with adult participants.

In the study by Saavedra and Silverman, the child participant (aged nine) was asked for consent. In accordance with ethical guidelines, his mother also consented to his participation. This study was potentially highly distressing, as it involved both real and imagined exposure to frightening stimuli. Furthermore, the boy could be considered vulnerable as his specific phobia is a recognised mental health condition. However, the intention of the researchers was to treat his phobia and improve his quality of life, which may justify the temporary distress caused during treatment.

The use of animals in psychological research

Although the Bandura study was conducted on humans, similar research could, and has, been done with animals. Clearly there are some reasons why this would be better: it removes the potential risk of causing short-term distress or long-term harm to children. In addition, although it is assumed that the children remained naive to the purpose of the activity, it is still possible that they believed that they were 'supposed' to copy the adult's behaviour. This would not be a risk if animals were used, and the possibility that some animals had been exposed to more aggression prior to the study could be controlled.

Conversely, there would be disadvantages. Although there are biological sex differences in the behaviours of animals, they do not acquire sex-typed behaviours that are a consequence of cultural factors in the way that children do. Because this has been shown to be important, an animal study would not be able to test such social influences.

The research by Fagen et al. was a controlled observation of the training and testing of a small group of elephants. Practically there were some advantages to working with these animals; they were already in captivity and familiar with their handlers. Psychologists working with animals in captivity have to meet requirement for suitable housing of these animals (Figure 4.9). In this study there is no evidence that the elephants were harmed as a result of the learning techniques of positive reinforcement and their housing and care was sufficient.

The study was conducted over a number of weeks and involved training on a near daily basis, which would have been impractical to achieve with a human participant. The elephants were also motivated by intermittent food rewards as part of the SPR training; again, motivating a human participant to continue with on-going trials might have been harder.

Figure 4.9: Is it right to keep animals in captivity for the purposes of research?

SELF-EVALUATION CHECKLIST

After studying this chapter, copy and complete a table like this:

I can	Needs more work	Almost there	Ready to move on	Coursebook	Workbook
state what is meant by the learning approach					
explain the psychology being investigated in the learning approach					
describe the main assumptions of the learning approach and link them to the studies					
use terminology relevant to the learning approach					
describe and evaluate the study by Bandura et al. (aggression)					
describe and evaluate the study by Fagen et al. (elephant learning)					

CONTINUED

I can	Needs more work	Almost there	Ready to move on	Coursebook	Workbook
describe and evaluate the study by Saavedra and Silverman (button phobia)					
apply relevant research methods to the learning approach					
consider issues and debates that are relevant to the learning approach.					

PROJECT

Bandura et al.'s study revealed that children are more likely to copy adults of the same sex, which reinforces differences in behaviour between girls and boys. We are exposed to many role models throughout our daily lives, for example our parents, older siblings, teachers and coaches. However, the media is also an important influence. Celebrities, actresses and actors in TV shows and advertising can also be role models who shape our behaviour (see Figure 4.10). For this reason, the media can be one way in which we learn stereotypical behaviours, through observation and imitation.

Working on your own or in a small group, you will collect data on sex stereotypical television advertisements and produce a short report.

1 Identify a media source to collect advertising data from. This could be a magazine aimed at young people, or an hour or two of television that contains advertisements.

2 Create a simple table in which to record your quantitative data. You will need to write down the product being advertised, and whether or not it shows sex stereotyping (could be stereotypical/not stereotypical/neutral or a rating score). For example, you could use something such as Table 4.6:

3 Watch or review your media advertising. If you are working with others, you might want to watch or review an advertisement together to ensure you agree how to categorise your data.

Name of product	Stereotypical	Non-stereotypical	Neutral
Laundry detergent	x		
Banking services			x
Sports drink		x	

Table 4.6: Example table for recording data

CONTINUED

4 Write a short report of your findings, using the following headings:

- Aim: What were you trying to find out?

- Method: How did you collect your data?

- Results: What did you find?

- Conclusion: Did you find what you expected?

Figure 4.10: Role models in advertisements can encourage stereotypical behaviour

EXAM-STYLE QUESTIONS

1 In their conclusion, Bandura et al. suggest that social imitation can speed up the learning of new behaviours as they can be acquired without the need for reinforcement, that is, without operant conditioning.

Suggest why acquiring new behaviours through social imitation would be quicker than through operant conditioning. **[2]**

2 If Bandura et al.'s study was performed today, the researchers would be required to obtain informed consent from both the children and their parents or guardians.

Explain why this would be necessary. **[3]**

3 The results of Bandura et al.s' study demonstrate several examples of sex-typed behaviours in the children.

Identify two examples of sex-typed behaviour in the children. **[2]**

4 **One** debate in psychology is over the use of animals in psychological research. This is demonstrated in the study by Fagen et al. (elephant learning).

a Explain what is meant by the guideline of 'choice of species and strain'. **[2]**

b The trainer in the study by Fagen et al. rewarded the elephants with chopped banana. Explain why positive reinforcement was used in this study. **[2]**

c Explain **one** benefit of Fagen et al.'s study. **[2]**

5 **Describe two** findings from the study by Fagen et al. **[4]**

6 **Evaluate** the strengths and weaknesses of the study by Fagen et al. **[8]**

7 Explain why the study by Saavedra and Silverman was carried out. **[2]**

CONTINUED

8   In the study by Saavedra and Silverman on button phobia, one technique for therapy used operant conditioning.

    a   Define what is meant by operant conditioning.   [1]

    b   Describe how operant conditioning was used to help reduce the boy's phobia in the study.   [2]

9   Describe the conclusions from the study by Saavedra and Silverman.   [2]

[Total: 32]

Additional references

Alexander, G. M., & Hines M. (2002) Sex differences in response to children's toys in nonhuman primates (Cercopithecus aethiops sabaeus). *Evolution and human behavior, 23,* 467–479.

Aserinsky, E., & Kleitman, N. (1955). Two types of ocular motility occurring in sleep. *Journal of applied physiology, 8,* 1–10.

Baron-Cohen, S., Jollife, T., Mortimore, C., & Robertson, M. (1997). Another advanced test of theory of mind: evidence from very high functioning adults with autism or Asperger syndrome. *Journal of child psychology and psychiatry, 38,* 813–822.

Desmond, T. & Laule, G. (1991). Protected-contact elephant training. In *AAZPA Annual Conference proceedings, 1991,* 606–613.

Do, S. L., & Schallert, D. L. (2004). Emotions and classroom talk: toward a model of the role of affect in students' experiences of classroom discussions. *Journal of educational psychology, 96,* 619–634.

Kimble, Gregory A. (1961). *Hilgard and Marquis' conditioning and learning.* 2nd ed., rev. Appleton.

Pavlov, I. P. (1927). *Conditioned reflexes; an investigation of the physiological activity of the cerebral cortex* (translated and edited by G. V. Anrep). Oxford University Press, Humphrey.

Pozzulo, J. D., Lindsay, R.C. L. (1997). Increasing correct identifications by children. *Expert evidence,* :126–132.

Pozzulo, J. D,, Lindsay, R. C. L. (1998). Identification accuracy of children versus adults: a meta-analysis. *Law & human behavior, 22,* 549–570.

Loftus, E. F., & Palmer, J. C. (1974). Reconstruction of auto-mobile destruction: an example of the interaction between language and memory. *Journal of verbal learning and verbal behavior, 13,* 585–589.

Watson, J. B., & Watson, R. R. (1921). Studies in infant psychology. *The scientific monthly, 13*(6), 493–515.

> Chapter 5
Social approach

LEARNING INTENTIONS

In this chapter, you will learn how to:

* describe and apply the concepts and terminology of the social approach and its main assumptions

* explain and apply the psychology being investigated in the social approach

* describe, evaluate and apply the three core studies from the social approach

* apply relevant research methods to the social approach

* consider issues and debates that are relevant to the social approach.

Introduction

The aim of this chapter is to introduce you to the social approach to psychology and to explore three core studies that illustrate this approach:

- **Milgram (obedience)** is based on the conflict between individual conscience and obedience to authority. It considers how far a person would obey instructions which involved hurting another person. The main psychology being investigated was obedience and social pressure.

- **Perry et al. (personal space)** investigates the effects of empathy and the social hormone oxytocin on social cues and personal space. The main psychology being investigated was interpersonal distance (personal space), social hormones and empathy.

- **Piliavin et al. (subway Samaritans)** considers bystander behaviour in real-life situations and factors that affect people's desire to help others, including diffusion of responsibility. The main psychology being investigated was bystander apathy and diffusion of responsibility.

GETTING STARTED

The social approach to psychology is concerned with many group processes that we are familiar with from our daily lives, including personal space, **obedience** and helping. Consider your normal interactions with others: Do you wave at your neighbour over the road or go and hug them? Are you more likely to turn down your music if a parent asks you to, or if your little sister asks? Do you offer your classmate a pen when they have lost theirs? Some of these social behaviours might seem so normal and everyday that you might wonder why psychologists are interested in them.

We are surrounded by **authority** figures, including parents, teachers and politicians, who make and enforce rules for us to follow. We do much of this without even noticing. For example, following signs which remind us to 'Keep off the grass' or 'Do not touch' are acts of obedience. Working with a partner, try to think of as many everyday examples of obedience as you can.

Now imagine you are walking to a friend's house and notice an older person about to cross the road into busy traffic. Perhaps you might stop and ask if they need help. Perhaps you would like to help but do not feel confident approaching them, or maybe you do not feel it is your place to help. You might even have felt bad about just walking away from the situation.

Think of how you would behave in this situation. Reflect on what you would do, and why.

KEY WORDS

obedience: following a direct order from a person or people in authority

authority: a person or organisation in a position of power who can give orders and requires obedience

MAIN ASSUMPTIONS IN CONTEXT

Humans as social actors?

Social psychologists are interested in understanding the factors that influence how we behave in social situations. The main assumptions of the social approach to psychology are that:

- Our behaviour, cognitions and emotions can be influenced by the actual, implied or imagined presence of others.

- All of our behaviour, cognitions and emotions can be influenced by social contexts, social environments and groups.

These assumptions introduce the idea that other people have an enormously powerful effect on how we live our lives. We might experience this in the different 'social roles' we play as students, children, workers, volunteers, etc. For example, a manager of a business may behave formally in their office environment, greet colleagues with handshakes and wear smart work clothes, and expect and enforce rules such as time-keeping. However, when that same individual visits their mother they change roles to a more informal one, greeting their mother with a hug, dressing in casual clothes and taking instruction about where to sit or what food to prepare.

Interestingly, the influence of others in not just limited to their actual presence. We may act as though others are with us, even when they are not. Feelings of excitement or anticipation before going to a party are linked to imagining the presence of our friends, and the fun and laughter we can share with them. These powerful influences on our thoughts, feelings and behaviour are collectively known as **social pressure**. Do you agree with the idea that all cognition and behaviour is influence by others? Are you the same 'self' in private, with friends and family, at school, work or in public?

KEY WORDS

social roles: these are the ways in which we behave as members of a social group. A person can have a number of different roles as they adapt their behaviour to meet expectations

social pressure: the influence of a person or group on another person or group

5.1 Core study 1: Milgram (obedience)

Milgram, S. (1963). Behavioural study of obedience. *Journal of abnormal and social psychology, 67*, 371–378.

The psychology being investigated

Social pressure is a term used to describe the influence of a person or group of people on another person or group. This might involve direct forms of influence such as orders, threats or demands, but may also involve the use of social approval or reward. Social pressure can take the form of feeling the needs to conform to the expectations of others, or to obey the directions of another person.

Many social psychologists consider obedience to be one of the most basic parts of the structure of our social worlds. An agreed system of authority and obedience is a necessary for humans to live and work together. However, the social pressure created by obedience to authority can also have negative consequences, including aggression towards others.

The concept of obedience, in particular **destructive obedience**, is of special interest to social psychologists. In Europe around the time of the Second World War, 11 million innocent people were systematically murdered on command by the Nazis during Adolf Hitler's regime (Figure 5.1). The Holocaust took the lives of people from a range of minority groups, including six million Jews. For such a large-scale atrocity to be possible required the obedience of many people, including most

KEY WORD

destructive obedience: obedience that has potential to cause psychological or physical harm or injury to another

Figure 5.1: Why did so many people obey the orders to commit mass murder in Nazi concentration camps?

ordinary citizens as well as Nazi officers and guards. Some of those who were later tried as war criminals in the Nuremberg Trials argued in their defence that they were 'just following orders'.

One theory used to explain the tragic events of the Holocaust is that German citizens possessed some defective personal traits which made such extreme levels of obedience possible. This is an individual argument which seems to suggest that Germans are somehow different from others; this is called the 'Germans are different' hypothesis.

ISSUES AND DEBATES

Individual and situational explanations consider whether the person's individual characteristics or the conditions of their environment are more influential on levels of obedience.

KEY WORD

individual-situational explantions: this is the debate about the relative influence or interaction of a person's unique physiology or personality (individual) and factors in the environment (situational) on thinking and behaviour

---

Background

Stanley Milgram, who was himself born into a Jewish family, sought to challenge this 'Germans are different' hypothesis. He proposed a situational explanation for

obedience; that many people who found themselves in a similar situation would harm or even kill other human beings under the orders of an authority figure.

Before his study, Milgram told psychology students and some of his own colleagues about the procedure he would use involving destructive obedience, and asked them how many participants would apply the maximum voltage shocks to another person. Those asked believed that less than 3% of participants would deliver the maximum voltage shock, with many stating they felt that no one would deliver such strong punishment.

Aim

The aim of this study was to investigate how obedient individuals would be to orders received from a person in authority. Specifically, Milgram wanted to know whether people show obedience even when it would result in physical harm to another person (destructive obedience). To test this, he developed a laboratory-based procedure which involved a researcher ordering the participant to give electric shocks to a victim.

Method

Research method and design

This study is a *controlled observation*. It took place in a laboratory setting where all the variables and measurements were controlled, while the behaviour of participants was observed and recorded. Milgram originally described his study as a laboratory experiment, however, it contained no manipulated (independent) variables. In this particular study, each participant underwent the same procedure and there was no control condition. However, he later replicated the procedure in other studies using different variations (e.g., using voice feedback from the 'victim') to allow comparisons to be made.

In this study, participants' levels of obedience were measured through observation. This was operationalised as the maximum voltage given in response to the orders. Observers also noted the participants' body language and any verbal comments or protests made throughout the procedure.

Sample

A newspaper advertisement was used to recruit 40 men between the ages of 20 and 50 years old. This meant it was a *volunteer sample*, composed of men living in the New Haven area of the USA. The participants came from a range of different backgrounds and occupations, representing unskilled workers, white collar workers and professionals.

Procedure

After responding to the newspaper advertisement, each participant was promised $4.50 for taking part. This was not conditional on their completing the study, but simply for being willing to participate. The study took place at Yale University, in a modern laboratory. The location was chosen in order to make the procedure seem legitimate, an important situational factor in obedience.

The participants arrived individually to the lab, and were then introduced to another man whom they believed to

be another participant. This man was in fact a **stooge or confederate**; he was a likeable, middle-aged man who worked for Milgram and had been trained in the procedure which followed. Both men were told that they would be allocated the roles of 'teacher' or 'learner' in what was to be an experiment about the effects of punishment on learning. They drew pieces of paper from a hat to determine the roles, but it was fixed so that the real participant was always allocated the role of teacher.

Next the participant was taken to another room, where the stooge was strapped to a chair and had electrodes attached to him by the experimenter. The participant was presented with the shock generator (see Figure 5.2), which consisted of rows of switches labelled with voltage readings ranging from 15 V to 450 V. The shock voltage was also labelled in ascending order with words such as 'moderate shock', to 'danger: severe shock' and for the final two switches 'XXX' (Figure 5.3).

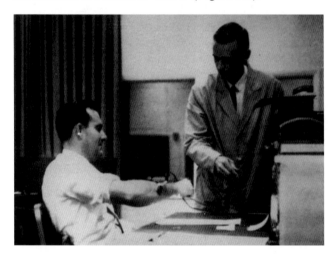

Figure 5.2: Milgram's participants were shown the shock generator before the procedure began

Figure 5.3: The simulated shock generator used in the study

The participant was told that although the shocks were painful, they were not dangerous. They were also then given an example shock of 45 V as a demonstration. After this, they were seated behind a wall so that they could hear but not see the stooge who was attached to the machine. Although the stooge 'learner' at no point in the procedure received any kind of shock, the elaborate machine was set up to convince the participants that they were really able to injure the learner. The experimenter remained with the participant; the same experimenter was used in each trial. He was a 31-year-old teacher who wore a grey technician's coat and behaved seriously throughout.

The participants were instructed in the 'memory' task, which involved reading pairs of words aloud to the learner, and subsequently testing the learner on their recognition of the words. Whenever the learner made a mistake, the participants were told by the experimenter to give him a shock by pressing a switch on the generator. They were ordered to increase the level of shock each time by 15 V for each error the learner made. Since the learner was a stooge, they could follow a pre-set plan of mistakes, deliberately giving the wrong answers at particular times.

Until 300 V were reached, the learner had remained silent when receiving the punishment. However, once the punishment level had reached 300 V and again at 315 V, the learner began to bang the wall in protest to the participant. After this time, the learner made no further noises and stopped responding to the memory task altogether. If the participants asked the experimenter what they should do, the experimenter insisted that they continue with reading the words aloud and punish the learner. Participants were told that no response from the learner counted as an incorrect answer and should also receive a shock. When participants protested at this, the experimenter continued to give them verbal prods in the sequence: Please go on / Please continue / The experiment requires that you continue / It is absolutely essential that you continue / You have no other choice, you *must* go on. These verbal prods or orders had a set wording, and were given in a standard order to any participants who protested the task.

The procedure was considered to be complete when the participant refused to give any more shocks, or when they had given the maximum 450 V available. One-way mirrors were used to record the physical behaviours of the participants, and observers noted any comments that participants made. After the procedure was complete, each participant was interviewed and the deception was fully explained to them. As part of the interview, participants were asked to estimate how painful they thought the final 450 V shock was, on a scale of 0–14 ('not at all painful' to 'extremely painful'). They were given the chance to meet the learner again, in order to reassure them that the learner was uninjured.

Results

Most participants were convinced that all aspects of the situation were real; that they were delivering electric shocks to another person and that the shocks were extremely painful. The *mean* estimate of the pain of the 450 V shock was 13.42 out of a maximum 14 (as reported in the debriefing interview), meaning that participants believed that they were causing serious pain.

RESEARCH METHODS

The *mean* is a measure of average calculated by dividing the sum of all participants' scores by the number of participants. Can you explain why the mean was the most suitable *measure of central tendency* for this study?

ACTIVITY 5.1

In this study, 368 V is the mean (average) shock administered by participants. The mode is a different measure of average: it represents the most frequently occurring score amongst a group of participants.

1   Using the data in Table 5.1, calculate the mode of the participants' shock scores.

2   What conclusion can you reach from this data?

Despite the findings being clear that participants believed the situation was real, participants showed extremely high levels of destructive obedience. The mean voltage given by participants was 368 V. All participants gave at least 300 V, and 65% gave the maximum 450 V shock (see Table 5.1). This is a startling contrast with the 0–3% obedience rate estimated by Milgram's students and colleagues before the study.

CONTINUED

However, the qualitative data collected in this study revealed that participants showed signs of tension when undertaking the procedure. Observers reported signs of nervousness in participants, which increased as they gave more powerful electric shocks. The participants were also frequently observed to be sweating, shaking and groaning, with 14 out of the 40 men showing signs of nervous laughter or smiling. One participant could not complete the experiment because he suffered a violent seizure, a result of the high level of stress he was experiencing.

The 40 male participants had been paid to take part in the study. Milgram also mentions that an additional 43 undergraduate students from Yale University completed the same experiment but without payment. Although details of this additional sample are not included in the original paper by Milgram, he does note that the undergraduates' results were very similar to those obtained by paid participants.

ISSUES AND DEBATES

The application of psychology to everyday life: this study shows us how likely it is that we will follow the orders of an authority figure, even when we feel uncomfortable with obeying. Think about how this might affect people in the military, or working in hospitals where they have to carry out orders which may conflict with their own consciences or personal beliefs.

Some participants protested at the orders, saying things like 'I don't think I can go on with this…I don't think this is very humane', and 'I'm gonna chicken out… I can't do that to a man, I'll hurt his heart'. Nonetheless, the verbal prods given by the experimenter generally persuaded the participants to continue. After the procedures ended, the participants showed visible signs of relief, wiped their faces, sighed and shook their heads. A small minority of participants, however, did not show elevated levels of stress and appeared calm during the procedure.

Voltage label	Voltage range (V)	Number of participants for whom this was maximum voltage
Slight shock	15–60	0
Moderate shock	75–120	0
Strong shock	135–180	0
Very strong shock	195–240	0
Intense shock	255–300	5
Extreme intensity shock	315–360	8
Danger: severe shock	375–420	1
XXX	435–450	26

Table 5.1: Distribution of participants' maximum shocks

Conclusion

Milgram's study supports the idea of a situational explanation for obedience. He identifies a number of factors that contributed to the high level of obedience recorded in his study. One of these factors is the perceived **legitimacy** of the study; the professional academic environment of the study and use of uniform by the experimenter. Another factor that might have encouraged obedience was that the participants had been paid to participate so they felt obliged to continue. Participants also believed that both they and the learner had freely volunteered to participate.

KEY WORD

legitimacy: the extent to which an authority figure (or organisation) is perceived as being worthy of obedience. For example, a police officer may appear to be more legitimate if they are wearing a badge and uniform

Milgram stated two main conclusions from this study:

- Individuals are far more obedient to authority than expected. This seems to be true for most people.

- Despite high levels of obedience, people find the experience of carrying out destructive acts under the orders of authority figures to be stressful. This is due to a conflict between two important social phenomena: the need to obey those in authority and the need to avoid harming other people.

Strengths and weaknesses

The method used in this study was a controlled observation. This means that it was possible to control extraneous variables in the environment, such as the age and appearance of the actor playing the stooge. As such the level of shock administered by each participant was not based on whether the participant felt more or less sympathetic towards different stooges (e.g. they might have been less willing to deliver shocks to an older individual). Also, the procedure was standardised throughout; the verbal prods used by the experimenter were the same each time. The standardisation of the procedure means the research was more *reliable*, because each participant went through exactly the same experience. The realistic design of the electric shock generator and the example shock given to participants improved the *validity* of the design, because it ensured that participants were convinced that the study was real and that their actions actually mattered.

The participants in this study were all men who came from the same local area. This could mean that the *sample* was low in *generalisability*. It would not be possible to predict what differences there might be in obedience levels between men and women, for example. However, Milgram carefully selected participants to ensure a range of ages and backgrounds. This means that the sample has greater external validity. It showed that even those with professional backgrounds who are more likely to be in positions of power are susceptible to obeying the commands of an authority figure.

The main measure of obedience was the voltage of shocks delivered. This is a quantitative measurement, which offered an *objective* record of obedience for each participant. It made it easy to compare the results of the participants and reach conclusions about the overall amount of destructive obedience seen in this study. However, the recorded voltages did not fully explain the experience of the participants. Observers also noted the participants' physical and verbal behaviour as they administered the shock. This provides a qualitative measure. Although this data is more *subjective*, it provided a richer understanding of the tension between wanting to obey orders and wanting to obey one's own conscience. Furthermore, interviews with the participants after the procedure also helped explain some of the participants' behaviour.

Ethical issues

This study had major ethical issues. Although participants had consented to take part in the research, they did not give their *informed consent* as they were told the study was about memory and punishment. Participants were also repeatedly deceived throughout the study. For example, participants were tricked into believing they had chosen the role of teacher by chance. Participants were able to exercise their right to withdraw, as some did ask to stop partway through giving shocks. However, many felt as though they had to keep going with the shocks out of obligation to the research and as a result of the verbal prods.

Ethical issues are particularly important to Milgram's research, which caused outrage at the time of its publication. In some ways this research can be considered harmful to the reputation of psychology. It might also lead to distrust by the general public who may not want to take part in future research studies.

Participants were not protected from psychological harm; many underwent visible and extreme distress, yet in only one trial was the procedure stopped. All participants were debriefed and told the true aim of the study, as well as being reassured that they had not done any real harm. However, there is the potential for lasting negative consequences to the participants, who may have felt distressed by their own behaviour.

ISSUES AND DEBATES

This study has the potential for application to everyday life. The findings suggest that situational variables are likely to influence how obedient people are to authority figures. This is important as it could be used to help reduce destructive obedience within organisations. For example, organisations could have whistle-blowing policies and training for staff so they can safely challenge orders or decisions that they think may be harmful.

CONTINUED

Individual and situational explanations for behaviour are also relevant to this study on obedience. The findings of the study challenge the idea that certain personalities may be more likely to be destructively obedient, because all the participants administered an intense shock of 300 V to the learner. Milgram attributed this behaviour to situational variables such as the legitimacy of the setting and the authority of the researcher. In other words, the study discredits the 'Germans are different' hypothesis, as this sample from a different culture was capable of showing high levels of destructive obedience. Further research in this area has investigated the influence of cultural differences on obedience.

Summary

Milgram's study investigated the extent to which ordinary people obey the orders of an authority figure when they involve physically harming an innocent person. All participants were willing to give high levels of electric shocks at the command of a researcher, with a significant majority of people willing to give the maximum shock level possible. This was a well-controlled observation collecting data using objective and reliable measurements. Qualitative data suggested that most participants showed signs of stress during the destructive obedience. The findings suggest that situational factors may be better at explaining obedience to authority than individual ones.

ACTIVITY 5.2

In a different study of destructive obedience, a researcher wanted to test whether nurses would obey the orders of a doctor they had never met before, even if this meant possibly harming their patients. In this study by Hofling et al. (1966), the nurses were given orders via telephone from a 'Dr Smith' to administer 20 mg of an unknown drug. This drug was actually harmless, but nearly all the nurses in the study followed the orders of Dr Smith and gave the drug to the patient, even though the label on the drug said 'maximum daily dosage 10 mg'.

CONTINUED

1 What explanations might there be for this kind of destructive obedience?

2 Research a different example of destructive obedience. Write a brief description and compare it to the one provided here.

Questions

1 Milgram collected both quantitative and qualitative data in this study.

   a Can you identify the quantitative and qualitative data discussed in this chapter?

   b Why are both types of data useful in understanding destructive obedience?

2 Why do you think the stooge and real participants chose slips of paper to 'allocate' their roles, when they could have been told by the experimenter which role to take?

3 What might the real participants have been thinking when the learner stopped responding to the task?

4 Why is validity so important in this study? Consider the evidence in Milgram's results that support the idea that the participant believed the study was real.

5.2 Core study 2: Perry et al. (personal space)

Perry, A., Mankuta, D., & Shamay-Tsoory, S. G. (2015). OT promotes closer interpersonal distance among highly empathic individuals. *Social cognitive and affective neuroscience, 10*(1), 3–9.

The psychology being investigated

Interpersonal distance (personal space) is an essential part of any social interactions. When we stand farther away from someone than expected, this sends a signal that we feel uncomfortable and less responsive. On the other hand, if we leave too little personal space, then the other person may feel uncomfortable or even threatened.

KEY WORD

interpersonal distance (personal space): the relative distance between people. It is the area of space around a person in which they prefer not to have others enter. It is like a bubble that moves with the person. This bubble may be larger or smaller depending on the social situation the person is in

The requirements humans have for personal space have been of great interest to social psychologists. Often we choose interpersonal distances based on our relationship to the person with whom we are interacting (Figure 5.4). Edward T. Hall introduced the idea of interpersonal distance in 1966, proposing the following different zones of space based on the preferences of middle-class Americans:

- Intimate: used between romantic partners or very close family members and involves all senses

- Personal: used with other people in most everyday interactions, in which we can see, touch and hear the other person

- Social: used in formal interactions with others, in which we may use louder voices, body movements and eye contact

- Public: used to keep distance from public figures (e.g. a person making a speech), in which a loud voice and body movements usually feature

Figure 5.4: People prefer physical closeness with family and friends, but greater distance from strangers

There are several factors that have been found to influence personal space requirements, in addition to how well we know the other person. Some of these factors are situational, such as culture (Beaulieu, 2004). Research has shown that different culture types show different personal space requirements; in no-contact cultures people touch less and stand further apart.

Psychologists are interested in testing other factors that may influence personal space behaviour. One such factor is the social *hormone* known as **oxytocin** (OT), which helps regulate social thinking and behaviour in humans and animals. OT can affect individuals in different ways dependent on their situation, individual attributes and culture. This means that as well as being associated with helping behaviour and **empathy**, OT has also been linked to lack of cooperation with out-groups and jealousy.

Empathy is the ability of one human to recognise and share the thoughts and feelings of another. The trait starts to develop in childhood and helps people cooperate with others, make friends and help those in trouble. Individual differences in empathy abilities suggest that this trait can shape how people process **social cues** (**social salience**), meaning that empathy may also be linked to personal space preferences.

KEY WORDS

oxytocin: a social hormone found in humans that heightens the importance of social cues and is linked to positive social behaviours such as helping others

empathy: how people respond to the observed experiences of others, seeing or imagining experiences from the other person's point of view and feeling concerned or upset for them

social salience: the importance or attention someone gives to cues from other people, e.g. body language, interpersonal distance and expressions

social cues: these are facial expressions or body language which people use to send messages to one another, for example a smile to indicate happiness

In this study, the researchers were able to test for the effects of OT by including a placebo. Placebos are given to participants in psychological experiments in order to provide a control condition, so the effects of the placebo can be directly compared to the effects of the treatment condition (in this case, OT).

Background

Perry et al. were interested in investigating how people's personal space preferences are affected by a few different factors. One of these is interpersonal distance; so, they measured people's preferences for different social figures so they could compare how close people want to be to strangers or friends, for example. Perry et al. believed this preference could be influenced by the action of social hormones on individuals' preferences, so they also looked at the effect of OT.

Specifically, Perry et al. tested whether people with different empathy abilities were influenced by OT in the same or different ways when asked about their personal space preferences. In psychology this is known as an **interaction effect** and the interaction between variables is represented by an '×', e.g. OT × empathy × condition.

Aim

The aim of this study was to test the **differential effect** of the social hormone oxytocin (OT) on personal space preference in relation to a person's empathy ability. The researchers believed that controlling for empathetic traits in individual participants would reveal the effect of OT on interpersonal distance choices. Perry et al. wanted to find out whether highly empathetic individuals would prefer closer distances while low empathy individuals would prefer greater interpersonal distances when given OT.

ISSUES AND DEBATES

Research suggests that empathy is an innate capacity, meaning that individuals are born with the ability to understand the thoughts and feelings of those around them. This relates to the nature side of the nature–nurture debate. However, this capacity is developed over time through interactions with others, for example between children and their parents. Through nurture, individuals develop empathy as they learn to identify and regulate their emotions.

KEY WORDS

interaction effect: the effect of two or more independent variables (e.g. OT × empathy × condition) on at least one dependent variable (e.g. personal space preference) in which the combined effect of the IVs is greater or less than each variable on their own

differential effect: when one or more individuals experience a difference in outcome when exposed to the same stimuli

Method

Research method and design

This study was a *laboratory experiment* conducted at the University of Haifa. This means it took place in an artificial environment. It used a mixed *experimental design* to allocate participants.

In both Experiments 1 and 2, the study used an independent groups design for the IV of 'empathy'. This IV was operationalised as two levels: 'high' or 'low'. Participants were categorised into different groups and could only be either a 'high' empathiser or 'low' empathiser. This IV was naturally occurring and was not manipulated by the researchers.

In both Experiments 1 and 2, the study used a repeated measures design, as all of the participants took part in both levels of the second IV of 'treatment'. The IV of treatment was operationalised in the experiment as: OT administered or placebo administered. This IV was manipulated by the researchers.

In Experiment 1 only there was a third IV known as 'condition'. This was also a repeated measures design and included the levels stranger, authority, friend and ball. There was no third IV in Experiment 2 as the participant was always asked to imagine their personal space in relation the same person. This means there was no manipulation of this part of Experiment 2.

The dependent variable (DV) was the personal space requirements of each participant. In Experiment 1, the DV was operationalised as the preferred distance measured between participant and approaching person/object. In Experiment 2 the DV was operationalised as preferred distance and angle between two chairs in a room.

Sample

54 male undergraduates from the University of Haifa, aged 19–32 years (mean age 25.29), participated in this experiment for course credit or payment. All participants had normal vision and no history of psychiatric or neurological disorders. Five participants were left-handed. Participants were divided into two groups based on their scores on the Interpersonal Reactivity Index (IRI), a 28-item self-report measure with four 7-item subscales all relating to empathy.

The High Interpersonal Reactivity group contained 20 participants with empathy scores greater than or equal to 40 and a mean age of 23.9 years. The Low Interpersonal Reactivity group contained 20 participants with empathy scores below 33 and a mean age of 25.9 years.

RESEARCH METHODS

Experimental design is the way in which participants in an experiment are allocated to the level(s) of the IV. A study that uses both an *independent measures* design and a *repeated measures* design can be described as 'mixed'.

Procedure

Participants attended the university in order to complete Experiment 1 and then again, a week later on the same day and time to complete Experiment 2.

OT administration

Participants were randomly administered a treatment of either a solution of 24 international units in 250 ml of intranasal OT or a placebo saline solution which did not contain the hormone. The nasal drops were self-administered by participants using a nasal dropper, under the supervision of the experimenter. The procedure used a *double-blind technique*; neither the participant nor experimenter knew whether the participant had received the OT or saline solution.

Assessment of empathy

After the solution was administered, participants completed the IRI online questionnaire. After completing this, participants were given nature magazines and waited in a quiet room for 45 minutes. The order of the experiments was *counterbalanced*

meaning that half the participants were undertook OT one week then saline the next week, and the other half first took saline on their first week and OT on their second.

RESEARCH METHODS

Double-blind: refers to an experimental procedure in which neither the participant nor the researcher are aware of which condition the participant is in, to prevent demand characteristics and act as a control to improve the validity of any data collected.

Counterbalancing is a technique used to overcome order effects in a repeated measures design. Each possible order of levels of the IV is performed by a different sub-group of participants. This can be described as an ABBA design, as half the participants do condition A then B, and half to B then A.

Experiment 1: The Comfortable Interpersonal Distance (CID) paradigm

This experiment used a modified version of an older, paper-based interpersonal space test known as the Comfortable Interpersonal Distance (CID) paradigm as shown in Figure 5.5. A circle was presented on a computer screen and participants were instructed to imagine themselves in the centre of the room with another person approaching them along a **radius**. The participant had to indicate by pressing the keyboard space bar at the point along the radius where they would want the person to stop their approach. The computer animation had options for the imagined other to be one of the following conditions: a close friend, stranger, authority figure or a rolling ball.

The animation stopped when the figures collided or the participant pressed the space bar. There were 24 trials for each figure and 96 trials in total. The researchers recorded the percentage of remaining distance from the total distance.

KEY WORD

radius: a straight line from any point on the circumference of a circle to the centre of the circle

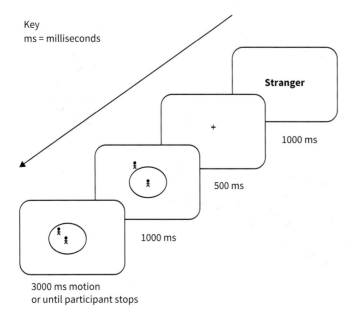

Key
ms = milliseconds

Stranger

1000 ms

500 ms

1000 ms

3000 ms motion
or until participant stops

Figure 5.5: The Comfortable Interpersonal Distance (CID) paradigm showing the name of the approaching figure (e.g. stranger) for 1 s, a fixation point for 0.5 s, the circular space with person at centre and approaching figure outside circle for 1 s then a 3 s animation of the figure approaching the person at the centre

ACTIVITY 5.3

Experiment 1 used the CID paradigm. This activity will allow you to replicate the CID test using a pen and paper. You will be able to collect data and produce a graph to show your results.

1   Draw a large circle on a blank page. Place a dot in the centre of the circle and draw a line from the dot to a point on the outside of the circle.

2   Imagine yourself as the dot and place a mark on the line for the personal distance you would want from another person – this could be your family member, a friend, an authority figure or a stranger.

3   Measure the distance for each mark you have made using a ruler.

4   Write down the measurement in a table.

5   Repeat steps 2–4 for each of the people (a family member, a friend, an authority figure, a stranger).

CONTINUED

6   Draw a bar chart to show your results.

7   Compare your results with the findings of Experiment 1: CID and write a short summary of your findings.

Peer assessment

Swap your graph from the Activity 5.3 with your partner and check their graph. Bar charts should contain the following:

• A bar chart with a suitable title

• Correctly labelled x-axis (name / type of person)

• Correctly labelled y-axis (distance in cm or inches)

• Correctly plotted data (check against the data table)

• No gaps between the bars of the bar chart

Give some feedback to your partner. Include one positive comment on the bar chart and one comment about how the chart could be improved next time.

Experiment 2: choosing rooms

Participants were told that after doing two runs of the experiment (placebo and OT) that they would be asked to sit in a room with another participant to discuss personal topics. Participants were informed they were going to be shown pairs of similar rooms and for each trial choose the one room they preferred. They were told that this information would be used to design a room according to their preferences.

The computerised stimuli were coloured pictures with two identical chairs in the middle, a table on one side, a cupboard, a plant, a lamp and a clock as shown in Figure 5.6. The experimental condition was preferred distance between chairs and consisted of the following stimuli:

• Distance between the chairs (20–140 cm (8–55 in) with intervals of 20 cm (8 in))

• Angle of the chairs positions (0°: both facing forwards, 45° each or 90°: facing each other)

Figure 5.6: An example of stimuli used in Experiment 2: choosing rooms

The control condition was preferred distance between table and plant and consisted of the following stimuli:

- Distance between the table and the plant (200–320 cm (80–125 in)) with intervals of 20 cm (8 in))

- Angle of the table and plant positions (0°: both facing forwards, 45° each or 90°: facing each other)

The experiment included 21 different pairs of chair distances, 21 different pairs of table-plant differences and three options for each pair of angles, repeated seven times to equal 21 pairs of comparative angles. Each participant was shown a total of 84 pairs, each repeated twice to equal 168 pairs overall.

The two picture sets were shown on a computer screen for 2 s and the participant had to select their preference. The mean preferred distance between chairs, between table and plant and the preferred angle for these furniture pairs was calculated.

Results

Experiment 1: CID

There were three IVs manipulated in Experiment 1: condition, treatment and empathy. The dependent variable of preferred distance was presented by Perry et al. as a mean percentage distance from the centre of the circle where the participant imagined themselves. A higher percentage means participants preferred a greater personal distance.

IV: condition

For Experiment 1: CID, there were differences found between preferred distances between stranger, authority, ball and friend (see Table 5.2) across all trials. This finding supports the idea that participants' need for personal distance increases the less well the approaching figure is known to them.

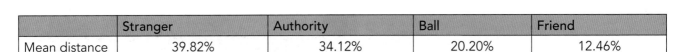

	Stranger	Authority	Ball	Friend
Mean distance	39.82%	34.12%	20.20%	12.46%

Table 5.2: Table showing results of Experiment 1: CID as mean percentage of participants preferred distance in the 'condition' variable

Interaction effect of IVs: treatment × empathy

OT was found to decrease the mean preferred distance from participant to other in the high empathy group but had the opposite effect in the low empathy group. This finding is shown in Table 5.3. The effect of OT on the low empathy group was to increase the preferred distance between self and other. This finding suggests that the administration of OT has a differential effect rather than the same effect on high and low empathisers.

	Oxytocin (OT) group	Control group-placebo
High empathy group	23.29%	26.11%
Low empathy group	30.20%	26.98%

Table 5.3: Table showing results of Experiment 1: CID as mean percentage of participants' preferred distance in the treatment × empathy interaction

---

ACTIVITY 5.4

In Experiment 1: CID the researchers recorded the percentage of remaining distance from the total distance. The results are presented in the study as a mean percentage distance in centimetres.

1   Explain the method that could be used to calculate the mean percentage distance in this study. You can use examples to support your explanation.

Table 5.3 shows the results of Experiment 1: CID in the treatment × empathy interaction.

2   Draw a bar chart to represent the data shown in Table 5.3. You must include a title, label the x- and y-axes, and plot the data to show the comparison between the variables.

3   Explain why a bar chart is the most appropriate way to plot the data.

Interaction effect of IVs: treatment × condition × empathy

There was also an interaction between the IVs of treatment, condition and empathy (see Table 5.4). With the placebo, high empathisers showed statistically significant differences between preferred distances from friend and authority, as well as friend and stranger. With OT, the same differences appeared, but there were also significant differences between ball and stranger and ball and authority. This finding could indicate that the ball is an invitation to social interaction, a cue which is enhanced with the treatment of OT for high empathisers.

	Oxytocin (OT) group	Control group-placebo
Stranger	39.73%	38.55%
Authority	30.55%	33.92%
Ball	14.42%	20.96%
Friend	8.49%	11.02%

Table 5.4: Table showing results of Experiment 1: CID as mean percentage of high empathisers by treatment and condition

Experiment 2: choosing rooms

For Experiment 2: choosing rooms, there were differences in preferences for chair distance but not for preferred angles. Participants in the high empathy group chose closer chair distances following OT administration than placebo administration. OT administration had the opposite effect for those participants in the low empathy group (see Table 5.5).

	Oxytocin (OT) group	Control group-placebo
High empathy group	78.07 cm (30.74 in)	80.58 cm (31.72 in)
Low empathy group	80.14 cm (31.55 in)	78.33 cm (30.84 in)

Table 5.5: Table showing results of Experiment 2: choosing rooms as preferred distance between chairs

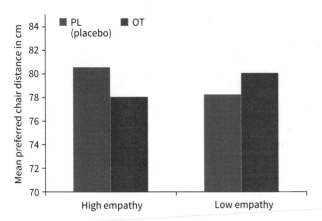

Figure 5.7: Graph showing results of Experiment 2: choosing rooms

Interaction between treatment and empathy was only present in the experimental condition (distance between chairs) meaning OT and empathy had no effect on choices of distance between the plant and table (see Figure 5.7). This finding supports the social salience hypothesis, as OT did not affect participants' general preferences, only the preferences that have a social context.

Finally, the results of both experiments were compared to establish a relationship. This comparison showed a moderate correlation between average distance chosen in the Experiment 1: CID under placebo treatment and average chair distance chosen in Experiment 2: under placebo treatment.

Conclusion

The administration of OT enhances social cues in opposite ways for individuals with different empathetic abilities, supporting the idea of social salience. People with low empathetic ability respond to OT with a preference for increased personal distance and those with high empathetic ability respond to OT with a preference for decreased personal distance.

The results also confirmed the findings of previous personal space research that people need less distance between themselves and their close friends than they need with strangers.

Strengths and weaknesses

Because this study took place in the artificial environment of a university, it lacks ecological validity. Participants' experience of personal space

with individuals who are actually known to them (or strangers) might not be the same as the decisions they made about personal distance in the study. Furthermore, participants were asked to judge their preferred distances using computer-generated images and to respond using keyboards. This meant that the tasks in both Experiment 1 and Experiment 2 lacked *mundane realism*. In everyday life, our choices about personal space are influenced by complex cues from others such as their facial expressions, tone of voice and gestures.

However, the study had good internal validity. The order of experiments was counterbalanced (half of the participants did Experiment 1 then Experiment 2; the other half did Experiment 2 and then Experiment 1) and this was used to prevent order effects. Extraneous variables were also controlled, as social interaction after OT or saline administration was minimised through use of the waiting room. Researchers overseeing the OT or saline administration were taking part in a double-blind procedure; therefore, participants should have been less subject to demand characteristics and the results free from researcher bias.

This study was a laboratory experiment with a highly standardised procedure. For example, the computer program projected the images of the room in Experiment 2 for a consistent 2 seconds each time. Likewise, the images were computer generated for maximum accuracy and consistency. This meant that the results were reliable; the experimental procedures could be repeated and expected to produce the same results.

Ethical issues

The study was ethically strong as written, informed consent was obtained from participants. The study was approved by the University of Hafia's ethics committee and The Hadassah Medical Centre, which was important for safeguarding the well-being of participants, researchers and the reputation of psychology. Participants reported no side effects from the OT or placebo that was administered in a painless manner, meaning they were protected from physical harm. The participants were deceived about the purpose of the task in Experiment 2, as no personal discussion ever took place. However, this deception was unlikely to cause them psychological distress. Participants were fully debriefed after the study and informed and told of the aim of the study.

Summary

Perry et al.'s study considered the effects of OT on personal space and empathy. It used two laboratory experiments involving a computer simulation of comfortable personal distance and choice of rooms with different layouts. This laboratory experiment also used questionnaires to collect data. Both experiments found an interaction between the effect of OT, empathy and interpersonal distance preference. The findings suggest that OT enhances social cues to produce an opposite effect on individuals with different empathic abilities.

Questions

5 The original version of the CID used paper and pencil.

   a What are the advantages of using the computerised version in the study by Perry et al.?

   b What limitations might there be to using the CID to measure personal space preferences?

6 Experiment 1: CID included the stimulus of a rolling ball as a control.

   a Why do psychologists use controls?

   b Which stimulus was used as a control in Experiment 2?

7 The participants in this study were aware that they were taking part in research. What ethical guidelines were followed in this study?

5.3 Core study 3: Piliavin et al. (subway Samaritans)

Piliavin, I. M., Rodin, J., & Piliavin, J. (1969). Good Samaritanism: an underground phenomenon? *Journal of personality and social psychology, 13*(4), 289–299.

The psychology being investigated

Social psychologists have studied the role of **bystanders** in emergency situations. A key trigger for research into **bystander apathy** was the murder of a young woman

Figure 5.8: Front-page newspaper article expressing outrage about witnesses to Kitty Genovese's murder

called Kitty Genovese (Figure 5.8) in New York City in 1964. After returning from her work during the early hours of the morning, Miss Genovese was followed and attacked by a man near her home. One witness had called down to warn off her attacker as Miss Genovese screamed that she was being stabbed. Her attacker was scared off but returned to continue the assault. It was alleged in news reports of the time that around 38 individuals living nearby either saw or heard what happened, but failed to prevent her murder. While it is impossible to say what each person saw or interpreted, the event triggered the interest of social psychologists who tried to understand different types of bystander behaviour.

> KEY WORDS
>
> **bystander:** a person who is present but not directly involved in a situation
>
> **bystander apathy:** when a bystander does not show concern for a person in need

One explanation for the lack of bystander helping was outlined by Darley and Latané (1968). They found that bystanders who believed that there were other people witnessing an emergency, such as over-hearing someone having an epileptic seizure, were significantly less likely to help than those who believed they were alone in hearing the event. The explanation for this is known as the 'diffusion of responsibility' hypothesis, in which an individual person's perceived obligation to help in a situation is reduced when other people are present. Alternatively, if we witness those around us assisting or 'modelling' helping behaviour, we may be more likely to imitate and engage in helping (as discussed in Section 4.1 of Chapter 4, in the study by Bandura).

There is also evidence to suggest that we are more likely to help some people than others. For example, we may be more willing to assist those whom we consider to be more similar to ourselves. Some studies have shown that bystander helping occurs more when victims are not seen as responsible for their circumstances (Schopler & Matthews, 1965). This may be because they create more feelings of sympathy from those around them.

KEY WORDS

diffusion of responsibility: when there are other people available to help in an emergency, an individual may be less likely to take action because they feel a reduced sense of personal responsibility

modelling: when we watch a person (model) perform the desired behaviour, e.g. helping behaviour

Background

Following on from previous laboratory-based studies on bystander apathy and helping, Piliavin et al. investigated whether people would demonstrate bystander apathy towards a person in need of help in a realistic setting.

The researchers wanted to test the diffusion of responsibility hypothesis to see whether the bystanders felt they had less responsibility to help when other people were present. Piliavin et al. were also interested in understanding the influence of a number of other situational factors on bystander behaviours.

Aim

The researchers aimed to study bystander apathy and diffusion of responsibility in a natural setting. Piliavin et al. also wanted to investigate the effect of four variables on helping behaviour or being a 'Good Samaritan':

- the type of victim
- the race of the victim
- the behaviour of a 'model'
- the size of the group of bystanders.

KEY WORD

Good Samaritan: this term originates from the New Testament in the Bible. It refers to a story of a Samaritan (person originating from ancient Samaria) who stops to offer help to an injured stranger. The term now refers to someone who offers help to others experiencing difficulty

Method

Research method and design

This study was a *field experiment*. This means it took place in a realistic environment; in this case, the New York City subway. The study used an independent groups design, as the trials were repeated on different days and involved different participants in each condition.

There were four independent variables (IVs) that corresponded to the factors outlined in the aims of the study. These were operationalised as:

- the type of victim: the levels were 'drunk' or 'ill' victim
- the race of the victim: the levels were black or white victim
- the behaviour of a 'model': the levels were a model who was either close to or distant from the victim helped, either early or late in the event
- the size of the group of bystanders: this level was the naturally occurring number of passengers present in the subway carriage.

The dependent variable (DV) was the level of bystander helping. In quantitative terms, this was operationalised as the time taken for the first passenger to help, as well as the total number of passengers who helped. The race, gender and location in the carriage of each helper were also recorded. Qualitative data was recorded in the form of verbal remarks made by passengers during each incident.

> RESEARCH METHODS
>
> A *field experiment* is a type of study that takes place in everyday locations, rather than the controlled environment of a laboratory. It still has an experimental design, meaning that independent variables are manipulated by the researcher, while the dependent variables are measured.

Sample

This study took place on the New York City subway. Participants were passengers travelling on an underground railway service between Harlem and the Bronx (areas of New York City) on weekdays between 11 a.m. and 3 p.m. We might consider this an opportunity sample as passengers were not deliberately selected for participation. The total estimated number of participants was 4450 people, of whom around 45% were black and 55% were white. The mean number of passengers per carriage was 43, and the mean number of people in the critical area (where the incident took place) was 8.5.

Procedure

Four teams of student researchers carried out the study using a standard procedure. On each trial, two male and two female students boarded the train using different doors. The female confederates sat in the area adjacent to the immediate 'critical' area where the incident took place (see Figure 5.9). They observed the passengers and recorded data during each trial. The male confederates took the roles of the victim and the model. The victim stood at the pole in the centre of the critical area, and the model remained standing throughout the trial.

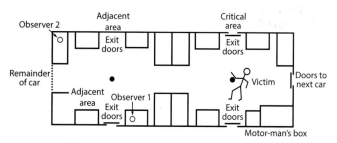

Figure 5.9: Layout of adjacent and critical areas of the subway carriage

Each trial used the same route that included a 7.5-minute gap between two stations. At approximately 70 seconds into the journey, the 'victim' staggered forward and collapsed. He remained lying on the floor looking upwards. If he received no help, the model would help him to his feet at the next stop.

> RESEARCH METHODS
>
> Even though this is a field experiment, there was some *standardisation* between trials and *controls* that ensured there were few differences between different conditions. For example, the 'victim' was always identically dressed and behaved in the same way for all trials.

The victim was played by different males during the study, but all were made to look similar. They were aged 26 to 35 years; three were white and one was black. They were dressed in identical, casual clothing (jacket, old trousers, no tie). On 38 out of 103 trials the victim smelled of alcohol and carried a bottle of alcohol wrapped in a brown bag. On the remaining 65 trials they appeared sober and carried a black cane. In all other ways they behaved identically.

The models were all white males aged 24 to 29 years of age, who were also dressed informally. When helping, the model raised the victim to the sitting position and stayed with him until the train reached the next stop.

Trials were split into the following conditions:

- Critical / early: model stood in critical area and waited 70 seconds to help victim

- Critical / late: model stood in critical area and waited 150 seconds to help victim

- Adjacent / early: model stood in adjacent area and waited 70 seconds to help victim

- Adjacent / late: model stood in adjacent area and waited 150 seconds to help victim

- No model condition: the model did not help the victim until after the trial was over and the train had reached the next stop

Results

Overall, the frequency of helping recorded in this study was much higher than had previously been reported in laboratory studies. Seventy-eight percent of victims received spontaneous help (i.e. helped before model intervened or in a no model condition), and in 60% of cases more than one person helped.

There were key differences in levels of helping between different conditions of the study, as seen in Table 5.6. In terms of the type of victim, participants were more likely to help the victim with the cane than the drunk victim (the cane victim received help in 62/65 trials; the drunk victim received help in 19/38 trials). In the cane trials, spontaneous helping also occurred earlier than in the drunk trials. For example, in all but three of the cane trials that were also model trials, helping occurred before the model could give assistance.

Trial	White victim		Black victim	
	Cane	Drunk	Cane	Drunk
No model	100%	100%	100%	73%
Model trial	100%	77%	–*	67%

*No model trials for the black 'victim' were run for the cane condition

Table 5.6: Percentage of trials in which help was given

In terms of race, both black and white cane victims were equally likely to receive help. However, there was some minor evidence of same-race helping in the drunk condition, with participants being more willing to offer help to those of their own race. In the drunk condition, black victims received less help overall. Although these results were not at statistically significant levels, they support research suggesting people are more likely to help those similar to themselves.

The result relating to the variable of sex was that the majority of helpers (90%) were male. Female passengers made comments such as, 'It's for men to help him', or 'I wish I could help him—I'm not strong enough.' This may suggest a difference between men and women in terms of bystander helping behaviour, or it may be a result of the victim always being played by a male.

The effect of modelling was difficult to analyse, because most of the helping that occurred was spontaneous. However, it appeared that early model intervention at 70 seconds was slightly more likely to result in helping behaviour than waiting until 150 seconds had passed.

Surprisingly and in contrast to previous research, this study found no evidence to support the diffusion

of responsibility hypothesis. In fact, there was some evidence to suggest that when more passengers were present, rates of helping were actually slightly higher. Looking at the graph in Figure 5.10 we can see that the hypothetical speed to respond for seven-person groups, as predicted by the diffusion of responsibility theory, is slower than for three-person groups. This is because in seven-person groups the responsibility should be diffused or shared between more individuals. In fact, natural seven-person groups were faster to respond than predicted, and faster to respond than the three-person groups. This directly opposes the prediction of diffusion of responsibility.

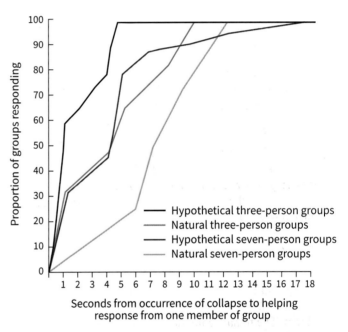

Figure 5.10: Graph showing the difference in helping behaviour between the groups

Piliavin et al. proposed a model of response to an emergency situation as an alternative to the diffusion of responsibility hypothesis to explain the findings of this study. This is termed the 'cost–benefit model' (Figure 5.11). This model suggests that witnessing an emergency raises

> **KEY WORD**
>
> **cost–benefit model:** involves a decision-making process in which a person weighs up both the advantages and disadvantages of helping. If it seems beneficial to help, then the person is more likely to do so; if the risks are too great, they may not help

an individual's level of arousal: their feelings of disgust and aversion, or even sympathy and courage. This heightened arousal level prompts individuals to respond to the situation, in order to reduce any difficult feelings. The cost–benefit model can explain the findings that a higher number of comments were made during trials without helping and that more comments were made during trials with a drunk victim. Observers also noted that in around 20% of trials, passengers actively moved away from the critical area where the incident was taking place. So, although less helping occurred due to disgust, the arousal of the participants prompted them to comment or move away instead.

Figure 5.11: Weighing up the pros and cons of helping

Conclusion

This study found that in a natural setting, many people would offer spontaneous help to a stranger, even in a group situation. This study found no evidence of diffusion of responsibility, but did identify several factors which influence an individual's decision to help:

- the type of victim (someone using a cane will be helped more than a drunk person)

- the gender of the helper (men are more likely to help than women)

- the similarity of the victim to the helper (people may be more likely to help members of their own race, especially if the victim is drunk)

- the duration of the emergency (the longer an emergency continues, the less likely it is that anyone will help, and the more likely it is they will find another way of coping with arousal).

Strengths and weaknesses

The method used in this study was a field experiment that used independent measures. This meant that it had good *ecological validity*; the participants were ordinary train passengers who were unaware they were taking part in the experiment. They would have behaved naturally as they believed the emergency situation to be real. However, one limitation of this method is that there is less control over extraneous variables (such as the weather conditions or train delays), which could affect the participants' behaviour and lower the *validity* and *reliability* of the study.

There are other methodological issues with the study. For example, the experimenters cannot be sure that participants only took part in the experiment once; as they used the same route each time there is a chance participants may have been exposed to more than one condition of the experiment. Suspecting that the emergency was a set-up might have made the participants more or less likely to offer help, creating *demand characteristics*.

The participants in this study were all subway passengers from New York City, which means that the sample is unrepresentative. It would not be possible to predict levels of bystander helping in other countries from this study. However, the design of the study meant that around 4500 individuals participated in the study, which included a mix of ethnicities and genders. This large sample therefore is likely to be more representative than a smaller sample or single trial of the experiment, which increases the generalisability of the findings.

The main recorded measure of bystander helping was the number of helpers and how long they took to help. This quantitative measurement ensured an objective record, made more reliable by the presence of two observers. The observers also recorded qualitative data including the remarks and movements made by the passengers during each trial. This allowed the researchers to understand the thoughts and behaviours associated with helping in more depth.

Ethical issues

This study raised serious ethical issues. First, participants did not give their consent to take part in the research, nor were they debriefed after the study had finished. Participants were deceived during the study, as they believed the victim had genuinely collapsed and needed help. They might have suffered psychological distress as a result of the study, guilt at not helping or concern about the well-being of the victim.

ACTIVITY 5.5

The study by Piliavin et al. was conducted in 1969. Typically, psychological research now has to be approved by an ethics committee. Imagine you are on an ethics committee and Piliavin et al. present the idea for their study.

1   Would you allow the study to be conducted in the way Piliavin et al. carried it out originally? Why or why not?

2   Describe some changes you would recommend to Piliavin et al. to help improve the ethical issues in this research.

3   Explain what other effects the changes you described might have on the validity or reliability of the research.

RESEARCH METHODS

Participants in this study were not aware they were taking part in research. This means they did not give their informed consent to participate. Why might this be an *ethical issue*, and how could it be overcome?

Summary

Piliavin et al.'s study considered different factors which affect bystander behaviour. It looked at how specific circumstances might make subway passengers more or less likely to help a man who had collapsed on a train. This was a field experiment involving a large number of participants. Quantitative measurements showed that victims who were ill were more likely to receive help than those who appeared drunk, and that the number of bystanders does not affect the amount of bystander helping. The findings suggest that diffusion of responsibility is not typical of bystander helping in natural environments.

Questions

8   The study by Piliavin et al. intended to use different participants for each of the trials.

a   Why can we not be sure that there were different participants in each of the trials?

b   Explain the possible effect on the results of the study if participants took part more than once.

9   Piliavin et al. found that people are more likely to help when they had watched a model help quite quickly after the victim collapsed. How might this finding be explained?

10 The validity of field experiments can be affected by extraneous variables. How did Piliavin et al. improve the validity of the study?

11 The participants in this study were unaware that they were taking part in research. What ethical issues does this lack of awareness raise?

Issues, debates and approaches

Application of psychology to everyday life

Milgram's study has important implications for understanding obedience in the real world. Previously it was believed that acts of extreme, destructive obedience such as the Holocaust had an individual explanation (i.e. that Germans were somehow very different from other people). However, Milgram's study as well as his later research (e.g. 1974) and other work inspired by his findings has shown that situational variables such as the legitimacy of authority can elicit destructive obedience in nearly anyone. A result of this is a raised awareness of the power of authority in the workplace. For example, some hospitals have introduced whistle-blowing policies to encourage reporting of mistakes by doctors or other senior staff in order to protect the safety and well-being of patients.

The findings from Perry et al. have important implications for those with social difficulties, for example, people with autism spectrum disorders or social anxiety disorder (see Chapter 6, Clinical psychology). Many people expect OT as a social hormone to have a universally positive effect. However, this research shows the effect of OT to be more complex as it was found to differentially enhance the importance of existing social cues. This means that administering OT as a treatment could actually cause further social difficulty.

Piliavin et al.'s study has interesting practical applications as well. It tells us about specific situational factors which may make bystanders more likely to help. For example, it may be useful to know that people may be more willing to help if they are of the same sex or race as the victim, or in a situation that they cannot easily just walk past. It shows us that a person in need may be more likely to get help from a stranger if they do not risk embarrassing, intimidating or disgusting them.

Individual and situational explanations

Milgram's research was particularly significant in highlighting the importance of situational factors in influencing how obedient we are to authority figures. Findings from his study showed that the majority of people will be destructively obedient if they feel that the authority figure is legitimate or the cause is worthy, for example. However, some individuals are more resistant to authority than others: not all participants inflicted the full voltage on the learner as directed. This suggests that there is a role for individual factors, which may affect overall levels of obedience as well.

Perry et al.'s study shows us that situational factors matter in our preferences for personal space, for example need for space depends on our relationship to the person we are interacting with. As well as interpersonal context, individual factors could also explain some differences in personal space requirements. Individual traits such as empathetic ability can explain why, even when people are exposed to the same levels of social hormone, their personal space needs differ.

SELF-EVALUATION CHECKLIST

After studying this chapter, copy and complete a table like this:

I can	Needs more work	Almost there	Ready to move on	Coursebook	Workbook
state what is meant by the social approach					
explain the psychology being investigated in the social approach					
describe the main assumptions of the social approach and link them to the studies					
use terminology relevant to the social approach					
describe and evaluate the study by Milgram (obedience)					
describe and evaluate the study by Perry et al. (personal space)					
describe and evaluate the study by Piliavin et al. (subway Samaritans)					
apply relevant research methods to the social approach					
consider issues and debates that are relevant to the social approach.					

PROJECT

Internationally, there are many organisations that celebrate and give awards for acts of helping. Typically, members of the public nominate ordinary people who have taken action to help others and to make the world a better place.

One example of these is Dena, the 92-year-old recipient of the Pride of Britain Award 2020:

92-year-old Dena is spending her retirement tending her garden allotment in the city where she has lived for 24 years. The great-grandmother has used her love of gardening to help criminals to learn new skills and repay their debt to society. Dena has taught allotment gardening to over 300 ex-young offenders as part of their community service orders, many of whom have since returned to education (see figure 5.12). *Source: www.prideofbritain.com, accessed 22nd January 2021*

Working on your own or with a partner, you will produce a poster, presentation or speech on a case of Good Samatianism/heroic helping. To complete the project, follow these steps:

1   Use the internet, other media or your own knowledge to identify a hero or Good Samaritan like Dena who has contributed to helping society in some way. This person can be of any age, race, gender, religion, social class or ability.

2   Using the information in this chapter on helping (see Section 5.3), your class notes and any other relevant resources, consider:

- The circumstances of the heroic act(s) of the Good Samaritan

- Possible reasons why the hero helped: consider why the hero took responsibility for helping, and the costs and benefits of helping for the hero

- Individual and situational explanations for the hero's behaviour

- Why other people may not have helped in the same way as this hero (bystander apathy)

3   Create your presentation using software if available or as a speech accompanied by visual aids. Include the information from your research, supported with suitable images to add interest.

4   Remember to give your audience an opportunity to ask questions during or after your presentation.

Figure 5.12: Volunteers like Dena help others to improve their lives through community projects

REFLECTION

After you have given your presentation, reflect on how it went. You might want to talk to your presentation partner about this, if you had one. Consider these questions when thinking about your presentation:

- What went well?

- What would you change for next time?

- What areas might you need to revisit in this chapter to strengthen your understanding?

EXAM-STYLE QUESTIONS

1   **Outline one** assumption of the social approach. [2]
2   The study by Milgram collected both quantitative and qualitative data.
    a   Outline **one** quantitative result from the study by Milgram. [2]
    b   Outline **one** qualitative result from the study by Milgram. [2]
3   The findings of the study by Milgram support the situational explanation for obedience.
    a   **Identify two** features of the situation which may have contributed to the high levels of obedience seen in this study. [2]
    b   **Explain** how the study by Milgram could be applied to real-life destructive obedience. [4]
4   **Evaluate** controlled observations as a research method using the study by Milgram. [6]
5   **Describe** the sample used in the Perry et al. study. [2]
6   **State** what is meant by the term 'personal space'. [1]
7   Outline **one** conclusion from the study by Perry et al. [2]
8   The study by Perry et al. was a laboratory experiment consisting of two experiments.
    a   Describe the **two** independent variables (IV) that were manipulated in both Experiment 1: CID and Experiment 2: choosing rooms. [4]
    b   Describe how the dependent variable was measured in Experiment 1. [2]
9   Evaluate the study by Perry et al. including **two** strengths and **two** weaknesses. [10]
10 Outline **two** ways in which the procedure used by Piliavin et al. was standardised. [4]
11 The aim of Piliavin et al.'s study was to test the diffusion of responsibility hypothesis.
    a   Describe what is meant by 'diffusion of responsibility'. [4]
    b   Explain whether the results of Piliavin et al.'s study support or contradict this hypothesis. [3]
12 Piliavin et al. carried out a field experiment. Outline **one** strength and **one** weakness of this research method in the study by Piliavin et al. [4]

[Total: 54]

COMMAND WORDS

outline: set out main points

state: express in clear terms

Additional references

Beaulieu, C. (2004). Intercultural study of personal space: a case study. *Journal of applied social psychology*, *34*(4), 794–805.

Darley, J. M., & Latané, B. (1968). Bystander intervention in emergencies: diffusion of responsibility. *Journal of personality and social psychology*, *8*(4p1), 377.

Hall, E. T. (1966). *The hidden dimension, Vol. 609*. Doubleday.

Hofling, C. K., Brotzman, E., Dalrymple, S., Graves, N., & Pierce, C. M. (1966). An experimental study in nurse–physician relationships. *The journal of nervous and mental disease*, *143*(2), 171–180.

Schopler, J., & Matthews, M. W. (1965). The influence of the perceived causal locus of partner's dependence on the use of interpersonal power. *Journal of personality and social psychology, 2*(4), 609.

> Issues and debates at A Level

From your AS Level you will have gained an understanding of some of the important debates and issues in psychology, including the application of psychology to everyday life, individual and situational explanations, nature versus nurture, and the use of children in psychological research. You will need to learn to apply these ideas to the new topics you explore at A Level as well as the Key Concepts discussed earlier. As the A Level course is based on applied topics, you will find that the 'applications to everyday life' are very obvious, so you can consider the extent to which these applications are useful and how valid and reliable you feel the research is that supports them.

In addition, you will also need to be able to consider four further issues and debates in relation to each of the specialist options:

1. Cultural differences

2. Reductionism versus holism

3. Determinism versus free-will

4. Idiographic versus nomothetic.

The first of these is the influence of cultural differences on the study of psychology. As you might notice, much evidence in psychological research is collected on narrow samples; exclusively or predominantly from one culture. The findings of such research may not apply to other cultures. For example, you will notice that students from Western universities are a popular choice of sample in psychological research. Consider how this could affect the results of research, given that these individuals are likely to be well-educated, relatively young and wealthy enough to access higher education. This would mean that any decisions based on the evidence would be potentially biased, or that we might reasonably expect there to be differences between participants from different cultures. Cross-cultural research in psychology is helpful in highlighting cultural differences within psychological phenomena.

The second debate at A Level is known as 'reductionism versus holism'. The term reductionism relates to the extent to which a psychological phenomenon (such as a feature of our emotions, thinking or behaviour) is explained by a theory or concept in terms of its most basic elements. In practice this means 'reducing' explanations to biological factors such as the actions of neurotransmitters (the chemicals that send messages between nerve cells) or genes. There is a huge focus on identifying specific areas of the brain or individual genes as 'responsible' for certain behaviours. This can be useful, especially in terms of diagnosis and treatment. However, in a wider sense, reductionism may refer to considering only some of many elements that are important in explaining a phenomenon, such as looking only at cognitive factors (to do with the way we think) and excluding biological or social ones. In contrast, holism relates to psychological theories which views things a whole; and argues that behaviour cannot be understood in terms of each individual part. The value of holism is that it can help psychologists recognise that multiple, interacting factors are involved in the phenomena they are trying to study, and that no single cause can always be found.

In addition, the determinism versus free-will debate can be applied to the specialist options you will encounter. 'Determinism' refers to the extent to which a psychological phenomenon, such as a feature of our emotions, thinking or behaviour, is governed by processes that are beyond our control. A 'deterministic' view suggests that we have little free will to choose how we feel, think or behave and that we are the product of biological, social or other environmental influences. For example if a person commits a crime, determinism would view this as an unavoidable result of their genetics or upbringing. On the other hand, freewill can be understood as the argument that people have choice in how they behave. A 'free-will view' suggests that to a greater or lesser extent humans can act freely, which also means they are responsible for their actions. So on the other hand, those who believe in freewill would argue that if a person committed a crime, it was entirely their own choice.

Finally, the **idiographic** versus **nomothetic** debate considers how psychologists construct theories and conduct studies. Idiographic research relies on qualitative data and gathering detailed data from individuals through case studies and unstructured self-reports. This type of research is popular in the psychodynamic approach or when studying people who have experienced brain damage, as it focuses on the unique experiences of the individual in great depth. However, a nomothetic approach to research is concerned with establishing 'laws' of psychology; principles that can be applied to all people. Such researchers achieve this through using experimental or observational methods which produce quantitative data which can be analysed to make statements or predictions about larger populations. Examples of nomothetic research may include research to test the effectiveness of drug treatments on a target population, or social experiments such as that of Milgram and Piliavin et al. you have studied at AS. These approaches can be seen as complementary; often an idiographic approach is suitable for unusual or new areas of research where little is known about the topic. Findings from idiographic studies can then help psychologists test ideas more robustly and on a larger scale.

> ### KEY WORDS
>
> **idiographic:** attempts to describe the nature of the individual
>
> **nomothetic:** attempts to establish general laws of human behaviour

> Research methods at A Level

You have covered a substantial amount of information regarding research methods in psychology within the AS Level Research Methods chapter and topic chapters so far. As well as the research methods you have studied at AS Level, you must be aware of the following aspects of research methods and how they can be applied to the specialist options.

Experiments

At AS Level, you learned about the different features and types of experiments. You also learned about **random allocation** as a technique researchers use to reduce the effect of individual differences between participants. Randomised Control Trials (commonly known as RCTs) are studies in which a number of similar people are randomly allocated to two or more groups. RCTs are typically used to test drugs or psychological treatments. The experimental group receives the intervention (e.g. a drug) and the control group has an alternative intervention or no intervention at all. RCTs often administer placebos (fake drugs that have no effect but look just like the real drug) to participants. Then the groups are monitored to see the effect, if any, of the intervention. The results of each group are statistically analysed to determine the effect of the intervention.

One advantage of using RCTs is that they are considered to be highly effective in reducing bias. One reason for this is that participants are unaware or 'blind' as to which condition they are taking part in (e.g., whether they are in the experimental or control group). In a double-blind trial, neither the participants nor researchers know which condition the participants are in. This further increases the validity of the results, as researcher and participant bias are controlled for.

There are some limitations to using RCTs, however. It can be challenging in practice to conduct large scale trials on a group of participants who are similar enough (e.g. controlling for age, sex, socioeconomic status, physical health, etc.). Also, RCTs are considered the 'gold standard' in medical research, but are less effective for measuring the effectiveness of psychological treatments. One reason for this is that there are a number of factors that can influence the effectiveness of a psychological treatment that are hard to control, whereas drugs may have a more universal biochemical effect.

Questionnaires

You have already studied questionnaires as one form of self-report. Questionnaires do not have to be administered in person; they can take the form of online or postal questionnaires that are sent to participants to complete individually.

One advantage of a postal questionnaire is that participants may feel more relaxed or willing to share information because they can complete the questionnaire privately and feel less identifiable to the researchers. Postal questionnaires are also a good way to reach a large sample of people very quickly and easily. However, postal questionnaires may not be representative of the population for practical reasons because some may get lost or be completed by people outside of the target population. The return rate is likely to be higher for questionnaires on topics that people have an interest in, which means the sample becomes self-selecting and less representative of the population as a whole.

Two common question types used in self-reports are rating scales and forced-/fixed-choice questions. These are both forms of closed questions in that the respondent cannot write an open, extended response. A rating scale is a tool for scoring items along a numerical dimension, such as agreement with an attitude statement (e.g. a 5-point scale in which 1 = totally disagree and 5 = totally agree). One type of rating scale is a Likert scale, which you studied at AS (see Chapter 1, Section 1.2). Forced choice items require respondents to provide an answer (e.g. yes or no) and fixed-choice items require a response but typically include a 'don't know' or 'not applicable' option.

The advantage of rating scales is that they allow respondents to indicate a degree of opinion (e.g. that they 'slightly agree' or 'totally agree' with a statement). This allows respondents to express more than simply 'yes' or 'no', which is a disadvantage of forced/fixed-choice questions. Both rating scales (such as Likert scales) and forced/fixed-choice items produce quantitative data that is straightforward to compare and analyse. However, these styles of items are not always well-designed and can be confusing to respondents if not properly designed. For example, respondents might read the rating scale the wrong way round and give the opposite answers to which they intended. Closed questions of this kind are only suitable when such definitive data is required. If more depth is needed, open questions may be more useful for researchers.

Psychometrics

A psychometric test is a form of self-report that use entirely objective scoring procedures. This means that no researcher is involved in making a judgement about the score to be given to any item on the test. Psychometric testing was initially designed to measure the concept of intelligence and has led to the development of modern IQ tests. The tests can now be used to measure many different concepts such as personality, memory and happiness. They are used widely in psychology in areas such as organisational and clinical psychology.

One major advantage to psychometric tests is that they are a standardised method of testing that produces reliable results. Psychometric tests are also highly useful in the real world. They are used by employers to help identify suitable candidates for job roles, for example. Another advantage is that they produce quantitative data that makes it easy to compare to the norms for the test. This means bias in scoring is reduced or eliminated.

There are a number of limitations to using psychometric testing. First, the tests only provide a snapshot of how the participant is thinking or feeling at that day and time; performance can be affected by mood or other factors. Participants in such tests are subject to a practice effect and can get better at IQ tests for example when they are familiarised with the type of questions the test contains. There are also problems with the validity of the tests themselves. Psychometric tests may lack face validity and not measure what they intend to measure, or they may be developed with specific populations that means they can be biased towards certain social or cultural groups.

Validity

Chapter 1 contains a thorough description of validity and how it can be used to evaluate studies. An additional type of validity that you should be aware of is temporal validity. This is a type of external validity meaning a judgement about whether the findings of research continue to be true over time. Temporal validity is high when such findings can be successfully replicated and shown to be similar at a later date. However, certain variables that were influential on people's thinking or behaviour in the past do not always continue to be important in future.

A judgement about temporal validity can be applied to evaluate research. One example of this is that a change in attitudes towards gender roles can occur over time. In the Pilliavin et al. study (subway Samaritans, see Section 5.3), female participants made comments that included 'it's for men to help him'. However, if stereotypical beliefs about the roles of men and women change over time, a study on helping conducted nowadays might find greater levels of female helping.

How could you evaluate the Milgram study (obedience) in terms of temporal validity? How valid do you think his findings would be within your current environment? Thinking about temporal validity in this way will be useful as you evaluate the specialist options in the following chapters.

> # Chapter 6
Clinical psychology

LEARNING INTENTIONS

In this chapter, you will learn how to:

- describe, evaluate and compare diagnostic criteria for schizophrenia and to describe and evaluate explanations and treatments of schizophrenia, including applying the findings of the topic area to the real world

- describe, evaluate and compare diagnostic criteria for mood disorders and to describe and evaluate explanations and treatments of mood disorders, including applying the findings of the topic area to the real world

- describe, evaluate and compare diagnostic criteria for impulse control disorders and to describe and evaluate explanations and treatments of impulse control disorders, including applying the findings of the topic area to the real world

- describe, evaluate and compare diagnostic criteria for anxiety disorders and fear-related disorders and to describe and evaluate explanations and treatments of anxiety disorders and fear-related disorders, including applying the findings of the topic area to the real world

- describe, evaluate and compare diagnostic criteria for obsessive-compulsive disorder and to describe and evaluate explanations and treatments of obsessive-compulsive disorder, including applying the findings of the topic area to the real world.

Introduction

This chapter will introduce you to a range of psychological disorders. You will learn about schizophrenia; mood disorders; impulse control disorders; anxiety disorders and fear-related disorders and obsessive-compulsive disorder. For each disorder you study you will learn about the main symptoms and the diagnostic criteria, according to the ICD-11 (the newest version of the International Classification of Diseases). You will also discover competing explanations for each disorder, looking at both biological and psychological explanations. Finally, you will learn about a range of different treatments that are used for each disorder.

Throughout the chapter, you will explore relevant psychological issues and debates and you will revisit research methods in relation to each topic. Key studies and example studies will be introduced throughout the chapter to aid your understanding and to add context. We will summarise example studies to give you a general understanding of what the study entailed and the key findings. We will look at key studies more closely, including looking in more detail at the context and aims of the study, all aspects of the design, and results and conclusions. We will also look at the strengths and limitations of these studies, as well as applying issues and debates to them. By the end of this chapter, you should have a good understanding of a range of psychological disorders, possible explanations for their onset and different treatments that are used.

GETTING STARTED

Clinical psychology focuses on diagnosing and treating psychological disorders. There are often many different approaches to explaining and treating a disorder, and the approaches you studied at AS Level are a good place to start.

The biological approach is one of the main approaches we will use when considering explanations and treatments of disorders. What might happen if certain neurotransmitters in your brain become imbalanced? How could this be treated using drug therapy? And what about genetics? Most psychological disorders are thought to be at least partly genetic, so what does this mean if someone has a family member with a disorder? We will also look at biological methods of study, with a focus on brain scans and blood tests. What are the strengths of these biological methods?

The social approach takes a contrasting approach to explaining psychological disorders, suggesting that they develop as a result of our interactions with the environment and with other people. How might a traumatic event lead to a psychological disorder? Might it be sensible to consider an interaction between biological and social factors in the cause (and therefore treatment) of a psychological disorder?

The cognitive approach offers great insight into the causes and treatments of psychological disorders too. What might happen if someone is processes information incorrectly? How might a disorder result from irrational thinking? And, importantly, how could this be treated? The cognitive approach offers one of the most successful treatments of psychological disorders, and it is based on correcting faulty thinking.

The learning approach can offer a sound explanation for some psychological disorders, particularly phobias. Consider what you know about classical and operant conditioning – how could this explain the development of a phobia? And if a phobia develops due to conditioning, how could it be treated?

Research methods that you have learned so far will also be relevant as you learn about clinical psychology. Most of what is covered in this chapter will be research methods you are already familiar with, but there will be some new methods and techniques to discover.

6.1 Schizophrenia

Diagnostic criteria

Psychotic disorders involve a major break from reality in which the individual perceives the world in a way that is vastly different to how others perceive it. Schizophrenia is a very severe type of psychotic disorder.

According to the **ICD-11**, schizophrenia is characterised by disturbances across many aspects of a person's thoughts, feelings, experience and behaviour. There are many symptoms that may be present in someone with schizophrenia but the ICD-11 states that there are some core symptoms:

- Persistent delusions: beliefs that an individual holds, which are not based in reality, for example falsely believing that someone is trying to harm you.

- Persistent hallucinations: sensory experiences, most commonly auditory (hearing things that are not there, for example hearing voices; see Figure 6.1) or visual (seeing things that are not there).

- Thought disorder: an inability to think, and therefore speak, in an organised manner.

- Experiences of influence, passivity or control – the belief that your thoughts or actions are influenced or controlled by someone or something external.

There are many other symptoms that may also occur, including:

- avolition (lack of motivation)

- **flattened affect** (blunted emotional expression)

- impaired cognitive function (reduced memory or attention)

- catatonia (lack of movement or speech).

These symptoms can be described as either 'positive' or 'negative'. In relation to symptoms of schizophrenia, these terms do not have the same meaning as they do usually; we are not referring to 'positive' as 'good' and 'negative' as 'bad'. The four core symptoms in the first list are all **positive symptoms**; the four other symptoms in the second list are **negative symptoms**.

A positive symptom describes an experience that is 'in addition to' or 'a distortion of' normal experience. For example, delusions are positive symptoms because they involve a distorted way of thinking and hallucinations are positive symptoms because they involve a distorted perception of the world.

Figure 6.1: An auditory hallucination (hearing voices) is one of the core symptoms of schizophrenia

A negative symptom is where level of functioning or experience falls below normal levels. For example, avolition is a negative symptom because a person's motivation levels are lower than would be considered normal and flattened affect is a negative symptom because the expression of emotion is less than would be expected.

For a diagnosis of schizophrenia to be made, symptoms must have persisted for at least one month and must not be due to another health condition (such as a brain tumour) or due to the effect of a substance or medication.

Example study

Aneja et al. (2018) carried out three **case studies** on individuals who all developed **early-onset** schizophrenia, where the symptoms began before the age of 18 years. Core study 1 describes a boy who began to show a decline in his academic studies and general behaviour from the age of 10, when his parents divorced; as a result, he and his mother moved in with his grandparents and he changed schools. From the age of 12 he had been hearing voices and as time went on, he believed his mother and other people were communicating with the voices. His behaviour became more erratic, and he muttered to himself and shouted at people who were not there. He barely slept and his level of self-care declined dramatically. In the following years, he was admitted to hospital several times and given a range of medications to attempt to get his worsening symptoms under control. The boy was diagnosed with early-onset schizophrenia and was released from hospital, on medication that kept his aggressive behaviours under control. However, he still suffered from negative symptoms such as apathy, social withdrawal and a resistance to going to school.

KEY WORD

early-onset: when a disorder starts at a significantly younger age than average. Schizophrenia typically starts during early adulthood so any development during childhood would be classed as early-onset

Types of delusion

There are many different types of delusion that someone with schizophrenia may experience. Some of the most common types of delusion are:

- **Persecutory delusion:** a strongly held belief that you are in danger, that you are being conspired against and that others are pursuing you to try to do you harm.

- **Grandiose delusion:** a strongly held belief that you are someone with special abilities or special powers, for example the belief that you are a superhero.

- **Delusion of reference:** a strongly held belief that events in the environment are related to you, for example the belief that a television programme is talking about you.

There is a range of other types of delusion, but they are all examples of a belief that is fully believed, despite strong evidence to contradict it.

KEY WORDS

persecutory delusion: a strongly held belief that you are in danger, that you are being conspired against and that others are pursuing you to try to do you harm

grandiose delusion: a strongly held belief that you are someone with special abilities or special powers, for example the belief that you are a superhero

delusion of reference: a strongly held belief that events in the environment are related to you, for example the belief that a television programme is talking about you

ACTIVITY 6.1

Make a crossword or wordsearch for the symptoms of schizophrenia. The clues should be descriptions of the symptoms and the words to either find in the grid, or to put into the crossword will be the names of the symptoms. Swap your crossword or wordsearch with someone else so you can have a go at completing each other's.

The use of the *case study* by Aneja et al. (2018) is beneficial as it allows for lots of detail to be gathered about this one participant. A range of *data collection techniques* can be used in a case study to gather both *qualitative* and *quantitative* data. To study one person, or a small group of people, in such depth allows for a deeper understanding and insight into their experience, increasing the *validity* of the research. One problem with the use of case studies is that, because the research focuses only on one person, or a small group of people, the results can't be *generalised* to the wider population; the study just tells us about that person (or those people) in their specific set of circumstances. Furthermore, the case study cannot be *replicated* as no two situations will be exactly the same. What could be the strengths of using interviews in a case study?

ISSUES AND DEBATES

The *use of children in psychological research* is a sensitive one. When children are used in research, for example the study by Aneja et al. (2018), the ethical issues need to be considered even more closely. It is more difficult for children to give fully informed consent to take part in research as they may not understand fully what is involved, so parents must give fully informed consent along with their children. Protection from harm is particularly important because children may respond to things differently to adults and they may find it difficult to communicate their feelings. This also applies to right to withdraw: a child may not understand fully that they can withdraw from the research, or they may not know how to express this effectively.

Key study: Freeman et al. (2003)

Freeman, D., Slater, M., Bebbington, P. E., Garety, P. A., Kuipers, E., Fowler, D.,... & Vinayagamoorthy, V. (2003). Can virtual reality be used to investigate persecutory ideation? *The journal of nervous and mental disease, 191*(8), 509–514.

Context

In the 1990s and early 2000s, **virtual reality (VR)** was a very new technology to be used in psychology. VR was primarily used to investigate spatial awareness and other cognitive skills, as well as social interactions. However, VR has also been shown to be useful in treating a range of different psychological disorders, including phobias and anxiety disorders. Research by Rothbaum et al. (2000) shows that people suffering from a range of phobias (including phobias of specific animals, objects and situations) have been successfully treated using VR. In this case VR is used to carry out exposure therapy, where the individual is gradually exposed to more fearful instances of their phobic stimulus until they no longer feel fear of the stimulus. VR has also been used to help reduce a fear of public speaking, with virtual people (avatars) being able to elicit anxiety and therefore provide an opportunity for the person to overcome their fear (Slater et al. 1999).

Main theories and explanations

Persecutory ideation is the belief (without any evidence) that other people are being hostile towards you, or that they have negative feelings towards you. Persecutory ideation is one of the most common symptoms of schizophrenia. Persecutory ideation can have a profoundly negative effect on someone's life as it can lead to complete social withdrawal and an inability to maintain usual activities due to fear of hostility from others. However, when someone is experiencing persecutory ideation as a symptom of schizophrenia it can be difficult to understand their experience due to the complex nature of the disorder. If VR can be used to develop a greater understanding of persecutory ideation in people without schizophrenia this could help develop a better understanding of persecutory ideation in those with schizophrenia. A better understanding could, in turn, lead to better ways of helping those with schizophrenia understand and learn to cope with their persecutory ideation.

KEY WORDS

virtual reality (VR): a computer-generated simulation where a person uses special goggles and a screen or gloves to interact with a three-dimensional environment. See Figure 6.2

persecutory ideations: the belief that people want to hurt you, despite there being no evidence to back this up

Figure 6.2: Virtual reality has been used to understand and help treat psychological disorders

Aims

The aim was to investigate whether participants without a history of mental illness have thoughts of a persecutory nature in virtual reality. The research also aimed to find out whether there are cognitive or emotional factors that predict the likelihood of persecutory ideation being shown in virtual reality. The researchers hypothesised that a small number of participants would have thoughts of a persecutory nature in virtual reality, and that these would be people with higher levels of emotional distress and paranoia.

Design

The sample consisted of 12 male and 12 female participants, all students, or administrative staff from University College London, UK, with an average age of 26 years. All participants had no history of mental illness. Participants were recruited using volunteer sampling, where participants responded to an advertisement within University College London.

A lab experiment was used, where participants were trained how to use the VR equipment and then asked to enter the virtual environment (a library scene) for 5 minutes. Participants were not told the research was investigating persecutory ideation, but were asked to explore the environment and try to form an impression of the people in the room and what those people may think of the participant. There were five avatars in the scene: three sat at one desk and two sat at another desk. Occasionally the avatars showed ambiguous behaviour, such as smiling, looking, talking to each other (see Figure 6.3).

After leaving the VR environment, participants were given a range of questionnaires. One questionnaire was the **Brief Symptom Inventory (BSI)**, which is a 53-item self-report measure designed to assess nine symptom dimensions over the last seven days. The symptoms measured include: **interpersonal sensitivity** (a tendency to focus on feelings of personal inadequacy or inferiority, and a feeling of marked discomfort during interpersonal interactions), depression (depressive disorder (unipolar)), anxiety, hostility and psychoticism. Other questionnaires were given, which measured anxiety and paranoia, as well as a 'sense of presence' (the extent to which the participant felt they were a part of the virtual world) and specific ideations of persecution. The questionnaires included closed questions, where participants gave their answer on a numerical scale (e.g. the measure of anxiety had 20 items each measured on a scale of 1–4). To allow for the possibility that the questionnaires after the virtual reality exercise may prime participants for persecutory thoughts, half of the participants (equal number of males and females) completed questionnaires both before and after the virtual reality experience. Semi-structured interviews were also carried out to find out the participants' thoughts and feelings about the virtual reality experience.

KEY WORDS

Brief Symptom Inventory (BSI): a 53-item self-report measure designed to assess nine symptom dimensions (such as hostility, anxiety and depression) over the last seven days

interpersonal sensitivity: a tendency to focus on feelings of personal inadequacy or inferiority, and a feeling of marked discomfort during interpersonal interactions

Figure 6.3: The virtual scene used in Freeman et al.'s study

Results, findings and conclusions

There was a significant correlation between scores on the paranoia questionnaire and the paranoia score given based on the interview. The results showed that, for the most part, participants had positive opinions about the avatars, but some had ideas of persecution. For example, for the item 'they were talking about me behind my back', 11 participants did not agree, eight agreed a little, three agreed moderately and two agreed totally. Some examples of the statements on the paranoia questionnaire can be seen in Table 6.1. There were no significant differences in the persecution scores between males and females, or between those who had questionnaires only after, or before and after the task.

In terms of predictive factors for persecutory ideation in VR, persecutory thoughts about the avatars did not significantly correlate with paranoia score. Higher

levels of interpersonal sensitivity and higher levels of anxiety were significantly correlated with higher levels of persecutory thoughts in VR. Freeman et al. concluded that people do attribute mental states to VR characters and, although these are usually positive, they can be persecutory in nature. People are more likely to show persecutory ideation if they show high levels of interpersonal sensitivity or anxiety.

'Positive'
'Friendly people just being friendly and offering a smile'
'People were nicer than real people'
'Part of a game (flirting but being shy)'
'It was nice when they smiled, made me feel welcome.'
'They looked friendly – that was my over all impression'
'I smiled and chuckled'
'Negative'
'They were very ignorant and unfriendly'
'Sometimes appeared hostile, sometimes rude'
'It was their space: you're the stranger.'
'They were telling me to go away'
'One person was very shy and another had hated me'
'The two women looked more threatening'
'Some were intimidating'

Table 6.1: Examples of some of the statements included in the paranoia questionnaire in Freeman et al.'s research

Evaluation

The study by Freeman et al. (2003) uses a specially designed VR program that allows for a *standardised* approach to assessment which increases the *reliability* of measurement. However, it compromises the *ecological validity* of the assessment, as it involves a simulated environment quite different from what we typically experience. It relies on *self-report* in that users of VR were asked to make comments about their experiences, which may lead to *response bias*. However, by using a combination of numerical scales and semi-structured interviews, the researchers were able to gather a combination of quantitative and qualitative data. This allows for data analysis to be carried out on the quantitative data while also allowing detailed information from the qualitative data. The use of a *control* where half the participants completed questionnaires both before and after the VR increases the validity, by ensuring the questionnaires themselves are not eliciting feelings of persecution.

The sample was relatively small (24), and all participants were from the same university (either students or administrative staff) so this is not a representative sample, which limits the *generalisability* of the results. However, there was an equal split of males and females so there is no *gender bias*.

The research was ethical in that participants gave *consent*, had the *right to withdraw* and were *debriefed* afterwards. Participants who scored high in anxiety or interpersonal sensitivity and those who reported persecutory ideation may be somewhat distressed by these outcomes, so a full and thorough debrief would be essential in order to *protect them from harm*.

It is important to consider *application to everyday life* with Freeman et al.'s study. On the one hand the findings of the study can be applied to everyday life by allowing a greater understanding of factors that may predict persecutory ideation. The findings that VR can be used effectively as a measure of persecutory ideation is also applicable to everyday life as this suggests VR could be used again to measure similar experiences. However, the application to everyday life is limited because the study used VR, not actual real-life situations. This study shows us how people respond and interpret behaviours and intentions in avatars in VR, but this cannot tell us for certain how people would respond to similar experiences in everyday life.

Explanations

Psychologists offer competing explanations for schizophrenia. We will discuss possible biological causes (genetics and biochemical) as well as a cognitive explanation.

Biological

Genetic

One biological explanation for schizophrenia is that genes or particular combinations of genes are passed on to offspring which may cause the disorder to develop. Three ways of investigating the genetic explanation for schizophrenia are **family studies**, **twin studies** and **adoption studies**.

Family studies show a general trend in the development of a disorder for individuals who have close family members (with whom they share a higher proportion of their genes) with that disorder. This research generally shows that if you have close family members

with schizophrenia you are more likely to also develop schizophrenia.

KEY WORDS

family study: a type of study investigating whether biological relatives of those with a disorder are more likely than non-biological relatives to be similarly affected

twin study: a type of study that compares sets of twins to analyse similarities and differences. This may include concordance for intelligence or mental disorders. Both monozygotic (MZ) and dizygotic (DZ) twins are studied, and their concordance rate is compared

adoption study: a type of study looking at the similarities between adopted individuals and their biological parents as a way of investigating the differing influences of biology and environment

This suggests that schizophrenia is at least partly caused by genetics. For example, as shown in Figure 6.4, Gottesman (1991) found that the likelihood of developing schizophrenia went from 1% in the general population, up to 48% if you have an identical twin with schizophrenia.

Twin studies are a useful way of studying the role of genetics in schizophrenia because they allow researchers to study the relative influences of nature and nurture.

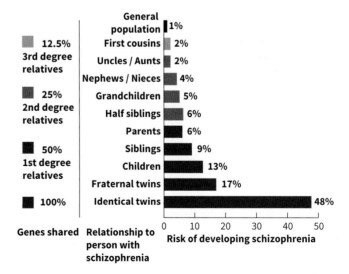

Figure 6.4: The results of the study by Gottesman (1991)

For example, identical or **monozygotic (MZ) twins** share their entire DNA, whereas non-identical or **dizygotic (DZ) twins** only share around 50% of their DNA. Research tends to show that the **concordance** of schizophrenia is higher in MZ twins than DZ twins, again, suggesting there is a genetic contribution. Hilker et al. (2017) carried out a twin study with over 30000 twin pairs in Denmark, using two national registers: Danish Twin Register and the Danish Psychiatric Central Research Register. They looked not only at those with a diagnosis of schizophrenia but also those with related disorders. Hilker et al. concluded that **heritability** of schizophrenia was 79%.

> **KEY WORDS**
>
> **monozygotic (MZ) twins:** identical twins, who share 100% of their DNA with one another
>
> **dizygotic (DZ) twins:** non-identical twins, who share approximately 50% of their DNA with one another
>
> **concordance:** the presence of a particular observable trait or disorder in both individuals between family members and within a set of twins; for example, the likelihood that one twin will have schizophrenia if the other twin has schizophrenia
>
> **heritability:** the extent to which the presence of a disorder (or a trait) is due to the genetic variance in the population, i.e. the extent to which it is inherited

Adoption studies allow us to truly separate out the influence of genetics and the influence of the environment, something that neither family studies nor twin studies have been able to do. This is achieved by comparing a child, raised by an adoptive family, with their biological parent, who they were not raised by. Tienari et al. (2000) found schizophrenia in 6.7% of adoptees with a biological mother with schizophrenia, compared to just 4% of a control group (adoptees born to mothers without schizophrenia). This suggests that, in line with family studies and twin studies, there is a genetic influence in the development of schizophrenia.

Biochemical (dopamine hypothesis)

The dopamine hypothesis essentially states that the brains of people with schizophrenia produce more dopamine than the brains of people without schizophrenia. Dopamine is a **neurotransmitter**, meaning it is a chemical substance which enables communication between two neurons. To allow the nerve impulse to pass between two cells, the neurotransmitter moves across a small junction known as a 'synapse' (see Figure 6.5).

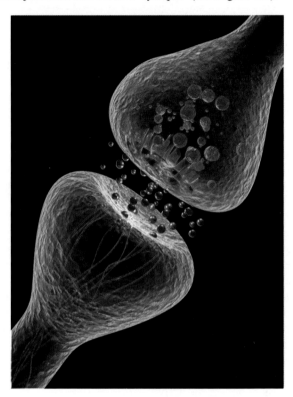

Figure 6.5: Neurotransmission is the transmission of nerve impulses from one neuron to another

The dopamine hypothesis identifies a link between excessive amounts of dopamine or dopamine receptors and positive symptoms of schizophrenia and related disorders. Research suggests that neurons that use the transmitter dopamine either fire too often, or send too much information. Additionally, research suggests that an excess of dopamine in particular brain regions can be related to certain symptoms. For example, an increase in dopamine in the Broca's region (responsible for formation of language) can impair logical speech, which is a classic symptom of schizophrenia.

> **KEY WORD**
>
> **neurotransmitter:** a chemical messenger that enables communication between the neurons in the brain

Evidence to support this theory comes from **drug trials** involving people with schizophrenia and people without the disorder. Drugs that increase the level of dopamine in the brain include amphetamines and cocaine. Large increases in dopamine production are correlated with an increase in the reporting of hallucinations and delusions. In people with schizophrenia, the drugs cause their positive symptoms to worsen. Patients with Parkinson's disease are often treated with a synthetic form of dopamine called L-dopa. If their dosage is too high, it also creates symptoms in these individuals identical to those in people with schizophrenia, such as hallucinations (Lindström et al., 1999).

Post-mortem studies and brain scans can also help us to understand the neurochemistry involved. Post-mortem studies have found that the brains of deceased individuals with schizophrenia have a larger number of dopamine receptors than those without the disorder. Wise et al. (1974) found that brain fluid from deceased patients had abnormally low levels of the enzyme that breaks down dopamine, suggesting that dopamine may have been present in excessive quantities.

Positron emission tomography (PET) scan analysis to measure the amount of dopamine activity in the brain indicates a greater number of receptors in the striatum, limbic system, and cortex of the brain in those with schizophrenia than in those without. Excessive dopamine activity in these areas may be linked to positive symptoms, while some research (Nestler, 1997) suggests that decreased dopamine activity in the prefrontal cortex of schizophrenia patients may correlate with negative symptoms such as flattened affect. See Figure 6.6 for a PET scan showing the differences in the dopamine activity of those with schizophrenia compared to those without schizophrenia.

> **KEY WORDS**
>
> **drug trial:** research studies where different drugs or medications are given to groups of people and their responses or outcomes are compared
>
> **post-mortem studies:** the examination of a person's brain after they have died, to investigate abnormalities that could explain symptoms or conditions they experienced when they were alive

> **KEY WORD**
>
> **positron emission tomography (PET) scanning:** a technique that uses gamma cameras to detect radioactive tracers, such as glucose that is injected into the blood. The tracer accumulates in areas of high activity during the scan, allowing them to become visible for analysis

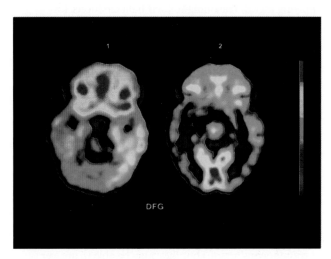

Figure 6.6: PET scans showing greater dopamine activity (deep purple) in the striatum, limbic system and cortex in the brain of an individual with schizophrenia (2) than one without schizophrenia (1)

Psychological

Cognitive

The cognitive explanation recognises that biological factors contribute in some way to the positive symptoms of schizophrenia. For example, Frith (2015) accepts the role of biochemical processes, brain structure and genetic influence on the disorder. However, since no single genetic, structural or biochemical cause has been identified as being responsible for schizophrenia, he looked for cognitive explanations of schizophrenia. This essentially means schizophrenia is viewed as involving faulty mental processes, rather than relying solely on physiological explanations.

Frith describes schizophrenia as an 'abnormality of self-monitoring'. This occurs when patients fail to recognise that their perceived hallucinations are in fact just inner speech (the kind of self-talk people normally experience). It leads them to attribute what they are hearing to someone else, e.g. a voice speaking to them from an external source. He tested this idea with patients with schizophrenia by asking them to decide whether items that had been read out loud were done so by themselves, an experimenter or a computer. Patients with schizophrenia who had incoherent speech as a symptom performed the worst at the task, which may be linked to memory and attention difficulties crucial for self-monitoring.

Frith suggests that another major positive symptom, delusional thinking, may also arise from a misinterpretation of perception. Those experiencing delusions may be applying logical reasoning to their hallucinations, for example. So, thoughts that are actually self-generated instead appear to be coming from an external source and become incorporated in the individual's set of beliefs. These failures in monitoring can lead to delusions of alien control, auditory hallucinations and thought insertion. On the other hand, inability to monitor the intentions of others can lead to delusions of paranoia and incoherence.

Frith explains that those experiencing negative symptoms such as avolition have difficulty generating spontaneous actions. This means that they may find it difficult to make decisions on how to behave or what to do without some sort of a prompt from someone or something else. For example, someone with negative symptoms may find it difficult to start a conversation with someone else (a spontaneous action) but they may be able to answer questions when asked (responding to a stimulus). This may arise in part due to an impaired theory of mind, which creates problems in recognising the intentions of others. A flattening of affect, lack of speech and social withdrawal all result from difficulties in monitoring their own mental states and the states of others.

RESEARCH METHODS

There are some methodological issues with *samples* in family, twin and adoption studies. The samples are often relatively small and not necessarily *representative* of the whole population. This is because there are not very many people who are part of a set of twins where at least one of the twins has schizophrenia. Hilker et al. (2017), however, recruited a vast sample of 30,000 twin pairs from two nationwide registers, ensuring a representative sample. How could the use of a control group increase the validity of twin or adoption studies? Some twin and adoption studies are *longitudinal*, which increases the validity as we can see potential diagnoses and changes in behaviour over time, which is far more useful than a *snapshot study* where we only look at the participants at one point in time.

ISSUES AND DEBATES

The *nature versus nurture* debate is particularly relevant to understanding explanations of schizophrenia and related disorders. Twin studies tend to suggest a genetic explanation for schizophrenia through higher concordance rates for MZ, rather than DZ, twins. However, it is difficult to isolate nature from nurture. It is likely that MZ twins are not only more genetically similar than DZ twins but are also more likely to be treated more similarly by others. This is because they are always the same gender (unlike DZs) and may look much more alike. DZ twins, although they are the same age and live in the same environment, may experience life more like ordinary non-twin siblings. This means that not all differences between MZ and DZ twins can be simply attributed to genetics. This is where adoption studies are particularly helpful: they are able to really allow us to consider the influence of nature (similarities with the biological parent) and nurture (similarities with the adoptive parent). How could the free will versus determinism debate be applied to explanations of schizophrenia?

Treatment and management

Schizophrenia can be especially difficult to treat because of the complexities and variety of symptoms. Schizophrenia can affect all areas of functioning and often consists of both positive and negative symptoms. Individuals may require treatment for **acute episodes** as well as help to manage independent living.

KEY WORD

acute episode: a period of time during which a person is suffering with psychotic symptoms, such as hallucinations or delusions

Biological

Biochemical treatments: typical and atypical antipsychotics

Before dopamine was identified as an explanation for schizophrenia in the 1950s, there was no treatment for schizophrenia; patients were just hospitalised in the hope symptoms would improve. During the 1950s, antipsychotics were developed, which work by reducing the activity of dopamine and as a result reducing symptoms. Antipsychotics are usually the first treatment given after a diagnosis of schizophrenia and they are usually continued to be used alongside psychological therapies such as **cognitive-behavioural therapy (CBT)**. There are two types of **antipsychotics**: typical and atypical.

> **KEY WORDS**
>
> **cognitive-behavioural therapy (CBT):** a treatment that incorporates aspects of cognitive and behavioural approaches to treating psychological disorders, such as schizophrenia
>
> **antipsychotics:** a type of medication that is used to treat psychotic disorders, such as schizophrenia, by affecting levels of neurotransmitters in the brain

Typical antipsychotics, also referred to as first generation, were developed in the 1950s. An example is chlorpromazine. They work by reducing the effects of dopamine and therefore reducing the positive symptoms of schizophrenia (mainly hallucinations and delusions). Typical antipsychotics are dopamine antagonists, which means that they block dopamine receptors so there is less dopamine activity. To be effective treatments, they must block a considerable proportion of dopamine activity. However, the downside to this is that there are many undesirable **side effects**.

> **KEY WORDS**
>
> **typical antipsychotics:** antipsychotics developed in the 1950s that reduce the effect of dopamine in order to reduce positive symptoms of schizophrenia
>
> **side effects:** any consequences of taking a medication, other than the intended one. These can range from mild to severe and can affect physical, emotional or cognitive functioning

Atypical antipsychotics, also referred to as second generation, were developed in the 1990s. An example is clozapine. Compared to typical antipsychotics, atypical antipsychotics have a lower risk of side effects, have a beneficial effect on negative symptoms as well as positive symptoms and have been shown to be effective for 'treatment-resistant' patients (those for whom other treatments have been ineffective). Atypical antipsychotics work by blocking dopamine, but unlike typical antipsychotics, they rapidly dissociate (they only block dopamine activity for a short period of time). The rapid dissociation allows for normal dopamine transmission to take place, which is what leads to less side effects.

> **KEY WORD**
>
> **atypical antipsychotics:** antipsychotics developed in the 1990s that affect dopamine levels in order to reduce both positive and negative symptoms of schizophrenia

The use of antipsychotic drugs has been thoroughly researched using **randomised control trials (RCTs)**. These trials are often **double-blind placebo controlled**, and consistently show that around 50% of those taking antipsychotic medication show significant improvement in their condition after four to six weeks. Around 30–40% show partial improvement; however, a substantial minority of those remaining patients show little to no improvement in their functioning.

Relapse rates, where a person's symptoms return after a period of time, using antipsychotics can be quite high. One reason for this is that patients are usually directed to keep taking medication after acute psychotic episodes, even in periods of remission (periods of time where they are not experiencing symptoms), albeit at lower doses. However, the medication can cause unpleasant side effects that, combined with a reduction in symptoms, can result in **non-adherence to medication**. Side effects for typical antipsychotics are common, and can be severe, for example extrapyramidal symptoms (EPSs) and tardive dyskenesia (TD). Both of these affect motor control and can result in involuntary spasms and abnormal movements of the face and body. Side effects for atypical antipsychotics tend to be less severe and can include weight gain, drowsiness and difficulties in concentration.

> **KEY WORDS**
>
> **randomised control trial (RCT):** a study where the participants are randomly assigned to either the treatment condition or a control condition
>
> **double-blind placebo controlled:** neither the patient, nor the psychologists directly involved with the patient, know who has been given the real drug and who has been given the placebo
>
> **non-adherence to medication:** this occurs when a patient goes against a physician's instructions for drug dosage, for instance by stopping taking their medication

Electro-convulsive therapy

Electro-convulsive therapy (ECT) is another biological treatment which has been applied to help alleviate symptoms of schizophrenia. For hundreds of years, inducing seizures by other methods had been used to treat psychiatric problems. By the 1930s it was mistakenly believed that schizophrenia was very rare in those who suffered from epilepsy, which inspired the first trials of ECT on patients with schizophrenia. Physicians Ugo Cerletti and Lucio Bini had discovered the potential for electricity to be used to induce seizures and unconsciousness by observing the effect electric shocks had on cattle. They modified this technique to be applied to humans; however, without the use of anti-anxiety drugs or anaesthetic, patients were often traumatised and suffered broken bones.

Modern ECT (see Figure 6.7) is a much more refined version of the traditional method, although it is still considered controversial. It involves passing electricity through the brain with the intention of inducing a seizure; the seizure is the 'treatment' rather than the electricity. Patients usually undergo a course of ECT treatments ranging from six to 12 sessions, although some may need fewer. It is typically given twice a week during the treatment period, or less commonly at longer intervals to prevent relapse of symptoms. Instead of applying ECT bilaterally (across both brain hemispheres), it is now applied unilaterally to the non-dominant hemisphere only, to reduce memory loss. Despite improvements to the technique, there are still significant risks involved to the individual. The procedure affects the central nervous system and cardiovascular system, which can be dangerous for those with pre-existing medical conditions. Memory loss is still a common side effect of ECT, but this is usually temporary. More serious but extremely rare side effects can include lasting neurological damage or even death.

There is still no generally accepted explanation for the effect ECT has on the treatment of mental disorders. One theory is that it affects post-synaptic responses to central nervous system transmitters. ECT is rarely used in the treatment of schizophrenia because of a lack of evidence to suggest it is more effective than other forms of therapy, such as antipsychotics. Evidence suggests that ECT can be effective during acute episodes of psychosis where fast, short-term improvement of severe symptoms is needed. There is also some evidence indicating it may be most effective for individuals experiencing catatonic symptoms (National Institute for Clinical Excellence (NICE), 2015).

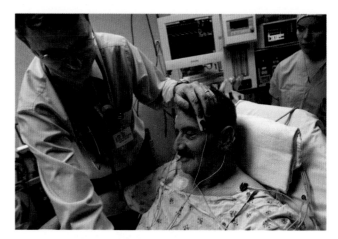

Figure 6.7: Modern ECT is much more refined than the traditional method but it is still considered to be controversial

Psychological

Cognitive-behavioural therapy

Cognitive-behavioural therapy (CBT) is an approach to the treatment of mental health disorders which incorporates principles of both the cognitive and behaviourist approaches to psychology. It departs from the behaviourists' strict focus on observable behaviour in order to recognise the influence of invisible cognitive processes on learning. CBT is a talking therapy designed to help people change through recognising and challenging the thoughts that underlie their behaviours. CBT is almost always used as a treatment alongside antipsychotic drugs, and often requires an initial treatment with antipsychotics to stabilise the patient enough to be able to engage in the therapy.

Example study

Sensky et al. (2000) carried out a *randomised control trial* to compare the effectiveness of CBT with a control group who engaged in 'befriending'. Befriending sessions included informal one-to-one discussions about hobbies, sports or current affairs. This comparison was used to test whether CBT itself is effective, rather than just the experience of talking to others. The sample included 90 patients aged 16–60 years, with a diagnosis of treatment-resistant schizophrenia. Patients received a mean average of 19 sessions of CBT or befriending over the treatment period. They were randomly allocated to either treatment condition, making this an independent groups design.

Each intervention was delivered by two experienced nurses. The CBT treatment followed distinct stages, including engaging with the patient and discussing the emergence of their disorder, before tackling specific symptoms. For example, those with auditory hallucinations engaged in a joint critical analysis with the nurse to challenge beliefs about the nature and origin of the voices. Patients kept voice diaries to record what they were hearing in order to generate coping strategies.

Participants were assessed by blind raters (meaning they did not know which condition the participants were in) before the start of their treatment, at treatment completion (up to nine months) and at a nine-month follow-up. They used a number of standardised, validated assessment scales such as the Comprehensive Psychiatric Rating Scale (CPRS) and Scale for the Assessment of Negative Symptoms (SANS). Results showed that immediately following the treatment period both groups showed a significant overall reduction in both positive and negative symptoms of schizophrenia. At the follow-up stage nine months later, the improvement in symptoms remained in those in the CBT condition but was no longer evident in the befriending condition. Sensky et al. concluded that CBT is an effective treatment for reducing positive and negative symptoms of schizophrenia and that the benefits continue for at least another nine months after the end of the treatment. See Figure 6.8 for a chart showing the findings of Sensky et al.'s research.

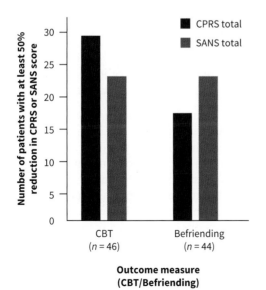

Figure 6.8: A bar chart showing the findings of Sensky et al. (2000)

RESEARCH METHODS

Sensky et al. (2000) used a *randomised control trial (RCT)* design, which increased validity. Assessors were blind to the treatment group they were assessing, which removes any *bias* they might have felt for or against the treatment. Also, since participants were from several different clinics across the UK, the sample was probably fairly *representative*. A further strength was that the nurses in both conditions were carefully trained and monitored, which ensured they used a standardised approach to the CBT. How does a standardised procedure increase reliability?

ISSUES AND DEBATES

The *idiographic versus nomothetic approach* can be applied here. For the most part, research into treatments takes a nomothetic approach, with the aim to make generalisations about effective treatments based on large sets of data. The use of randomised control trials, such as that carried out by Sensky et al., allow psychologists to gather large amounts of data about how effective a treatment is, compared to a placebo. This takes a nomothetic approach because the aim is to find a treatment that is most likely to work for most people, based on the data available.

ACTIVITY 6.2

Design a study to compare the effectiveness of two treatments of schizophrenia.

Questions

1   According to Freeman et al. (2003), what are some of the main predictors of persecutory ideation in VR?

2   Twin studies show that, although there is a genetic influence in the development of schizophrenia, this is never shown to be 100%. Influences from the environment must therefore play a part as well. How does this contribute to our understanding of the nature versus nurture debate in psychology?

3   Which explanation for schizophrenia fits best with using antipsychotics as a treatment?

6.2 Mood (affective) disorders: depressive disorder (unipolar) and bipolar disorder

Diagnostic criteria

Mood disorders refer to a group of disorders including bipolar and depressive disorder (sometimes referred to as unipolar depressive disorder). Mood disorders are characterised by episodes of particular types of mood over time. Mood episodes can include depressive, manic, mixed and hypomanic episodes. Mood episodes are not diagnosable in their own right but are the main components of most mood disorders.

Depressive disorder (unipolar)

Depressive disorder is characterised by depressive mood (feeling sad, irritable or empty) or loss of pleasure. This will be accompanied by other symptoms that affect the individual's ability to function, such as difficulty concentrating, excessive feelings of worthlessness or guilt, recurrent thoughts of death, or changes to eating or sleeping patterns. A diagnosis of depressive disorder can only be made if the individual has never experienced a manic, mixed or hypomanic episode, as these would indicate bipolar disorder instead.

Single episode depressive disorder is characterised by the presence of one depressive episode, without history of previous episodes. Recurrent depressive disorder is diagnosed when there are at least two depressive episodes separated by several months or more without a significant mood disturbance. A depressive episode is a period of at least two weeks, during which time there is almost daily depressed mood or decrease in interest in activities.

Bipolar disorders

There are two types of bipolar disorder: type 1 and type 2. Both are **episodic mood disorders**, but they are distinct from each other due the *types* of mood episodes experienced.

- Type 1: defined by the occurrence of at least one manic or mixed episode. A **manic episode** lasts at least one week and is characterised by an extreme mood – usually feeling euphoric but also

irritable and involves high levels of activity and/ or feelings of increased energy. Individuals will often show rapid speech, impulsivity, reckless behaviour and extremely high self-esteem, as well as rapid changes between mood states. A **mixed episode** is characterised by a mixture or rapid alternating between manic and depressive states on most days during a two-week period. Most often manic or mixed episodes alternate with depressive episodes over time. A **depressive episode** lasts at least two weeks and involves depressed mood or lack of interest in usual activities for most of the day, nearly every day. Other symptoms may include changes to sleep and appetite; feelings of worthlessness, guilt or hopelessness; difficulties concentrating and suicidal thoughts.

KEY WORDS

episodic mood disorder: a condition characterised by episodes of time where mood is either very low or very high

manic episode: a period of at least week where mood is extremely high

mixed episode: a period of two weeks where there is a mixture of manic and depressive states

depressive episode: a period of at least two weeks, which involves depressed mood or lack of interest in usual activities for most of the day, nearly every day

hypomanic episode: a less extreme version of a manic episode, which involves several days of persistent elevated mood or increased irritability

---

- Type 2: defined by the occurrence of one or more **hypomanic episodes** and at least one depressive episode. A hypomanic episode is a less extreme version of a manic episode and involves several days of persistent elevated mood or increased irritability, along with increased activity or increased energy levels. Behaviours shown will be lesser versions of those in a manic episode, for example increased talkativeness, increased self-esteem and impulsivity. These behaviours will be significantly different to the individual's usual behaviour but will not cause marked impairment to functioning. There is no history of manic or mixed episodes.

Measures: Beck Depression Inventory

One way that depressive disorder is commonly measured by healthcare professionals is through **psychometric testing**. A good example of this is the Beck Depression Inventory (BDI). This 21-item self-report measure assesses attitudes and symptoms of depressive disorder and is one of the most widely used tools for detecting depressive disorder. Each item in the inventory consists of at least four statements, and the person taking the test must choose the one statement that best fits how they have been feeling during a recent period of time. This may be the past week or two weeks, depending on the version of the test that is being used. An example item is given here (Beck, 1979, page 398), with the corresponding score listed in brackets:

I get as much satisfaction out of things as I used to (0)

I don't enjoy things the way I used to (1)

I don't get real satisfaction out of anything anymore (2)

I am dissatisfied and bored with everything (3)

KEY WORD

psychometric testing: a method of measuring personality traits, emotional states or other experiences by using sets of questions and numerical scales

Other items relate to the known symptoms of depressive disorder; feelings of guilt and hopelessness and physiological symptoms such as fatigue and weight loss. The total score across the test is used to determine the severity of the disorder, with a score of 10 being the minimum for diagnosing mild depression, 19–29 moderate depression and a score or 30 or more indicating severe depression.

Since its initial introduction, this influential tool has been updated twice. The current version BDI-II was issued in 1996 and, while retaining the same structure as the original, has been revised to include the symptoms of increase of appetite, loss of appetite and fatigue.

ACTIVITY 6.3

Imagine you are designing a new measure of depressive symptoms. Using your knowledge of depressive disorder, and the BDI to help you, come up with five items that you would include in your measure.

RESEARCH METHODS

The BDI is a robust instrument; numerous studies have demonstrated that it has high levels of reliability and validity. This means it is fairly accurate and consistent in measuring the severity of an individual's level of depressive disorder. It is a quantitative measurement, as it provides a numerical score for each person. This gives it a level of *objectivity* that could not be achieved through an unstructured interview. Although it cannot capture the detail and richness that a less structured approach would offer, it is a tool that allows clinicians treating those with depressive disorder to measure improvement or deterioration of their condition over time or with treatments. However, as a self-report, there is a risk that validity may be reduced as the person taking the test may either exaggerate or play down their symptoms.

ISSUES AND DEBATES

One relevant issue here is that of *cultural differences*. A measure, such as the BDI, that has been devised in one culture cannot necessarily be used appropriately in other cultures. Most assessment tools such as the BDI are created in Western cultures, by Western researchers and are tested on Western participants. If they are then used to gather information from people in different cultures this may decrease the validity of the measure as it may not have the same meaning in different cultures. Symptoms of depressive disorder may vary between cultures, and so may the language used to describe these symptoms. Therefore, the measure used to assess depressive disorder should account for these differences.

Explanations

There are many different factors that are thought to contribute to the onset of depressive disorder, including environmental factors, such as experiencing a trauma, and biological factors, such as genetics and brain chemistry.

Biological

Biochemical

Brain chemistry is concerned primarily with levels of different neurotransmitters in the brain. There isn't just one neurotransmitter that can be attributed to depressive disorder; it is very complex, and several neurotransmitters have been identified as being associated with depressive disorder. Two of the main ones are dopamine and serotonin.

Dopamine carries signals in parts of the brain responsible for, among other things, feelings of motivation and pleasure. So, it makes sense that if levels of dopamine are reduced, feelings of motivation and pleasure would be affected. As we know, core symptoms of depressive disorder are low mood, lack of interest or enjoyment in usual activities and lack of motivation. Research shows that low levels of dopamine are often found in those suffering from depressive disorder. Furthermore, anti-depressants reduce symptoms of depressive disorder by increasing dopamine levels, which supports the theory that low dopamine levels were the cause of the depressive symptoms.

Serotonin is a neurotransmitter that regulates sleep and appetite as well as mood and anxiety. When serotonin levels are normal, mood and anxiety levels are balanced. However, when serotonin levels reduce, this can lead to low mood, anxiety and disruption to sleeping and eating patterns, which are all symptoms of depressive disorder. Evidence for the role of serotonin in depressive disorder comes from the fact that the most common anti-depressants are SSRIs (see the text on 'treatment and management' in Section 6.2), which work by increasing serotonin levels.

Genetic

First-degree relatives such as parents and siblings share 50% of their DNA. Just like physical illnesses, some mental disorders are thought to have a genetic basis, meaning they can be transmitted from one generation to the next. Current evidence for bipolar and depressive disorder suggests that there is at least some genetic explanation for why some individuals are more at risk of developing such disorders.

Key study: Oruč et al. (1997)

Oruč, L., Verheyen, G. R., Furac, I., Jakovljević, M., Ivezić, S., Raeymaekers, P., & Broeckhoven, C. V. (1997). Association analysis of the 5-HT2C receptor and 5-HT transporter genes in bipolar disorder. *American journal of medical genetics, 74(5), 504–506.*

Context

As with other psychological disorders, the cause of bipolar is very complex. There is thought to be a combination of biological and psychological factors associated with the onset of bipolar disorder. Psychological triggers may include a traumatic event, such as a breakdown of a relationship or death of a loved one, or other environmental factors such as physical illness or sleep disturbances. Biological explanations focus primarily on brain chemistry and genetics. If levels of certain neurotransmitters in the brain are too high or too low this can lead to a psychological disorder. For example, serotonin dopamine and noradrenaline are three neurotransmitters thought to be associated with bipolar disorder. Previous research has shown that genetics is at least partly responsible for the development of bipolar disorder. However, research to try to identify specific genes that are responsible for bipolar disorder is very difficult due to the complex inheritance patterns and the difficulties in precise diagnoses (McGuffin et al., 1994).

Main theories and explanations

Bipolar disorder is thought to be one of the most likely psychological disorders to be inherited. Genetic factors are considered to account for up to 80% of the cause of bipolar disorder. However, there is little understanding about the specific genes that are associated. One way of trying to identify which genes are associated with a disorder is to look at the neurotransmitters that are involved with the disorder and working back from there. In the case of bipolar disorder, we know that dopamine, noradrenaline and serotonin are all neurotransmitters that are associated with the onset. In order to look at which genes may be involved in the onset of bipolar, therefore, we can look at genes that are involved in these biochemical pathways in the brain. Specifically then, the suggestion is that, if lower serotonin activity is implicated in the origin of bipolar disorder, it is a logical step to investigate the genetic factors that are involved in serotonin levels.

Aims

The aim of the research is to investigate whether the genes encoding for certain serotonin receptors and serotonin transporters could be involved in susceptibility to bipolar disorder.

Design

Forty-two unrelated patients with bipolar disorder type 1 from two Croatian hospitals were recruited. There were 25 females and 17 males, with an age range of 31–70 years. Sixteen of these patients had a first-degree relative who had been diagnosed with a major affective disorder such as bipolar disorder. This information was collected from participants and their family members, with diagnosis confirmed through medical records. There was a control group of 40 participants, with no personal or family psychiatric history. A matched pairs design was used: where participants in the control group matched the patient sample in terms of age and sex. DNA testing was carried out with participants to test for **polymorphisms** (variations) in the genes responsible for a particular serotonin receptor and serotonin transporter. These genes were chosen because alterations in them can lead to disturbances in specific biochemical pathways with known links to depressive disorders. The results of the DNA analysis were compared between participants to look for significant factors.

Results, findings and conclusions

Results of the testing showed that there were no significant associations in the sample. This means that participants with bipolar were not significantly more likely to have polymorphisms of the genes under investigation than the control group. It also means that those with a family history of mood disorder were no more likely to have polymorphisms in these genes than other participants. However, serotonin as a neurotransmitter is understood to be **sexually dimorphic** (there are differences between men and women). So, when participants were analysed separately by gender, results showed that polymorphisms for both genes were more common in women with bipolar than in the control group. This analysis suggested that polymorphisms in these genes could be responsible for an increased risk of developing bipolar disorder in females only.

KEY WORDS

polymorphism: a variation in a gene or genes

sexually dimorphic: any differences between males and females of any species that are not just differences in organs. These differences are caused by inheriting either male or female patterns of genetic material

Evaluation

The study by Oruč et al. (1997) is limited in terms of its *sample size*, meaning it is difficult to generalise from the results. Typically, genetic studies require fairly large samples for accurate and valid analysis to take place. Establishing the importance of the serotonin-related genes in increasing risk of depressive illness in females would require a larger sample. Furthermore, the researchers pointed out that some participants in the control group were still young enough that they could be susceptible to bipolar disorder but it has not developed yet. This means the findings might have changed if the researchers had used an older population and so age is an *extraneous variable*. A strength of the study is that it collected DNA samples which were analysed in a laboratory setting with automated equipment, which increases the validity of the measurement and removes *researcher bias*.

Application to everyday life should be considered in relation to Oruč et al.'s study. Any research that helps develop our understanding of the causes of psychological disorders is really significant because the more we understand about the causes the more that can be done to help those at risk. Understanding that there may be a genetic influence in the onset of bipolar disorder means that family members of someone who has been diagnosed with the disorder could be screened or offered advice and guidance on signs to look for, and positive steps to take.

The Oruč et al. (1997) study raises the *determinism versus free will* debate, since it investigates the influence of genes and we cannot change our DNA. It suggests that individuals with a family history of bipolar disorder are at a greater risk of developing a similar disorder. This removes the impact of free will, and the idea that we have some control over the decisions we make and the circumstances in our lives. However, in this case, the findings of Oruč et al. suggest only a small genetic susceptibility for females; this indicates there must be other causes of the disorder, which may or may not be genetic in origin.

Psychological

Beck's cognitive theory of depression

Cognitive theorists such as Beck (1979) believe that the negative views held by someone with depression form a reality for that person, even if they seem far-fetched to others. The reason for the individual's low mood and physiological symptoms is an underlying process of incorrect information processing.

Another term for this irrational thinking is 'cognitive distortion'. According to Beck, cognitive distortion is when a person tends to see things in a negative way (a negative bias). This develops as a result of negative experiences during childhood, leading to negative **schemas**. When faced with events or experiences throughout their life, the person's negative schema is 'activated' (their bias affects their processing) and they expect things to turn out badly. The result of cognitive distortion is the emotional, cognitive and behavioural symptoms typical of depressive disorder.

KEY WORD

schemas: units of knowledge about the world. As we grow and learn, information from our senses is arranged meaningfully in our minds; it helps us to categorise new experiences and details. Our individual systems of schema underlie virtually all cognition, such as reasoning, memory and perception

Cognitive processes involved in depressive disorder can be understood to form a triad, as seen in Figure 6.9.

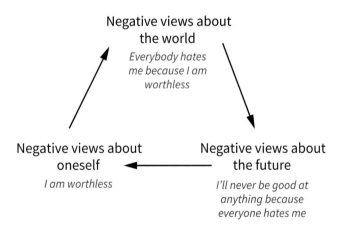

Figure 6.9: Beck's cognitive triad

The first component of this model relates to the individual's view of themselves. Unpleasant experiences are attributed internally, meaning that the individual thinks that they are worthless and not capable of being happy. Second, the individual perceives the world as presenting them with insurmountable obstacles to happiness and well-being. They misinterpret external forces as being against them. The third component

is a negative view of the future; when considering undertaking a specific task in future, the person anticipates failure or rejection.

Learned helplessness and attribution style

Learned helplessness was developed by Seligman and his colleagues in the 1960s. Learned helplessness is a state that occurs as a result of a person having to endure an unpleasant situation when they perceive the unpleasantness to be inescapable. In theory, the individual learns that they are unable to control the situation and prevent suffering, so they eventually stop trying to resist it. Seligman believed that learned helplessness could explain depressive disorder. His view was that depression was a direct result of a real or perceived lack of control over the outcome of your situation.

Learned helplessness is the basis of 'attributional style' or 'explanatory style'. As life experiences teach us to develop trust or distrust in our environments, so we develop particular patterns of thinking towards the world and ourselves. A person who has had a difficult upbringing, or experienced parental loss, for example, might be more likely to perceive a lack of control over the negative events in their lives (learned helplessness), and subsequently be more inclined towards a negative attributional style. This means they will consistently view things that happen in the future as internal, stable and global. If something bad happens they might think it is their fault (internal), or that it will stay this bad forever (stable) and that it means more things are likely to go wrong now (global).

KEY WORD

attribution: the cognitive process by which individuals explain the causes of behaviour and events. Our attributions may be faulty or biased: tending to always look to specific causes for behaviour on the basis of our previous life experience

Example study

Seligman et al. (1988) investigated how well attributional style could predict depressive symptoms. Thirty-nine patients with depressive disorder (unipolar) and 12 patients with bipolar disorder participated in the study during a depressive episode. All the participants came from the same outpatient clinic, included a mix of genders, and had a mean age of 36 years. They were compared with a non-clinical control group of ten participants. At the start of the study, participants completed a short form of the BDI to assess severity of symptoms. They then completed an Attributional Style Questionnaire consisting of 12 hypothetical good and bad events. The participants had to make causal attributions for each one (they needed to say what or who they think was responsible for the event) and then rate each cause on a seven-point scale for internality, stability and globality.

Both the bipolar and unipolar participants were found to have more pessimistic, negative attributional styles than the non-patient control group. This means they tended to attribute more of the negative events to themselves (internality), tended to view negative things as being more permanent (stability) and tended to see negative things as affecting many areas of their life (global). The more severe the depression score on the BDI, the worse the pessimism on the Attributional Style Questionnaire. For those with unipolar depressive disorder undergoing cognitive therapy, an improvement in attributional style correlated with an improvement in BDI scores. This suggests that the way we make attributions is an important mechanism underlying the experience of unipolar depressive disorder.

RESEARCH METHODS

Seligman et al. (1988) used standardised questionnaires to assess participants. The *Attributional Style Questionnaire* and BDI are considered to be valid and reliable measurement tools. However, the link between BDI and positivity of attribution was correlational, meaning it is impossible to determine *cause and effect* in this research. Rather than, as Seligman suggests, attributional style predicting symptoms, it could be that an improvement in symptoms could predict a change in attributional style. Alternatively, there could be a third factor (such as an effective treatment) that influences both attributional style and BDI score.

ISSUES AND DEBATES

The biological explanation for mood disorders reflects the influence of nature in the *nature versus nurture* debate. As particular genes and biochemicals are implicated in developing these illnesses, biology is seen as the primary cause. One example of this is the study by Oruč et al., which showed a possible genetic cause for bipolar disorder in the female population. This, however, ignores the nurture side of the nature versus nurture debate, which instead suggests environmental causes for mood disorders such as adverse life events or learned helplessness. Although these explanations are often thought to be opposing, it is perhaps sensible to look at how the explanations interact. Someone may inherit a genetic predisposition to a mood disorder but this may only develop if it is triggered by an environmental influence such as a traumatic event.

ACTIVITY 6.4

This activity relates to the section on Explanations in Section 6.2.

Laura has a six-month old baby boy and has just found out that her brother has been diagnosed with depressive disorder. Laura remembers reading somewhere that depressive disorder is genetic and now she is worried her baby will grow up to have depressive disorder.

She writes to her friend, who she knows studies psychology, to tell her about her concerns.

Your activity is to write a letter back to Laura in response to her concern. In your letter, you should use the information in Section 6.2.

The aim of the letter should be to offer reassurance to Laura but should include a full range of information.

As you are writing in the form of a letter to a friend, have a think about the language you use. The language could be fairly informal and friendly.

Also, you are writing to someone who doesn't have knowledge of psychology so try to write in a way that makes the material easy to understand.

CONTINUED

In your letter, you might like to include:

- some evidence for a genetic explanation of depressive disorder

- at least one other explanation of depressive disorder

- evidence from at least one study.

You could also:

- include discussion of the nature versus nurture debate

- (for more of a challenge) research the interactionist approach to explaining depressive disorder and include that in your letter.

Peer assessment

When you have completed your letter to Laura, swap letters with someone else and read theirs. You need to give them feedback on their letter in the following way:

- One part that you thought was particularly well-written

- One part that you think is a good idea but could be explained more clearly

- A suggestion of one thing you feel they could add to their letter

When you have done this, read and discuss each other's feedback and make any changes to your letter.

Treatment and management

Biological

There are numerous biochemical treatments for depressive disorder. As a group they are commonly known as anti-depressant drugs. Each works in slightly different ways, though they have a similar effect on particular neurotransmitter levels in the brain.

Tricyclics were first introduced in the 1950s and are still used today, although usually only when other treatments have failed. Tricyclics increase levels of serotonin and norepinephrine in the brain by stopping them from being reabsorbed. The increase in levels of these neurotransmitters reduces symptoms of depressive disorder. Tricyclics are effective when compared to other anti-depressants but tend to have more side effects than more modern alternatives such as SSRIs. Side effects of tricyclics include drowsiness, nausea and vomiting, blurred vision and weight gain.

Monoamine oxidase inhibitors (MAOIs) inhibit the work of an enzyme known as monoamine oxidase. This enzyme is responsible for breaking down and removing the neurotransmitters norepinephrine, serotonin and dopamine. Thus, MAOIs prevent these neurotransmitters from being broken down, and allow them to remain at higher levels in the brain. There has been evidence from as early as the 1950s that MAOIs are effective. However, they have numerous side effects such as headaches, drowsiness/insomnia, nausea, diarrhoea and constipation. This type of anti-depressant can cause patients issues with withdrawal. MAOIs may interact with other medications, such as pain medications and other anti-depressants, which may lead to negative side effects such as high blood pressure or headaches. For this reason, MAOIs now tend to be used to treat depressive disorder only when other anti-depressants or treatments have been unsuccessful.

KEY WORDS

inhibit: to hinder or prevent. In neuropsychology, inhibition occurs when a chemical or chemical process is reduced or stopped

withdrawal: the physical or mental negative effects on a person when they stop taking or reduce some medications. Symptoms can be relatively mild or can be severe

More recently developed anti-depressants include the group known as selective serotonin reuptake inhibitors (SSRIs). SSRIs act on the neurotransmitter serotonin to stop it being reabsorbed and broken down once it has crossed a synapse in the brain. This means that serotonin levels in the brain are increased, which reduces the symptoms of depressive disorder. SSRIs are now the most commonly prescribed anti-depressant drug in most countries. They tend to have fewer and less severe side effects than MAOIs and tricyclics, although different individuals may respond better to particular drugs.

Having fewer side effects is important both because it will improve the quality of life for patients and because side effects can lead to patients stopping their treatment. Therefore, drug therapy with fewer side effects means patients are more likely to continue their treatment and so the drugs will be more likely to be effective.

Numerous large clinical studies have provided evidence that tricyclics, MAOIs and SSRIs are more effective treatment for depressive disorder than placebos. However, there is growing evidence to suggest that the impact of these drugs on individuals is far more noticeable in patients with moderate to severe symptoms, and less so in patients diagnosed with mild depressive disorder (Fournier et al., 2010).

Psychological

Beck's cognitive restructuring

Cognitive restructuring aims to gain 'entry into the patient's cognitive organisation' (Beck, 1979). It is essentially a talking therapy, based on one-to-one interactions between the patient with depressive disorder and their therapist. It involves techniques, such as questioning, to identify illogical thinking, and talking through ways of changing the patient's way of thinking.

Cognitive restructuring as a form of therapy begins with explaining the theory of depressive disorder to the patient (see the text on Beck's cognitive theory of depression in Section 6.2). The explanation of the triad is an important part of therapy as it enables the patient to understand that their way of thinking about themselves and the world contributes to their depressive disorder. A further stage is to train the patient to observe and record their thoughts; this is critical for helping them to recognise irrational or inaccurate beliefs and statements.

Once the individual can recognise their own cognitions, the therapist helps them to understand the link between their thoughts, affect and behaviour, and how each influences the others. The patient is often directed to try to 'catch' automatic, dysfunctional thoughts and record them. This is practised outside therapy sessions, to help them identify such thoughts as they occur in a real-life context. Such thoughts can be discussed and challenged in therapy, to explore with the patient whether they really are an accurate reflection of reality.

The purpose of this 'reality testing' for patients is to investigate and begin to notice negative distortions in thinking for themselves. The therapist can then use techniques such as 'reattributing' where they discuss whether the cause of problems or failures the patient has experienced are internal or external. As a result of this, the patient can reframe their thinking about an upsetting situation and perhaps realise that they were not responsible for it. Ideally, the therapy finishes when the patient is able to employ cognitive restructuring for themselves and can see a reduction in their depressive symptoms.

Cognitive therapy is now a well-established way to manage depressive disorder, particularly in cases where drug treatment is unsuitable. Wiles et al. (2013) showed that it can reduce symptoms of depression in people who fail to respond to anti-depressants. A group of 469 individuals with depressive disorder were randomly allocated either continued usual care (including on-going anti-depressants) or care with CBT. Those who received the therapy were three times more likely to respond to treatment and experience a reduction in symptoms.

Ellis's rational emotive behaviour therapy (REBT)

Rational emotive behavioural therapy (REBT) is a psychological approach to treatment based on the principles of stoicism. Stoicism is a philosophy, and one of the principles is that in most cases, an individual is not directly affected by external things but by their own *perception* of external things. Albert Ellis (1962) placed this belief at the core of his theory on how depressive disorder should be recognised and treated. He argued that a person becomes depressed because of internal constructions; because of their perceptions and attitudes towards things that happen to them in their lives.

> **KEY WORD**
>
> stoicism: a philosophy where one of the principles is that the individual is not directly affected by external things but by their own *perception* of external things

Components	Description	Example
A Activating event	Adversity in one's life (not directly the cause of emotional upset or negative thinking)	Unsuccessful at a job interview
B Beliefs about event	Beliefs about the activating event that lead to emotional and behavioural problems	'I'll never get anywhere' 'I'm just not good enough'
C Consequences	Emotional and behavioural responses, resulting from beliefs	Feeling sad, tearful, or angry Withdrawal from friends and family Refusal to apply for other work

Table 6.2: The ABC model of psychological change

In REBT, the therapist helps individuals to understand the process known as the ABC model (see Table 6.2). The most important element of the model is 'B', one's beliefs about the event. This is because, while we all experience adversity and setbacks to some degree, Ellis argues that it is how we think about those experiences that have greatest impact on our emotional well-being and behavioural outcomes. People who consistently develop negative, fixed or irrational beliefs are at greater risk of depressive disorder.

The goal of therapy therefore is to help individuals create and maintain constructive, rational patterns of thinking about their lives. This means identifying and changing thoughts which lead to guilt, self-defeat and self-pity, or negative behaviour such as avoidance, withdrawal and addiction. The main way this is achieved is through a process known as 'disputing'. The REBT therapist forcefully questions irrational beliefs using a variety of different methods to reformulate dysfunctional beliefs.

Thus, the therapist enables the individual to recognise that whatever setbacks they might experience, they can choose how they think and feel about it. Individuals must begin to see that the consequences (C) they experience are only partly a result of an activating event (A). They then must accept that holding on to negative and self-defeating beliefs (B) is a destructive tendency, but one that can be changed by challenging the beliefs and replacing them with healthier thoughts. Ellis argues that the tendency to hold on to irrational and unhealthy beliefs is ingrained in people over time, and so REBT has a great focus on the present, with little concern for exploring past experiences (as psychoanalysis would do).

Lyons and Woods (1991) conducted a **meta-analysis** of 70 REBT outcome studies. They examined a total of

236 comparisons of REBT to baseline, control groups or other psychotherapies. They found that individuals receiving REBT demonstrated significant improvement over baseline measures and control groups. Recent research comparing the effectiveness of REBT to anti-depressants suggests that both methods of treatment are equally effective in relieving symptoms of depressive disorder (Iftene et al., 2015).

KEY WORD

meta-analysis: data from a range of studies into the same subject are combined and analysed to get an overall understanding of the trends

RESEARCH METHODS

Studies in this section investigating the effectiveness of anti-depressants such as tricyclics, MAOIs and SSRIs consist of generally well-controlled experimental research using large samples, which is highly *replicable*. Similarly, research considering the use of cognitive therapy and REBT such as Wiles et al. (2013), Lyons and Woods (1991) and Iftene et al. (2015) also include the use of control groups. This increases the validity as it allows researchers to be confident in identifying cause and effect. For example, Lyons and Woods assessed results between those receiving REBT and the control group who did not receive the therapy. In what ways would a case study be a useful way of measuring the effectiveness of treatments of depressive disorder?

ISSUES AND DEBATES

Individual versus situational explanations are highly relevant to this topic. All the forms of treatment outlined in this section focus on the individual's requirements. For example, the individual is considered to have problematic levels of neurotransmitters that require correction through anti-depressant usage, or irrational thinking that needs to be challenged. Little consideration is given to changing situational factors that may contribute to depressive disorder, such as trying to alleviate social isolation.

Biological versus psychological treatments is a really important consideration for all psychological disorders. There is usually some form of drug treatment and some form of psychological therapy for any disorder; in this case there are a range of different anti-depressants (biological treatments) and cognitive restructuring and REBT (psychological treatments). Biological treatments are beneficial because, compared to psychological treatments, they are cheaper, work more quickly and are easier for the patient and whoever is administering the treatment. This makes them a good option for treatment, usually at least in the first instance. However, almost all drug therapies can have side effects, which can be mild to severe. Although this is not pleasant for patients taking them, the main problem is that, if the side effects are unpleasant enough, the patient may decide to stop taking the medication. This will of course mean that they cannot work effectively, and symptoms are likely to return. Psychological therapies, in contrast, are more time-consuming and expensive, and do require the patient's effort and participation. However, when psychological treatments are effective the benefits are great; the results tend to be long-lasting as they tend to deal with the actual cause of the problem, and what is learned can be used again at a later date if necessary. In addition, there are of course no side effects and in fact having taken part in psychological therapy can have a positive impact on the patient's self-esteem and outlook.

Questions

4 Consider whether you think the BDI is a useful tool. Can it help us to understand what it is really like to experience depressive disorder (unipolar)? Why or why not?

5 The research by Oruč et al. (1997) shows a genetic predisposition towards bipolar depressive disorder and related disorders. What alternative explanations might there be to explain why two family members develop the same disorder?

6 You are part of a football team and your team has just lost a match. How might you feel about this in terms of why it happened and what might happen in the future? What might someone with a negative attributional style consider to be the reason behind this failure and the expectations for the future?

6.3 Impulse control disorders

Diagnostic criteria

According to the ICD-11, impulse control disorders are characterised by the repeated inability to resist the impulse or urge to carry out a behaviour. This behaviour will feel rewarding to the person in the short-term but will have long-term negative consequences such as harm to themselves or others, distress about the behaviour or significant impairment to some aspect of their life such as their family, friendships or work life. There are a range of different impulse control disorders, each with specific behaviours. We will look at kleptomania, pyromania and gambling disorder.

Kleptomania is characterised by a powerful impulse to steal (see Figure 6.10). This impulse is very hard to resist and the person will often steal things as a result. Before

KEY WORD

kleptomania: a disorder characterised by a powerful impulse to steal. This impulse is very hard to resist and the person will often steal things as a result

theft occurs, there is an intense feeling of tension or affective arousal and, during or immediately following the theft, there are feelings of excitement, gratification or relief. The stealing is not intended to achieve any motive such as for monetary gain and for a diagnosis to be made there must not be another obvious explanation for the behaviours, such as any other behavioural or mental disorder, substance use or intellectual impairment.

Figure 6.10: Kleptomania is characterised by a powerful impulse to steal

Pyromania is characterised by a powerful impulse to set fires (see Figure 6.11). This impulse is very hard to resist, which results in many acts of, or attempts at, setting fire to property or other objects. An increasing sense of tension occurs directly prior to fire-setting and a sense of pleasure, excitement or gratification is felt during and immediately after the act, as well as while witnessing the effects or participating in the aftermath. Additionally, there is fascination or preoccupation with fire and related stimuli, such as watching or building fires, or with firefighting equipment. There is no intelligible motive such

> KEY WORD
>
> **pyromania:** a disorder characterised by a powerful impulse to set fires. This impulse is very hard to resist, which leads to the person persistently setting fires

as monetary gain, sabotage or revenge, and for a diagnosis to be made there must not be another obvious explanation for the behaviours, such as any other behavioural or mental disorder, substance use or intellectual impairment.

Figure 6.11: Pyromania is characterised by a powerful impulse to set fires

Gambling disorder involves a pattern of persistent or recurring gambling behaviour either online or offline (see Figure 6.12). It is characterised by:

- impaired control of the gambling in terms of, for example, length of time spent gambling or how much money is being spent

- gambling being given priority over other activities or interests

- gambling continuing or increasing despite negative consequences.

The gambling results in significant distress or significant impairment to important areas of functioning such as family life, friendships or work life. Usually, for a diagnosis, the gambling behaviour and other features would be present for at least a year, but this can be for a shorter duration if all diagnostic requirements are met, and symptoms are severe.

> KEY WORD
>
> **gambling disorder:** a disorder involving a pattern of persistent or recurring gambling behaviour either online or offline

Figure 6.12: Gambling disorder involves a pattern of persistent or of recurring gambling behaviour

ACTIVITY 6.5

Malia is worried that her husband may have gambling disorder. Malia is hoping he will agree to see a professional in order to make a diagnosis, but she wonders if she is overreacting as she isn't quite sure what is necessary for a diagnosis to be made. Write a summary of what Malia needs to look out for: focus on how she can distinguish between whether her husband just gambles (which she doesn't like, and would like him to stop doing anyway) or whether he may actually be diagnosable with gambling disorder.

Measures (Kleptomania Symptom Assessment Scale)

Diagnosis of these disorders can be made with a clinician using an appropriate self-report measure. One such measure for the diagnosis of kleptomania is the Kleptomania Symptom Assessment Scale (K-SAS). See Figure 6.13 for an example of the items in the K-SAS.

If you had urges to steal during the past WEEK, on average, how strong were your urges? Please circle the most appropriate number:

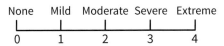

None	Mild	Moderate	Severe	Extreme
0	1	2	3	4

Figure 6.13: K-SAS is a measure used for the diagnosis of kleptomania and includes items such as this

This is an 11-item self-rated scale that measures impulses, thoughts, feelings and behaviours related to stealing. The individual taking the assessment is asked to consider the question in relation to the past seven days. Each item is rated on a point-based scale, typically 0–4 or 0–5 (0 = no symptoms, 4 or 5 = severe, frequent or enduring symptoms), with the highest scores reflecting the greatest severity and duration of symptoms.

RESEARCH METHODS

The *K-SAS* has scored well for *test–retest reliability*. It has also been compared with other validated tools such as the Global Assessment of Functioning Scale and found to have good **concurrent validity**. However, it relies on self-report, which means there could be *response bias*, as individuals may feel ashamed of their behaviour and may under-report symptoms. Nonetheless, it provides quantitative data, which makes it easy to compare the outcomes of interventions as we shall see in the next section

KEY WORD

concurrent validity: a way to judge validity by comparing measures of the same phenomenon in different ways at the same time to show that they produce similar results in the same circumstances

ISSUES AND DEBATES

The *idiographic versus nomothetic* approach can be applied to the research we have looked at into impulse control disorders. Assessment scales such as K-SAS are designed to gather large amounts of data and collect an understanding of universal symptoms and experiences for people with a particular disorder.

This takes a nomothetic approach with the aim to make generalisations about symptoms based on large sets of data. It is important to remember, however, that symptoms and individual experiences can vary significantly for those diagnosed with impulse control disorders so a consideration of an idiographic approach may be beneficial too.

Explanations

We considered the function of the neurotransmitter dopamine in relation to schizophrenia earlier in this chapter. It has also been linked to impulse control disorders.

Biological

Dopamine

Dopamine is sometimes referred to as a 'happy' chemical. This is because its release is triggered by rewarding stimuli, such as engaging in enjoyable behaviours. So, when someone with kleptomania steals something, their reward centres are stimulated and release dopamine. When these behaviours become compulsive, however, levels of dopamine in the striatum are reduced. The striatum is an area of the brain that is responsible for reward and behavioural control, and so deficiency in dopamine can lead to the continuation of compulsions and addictions. The person with kleptomania will then increasingly engage in stealing behaviours. This mechanism is otherwise known as 'reward deficiency syndrome' (Comings & Blum, 2000) and may also explain other forms of addiction.

Kleptomania is a possible side effect of using synthetic dopamine for treatment of disorders such as Parkinson's. There is also some evidence that symptoms of gambling disorder and compulsive shopping emerge alongside the use of these drugs, which further suggests a relationship between dopamine and impulse control disorders.

Psychological

Behavioural: positive reinforcement

An alternative explanation for these disorders also relates to the idea of rewards. Rather than a biological focus, the behavioural approach considers the action of the person involved in the compulsive behaviour, whether it is setting fires, shoplifting or gambling. One behavioural theory that can account for these patterns of behaviour is 'positive reinforcement'.

Positive reinforcement is one aspect of operant conditioning. Positive reinforcement occurs when someone's learned behaviour is a result of previous trials of that behaviour. Take, for example, a person who is given a scratch card for their birthday and wins, which encourages them to buy more scratch cards. The enjoyment of winning acts as a positive reinforcer (a reward that increases the likelihood of their repeating the behaviour).

You might wonder why gamblers don't stop playing once they start losing. This can be explained by the 'schedules of reinforcement' they receive while gambling. Instead of constant positive reinforcement, most betting games involve a lot of losing! Some fruit machines, for example, may pay out only one in every 500 plays. In other words, gambling on a fruit machine involves partial positive reinforcement: you do not receive a reward each time. This reduces the chance that the player will ever feel fully satisfied with their reward, and means they are much more likely to keep playing in the mistaken belief that they will make up the money that they have lost. They believe that the pay out could happen if they play just one more time, and so on.

Cognitive: Miller's feeling-state theory

A third explanation for impulse control disorders is the feeling-state theory. It relies on underlying thoughts about particular behaviours to explain obsessions. Miller (2010) uses this cognitive approach to explain how intense, positive feelings can become linked with specific behaviours such as gambling. Miller proposes that impulse control disorders are caused because these links (between positive feelings and specific behaviours) form a 'state-dependent memory', which he refers to as a feeling-state (see Figure 6.14).

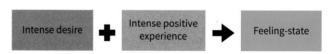

Figure 6.14: Miller's feeling-state theory

The feeling-state is all the sensations, emotions and thoughts a person experiences in relation to a particular event. It can also include physiological arousal (e.g. increased heart rate, release of adrenaline). It is this feeling-state composed of the positive emotions and memory of the behaviour that leads to impulse control problems. If a person's feeling-state about starting a fire is 'I am a powerful human being', combined with the positive emotions, physiological arousal and memory of setting the fire, then this could create a compulsion for fire-setting behaviour.

These feeling-states persist over time and different circumstances, so even early positive feeling-states can affect later behaviour. It is also important to note that normal behaviours that occur in moderation only become problematic because of fixated, intense feeling-states. Miller argues that an underlying negative thought or experience is most likely to create the feeling-states that lead to impulse control disorders. For example, the person with pyromania who has the feeling-state 'I am powerful' when setting a fire may have underlying negative beliefs about themselves, such as that they are weak or unimportant. This makes the feeling-state achieved during the act of fire-setting highly intense and desirable. However, further negative beliefs occur when the behaviour goes out of control, typically because behaviours such as gambling, stealing and setting fires have highly negative consequences for the individual and those around them. Table 6.3 summarises the three sets of beliefs associated with these disorders.

Belief type	Example of belief
Negative belief about oneself or the world	'I'm a loser'
Positive belief created during event (e.g. gambling)	'I'm a winner'
Negative belief created from out-of-control behaviour	'I mess up everything'

Table 6.3: Beliefs associated with impulse control disorder

RESEARCH METHODS

Research into brain structure or brain chemistry, such as dopamine levels, for example research by Comings and Blum (2000), has many strengths. The use of brain scans (such as PET scans or fMRI scans) is *scientific* and *objective*; we can actually see which parts of the brain are active or not active. It does not rely on *subjective* interpretation from the researcher or on self-report from participants, so this increases the validity of the research. Technological advances allow us a much greater understanding of the human brain and, as a result, of human behaviour, and the scientific approach allows for high levels of validity and reliability. How would psychologists have investigated brain changes before brain scans?

KEY WORD

fMRI (functional magnetic resonance imaging): a scanning technique used to measure activity in the brain by tracking the changes in flow of oxygenated blood. When a part of the brain is active it requires more oxygen so there will be an increased blood flow to that area

ISSUES AND DEBATES

The *individual versus situational debate* is relevant to the biological and cognitive explanations, as the biochemical account of impulse control explains addiction as relating to individual impairment of brain function. The cognitive explanation for impulse control disorders reflects a more balanced view, considering both individual and situational factors. For example, some experiences will be stimulating, rewarding or upsetting (situational influence), but as individuals we each develop our own feeling-states in relation to these, which lead to overall patterns of behaviour.

Treatment and management

As we have seen, impulse control disorders involve habitual, compulsive behaviours that the individual finds rewarding but which may also be highly detrimental, to both themselves and others. Here we will consider several ways of managing these disorders.

Biological

Research suggests that one successful treatment of gambling disorder is a group of drugs called **opiate antagonists**. The key study by Grant et al. explores this method of treatment.

Key study: Grant et al. (2008)

Grant, J. E., Kim, S. W., Hollander, E., & Potenza, M. N. (2008). Predicting response to opiate antagonists and placebo in the treatment of pathological gambling. *Psychopharmacology*, *200*(4), 521.

Context

There are a range of different treatments that can be used to treat people with pathological gambling (PG), with varying degrees of success. Psychological therapies such as covert sensitisation and imaginal desensitisation (see the next section) work by changing the thoughts of the client, in order to bring about behavioural change. Drug therapy is a biological treatment that can be used to treat those with PG. Previous research, such as that carried out by Kim et al. (2001) has shown that opiate antagonists can be a successful treatment for (PG). There are, however, individual differences in responses, and between 10 and 30% of patients treated with opiate antagonists do not show significant improvement (Kim et al. 2001). Although these findings suggest there are individual differences in the effectiveness of opiate antagonists as treatment for PG, no previous research had been carried out to examine predictors to treatment outcome in PG.

Main theories and explanations

Opiate antagonists are a group of drugs that have been traditionally used to treat substance abuse. When someone suffers from substance abuse, the reward centres in the brain are activated by the drug or alcohol use, which then makes the person crave the drug or alcohol more and more. The same happens when someone with PG engages in gambling behaviour; the reward centres in their brain are activated. Opiate antagonists work by reducing the response of the reward centre in the brain. This reduces the urge to engage in addictive behaviours, such as gambling and drinking alcohol, and extends the periods of abstinence (when the addictive behaviour is not carried out). An example of a commonly used opiate antagonist is nalmefene.

Opiate antagonists have been shown to be effective treatments for alcohol dependence, particularly for people with strong alcohol cravings, a family history of alcoholism and a euphoric response to alcohol (O'Brien 2005, Monterosso et al., 2001). Alcohol dependence is genetically linked to PG, and the two often occur alongside each other.

Aims

The research aimed to identify clinical variables associated with treatment outcome in PG subjects receiving opiate antagonists. The researchers hypothesised that a family history of alcoholism and stronger urges to gamble would be associated with positive outcomes for those treated with opiate antagonists. They also hypothesised that people with less severe PG would be more likely to respond positively to a placebo than those with more severe PG.

Design

Two double-blind placebo clinical trials (lasting 16 weeks and 18 weeks) were carried out on 284 patients with PG who had gambled in the last two weeks. The sample included an approximately equal number of men and women; all participants were from the USA.

An independent groups design was used, where participants in each trial were randomly assigned to one of four conditions: placebo, or nalmefene doses of 25 mg/day, 50 mg/day or 100 mg/day in one trial and, similarly in the other trial: placebo, or naltrexone (another type of opiate antagonist) doses of 50 mg/day, 100 mg/day or 150 mg/day. Across both trials, approximately 25% of the participants were given a placebo, to act as a control. The trials were double-blind so neither the participants nor the investigators knew who was taking the placebo and who was taking the active drugs (see Figure 6.15).

Clinician-administered scales and semi-structured interviews were used to gather data. The **Yale-Brown Obsessive Compulsive Scale Modified for Pathological Gambling (PG-YBOCS)** was the main measure used. This is a clinician-administered scale to assess gambling severity by assessing symptoms over the previous seven days, in terms of both gambling urges/thoughts and gambling behaviour. Other scales were also administered, assessing the participants on psychological functioning, anxiety and depressive disorder (unipolar). Semi-structured interviews were used to gather family history, particularly relating to first-degree relatives with alcoholism.

> ### KEY WORDS
>
> **opiate antagonists:** a group of drugs that have traditionally been used to treat substance abuse. They work by blocking the reward centres in the brain that are activated by drug or alcohol use
>
> **Yale-Brown Obsessive Compulsive Scale Modified for Pathological Gambling (PG-YBOCS):** a clinician-administered scale to assess gambling severity by assessing symptoms over the previous seven days, in terms of both gambling urges/thoughts and gambling behaviour

Results, findings and conclusions

Treatment response was defined as at least a 35% reduction in PG-YBOCS total score for at least one month following treatment. Results showed that the variable most strongly associated with a positive response to opiate antagonist treatment was a family history of alcoholism. This, combined with the knowledge that opiate antagonists can be an effective treatment for alcohol dependence, suggests there may be a genetic influence on the response to opiate antagonist treatment. For those receiving a higher dose of opiate antagonists, intensity of gambling urges was associated with a positive response to treatment. With those receiving a placebo, younger age was associated with a more positive response; presumably because the gambling urges and behaviours were less ingrained than in older patients so the placebo was more easily able to work. Contrary to expectations, those with less severe PG did not respond more positively to placebo.

The researchers concluded that a family history of alcoholism and strong gambling urges seem to predict a positive response to opiate antagonists in treatment of PG. Although further research should be carried out to investigate whether there are genetic or other specific factors involved, this is really useful in determining who may respond best to opiate antagonist treatment.

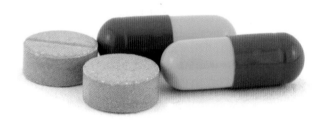

Figure 6.15: Placebos are used as a control when testing the effectiveness of drug treatments

Evaluation

Grant et al. (2008) used a double-blind trial, so neither the experimenter nor participant knew which drug or placebo they were receiving. This eliminated the possibility of *participant* or *researcher bias* and increased the validity of the results. The data collected in this study were quantitative; using this objective measurement made it easy to compare improvement of symptoms through the standardised Y-BOCS. However, as with all experiments involving placebos, there are *ethical issues* around deceiving participants into believing they are receiving real drug treatment. When a participant is deceived in any way there is an ethical consideration, particularly if the deception may lead to distress, embarrassment or any form of harm to the participant. When using deception in a placebo trial this means that some of the participants are not receiving the real drug so there is a risk to their health as they will not benefit from the treatment. However, before entering a placebo trial, participants will be informed of the process and it will be made clear that if they consent to take part in the trial, they may receive the actual drug or they may receive the placebo.

The study by Grant et al. (2008) shows *application to everyday life* by showing the effectiveness of opiates in treating individuals with a gambling disorder. It gives us an idea of which individual circumstances might make this treatment most effective. This could have a hugely beneficial impact on the treatment of patients; by understanding factors that can predict a positive response to certain treatments this makes it more likely for a successful treatment to be found more quickly.

Psychological (cognitive-behavioural therapies)

As we have learned, cognitive and behavioural therapies may rely on changing distortions in the thoughts and feelings of clients, in order to bring about behavioural change. We will discuss two types of therapy that have been used to treat impulse control disorders: covert sensitisation and imaginal desensitisation.

Covert sensitisation

The covert sensitisation procedure involves conditioning, in which an unpleasant stimulus such as nausea or an anxiety-producing image is paired with an undesirable behaviour in order to change that behaviour. It therefore draws on classical conditioning and is less concerned with underlying reasons regarding the origin of behaviour.

Example study

Glover (1985) describes one case study using covert sensitisation to treat an instance of kleptomania. A 56-year-old woman with a 14-year history of daily shoplifting who was seeking help for her behaviour took part in this therapy. Her behaviour started after her husband was convicted of embezzlement (stealing money from his workplace). Finding it difficult to forgive him, the woman had then become isolated from their close friends, reluctantly taken a low-status job, and become depressed. Compulsive thoughts of shoplifting entered her head each morning, which were repulsive but nonetheless impossible to resist. Her shoplifting was without purposeful gain. For example, she once stole baby shoes, despite not having anyone to give them to.

Glover reports that the woman sought treatment for her disorder. The treatment involved using the imagery of nausea and vomiting to create an unpleasant association with stealing. The woman underwent four sessions at two-weekly intervals. For the first two sessions, muscle relaxation was used to enhance her ability to immerse herself in the visualisation. Increasing nausea visualisation was used over each session; she imagined vomiting as she lifted the item to steal and attracting attention and disgust of those around her. She practised these visualisations outside the formal sessions as 'homework'. During the last session, she imagined the sickness going away as she replaced the item and walked away without shoplifting. The participant learned to associate the unpleasant sensations of vomiting with the undesirable stealing behaviour. At a 19-month check-up she had decreased desire and avoidance of the stealing, with just a single relapse. Additionally, she reported improvements in her self-esteem and social life.

KEY WORD

muscle relaxation: used in therapies to relieve tension from within the body and mind. It can be induced using medication, visualisation exercises or repetition of calming phrases

Imaginal desensitisation

Imaginal desensitisation therapy relies on the use of images to help individuals who have specific types of impulse control disorders, such as gambling disorder and kleptomania.

Example study

Blaszczynski and Nower (2003) describe imaginal desensitisation therapy and explore some evidence of its effectiveness.

First, the therapist teaches a progressive muscle relaxation procedure, as seen in Figure 6.16. Clients must then visualise themselves being exposed to a situation that triggers the drive to carry out their impulsive behaviour. So, for example, a gambler might be instructed to imagine they are coming back from a long, stressful day at work. They are then asked to think about acting on the impulse to gamble, then to mentally leave the situation. This should all be done in a state of continued relaxation, without having acted on the impulse to gamble. The sessions are often audio-recorded to assist with practising the technique outside therapy sessions.

Imaginal desensitisation has been found to be effective in several studies. It has been shown to reduce the strength of a compulsive drive by reducing levels of psychological and physiological arousal associated with these disorders. In those with gambling disorders, for example, imaginal desensitisation was found to significantly decrease arousal and anxiety levels associated with gambling impulses, even at a five-year follow-up. Clients who have undertaken the therapy generally also report that they feel better able to control their impulses.

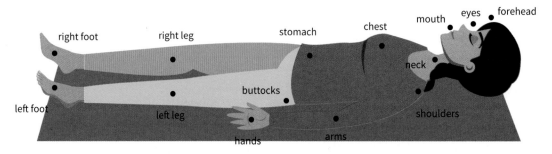

Figure 6.16: Progressive muscle relaxation is used in therapies to relieve tension from within the body and mind

The study by Glover (1985) shows how covert sensitisation can be used effectively to reduce symptoms of kleptomania over several months. However, this research is a case study, meaning it cannot be generalised to a larger number of people. Also, as the study is about an individual with kleptomania, we cannot be sure the improvements would be as good for other impulse control disorders.

Furthermore, the follow-up interview with the participant occurred within a year post-treatment; a longer-term review could check for relapses in behaviour. Also, it is the therapist who is assessing the participants, meaning they may be *biased* in reporting improvements as a result. However, the main strength of this study is that it allows for the collection of in-depth qualitative data that help us understand the experience of the person undergoing treatment.

ISSUES AND DEBATES

The treatments we have explored in this section can be *applied to everyday life*. In addition to the key study by Grant et al. investigating the effectiveness of opiates, the cognitive-behavioural treatments we have explored can be used in conjunction with drug therapy or to improve the symptoms of those with treatment-resistant impulse control disorders. How could the nature versus nurture debate be applied to treatments of impulse control disorders?

ACTIVITY 6.6

We have looked at biological and psychological explanations for impulse control disorders. How might we look at an interactionist approach, where a disorder is explained by the interaction between the biological and psychological explanations? Consider what you have learned about the explanations for impulse control disorders and summarise how the two approaches could interact to explain the development of an impulse control disorder.

Questions

7   Consider how gambling behaviour might create conflict in the gamblers' lives. Give examples of how social, family and occupational areas of functioning might be impacted.

8   The K-SAS is an example of a self-report measure. Consider the advantages and disadvantages of using this tool to diagnose kleptomania.

9   Dopamine has been shown to be an important neurotransmitter implicated in these disorders. Consider the principle of cause and effect: could we say for certain that reduced dopamine causes symptoms of impulse control disorders? Why or why not?

6.4 Anxiety disorders and fear-related disorders

Diagnostic criteria

Anxiety disorders and fear-related disorders are characterised by excessive fear and anxiety and related disturbances to behaviour. Symptoms are severe enough to result in significant distress or to significantly impair one or more important areas of functioning, such as family, social or occupational. The distinction between fear and anxiety is important: fear is a response to perceived imminent threat in the present, whereas anxiety is more focused on perceived anticipated threat in the future. Anxiety and fear-related disorders are usually differentiated by the specific stimulus that triggers the fear or anxiety. We will look at the ICD-11 criteria for three such disorders: generalised anxiety disorder, agoraphobia and specific phobia (blood-injection-injury (BII)).

Generalised anxiety disorder (see Figure 6.17) is characterised by marked symptoms of anxiety for the majority of days, over a period of at least several months. The anxiety may be a general feeling of apprehension or may be worry focused on multiple everyday events such as health, family, finances or work. Related symptoms such as muscular tension, sleep disturbance, difficulty concentrating, or irritability may also present. Symptoms result in significant distress or significant impairment in one or more important areas of functioning such as family, social or occupational. For a diagnosis to be made the symptoms must not be due to another medical condition or the effect of substance or medication.

Figure 6.17: Generalised anxiety disorder is characterised by marked symptoms of anxiety over a period of several months or more

Agoraphobia is characterised by excessive fear or anxiety in response to situations where escape might be difficult or help might not be available, such as using public transport, being in crowds or being outside the home alone (see Figure 6.18). The person will be afraid of having specific negative outcomes, such as panic attacks or other embarrassing symptoms in a public place. When possible, these situations are actively avoided and only entered under specific circumstances or endured with extreme distress. The symptoms persist for several months and are severe enough to result in significant distress or significant impairment to one or more important areas of functioning.

Figure 6.18: Agoraphobia involves excessive fear or anxiety such as when in a crowded place

Specific phobia (BII) is characterised by excessive fear or anxiety that occurs consistently when exposed to, or in anticipation of, a specific stimulus: in this case, the exposure to or anticipation of the sight of blood, injection or injury. The fear or anxiety will be disproportionate to the actual danger and the phobic stimulus will be avoided where possible or endured with intense fear or anxiety. The symptoms persist for several months and are severe enough to result in significant distress or significant impairment to one or more important areas of functioning.

Measures

The Generalised Anxiety Disorder 7 (GAD-7)

Questionnaire is a screening test often used to enable further referral to a **psychiatrist** or counsellor. It has seven items that measure the severity of anxiety. These include 'Feeling nervous, anxious or on edge', 'Being so restless that it is hard to sit still' and 'Feeling afraid as if something awful might happen'. Similar to the Blood Injection Phobia Inventory (BIPI), individuals are asked to provide a score between 0 and 3 for each item; however, in this test the scores refer to the frequency of occurrence of symptoms (0 = not at all, 1 = several days, 2 = more than half the days and 3 = nearly every day). This tool is typically used by general practitioners and in primary care settings rather than by specialists. As such, it can be described as a screening tool, useful for recommending further referral rather than providing the level of detail needed for a formal diagnosis.

The Blood Injection Phobia Inventory (BIPI)

The **Blood Injection Phobia Inventory (BIPI)** is a way of measuring this specific phobia. The self-report measure lists 18 possible situations involving blood and injections (see Table 6.4 for an example). For each situation the individual is asked to evaluate different reactions they might experience for that situation. These include

> **KEY WORDS**
>
> **psychiatrist:** a doctor with specialised medical training to deal with the diagnosis and treatment of disorders. (Most psychologists are not medical doctors)
>
> **Blood Injection Phobia Inventory (BIPI):** a self-report measure of BII phobia

cognitive, physiological and behavioural responses. They are then asked to rate on a scale of 0–3 the frequency of each symptom (0 = never, 1 = sometimes, 2 = almost always, 3 = always).

Example situation	Example cognitive response (rated 0–3)
When I see blood on my arm or finger after pricking myself with a needle	I don't think I will be able to bear the situation
	I think I am going to faint
	I think that something bad is going to happen to me

Table 6.4: Extract from the Blood Injection Phobia Inventory (BIPI) (adapted from Mas et al., 2010)

Example study

Mas et al. (2010) carried out research to see whether the BIPI could discriminate between those diagnosed with BII phobia and those who were not. They also wanted to investigate whether blood phobia was a one-dimensional construct, or whether it was influenced by a range of stimuli (such as other medical procedures) and responses (cognitive, biological and behavioural). Finally, the research aimed to find out whether the BIPI could identify a change in people with the phobia, as a result of therapy. They studied 39 participants diagnosed with BII phobia and a control group matched on age and gender. As well as the BIPI, participants completed the Fear Questionnaire (FQ; Marks & Matthews, 1979) designed to measure agoraphobic fear, social anxiety and blood-injection-injury phobia.

Results showed that the BIPI had excellent reliability and internal consistency as well as good *concurrent validity* with the subscale of blood phobia of the FQ. The BIPI also clearly discriminated between those diagnosed with blood-injury-injection phobia and those who were not. Finally, the BIPI was found to be a sensitive tool in identifying therapeutic improvement. Participants completed the BIPI before and after undergoing treatment for their phobia and the BIPI scores indicated a notable reduction in the severity of the phobia following treatment.

RESEARCH METHODS

In this section, we have considered two assessment tools for measuring symptoms of anxiety and related disorders: the BIPI and the GAD-7. Both the GAD-7 and the BIPI have been shown to have good *concurrent validity* with other measures, and thus are valid and reliable instruments for assessing anxiety and blood phobia respectively (Mas et al., 2010, Spitzer et al., 2006). However, both measures rely on the accuracy of the individual's self-reporting of symptoms. If a person is having a particularly 'bad' day (perhaps they have accidentally cut their finger that morning), then their BIPI score might be distorted by this.

Both measurement tools described here can be considered to be *psychometric* assessments. This means they analyse one dimension of a person's thinking, behaviour and emotions, e.g. towards blood in the case of the BIPI. This type of assessment can be controversial; it relies on a single quantitative measurement of what is actually a complex and all-consuming lived experience for individual sufferers. Some psychologists might feel that these assessments alone do not tell us enough about what it is like to have a specific phobia, and how symptoms may change over time and with treatment.

ISSUES AND DEBATES

Cultural differences can be considered in relation to methods of measuring psychological disorders. Many psychological disorders have been found to have slightly different symptoms for people in different cultures. There is a concern about the validity of using the same diagnostic criteria for people across all cultures. Blood-injury-injection phobia is a particular example where there may be cultural differences in people's experiences. The phobia relates mainly to blood tests and other similar procedures such as injections, so it may

CONTINUED

not have as much relevance in some non-Western cultures where medical procedures such as this are rare or not present at all. Similarly, symptoms of general anxiety disorder and agoraphobia will be very different for those in some cultures, where, for example, public transport or busy shopping centres are not part of everyday life. It is not to say that these disorders may not be present across all cultures but that the specific ways they present may differ between cultures so the measures used may need to be amended to account for this.

Explanations

Biological

Genetic

The genetic explanation suggests that we are born prepared to fear certain objects. In other words, there are particular stimuli in the environment that may pose a threat to survival that we are more genetically set up to avoid. This is transmitted in our DNA through the generations to help our survival.

Example study

Öst (1992) carried out a study included 81 individuals with blood phobia and 59 individuals with injection phobia. These were also compared with a sample of other participants who had been diagnosed with different specific phobias, such as animal, dental and claustrophobia (fear of small spaces). Participants underwent a screening interview with a clinician and completed a self-report questionnaire on the history and nature of their phobia. This included discussing the impact the phobia had on their normal lives, as well as giving ratings to particular situations that might trigger a fearful response.

Participants also underwent a behavioural test. Those with blood phobia were shown a 30-minute silent colour video of surgery being performed. They were told not to close their eyes but to try to watch for as long as they felt they could. The experimenter tracked gaze direction and if participants looked away or stopped the video using a remote control, the test would be terminated. The injection phobic test was 'live' and involved 20 steps, from the individual's fingertip being cleaned, to having a fingertip prick performed on them. Each step was described to the subjects, who had to say whether or not it was OK to perform. If they said 'no' the test ended.

The measures included a score relating to the percentage of maximal performance (e.g. how long they watched the video), the experimenter's rating of the patient's fainting behaviour (0 = no fainting and 4 = fainting), and a self-rating of anxiety (0 = not at all anxious and 10 = extremely anxious). Participants also completed a questionnaire on their thoughts during the test and had their blood pressure and heart rate monitored. This is because the fainting associated with these phobias has been found to be related to changes in blood pressure and heart rate.

The family histories of participants revealed that around 50% of those with blood phobia had one or more parents who also had blood phobia. Similarly, for those with injection phobia, 27% had at least one parent who has also had injection phobia. Around 21% of those with blood phobia also reported having at least one sibling who shared the disorder. Another key finding of this study is that a high proportion of the participants with blood phobia and injection phobia had a history of fainting when exposed to their respective phobic stimuli (70% of those with blood phobia and 56% of those with injection phobia). These results are much higher than those participants with other specific phobias or anxiety. Öst concluded that there seemed to be a strong genetic link for these phobias, which are more likely than other phobias to produce a strong physiological response (fainting).

Psychological

Behavioural including classical and operant conditioning

One behavioural explanation for phobias is based on classical conditioning. An individual may develop a phobia of a harmless stimulus if it is paired with a frightening experience. For example, a person might develop agoraphobia following an assault or mugging (being a victim of robbery) in public.

In what is now thought to be a controversial study, Watson and Rayner (1920) used the principles of classical conditioning to create a phobia in a young boy. A normal, healthy 9-month-old infant known as 'Little Albert' was the participant in their case study (see Figure 6.19).

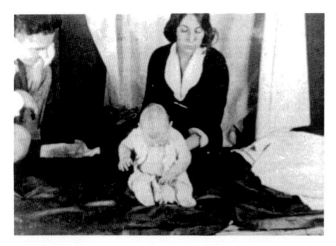

Figure 6.19: Little Albert was the subject of Watson and Rayner's case study into classical conditioning and phobias

Prior to the conditioning, he was shown a range of different stimuli. These included a white rat, a rabbit, a dog, a monkey, masks with and without hair, cotton wool, burning newspapers, etc. He reacted normally and neutrally throughout with no outward signs of fear. The white rat was chosen as the neutral stimulus (NS). They also placed a metal bar above and behind Albert's head and struck it loudly with a hammer. This was the unconditioned stimulus (UCS) as it produced an unconditioned response of fear (UCR) in the boy.

The next phase was the conditioning (see Table 6.5). When Albert was shown the rat, he began to reach for it, but just as his hand touched the animal the researchers made a loud noise by striking a hammer against a metal bar just behind his head. Understandably this made the infant very distressed. Watson and Rayner repeatedly paired the loud noise with presentation of the white rat over several trials one week after the initial trial. Eventually Albert only had to see the rat and he began to show a fearful response (crying, trying to move away from it). The white rat had become a conditioned stimulus (CS), producing a conditioned response (CR) of fear. The researchers wanted to see if Albert's fear of the rat was generalised to other similar-looking animals or items. When presented with a rabbit he also had a similarly distressed reaction. These results suggested that fear could indeed be learned through classical conditioning.

We have seen how classical conditioning can explain how a phobia can begin. To understand how phobias can be maintained, however, we need to look at another form of conditioning: operant conditioning. Operant conditioning is based on the principle of learning through consequences. So, if you are punished for a behaviour, you will be less likely to repeat the behaviour. However, if you carry out a behaviour and you get a reward, you will be likely to repeat the behaviour again (reinforcement). **Negative reinforcement** is an important feature of operant conditioning and it is this which can best explain how phobias persist. Negative reinforcement is the increased

---

KEY WORD

negative reinforcement: an increased likelihood of repeating the behaviour, due to the removal of something negative or unpleasant

---

Before conditioning	unconditioned stimulus (UCS)	→	unconditioned response (UCR)
	Loud noise of metal bar		Fearful crying and avoidance
During conditioning	neutral stimulus + unconditioned stimulus (NS) + (UCS) White rat + loud noise	→	unconditioned response (UCR) Fearful crying and avoidance
After conditioning	conditioned stimulus (CS) White rat or similar animal/item	→	conditioned response (CR) Fearful crying and avoidance

Table 6.5: Stages of Little Albert's classical conditioning

likelihood of a behaviour being repeated, due to the removal of something negative or unpleasant. In terms of a phobia, the avoidance of the phobic stimulus reduces the fear, so it is therefore rewarding, and the avoidant behaviour will be repeated. This leads to a continuation of the phobia because, by avoiding the stimulus you are not allowing yourself the opportunity to see that there is little to fear. For example, an individual develops a phobia of ducks after being chased by a duck (thus forming an association through classical conditioning). As a result, the person avoids parks, farms, etc. where ducks are most likely to be encountered, so that they can avoid the fear they would feel in the presence of ducks (negative reinforcement). However, most ducks are not aggressive or scary so meeting other ducks may act as a way of **counterconditioning** and overcoming the phobia. So, although rewarding in the short-term, the avoidance behaviour actually allows the phobia to persist.

KEY WORD

counterconditioning: replacing a conditioned response, such as fear, with another response, such as a feeling of calm

Psychodynamic

Freud suggested that anxiety and fear can result from the impulses of the id, usually when it is being denied or repressed. Phobias are one way this internal conflict can manifest in human behaviour. According to Freud's theory of psychosexual stages, such sources of conflict are common at different times in our development. The phobic object comes to symbolise the conflict typical of the stage.

Example study

Freud (1909) offered an account of a boy who was suffering from a phobia of horses and a range of other symptoms to illustrate the Oedipus complex. Little Hans was a five-year-old Austrian boy whose father had referred the case to Freud and provided most of the case detail; Hans met Freud no more than twice during the period of the study (see Figure 6.20).

When he was three, Little Hans had developed an intense interest in his penis. He frequently played with himself, which angered his mother who threatened to

cut it off. This upset the boy and he developed a fear of castration. Around this time, Hans' younger sister was born, and his mother was separated from him in hospital. He also witnessed an upsetting incident where a horse fell and died in the street.

Quite soon after this time, Little Hans' horse phobia emerged. He was particularly worried that he would be bitten by a white horse.

Figure 6.20: Little Hans' phobia of horses was the subject of a case study by Freud

Hans' father felt this concern was related to horses' large penises. Conflict began to emerge between Hans and his father, who had begun denying him the chance to get into his parents' bed in the mornings to sit with his mother. Hans' phobia lessened as he reached the age of five. His father reported Hans had experienced two notable fantasies at this time. One was that he had several children of his own with his mother and imagined that his father was in fact his grandfather. He also fantasised that a plumber had come and removed his penis and replaced it with a new, larger one.

Freud felt that the object of fear, the horse, represented Hans' father. Hans was particularly afraid of white horses with black nosebands, which symbolised his moustached father. The anxiety Little Hans experienced was related to his castration fear from his mother's threat and the banishment of Hans from his parents' bed. Freud argued that the Oedipus complex was further supported by the two fantasies, which represented the dynamic of the three-way relationship between Little Hans and his parents.

RESEARCH METHODS

Ethical considerations should be taken into account particularly when looking at Watson and Rayner's study into Little Albert. The fact that Watson and Rayner's research was carried out on a child means that ethical issues are particularly important. It could be argued that Watson and Rayner did not protect Little Albert from harm. Little Albert was deliberately and repeatedly exposed to fearful experiences to create phobias, which would have lasting damage. However, it is important to remember that Little Albert's parents consented for him to take part in the research, with a full understanding of what was going to take place.

Both the studies by Watson and Rayner (1920) and Freud (1909) were case studies. This means we cannot reasonably generalise about the acquisition of phobias from Little Albert's or Little Hans' experiences alone. However, Watson and Rayner conducted a number of trials using different stimuli to check whether Albert was a particularly fearful boy and controlled for any changes that occurred during the study. As Albert appeared healthy and confident, it may well be that phobias could be acquired by other children in the same way. Freud's study lacked objectivity as he was a friend of Hans' father, who also provided him with the case study detail. This research lacks validity as it may be subject to bias in an attempt to fit Freud's existing theories about the subconscious and psychosexual stages.

In comparison, the research by Öst could be considered more objective, because it used standardised behavioural tests and interviews with larger groups of participants. His findings could be generalised more easily and had better levels of control. However, the study was **cross-sectional** and did not consider the different participant's experiences in depth.

Freud's case study of Little Hans takes into account Hans' fears, dreams, conversations and fantasies over a number of years to trace the origin and resolution of his horse phobia. Use of longitudinal research in this way can build an in-depth picture of a participant's experience, which can help us to get a better understanding of causal factors in specific phenomenon, such as the development of phobias.

ISSUES AND DEBATES

All the explanations we have seen in this section can be seen to be *deterministic*. The genetic explanation suggests that if you have a close family member with blood phobia you are at significant risk of developing it yourself. If a condition is thought to be genetic it suggests that *free will* is not involved and that an inheritance of a certain gene, or combination of genes, will make you more likely to develop the disorder.

Similarly, the behaviourist and psychodynamic explanations are also deterministic. The behaviourist approach suggests that if you are subject to conditioning where an association is made between a feared stimulus and a neutral stimulus, a phobia will develop. The psychodynamic approach proposes that anxiety and fear-related disorders develop due to unresolved conflicts during childhood. Again, this is deterministic as the suggestion is that if you experience this unresolved conflict, anxiety or fear will develop and there is little that can be done to overcome or avoid it.

It is important to consider that no gene has been found to be anywhere near 100% predictive of anxiety or fear-related disorder, that not everyone who experiences a fearful situation then develops a phobia and that evidence for unresolved conflicts during childhood is unscientific and retrospective so cannot be used to make predictions or determine the onset of anxiety or fear-related disorder.

Treatment and management

Behavioural therapy: systematic desensitisation

Systematic desensitisation is a way of reducing undesirable responses to particular situations. This makes it a particularly appropriate way of managing phobias, such as agoraphobia. Its principles are based within behavioural psychology; it holds the assumption that nearly all behaviour is a conditioned response to stimuli in the environment. If a phobia can be learned as in the case of Little Albert (Watson & Rayner, 1920), then it can also be unlearned.

This is referred to as counterconditioning. Systematically desensitising a patient requires that a once frightening stimulus should eventually become neutral and provoke no real anxiety.

Wolpe (1958) introduced the idea of 'reciprocal inhibition', which is the impossibility of feeling two strong and opposing emotions simultaneously. The key to unlearning phobic reactions through systematic desensitisation is to put the fearful feelings associated with a phobic stimulus directly in conflict with feelings of deep relaxation and calm. A therapist practising systematic desensitisation follows particular stages that are outlined next:

- The therapist teaches the patient relaxation techniques. These can be progressive muscle relaxation exercises, visualisation or even anti-anxiety drugs.

- The patient and therapist work together to create an anxiety hierarchy (see Table 6.6 for an example relating to agoraphobia). This is a list of anxiety-provoking situations relating to the specific phobia that increase in severity. The list is unique to the individual who works through *in vitro* or *in vivo* exposure to each stage in turn. In Table 6.6, the patient begins with in vitro exposure – imagining the scenarios – and then moves on to in vivo exposure – facing the stimuli in real life (see Figure 6.21).

- At each stage of the anxiety hierarchy, the patient is assisted to remain in a calm, relaxed state using their chosen technique. The patient does not move on to the next stage in the hierarchy until they report feeling no anxiety in relation to their current stage.

KEY WORDS

in vitro: instances where exposure to the phobic stimulus is imagined, such as through a visualisation exercise

in vivo: instances when the individual is directly exposed to the stimulus in real life

Stage	Situation relating to agoraphobia
1	Picturing walking to the end of your front path
2	Picturing being in a quiet shop alone
3	Picturing being in a busy supermarket
4	Stepping outside from door
5	Walking to the end of your path
6	Walking to the shop on the corner
7	Going into the shop on the corner and buying one item
8	Walking to the main supermarket and looking inside
9	Stepping inside the supermarket
10	Buying items in the supermarket

Table 6.6: An anxiety hierarchy for agoraphobia

As the two emotions of fear and calm are incompatible, the fearful response to the stimuli is gradually unlearned and will no longer produce anxiety in the patient. There is good research evidence to support the effectiveness of systematic desensitisation in treating phobias such as agoraphobia (Agras, 1967) and fear of snakes (Kimura et al., 1972). However, since the 1970s and 1980s, this form of therapy has declined in popularity and other treatments which involve more direct forms of exposure are now more commonly used.

Figure 6.21: The aim of someone being treated for agoraphobia might be to visit a crowded place or a busy supermarket

Key study: Chapman and DeLapp (2014)

Chapman, L. K., & DeLapp, R. C. (2014). Nine session treatment of a BII phobia with manualized cognitive behavioral therapy: an adult case example. *Clinical case studies*, *13*(4), 299–312.

Context

Existing evidence suggests that CBT can be an effective treatment of specific phobias, including BII phobia (Antony et al., 2001). Most phobias can be successfully treated with a therapeutic approach to reduce the fear-response in the patient. For most phobias, any physical symptoms are directly associated with fear (shaking, sweating, nausea), so once the fear response is treated the patient is able to face their phobic stimulus.

However, effective treatment of BII phobia is considered to require more than just a therapeutic approach to reduce the fear response in the patient. As discussed previously, BII phobia is associated with an increased likelihood of fainting when exposed to the phobic stimulus. Therefore, treatment for BII phobia also requires the need to teach strategies focusing on staying conscious instead of fainting when faced with their feared stimuli.

Main theories and explanations

CBT is an effective treatment for a range of phobias because it enables the individual to challenge their irrational thoughts and replace them with more rational ones. The rational thinking leads to changes in behavioural and emotional responses, which can be practised until the phobia is treated.

The introduction of behavioural therapy for anxiety disorders such as systematic desensitisation paved the way for further forms of treatment, including applied tension. This form of treatment involves applying tension to the muscles, in an effort to increase blood pressure throughout certain areas. As you may remember, blood phobia in particular is associated with lowered blood pressure and fainting. By training individuals with blood phobia to increase muscle tension, the aim is to reduce instances of fainting and other unpleasant responses when exposed to medical procedures such as **phlebotomy** (taking blood samples).

> **KEY WORD**
>
> **phlebotomy:** the process of taking a sample of blood

Aims

The aim of this case study was to investigate whether BII phobia could be successfully treated using CBT and applied muscle tension.

Design

A case study was used to gather in-depth detail about one individual, known as 'T'. He was a 42-year-old white male, diagnosed with BII phobia. The researchers used interviews to gather a detailed life history from T, involving information about several challenging times in his life. These included witnessing the deaths of several family members, living with a highly anxious grandmother who used a scanner to listen to emergency dispatch calls throughout the day, and witnessing other family members faint during medical procedures. Questionnaires were also administered, including measures of anxiety and depression (the Beck Anxiety Inventory (BAI), the Beck Depression Inventory (BDI)) and a measure of general satisfaction across several areas of life (the Quality-of-Life Satisfaction Questionnaire (Q-LES-Q)). The Blood-Injection Symptom Scale (BISS) was given to test if T met the criteria for a diagnosis of BII phobia, which he did. T was also diagnosed with major depressive disorder (recurrent, in full remission) based on an episode in college.

T then underwent nine sessions of CBT and applied muscle tension. During CBT, T was educated about how common phobias are and he created a fear hierarchy, which he worked through. T was introduced to the Subjective Unit of Discomfort Scale (SUDS), which was used to give ratings of his anxiety (from 0–100) at different stages of the hierarchy exposure.

Results, findings and conclusions

Before undergoing treatment, the results of T's self-assessments showed he had severe anxiety, minimal depressive symptoms, and overall good health in most areas of life. He showed intense fear and anxiety surrounding blood and injections. Throughout the therapy sessions T was able to experience each stage of his fear hierarchy, without his SUDS becoming too high. This ended with him having blood taken (SUDS of 40 out of 100 initially, then soon dropping to 'nothing') with only minimal applied muscle tension used. At 4, 10 and 12 months post-treatment, T reported back on his progress and, as well as having been to several medical appointments, results of the self-report measures showed that his anxiety levels had dropped significantly and that he no longer showed fear or terror to medical-related stimuli. In short, he no longer had the phobia, and reported having 'never felt better'.

This demonstrates the successful treatment of blood-injection-injury phobia using CBT and applied muscle tension. Before treatment, the subject passed out during phlebotomy procedures and experienced extreme anxiety and panic when exposed to other medical procedures and related experiences. Following treatment, and for at least 12 months afterwards, he was able to engage in medical procedures with minimal symptoms.

Evaluation

A case study was used that allows the participant to be studied in great detail and can give us a detailed understanding of the specific circumstances surrounding them. However, a key weakness of a case study comes from the difficulties in generalising the results. A case study tells us only about the particular person who has been studied and so the results cannot be generalised to the wider population, which limits the *usefulness* of the study. Furthermore, a case study cannot be *replicated* as there won't be another person with the exact same set of circumstances to allow a replication of the study, so results cannot be checked for reliability. Why do you think a case study was chosen by Chapman and DeLapp?

Many different techniques were used to gather information, including the BAI, BDI, Q-LES-Q and BISS; all of which provide quantitative data to allow for statistical analysis to be carried out, and for data pre- and post-treatment to be compared. In addition, there were detailed *interviews* carried out to gather qualitative data in the nature of a full history of T's life. A weakness, however, of all of these measures is that they rely on *self-report* so this may lead to inaccurate information. This may be due to *social desirability*, subjective interpretation, or misremembering of *retrospective* data; this decreases the validity of the findings.

The findings of the study by Chapman and DeLapp can be *applied to everyday life*. Treatment of any phobia is important and will of course improve the quality of life of the patient. But finding a successful treatment for blood phobia is particularly significant due to the importance of attending medical procedures when necessary. Someone with, for example, a phobia of the sea, could, relatively easily, avoid the sea and still live a fulfilling and otherwise healthy life. However, a blood or related phobia could have serious repercussions on the patient's health if they avoid medical interventions.

RESEARCH METHODS

Most research into the effectiveness of treatments for anxiety and fear-related disorders relies on *self-report* from the patient, pre- and post-treatment. This is beneficial as it allows us to get an understanding of the patient's feelings and symptoms in what is a very *subjective* experience. However, the disadvantages of self-report may reduce the validity of the findings due to *social desirability*, where the patient feels that they should report an improvement of symptoms even if it is not fully the case. Finally, there is the problem of the use of self-report questionnaires or other assessment measures, where patients may misinterpret questions, or the use of *forced choice* options may lead a patient to give an answer that is not a true or accurate reflection of how they really feel.

ISSUES AND DEBATES

The treatments we have explored in this section can be *applied to everyday life*. As well as the key study by Chapman and DeLapp, the research into systematic desensitisation can be applied to everyday life as it can be used as a non-drug treatment to help treat or reduce the severity of phobias and therefore help patients to regain a higher quality of life. The methods they learn during the treatment can be used again if needed, so this can offer a long-term solution to their problem.

Questions

10 Freud suggested Hans' phobia of horses was caused by his Oedipus complex. Can you suggest an alternative explanation?

11 Systematic desensitisation is based on the theory of classical conditioning. Can you explain, using the correct psychological terms, the process by which a phobic response is unlearned?

12 Consider the case study carried out by Chapman and DeLapp. In what ways are their findings useful? And how might the usefulness of their findings be limited?

6.5 Obsessive-compulsive disorder

Diagnostic criteria

Obsessive-compulsive disorder (OCD) is characterised by the presence of persistent obsessions or compulsions, or most commonly both. Obsessions are unwanted, repetitive thoughts (e.g. of contamination), images (e.g. of violent scenes) or urges (e.g. to stab someone). Obsessions are intrusive and commonly associated with anxiety. Compulsions are repetitive behaviours (e.g. washing or checking) or mental acts (e.g. repeating words silently) that the individual feels driven to perform, as a response to an obsession. The individual feels that these must be carried out according to rigid rules.

For a diagnosis to be made the obsessions and compulsions must take up more than an hour per day and must result in significant distress or significant impairment to one or more important areas of functioning, such as family, social or occupational. There are many different types of obsession and compulsion; some are shown in Table 6.7.

Example study

Rapoport's (1989) case study 'Charles'. Charles was a 14-year-old boy with OCD who spent three hours or more each day showering, plus at least another two hours getting dressed. He had elaborate and repetitive routines for holding soap in one hand, putting it under water, switching hands and so on. His mother contacted Rapoport (1989) after this behaviour had been going on for around two years. Before this, Charles had been a good student with a particular interest in the sciences. He had had to leave school because his washing rituals were making it impossible for him to attend on time. He had also been in and out of hospital for his condition, and had already received standard treatments of medication, behavioural therapy and psychotherapy.

Obsessions	Compulsions
Fear of deliberately harming oneself	Frequent and excessive handwashing
Fear of illness or infection	Putting things in order (e.g. all labels on food in cupboard facing same way)
Fear about harming or killing other people	Checking things repeatedly (e.g. checking oven 20 times to ensure it is 'off' before leaving home)
Fear of accidentally injuring oneself or others	
Strong desire for order and symmetry	Repeating words to oneself or repetitive counting

Table 6.7: Different types of obsession and compulsion

Charles was, however, still utterly obsessed with the thought that he had something sticky on his skin that had to be washed off. In an attempt to help her son overcome this worrying thought, his mother had helped him clean his room and kept things he touched clean with rubbing alcohol. He had only one friend because his rituals left him little time to leave the house. He underwent a drug trial for clomipramine (a type of anti-depressant), which gave effective relief of his symptoms; he was able to pour honey, for instance. Yet after a year, he had developed a **tolerance** for his medication (the effectiveness of the medication started to reduce as his body got used to it over time). Charles relapsed and returned to ritualistic washing and dressing.

Measures

There are several tests used to assess obsessive-compulsive disorders. We will consider two in this section.

Maudsley Obsessive-Compulsive Inventory (MOCI)

The MOCI is a short assessment tool that contains 30 items that are scored either 'true' or 'false'. It assesses symptoms relating to checking, washing, slowness and doubting. It takes around 5 minutes to complete and produces scores that range between 0 and 30. Example items (Hodgson & Rachman, 1977, page 391) include:

- I frequently have to check things (gas or water taps, doors, etc.) several times. (Checking)

- I am not unduly concerned about germs and diseases. (Washing)

- I do not take a long time to dress in the morning. (Slowness)

- Even when I do something very carefully, I often feel that it is not quite right. (Doubting)

The MOCI was designed as a quick assessment tool for clinicians and researchers, rather than a formal diagnostic tool.

Yale-Brown Obsessive Compulsive Scale (Y-BOCS)

The Yale-Brown Obsessive Compulsive Scale (Y-BOCS) developed by Goodman et al. (1989) is a widely used test designed to measure the nature and severity of an individual's symptoms. The Y-BOCS involves a semi-structured interview that takes around 30 minutes to conduct. It also involves a checklist of different obsessions and compulsions (see Table 6.8), with a ten-item severity scale. The severity scale allows individuals to rate the time they spend on obsessions; how hard the obsessions are to resist and how much distress the obsessions cause. The checklist can be used to help plan treatment or to assess how treatment is progressing. Scores range from 0 (no symptoms) to 40 (severe symptoms). Individuals with scores above 16 are considered in the clinical range for OCD.

Obsessions	Aggressive, Contamination, Sexual, Hoarding, Religious, Symmetry, Body-focused, Other
Compulsions	Cleaning, Washing, Checking, Repeating, Counting, Ordering/arranging, Hoarding, Other

Table 6.8: Y-BOCS obsessions and compulsions categories

RESEARCH METHODS

The reliability and validity of assessment tools such as the MOCI and Y-BOCS have been evaluated in a number of studies. They have good levels of concurrent validity; meaning that individuals will score similarly on different tests for obsessive-compulsive disorder (Esfahani et al., 2012). They also both offer good test–retest reliability, meaning that individuals who repeat the measures at different times are likely to get the same results. This is important for researchers wanting to use the tools in trialling psychological interventions as the measures need to be consistent to allow for changes to be seen.

Both tests use a self-report measure, however, which means that they rely on the individual to give accurate and honest answers to each item. This can be quite a subjective process for several reasons. For example, those who are resistant to treatment or fear being thought of badly might downplay the severity of their symptoms. It can therefore be difficult for researchers or clinicians to obtain a true picture of the nature of someone's condition.

The case study (Rapoport, 1989) is useful in helping us understand the experience of OCD in everyday life. The experience of Charles and his mother demonstrates the impact of compulsive behaviours on normal functioning, such as the extremely lengthy washing rituals that prevented the young man from attending mainstream schooling. It can also highlight the unique obsessive thoughts (e.g. Charles' 'stickiness') that are symptomatic of these disorders.

Explanations

Biological

Biochemical

We have seen previously in this chapter that dopamine is an important neurotransmitter for a range of psychological disorders, and this is also the case for OCD. Research shows that those with OCD tend to have abnormally high levels of dopamine. Research by Szechtman et al. (1998), shows that if you increase dopamine levels in rats, they will show repetitive movements that reflect the compulsive behaviours of individuals with OCD.

Another neurotransmitter we have seen in the biological explanations throughout this section is serotonin. Research tends to show that individuals with OCD have lower than normal levels of serotonin in their brains. This research is supported by evidence that shows that anti-depressants that work specifically on increasing levels of serotonin (e.g. SSRIs: see section on Treatment and management in Section 6.3 for more detail) are more effective treatments for OCD, than anti-depressants that have less effect on serotonin (Pittenger & Bloch, 2014).

A third biochemical explanation of OCD relates to the influence of oxytocin. Oxytocin is commonly referred to as the 'love hormone', because it is involved in enhancing trust and attachment. However, oxytocin has also been shown to increase distrust and fear of certain stimuli, particularly those that might pose a threat to survival. There is mixed evidence for the role of oxytocin in the development of OCD. By analysing cerebral spinal fluid and patient accounts of behaviour,

Leckman et al. (1994) found that some forms of OCD were related to oxytocin dysfunction. However, there is also contrasting evidence; for example, den Boer and Westenberg (1992) found no evidence of a link between oxytocin and OCD. They used a double-blind, placebo-controlled study of 12 patients with OCD. Half were given syntocinon (synthetic oxytocin) through a daily nasal spray and half were given a placebo. No reduction in obsessions or compulsions was reported in either group, suggesting that there does not appear to be a link between oxytocin and OCD.

Genetic

Recent research suggests that OCD may have a genetic basis. Monzani et al. (2014) carried out a large-scale twin study and found a significantly higher concordance rate for MZ twins (52%) compared to DZ twins (21%). Remembering that MZ twins share 100% of their genes and DZ twins share around 50% of their genes, these findings suggest a genetic influence for OCD, with an overall heritability estimated to be 48%.

Much research has been carried out to investigate which specific genes are implicated in OCD, but no conclusive evidence has been found. Knowing that low levels of serotonin seem to be related to OCD, it makes sense to consider the role of genes responsible for serotonin levels, one of which is the SERT gene. Ozaki et al. (2003) found a mutation of the SERT gene, leading to lower levels of serotonin, in six members of two unrelated families who had OCD.

Mattheisen et al. (2015) conducted a large-scale study involving 1406 patients with OCD and other members of the general population to analyse and identify genes that may be linked to OCD symptoms. The gene PTPRD was implicated, along with a gene called SLITRK3, both of which interact to regulate particular synapses in the brain.

We certainly don't have any definitive answers surrounding which genes are implicated in OCD, and the range of different research findings shows how complex the genetic influence is. However, what the evidence does show is that OCD runs in families and is more concordant in identical than non-identical twins so there does seem to be some genetic influence.

Psychological

Cognitive (thinking error)

As you have discovered, OCD is composed of two aspects: cognitive obsessions and behavioural compulsions. The cognitive explanation considers that obsessive thinking is based on faulty reasoning (Rachman, 1977). For example, the belief that hands are covered in harmful germs that could kill is due to errors in thinking. These mistakes in cognition can also worsen under stressful conditions. Compulsive behaviours are the outcome of such erroneous thinking, attempts to alleviate the unwanted thoughts and the anxiety they create.

Behavioural (operant conditioning)

Compulsive behaviour can be explained through the principles of operant conditioning. Engaging in behaviour such as handwashing may alleviate the obsession over germs, albeit temporarily. The handwashing has become a negative reinforcer because it has relieved something unpleasant (the worrying obsessive thoughts). It is also a positive reinforcer, because the person is 'rewarded' by knowing that they have clean hands (see Figure 6.22). The influence of negative and positive reinforcement can shape obsessive-compulsive behaviours, meaning they are *learned* behaviours.

Figure 6.22: A common compulsion in those suffering with OCD is handwashing

Psychodynamic

The psychodynamic approach explains OCD through looking at unconscious beliefs and desires. Psychodynamic theorists claim that symptoms of OCD appear as a result of an internal conflict between the id and the ego. Freud suggested that such conflict arises in the anal stage of psychosexual development, around the time most children begin toilet training.

This process may involve tension between children and their parents, who may wish to control how and when the child defecates or urinates, against the child's wishes. In an attempt to regain control the child may soil themselves (referred to as anally expulsive), which causes upset and arguments. Alternatively, the child may fear harsh responses from their parents and retain faeces or urine (referred to as anally retentive) to regain control.

According to the psychodynamic approach, both these behaviours can lead to later behavioural disturbances, as the individual has become 'fixated' in this stage. Essentially, the argument is that obsessive thoughts that come from the id disturb the rational part of the self (the ego) to the extent that it may lead to compulsive cleaning and tidying rituals later in life, in order to deal with the earlier childhood trauma.

RESEARCH METHODS

The biological explanations each have strengths and weaknesses. The scientific analysis used in identifying genes relating to OCD is objective and usually conducted under well-controlled laboratory conditions. This also makes it highly *replicable*. However, it does not offer a complete picture in that it cannot explain why some individuals may carry genes that are implicated in OCD, yet never develop symptoms.

Biochemical explanations such as the oxytocin hypothesis are also supported by laboratory-based studies. However, it is difficult to establish a *cause-and-effect* relationship between the hormone and OCD symptoms.

Cognitive-behavioural accounts fit well with the experience of OCD symptoms reported by individuals with the disorder. However, much research in this area relies on self-report, including measures such as the Y-BOCS or MOCI. This introduces bias as individuals may deliberately

CONTINUED

or inadvertently mislead researchers. Why might this particularly be the case for people with disorders such as OCD?

The psychodynamic explanation, by contrast, is not supported by empirical research. This is because you cannot accurately measure or control the variables involved. It means it would be difficult to demonstrate a cause-and-effect relationship between harsh parenting during toilet training and a child's later compulsive washing, for example.

ISSUES AND DEBATES

Biological and cognitive-behavioural explanations focus on the *individual* and their hormonal abnormalities or faulty thought processes (Rachman, 1977). This ignores the role of *situational* factors and can also be considered *reductionist*. The psychodynamic explanation, however, places more emphasis on early social relationships and considers the effect these can have on an individual's development.

Likewise, the genetic and biochemical accounts both rely on physiological factors (genes, hormones and neurotransmitters) which are *biological explanations*. By contrast, the cognitive-behavioural and psychodynamic explanations suggest compulsions result from learned behaviour or from experiences in childhood, offering a *psychological*, rather than biological *explanation*. These explanations can all be considered to be *deterministic*; we have no free will to influence our genetic make-up, brain chemistry, early experiences or the automatic learning processes that may lead to developing OCD.

Treatment and management

Biological

SSRIs

OCD can be treated with a range of different drug therapies, including anti-depressants and anti-anxiety medication. The most used medications to treat OCD are SSRIs. We considered the use of SSRIs in treating

depressive disorder earlier on (section on Treatment and management in Section 6.2). They have also been used to treat OCD. These medications work by blocking the serotonin from being reabsorbed once a message has been passed from one neuron to another, meaning that serotonin levels remain higher. In a meta-analysis, Soomro et al. (2008) reviewed the results of 17 studies (with a total of 3097 participants) which compared the effectiveness of SSRIs with placebos. The studies used Y-BOCS to measure OCD symptoms. In all studies SSRIs as a group were more effective than placebos at reducing OCD symptoms 6–13 weeks after treatment. The effect of taking SSRIs to treat OCD is that they reduce the severity of obsessive-compulsive symptoms as they seem to lessen the anxiety associated with the disorder. They have been shown to work in individuals with and without depressive disorder, although generally a higher dosage of medication is given to treat OCD than is used to treat depressive disorder, as it has been shown to be more effective (Pampaloni et al., 2009).

Psychological

Exposure and response prevention (ERP)

Exposure and response prevention (ERP) is a form of CBT. Individuals are exposed to stimuli that provoke their obsessions and the associated distress, while at the same time they are helped to prevent their compulsive behaviours. For example, an individual may be exposed to a door handle, which would elicit obsessions surrounding dirt and germs, along with a strong desire to carry out a compulsion such as handwashing. The individual is helped to not wash their hands but instead to tolerate the anxiety and learn to accept their obsession and become **habituated** to it (to get used to it). The key thing is to prevent the compulsive behaviour as a response to the obsessive thought. This helps the individual to learn that the uncomfortable feelings will eventually go away even without preforming a compulsive behaviour.

Example study

Lehmkuhl et al. (2008) researched the application of this form of treatment in a case study with a 12-year-old boy referred to as Jason who had both OCD and autism

KEY WORDS

habituated: when a person becomes accustomed to something. When someone is frequently exposed to a certain stimulus then over time, they become used to it

spectrum disorder (ASD). Approximately 2% of children with ASD are also diagnosed with OCD. It can be difficult to distinguish ASD rituals and behaviour from compulsive behaviour seen in OCD; however, cleaning, checking and counting tend to be common in those with OCD. Jason had been diagnosed with high-functioning autism (normal IQ score), and experienced contamination fear, excessive handwashing, counting and checking. He would spend several hours each day engaged in compulsive behaviour and reported significant anxiety when prevented from completing his rituals. Jason attended ten 50-minute CBT sessions over 16 weeks. Some of the ERP techniques were modified to meet Jason's specific ASD needs; he was not asked to do visualisation exercises as he would find it impossible to imagine pretend situations. Jason first identified feelings of distress and with the help of the therapist, learned coping statements for when he felt anxious (e.g. 'I know that nothing bad will happen…').

The next step involved exposing Jason to stimuli which he felt were contaminated and produced feelings of anxiety or disgust. These include common objects such as door handles and elevator buttons. The exposure involved Jason being asked to touch these items, and repeatedly to do so until he became habituated, and his anxiety levels dropped. Exposures became increasingly difficult, so that Jason was engaging in behaviours that held increasing anxiety for him. In between sessions, he practised this exposure through specific tasks in his normal environment, handing out papers in a classroom or using 'contaminated' items at home.

After completing his therapy, Jason's score on the Y-BOCS had dropped from a severely high pre-therapy score of 18 to just 3, well within the normal range. At a three-month follow-up his score remained low, and both he and his parents reported a significant improvement in both his OCD symptoms and his participation in school and social activities.

Cognitive-behavioural therapy (CBT)

We have learned about CBT as an effective treatment throughout this chapter and the basic principles are no different when using CBT to treat OCD. CBT works by understanding and then challenging the irrational thoughts held by the individual to bring out positive change in their emotional and behavioural responses.

Key study: Lovell et al. (2006)

Lovell, K., Cox, D., Haddock, G., Jones, C., Raines, D., Garvey, R.,... & Hadley, S. (2006). Telephone administered cognitive behaviour therapy for treatment of obsessive compulsive disorder: randomised controlled non-inferiority trial. *British medical journal, 333*(7574), 883.

Context

Vast amounts of research, including from the National Institute for Clinical Excellence (NICE) in the UK, have shown that CBT can be a very effective treatment for those suffering with OCD. CBT traditionally requires a face-to-face session (45–60 minutes) once a week for several weeks. Carried out in this traditional way makes CBT an expensive treatment and also makes it very time-consuming, which results in long waiting lists.

Not only does this mean that patients will need to wait a long time to receive treatment, it also means that during this waiting time there is the potential for their OCD to become more severe, which in turn may mean that it will be more difficult to treat and therefore take longer, which will add to the waiting time for others. There have been many attempts to try to ease waiting times and make CBT more accessible. Two of these approaches are computerised CBT and facilitated self-help, both of which have been shown to be helpful to some extent.

Main theories and explanations

Offering CBT over the phone can be beneficial in several ways. By offering shorter telephone sessions this would reduce the waiting lists experienced by the provision of the traditional face to face sessions. This would benefit not only the patients by reducing the length of time they need to wait for treatment, but will also relieve the pressure on resources for whoever provides the CBT. As well as the reduced waiting time, telephone CBT can offer a more accessible way for patients to be treated. Some patients may not have their own transport, or be able to afford to pay for public transport to attend a face to face appointment each week. In addition, it may be more difficult to fit in a face to face appointment around work, family or other commitments, whereas a telephone call would be easier to manage and would take less time. In addition to these general difficulties faced to attend face to face appointments it is important to consider that people suffering from OCD are likely to find it difficult and anxiety-provoking to travel and go to a new environment for a face to face appointment. Mohr et al. (2000) suggested that CBT delivered by phone has been increasing, which offers more accessible support to those who cannot attend a clinic. Research by Taylor et al. (2003) has shown that, compared to face-to-face CBT, telephone delivered CBT can be an effective, and less expensive, treatment for individuals with OCD.

Aims

The aim was to compare the effectiveness of CBT carried out by telephone with CBT carried out face to face, in the treatment of OCD. It was hypothesised that outcomes would be similar for both methods used.

Design

A randomised controlled trial was used to compare exposure therapy and response prevention delivered by traditional 60-minute face-to-face sessions, or by shorter telephone sessions (up to 30 minutes each). Ten weekly sessions were provided for participants in each condition.

The sample consisted of 72 participants, diagnosed with OCD, and aged between 16 and 65 years old. All participants were from the UK and attended one of two outpatient clinics. Participants all scored at least 16 on the Yale-Brown obsessive-compulsive checklist (self-report version; Y-BOCS) and did not suffer from substance misuse or other conditions such as severe depressive disorder. Participants were randomly assigned to either the telephone or the face-to-face condition, making this an independent measures design.

Two experienced therapists carried out the treatments (one at each clinic carried out both types). Consistency of treatment was maintained by use of therapist manuals, fortnightly supervision sessions and four-monthly training days.

Prior to treatment, all participants were assessed twice, four weeks apart, using the Y-BOCS to measure the severity of their OCD and Beck Depression Inventory (BDI), to measure feelings of depressive disorder. Participants were then assessed, using these measures, immediately after treatment and then at one-, three- and six-month follow-ups. Patients were also given a client satisfaction questionnaire. The researchers who assessed the participants before and after treatment did not know which condition they were in, to protect against any potential bias from the researchers.

Results, findings and conclusions

Results (see Figure 6.23) showed that the mean Y-BOCS score prior to treatment was 25 (indicating OCD of marked severity). Prior to treatment there was no significant difference between the mean scores for Y-BOCS or the BDI between the two conditions. At all four time points (immediately after treatment, one month later, three months later and six months later) clinical outcome was equivalent for each condition. Mean scores on the Y-BOCS dropped significantly between the

initial scores and those following treatment. Treatment was classed as 'clinically relevant' if the Y-BOCS mean pre-treatment score dropped by two standard deviations or more after treatment. This was found to be the case in 72% of the patients (77% in the telephone condition and 67% in the face-to-face treatment condition). Scores on the client satisfaction questionnaire showed that patients were very satisfied with their treatment and that these results were similar across both treatment conditions.

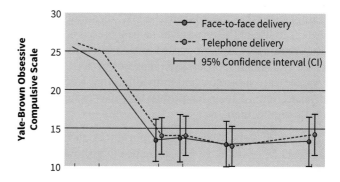

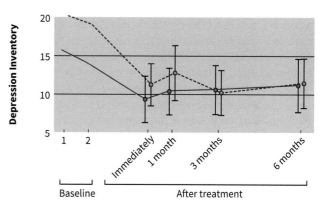

Figure 6.23: The change in scores on the Y-BOCS and BDI for first visit to six-month follow-up in the study by Lovell et al. (2006)

The researchers concluded that clinical outcome of CBT delivered by telephone was equivalent to CBT carried out face to face at all four time points. Additionally, participants reported similarly high levels of satisfaction across both treatment conditions. This suggests that patients with OCD may benefit equally from CBT delivered over the phone, with reduced contact time, as with traditional face-to-face CBT.

Evaluation

The research by Lovell et al. (2006) used an *independent measures* experimental design in which participants were randomly allocated to one of two conditions. Random allocation to the conditions removed the possibility of researcher bias (the researchers didn't choose who to put in which condition) The face-to-face CBT group acted as the control group for the experiment, meaning researchers could compare the effectiveness of telephone therapy to standard face-to-face CBT. The duration of the therapy was kept the same in both conditions, and outcomes were measured using the same validated scales. This meant the study had high levels of validity and reliability. However, the study used a relatively small sample, and they are all from the UK, meaning the extent to which the results can be generalised is limited. Self-report measures were used, which can lead to lower validity as the responses given may not be accurate. Answers are subjective and individuals may not give a true account of their symptoms: they may exaggerate or downplay them.

Lovell et al.'s study has really important applications to real life. Lovell et al. have evidence that shows that a cheaper and more accessible alternative to traditional CBT can be equally as effective as the face-to-face approach. This has implications first to providers, such as the NHS in the UK: if there is less contact time required with therapists then this means over-the-phone CBT is a more cost-effective approach, which means funds will stretch further. Over-the-phone CBT also benefits the patients because it increases the accessibility. As the individual doesn't need to attend a clinic, it will be, at the very least, easier for them, but could also potentially overcome huge obstacles as some individuals with OCD may struggle to leave their home. Another benefit to patients is that over-the-phone CBT will lead to shorter waiting lists so patients can get the help they need sooner.

The study by Lovell et al. (2006) raises the debate of *biological versus psychological treatments*. As we have discovered throughout this chapter, both biological treatments, such as antipsychotics and anti-depressants, and psychological treatments, such as CBT and systematic desensitisation have strengths and weaknesses. Lovell et al. (2006) investigate the effectiveness of CBT face to face compared to via the phone, however this purely focuses on psychological treatments. Psychological treatments may be considered to be superior to biological treatments in that they help the patient deal with the source of the problem; allow them to learn techniques that they can use again if necessary; and allow the patient to take responsibility for their treatment. In comparison, biological treatments are generally quicker, easier, and cheaper, which can make them a more appealing

option. Lovell et al.'s research into a method of administering CBT that is quicker and therefore cheaper than other ways of administering CBT, is a great way to mitigate these factors.

CONTINUED

In terms of *individual vs situational explanations*, the use of SSRIs to manage OCD treats only one aspect: the individual's serotonin uptake. This treatment does not alter their environment or take into consideration what might have caused the OCD symptoms to emerge in the first place. In this way SSRIs can be seen as limited and, instead, ideally, treatment would consider both individual and situational factors.

Questions

13 Compare the two assessment tools (MOCI and Y-BOCS) outlined in this section. What are the advantages or disadvantages of each?

14 Freud suggests that OCD appears as a result of unresolved conflicts during childhood. Why might it be difficult to investigate this?

15 Why do you think Lovell et al. (2006) did not include a third group of OCD patients who received no therapy during the experiment?

SELF-EVALUATION CHECKLIST

After studying this chapter, copy and complete a table like this:

I can	Fully confident	Fairly confident	Need to revisit	Workbook	Coursebook
describe diagnostic criteria for schizophrenia					
describe, evaluate, compare and apply explanations of schizophrenia					
describe, evaluate, compare and apply treatments of schizophrenia					
describe diagnostic criteria for mood disorders					
describe, evaluate, compare and apply explanations of mood disorders					
describe, evaluate, compare and apply treatments of mood disorders					
describe diagnostic criteria for impulse control disorders					
describe, evaluate, compare and apply explanations of impulse control disorders					
describe, evaluate, compare and apply treatments of impulse control disorders					
describe diagnostic criteria for anxiety disorders and fear-related disorders					

CONTINUED

After studying this chapter, copy and complete a table like this:

I can	Fully confident	Fairly confident	Need to revisit	Workbook	Coursebook
describe, evaluate, compare and apply explanations of anxiety disorders and fear-related disorders					
describe, evaluate, compare and apply treatments of anxiety disorders and fear-related disorders					
describe diagnostic criteria for obsessive-compulsive disorder					
describe, evaluate, compare and apply explanations of obsessive-compulsive disorder					
describe, evaluate, compare and apply treatments of obsessive-compulsive disorder.					

PROJECT

Your task is to create a poster, leaflet or presentation describing and evaluating one of the treatments you have learned about in this chapter. You can work in pairs or small groups to complete this task.

In your pairs, select one of the treatments you have learned about in this chapter. You could either choose the one you find the most interesting, or the one you feel you understand the most. Or, if you want to challenge yourself, you could pick a treatment that you found a bit more difficult to understand or that you find more difficult to remember.

Next, you need to choose what item to produce. This could be either a poster, leaflet, presentation or something else if you prefer.

Whichever way you choose to present your information you must make sure to include the following:

- The name of the treatment and the disorder it is used to treat.

- A brief description of the disorder (just a few points).

- A brief summary of the explanation for the disorder that best fits the treatment you have chosen. For example, if you have chosen antipsychotics as a treatment for schizophrenia you would describe the dopamine hypothesis as the explanation. If you have chosen Beck's cognitive restructuring as a treatment for depressive disorder (unipolar) you would describe Beck's cognitive theory as the explanation.

- A detailed description of the treatment, focusing on how it works and relating it back to the explanation you summarised previously.

CONTINUED

- A study that relates to your chosen treatment (if you wish to).

- Evaluation of the treatment. This can include:

  - research methods

  - issues and debates

  - Alternative treatments (if you have chosen a biological treatment, you might challenge it with a psychological treatment)

  - Any other strengths or weaknesses of the treatment

Make sure to plan your work before you start. You should also consider illustrations and choice of colour to make your presentation eye-catching.

Finally, plan how to present this to the rest of the class. It is important to plan and rehearse the presentation, so it goes smoothly when you present to your audience.

The presentation to the rest of the class is important, not only as part of your project but also so that everyone can benefit from each other's work.

REFLECTION

Once you have completed the project, it is important to spend some time thinking about what you did well and why it worked well, as well as considering anything that didn't work so well and why that might be so that you can improve your strategy for future tasks.

Consider the following points about how you worked as a team on your project:

- How did you work as a team? Did you or your partner take the lead role, or did you work equally together?

- In what ways did this work and in what ways could you change and improve things next time?

- Did you have any disagreements with your partner? If so, why do you think that was? How did you resolve the disagreement and what have you learned from it?

EXAM-STYLE QUESTIONS

1 a **Define** the term 'positive symptom' in schizophrenia and give **one** example of a positive symptom. [2]

   b Define the term 'negative symptom' in schizophrenia and give **one** example of a negative symptom. [2]

2 a **Describe** the genetic explanation of schizophrenia. [4]

   b Choose **two** other explanations of schizophrenia, and compare them. [6]

3 a Briefly describe Beck's cognitive theory of depression. [2]

   b Describe learned helplessness and attributional style as an explanation for depressive disorder (unipolar). Use a study to help explain your answer. [4]

4 a Describe tricyclics, MAOIs and SSRIs as treatments for depressive disorder (unipolar). [6]

   b **Compare** any **two** of these treatments. [4]

COMMAND WORDS

define: give precise meaning

compare: identify/comment on similarities and/or differences

CONTINUED

5 a Describe the diagnostic criteria for each for the following:

    i kleptomania [3]

    ii pyromania [3]

    iii Gambling disorder. [3]

b **Evaluate** K-SAS as a measure of kleptomania. [4]

6 a Answer the following questions about the key study: treating pathological gamblers with drugs and placebo: Grant et al. (2008):

    i Describe the sample. [2]

    ii Describe what is meant by a placebo, and why it was used in the study. [4]

    iii State the results of the study. [2]

    iv Evaluate the study. [4]

b Describe **one** psychological treatment for impulse control disorders. Use a study to help explain your answer. [6]

7 Consider the determinism versus free will debate in relation to the explanations of anxiety and fear-related disorders. [6]

8 a **Explain** systematic desensitisation as a treatment for agoraphobia. [4]

b Answer the following questions about the key study: treating 'medical procedure' phobia with applied tension: Chapman and DeLapp (2014):

    i Outline the aim of this study. [2]

    ii Identify the research method used. [1]

    iii **Give one** strength and **one** weakness of this research method in relation to this study. [4]

    iv Identify **two** of the self-report questionnaires used for data collection. [2]

    v Give **one** strength and **one** weakness of using these questionnaires. [4]

9 a **Analyse two** measures used to assess OCD. [4]

b Evaluate the use of psychometric tests such as those used to assess OCD. [6]

10 a Briefly **outline** the procedure and findings of the key study: CBT for obsessive-compulsive disorder: Lovell et al. (2006). [4]

b Evaluate the study by Lovell et al. (2006). [10]

[Total: 108]

COMMAND WORDS

analyse: examine in detail to show meaning, identify elements and the relationship between them

outline: set out the main points

Additional references

Agras, W. S. (1967). Transfer during systematic desensitization therapy. *Behaviour research and therapy*, 5(3), 193–199.

Aneja, J., Singhai, K., & Paul, K. (2018). Very early-onset psychosis/schizophrenia: case studies of spectrum of presentation and management issues. *Journal of family medicine and primary care*, 7(6), 1566.

Beck, A. T. (Ed.). (1979). *Cognitive therapy of depression*. Guilford Press.

Blaszczynski, A., & Nower, L. (2003). Imaginal desensitisation: a relaxation-based technique for impulse control disorders. *Journal of clinical activities, assignments & handouts in psychotherapy practice*, *2*(4), 1–14.

den Boer, J. A., & Westenberg, H. G. (1992). Oxytocin in obsessive compulsive disorder. *Peptides*, *13*(6), 1083–1085.

Comings, D. E., & Blum, K. (2000). Reward deficiency syndrome: genetic aspects of behavioral disorders. *Progress in brain research*, *126*, 325–341.

Ellis, A. (1962). *Reason and emotion in psychotherapy*. Lyle Stuart.

Esfahani, S., Motaghipour, Y., Kamkari, K., Zahiredin, A., & Janbozorgi, M. (2012). Reliability and validity of the Persian version of the Yale-Brown Obsessive-Compulsive Scale (Y-BOCS). (English). *Iranian journal of psychiatry and clinical psychology*, *17*(4), 297–303.

Fournier, J. C., DeRubeis, R. J., Hollon, S. D., Dimidjian, S., Amsterdam, J. D., Shelton, R. C., & Fawcett, J. (2010). Antidepressant drug effects and depression severity: a patient-level meta-analysis. *Journal of the American Medical Association*, *303*(1), 47–53.

Freud, S. (1909). Analysis of a phobia in a five-year old boy. *The Standard Edition of the Complete Psychological Works of Sigmund Freud*, *10*(3). Hogarth Press.

Frith, C. D. (1992). *The cognitive neuropsychology of schizophrenia*. Psychology Press.

Glover, J. H. (2011). A case of kleptomania treated by covert sensitization. *British journal of clinical psychology*, *24*(3), 213–214.

Goodman, W. K., Price, L. H., Rasmussen, S. A., Mazure, C., Fleischmann, R. L., Hill, C. L., ... & Charney, D. S. (1989). The Yale-Brown Obsessive Compulsive Scale: I. Development, use, and reliability. *Archives of general psychiatry*, *46*(11), 1006–1011.

Gottesman, I. I. (1991). *Schizophrenia genesis: the origins of madness*. WH Freeman/Times Books/Henry Holt & Co.

Hilker, R., Helenius, D., Fagerlund, B., Skytthe, A., Christensen, K., Werge, T. M., ... & Glenthøj, B. (2017). Is an early age at illness onset in schizophrenia associated with increased genetic susceptibility? Analysis of data from the Nationwide Danish Twin Register. *eBiomedicine*, *18*, 320–326.

Hodgson, R. J., & Rachman, S. (1977). Obsessional-compulsive complaints. *Behaviour research and therapy*, *15*(5), 389–395.

Iftene, F., Predescu, E., Stefan, S., & David, D. (2015). Rational-emotive and cognitive-behavior therapy (REBT/CBT) versus pharmacotherapy versus REBT/CBT plus pharmacotherapy in the treatment of major depressive disorder in youth: a randomized clinical trial. *Psychiatry research*, *225*(3), 687–694.

Kim, S. W., Grant, J. E., Adson, D. E., & Shin, Y. C. (2001). Double-blind naltrexone and placebo comparison study in the treatment of pathological gambling. *Biological psychiatry*, *49*(11), 914–921.

Kimura, H. K., Kennedy, T. D., & Rhodes, L. E. (1972). Recurring assessment of changes in phobic behavior during the course of systematic desensitization. *Behaviour research and therapy*, *10*(3), 279–282.

Leckman, J. F., Goodman, W. K., North, W. G., Chappell, P. B., Price, L. H., Pauls, D. L., ... & Cohen, D. J. (1994). The role of central oxytocin in obsessive compulsive disorder and related normal behavior. *Psychoneuroendocrinology*, *19*(8), 723–749.

Lehmkuhl, H. D., Storch, E. A., Bodfish, J. W. & Geffken, G. R. (2008) Brief report: exposure and response prevention for obsessive compulsive disorder in a 12-year-old with autism. *Journal of autism and developmental disorders*, *38*(5), 977–981.

Lindström, L. H., Gefvert, O., Hagberg, G., Lundberg, T., Bergström, M., Hartvig, P., & Långström, B. (1999). Increased dopamine synthesis rate in medial prefrontal cortex and striatum in schizophrenia indicated by L-(β-11C) DOPA and PET. *Biological psychiatry*, *46*(5), 681–688.

Lyons, L. C., & Woods, P. J. (1991). The efficacy of rational-emotive therapy: a quantitative review of the outcome research. *Clinical psychology review*, *11*(4), 357–369.

Mas, M. B., Jiménez, A. M. L., & San Gregorio, M. Á. P. (2010). Blood-injection Phobia Inventory (BIPI): development, reliability and validity. *Anales de psicología*, *26*(1), 58–71.

Mattheisen, M., Samuels, J. F., Wang, Y., Greenberg, B. D., Fyer, A. J., McCracken, J. T., ... & Nestadt, G. (2015). Genome-wide association study in obsessive-compulsive disorder: results from the OCGAS. *Molecular psychiatry*, *20*(3), 337–344.

McGuffin, P., Owen, M., O'Donovan, M., Thapar, A., & Gottesman, I. (1994). *Seminars in psychiatric genetics*. London: College Seminars Series, 110–127.

Miller, R. (2010). The feeling-state theory of impulse-control disorders and the impulse-control disorder protocol. *Traumatology*, *16*(3), 2–10.

Mohr, D. C., Likosky, W., Bertagnolli, A., Goodkin, D. E., Van Der Wende, J., Dwyer, P., & Dick, L. P. (2000). Telephone-administered cognitive–behavioral therapy for the treatment of depressive symptoms in multiple sclerosis. *Journal of consulting and clinical psychology*, *68*(2), 356.

Monterosso, J., Flannery, B. A., Pettinati, H. M., Oslin, D. W., Rukstalis, M., O'Brien, C. P., & Volpicelli, J. (2001). Predicting treatment response to naltrexone: the influence of craving and family history. *The American journal on addictions*, *10*(3), 258–268.

Monzani, B., Rijsdijk, F., Harris, J., & Mataix-Cols, D. (2014). The structure of genetic and environmental risk factors for dimensional representations of DSM-5 obsessive-compulsive spectrum disorders. *Journal of the American Medical Association: psychiatry*, *71*(2), 182–189.

National Institute for Clinical Excellence (NICE) (2015). Guidance on the use of electroconvulsive therapy. Retreived from www.nice.org/guidance/ta59.

Nestler, E. J. (1997). Schizophrenia–an emerging pathophysiology. *Nature*, *385*(6617), 578–579.

O'Brien, C. P. (2005). Anti-craving (relapse prevention) medications: possible a new class of psychoactive medication. *The American journal of psychiatry*, *162*, 1423–1431.

Öst, L. G. (1992). Blood and injection phobia: background and cognitive, physiological, and behavioural variables. *Journal of abnormal psychology*, *101*(1), 68–74.

Ozaki, N., Goldman, D., Kaye, W. H., Plotnicov, K., Greenberg, B. D., Lappalainen, J., ... & Murphy, D. L. (2003). Serotonin transporter missense mutation associated with a complex neuropsychiatric phenotype. *Molecular psychiatry*, *8*(11), 933–936.

Pampaloni, I., Sivakumaran, T., Hawley, C. J., Al Allaq, A., Farrow, J., Nelson, S., Fineberg, N. A. (2009). High-dose selective serotonin reuptake inhibitors in OCD: a systematic retrospective case notes survey. *Journal of psychopharmacology, 28,* 596–602.

Pittenger, C., & Bloch, M. H. (2014). Pharmacological treatment of obsessive-compulsive disorder. *Psychiatric clinics*, *37*(3), 375–391.

Rachman, S. (1977). The conditioning theory of fear acquisition: a critical examination. *Behaviour research and therapy*, *15*(5), 375–387.

Rapoport, J. L. (1989) *The Boy Who Couldn't Stop Washing*. New York: Plume.

Rothbaum, B. O., Hodges, L., Smith, S., Lee, J. H., & Price, L. (2000). A controlled study of virtual reality exposure therapy for the fear of flying. *Journal of consulting and clinical psychology*, *68*(6), 1020.

Sensky,T., Turkington, D., Kingdon, D., Scott, J. L., Scott, J., Siddle, R., O'Carroll, M. & Barnes, T. R. (2000). A randomized controlled trial of cognitive-behavioral therapy for persistent symptoms in schizophrenia resistant to medication. *Archives of general psychiatry*, *57*(2), 165–172.

Slater, M., Pertaub, D. P., & Steed, A. (1999). Public speaking in virtual reality: facing an audience of avatars. *IEEE computer graphics and applications*, *19*(2), 6–9.

Soomro, G. M., Altman, D. G., Rajagopal, S., & Browne, M. O. (2008). Selective serotonin re-uptake inhibitors (SSRIs) versus placebo for obsessive compulsive disorder (OCD). *Cochrane database of systematic reviews*, (1).

Szechtman, H., Sulis, W., & Eilam, D. (1998). Quinpirole induces compulsive checking behavior in rats: a potential animal model of obsessive-compulsive disorder (OCD). *Behavioral neuroscience*, *112*(6), 1475.

Spitzer, R. L., Kroenke, K., Williams, J. B., & Lowe, B. (2006). A brief measure for assessing generalised anxiety disorder: the GAD-7. *Archives of internal medicine*, *166*(10), 1092–1097.

Taylor, S., Thordarson, D. S., Spring, T., Yeh, A. H., Corcoran, K. M., Eugster, K., & Tisshaw, C. (2003). Telephone-administered cognitive behavior therapy for obsessive-compulsive disorder. *Cognitive behaviour therapy*, *32*(1), 13–25.

Tienari, P., Wynne, L. C., Moring, J., Läksy, K., Nieminen, P., Sorri, A., ... & Miettunen, J. (2000). Finnish adoptive family study: sample selection and adoptee DSM-III-R diagnoses. *Acta psychiatrica Scandinavica*, *101*(6), 433–443.

Watson, J. B., & Rayner, R. (1920). Conditioned emotional reactions. *Journal of experimental psychology*, *3*(1), *1*.

Wiles, N., Thomas, L., Abel, A., Ridgway, N., Turner, N., Campbell, J., ... & Lewis, G. (2013). Cognitive behavioural therapy as an adjunct to pharmacotherapy for primary care based patients with treatment resistant depression: results of the CoBalT randomised controlled trial. *The lancet*, *381*(9864), 375–384.

Wise, C. D., Baden, M. M., & Stein, L. (1974). Post-mortem measurement of enzymes in human brain: evidence of a central noradrenergic deficit in schizophrenia. *Journal of psychiatric research, 11,* 185–198.

Wolpe, J. (1958). Psychotherapy by reciprocal inhibition. *Conditional reflex: a Pavlovian journal of research & therapy*, *3*(4), 234–240.

> Chapter 7

Consumer psychology

In this chapter, you will learn how to:

- describe, evaluate and compare research into the influence of the physical environment in consumer psychology, including applying the findings of the topic area to the real world

- describe, evaluate and compare research into the influence of the psychological environment in consumer psychology, including applying the findings of the topic area to the real world

- describe, evaluate and compare theories behind consumer decision-making, including applying the findings of the topic area to the real world

- describe, evaluate and compare psychological theories on selling, buying and gifting of products, including applying the findings of the topic area to the real world

- describe, evaluate and compare research into advertising, including applying the findings of the topic area to the real world.

Introduction

This chapter will introduce you to a range of different aspects of consumer psychology. You will learn about the importance of the physical environment, in terms of how the look, sound and smell of a store or restaurant influence a consumer's behaviour. You will learn about the importance of the psychological environment, in terms of finding your way around a shopping centre, the design of a menu and the effect of personal space. You will also find out about different theories to explain our decision-making processes and the mistakes we can make. The product itself will be explored, in terms of how it is presented and how it can be sold effectively. Finally, you will learn different types of advertising technique and how this leads to brand awareness.

Throughout the chapter, you will explore relevant issues and debates and you will revisit research methods as they relate to each topic. We will look at example studies throughout the chapter, where we will summarise the study, including the key findings, and use this to help understand the topics. We will also look at five key studies in more detail, and will consider the background and context to the study as well as details about the procedure, results and conclusions. We will also evaluate the key studies in terms of both methodological evaluation and relevant issues and debates. When you have finished this chapter, you should have a good understanding about consumer psychology and understand how the research can be applied to everyday life.

GETTING STARTED

What is consumer psychology? This is a relatively new area of applied psychology which looks at why and how individuals and groups engage in consumer behaviours (Boyd-Jannson, 2010). A consumer is anyone who purchases goods or services, so this could relate to people shopping in supermarkets, eating and drinking in restaurants or buying cars from a dealership.

You may be able to think of some applications already based on the psychology you learned in your AS course. Social psychology may be relevant when considering issues such as attitudes and how these attitudes may be changed, as well as the effects of other people on our consumer behaviours. Can you think of ways in which other people might influence your consumer behaviour? How might other people affect what you buy, where you shop or how much you spend?

The learning approach is also important in considering how advertisers might use knowledge about classical and operant conditioning to develop successful advertising techniques. Thinking about what you know already about classical and operant conditioning, how might this relate to advertising? What associations might be made? What responses might happen?

Aspects of the cognitive approach such as memory and decision-making are also crucial in understanding how individuals make sense of advertisements and other marketing techniques. Why is memory important in advertising? Think of

some adverts that you can easily recall: why can you remember them so well? Are there adverts that you can remember but don't remember what they are advertising? Why might this happen?

Finally, although there is little biological research in this chapter, some recent research has made use of fMRI technology to see if it is possible to predict the decisions that we might make before we respond to questions. EEG scanning has been used to measure our frustration levels when viewing adverts. Eye-scanning has been used to measure where we look on a shelf when choosing a product. What are the strengths of these biological methods?

Much of the research that we will be covering in this chapter uses research methods that will be familiar to you from other parts of your course. The same evaluation issues will also be relevant to this research. As consumer psychology relates to behaviour in the real world, it is particularly important to consider this when looking at *laboratory experiments* compared to *field experiments*. Why is it particularly an issue to use laboratory experiments when investigating consumer psychology? Why might it be then that field experiments aren't always used to study consumer psychology?

Before reading any further, think about all the psychology that you have learned so far. Make a note of all the things you can think of that might be relevant to the study of consumer behaviour.

7.1 The physical environment

The physical environment of a shop or restaurant is an important influence on the atmosphere of the place, and will be a big part of what makes a consumer enjoy their experience. The physical environment refers to the interior and exterior design of the setting, as well as other factors that influence the ambience, such as sound and scent.

Retail store design

Types of store exterior design

Before even entering a shop, there are exterior design features which influence the views and feelings of the shopper. Exterior features including storefront, window displays and landscaping are all important in making a positive impression on potential customers. These features are particularly important for small, independent shops that cannot rely on their big brands to draw in customers.

Most research into the influence of store exteriors uses the **stimulus-organism-response (S-O-R) model** (Babin et al., 2003), which assumes that the stimuli, such as physical environment, affects consumer's attitude, which further affects behaviour (see the section The effect of ambience: the pleasure-arousal-dominance (PAD) model for more detail).

In terms of landscaping, evidence tends to show that the presence of vegetation positively influences the moods of respondents who live in an urban setting (Sheets & Manzer, 1991) so it is logical that a shop with landscaping outside would give a positive impression. Chebat and Morrin (2007) used plants and flowers to decorate malls and found this to have positive effects on shoppers' perception of the environment and on their perception of the quality of the products.

In terms of window displays, this is the best chance a shop has of showing potential customers what they can expect in the store. Edwards and Shackley (1992) found that sales were higher for stores that used window displays compared to stores that did not, and that a larger window display is more effective than a smaller one. A successful window display was aesthetically pleasing, used lighting effectively, had a theme and used warm colours.

Example study

Mower et al. (2012) investigated the effects of both window display and landscaping on consumer responses in terms of liking, mood and patronage intentions (whether they intended to go into the shop, buy anything from the shop, recommend the shop and revisit the shop). An online survey was conducted with a sample of 180 students (mostly female) from an American university. Participants were asked to imagine they need to buy a new pair of jeans, then they logged onto a website and read a description of a store exterior of a small clothes shop. All descriptions included detail of the building, but they varied as to whether they included descriptions of window displays, or not, and descriptions of landscaping, or not, to test the effects of these variables. Results showed that the presence of a window display and landscaping both positively influenced liking of the store exterior as well as intention to shop there. Furthermore, liking of store exteriors increased pleasure and arousal experienced, which in turn led to increased patronage intentions (see Figure 7.1)

Figure 7.1: An attractive store exterior influences consumer satisfaction

Types of store interior design

The interior design of the store is also significant in influencing consumer behaviour. There are three main layouts that can be used in stores (see Figure 7.2):

- Grid: the grid is the layout that is used in most supermarkets and other convenience stores. Products are displayed in long aisles, and customers weave up and down the aisles. Impulse items (such as treats) tend to be at the front and essential items (such as milk or rice) tend to be at the back. This is so that customers need to walk past other items such as impulse items on the way to get the essentials they need, which encourages them to spend more. The grid allows all similar items to be grouped together, and to keep different items apart; making it easier to shop where there are a range of different types of item, such as a supermarket. The grid is beneficial because it is easy and familiar to customers, allows for predictable traffic flow to help decide where to put promotions, and it is easy to construct shelving, etc. in this layout. The downsides to a grid layout may include confusion for customers if they don't understand the grouping of items, frustration if it is not possible for customers to go directly to the item they need, and the lack of creativity or interest of the layout.

- Freeform: as the name suggests, the freeform layout does not follow any specific rules or criteria, and customers are not deliberately forced to go in any direction. Customers are encouraged to wander and browse the items in the shop, often leading to impulse buys. It is best suited to shops with less merchandise but perhaps of higher value, such as boutiques or gift shops. If done well, a freeform layout can be a really positive experience for the customer, but it can be difficult to get right and can be cluttered or be confusing to the customer.

- Racetrack: the racetrack is designed so that the route taken by customers takes the form of a loop from the starting point, all the way around the store and past all the merchandise through to the check outs and the exit. This is used famously by IKEA, and other department stores. The main positive of a racetrack layout is that it leads to maximum exposure of merchandise to customers, encouraging more purchases. It also allows for a predictable traffic pattern, making it easy to place promotions and high-end products where they will be most visible. The downsides of a racetrack, however, is that customers are not able to browse as they wish, and they may find it frustrating and time-consuming if they are intending to buy specific items.

Grid layout:

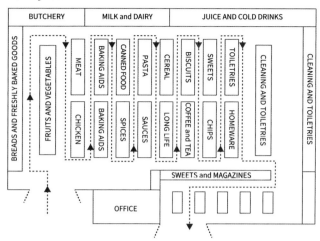

Freeform layout:

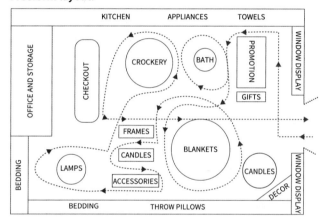

Racetrack layout:

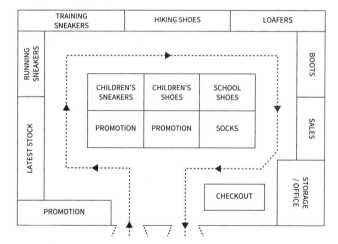

Figure 7.2: Grid, freeform and racetrack are three forms of store interior design

Work in pairs to design a high-end gift shop. Describe each feature of your shop and the justification for it. Remember to consider the sort of shop you are designing and who you are expecting your customers to be. Include features that relate to the exterior and interior of your shop.

Example study

Vrechopoulos et al. (2004) manipulated the layout of a virtual grocery store to reflect the three main layouts used in physical supermarkets: grid, freeform and racetrack. They proposed four *hypotheses*, based on the assumption that research findings based in physical shopping will also apply to virtual shopping:

- Hypothesis 1 Consumers will perceive the grid layout to be most useful for planned purchases.

- Hypothesis 2 Consumers will perceive the freeform layout to be easier to use in general.

- Hypothesis 3 The racetrack layout will be more entertaining than the other two layouts.

- Hypothesis 4 Consumers will spend more time shopping in the freeform layout.

To make the transition from real-life layouts to web-based shopping experiences there were several steps taken. The three layout patterns were analysed and the key features of each were transferred to a web-based virtual store layout. Other characteristics such as background colour, product images, speed and so on were kept the same across the three layouts. As a result of the analysis and transformation, the three store layouts were represented online as described:

- Grid: this involved a hierarchical structure (e.g., select product category, then select product subcategory, then select final product).

- Freeform: this involved being able to reach the desired products immediately, through either a search button or by selecting an item displayed on the page.

- Racetrack: customers are forced to navigate through specific paths to reach their desired products. Each page has a choice of two 'corridors' and customers must select one of these to continue in their search for their product.

One hundred and twenty participants were recruited from both Greece and the UK to take part in a laboratory experiment where they were given a planned shopping task with money to spend and completed this task in one of the three virtual store layouts. Each participant was given a budget of £20 (or 12 000 Greek drachmas) and whatever was 'purchased' during the experiment was subsequently purchased by the researchers and physically delivered to the participants.

The online store offered mainly European brands (e.g. Coca-Cola and Pringles) but also included some own-brand products. To make the online experience as similar to a real-life shopping trip as possible, participants were given a blank shopping list and information about what was available in the store in order to plan their purchases.

The results showed that the freeform layout was significantly more useful for finding items on a shopping list. It was also reported to be the most entertaining to use. The grid layout was reported to be significantly easier to use than the other two layouts (with the racetrack layout the hardest to use). Finally, the layout significantly affected the length of time that customers spent shopping, with the racetrack and freeform layouts engaging shoppers for longer, as would be predicted by conventional retail theory.

None of the researchers' hypotheses were found to be supported. Since the hypotheses were based on research into real-life shopping experiences, this suggest that such theories cannot be readily applicable to online grocery retail and that customers visiting a virtual grocery store prefer a hierarchical/tree structure. Such a structure is only provided by a grid layout which was perceived as the easiest to use. Shopping behaviour was also facilitated by being able to reach any place in the store directly (that is from the home page or from any other 'place' in the store). This was only provided by the freeform layout which was perceived as the most useful for conducting planned purchases.

Much research into the effect of store exterior design, such as Mower et al. (2012), has been carried out using *self-report* methods, such as surveys and *questionnaires*. These are a useful tool to use as they allow researchers to understand the thoughts and feelings of a consumer, rather than just viewing their behaviour. However, the main problems with these methods are that participants may not give an accurate or true account of their thoughts and feelings, or they may misunderstand the questions, thus reducing the *validity*. Furthermore, as Mower et al. asked participants hypothetical questions about the influence of store exterior on their purchase intentions, their research doesn't tell us about the influence on consumers' actual behaviour, so it lacks *ecological validity*. How could the ecological validity be increased? Vrechopoulos et al. (2004) used a laboratory experiment, with a virtual store, and, although this too lacked ecological validity, it had high *control* of variables, which increased the validity, and used a *standardised* procedure, which increased the *reliability*.

ISSUES AND DEBATES

Application of psychology to everyday life is relevant in research into retail store design because all the research is aimed at trying to understand consumer perceptions and feelings and the impact that these have on consumers' purchases. The findings of this research can be used to inform and advise owners of shops to allow them a better understanding of how to attract customers and therefore increase their profit.

Sound and consumer behaviour

Key study: North et al. (2003)

North, A. C., Shilcock, A., & Hargreaves, D. J. (2003). The effect of musical style on restaurant customers' spending. *Environment and behavior*, 35(5), 712–718.

Context

Research has shown that many factors, such as lighting, decoration and smell, can influence the atmosphere of retail environments. More specifically, research has shown the effect of different genres of background music in restaurants on customers' spending. Creating a certain atmosphere with the right genre of music can encourage people to spend more money, when compared to there being no music at all, as well as compared to other genres. North and Hargreaves (1998) investigated the effect of music genres on perception of a student cafeteria and intention to spend money. Classical music led to a perception of the cafeteria as being more upmarket and led to customers claiming they would spend more money, when compared to no music playing, or to other genres. Participants listening to classical music claimed they would spend 20.5% more than if no music was playing, 18.8% higher than easy listening music, and 3.7% higher than pop music. However, this research looked only at *intentions* to purchase, not actual spending.

Main theories and explanations

There are different explanations as to why music genres affect customers' spending. It can be as simple as the fact that if you are in a shop or a restaurant where there is music playing that you like, you will be more likely to stay for longer, and as a consequence, spend more. Other explanations suggest that the genre of music being played should encourage a particular mood in order to encourage spending. This may be a case of music to excite and arouse the customer, perhaps to encourage impulsive purchases, or it may be to relax the customer so they spend their money more freely. Research such as North and Hargreaves (above) suggests that customers in a retail environment, such as a restaurant, associate classical music with more affluence and wealth and so it **primes** them to spend more money.

KEY WORD

primed: you are 'ready' or 'prepared' to act in a certain way in a particular scenario

Aims

The aim of the study was to investigate the effect of musical style on the amount of money customers spent in a restaurant. It was predicted that classical music would lead to customers spending more money than pop music. The researchers were unsure of the effect of no music relative to classical music or pop music.

Design

The study was a field experiment, carried out at a restaurant. For one week there was classical music being played, for one week there was pop music being played and for one week there was no background music. The volume of the music remained consistent, and two 76-minute CDs were made for each condition, each featuring well-known classical or pop music. Aside from the change in music, all other aspects of the restaurant remained the same, including lighting, temperature and menu. The time spent between being seated and paying the bill was recorded, as this would affect the amount of money spent. Customer bills were collected and analysed, and an experimenter collected these data while working as a waitress in the restaurant.

The sample was made up of 393 customers who ate at the restaurant between February and March 2002. There was an approximately equal number of males and females, and approximately the same number of participants in each condition. Opportunity sampling was used: participants were customers who ate at the restaurant during the time of the research. The study used an independent measures design; where each participant was exposed to only one of the music conditions.

The *independent variable* was the background music played at the restaurant: pop music, classical music or no music. The *dependent variables* were spending on starters, main courses, desserts, coffees, bar drinks, wine, total spend on food, total spend on drinks and total overall spend.

Results, findings and conclusions

Results showed that for starters, coffee, total food and total overall spend, there was a significant difference in spending between conditions; for each of these categories, spending was highest in the classical music condition.

The researchers concluded that classical music led to significantly higher spending in restaurants, when compared to pop music or to no music. The results are in line with expectations, based on previous research.

Evaluation

North et al. used a field experiment, which has high ecological validity as it was carried out in a real-life setting so we can apply the results beyond the research setting. The experiment was also highly controlled as the researchers ensured all other aspects of the restaurant stayed the same throughout, and the music was played at the same volume, using the same set up of two CDs for each condition. This high level of control increases

the validity of the study as we can be more confident that the change in money spent was due to the change in music genre, rather than anything else. There was a large sample of almost 400 participants, allowing for large amounts of data to be collected, again increasing the validity of the study. Application to real life is relevant for North et al.'s research because it is investigating the way in which music affects how much money customers would spend in a restaurant. This was carried out over a series of nights at a real restaurant and the results clearly showed that customers spend more money when they are listening to classical music. This has implications for real life because restaurant owners and managers can use this information to make changes to their restaurant to help to increase their profit.

The effect of background noise on the perception of food taste

There is much evidence to show that background sounds associated with food can influence our experience of eating, in terms of taste and other properties, such as 'crispiness'. Zampini and Spence (2004) found that manipulating the sound made by biting a crisp (potato chip) (by recording it, making it louder and playing that sound through headphones) affected ratings of crispness and freshness. Broadly speaking, the evidence tends to show that sounds that are connected to the food (e.g. the sound of biting a crisp) influence experience of eating and tasting the food.

Example study

Woods et al. (2011) investigated whether sounds *not* directly associated with eating could still influence a person's perception of food. Forty-eight participants took part in Study 1, and each participant completed 25 trials, in each of three conditions. Participants sat at a table with their eyes closed and wearing headphones and were given bite-sized pieces of different foods to eat. There were three conditions: loud white noise, quiet white noise and no white noise, and the order of these conditions was *counterbalanced*. For each condition there were soft and hard foods in both salty and sweet tastes (salty; cheese and crisps; sweet; flapjack and biscuit) (see Figure 7.3). After eating each piece of food, participants were asked to rate the food for intensity of sweetness, saltiness and liking.

Results for Study 1 showed that sweetness and saltiness were both rated lower in the loud condition than in the quiet condition. Soft and hard foods were not affected differently, so it is concluded that background noises affect both soft and hard foods equally. Food liking appeared to be lowered by loud background noise, but this was not shown to be statistically significant. The researchers concluded that taste was reported to be less intense when in the noisy condition. Importantly, this was the case for both crunchy and soft food, so it does not appear to be linked to sounds associated with food or eating (see Zampini & Spence, 2004).

Figure 7.3: Does background noise affect taste perception?

Why does sound influence taste?

We will explore four different explanations for the effect of sound on taste.

A direct interaction between **sensory cortices**: each of our senses are processed in specific parts of our **cerebral cortex** and are generally processed independently of each other. However, some evidence (Teichert & Bolz, 2018) suggests that these sensory cortices can interact, for example, the area responsible for processing taste may interact directly with the area responsible for sound. Wesson and Wilson (2010) found that playing a continuous tone activated 19% of neurons in the **olfactory tubercle** of rats (usually associated with processing odour/taste). Furthermore, the response of 29% of these neurons to odour was changed when the tone was played, thus showing a direct effect of sound on odour. This could explain why sound can influence our experience of taste; the two senses are not processed completely independently of each other.

- **A cross-modal contrast:** a contrast effect is a cognitive bias where our perception of something is distorted when we compare it to something else. By enhancing the differences between the two things, our perception is distorted. For example, a drink tastes sweeter when drunk straight after something that is less sweet, compared to when you drink it after something sweeter. In terms of the effect of noise on taste, this explanation proposes that this contrast effect can occur across the senses. So, this would explain why, for example, hearing a loud noise might impair your ability to perceive a taste as intensely as you would without the loud noise.

- **Attentional:** this explanation suggests that the presence of a loud noise takes attention away from the taste experience, and this is responsible for the influence of noise on taste. Research by Boyle et al. (2006) shows that ratings of pain were lower when people experience loud background noise, compared to no noise. This suggests that the background noise distracts attention and therefore reduces the perception of pain. The same could be applied to the effect of noise on taste: a loud noise distracts attention and therefore reduces the ability to fully perceive taste.

- **Implicit association:** this explanation is based on the suggestion that certain types of noise are associated with certain tastes, although the cause for this is not yet known. Crisinel and Spence (2010) found that the names of bitter foods (such as coffee) and salty foods (such as crisps and salt) were associated with low pitch sounds. Sweet foods (such as sugar and honey) and sour foods (such as lime and lemon) were associated with high-pitch sounds. Therefore, it could be that different types of background noise could affect tastes differently, depending on their association.

RESEARCH METHODS

The study by Woods et al. used *repeated measures design*, where each participant completed 25 trials in all three conditions. The results could then be compared for each participant in each condition, thus removing the effect of *participant variables* and increasing the validity of the study. Furthermore, the study used counterbalancing, where the order of the conditions was different for different participants, to remove *order effects*. What would change if the researchers used an independent groups design instead?

ISSUES AND DEBATES

Individual versus situational explanations is relevant to the research in this section. For example, Woods et al. investigated the effects of background noise on taste, so they were studying situational explanations for our experiences. The results showed that sound did indeed influence our experience of taste and there were several explanations proposed to explain this, all of which focus on situational explanations. This suggests that our taste experience can be explained at least partially as a result of situational factors. However, individual factors might also be important, but these were not explored in this research.

Retail atmospherics

The effect of ambience: the pleasure-arousal-dominance (PAD) model

The pleasure-arousal-dominance model (**PAD model**) was developed by Mehrabian and Russell (1974) to demonstrate the way physical environments influence people through their emotional impact. Mehrabian and Russell proposed three dimensions of individuals'

emotions that influence their response to an environment: pleasure, arousal and dominance. Pleasure relates to the extent to which the consumer feels happy, content or satisfied. Arousal relates to the extent to which the consumer feels stimulated or excited. Dominance refers to the person's feeling of being in control.

Donovan and Rossiter (1982, cited in Mehrabian & Russell, 1974) applied this model to retail environments and concluded that dominance wasn't significantly relevant. They found, however, that pleasure and arousal interact. If the **ambience** (atmosphere) of a shop leads to an interaction of feelings of happiness and satisfaction (pleasure) and excitement and stimulation (arousal) the consumer is more likely to show 'approach' behaviours. These 'approach' behaviours include the desire to enter and explore the shop, to interact with staff and other customers and to be satisfied with the environment. However, if the ambience leads to feelings of dissatisfaction and boredom, the consumer is more likely to show 'avoidance' behaviour and choose not to spend time and money in the shop. Approach behaviours of course make a consumer more likely to make purchases and become loyal customers who return in the future.

KEY WORDS

PAD model: a model designed to demonstrate how physical environments influence people through emotional impact: pleasure, arousal and dominance

ambience: the atmosphere or 'feel' of a place, often affected by sound, scent and sight

The effects of odour on shopper pleasure-arousal-dominance

The background scent of an environment has become more and more important in recent years; with most retail environments using some sort of scent to encourage customers in and to increase their sense of satisfaction with their shopping experience. The scent can range from simple air fresheners to advanced aroma technology, and some companies (such as bakeries and cafes) have released synthetic scents (artificial scents of, e.g., baking and fresh coffee) to attract customers (Hunter, 1995).

Example study

Chebat and Michon (2003) investigated the influence of ambient odours on mall shoppers and compared the PAD model to a cognitive theory of emotions (Lazarus, 1991). A shopping mall in Canada was used in this study; in the control week nothing was changed (there was no ambient odour), and in the following week a light, pleasing scent was diffused into the mall's main corridor. A citrus scent was used as previous research has suggested that citrus is an effectively pleasing scent (Spangenberg et al., 1996). A sample of shoppers in each week were asked to complete a questionnaire about their shopping trip but were not told the purpose of the study.

As we have discussed, the PAD model suggests that ambient odour would influence consumers' mood, and therefore their approach/avoidance behaviours through the interaction between pleasure and arousal. In contrast, Lazarus' cognitive theory proposes that the ambient odour is perceived by consumers, but that this doesn't lead to a change in mood.

Chebat and Michon's study found that, although ambient scent increased arousal in consumers, it did not increase feelings of pleasure. It was found that pleasure and arousal do not mediate the effects of environmental cues on perceptions and behaviours. The findings did, however, support the cognitive model: that a light and pleasant ambient odour directly influenced consumers' perception of the shopping environment and product quality. Overall, this study has shown that a light and pleasant background odour does have a positive effect on consumers' perception of the shopping environment. However, it does not support the PAD model, it instead suggests that odour has a direct effect on perception without an influence on mood.

The effects of crowding on shopper pleasure-arousal-dominance

Crowding is just one of many physical aspects of a shopping environment that has been shown to affect the experience of the consumer. Perceived crowding occurs when a person's demand for space is exceeded by the supply (Stokols, 1972). Crowding will be affected by anything that restricts the amount of space a person requires or desires. Spatial crowding relates to the number of physical objects, whereas human crowding relates to the amount of people in a space (see Figure 7.4). Research by Eroglu and Machleit (1990) shows that perceived crowding can influence decisions about where to shop, as well as satisfaction with shopping experience.

KEY WORDS

spatial crowding: a person's demand for space is not met due to the high number of physical objects in a space

human crowding: a person's demand for space is not met due to the high number of people in a space

Figure 7.4: Human crowding can affect a person's satisfaction levels

Example study

Machleit et al. (2000) investigated how perceived crowding influenced the shoppers' satisfaction, and whether this relationship was moderated by emotions. A set of three studies were carried out. There were two field experiments, where samples of students and non-students were asked to complete a questionnaire about their shopping experience across a range of retail environments. There was one laboratory experiment, where students were asked to imagine they were going to a bookstore and then shown a video clip of the store, with spatial and human crowding density manipulated. Following this, they were asked to complete a questionnaire about their thoughts, feelings and perceptions of the bookstore.

The results of all three studies show that the effect of crowding on shopping satisfaction is complex. Perceived crowding, both in terms of spatial and human crowding, lowers satisfaction, and this effect is greater for spatial crowding.

In terms of the PAD model, the results of the two field studies show that emotions can partially mediate the effect of crowding on satisfaction. When pleasure and arousal are included as **mediating factors**, the crowding–satisfaction relationship (for both spatial and human crowding) drops but is still significant. This means that pleasure and arousal do appear to have some mediating effect on the influence of crowding on satisfaction but that there are other important factors as well, such as expectation and tolerance.

KEY WORD

mediating factors: any variable or process that affects the relationship between the stimulus and the response

RESEARCH METHODS

Machleit et al.'s use of two field experiments and one laboratory experiment is a good way of investigating perceived crowding as it enabled them to benefit from the strengths of both types of experiments. There is usually a trade-off between lab and field experiments in terms of ecological validity and control. A field experiment has high ecological validity and tells us about how people behave in a real-life setting, which is particularly important when investigating something such as consumer behaviour as it means we can *generalise* the findings more confidently beyond the research setting. However, the downside is that field experiments lack the high level of control achieved by laboratory experiments. By using both types of experiments, Machleit et al. have been able to get the best of both worlds, while understanding the weaknesses of each experiment type.

ISSUES AND DEBATES

Cultural differences are relevant in this section because it considers retail atmospherics. The research focuses on the influence of odour in a shopping mall and crowding across a range of different shops in Canada and the USA. It is important to consider the fact that these are two large Western developed cultures where large shopping malls and a wide range of different shops are the norms, and where shopping is considered a leisure activity, as well as part of daily life.

CONTINUED

In some cultures, however, shopping malls would not exist and any shops that were present would be smaller and based on need rather than leisure. Therefore, the findings of this research would not be applicable to all cultures.

Questions

1   Mower et al. (2012) investigated the effect of store exterior on consumer response using an online survey and a website with images of a store. How could you investigate the effects of store exterior in a real-life setting?

2   North et al. (2003) made sure they kept the volume of the music consistent, as well as using well-known music for both conditions. Why are these variables important?

3   Background noise has been shown to affect perception of food taste. Think of another situational factor that may affect perception of food taste and briefly outline how you would investigate this.

7.2 The psychological environment

Environmental influences on consumers

Wayfinding in shopping malls

Wayfinding refers to our ability to know where we are and to plan a route to where we are going. Certain tools can help us with wayfinding, for example to find our way around a shopping mall, we may rely on maps and signs.

KEY WORD

wayfinding: refers to our ability to know where we are and to plan a route to where we are going. Certain tools can help us with wayfinding, for example to find our way around a shopping mall, we may rely on maps and signs

Weisman (1981) identified four groups of environmental variables that can help with wayfinding: visual cues or landmarks within or outside of a building; architectural differences between different parts of a building; the use of signs and room numbers; **building configuration**. A trip to a shopping mall is likely to involve visiting several different shops and so the ease of which a consumer can find their way around will have a direct impact on the satisfaction they experience (Arthur & Passini, 1992).

KEY WORD

building configuration: the overall size and shape of a building, and the way the building is laid out

Example study

Dogu and Erkip (2000) aimed to investigate how spatial factors, such as signs and maps, could aid wayfinding within a shopping mall. The *case study* was carried out in a shopping mall in Ankara, Turkey, where the spatial layout was analysed, and questionnaires were given to shoppers. The shopping mall was categorised and evaluated in terms of architecture, graphics and verbal information. In terms of architecture, there is a central atrium at the main entrance, with many shops leading off the main corridor (see Figure 7.5). The layout is almost symmetrical and there are three other entrances, and three floors. There are circular corridors on each level, which indicate the direction of travel. Elevators and escalators connect the three floors. Graphic information all follows the same consistent style and is almost all based on **pictographs** rather than text (aside from 'WC' and 'Exit'). Door numbers are confusing; all shops on the ground floor are numbered in the '100's but not all shops on the second floor are in the 200s, nor are all shops on the third floor in the 300s. Also, numbers are not all in order as some shops were split later, so numbers have been added later are out of order. This of course makes wayfinding more difficult. The 'You Are Here' map and directory are just across from the main entrance, but they sit parallel to the direction of approach so are not very easy to see. The

KEY WORDS

pictographs: a way of providing information using images only

bureaucratic hierarchy: decisions are made based on who pays the most money; so, the businesses that pay the most money will get the best spaces

directory is confusing and illogical, perhaps because it is organised in a **bureaucratic hierarchy** (those who pay the most money or are most important get the best spaces) rather than in a way that logically helps with wayfinding. In terms of verbal information, the information desk sits prominently in the main atrium and security guards are helpful when approached.

Questionnaires asked about participants' views of the shopping mall in terms of wayfinding, focusing on all the areas described previously. Results showed that, although signage was not seen as more important than building configuration for wayfinding, there was a significant relationship between the evaluation of the shopping mall for wayfinding and its signage system. Those who found wayfinding easy found the signage to be significant, but many didn't notice the signs and others found them insufficient. Most respondents found 'You Are Here' maps to be useful, but 47% didn't believe there were any in this mall (demonstrating that they are not placed in a very visible or accessible way). There was a slight relationship between door numbers and wayfinding, but none of the architectural characteristics were significant for wayfinding. The researchers concluded that the most important feature that helped with wayfinding was signage. Other features, such as building configuration, visual access and use of circular paths, appeared to influence individuals differently, so would benefit from further research.

Figure 7.5: The shopping mall in Ankara that was the subject of Dogu and Erkip's case study

Spatial movement patterns

Shopper behaviour has been researched in different contexts, and research has shown that the purpose of the trip and the shopper profile can influence movement and behaviour patterns. There are different types of shopping trip that have been identified based on whether the trip is a big weekly shop, or just popping in for certain things. There are also different types of shopper identified: some who have a list and are focused on what they need, and others who wander up and down aisles and see what they fancy. The types of trip and the type of shopper will affect the sort of movement pattern that is used.

Example study

Gil et al. (2009) examined patterns of shopper movement and behaviour in a supermarket. They tracked movements of over 480 shoppers, and interviewed them after their visit, to produce shopper profiles. The study is non-experimental because the researchers did not manipulate any variables. The researchers were interested in whether store layout has an impact on shopper behaviours, specifically movement patterns, shopping duration and interaction with products. They aimed to identify distinctive movement patterns and to see if these patterns can be associated with certain shopper groups.

Shoppers were initially approached to take part in a survey, and basic information (such as age, gender and size of group) was recorded. CCTV (video surveillance often used in shops for security) was used to track their journey around the shop, using a coloured tag to identify them. As they left the store, they were given a more detailed interview. The interview covered a range of topics, asking the shopper about the purpose of their trip, their use of a shopping list, satisfaction with their shopping and the amount of money spent. Participants were also asked about more general shopping habits such as the frequency of shopping trips. The CCTV recordings were processed to extract data on the store areas visited, the time spent in each area and the type of product interactions. The researchers concluded that, as expected, shopper behaviour is strongly affected by the location of products within the store. Also as expected, some areas are more popular than others, with milk, fruit and vegetables, and bread being the busiest and non-food and baby products being the least busy.

A more interesting result is that it is possible to identify four distinct patterns of movement around the store:

- Short trip: a short, simple trip for a few targeted items, and not necessarily visiting the most popular products (32 shoppers).

- Round trip: moving up and along the top corridor, then returning along the main corridor with detours into various aisles (173 shoppers).

- Central trip: using the main corridor for entering and exiting the building, and moving down various aisles, mostly the top aisles initially then the bottom aisles on the return (110 shoppers).

- Wave trip: linear progression along the main corridor, zigzagging through the aisles and mostly exiting near the far end of the store (166 shoppers).

Figure 7.6 shows these four patterns of movement.

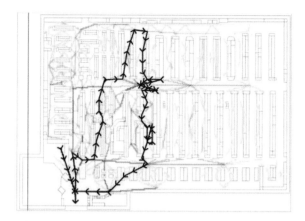

Short trip (32)

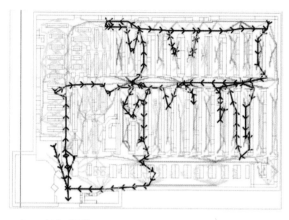

Round trip (173)

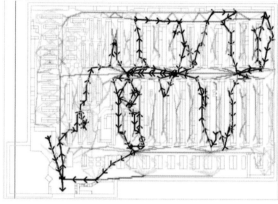

Central trip (110)

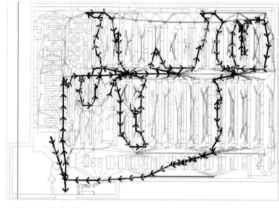

Wave trip (166)

Figure 7.6: Short trip, round trip, central trip, wave trip

There were no significant differences in the types of people making each type of trip. It instead appears to represent individual preference.

Of further interest was the identification of five types of spatial behaviour patterns:

- The Specialist

  - focusing on a few products and spending a lot of time with each product, though not necessarily resulting in a purchase.

  - These shoppers are mainly on 'top-up' or 'non-food' mission.

  - 19 shoppers, 25% males, 58% use baskets, 85% shop for less than 20 minutes.

- The Native

  - A long trip visiting relevant aisles, and interactions are most likely to lead to purchases.

  - They are mainly on 'main' or 'top-up' mission.

  - 161 shoppers, 98% use a trolley, 90% are satisfied with their shopping experience.

- The Tourist

  - Fast-moving shoppers who don't stray too far from the entrance and tend to stay on the main corridor.

  - They look more than buy and some are on 'non-food' mission.

  - 101 shoppers, 80% have short or medium trips, 35% are of the mature profile, only 28% are very satisfied with their experience.

- The Explorer
  - The longest trip, visiting all aisles in the store and often visiting places more than once.
  - This involves spending a long time with products and buying a lot and involve a 'main' shopping mission.
  - 67 shoppers, 62% females shopping alone, 87% take a trolley, 43% have a shopping list (highest of all categories).
- The Raider
  - Involving fast movements and fast decisions, showing preference for the main corridor but going where necessary.
  - These have the highest proportion of male shoppers and are on 'top-up' or 'food for tonight' missions.
  - 113 shoppers, 33% male (biggest proportion of all categories), 100% walking at medium or fast speed.

Gil et al. concluded that this information about shopper behaviour could be further investigated in other stores with other layouts.

RESEARCH METHODS

Dogu and Erkip (2000) used a case study to find out about factors that affect wayfinding in a shopping mall. The use of a case study means that the researchers could gather lots of detailed information about the shopping mall and this can give a really good insight into a range of factors. However, the problems with using a case study is that it is just focusing on this one shopping mall, so the results cannot be fully generalised to other shopping malls, as they are all unique. Case studies can be criticised for lacking reliability because they cannot be *replicated* due to the unique nature, so there is no way to test if their results would be found again.

Gil et al. (2009) used a different approach in their work: by using a non-experimental design where no variables were manipulated. This means that they are just gathering data from people's normal everyday lives. The use of CCTV allowed for consumers to be tracked, and they also

CONTINUED

used interviews to find out about consumers' experience. The interviews provided information about the shoppers' intentions and experiences of the shop that, combined with the CCTV tracking, allowed the researchers to get a good understanding of different shopper behaviour.

ISSUES AND DEBATES

The studies carried out by Gil et al. and by Dogu and Erkip both take a holistic approach in their research. They both use a range of different approaches in their investigation in order to try to gather as full and holistic understanding as possible. Gil et al., for example, used CCTV tracking to measure observable behaviour of the customers in the shop, but then they also used interviews to understand the customers' attitudes, thoughts and feelings, making the approach holistic. Similarly, Dogu and Erkip carried out a case study on a shopping mall so they could look in detail at all aspects of the spatial layout, as well as giving questionnaires to customers to get an understanding of their attitudes and feelings about the mall. How could individual versus situational explanations be applied to environmental influences on consumer behaviour?

Menu design psychology

Eye-movement patterns, framing and common menu mistakes

The menu is the most important marketing tool for a restaurant, so it is vital for owners and managers to understand how it can be used to increase sales and improve customer loyalty (see Figure 7.7). There are many common mistakes that can be made with menus, as well as many clever tips to encourage sales of key items. Key items may be those with the biggest profit margins, signature dishes, or those that are quick and easy to prepare. These mistakes and tips are discussed in the paper by Pavesic (2005).

Figure 7.7: The menu is an important marketing tool for a restaurant

Example study

Pavesic (2005) reported that the average time spent reading a menu is 109 seconds. This is an important piece of information for someone designing a menu. The use of **eye tracking** can inform us of the typical way in which customers will look at a menu, and this can be used to determine where to place certain items. See Figure 7.8 for eye tracking in Pavesic's study. The pattern of **eye movement** is not fixed, however, and can be amended and directed by '**eye magnets**'. 'Eye magnets' are anything that draws someone's attention to particular menu items. This may be a box around the item, a different coloured background, a larger or bolder font, or a photo or illustration. These all work by directing the eye movement to the item you would like to encourage your customers to buy. '**Framing**' is a method of drawing the customers' eyes to a certain part of the menu and works by grouping certain menu items together. This can be achieved by using a border or box, or by placing similar items in a confined space in the menu, for example, placing all the appetisers in one box encourages customers to read them all as a unit.

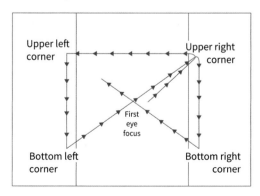

Figure 7.8: Eye-movement patterns (Pavesic, 2005)

As well as the features described above, which have a positive impact, there are also some features of menu design that can have a negative impact. Features that have a negative impact are also discussed by Pavesic. These include:

- Inadequate management commitment: not investing enough time and effort into making sure the menu design is as good as it could be, and not realising how important an asset it can be.

- Hard to read: crowded pages or poor choice of font size and style or colour of paper.

- Overemphasising prices: diners can dismiss certain items based purely on price if this is not considered.

- Poor use of space: this includes not using the front and back cover effectively, for example it is important to include details about the restaurant on the front page.

- Incongruence: if the menu doesn't fit the ambience of the restaurant in terms of style, décor, etc. it isn't going to work very well. If someone were to read your menu somewhere else, it should give them a feel for the type of place it represents.

KEY WORDS

eye tracking: a method using a computer to record the pattern of eye movement of a participant

eye magnets: anything that interrupts eye-movement patterns and draws attention to a particular item

framing: the use of borders or boxes to group certain items together and draw a customer's eye to them

The primacy and recency effects and menu item position

The **primacy effect** and **recency effect** are two effects found in memory research, which show that, if you are recalling a list of words, the words at the start and end of the list are more likely to be remembered than those in the middle of the list. The same theory has been investigated in relation to item position on a menu: are items at the start and end of the menu more likely to be purchased?

KEY WORDS

primacy effect: an effect found in memory research, which shows that, when recalling a list of words, you are more likely to recall words from the start of the list than those from the middle

recency effect: an effect found in memory research, which shows that, when recalling a list of words, you are more likely to recall words from the end of the list (the most 'recent') than those from the middle

Example study

Dayan and Bar-Hillel (2011) reported two studies which manipulated the position of items on a menu to increase or decrease the frequency of choice. They predicted that items at the beginning and end of the menu would be more likely to be ordered.

In the first study, 240 students were *randomly allocated* to four conditions. These were four different menu designs, differing only in terms of order of item presentation within each category. The menus all offered four appetisers (A), ten entrées (main courses, E), six soft drinks (S) and eight desserts (D).

The names of the items and their descriptions were copied from an Israeli pizza chain. No prices were displayed. The four menus (in Hebrew) presented the items in different orders within each category:

- baseline: arbitrarily ordered (no particular order)

- mirror: complete reverse of the baseline

- inside out baseline: reversed the baseline order within the top and bottom half of each category separately, therefore turning middle items into top/bottom items and vice versa

- inside out mirror: as for the inside out baseline but reversing the mirror version.

The participants were each given one version of the menu and asked to choose one item from each of the categories. The results showed that participants were significantly more likely to select items at the beginning or end of the list than they were to select items placed in the middle. Overall, the advantage of being listed at the beginning and end was 56% (i.e. items listed at the beginning or end were 56% more likely to be chosen than items listed in the middle).

There was no significant difference in the impact of the primacy effect and the recency effect; the number of items chosen from the beginning of the list and those chosen from the end of the list were almost exactly the same.

These results were convincing, but the researchers were aware that this only represented a hypothetical choice rather than one made in a real restaurant. To address this criticism, they conducted a second study in a small coffee shop in the centre of Tel Aviv over 30 days. The coffee shop had 60 items on the menu in three categories: coffee, soft drinks and desserts.

The baseline menu (the coffee shop's standard menu) was alternated with the inside out version which changed the position of items in the three categories by exchanging items from the two ends of the category with items from the middle. Staff recorded orders made during this time and data from any customers who ordered without reference to a menu were excluded. There were 459 orders from the baseline menu and 492 from the inside out menu.

The *mean* advantage in this study was 55% and the results confirmed the findings from Study 1. In Study 2 there was an even larger gain when an item was moved from the exact middle to the extreme end (55%) than when moved from the near middle to the near end (51%). The results also seemed to suggest an advantage (59%) from being in the top half of the category although this study did not use a mirror condition.

This research provides evidence that it is beneficial to place items at the beginning or end of the category if you want them to be ordered more often. This is most likely to be used to encourage sales of higher profit items, but the researchers also suggest that there may be practical implications from this study in terms of manipulating people's choices towards healthier options (see Figure 7.9).

Figure 7.9: Putting salads and other healthy options at the start and end of a menu could have implications for healthy eating

Menu style	Description of dish
French style menu (1)	Consomme julienne
English with French menu (2)	Clear soup garnished with a julienne of vegetables
Seasonal menu (3)	Spring vegetables garnished in a fresh clear soup
Elaborate style menu (4)	A delicious flavourful clear soup garnished with the freshest, most tasty vegetables
Organic style menu (5)	Naturally grown ingredients made into a crystal clear soup served with organic slivers of vegetables

Table 7.1: The words used to describe the same dish across five menus in the study by Lockyer (2006)

The effect of food name on menu item choice

We have considered the effect of menu design in terms of layout, font, and use of boxes, and we have considered the effect of item position on a menu. Last, we are going to discover whether the *name* that is given to a dish can influence how likely it is to be purchased.

Example study

Lockyer (2006) used focus groups, followed by a survey, to gather data on the effect that different words on a menu have on the food that people want to buy. The four focus groups were made up of 48 self-selecting participants (of a mix of gender, age and income) who responded to a letter asking them to take part in the research. The survey was used to measure the validity of the findings of the focus groups and the 200 usable responses were those returned from approximately 1800 that were sent out to homes in the local New Zealand area (also a mix of gender, age and income).

In the focus groups, participants were presented with five different style menus, each including the same dishes but described in very different ways. See Table 7.1 for example wording of one of the dishes described on each of the five different menus.

The participants were asked, on a scale of 1 (most appealing) to 5 (very unappealing) how appealing each menu was to them. Results were mixed, but there were no statistical differences based on age, gender or income. 42% of participants rated menu 1 (French style) as 'very unappealing', 42% rated menu 3 (seasonal menu) as the one with the highest appeal, whereas menu 5 (organic style) was rated as 'very appealing' by 27% and 'very unappealing' by 22% of participants. Lockyer now wanted to find out the reasons behind the participants' preferences so he asked them to write their reasons for finding menus appealing and unappealing and then used these notes and their ratings for a group discussion.

A **content analysis** was carried out, which involved the discussions being transcribed and a computer program used to count how often, and in what groupings, certain words were used. Content analysis allows researchers to turn qualitative data (such as verbal discussions) into quantitative data (the most common words and terms used) so that the information can be analysed and

> **KEY WORD**
>
> **content analysis:** is a research tool used to measure and analyse the presence of certain words or terms in qualitative data, such as verbal discussions or text

better understood. The content analysis showed certain groups of words that can tell us about the participants' opinions. The words 'fresh, interesting' were grouped together, telling us that the words used can give a definite feeling for the menu, and that the items on the menu were both 'fresh' and 'interesting'. Words such as 'trends, organic, season' and 'pure, natural, products' were grouped together, indicating the importance of current trends towards the importance of organic and fresh ingredients. The occasion for the meal influenced the importance of the general 'feeling' of the menu, with the words 'mystique' and 'occasion' being grouped together. Finally, words such as 'produce, actually, expect' and 'understand, language, clear' were grouped together, suggesting that the group found it important that the language was clear and that it actually described what the dish would be.

As the focus groups suggested that the occasion for the meal would influence the menu choice, the survey asked respondents to say which menu items they would choose for different occasions, such as family reunion, romantic dinner, business meeting or dinner with their mother-in-law. The participants were also asked to comment on the reasons for their choices, and a content analysis was carried out to identify the most common reasons for each menu choice. Unlike in the focus group, the survey found menu 4 (elaborate style) to be the most selected for all the dining experiences. For meal with their mother-in-law menu 5 was the joint top choice and for a business meeting menu 3 was the joint top choice. Reasons for the choice of a chicken dish from each menu include:

- Menu 1: Poulet sauté chasseur: 'feels romantic', 'sounds sophisticated'

- Menu 2: Chicken sautéed in butter and served with sauce chasseur: 'sounds delicious', 'appears to have the nicest flavour'

- Menu 3: Spring chicken cooked and served in a new season mushrooms, shallot and tomato flavoured sauce: 'not too fussy', 'tells me basically what I get'

- Menu 4: The most tender chicken cooked till golden and sewed with a delicious sauce finished with tomatoes, shallots and mushrooms: 'mouth-watering', 'chicken sounds tender'

- Menu 5: Free range organic chicken cooked and served with mushrooms, shallots and tomatoes in a naturally produced sauce: 'organic', 'I like to know what I'm eating'

These examples show that the way in which the dish is described has an impact on the potential diner, and influences their perception of the dish.

Overall, the results of Lockyer's research show that the words used on a menu do have an impact on the likelihood of potential diners to choose a dish. Most participants showed a preference for items on the menu that were clear, tasty and described as fresh and natural. There were, however, broad differences in the preferences of the participants so further research is required to investigate this further.

ACTIVITY 7.2

Create a menu for a new café, which is focusing on promoting healthy eating.

Use research by Lockyer, Dayan and Bar-Hillel, and Pavesic to help you.

You should consider the use of descriptive names, position on the menu, and menu design features that have a positive impact to encourage sales of healthier options.

RESEARCH METHODS

Dayan and Bar-Hillel (2011) carried out a laboratory experiment, which allows for high levels of control, increasing the validity and the reliability of the study. However, participants were asked to look at a menu and make hypothetical choices, which lacked ecological validity as it was not showing the decision-making of customers in real restaurants. To deal with the lack of ecological validity, the researchers followed this study with a field experiment where they changed the order of the menu for a café to measure the effects on customers' orders. These results supported the findings of their first experiment, showing that the results could be generalised to real life.

Research into menu design can be applied to everyday life because it focuses on how an effective menu design works, the importance of the order of food items on the menu, and even research into the effect of naming the food differently. This evidence is only really important and useful when it is applied to real life and used by restaurants and cafes to make changes to their menus and see the effect it has on their businesses. It is particularly useful because they can hopefully benefit greatly from what are relatively simple and low cost changes, compared to other aspects of their restaurant.

Consumer behaviour and personal space

Personal space at restaurant tables

Personal space refers to the area surrounding a person, which they consider to be psychologically theirs (as discussed in Chapter 5). Personal space is extremely important to most people, and people will feel discomfort, anxiety or anger if their personal space is invaded. Personal space is an important consideration for any restaurant: there needs to be a balance between the comfort of the customer and the profit of the restaurant. In simple terms, the closer diners can sit to each other, the more diners you will be able to fit in your restaurant and therefore (in theory) the more profit you will be able to make. However, customers will not want to feel that they are crowded, or that their personal space is being invaded as this will lead to a negative experience.

Hall outlines four zones of physical distance that people may feel comfortable with, depending on the circumstances (see Figure 7.10):

- Intimate distance: less than 18 inches (46 cm). For touching or whispering, and with people we have a close, most likely romantic connection to

- Personal distance: 18 inches–4 feet (46–122 cm). For interactions between good friends and family

- Social distance: 4–12 feet (1.2–3.7 m). For interactions with acquaintances

- Public distance: 12 feet (3.7 m) or more. For public speaking or formal interactions

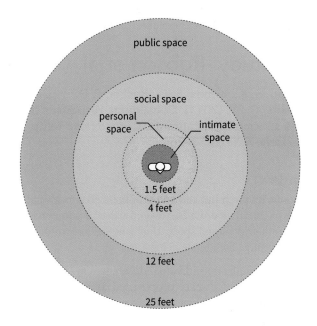

Figure 7.10: Hall's four zones of personal space

This shows how complicated personal space considerations can be in a restaurant, because people will feel more comfortable seated closer to someone that they are intimate with, than they would a friend, and certainly than they would a stranger.

Responses to the invasion of our personal space can be explained with reference to three concepts: *overload*, *arousal* and *behaviour constraint*. The concept of overload suggests that we maintain our personal space to reduce (and to maintain control over) the amount of information that needs to be dealt with. If people are too close, we must process information relating to their features, their smell, their body heat and possibly even their touch. This produces an overload of information to process as well as a lack of control over the information that we process, producing feelings of stress.

The invasion of personal space can also be explained by the concept of arousal. When our personal space is invaded, we may feel a heightened sense of arousal. Our response may be positive (such as at a concert, or if someone hugs you) or it may be negative (such as a stranger sitting too close).

The invasion of personal space can also be understood in terms of behaviour constraint, which refers to having your freedom to choose how to behave being taken away. Research shows that crowds behave very differently from individuals, often leading to increased aggression and a decrease in prosocial or helping behaviours. It is possible that the stress experienced by lack of personal space may be responsible for these changes in behaviour.

Key study: Robson et al. (2011)

Robson, S. K., Kimes, S. E., Becker, F. D., & Evans, G. W. (2011). Consumers' responses to table spacing in restaurants. *Cornell hospitality quarterly, 52*(3), 253–264.

Context

Previous research has shown that diners need personal space so that they don't feel overcrowded; if someone invades their personal space, they will feel uncomfortable and may show avoidance behaviours.

There are significant individual differences in terms of how much personal space people need. It is generally found that men and older people require more personal space than women and younger people. The people you are with will also affect the amount of personal space you require as well, with larger groups requiring more space per person than smaller groups (Knowles and Bassett 1976). Personal space also varies between cultures, and between situations. Not only does personal space vary between individuals, cultures and situations, it also varies spatially. This means that personal space isn't like a round bubble that surround a person in the centre, but that the amount of personal space a person requires varies depending on their position. Personal space generally tends to be narrower on either side, but broader in front or behind a person (Hayduk 1981), so an individual would be happier having someone sit or stand close by next to them rather than directly in front or behind them.

Main theories and explanations

When designing a restaurant there is a balance to be struck between fitting in as many tables and chairs as possible and making the restaurant a pleasant place to be. It makes sense that, from a financial point of view, the more tables and chairs you have in your restaurant, the more customers you can fit in and therefore the money you can make. However, research into personal space is an important consideration because if people feel that their personal space is being invaded they will feel uncomfortable and will be less likely to stay for a long time (and therefore spend less money) and will be less likely to return to the restaurant or to recommend it to others.

Robson et al. hoped to develop the research into the importance of personal space in diners by looking more specifically at the space *between* tables rather than previous research that has mostly focused on distance between individual chairs or spacing around a table (Sommer 1969).

Aims

The researchers aimed to find out how diners perceive specific table distances during particular dining experiences, and the impact that those perceptions have on attitudes and preferences. Their aim was to give the restaurant industry guidance on appropriate table distances.

Design

A web-based questionnaire was used to gather diner responses to images of restaurant tables at different distances (see Figure 7.11). The independent variables were table spacing (6, 12 or 24 inches (15, 30 or 60 cm)) and scenario (business, friend or romantic). The dependent variables were the measures of emotional and behavioural responses measured by Likert-type scales. Participants were randomly allocated to one of the nine conditions (combinations of three table spacings and three scenarios). The same images, distances and statements were used for each participant in each condition, to control for any extraneous variables.

Figure 7.11: Image similar to those shown in Robson et al.'s study 6-inch table spacing

The sample consisted of just over 1000 participants from the USA, with a good balance of gender and location of residence (urban, suburban or rural), and a range of age and ethnicity. The *sampling technique* was volunteer sampling.

The first part of the questionnaire asked about gender, age, ethnicity, place of residence, restaurant use frequency and whether they had worked in the restaurant industry. The second part measured emotional, intentional and anticipated behavioural reactions to images of two tables 6, 12 or 24 inches apart. Participants were told to imagine they were in one of three scenarios: business, dining with a friend or a romantic scenario. Likert-type scales (1 = strongly disagree, 7 = strongly agree) were used on a series of 32 statements about their emotional and behavioural responses to the images of the table spacings. The statements relating to emotional responses were derived from the Stress Arousal Check List (SACL): an instrument that accurately reflects a respondent's stress and arousal and clearly differentiates between the two. The statements that relate to behavioural responses included questions around the constructs of perceived control, physical and sensory privacy, goal blocking and general comfort. Perceived crowding was also measured.

Results, findings and conclusions

Results showed significant differences across almost all responses for tables at 6-, 12- and 24-inches distance. Close table spacing made respondents feel less private, more crowded, less likely to have a positive experience and more dissatisfied with their assigned table. Those with the 6-inch distance were also more concerned about being overheard or about disturbing other diners. Arousal score did not vary significantly between table spacing, but stress levels were significantly higher for the 6-inch spacing, and feelings of control and comfort were markedly lower than for wider spaced tables.

The proposed scenario had a significant influence on dining satisfaction. Those imagining a romantic scenario showed significantly higher stress, less control and more discomfort with the 6-inch spacing than 12- and 24-inch. Dining while on business did not affect responses to tight table spacing except in terms of comfort. Dining with a friend prompted moderate stress and discomfort for tight spacing. There were significant differences between genders; in general women showed significantly more stress, less control and greater discomfort than men, whereas men felt more arousal at each distance. Frequent diners showed more comfort across all table spacings than those who dined out less frequently. There were some apparent differences in response across age, location and ethnicity, but these were not consistent and there were no significant interactions.

The researchers conclude that diners feel strongly negatively towards tightly spaced tables of 6 inches,

in terms of feeling uncomfortable, overcrowded and generally negative about the restaurant. 70% of diners said they would have been asked to be re-seated if they had been seated so closely to another table. The common spacing of 12 inches was also less desirable than those spaced further apart, especially for those imagining a romantic scenario. This is important for those in the restaurant business, as those who are seated uncomfortably are likely to stay for less time (and likely to spend less money), are less likely to return and less likely to recommend the restaurant to others.

Evaluation

Robson et al.'s study had a large sample, with over 1000 participants. Most importantly, the sample had a good balance of gender and location of residence (urban, suburban or rural), and a range of age and ethnicity. This is a representative sample, so the results can be generalised to the wider population. However, all participants were from the USA so the results may not be applicable to people from other cultures. The use of Likert-type scales is beneficial as it collects *quantitative data*, allowing the data to be compared and analysed. However, the disadvantage of using Likert-type scales is that they don't allow participants to offer more detailed answers, and they rely on *subjective* interpretation of the scales. How might *qualitative data* have been collected?

Robson et al.'s study into personal space in restaurant tables is relevant to application to real life as the findings can be used to help restaurants appeal to their customers. However, alongside this, it is particularly important to consider cultural differences as the study was carried out in the USA. Research shows that there are significant differences across cultures in terms how much personal space individuals are comfortable with (Lomranz, 1976). It is important, therefore that anyone wishing to use this research to help them make decisions about the layout of their restaurant should consider the implications of cultural differences. Restaurants in different cultures may not be able to use these findings confidently so it may be beneficial to consider further research within their own culture as well.

Defending your place in a queue

Another issue that is related to personal space is the way that people behave when they are in a queue. Research has shown that people are very protective of their position in a queue and there are certain expectations that we have about the behaviour of other people in the queue. For example, someone pushing into a queue goes

KEY WORDS

social structure: a system where there are certain rules and expectations that people are expected to follow when they are part of this system

confederate: someone who is involved in the study but acts as if they are not

Figure 7.12: A queue is a social system and intruders are not acceptable

against the behaviour that most people expect, and is seen as unacceptable. However, there are many factors that may influence a person's response to someone pushing into a queue. The nature of the intrusion is important, as is the number of people who are intruding. We need to also consider the **social structure** of a queue.

ACTIVITY 7.3

Before reading the example study by Milgram et al., consider how *you* would react if someone pushed in front of you in a queue. What might you say or do? What factors would affect how you reacted? Think about how they pushed in, what you were queuing for, how long you had been queuing, how other people reacted, as well as any other factors. How do you think *most* people would react to someone pushing into a queue? When you have come up with your own ideas discuss with a partner.

Example study

Milgram et al. (1986) carried out a series of field experiments in a range of settings in New York City, such as train stations, convenience shops, etc. A **confederate** calmly approached a point between the third and fourth person in the queue and said in a neutral tone 'excuse me; I would like to get in here'. The confederate would then simply join the queue without waiting for a response. If the confederate was explicitly asked to leave the queue they would do so, otherwise they would remain for 1 minute before leaving. An observer stood nearby, ready to record physical, verbal and non-verbal reactions to the intrusion. There was a total of 129 intrusions carried out and observed.

The researchers also varied the number of intruders: sometimes one and sometimes two. They also used buffers: these were confederates who passively occupied a position between the point of intrusion and the next

naive queuer (the next person who is unaware of the study taking place). This was designed to see if the responsibility for objecting would be displaced from the person immediately at the point of intrusion to others. In some conditions, two buffers were used standing immediately behind each other. Therefore, there are two independent variables: number of intruders (one or two) and number of buffers (zero, one or two) resulting in six *experimental conditions* (see Figure 7.12).

Results showed that queuers behind the intruder were far more likely to object than those who were ahead of the intruder. Two intruders provoked a much greater reaction than one, and buffers dampened the queue's response to the intruder. Verbal objections (from polite to hostile, demanding the intruder leave or go to the back of the queue) were the most common, occurring in 21.7% of queues. Generalised expressions of disapproval were also included in this category and included more tentative comments such as 'excuse me, this is a queue'. Physical action (such as tapping the shoulder, tugging a sleeve or even pushing the intruder out of the queue) against the intruder happened in 10% of queues. This type of response normally originated from the person standing immediately behind the intruder. Non-verbal objections included disapproving looks, hostile glares and gestures to the intruder to move to the end of the queue. They occurred in 14.7% of queues.

Milgram et al. conclude that the queue is considered to be a social system with a shared set of beliefs governing the behaviour of the participants. The queue acts as a way of instilling social order: individuals who are waiting for a service expect that those who approach after them will wait their turn. Most people believe that it is not acceptable to break the expected norms and push into a queue. We would all rather buy our ticket (or whatever we are queuing for) without waiting but we accept that if we were the ones waiting, we would expect others to take their place in the queue. We accept this social system and follow the rules. If someone were to push into a queue, it is not just the extra time an individual would need to wait that is the problem: depending on the nature of the queue it could only add seconds to a wait time. It is more than that; the anger and frustration felt comes from the injustice surrounding the fact that someone violated the rules of the social system (the queue) (Cooley, 1902).

A social system needs to be defended, otherwise order cannot be maintained. So, if there is a threat to the order of the system, by someone intruding, those in the queue must defend themselves. As Milgram's study showed, the queue does not act as a whole and defend their queue; instead it is thought to be the responsibility of those behind the intruder, and very much so of the individual directly behind the intrusion. Finally, the defence of the queue is almost always normative (based on expectations of the group), with individuals most likely to simply point out 'this is a queue' or tell the intruder 'you can't push in here'.

RESEARCH METHODS

The use of *observation* to gather data in Milgram et al.'s study has both strengths and weaknesses. *Covert observation* allows the observer to record people's natural behaviour, as they do not know they are being observed so they won't change their behaviour as a result. However, with covert observations there are *ethical issues* because, if people don't know they are being observed they cannot give *informed consent* and there is the issue of *deception*. Observation is also a way of measuring how people actually respond in a situation, as opposed to a self-report method where people may give a socially desirable answer about how they think they would respond to someone pushing into a queue. A weakness of the observation is that it is subjective, and the observer may miss something. Observer bias may occur, where the person involved in the research is more likely to interpret something in a way that it confirms the hypothesis. This reduces the reliability of the observation, particularly as there was only one observer so there is nobody to compare results with to check for *inter-observer reliability*.

ISSUES AND DEBATES

Research into personal space and queuing are particularly subject to cultural differences as they are both behaviours that vary between cultures. Milgram et al.'s research into queue jumping was carried out in New York City, so the results may only be representative of the city itself but would likely apply to the rest of the USA fairly accurately. However, other cultures around the world would likely respond differently when faced with someone intruding into their queue, so the results should be generalised with caution.

The research by Robson et al. highlights the importance of individual explanations when considering personal space. The research showed that factors such as gender, age and ethnicity were all important influences on someone's feelings about personal space. This is an important consideration in comparison to the more likely consideration of situational factors, such as whether the meal is romantic or business.

Questions

4 Dogu and Erkip found that most respondents found 'You Are Here' signs to be helpful but 47% did not believe there were any at that mall. How should someone designing a mall use this information to aid in their design?

5 Gil et al. used CCTV footage to track the routes taken by customers and also interviewed the customers as they left the shop. Why was it important to use both approaches?

6 Robson et al. considered the importance of personal space when designing a restaurant. What are the costs and benefits of having tables closer together or further apart, and what factors need to be taken into account?

7.3 Consumer decision-making

Consumer decision-making

Models of consumer decision-making

There are many different models of consumer decision-making, here we will consider three: **utility theory**, **satisficing** and **prospect theory**.

Utility theory was proposed by Von Neumann and Morgenstern (1944) cited in Von Neumann and Morgenstern (2007). The theory suggests that, when making a decision, consumers make the decision rationally. The decision is based on optimising the likely outcomes of their actions. For example, if you were deciding on a new car, utility theory would predict that

you would evaluate every available car against all the important variables (cost, size, mileage, make, etc.) and then select the car that scored highest on all of these variables (see Figure 7.13). However, in reality this is not practical, and it is unlikely that consumers are as rational as this model predicts or even that they are aware of the process of decision-making within a retail environment.

Simon (1956) proposed an alternative model called satisficing in which he describes consumers as getting 'approximately where they wanted to go' and then stopping the decision-making process. Continuing the example of buying a new car, from a satisficing point of view, you might look at a few cars and stop the process when you find one that is 'good enough'. Although this model may explain behaviour more accurately than utility theory, it still does not offer a good predictor of consumer behaviour that can be effectively used in a retail environment.

Prospect theory was developed by Kahneman and Tversky, in the 1970s. Their theory added two new concepts to the explanation of consumer decision-making; these were value (rather than utility in the earlier utility model) and endowment, which is when an item is more precious when owned than when owned by someone else. This suggests that people value gains and losses in different ways and are more likely to base their decisions on perceived likelihood of gains rather than perceived likelihood of losses. For example, we buy a lottery ticket because we might win, not because we are highly likely to lose.

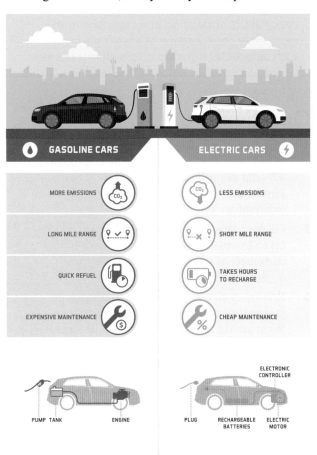

Figure 7.13: Utility theory suggests that we make decisions rationally, selecting products that score highest on all the variables

> ### KEY WORDS
>
> **utility theory:** the theory that a decision is made rationally and that a person makes a decision based on optimising the likely outcomes of their actions
>
> **satisficing:** the theory that a decision is made based on finding an option that is 'good enough' and then stopping
>
> **prospect theory:** this model proposes that people consider that an item is more precious when they own it, and that gains and losses are considered differently

Strategies of consumer decision-making

The next development in consumer decision-making was the identification of several possible consumer decision-making strategies that could be exploited by those working in consumer fields. These are described as: **compensatory strategies, non-compensatory strategies** and **partially compensatory strategies** (Green et al., 1973). Consumers may use any of the strategies, and may vary between strategies, depending on the individual and depending on the purchase.

KEY WORDS

compensatory strategies: a strategy where the value of one attribute can be allowed to compensate for another

non-compensatory strategies: a strategy where each attribute is evaluated individually

partially compensatory strategies: a strategy where items are considered in relation to one another in terms of important attributes

---

In compensatory strategies, a consumer will allow the value of one attribute to compensate for another. Again, in terms of buying a new car, you might decide that a very low mileage compensates for the fact that this was not your first choice of make or your preferred colour. Alternatively, you may choose the car based on the colour, allowing this to compensate for the high mileage.

Richarme (2005) describes two compensatory strategies:

- Equal Weight Strategy, where attributes are seen as being equally important. For example, someone buying a car might find mileage and colour to be of equal importance.

- Weighted Additive Strategy, where some attributes are seen as more important than others. For example, someone might value the low mileage on a car much more highly than the make or the colour.

In non-compensatory strategies each attribute is evaluated individually, rather than allowing one variable to compensate for another. So, in terms of buying a new car, even if it was a good price, the ideal make and had a low mileage, it would be immediately discounted if it was not the correct colour.

Simon suggests that there are three non-compensatory strategies:

- Satisficing: the first product to meet the basic requirements is chosen and no further consideration takes place. For example, if an essential piece of household equipment fails, such as a kettle, someone might simply purchase the first kettle they see.

- Elimination by aspects: this strategy sets a 'cut-off' value for the most important attribute and then allows everything that meets that attribute to remain under consideration. The remaining items are then assessed against the next attribute and so on. For example, when buying a kettle, you might decide on the minimum capacity so anything of at least that capacity is considered, then you might consider another factor, such as efficiency, for the remaining kettles.

- Lexigraphic: the most important attribute is evaluated and if one item is considered superior in terms of this attribute, this immediately stops the decision-making process, and the item is chosen. If one item does not emerge as superior on the most important attribute, then the consideration moves to the next attribute and so on. For example, you need to buy a kettle but have a large family so you decide you will get the kettle with the biggest capacity, and won't consider other factors.

Consumers may use a partially compensatory strategy, a middle ground between compensatory and non-compensatory.

Two partially compensatory strategies are:

- Majority of Conforming Dimensions: an individual using this strategy would evaluate two products against all relevant attributes and keep the one that does best. This one is then compared to the next product and so on until there is only one product left. For example, you might look at two kettles and compare them on price, and disregard the more expensive one, then compare the cheaper one with another and so on.

- Frequency of Good and Bad Features: all products are compared to the appropriate cut-off values and the product that has the most positive features exceeding the cut-off values will be chosen. For example, comparing all kettles on important factors, such as capacity, efficiency and price, and choosing the one that looks the best across all factors.

Decision-making strategies applied to internet shopping

In the previous section we looked at the three decision-making strategies (compensatory, non-compensatory and partially compensatory) used by consumers. Here we will consider how those three strategies apply to internet shopping, and specifically to website design.

Example study

Jedetski et al. (2002) were interested to discover the decision-making strategies used by consumers buying online. It was predicted that consumers would use compensatory strategies when buying from a website designed to allow comparison of items but would use non-compensatory strategies when this wasn't available. They also predicted that the number of alternatives available would influence which decision-making strategy was used. Each of the 24 participants was asked to read a document about the decision-making strategies (three compensatory and three non-compensatory strategies) and then given a quiz to test their understanding. Participants then went to one of two websites, each with quite different designs, and were shown how lists of alternatives could be found, refined and so on, and were asked to speak aloud their process as they made a decision on which item they would buy. Immediately afterwards, the participant was given a questionnaire about their decision-making strategy, how satisfied or frustrated they were and how confident they felt about their decision. The experimenter recorded information about which item was selected, how many alternatives there were and how long the decision took. This was repeated for four different items for each participant (although each participant used only one website).

Results showed that, as expected, participants used significantly more compensatory strategies on CompareNet (a website design that uses technology allowing comparisons of items to be made) and more non-compensatory strategies on Jango (a website design that does not allow comparisons of items). Furthermore, the number of alternatives affected strategies used: with participants using more compensatory strategies for items with fewer than 30 alternatives and more non-compensatory strategies for items with more than 100 alternatives. There was not a significant difference between compensatory and non-compensatory strategies in terms of confidence, satisfaction, frustration, perceived time or actual time. Participants were, however, more satisfied when using CompareNet than when using Jango; suggesting that website designs that use technology for comparisons are more satisfying for consumers.

RESEARCH METHODS

Jedetski et al. (2002) used an independent measures design, where each participant used only one of the two websites for their task. Results were then compared between the groups of participants in each condition. One strength of an independent measures design is that there is no risk of order effects (as could be the case with repeated measures) and it is less likely the participants will work out the aim of the experiment (as they could do with repeated measures), both of which increase the validity of the experiment. However, one weakness of independent measures is that one group of participants is compared to another group or participants, instead of being compared to themselves. This means that participant variables could affect the results; it could be that the participants in one condition just happen to be different in terms of their decision-making styles for example. Finally, a limitation recognised by Jedetski et al. was the fact that participants were informed of the different decision-making strategies before the main task. This was done so that the participants could describe the strategy they were using, but it had the negative consequence of reducing the ecological validity of the study. By learning about the strategies first, this meant that we are less likely to be seeing the natural way in which the participants would have carried out this task in a real-life situation.

ISSUES AND DEBATES

Research into the different models of consumer decision-making take a nomothetic approach. The models aim to offer a universal set of rules explaining why the population behaves in a particular way and uses research to gather lots of data to make these proposals. This can be a useful approach as it enables us to have a good understanding about the way people will likely behave, and to allow predictions and expectations. Furthermore, because the research is based on gathering large amounts of data, it is likely to be accurate for the most part. However, this contrasts with an idiographic approach,

CONTINUED

which looks at everyone as an individual and would seek to find out detail about an individual's personal circumstances to truly understand their behaviour. This would, of course, allow for a more specific and highly accurate account for an individual's behaviour but doesn't allow for the practical aspects of a nomothetic approach. Why should cultural differences be considered when investigating consumer decision-making?

Choice heuristics

Heuristics

We are constantly making decisions and have developed cognitive processing strategies or shortcuts to help us make decisions more easily. These are called **heuristics**. We are likely to use different heuristics for different sorts of decisions, and may use more than one for a particular decision. Heuristics are usually helpful as they aid our decision-making, but they can also lead to errors in judgement.

KEY WORD

heuristics: mental shortcuts that can help us when making decisions but can lead to errors in judgement

Availability heuristics

Availability heuristics are mental shortcuts based on how easy it is to bring something to mind. They are often useful ways of thinking about situations and can be beneficial, for example, by making us more cautious in dangerous situations as we can easily bring examples of negative outcomes to mind. However, this is often based on inaccurate information or faulty thinking.

Hoyer et al. (2010) suggest that if you had bought a DVD player that kept breaking down, your 'available' perception of that brand is likely to be a negative one, so you would be unlikely to purchase from that company again. Communication from others might also create an availability heuristic. If your friend had problems with a particular make, then this information is likely to influence your thinking even though this may be an isolated instance. This occurs because we ignore base rate information – how often something

really occurs – in favour of information that is readily available or easily memorable.

Representativeness heuristics

Representativeness heuristics are mental shortcuts that allow us to make judgements by making comparisons with the best-known (most representative) example of a category. If, for example, we are looking for a mobile phone, we are likely to compare a newly released model to the current market leader. If it appears similar, then we are likely to assume that this is also a quality product. Manufacturers take advantage of the fact that we use this heuristic, by making products (or their packaging) look like an established product so that the consumer assumes they will be similar.

Recognition heuristics

Recognition heuristics are used when we are, for example, choosing between two items or two brands. In this case if you are familiar with one of them (you recognise it), but not the other, you will assume the recognised one has more value, and it will therefore be chosen. For example, choosing between brands of mobile phones, if the specification and details are exactly the same for two phones but one of them is a familiar brand, you will choose that one over the other.

Take-the-best heuristics

Take-the-best heuristics allow a decision to be made based on one single 'good' reason only. When choosing between several options the decision-maker will make their choice based on one attribute that seems to best discriminate between the items, ignoring other information that is available. In the example of buying a mobile phone, there are lots of factors that are important (price, camera, appearance, size, etc.) but the 'take-the-best' heuristic would mean you would base your decision on the one factor you think is most important, ignoring all others, so you might choose the phone that has the best camera, regardless of anything else.

Anchoring

Anchoring describes our tendency to give the most importance to the first bit of information we receive about something, regardless of what further information we gather. This means that the decisions we make are based on adjustments of that first piece of information, but that that starting point has a huge impact on the final decision. For example, you are going to buy a new car and you see online what the average price for that car is. If you go to the dealership and the price is slightly under that price you will jump at the chance to spend that money. However, if you had seen a lower price online you would likely have bargained the price down and saved yourself some money.

ACTIVITY 7.4

Imagine you are buying a new mobile phone, which heuristics do you think you would use? How do you think they would help in your decision-making?

Point of purchase decisions

There are many factors that can influence our decision-making at the point of purchase. These include multiple unit prices and suggestive selling. Multiple unit prices involve offering a reduced price if you buy several of an item, for example a bottle of water might cost $1 per bottle but the multiple unit price could be $4 for five bottles. This can work in retail environments to increase sales by making consumers see a larger than normal purchase as attractive. It can even work when there is no price difference per item, e.g. a product may have a sign saying, 'On Sale – 6 cans for $3', which is more effective than a sign saying, 'On Sale – 50c', even though the price per item is the same. This effect may be due to customers expecting the multiple unit price to be cheaper.

Suggestive selling involves anything where the customer has something 'suggested' to them in order to encourage sales. This could be displaying earrings that match a necklace and a suggestion that the two are bought together, or a waitress suggesting a diner might like a salad with her main course.

KEY WORDS

multiple unit prices: a promotion where a reduced price is offered if you buy several of an item

suggestive selling: an attempt to encourage sales by 'suggesting' something to the customer, e.g. earrings that match a necklace

Example study

Wansink et al. (1998) examined factors that might influence how many units of a product a consumer chooses to buy.

They suggested how point of purchase promotions could increase sales. The paper reported on two field

experiments and two laboratory experiments (we will look at one of each), investigating the effect of multiple unit prices and suggestive selling.

Wansink et al. (1998) conducted a one-week field experiment comparing multiple-unit pricing with single-unit promotional pricing in 86 stores. The same size shelf label was used, and it displayed the original price (99 cents) as well as either the single-unit promotion price (75 cents) or the multiple unit price (2 for $1.50). Thirteen common food items were included in the experiment.

The results showed that multiple unit promotional prices resulted in a 32% increase in sales over the single-unit control. For 12 of 13 products, sales were higher with multiple unit pricing, and for nine products the difference was statistically significant (see Figure 7.14).

Figure 7.14: Multiple unit prices encourage consumers to spend more

However, because no self-report data were gathered, we can't be sure of the reasons for the increased sales (it could be that the shoppers were confused). Furthermore, because data only showed sales, not how many items each customer bought, we don't know if more people bought the items or if the same number of customers bought more items.

The next study examined the effect of suggestive selling: in this case, in the form of suggesting a new and innovative way to enjoy the items, such as 'Snickers bars – buy them for your freezer'. It also examined the effect of these suggestive selling slogans when accompanied with or without a price discount.

The study involved a shopping scenario, where 120 undergraduates were offered six well-known products at one of three price levels: an actual convenience store price (no discount), a 20% discount and a 40% discount. Participants were given suggestive selling claims that included either no product quantity anchor ('Snickers bars – buy them for your freezer') or an explicit product quantity anchor ('Snickers bars – buy 18 for your freezer'). Participants were given no indication whether the price was a discount and were asked to provide purchase quantity intentions for all products.

The results showed that both the suggestive selling and the discount level increased purchase quantity intentions, and that the suggestive selling increased intended purchase quantities even without a discount. Including the product quantity anchor increased purchase quality intentions, and this was effective even without a discount.

Decision-making styles

Earlier in this section we looked at different heuristics that are involved in decision-making, and we are now going to revisit the recognition and take-the-best heuristics, alongside five decision-making styles.

According to Scott and Bruce (1995) there are five decision-making styles:

1   Rational: making decisions in a logical way, where various options are considered to achieve a specific goal.

2   Intuitive: making decisions that 'feel right'; trusting your intuition.

3   Dependent: consulting others and relying on their assistance when making a decision.

4   Avoiding: putting off decisions or making decisions only at the last minute.

5   Spontaneous: making quick and impulsive decisions.

The instrument devised by Scott and Bruce to measure decision-making styles does not assign everyone to one style. Instead, it gives each person a score in each dimension, indicating how much their individual style resembles each of the five styles.

The use of a heuristic has been shown to be influenced by the task and context (situational factors: Payne et al., 1993) and by personal factors, such as intelligence and personality traits (e.g. neuroticism). Time pressure is a particular factor that has been shown to increase the likelihood of using a heuristic (Hilbig et al., 2012).

Example study

del Campo et al. (2016) were interested to study the relationship between heuristics and decision-making styles, as this specific relationship has not been researched

previously. Their study included two experiments: one in Vienna and one in Madrid. In total, there were 320 participants, with a wide range of ages and approximately equal split of men and women. Participants were asked to complete a computer-based task where they were asked to choose between five different options of eggs and were either given a time pressure (40 seconds to make the decision) or no time pressure. Four of the egg options were designed to target a particular heuristic or type of response: one targeted the take-the-best heuristic, one the recognition heuristic, one triggered an emotional response and one required higher cognitive processing. The fifth option did not target a specific behaviour (see Figure 7.15). Following the task, participants were given a questionnaire asking questions about their reasons for the decision, their buying behaviours, their attitudes to the products and so on. Each participant also completed Scott and Bruce's instrument to determine the dimensions of their decision-making style.

Price: **only 2.99 Euro**
Raising: free-range
Quality Grade: A
Country of Origin: Austria
Shelf Life: 2 Weeks
Quantity: 6 eggs

"Take-the-best" stimulus

Price: 3.19 Euro
Raising: free-range
Quality Grade: A
Country of Origin: Austria
Shelf Life: 2 Weeks
Quantity: 6 eggs

"Recognition" stimulus

Price: 3.19 Euro
Raising: free-range
Quality Grade: A
Country of Origin: Austria
Shelf Life: 2 Weeks
Quantity: 6 eggs

"Emotional" stimulus

Price: **3.10 Euro**
Raising: free-range, **with additional information** on raising of chicken
Quality Grade: A/**extra large**
Country of Origin: Austria, **of guaranteed origin**
Shelf Life: 2 Weeks
Quantity: 6 eggs
Additional information: GM-free, salmonella-free, animal rights tested, free of toxins, hygiene programme

"Cognitive" stimulus

Price: 3.19 Euro
Raising: barn/deep litter
Quality Grade: B
Country of Origin: Austria
Shelf Life: 2 Weeks
Quantity: 6 eggs

"Filler" stimulus

Figure 7.15: The different egg carton designs use by del Campo et al. (2016)

Results showed that there were many differences between the two experiments, so these cultural differences need to be further investigated. In the Vienna Experiment, time pressure led to a significant shift from 'cognitive' to 'take-the-best' options, however, this was not the case in the Madrid Experiment, which suggests there is only limited evidence that time pressure increases the likelihood of using heuristics. Furthermore, in the Vienna Experiment, those who scored high on the spontaneous style were more likely to choose the 'recognition' product than the 'cognitive' one, as expected. Unexpected, however, is that those who scored high on the rational style chose the 'take-the-best' option more often than the 'cognitive' one, regardless of time pressure. In Madrid, those scoring high in the rational decision style were less likely to choose the 'take-the-best' product, compared to the 'cognitive', without time pressure, but this is reversed with time pressure.

RESEARCH METHODS

The first study by Wansink et al. was a field experiment, so it had high ecological validity and showed people's consumer behaviour in a natural setting. However, because it did not involve any self-report, there are no qualitative data so we cannot know about the thoughts or feelings that the consumers were experiencing. This limits how useful the study is because only quantitative data were gathered (in terms of how many purchases were made), but we cannot know the reasons behind the change in purchases. Their second experiment is flawed because they only included students, so we cannot generalise the results to the wider population. This is particularly important for an area such as consumer behaviour, because people from different sorts of households and with different budgets and priorities will be expected to show different consumer behaviour. How could Wansink et al. have improved their study?

ISSUES AND DEBATES

Research into point of purchase decisions, such as that by Wansink et al., is particularly applicable to real life because it shows the effectiveness of different promotions and selling techniques. This is useful for shop owners as they can use the information gathered from this research to maximise

CONTINUED

sales and profit, and to target certain products that they may, for example, have an excess of. The information could also be useful for consumers, however, because this would allow them to understand the psychology behind these promotions and it may help them to think about whether they are really going to benefit from the offers or not.

Mistakes in decision-making

Thinking fast and thinking slow/System 1 and System 2

Kahneman's (2011) book *Thinking, Fast and Slow* presents his 40 years of research into the theory of thinking and has been summarised and reviewed by Shleifer (2012). According to Kahneman, there are two different systems used for thinking: **System 1** and **System 2**. System 1 thinking corresponds to 'thinking fast', involving automatic, intuitive, unconscious and effortless thinking. System 1 thinking relies on associations and heuristics, rather than on statistical analysis or consideration of evidence. On the other hand, System 2 thinking corresponds to 'thinking slow', it is conscious, controlled and deliberate. System 2 thinking relies on statistical analysis and requires time and attention so it is costly to use. Kahneman and Tversky claim that System 1 describes 'normal' decision-making and is the approach most of us take to making decisions, most of the time. This not only applies to small and insignificant decisions but also to bigger decisions such as investments and purchases. System 1 is useful because it is quick and effortless so it allows for our lives to be easier. Often, System 1 thinking works out well, but because of the lack of deliberate and conscious thought, sometimes it can lead to errors. This does not mean that we are incapable of System 2 thought, but that we don't use it very often. This may be why it is so difficult to make accurate predictions about decision-making.

KEY WORDS

System 1 thinking: 'thinking fast', involving automatic, unconscious thinking, which is non-statistical and uses associations

System 2 thinking: 'thinking slow', involving conscious controlled thinking, which is deliberate and costly to use

An example to demonstrate the difference in System 1 and System 2 thinking comes from one of Kahneman and Tversky's best-known experiments. In the experiment, Americans were asked to respond to this statement: 'Steve is very shy and withdrawn, invariably helpful but with very little interest in people or in the world of reality. A meek and tidy soul, he has a need for order and structure, and a passion for detail.' Is Steve more likely to be a librarian or a farmer?

The most common response would come from System 1 thinking. Steve is more likely to be a librarian than a farmer because he sounds more like a librarian than a farmer. However, this has ignored the facts that there are at least five times as many farmers in the USA as there are librarians, and that male librarians in the USA are even less common. Therefore, a response from the System 2 approach would be that it is much more likely that Steve is a farmer, rather than a librarian.

Kahneman claims that adding two and two, completing the words 'bread and...' and driving a car on an empty road are all examples of System 1 thinking. They require a quick, intuitive response with little effort, and usually get the right answer. However, the previous example of Steve shows that System 1 can sometimes lead to errors.

There are some difficulties when considering System 1 and System 2 thinking. First, the parameters of these systems will vary between people. Kahneman uses an example of calculating 20 × 20 to demonstrate that, for some people (such as mathematicians) this is a System 1 effortless task, whereas for others it would rely on System 2, effortful thinking. Another difficulty with the systems is that we focus on the errors that tend to occur as a result of System 1 thinking, however, System 2 is not flawless, and can also lead to errors. Considering the example of 20 × 20, even using System 2 and spending time and effort on the calculation, some people will still make an error. Therefore, if we see an error in thinking or decision-making, it is not obvious whether the error is due to System 1, System 2 or a combination of the two. A third problem with the relationship between System 1 and System 2 comes from the idea that most of the information that is considered during System 2 comes from System 1. If the full or correct information is not 'sent' from System 1 to System 2 then what prompts System 2 to engage? To use the example of Steve, what would actually trigger someone to engage System 2 thinking and consider the ratio of male librarians to farmers? There are many questions that remain unclear or unanswered in terms of how the two systems are distinguished from another and how they work with one another.

Choice blindness

Key study: Hall et al. (2010)

Hall, L., Johansson, P., Tärning, B., Sikström, S., & Deutgen, T. (2010). Magic at the marketplace: choice blindness for the taste of jam and the smell of tea. _Cognition_, _117_(1), 54–61.

Context

Choice blindness is an example of an error in decision-making. This occurs when someone doesn't notice the difference between what they have chosen and the outcome they get. Johansson et al. (2005) investigated choice blindness by asking participants to select which of two photos of women's faces they found most attractive. The photos were then surreptitiously swapped over, and the participant was asked to defend their choice and explain why they found their chosen photo more attractive (while being presented with the other photo). Participants only noticed that there was something wrong with their choice in 26% of trials.

If the processing of faces was subject to choice blindness it is reasonable to expect that the same could be applied to other visual processing. However, Hall et al. were interested to discover whether choice blindness extended beyond human faces and other visual processing. They were interested in whether choice blindness would apply to other decision-making, and specifically, would it apply to consumer decision-making in a real-life setting.

> **KEY WORD**
>
> **choice blindness:** refers to a person's inability to notice mismatches between intention and outcome in a decision

Main theories and explanations

Choice blindness is a complex phenomenon, without a clear explanation. There has been a great interest in the importance of implicit or 'non-conscious' influence in consumer decision-making. One example of an implicit influence is preference fluency; how easy or difficult the consumer perceives the choice to be. Another implicit influence is placebo effect of marketing, where people tend to believe that a product will be less effective if it is purchased at a reduced price.

As well as these implicit influences, our decision-making is also affected by explicit influences, in other words making a decision based on what you actually see and hear relating to the product itself. Choice blindness then is interesting because it considers the interaction between explicit choices (the decision you make initially) and implicit changes (the surreptitious switching of your choice). Studying choice blindness allows us to gain insight into the decision-making processes that occurred at the time, as well as the extent to which we are consciously aware of these afterwards.

Aims

The aim was to investigate whether choice blindness would be shown with consumer decision-making in a naturalistic setting.

Design

The study was a field experiment, where a tasting venue was set up at a supermarket. The sample consisted of 180 participants, of which 118 were female, and with an age range of 16–80 years, at a supermarket in Sweden. This was opportunity sampling, as participants were asked if they would like to be involved in a quality control test for pairs of teas and jams (see Figure 7.16). Each participant was asked to taste the jam and smell the tea and say which of each pair they preferred. For each participant either the jam or the tea condition was manipulated. Half were told they would receive the chosen tea or jam as a thank you gift. For each participant, the order of presentation, the type of manipulation and which jams and teas were used were randomly allocated.

Figure 7.16: Participants tasted pairs of jams and chose their favourite

Experimenter 1 asked the questions, took notes and managed the recording device, while experimenter 2 conducted the preference test. In the manipulated condition the participant was presented with the two jars of jam or tea and asked to sample the first one and rate how much they liked it on a scale of 1–10. While they were rating it, experimenter 2 surreptitiously turned the jar upside down so that now the other sample was present (this was created by having two jars attached to each other bottom to bottom, each with a screw on lid and a paper label covering the join so it looked like a normal jar). The participant was asked to sample the other option and again while rating it, experimenter 2 turned it upside down. Participants were now asked to taste their preferred sample again, defend their choice, and indicate on a ten-point scale how difficult they found the decision and how confident they were in their choice. After the participant had completed the tea and jam pairing, they were asked if they felt there was anything odd or unusual about the set up or about the sampled alternatives. They were then fully *debriefed* and had the full aim explained, and were asked again if they suspected any manipulation.

There were three criteria for detection of the manipulation: concurrent detection (if the participant noticed anything unusual immediately after tasting or smelling the manipulated jam or tea), retrospective detection (where the participant claimed to have noticed the deception after the experiment, either before or after debriefing) and sensory-change detection (where, even if the participants did not report noticing anything, they made any comments about the change in taste or smell after the manipulation). Those with a concurrent detection completed the taste study but their results were not included in the results analysis.

Results, findings and conclusions

Only 14.4% of the jam and 13.8% of the tea trials were detected concurrently, 6.2% of the jam and 6.9% of the tea trials were detected retrospectively, and 12.4% of the jam and 11.5% of the tea trials were recorded as sensory-change detection. In total, 33.3% of the manipulated jam trials and 32% of the manipulated tea trials were detected. In contrast to predictions, those offered the tea as a gift were less likely to detect any manipulation than those who were not offered a gift. There were no differences based on incentives for jam. There were no differences in perceived ease of distinguishing between the two samples, or confidence in decision (for tea or jam) between the non-manipulation trials and the manipulation trials where there was no detection. Overall rating for perceived ease of distinguishing between the two samples, and confidence rating, was notably high for both jam and tea.

The results supported the main prediction: no more than a third of manipulation trials were detected by participants. This shows that, for most trials, participants were blind to the mismatch between intended and actual outcome of their choice, and instead believed that the taste or smell in their final sample matched their initial choice. Furthermore, in two-thirds of detected trials, participants didn't react at the time of tasting the manipulated sample, instead this only happened later, or through an expression of sensory change. Even for vastly different tastes such as cinnamon-apple and grapefruit, or smells such as mango and Pernod (strong aniseed smell), detections were made in less than half of trials, and no more than one-fifth were detected concurrently. One aspect that makes the findings so interesting is that, for non-manipulated trials and for non-detected manipulated trials the ease of distinguishing between the two samples scored high on the ten-point scale (7.3 for jam and 8.0 for tea). This shows that the non-detection could not just be that participants found it difficult to tell the samples apart; in fact, they found it easy to distinguish between the two, but they still could not detect the manipulation. Finally, although some may argue that this is a low-stakes decision, those who were offered the free gift were actually less likely to notice the manipulation than those who were not offered a gift. This suggests that choice blindness still remains at a significant level even when faced with real-world consequences.

Evaluation

Hall et al. used opportunity sampling for their field experiment. They set up a tasting stall at a supermarket and asked passers-by to take part in taste-testing. A strength of opportunity sampling is that it is quick, easy and convenient. By using whoever happens to be present it means the researchers don't need to spend time and resources trying to get a sample of participants, as with some other methods. Another strength is that there is likely to be a reasonable spread of people; in the case of Hall et al. there was an age range of 16–80, and a mix of men and women. A weakness of opportunity sampling, however, is that you don't have control over who the sample will be so you cannot ensure it is fully representative, or that there are any particular types of people. The use of **pilot testing** allowed for the researchers to use samples of jam and tea that they knew were easy to distinguish from one another. This is really important for increasing the validity of the study as we can be confident that the reason for participants not

noticing a manipulation was not just that it was hard to distinguish between the two, but instead that it was due to choice blindness.

Hall et al.'s research is applicable to real life because it helps us to understand the role of choice blindness. Although this was a low-stakes situation, where there were not any repercussions because of the choice blindness, it is still an important phenomenon to be aware of. There could be situations in real life where the stakes are higher and possible repercussions could be significant so understanding choice blindness may be relevant. For example, if somebody was a witness to a crime and they incorrectly identified a suspect from a set of photos, but then at trial they defended their choice, despite possible evidence to the contrary.

Consumer memory for advertising

Advertising is a really important tool for selling products, but adverts can only work if consumers remember them. It was first thought that memory simply fades over time, so if you view an advert one week you may have forgotten it by the following week because of the time that has passed (Zielske & Henry, 1980). However, there is much evidence to suggest that forgetting is not simply due to the passing of time but that it is more to do with the additional learning that happens during that time (McGeoch, 1932). Research shows that people are more likely to be able to remember information for a period of time if relatively little learning takes place in the interim (Roediger & Crowder, 1976). There are two types of interference that may affect a consumer's memory: **retroactive interference**, where new information is learned that makes it harder to recall earlier information, and **proactive interference**, where prior learning can interfere with a person's ability to learn and recall new information. **Retrieval failure** is generally accepted as

---

KEY WORDS

retroactive interference: this is the process that occurs when information is hard to recall because of new information that is learned

proactive interference: this is the process that occurs when information is hard to recall because of previous learning that has taken place

retrieval failure: when forgetting occurs due to either retroactive or proactive interference

one of the main causes of forgetting: the information is stored in long-term memory, but the difficulty is accessing the information again. Information is accessed by using cues to help find the correct information so, if more similar information has been learned, it will make it harder to retrieve the specific memory you are trying to recall.

McKinney (1935) investigated the role of retroactive interference in advertising by asking participants to study one full-page magazine advert. Then half of the participants were given a rest period while the other half were given two more adverts to learn (the 'work' condition). Participants were then given a cued recall test (where they were given cues to help trigger their memory) and results showed that those in the rest condition were more likely to remember the slogan of the advert (94%) than those in the work condition (72%), suggesting that the subsequent learning interfered with the ability to recall the original advert. Blankenship and Whitely (1941) investigated proactive interference in advertising by asking participants to learn either one list of 18 store items and prices, or to learn the list, after also learning a previous list. Their results showed that, 48 hours later, those who only had to learn the list were more likely to recall the items than those who had also learned a previous list, suggesting it is the previous information that interfered with the recall of information.

Example study

Burke and Srull (1988) aimed to discover whether a consumer's ability to recall distinctive brand informatin from an advert would be hindered if they subsequently view an advert for another similar product by another brand, or for another item by the same brand. They were also interested in how memory was affected by the consumer's **information processing objective** (the reason why they were looking at the advert). The researchers reported on three experiments, of which we will look at the first two. In Experiment 1 participants were shown 12 adverts (three of which were the target adverts they would later be asked to recall, which were presented near the beginning of the series) and the information processing objective was manipulated by asking participants to either decide how likely they

would be to buy that product, or how interesting they thought the advert was. The 12 adverts were either similar products by different brands, different products by the same brand, or a range of different products and brands. Following viewing, participants were given a questionnaire about magazine and television viewing habits as a **distractor task** and were then given a surprise recall test where they were given the brand name and product number of each of the target adverts in turn and were given 2 minutes to recall any information about the advert.

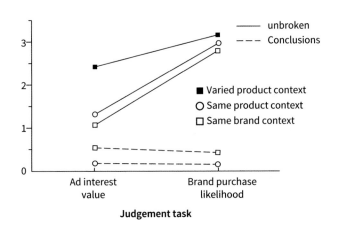

Figure 7.17: Results from Burke and Srull's Experiment 1 (1988)

Results showed that participants recalled on average twice as much when they had been asked to rate intention to purchase, rather than just rating the advert on interest, suggesting that purchase intention leads to closer attention being paid (see Figure 7.17). Results also showed that recall was significantly lower for those who subsequently viewed adverts for similar products or the same brand (compared to those who viewed a range of product adverts). This shows retroactive interference because the new learning (the adverts that were viewed after the target advert) interfered with the ability to recall information about the target advert. However, information processing objective (whether the consumer was looking to decide on purchase intent or just rating the advert on interest) mediated this effect and results showed that the memory of participants looking at an advert with a purchase intent was less likely to be affected by interference from other adverts.

Experiment 2 was designed the same way, but was intended to investigate proactive interference. As such in Experiment 2 the target adverts were presented later in the series, to see if earlier information interfered with recall of target adverts. Results were similar to Experiment 1: those rating on purchase intention recalled more information and those viewing similar product adverts remembered less information correctly. However, unlike in Experiment 1, Experiment 2 did not find that information processing objective had a significant mediating effect on the influence of similar product adverts.

RESEARCH METHODS

Burke and Srull's use of laboratory experiments offers a highly controlled method, giving high validity and reliability. Validity is high because extraneous variables are controlled so we can be confident that any changes in response by the participants will be due to the change in the independent variables. For example, adverts were shown in a specific order, and for the same length of time so we know that changes in recall can't be due to some participants viewing the material for longer. This increases the validity. Reliability is also high because of the standardised procedure used. Each participant followed the exact same procedure in terms of the instructions they were given, the times, the order, the distractor task and the cues used in the recall test. Therefore, because everything was kept the same for each participant, we can be confident of consistent, reliable results.

ISSUES AND DEBATES

Research into the two thinking systems (System 1 and System 2), and the way this impacts our decision-making can be seen to be deterministic. The suggestion is that System 1 (thinking fast) is automatic and unconscious and that we use it almost all the time. This has been used to explain why we may make errors in decision-making. This is deterministic because it suggests that errors in decision-making happen because we are automatically using System 1 thinking, rather than System 2 (thinking slow). However, one could argue that this explanation ignores free will and that we are responsible for our own actions and our own decision-making so if we make an error that is due to our free will, and our choice not to engage in System 2 thinking. How could the *idiographic versus nomothetic* approach be applied to research into mistakes in decision-making?

Questions

7   Why is a nomothetic approach useful in research into decision-making strategies?

8   What may be the advantages and disadvantages of using heuristics when making decisions?

9   Hall et al. recorded three different criteria for detection of manipulation. Why was this?

7.4 The product

Packaging and positioning of a product

Gift wrapping

This section will look at gift wrapping, which is used in many cultures around the world to signal that an object is a gift. There is no ambiguity. This means that the beliefs of both the giver and the recipient are important: a wrapped gift means that each knows exactly the roles that they are supposed to play. We will consider the beliefs of the giver and the recipient, why gifts are wrapped and types of wrapping.

Porublev et al. (2009) suggest that gifts can be presented in one of three ways: unwrapped, wrapped in a non-traditional manner where it may be difficult to determine that the gift is actually a gift (such as in a bag) or wrapped in a traditional manner. Howard conducted a study in which he examined how the appearance of a gift influenced mood. He found that people were happier when presented with a traditionally wrapped gift than with either a non-traditionally wrapped or an unwrapped gift. Unwrapped gifts can be acceptable, for example, if you were invited to a dinner and took a box of chocolates as a gift, you would probably not wrap it, but if it was being given as a birthday present you probably would.

In the study by Porublev et al., three data collecting techniques were used: (1) observations conducted at a Christmas gift-wrapping stall; (2) 20 in-depth interviews where respondents were asked to reflect on gift wrapping (including questions such as 'Do you prefer to receive gifts that are wrapped or unwrapped?', 'In what instance do you wrap gifts?', 'In what instance do you not wrap gifts?') and (3) six workshops where, in pairs, participants were asked to wrap two gifts, one for someone they were close to and one for an acquaintance, and to have a conversation about gift wrapping while doing so.

Results from both the workshops and the interviews revealed that most participants preferred to receive a gift that was wrapped and that there were clear expectations of what a gift should look like.

The researchers used qualitative data to support their findings that gifts should be wrapped. For example, one of their participants said '*I prefer wrapped. I like the reveal … I like a gift under any circumstances, but it does mean somebody's taken a little bit of extra time and put extra thought into it.*' Participants also identified that gift wrapping was traditional, and that people probably do it without thinking too much about why they are doing it: it is just 'what you do' (see Figure 7.18).

Figure 7.18: Gift wrapping is important for both the giver and receiver

There was also a preference for a gift to look like a gift. An analysis of the gifts created in the workshops showed that all 24 of them looked like gifts, with traditional wrappings: paper, decorative bags with ribbons, bows and other embellishments. It was suggested that this indicates social expectations of what a gift should typically look like. Participants in the gift-wrapping task reported 'playing it safe' with wrapping the gift for an acquaintance. However, when wrapping a gift for a close friend or family member they were able to relate this directly to the person, choosing colours and patterns that they knew the person would like. The researchers concluded that gifts should be wrapped because wrapped gifts make it easier for the exchange to occur because they 'enable the giver and receiver to fall into their roles without any confusion as to the purpose of the exchange'.

> ### ACTIVITY 7.5
>
> Imagine you were asked to take part in the workshop set up by Porublev et al. Draw and label a picture of how you would wrap up a gift for someone you are close to, and for someone who was just an acquaintance. What are the key differences? Why?

Key study: Becker et al. (2011)

Becker, L., van Rompay, T. J., Schifferstein, H. N., & Galetzka, M. (2011). Tough package, strong taste: the influence of packaging design on taste impressions and product evaluations. *Food quality and preference,* *22*(1), 17–23.

Context

The food package design is an important aspect of any product as it is what consumers will first see of a product. When making a decision about which product to buy, a consumer is often faced with a huge array of options, so it is important for a product to stand out and to appeal to a customer. Previous research in this area has shown that product design helps aid a decision in the absence of information about a product, for example when a new product becomes available.

There are many factors related to food package design that have been shown to influence consumers' perceptions of the product, in terms of taste, quality and price expectations. Not only can product packaging affect our *perception* of a product, research has also shown that it can have an effect on our *actual* experience of the product. There are several different features of packaging design that need to be considered, two of which are the colour and the shape.

Main theories and explanations

Evidence shows that consumers often base their purchase decisions on the visual appearance of the product, either the packaging or the item itself if it is visible (Bloch 1995). Colour of packaging has been specifically shown to influence consumer's taste perceptions. For example, research by Hine (1995) showed that adding 15% more yellow to the green colour of a 7-Up (a fizzy drink) can led to participants experiencing the taste of the drink as more lemony (even though the drink remained unchanged).

Packaging shape has also been shown to have an effect on consumer's perception. For example, Berlynne (1976) found that angular shapes tended to induce associations with energy, toughness and strength, whereas rounded shapes tended to be associated with approachability, friendliness and harmony. Research has also shown that packaging shape influences consumer's perception of the quality of the product and, consequently their price expectations (Chitturi et al. 2019).

Aims

The aim was to investigate the effect of packaging shape and colour on consumers' perception of the product. There were four hypotheses:

Hypothesis 1: An angular, rather than rounded, package will lead consumers to experience the product taste as more intense.

Hypothesis 2: A highly saturated, rather than lowly saturated, coloured packaging will lead to consumers experiencing the product taste as more intense.

Hypothesis 3: Shape–colour congruency (angular shape and highly saturated colour or rounded shape and lowly saturated colour) will lead to a more positive overall product attitude than shape–colour incongruency (angular and lowly saturated colour or rounded and highly saturated colour).

Hypothesis 4: All predicted effects will be greater for those with a sensitivity to design compared to those indifferent to product design.

Design

A field experiment was used, where participants were approached and asked to take part in a 'taste test' for a new brand of yoghurt. There were 151 participants, who were customers of a large German supermarket. There was an equal split of men and women and an age range of 15–81 years. Participants were approached at the entrance to the supermarket, so this was opportunity sampling. The *experimental design* was *independent measures*, where each participant was in one condition only.

Pretesting was used to design an angular and rounded shape and a highly saturated (high intensity of colour) and lowly saturated (low intensity of colour) colour packaging. A (different) set of participants were asked to rate three variations of angular and three different variations of rounded shapes on a range of different items, to identify the pair of shapes that led to the greatest difference in ratings. The same process was applied with two pairs of saturations of lemon-green. These pre-tests lead to the four lemon yoghurt product variants that were used in the main experiment: these are shown in Figure 7.19.

Each participant was shown a 20-second 3D clip on a laptop of one of four package variants and were then given a sample to taste (the same sample was used for all participants). Participants were then asked to complete a computer-presented questionnaire, using a seven-point Likert-type scales to assess their taste experience, product evaluation and price expectation, as well as a scale to assess their sensitivity to design.

Figure 7.19: The four lemon yoghurt packaging variants used by Becker et al. (2011)

Results, findings and conclusions

An analysis was carried out to see if package shape and colour had a significant effect on perceived packaging potency ('This product package strikes me as potent'). Potent means powerful, intense or strong. The effect of packaging shape was significant, with an angular shape being perceived as more potent. However, there were no significant overall effects of colour on packaging potency, except for participants with high design sensitivity (where highly saturated colour packaging was perceived as more potent). Results showed that neither packaging shape nor colour had a significant overall effect on intensity of taste experience, except for those with a high sensitivity to design, where an angular shape did have a significant effect on intensity of taste experience. Product colour did not have a significant effect on overall attitude to the product, but an angular shape did lead to a significantly more positive attitude than the rounded shape. Finally, in terms of price expectation, an angular packaging led to a significantly higher price estimate than a rounded shape, and the lowly saturated colour led to a marginally higher price estimate than the highly saturated colour. Further analysis showed that the angular shape led to a higher price estimate because it was perceived as more potent.

The results showed that packaging colour and shape may influence product potency perceptions and that this may in turn lead to higher price expectations. Specifically, the results showed that an angular shaped package may lead to an intense taste experience, supporting the idea of a cross-modal (across the senses) correspondence (Schifferstein & Spence, 2008), and that this is particularly the case for those who are sensitive to design. Packaging colour did not have the expected effect on taste or product evaluation, so perhaps the variation was too subtle to have an impact: this could be investigated further. This research has important implications as it shows that it is important to design the 'right' package for the 'right' taste. Of particular practical importance is the finding that lowly saturated colour packaging led to a higher price expectation than highly saturated colour packaging. This goes against a common strategy used in promotions or sale items where the tendency is to use highly saturated colour packaging to draw attention to the product, but this may have the unintended effect of associating the product with 'cheapness' or low quality.

Evaluation

A field experiment was used, so there is high ecological validity, meaning the results of the study can be applied beyond the research setting. The participants did not know the true aim of the experiment, which means there was less chance of *demand characteristics* and the risk of participants changing their behaviour accordingly, thus increasing the validity of the results. The study used a good-sized sample with a balance of gender and wide range of ages, which means the results can be generalised to the wider population. However, all participants were from the same area in Germany so results may not be applicable to other cultures. The study used a standardised procedure, where all participants experienced the same instructions, the same video clips, were given the same sample to taste and were given the same set of questionnaires to answer, thus increasing the reliability of the study. Quantitative data were gathered using the seven-point Likert-type scales, meaning the results can be compared and analysed. However, a lack of *open questions* means that there were no qualitative data, so we do not have details about the participants' thoughts and feelings or their reasons for the answers they gave.

Becker et al.'s research can be applied to everyday life because it has demonstrated consumers' views on food packaging and the implications that has for the perception of the product itself. This can be used by food package designers as a useful tool to guide decision-making in terms of shape and colour of the package. Packaging is one of the main components that a customer will use to make a purchase decision about a food item, so using information gained from research such as Becker et al. will be a valuable asset.

Attention and shelf position

Where a product is on a shelf can be a significant indicator of how likely it is to be selected for purchase. The amount of time a consumer pays attention to an item, and how likely they are to buy that item has been shown to be influenced by where it is in the array of products, as investigated by Atalay et al. (2012).

Example study

Atalay et al. (2012) used eye-tracking technology to identify the customer tendency to choose the option in the centre of the array (a variety of different versions or brands of the same item presented together). It was important to ensure the item in the centre of the array was not just selected because it was also in the participants' centre of vision, so to test this, Study 1 was split into Study 1A and 1B.

Study 1A involved participants looking at a screen to make a decision about a product, while a discreet infra-red camera recorded their eye gaze and tracked the exact location of **eye fixations** (the location of where their eyes focused) on the screen.

Participants reviewed two product categories: vitamin supplements and meal replacement bars. Two separate **planograms** were displayed. A planogram is a diagram that shows how and where specific retail products should be placed on retail shelves or displays to increase customer purchases. *Planogramming* is a skill used in merchandising and retail space planning. There were three brands and each brand appeared three times. Participants were asked to carefully review each product on the screen as if these were on the shelf in a shop. They were asked to hit the enter key when they had finished reviewing the products and were ready to make a choice. Once they hit the enter key, the stimulus disappeared from the screen to ensure that any further visual processing was stopped. Participants indicated their choice by ticking the box that matched the position of the product on a 3 × 3 matrix that mirrored the planogram.

Results of Study 1A showed that brands in the centre received more frequent eye fixations and overall were looked at for longer. This was particularly the case nearer to decision time; an effect that is known as the **central gaze cascade**. Further analysis revealed that products placed in the centre were chosen more often and this choice was unrelated to other inferences made about the product and was solely related to increased visual attention.

Study 1B was identical except that the shelf arrays were presented to either the left or right of the computer screen so that the item in the centre of the array was not also in the centre of the visual field. Results for Study 1B were the same as for Study 1A, which shows the item being central in the array (shelf position) is the important factor, not just the position in the visual field.

Study 2 was conducted to see if the results could be replicated in a more realistic context, rather than on a screen. Participants were asked to select one item from a set of three fictitious brands of energy drink.

Participants were tested one at a time and were positioned in the middle of the display so that the category they were asked to choose from was to their left or their right (but never exactly in the centre of their visual field). They were not allowed to reposition themselves (which would have put the category in the centre of their visual field) and were simply asked to review the items and to choose one of the energy drinks.

Results showed that the centrally located brand within a product category is more often chosen even when it is not in the centre of the visual field. This again shows just how robust the central gaze effect is and that it is not a product of screen-based presentation.

A study in a real shop also confirmed that the centrally located item is chosen more often, even when this is not the centre of the visual field (see Figure 7.20).

Interestingly, although the brand in the centre was chosen more often and received more visual attention, it was not evaluated any more positively than the other items. This suggests that more research is required to investigate why the central brand is chosen most often.

KEY WORDS

eye fixations: recordings of where participants focused on the screen

planogram: a diagram that shows how and where specific retail products should be placed on retail shelves or displays in order to increase customer purchases

central gaze cascade: the tendency to focus more and more attention on the central option immediately before the decision is made

Figure 7.20: Being in the centre of a shelf array increases the likelihood of an item being purchased

RESEARCH METHODS

Atalay et al.'s study had high validity because they used different studies to test that changes to the dependent variable are truly because of the independent variable. Study 1A appeared to show that items in the centre of the array were chosen more often, but because those items were also in the centre of the field of vision, the researchers carried out Study 1B to check what influenced the choice. Study 1B adjusted the view so that items in the centre of the array were not in the centre of the field of vision as well; the fact that those in the centre of the array were still chosen most often increases the validity. Furthermore, by carrying out a similar study in real-life the researchers were able to increase the ecological validity of their findings; they have shown that these findings do not just occur in computer-based laboratory studies but also in real-life settings.

ISSUES AND DEBATES

Research into the effect of shelf position takes a nomothetic approach, where a universal set of rules has been suggested to explain the behaviour of everybody. This is based on gathering large amounts of data. In the case of Atalay et al., they gathered data using eye tracking, which is a scientific and **objective** measure but does not consider the individuals' thoughts, feelings and attitudes. Consideration of everyone's individual thoughts and feelings would follow a more idiographic approach, where everyone would be considered independently and a range of factors relating to them would be considered. For research into consumer psychology, a nomothetic approach is the most useful and practical as it allows retailers to design and lay out their stores in a way that will be successful for most of their customers.

Selling the product

Sales techniques

There are several strategies that can be used to sell a product: customer-, competitor- and product-focused. Each of these strategies will have an effect on the buyer–seller relationship. With a **customer-focused sales technique**, the seller looks carefully at potential customers, identifies what they want and tailors their sales techniques to match these needs. This is sometimes called 'solution-selling' and advertisements based on solution-selling highlight exactly how the product suits the customer. For a customer-focused sales technique to be effective the seller requires as much information about the customers and their needs as possible. They also need to think about having a long-term, positive buyer–seller relationship, not only because loyal customers will spread the word and advertise the business for the seller, but also because satisfied customers will return. If a car dealer listens carefully to what a customer says they need and finds a car that perfectly suits their needs, there is every chance that this customer will come back next time they are buying a car and would recommend the dealer to friends.

The second strategy is the **competitor-focused sales technique**, where the seller focuses on how they compare to their competitors (see Figure 7.21). This is common in supermarkets for example, where advertisements regularly draw direct comparisons between prices in different shops. Competitor-focused sales techniques are also essential if your product is relatively similar in price to your competitors. In this case, the retailer needs to convince the customer of other advantages of buying from them, so the buyer–seller relationship will be focused around customer service, after-sales care or guarantees.

The final strategy is the **product-focused sales technique**, where the needs of individual customers are ignored, and the focus is primarily on producing or selling a quality product (see Figure 7.22). The assumptions are that if you have the best product then the customers will come to you and that creating a new, high-quality product could even create a customer need that did not exist before. Apple is a perfect example of an organisation which focuses on the product. This

KEY WORDS

customer-focused sales technique: the seller looks at potential customers and considers their wants and needs

competitor-focused sales technique: the seller focuses on how they compare to their competitors

product-focused sales technique: the focus is primarily on the quality of the product

strategy will have a negative effect on the buyer–seller relationship because the individual buyer is not seen as important to the seller.

In reality, however, it is not easy to separate out these techniques. A customer-focused sales pitch may well include elements of competitor comparison as well as product quality.

Figure 7.21: In the competitor-focused sales technique, the seller focuses on how they compare to their competitors

Figure 7.22: In the product-focused sales technique, the seller focuses on selling a quality product

Interpersonal influence techniques

The **disrupt-then-reframe (DTR) technique** is intended to confuse consumers with a disruptive message and then reduce this confusion (or ambiguity) by reframing the message. For example, Davis and Knowles (1999) asked participants if they would like to purchase Christmas cards sold by a charity. In some of the conditions, the experimenters used the DTR technique by saying 'The price is 300 pennies ... I mean 3 dollars'. The use of this technique doubled sales. Fennis et al. (2004) also showed that using the DTR technique reduced the number of counterarguments and disagreements from customers.

An important factor that may influence the likelihood of the DTR technique being effective is the customer's **need for cognitive closure (NFCC)**. This refers to the extent to which the customer has the 'desire for a firm answer to a question and an aversion toward ambiguity' (Kruglanksi & Webster, 1996). Someone who is high in NFCC will be unsettled by the confusion and ambiguity caused in the DTR technique so will be keen to grab on to any information that eases that ambiguity. The reframing that follows the confusion in the DTR technique will make the customer more likely to make a quick decision, as a way of reaching closure, and therefore they will be more likely to agree to a purchase. However, those low in NFCC are not as concerned by ambiguity so will be less motivated to ease that ambiguity and therefore less likely to be susceptible to the DTR technique.

> ### KEY WORDS
>
> **disrupt-then-reframe' (DTR) technique:** a technique intended to confuse consumers with a disruptive message and then reduce this confusion (or ambiguity) by reframing the message
>
> **need for cognitive closure (NFCC):** the extent to which the customer has a dislike of ambiguity and a desire for a firm answer to a question

Example study

Kardes et al.'s (2007) study involved two field experiments and one laboratory experiment to discover the effect of DTR on monetary contributions, and to discover whether NFCC affected the success of the DTR technique. Study 1 was a field experiment conducted in a European supermarket. The researchers set up a sales stand presenting a special offer on candy (sweets). Confederates would approach customers and tell them that 'as Christmas is approaching, these boxes of Christmas candy are on special offer today'. In the DTR condition, the confederate would then say, 'The price is now 100 eurocents (followed by a two second pause), that's one euro. It's a bargain.' In the *control condition* (reframe only) the confederate would simply say 'The price is one euro. It's a bargain!' The confederate then observed the customer response. Adding one or more boxes of candy to their shopping cart was recorded as complying with the sales request.

A total of 147 customers listened to the whole presentation and 54% subsequently bought candy. However, 65% of those in the DTR group bought candy compared with 44% of those in the control group.

Experiment 2 was also a field experiment. A male confederate claimed to be from a fictitious student interest group and approached students on the campus of a Dutch university, asking them to join the group for a small cost (three euros). Half of the students were exposed to a DTR message and the other half were not. After the request had been made, the participant was also asked to complete a 20-item scale measuring NFCC. In the DTR group, participants were told that 'You can now become a member for half a year for 300 eurocents. (followed by a two second pause) That's three euros. That's a really small investment.' In the control group (reframe only), they were told that 'You can now become a member for half a year for three euros. That's a really small investment.'

Overall, 22% of the students approached agreed to become a member, with 30% of those in the DTR group agreeing to join compared with only 13% of the control group. Compliance also increased as NFCC increased: 43% of high NFCC individuals complied in the DTR condition compared with only 17% in the control condition. Although there was a slight difference for low NFCC individuals (16% versus 9%) this difference was not significant. As predicted the DTR effect was stronger for those who were high in NFCC.

The final experiment examined this further. Participants were randomly assigned to one of three conditions: DTR, reframe only or disrupt only. Participants were shown one of three videos. In the DTR condition the video showed a male actor stating that research is essential to the quality of education at university and that money is necessary for research. For these reasons, he continued, the Student Advocacy Council is arguing for 'an increase in tuition of 7500 pennies. (followed by a two second pause.) That's $75, it's a really small investment.' In the reframe only condition, the participants heard the actor argue for 'an increase in tuition of $75; it's a really small investment' and in the disrupt only condition they heard 'an increase in tuition of 7500 pennies'.

All participants then completed the NFCC scale. Participants were then asked to complete a series of other scales measuring perceived ambiguity, attitudes and behavioural compliance.

The analysis of these data is complex, but the key findings are as follows. When NFCC was low, the DTR manipulation had no effect on perceived ambiguity. But when NFCC was high, the disruption manipulation was successful in increasing ambiguity and the reframing was successful in decreasing ambiguity. When NFCC was high, more favourable attitudes towards the tuition increases were formed in the DTR condition than in the reframe only condition, which in turn produced more favourable outcomes than the disrupt only condition. When NFCC was low, the DTR technique was no more effective than the reframe only technique but was more effective than the disrupt only technique. Overall, the findings suggest that the DTR technique was more effective as NFCC increased. This was also found when analysing the behavioural measures.

The researchers conclude that the effectiveness of the DTR technique increases as the NFCC increases and that disruption motivates consumers to accept a reframed message that aids closure through the reduction of ambiguity.

Cialdini's six ways to close a sale

Most techniques for closing a sale (when the customer buys the product) involve psychological principles drawn from social psychology and persuasion techniques. Cialdini (1984) cited in Cialdini 2006 suggests that there are six ways to close a sale:

- Reciprocity: if someone gives us something, we have to give them something in return. So free samples in a supermarket or the promise of a free gift with our purchase (common with cosmetics and beauty products) is more likely to make us agree to buy something.

- Commitment and consistency: if you can persuade someone to make a small commitment, then you will increase the likelihood that they will make a larger commitment. For example, if an online retailer can get someone to sign up to their newsletter (which costs nothing) they increase the chances of that person buying something in the future. If signing up to something implies a commitment (to exercise more, to de-clutter or learn a new skill) then making associated purchases is consistent with this initial commitment. Free returns can also increase commitment: they might make a customer think they could order several items and then decide which ones to send back, however, in reality, they are likely to keep all of them.

- Liking: liking may sound obvious, but it goes beyond the actual product. If we like the salesperson, or the friendliness of a store, then we are more likely to purchase from that store. If a product has been endorsed by a celebrity and we like that celebrity, then we are more likely to purchase the product. Consider, for example, how many brands of celebrity perfumes there are. Another way to create liking is to use social media such as Facebook to show you that your friend likes a product or has just bought a product. Hotel booking sites will tell you that 'five rooms have been booked in this hotel in the last hour' (see Figure 7.23) and online auction sites such as eBay will tell you how many views an item has had. All this creates liking for the product through associations and this can help to achieve a sale.

- Authority: we know that authority is powerful. The experimenter in the lab coat was thought to be partly responsible for the high levels of obedience in the infamous Milgram experiment (Chapter 5) and authority is equally effective in persuading us to buy. Product advertising which includes 'scientific' or 'expert' evidence will convince us to buy.

- Social proof: we like to have our decisions 'supported' by others. Knowing that lots of other people have bought a particular item or booked into the same hotel can act as 'proof' that we are making the right decisions. For example, fashion websites suggest 'best sellers' to convince us to buy products. Looking at the reviews left by other people on sites such as Amazon is also very influential, and many manufacturers will offer free products to customers in return for a review. The principle of reciprocity (above) is likely to mean that we will write a positive review in these circumstances.

- Scarcity: if we think that we might miss out on something, we are likely to make a purchase, even on something we didn't know we wanted (see Figure 7.24). Shops will often have 'last few days' signs to encourage us to buy now and online retailers make increasing use of limited time sales, such as 'Black Friday' in the USA, which is spreading to other countries.

Figure 7.23: Seeing how many other customers have bought a product creates 'liking' for the product through associations and encourages us to buy it

Figure 7.24: Thinking we might miss out on something creates 'scarcity' and encourages us to buy now

RESEARCH METHODS

Kardes et al.'s use of field experiments is useful as it tells us about how people behave in real-life settings. Asking passers-by to buy a product without the participants knowing they are part of an experiment is the best way to ensure we are seeing their genuine behaviours and responses. Not only does this give us high ecological validity, meaning we can confidently apply the findings outside of the research setting, it also reduces the risk of demand characteristics. If participants knew they were taking part in a psychological experiment, it would be easy for them to work out the aim and therefore potentially change their behaviour accordingly, which would reduce the validity of the experiment. What might be the problem with the opportunity sample of shoppers?

ISSUES AND DEBATES

Research into selling a product can be applied to real life in two important ways. First, this research will be useful for retailers, so that they can understand how best to approach making and completing sales. This is particularly important for retailers who have strong competition. Knowing which techniques are likely to be effective for particular situations and customers could improve training of staff and hopefully increase sales. However, this information can also be useful for consumers. If customers are more informed about the psychology behind the sales techniques, and the way in which this is likely to be successful, the consumer can make sure that they are only making purchases they are happy with and are not being convinced to buy something they don't want, or at a price they are unhappy with.

Buying the product

The Engel Kollat Blackwell model of buyer decision-making

The Engel Kollat Blackwell (EKB) model (1968) was developed as a way of describing the active information-seeking and evaluation processes of the consumer when making a decision. The model looks at the buyer's decision-making process and describes five activities that occur over time:

1 Problem recognition: the consumer will realise there is a difference between their actual state and their ideal state, i.e., they will recognise that there is a problem that needs solving.

2 Information search: the consumer will try to gather information from a range of sources and will likely accept information that is consistent with their previously held beliefs or attitudes. Stimuli may catch their attention, be received and then stored in memory.

3 Alternative evaluation: alternate brands will be evaluated, and different factors will be considered depending on the consumer's underlying motives and beliefs.

4 Choice: the choice will depend on the consumer's intention, attitude and circumstances and will likely be influenced by the views of others, such as friends and family.

5 Outcome: after the purchase, consumers will either feel positive or negative about the product. If the consumer feels positive they will likely repeat purchases and become a loyal customer. If the consumer feels negative about the product they will be unlikely to return.

Deciding where to buy

Deciding what shop to go to depends on many factors, relating to the product that is to be purchased, the shop itself and the shopper. In a study of store choice behaviour for those buying audio equipment, Dash et al. (1976) found that pre-purchase information about the brand influenced store choice. Those with high level pre-purchase information tended to shop in speciality stores, whereas those with low level pre-purchase information tended to shop in department stores. The store is chosen based on the level of confidence the consumer has about the store, in terms of the nature and quality of the product and service they would receive. Furthermore, the type of trip will affect the store decision, with small top-up trips leading to local choices but bigger grocery shops being selected for main weekly shops (Kahn & Schmittlein, 1989). In terms of the shopper themselves, Dodge and Summer (1969) found that store choice was influenced by socioeconomic background, personality and past purchase experience. Age is also influential (Lumpkin and Robert 1985), with older people viewing shopping as a recreational activity so entertainment value is important, but with less of a focus on cost or proximity to home.

Example study

Sinha et al. (2002) wished to discover more about the factors that influenced shoppers' choice of shops. At exits of a range of different shops (grocery, chemist, lifestyle, books and music, clothes and so on, see Figure 7.25) in an Indian town, shoppers were given a structured questionnaire including a mix of open questions and statements measured on a Likert-type scale, asking about their shop choice and the reasons behind it. Using an open question, many reasons were given for shop choice, with the main two factors being convenience and merchandise (70% gave these as their first reason). Ambience, patronised store (they have visited it before) and service were other important factors. Participants were encouraged to give three reasons for their store choice, but only 40% managed to provide three reasons and most could provide only one or two. Convenience was most important for groceries, chemists and lifestyle shops, whereas merchandise was more important for shops selling durables, books and music, clothes and accessories. The effect of age was of weak significance: proximity and merchandise were the primary factors across age groups, with those aged 30–40 and 41–50 years showing a higher preference compared to those in other age groups. Merchandising was also important for those aged 25–29, and ambience was also important for those aged 25–29 and 30–40 years. Gender also had an impact of store choice, with men more likely to choose a shop based on proximity and women more likely to make a choice based on merchandise. The motive for shopping was also different for genders, with men viewing it as a chore that needs to be completed as quickly and easily as possible whereas women prefer to spend more time and effort shopping. Further analysis shows that proximity of the store is valuable, but shoppers would be willing to travel further for a store that offers good value merchandise and, to a lesser extent, a good ambience.

Figure 7.25: Specific shops are visited for specific requirements, according to Sinha et al. (2002)

ACTIVITY 7.6

Working in pairs, design a questionnaire that you could give to people visiting a particular shop, in order to find out their reasons for choosing that shop. You could use a mixture of open and closed questions but make sure you include Likert-type scales

Post-purchase cognitive dissonance

Cognitive dissonance refers to the feeling of discomfort that comes from holding two conflicting beliefs, or from behaving in a different way to your beliefs. When there is a difference between beliefs and behaviours something needs to change to reduce or eliminate the dissonance. Factors that increase the likelihood of cognitive dissonance involve:

- The type of belief: the more personal the belief is the more likely there is for dissonance to occur. For example, buying an engagement ring has huge sentimental importance so finding out your partner doesn't like the ring, or having regrets about the purchase will lead to higher levels of cognitive dissonance.

- The value of the belief: the more important the belief is, the greater the chance of cognitive dissonance. For example, having strong beliefs about the environment and buying a car that you later find out is bad for the environment.

- The size of the disparity: the greater the distance between the two opposing beliefs or behaviours, the greater the chance of cognitive dissonance. For example, if you believe you should always be very strict and careful with money but then get talked into buying a high brand mobile phone that costs hundreds of dollars, when you know that a cheaper option would be just as good.

KEY WORD

cognitive dissonance: the feeling of discomfort that comes from holding two conflicting beliefs, or when there is a conflict between beliefs and behaviours

Example study

Nordvall (2014) wished to find out whether cognitive dissonances would occur when participants were choosing between organic and non-organic food. This was of interest because most research into cognitive dissonance has focused on high involvement shopping (for important purchases such as a car), whereas Nordvall wanted to investigate whether the same findings would occur for low involvement shopping (such as grocery shopping).

Nordvall asked 100 participants (male and female) to complete an individual virtual shopping spree that took about 20 minutes. Nordvall used a rate-choose-rate method to measure cognitive dissonance, where participants were asked to rate items, then choose items, and then rate them again after they had made their decision. In the first phase, participants were shown a total of 50 common grocery items one at a time (25 organic and 25 non-organic) and were asked to rate how frequently they purchased each item on a seven-point scale from 1 ('never buy') to 7 ('buy very often'). This measure was used rather than measuring the 'desirability' of an item as groceries are unlikely to be considered 'desirable' or not. Pairs of items (one organic and one non-organic) that were initially scored similarly (up to two points difference on the seven-point scale) were then presented again and the participant was asked to choose which product to put into their shopping basket. It is suggested that this task would cause dissonance in the participant because they had previously rated the items as being a similar preference, so being forced to choose one item and reject an equally liked item would cause a feeling of unpleasantness.

The second rating phase asked the participants to rate each of the items again, on the same seven-point scale, but this time they were reminded whether this was the chosen item or the rejected item. Participants were also asked to select from a list of reasons why they chose their chosen item, with reasons offered such as price, environment and health.

Nordvall expected that there would be two ways in which participants would try to reduce their cognitive dissonance. First, it was expected that participants would give their chosen item a higher score and the rejected item a reduced score in the second rating phase. Research has also shown that giving a reason for your choice helps to reduce cognitive dissonance, which was also part of the second rating phase.

Results showed that there was a significant increase in the rating given for the chosen item between the first rating

and second rating (mean score of 2.62 before the item was chosen and a mean score of 2.9 after the item was chosen). This shows that respondents tried to reduce their cognitive dissonance by increasing the rating for their chosen item. However, it was also expected that participants would decrease the rating of their non-chosen item, but this was found to not be the case. Total reduction of dissonance can be measured by combining the increased rating of the chosen item with the decreased rating of the non-chosen item. Results showed tendencies for dissonance reduction, but the findings were not significant. There was little difference in reduction of dissonance whether or not the organic or non-organic item was chosen. When the non-organic item was chosen, 'price' was the most common reason given, followed by 'physical appearance' (although further investigation is required to determine whether this term was interpreted as meaning 'more attractive' or 'looked familiar'). When participants chose the organic item, the most common reasons were 'environmental concerns' and 'animal welfare'. A questionnaire was also given to participants, asking questions about social responsibility (relating to things like caring about the world, the environment, animal rights, etc.) and results showed that these participants scored higher than average on social responsibility. This makes it surprising then that participants did not choose the organic option more often (which would be a more socially responsible choice), therefore showing a discrepancy between attitudes and behaviour. It is suggested that the participants' ability to rationalise their decision by reducing the cognitive dissonance explains why they may keep making decisions that differ from their values and attitudes.

RESEARCH METHODS

Sinha et al. used a mix of open and closed questions to gather data about people's shop choices. Open questions gathered qualitative data, allowing detailed answers and a good understanding of the participants' thoughts and feelings. Closed questions used Likert-type scales asking participants to what extent they agreed with statements. This leads to useful quantitative data that are easy to compare and analyse, and ensure that all areas of interest are covered relatively quickly and easily. The study gathered participants from a range of different shops, which increases the usefulness and validity of the research as it tells us about store choice across a variety of different requirements. Lastly, asking participants about their store choice for the

CONTINUED

particular trip they were making was important in terms of validity. By asking reasons for store choice in this particular instance the researchers were more likely to gather valid data, compared to if they gave out questionnaires in a laboratory setting and asked for hypothetical store choices for hypothetical trips.

ISSUES AND DEBATES

Sinha et al. carried out their research in an Indian town, in response to the limited amount of research into retail behaviour in India. The issue of cultural differences is, of course, extremely important for this research; it was in fact the reason that the research was carried out. Sinha et al. were aware that the vast amount of research that had been carried out into retail behaviour was conducted in Western cultures, primarily America. They felt that the findings were not necessarily generalisable to people from India, so they carried out their own research to investigate retail behaviour (specifically store choice) in India. Interestingly, the findings broadly supported previous research findings so it may be that cultural differences in retail behaviour are not as large as some may think. How might the individual versus situational explanation be applied to research into buying the product?

Questions

10 Atalay et al. used eye tracking to investigate the impact of shelf position on purchase decision. Why might it be that the products in the centre of the array are chosen more often than other alternatives?

11 Kardes et al. used two field experiments and one laboratory experiment. Why might they have chosen to do this?

12 Sinha et al. gave people a questionnaire about shop choice as they left a range of shops. Briefly outline another way you could investigate factors that influence shop choice.

7.5 Advertising

Types of advertising and advertising techniques

The Yale model of communication

The Yale model of communication was developed by Hoveland et al. (1953, cited in McGuire, 1996), initially to try to understand wartime **propaganda** during the Second World War. The basic idea of the model can be summarised as 'who said what to whom?' It has been used effectively since then to understand variables that might influence the comprehension, acceptance and retention of persuasive messages. McGuire (1996) refined the model and broke it down into six stages: presentation, attention, comprehension, yielding, retention and behaviour. In effect, a message must be presented, drawn attention to and then understood by the audience for an attitude change to take place and be remembered.

According to the Yale model of communication there are five important factors in determining whether an attitude change (and consequently a behaviour change) will occur:

1 The source of the message: a message is more likely to be paid attention to, and an attitude is more likely to change as a result, if the message is perceived as coming from someone with credibility. This would include someone who is seen as an expert in the field, so, for example, adverts for skincare may use a 'skincare expert' in a white coat to talk about the importance of a particular feature of the product. The same information would not be seen as being as credible, and so would have less persuasive impact, if it came from someone without expertise. The source of the message is also more likely to be effective if they are deemed as 'trustworthy', which may or may not be related to their apparent expertise. It is important to say that it is the audience's *perception* of the speaker that is important: what matters is whether an audience perceives a speaker to be trustworthy or an expert.

KEY WORD

propaganda: when information is spread in support of a cause; it is often seen in a negative light, where false claims are made, and incorrect information is spread

2 The content of the message: it is ultimately important that the desired aim of the message is made clear, and the argument is strong. However, a message where two sides of an argument are presented is more effective in leading to attitude change than one that only shows one side of the argument. For example, adverts for baby formula will tend to discuss breast-feeding as an option for feeding a baby and will then talk about formula as an alternative option and will then focus on the benefits of formula. Evidence is also an important part of an effective message: the use of statistics or results of research is likely to convince an audience and therefore lead to attitude change.

3 The channel or mode of delivery of the message: the channel through which a message is delivered may have an effect on how persuasive a message is. A message may be delivered verbally or in written form. The message may be delivered via the television, or other media such as newspapers or, in more modern times the internet or social media. The effectiveness of the delivery mode will vary for different audiences, for example use of social media or television is more likely to be effective for a younger audience, but the use of the radio or newspaper may be more effective for an older audience.

4 The audience of the message: age affects the likelihood of an attitude change. Those aged 18–25 are most likely to be persuaded and those who are older are less likely to be persuaded. A less intelligent audience may be more likely to be persuaded as they are less likely to understand the information themselves so will be more likely to rely on an expert. However, for an intelligent audience it is possible to persuade them, but in this case, it is essential for the argument to be valid and based on evidence.

5 The effect the message has: if an audience pays attention to a message, and retains the information then the message can have a range of different effects. First, the message can affect the opinions and thoughts of the audience. If an audience has paid attention to the message and the message is persuasive enough it may lead to the audience changing their attitude or beliefs. This is a good start, but for the message to be truly effective it is necessary for the effect to go beyond internal thoughts and opinions and to lead to behavioural changes. If a message is persuasive enough to change the behaviours of its audience it has been truly effective.

Advertising media

Advertising can use a range of different media, from the more traditional media of print and television to the more recent additions of internet and smartphones. Research has suggested that, although newspapers are read far less now than they used to be, advertising is less effective over the internet than through paper formats (Lindstädt & Budzinski, 2011). It has been suggested that this is due to 'banner blindness' (see Figure 7.26); the tendency to avoid looking at banners when viewing websites (Benway, 1998). Hervet et al. (2011) found that 63.3% of banners were not looked at, compared to research by Lohse (1997) who found that only 10% of adverts were not looked at when presented on a printed medium. The effectiveness of different types of advertising media is investigated by Ciceri et al. (2020).

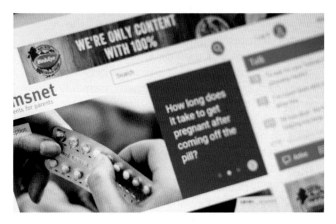

Figure 7.26: Banner blindness: the tendency to avoid looking at banners when viewing websites

Example study

Ciceri et al. (2020) used a mock newspaper for each of three mediums: a website displayed on a laptop computer, a printed paper edition, and a PDF file to be viewed on a tablet. Twenty-five real static adverts were included in each version. Each of the 72 participants was asked to read the newspaper, at their own pace, on one of the three media, while eye tracking and EEG

KEY WORD

banner blindness: the tendency to avoid looking at banners containing adverts, when viewing websites

measurements were taken. EEG is a method in which electrodes are placed on the scalp to measure cortical activity as a response to changing stimuli. The EEG was designed to measure the level of frustration felt by participants when viewing the adverts.

Once the newspaper task was completed, it was followed by a distraction task for an hour and then a memory recognition task, where participants were shown 50 adverts (25 were the ones they had seen and 25 were unseen) and were asked to say whether they had seen each advert.

Results from eye tracking showed that there was a significant difference in the amount of **fixation time** on adverts between the three media, with the most time being spent on tablets and the least time being spent on the website. These findings were supported by the recognition task, which found more accurate recall was found for those viewing the tablet, and least accurate recall for those viewing the website. EEG results showed that, when viewing adverts, participants were less frustrated when viewing them on the tablet and the paper, but more frustrated when viewing them on the website. This could be due to the acceptance that adverts are part of a newspaper (when viewed on paper or on tablet) but that advertising on the internet is perceived as irritating. Overall, the results for tablet and paper were not significantly different but viewing on websites was found to be significantly different from tablets across all measures. This study shows the importance of considering the media that is being used for advertising, and that marketing should consider the implications of this.

KEY WORD

fixation time: in an eye-tracking study, the amount of time the participant focuses attention on the stimulus

---

Lauterborn's 4Cs marketing mix model

Lauterborn (1990) proposed the 4Cs marketing mix model, as illustrated in Figure 7.27, as a more customer-focused take on the classic marketing mix model where the main 4Ps relate to product, price, place and promotion. Instead, Lauterborn proposed the following key issues in marketing:

- Consumer wants and needs (corresponding to 'product' in the 4Ps): moving the focus away from the product and instead basing decisions on what the consumer actually wants and needs.

- Cost to satisfy (corresponding to 'price'): this is more complex than simply the purchase price. Cost to satisfy considers a range of factors that, as well as price, also includes the time taken to make the purchase, the cost of conscience to use the product, the cost of moving to a new product and of not selecting an alternative.

- Convenience to buy (corresponding to 'place'): nowadays most purchases can be made online so the convenience to buy is higher than ever. There is no need to go to a physical shop and online baskets and trolleys can be saved and returned to with ease.

- Communication (corresponding to 'promotion'): rather than promotion, which is very much a one-way system of communication from the company to the customer, communication suggests a two-way conversation between the company and the customer, and this has increased significantly as digital marketing has developed.

Figure 7.27: Lauterborn's 4 Cs marketing mix model

RESEARCH METHODS

Ciceri et al. used a laboratory experiment to investigate advertising in different types of media. This has important strengths as it allows the researchers to have control over variables, so they can be fairly certain that the change in cued recall of adverts is because of the different forms of media, rather than anything else. This increases the validity of the study. It also means the study has high reliability because it can be easily replicated, with the same procedure being used. However, a weakness of using a laboratory experiment is that it lacks ecological validity, which means we need to use caution when generalising the results beyond the research setting, so it may not be a true reflection of how people relate to adverts in real life.

ISSUES AND DEBATES

Research into advertising, such as the Yale model of communication, Ciceri et al.'s research into advertising on different types of media and Lauterborn's 4 Cs marketing model all have significant application to everyday life. Advertising is everywhere, and it is the best marketing tool there is, so any research into how to produce an effective advert is going to be extremely useful for those who market almost any type of product. The way in which advertising works has changed over the years, particularly in terms of technological changes to media, but also changes to the way the 'relationship' between the seller and the consumer should be viewed. It is therefore important for marketing teams to be up to date with new research and use these findings to produce the most effective and successful adverts they can.

Advertising–consumer interaction

Key study: Snyder and DeBono (1985)

Snyder, M., & DeBono, K. G. (1985). Appeals to image and claims about quality: understanding the psychology of advertising. *Journal of personality and social psychology, 49(3), 586.*

Context

There are many different types of advert and different approaches to advertising. There is not one type of advertising that will always be the most successful (if there was, then everyone would use it all the time!). The product itself is one thing that will affect which type of advert to use, whether it is a luxury item, or a budget item, or whether it is a practical and useful item or whether it is purely for fun. For example, an advert for a high budget, luxury item might focus on all of the reasons why this product is worth its money, and why the consumer should want to spend their money on it. In contrast, a lower-cost, budget item might emphasise that low cost in its advertising and use the price as the selling point.

However, the product itself isn't the only thing that affects how successful an advert will be, this also depends on the consumer. Research suggests that the extent to which different types of advert are successful is in part due to the personality of the consumer (Fox 1984). One of these personality differences, which will be investigated by Snyder and DeBono, is levels of self-monitoring.

Main theories and explanations

High self-monitoring individuals are those who strive to be the type of person required for any situation they are in. They adjust their behaviour to fit in to different social situations and their behaviour changes from situation to situation (Snyder and Monson 1975). **Low self-monitoring** individuals are people who do not tend to amend their behaviour to fit into different social situations. Instead, they are guided by their own attitudes and feelings, so there will be correspondence between their private attitudes and their actual behaviour (Snyder and Swann 1976).

KEY WORDS

high self-monitoring: an individual who strives to be the type of person required for any social situation, so they adjust their behaviour from situation to situation

low self-monitoring: an individual who does not amend their behaviour to fit into different social situations; instead they are guided by their own attitudes and feelings

'soft-sell' approach: the product image is central to the marketing approach

'hard-sell' approach: the product quality is central to the marketing approach

Previous research has shown that advertising can be successful using either a **'soft-sell' approach** or a **'hard-sell' approach** (Fox 1984). In a 'soft-sell' approach the product image (focusing on the effect the product may have on a person's status or the way in which others may see them) is central, for example, in advertising a brand of coffee, the handsome well-dressed man who is drinking the coffee is the focus. In a 'hard-sell' approach the product quality is central, so when advertising a new brand of coffee, the focus would be on the quality of its taste or information about the quality of the blend that is used. The researchers were interested to see whether low self-monitoring individuals and high self-monitoring individuals are susceptible to different types of advert.

Aims

The aim of Study 1 was to investigate whether high and low self-monitoring individuals will respond differently to two different advertising strategies: those that focus on a product's image and those that focus on a product's quality.

Study 2 aimed to determine whether the type of advert (focused on product image or product quality) used would affect the amount a consumer was willing to pay.

Study 3 aimed to find out whether these differences between high and low self-monitoring individuals extended further and would actually influence the likelihood of consuming a product.

Design

In Study 1, participants (male and female undergraduates from an American university) were given the Self-monitoring Scale to complete, and based on their scores, half of the 50 participants were categorised as low self-monitoring and half were categorised as high self-monitoring. Three sets of magazine adverts were created, with each set containing two adverts for one of three products: whisky, cigarettes or coffee. For each of the two adverts the picture was the same, but the slogan was varied, to relate to either the image of the product or the quality of the product. A laboratory experiment was used, where participants were asked to look at all three sets of two adverts, with the order

of presentation being counterbalanced (to account for order effects). Participants were then asked to complete a 12-item questionnaire, asking them to make evaluative comparisons between the two adverts for each set.

Study 2 used 40 participants (with the same features as in Study 1) and the same six adverts as used in Study 1. However, here the participants were in groups of three to four and they were randomly assigned to be shown either the three product-quality oriented adverts or the three product-image-oriented adverts. Participants were asked to complete a questionnaire after each advert, with the critical item being 'How much would you be willing to pay for this product?' and were given a range of prices to choose from.

Study 3 used a similar pool of 40 participants as the previous two studies. In this study, an experimenter (blind to the self-monitoring score of the participant) phoned each participant and claimed to be a market researcher asking whether they would be interested in trying a new shampoo. He then delivered one of two messages about the shampoo: an image message or a quality message. The image message reported that lab tests showed that, compared to other brands, the shampoo was rated as average for how it cleans your hair, but above average on how it makes your hair look. The quality message reported that laboratory tests showed that, compared to other brands, the shampoo was rated as average for how good it makes your hair look, but above average for how clean it gets your hair. Participants were then all asked which response best described how willing they were to use the shampoo: definitely not, probably not, unsure, probably yes, or definitely yes, and to give a percentage indicating how willing they were to use the shampoo (0% being not at all and 100% being definitely willing).

Results, findings and conclusions

Results of Study 1 showed that, as expected, high self-monitoring individuals reacted more positively towards the image-focused advert than did low self-monitoring individuals. In contrast, low self-monitoring individuals were more favourable towards the product-quality focused adverts. This was the case for all three of the products advertised.

Study 2 showed that, as expected, high self-monitoring individuals were willing to pay more for products if they were advertised using an image orientation than if they were advertised with a quality orientation. Low self-monitoring individuals were willing to pay more for products that were advertised with a focus on quality rather than image. These results were particularly strong for the whisky adverts, but less so for the coffee and less again for the cigarettes.

Results of Study 3 showed that high self-monitoring individuals were more likely than low self-monitoring individuals to try the shampoo if they believed it would leave their hair looking good. Low self-monitoring individuals were more willing than high self-monitoring individuals to try the shampoo if they believed it would leave their hair very clean.

From Study 1 it can be concluded that high self-monitoring individuals and low self-monitoring individuals have different preferences toward product-oriented and image-oriented adverts. From Study 2 it can be concluded that this difference in preference influences the price that a consumer would be willing to pay for a product, Finally, Study 3 confirmed that these differences between low self-monitoring and high self-monitoring individuals were also shown in their willingness to use a product. High self-monitoring individuals were more willing to try a product based on the images associated with it (if shampoo made their hair look good) whereas low self-monitoring individuals were more willing to try a product based on the product's quality (if the shampoo cleaned their hair well) (see Figure 7.28).

Figure 7.28: Low self-monitoring individuals would be more likely to try shampoo if it cleaned their hair well

Evaluation

A laboratory experiment was used for Studies 1 and 2, which allowed high levels of control over variables, increasing the validity of the study. Furthermore, each set of adverts used the same images, and the only change was the slogan, so we can be certain that the change in response to the adverts must be because of the slogan itself rather than anything else. The studies have high reliability as all aspects of the procedure were kept the same, allowing it to be easily replicated. Counterbalancing was used in relation to the order of presentation of the adverts.

This increases the validity as it removes the potential issue of order effects. However, Studies 1 and 2 lack ecological validity because participants were asked to view the adverts and comment on them: this does not reflect the effect of adverts in real life. Study 3 was a field experiment where participants thought they were speaking to a market researcher and hearing genuine advertising. So, in this case, when they said how likely they were to try the product we can be more confident that this reflects real-life behaviour and therefore has more ecological validity.

Application to everyday life is relevant to Snyder and DeBono's research because, not only did they investigate the effects of level of self-monitoring on preference for advert, but they also went two steps further and investigated whether this would also influence how much an individual would pay for a product and, finally, how likely they would be to try a product. These last two stages are key to application to real life as the amount someone is willing to spend on a product and how likely they are to try it are what really matters in the real world of advertising and selling products. Advertising campaigns could be produced to account for both high and low self-monitoring individuals, to try to maximise sales.

Product placement in films

Product placement is where a branded product is given a prominent position within a scene in a television or film. This might include the characters drinking a branded soft drink or eating a branded chocolate bar. Although product placement is thought to be highly influential, there are remarkably few studies that examine the effectiveness of product placement.

Product placement may work in two ways: through mere exposure and through the use of reminders.

Mere exposure involves the product being on display repeatedly during scenes in the film or television programme. Research shows that repeated exposure to an object leads to an increased positive feeling toward that object (Harmon-Jones & Allen, 2001). The mere exposure effect works even when the individual is unaware that they were exposed to the object, as is often the case in product placement. For example, somebody may watch a television programme where people are eating a particular brand of cereal and this may influence their choice to buy that same brand of cereal when they next go shopping, without realising why.

Product placement can also work effectively with the use of reminders. Instead of mere exposure, reminders can work if an individual has already been exposed to a product. Product placement can then act as a reminder to them, which increases the positive feeling toward that product, and the choices they are likely to make. This is demonstrated in more detail in the example study by Auty and Lewis (2004).

Example study

Auty and Lewis (2004) aimed to investigate the effect of product placement on children's subsequent choices, and to see whether the age of the child influenced the effect of product placement.

Two age groups of children took part in the study: 6–7-year-olds and 11–12-year-olds. The 6–7-year-olds were selected as limited processors, who struggle to use storage and retrieval cues, even when prompted. The 11–12-year-olds were selected as cued processors, who can use cognitive strategies to retrieve information, but require prompting to do so.

KEY WORD
product placement: when a branded product is given a prominent position within a scene in a television programme or film

Participants were 105 children from state schools in the UK. They were randomly allocated to either the experimental group or the control group. Children in the experimental group were shown a short clip from the film *Home Alone*. The clip showed the family around the table eating pizza and drinking milk and Pepsi (a branded fizzy drink). Pepsi is also mentioned by name in the dialogue. The control group were shown a similar length clip from the same film, in which Kevin, the main character in the film, is shown eating macaroni cheese and drinking milk.

After watching the film clip the children were questioned individually and were first asked if they would like to help themselves to a drink from the table where two small cans of Pepsi and two small cans of Coca-Cola were set up (see Figure 7.29).

In the experimental group, the children's choice of drink was recorded while the child was being asked to describe as much as they could remember about the film. If they did not mention the Pepsi specifically, they were given a series of prompts to help them recall the brand of drink, and the number of prompts was recorded. They were also asked if they had seen the film before and, if so, how many times.

The control group followed a similar procedure. They were also asked about what was drunk in the clip to see if prior viewing of the film brought about mistaken identification of Pepsi as the drink being consumed.

Results showed that the product placement had an effect. Children in the experimental group were more likely to choose Pepsi (a **ratio** of 62:38) compared with the control group (a ratio of 42:58).

Figure 7.29: Children in the experimental condition were more likely to choose Pepsi than Coca-Cola

There was no statistically significant difference between the age groups in terms of their ability to recall Pepsi, although the younger age group required more prompts to get there (mean number of prompts was 4.43 for the younger group and 2.06 for the older group). However, results showed that the more times the children had seen the film, the fewer prompts were needed to name Pepsi. In terms of drink choice, children who had seen the film previously were significantly more likely to choose Pepsi as their drink if they were in the experimental group (and saw Pepsi in the clip that day) than if they were in the control group (and did not see Pepsi in the clip that day). This shows the important effect of reminders: previous exposure to the brand (those who had seen the

film before) only influenced drink choice for those who had been reminded of the Pepsi in the clip they viewed that day. This experiment clearly shows that product placement is effective: those who had seen Pepsi in the film clip were significantly more likely to choose Pepsi than those who hadn't seen it in the film clip (and this effect was even greater for those who had also seen the film previously).

KEY WORD

ratio: the proportionate number of one item compared to another item

RESEARCH METHODS

Auty and Lewis used an implicit preference test, where the child made a choice between the two drinks on offer, as well as interviews. This allowed them to gather quantitative data from the implicit preference test, so that data could be easily compared and analysed, as well as qualitative data from the interview. This allowed for more information to be gathered, so that a more detailed understanding could be gained. This increases the validity of the results. The interview was *semi-structured*, whereby the children were asked about the film but if they did not spontaneously name the branded drink, they were given an identical set of prompts, used in the same order. This increases the reliability of the results because the same format was used for all participants, which allows the research to be replicated. Why was it better to use an interview rather than a questionnaire in the study by Auty and Lewis?

ISSUES AND DEBATES

Research into product placement in films, such as Auty and Lewis, can be seen as being deterministic because it suggests that an individual's behaviour (e.g., what drink to choose) has been determined or influenced by the film they have watched. The results of research such as Auty and Lewis appear to suggest that this is the case: that someone who viewed a film

CONTINUED

where Pepsi was prominent was significantly more likely to choose Pepsi than Coca-Cola. However, this does ignore the factor of free will; that people are not just subject to external forces but that they are responsible for their own decisions and actions so can decide freely which drink to choose, for example. Results of Auty and Lewis are significant, but they are not unanimous; not everybody who had viewed product placement of Pepsi then selected it as their drink, suggesting free will is also playing a part.

Brand awareness and recognition

Brand recognition in children

Brand recognition in children is thought to be acquired in the early years and can be explained through learning theory. Gresham and Shimp (1985) suggest that classical conditioning (learning through association, see Section 4.3 in Chapter 4) is the most widely used mechanism to influence consumers' brand attitudes. Classical conditioning involves pairing two stimuli and creating a conditioned response. In advertising, classical conditioning can work in two ways: by associating a brand with a positive feeling, and by associating a product with its logo (Schachtman et al., 2011).

Brand recognition in children can develop over time with repeated pairings, for example if a child regularly sees an advert on television for McDonald's where the logo and the name is presented alongside a film of the restaurant and the food, the different components will eventually become associated so that the logo alone can be recognised as the McDonald's brand.

To measure children's understanding of advertising, researchers have focused on two dimensions of brand awareness: 'knowing the brand' and 'remembering the brand' (Fischer et al., 1991). Children's knowledge of brands can be measured in terms of brand logo, brand character and brand advertisement.

KEY WORDS

brand recognition: the ability for consumers to recognise a brand from visual or auditory cues such as logos or slogans

brand awareness: the extent to which consumers are familiar with a brand

Example study

Fischer et al. (1991) wanted to investigate brand awareness in children, so they developed a game technique to measure the recognition level for brand logos. They gathered 22 brand logos from a range of products, including ten children's brands (such as Disney, Disney Channel, McDonald's and Cheerios (a breakfast cereal)), seven adult brands (such as Ford, Apple and Kodak) and five cigarette brands.

Each logo was printed on a card and no information was included that might give clues to the product (e.g., no cigarettes were shown in cigarette logos). Recognition was measured by asking the children to match the 22 logo cards to one of 12 product categories pictures on a game board (e.g., cigarettes, television, cereal).

The study involved 229 children, aged 3 to 6 years old, from the USA.

The results showed that, not surprisingly, the children showed good recognition rates for the children's brand logos. This ranged from 91% for the Disney Channel (see Figure 7.30) to 25% for Cheerios.

All cigarette brands were well recognised, with one brand being recognised by over half of the children. Other adult products were recognised between 16% and 54% of the time, with car brand logos being recognised the most.

Recognition increased with age for children's brands, cigarette brands and adult brands. There was no effect from race or gender. Children from homes where parents smoked were more likely to recognise cigarette logos.

The researchers concluded that children demonstrated high recognition rates for products targeted at both children and adults. It would be expected that American children would recognise McDonald's or Disney, for example. It is even reasonable that they would recognise adult brands, such as car manufacturers, as these advertise regularly on television. However, it is surprising and worrying that children would recognise cigarette brands so well, especially considering that cigarette brands have not been allowed to advertise on television in the USA for many decades, including before the study took place. The researchers claim that this shows the power of 'environmental advertising' such as billboards, sponsorship displays, T-shirts and other items.

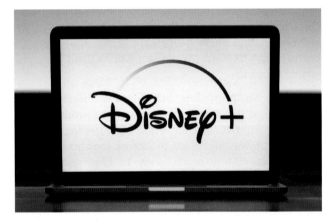

Figure 7.30: Fischer et al. found that 91% of children could recognise the logo for the Disney Channel

Brand awareness, brand image and effective slogans

Example study

Kohli et al. (2007) have reviewed many other articles and industry publications and aimed to produce a set of guidelines for creating an effective slogan. They consider the different types of slogan (such as jingle versus non-jingle, or simple versus complex) as well the functions of slogans (to enhance brand awareness and positively affect brand image). Brand name, logo and slogan are three key elements of a product (see Figure 7.31). The brand name is the product's key identity and cannot be easily changed. The logo acts as a visual cue to allow faster processing and universal brand recognition across languages and cultures. For example, the golden arches of the McDonald's logo can be recognised around the world. A logo will rarely be changed significantly

but may be modified or updated occasionally to stay modern. Lastly, the slogan is very important as it can communicate so much more than the one- or two-worded brand name or the image-based logo. Slogans can be more easily changed and updated. Pepsi, for example, has changed its slogan numerous times in 100 years, from 'Cures everything, Relieves exhaustion' in 1902 to 'Generation Next' in 1998 and to 'For the love of it' in 2019.

Figure 7.31: The brand name, logo and slogan are three key elements of a product's identity

KEY WORDS

brand name: the name used by a company to distinguish its products or services from other companies' products or services. It is the company's key identity and cannot be easily changed

logo: a symbol used by the company's to act as a visual cue to allow faster processing and universal brand recognition across languages and cultures

slogan: a short memorable phrase used in advertising a product

In the UK, several confectionary brands have changed their names. Opal Fruits became Starburst and Marathon became Snickers. However, they kept the same packaging design and colours, so they were still easily recognisable on the shelf. Brand knowledge is, of course, essential and there are two key elements of this: brand awareness and brand image. Brand awareness is determined by brand recall and brand recognition. Brand recall is the consumer's ability to remember the brand without any help (such as prompts or cues). Brand recognition, on the other hand, is easier as it requires a brand being identified from a provided list. Brand image tends to be assessed by measuring the type and strength of brand associations.

Slogans have two main functions: to enhance brand awareness and to positively affect the brand image. The effects that slogans have on brand awareness have been investigated through 'priming' effects. This refers to the idea that exposure to something can influence behaviour or thoughts at a later date. If a slogan talks about a particular attribute of a product, for example the taste, and if this slogan is heard repeatedly then when you are asked to rate the product on a range of attributes, you are likely to rate taste more highly than if you hadn't heard the slogans (Boush, 1993).

As a result of their research, Kohli et al. produced a set of guidelines for creating an effective slogan:

- *Keep your eye on the horizon*: brand strategy is about where you are and, more importantly, where you are going. It is important not to create a slogan that defines a brand too narrowly: it should be able to be used for years and to accommodate scope for change.

- *Every slogan is a brand positioning tool*: the slogan should position the brand (present it in an effective way) based on features or benefits in a clear manner.

- *Link the slogan to the brand*: it may sound obvious, but it is important that the slogan is linked to the brand and should be used on advertising as well as packaging. The consistent message is key, and the slogan should evoke the brand name; an obvious way to do this is by including the brand name in the slogan.

- *Please repeat that*: different adverts tend to be used during an advertising campaign, with the slogan being the one totally consistent feature. The repetition is essential in order to make the slogan memorable and, in turn, lead to a consistent brand image.

- *Jingle, jangle*: two different types of slogan are jingle (a short and memorable song) and non-jingle (written or spoken) slogans. Slogans are often presented as jingles as this is thought to do a better job of enhancing memory and recall. Yalch (1981) investigated this by presenting participants with a list of commonly used advertising slogans (some jingle slogans and some non-jingle slogans) and asking them to say which brands were associated with which slogans. When asked to name the brands without cues, Yalch found that brands with jingle slogans were more easily recalled than brands without jingles. However, when a recognition task was used instead (where a list of names of brands were provided), there were no significant differences between jingle and non-jingle slogans. However, jingles should be used with care as there is also some evidence that music can interfere with other cognitive processing. They may be better suited to small companies with limited budgets who are primarily looking to advertise on radio.

- *Use slogans at the outset*: slogans are such a significant component of brand identity that they must be used right from the start of marketing. A brand's image is primarily created early in the marketplace, so a slogan needs to be used to make the most of the early opportunity.

- *It's okay to be creative*: most slogans were kept simple because this makes them easier to recall. However, evidence suggests that slogans that are moderately complex (in terms of structure or content) require a deeper level of processing, which may lead to better recall than simpler ones.

RESEARCH METHODS

Fischer et al. carried out their study in the children's classroom. The use of a natural setting was particularly important for children as it would make them more likely to feel relaxed and to demonstrate natural behaviours, as well as being more likely to perform well in the task. Despite the natural setting there were still high levels of control and a standardised procedure was used. Each child was given the same set of instructions, was shown the same set of adverts and was given the same set of categories to sort the adverts into, thus increasing the reliability of the research. Also, using a matching task in the form of a game increases the validity of the results. Usual methods for brand recognition involve written questionnaires but this would likely make it much more difficult for young children so it may not give a clear and accurate account of their knowledge.

ISSUES AND DEBATES

The use of children in psychological research is a sensitive issue. When children are used in research, for example the study by Fischer et al., the ethical considerations need to be considered even more closely. It is not as easy for children to give fully informed consent to take part in research as they may not fully understand what is involved, so parents give consent alongside their children. *Protection from harm* is particularly important because children may respond to things differently to adults and they may find it difficult to communicate their feelings. This also applies to *right to withdraw*: a child may not understand fully that they can withdraw from the research, or they may not know how to express this effectively.

Questions

13 Lauterborn's 4 Cs marketing model shifts the emphasis of marketing from the product to the customer. Why might he have suggested this?

14 In Auty and Lewis's study into product placement, why did they have a control group who watched a different scene from *Home Alone*?

15 Using Kohli et al.'s research to help, explain why slogans are such an important feature of a brand.

SELF-EVALUATION CHECKLIST

After studying this chapter, copy and complete a table like this:

I can	Fully confident	Fairly confident	Need to revist	Coursebook	Workbook
describe, evaluate, compare and apply research into retail store design					
describe, evaluate, compare and apply research into sound and consumer behaviour					
describe, evaluate, compare and apply research into retail atmospherics					
describe, evaluate, compare and apply research into environmental influences on consumers					
describe, evaluate, compare and apply research into menu design psychology and consumer behaviour					
describe, evaluate, compare and apply research into personal space					
describe, evaluate, compare and apply research into consumer decision-making in terms of decision-making and choice heuristics					

CONTINUED

I can	Fully confident	Fairly confident	Need to re-visit	Coursebook	Workbook
describe, evaluate, compare and apply research into mistakes in decision-making					
describe, evaluate, compare and apply research into the product in terms of packaging, positioning and placement					
describe, evaluate, compare and apply research into selling the product and buying the product					
describe, evaluate, compare and apply research types of advertising and advertising techniques					
describe, evaluate, compare and apply research into advertising–consumer interaction					
describe, evaluate, compare and apply research into brand awareness and recognition					

PROJECT

Your task is to market a new restaurant! You will need to consider what you have learned throughout this chapter and use your new knowledge to help make the restaurant a success.

You can work in pairs or small groups.

Before you start you need to consider:

- What sort of restaurant it will be?
- What sort of food and drink you will offer?
- Whether it is high-end or low budget?
- Who your customers will be?

Your project must include:

- The restaurant brand:
  - A catchy name
  - A logo that relates to the name
  - A slogan
- An advertising campaign:
  - Sketch a magazine advert for your restaurant: remember to include your restaurant's name, logo and slogan.
  - Use a storyboard to plan out a TV advert.
  - Make sure the two different adverts tie in with each other so there is a consistent message.

CONTINUED

- A menu:

  - Consider how the menu will be laid out, and the order of your items.

  - Think about how to use boxes, headings, etc. effectively.

  - Think about the size and colour of the menu and the size and colour of the writing.

- Make sure your menu reflects the atmosphere and the style of the restaurant.

When you have produced all the above you need to write out the reasons for the choices you have made to convince the restaurant owners that you are the best people to market their restaurant. Use theories and studies you have learned throughout the chapter to explain your choices.

Peer assessment

Finally, join up with another pair or group and share your projects with each other. Talk through the restaurant brand, advertising campaign and menu you have created and explain your justifications to the other pair. Then swap over and look at the other pair's project and their justifications.

As a group, discuss what you think you each did well, and what you could have done differently. Discuss differences in your projects and the reasons for those differences.

EXAM-STYLE QUESTIONS

1   Name and briefly **outline three** types of store interior design layouts. [3]

2   **Describe** the following features of the study into musical style and restaurant customers' spending by North et al. (2005):

   a   The aim/hypotheses [2]

   b   The sample [2]

   c   The results and conclusions [3]

3   Use a study to **analyse** the effects of crowding on shopper satisfaction. [4]

4   a   What is meant by the primacy and recency effects in terms of menu item position? [2]

   b   How might the issue of application to everyday life be relevant to research into menu design? [4]

5   a   In their study into consumer responses to table spacing, Robson et al. (2011) used Likert-type scales to gather data. Give one strength and one limitation of using Likert-type scales for research such as this. [4]

   b   i   Describe the sample used by Robson et al. (2011). [2]

      ii   Give **one** strength of the sample used by Robson et al. (2011). [2]

6   **Explain** how cultural differences may be an issue in research relating to personal space and queue jumping. [4]

COMMAND WORDS

outline: set out the main points

describe: state the points of a topic / give characteristics and main features

analyse: examine in detail to show meaning, identify elements and the relationship between them

explain: set out purposes or reasons / make the relationships between things clear / say why and/or how and support with relevant evidence

give: produce an answer from a given source or recall/ memory

CONTINUED

7 a Name **three** models of consumer decision-making. [3]

  b Describe and compare these **three** models of consumer decision-making. [6]

8 Name and briefly describe three heuristics used in decision-making. [3]

9 a Describe the procedure of Becker et al.'s (2011) study into food packaging design and taste perception. [4]

  b **Give one** strength and **one** limitation of the Becker et al.'s study [4]

10 a Briefly describe the procedure and findings of **one** study into brand awareness in children. [4]

  b **Evaluate one** study into brand awareness in children. [10]

[Total: 70]

Additional references

Arthur, P., & Passini, R. (1992). *Wayfinding: people, signs, and architecture.* McGraw-Hill.

Atalay, A. S., Bodur, H. O., & Rasolofoarison, D. (2012) Shining in the center: central gaze cascade effect on product choice. *Journal of consumer research, 39*(4), 848–866.

Auty, S. G., & Lewis, C. (2004). Exploring children's choice: the reminder effect of product placement. in *Psychology and marketing, 21*(9), 697–713.

Babin, B. J., Hardesty, D. M., & Suter, T. A. (2003). Color and shopping intentions: the intervening effect of price fairness and perceived affect. *Journal of business research, 56*(7), 541–551.

Benway, J. P. (1998). Banner blindness: the irony of attention grabbing on the World Wide Web. *Proceedings of the human factors and ergonomics society 42nd annual meeting, 1,* 463–467

Berlyne, D. E. (1976). Psychological aesthetics. *International journal of psychology, 11,* 43–55.

Blankenship, A. B., & Whitely, P. L. (1941). Proactive inhibitions in the recall of advertising material. *Journal of social psychology, 13,* 311–322.

Bloch, P. H. (1995). Seeking the ideal form: product design and consumer response. *Journal of marketing, 59,* 16–29.

Boush, D. M. (1993). How advertising slogans can prime evaluations of brand extensions. *Psychology of marketing, 10*(1), 67–78.

Boyle, Y., Bentley, D. E., Watson, A., & Jones, A. K. (2006). Acoustic noise in functional magnetic resonance imaging reduces pain unpleasantness ratings. *Neuroimage, 31*(3), 1278–1283.

Boyd-Jansson, C. (2010). *Consumer psychology.* Maidenhead: Open University Press.

Burke, R. R., & Srull, T. K. (1988). Competitive interference and consumer memory for advertising. *Journal of consumer research, 15*(1), 55–68.

Chebat, J. C. & Michon, R. (2003) Impact of ambient odors on mall shoppers' emotions, cognition, and spending: a test of competitive causal theories. *Journal of business research,* 56(7), 529–539.

Chebat, J. C., & Morrin, M. (2007). Colors and cultures: exploring the effects of mall décor on consumer perceptions. *Journal of business research, 60*(3), 189–196.

Chitturi, R., Londono, J. C., Amezquita, C. A. (2019). The influence of color and shape of package design on consumer preference: the case of orange juice. *International journal of innovation and economic development, 5*(2), 42–56.

Cialdini, R.B. (2006). *Influence: the psychology of persuasion, revised edition.* New York: William Morrow.

Cooley, C. H. (1902). Looking-glass self. *The production of reality: essays and readings on social interaction, 6,* 126–128.

Crisinel, A. S., & Spence, C. (2010). A sweet sound? Food names reveal implicit associations between taste and pitch. *Perception, 39*(3), 417–425.

Dash, J. F., Schiffman, L. G., & Berenson, C. (1976). Information search and store choice. *Journal of advertising research, 16*(3), 35–40.

Davis, B. P., & Knowles, E. S. (1999). A disrupt-then-reframe technique of social influence. *Journal of personality and social psychology, 76*(2), 192.

del Campo, C., Pauser, S., Steiner, E., & Vetschera, R. (2016). Decision making styles and the use of heuristics in decision making. *Journal of business economics, 86*(4), 389–412.

Dodge, R. H., & Summer, H. H. (1969). Choosing between retail stores. *Journal of retailing, 45*(3), 11–21.

Dogu, U., & Erkip, F. (2000). Spatial factors affecting wayfinding and orientation: a case study in a shopping mall. *Environment and behavior, 32*(6), 731–755.

Edwards, S., & Shackley, M. (1992). Measuring the effectiveness of retail window display as an element of the marketing mix. *International journal of advertising, 11*(3), 193–202.

Engel, J. F., Kollat, D. T., & Blackwell, R. D. (1968). *Consumer behavior.* New York: Holt, Rinehart & Winston.

Eroglu, S. A., & Machleit, K. A. (1990). An empirical study of retail crowding: antecedents and consequences. *Journal of retailing, 66*(2), 201.

Fennis, B. M., Das, E. H., & Pruyn, A. T. H. (2004). 'If you can't dazzle them with brilliance, baffle them with nonsense': extending the impact of the disrupt-then-reframe technique of social influence. *Journal of consumer psychology, 14*(3), 280–290.

Fischer, P. M., Schwartz, M. P., Richards, J. W., Goldstein, A. O., & Rojas, T. H. (1991). Brand logo recognition by children aged 3 to 6 years: Mickey Mouse and Old Joe the Camel. *Jama, 266*(22), 3145–3148.

Fox, S. R. (1984). *The mirror makers: a history of American advertising and its creators.* University of Illinois Press.

Gil, J., Tobari, E., Lemlij, M., Rose, A. & Penn, A. R. (2009) The differentiating behaviour of shoppers: clustering of individual movement traces in a supermarket. In Koch, D., Marcus, L. & Steen, J. (eds) *Proceedings of the 7th International Space Syntax Symposium.* Royal Institute of Technology (KTH): Stockholm, Sweden.

Green, P. E., Wind, Y., & Jain, A. K. (1973). Analyzing free-response data in marketing research. *Journal of marketing research, 10*(1), 45–52.

Gresham, L. G., & Shimp, T. A. (1985). Attitude toward the advertisement and brand attitudes: a classical conditioning perspective. *Journal of advertising, 14*(1), 10–49.

Harmon-Jones, E., & Allen, J. J. (2001). The role of affect in the mere exposure effect: evidence from psychophysiological and individual differences approaches. *Personality and social psychology bulletin, 27*(7), 889–898.

Hayduk, L. A. (1981). The permeability of personal space. *Canadian journal of behavioural science /Revue Canadienne des sciences du comportement, 13*(3), 274.

Hervet, G., Guérard, K., Tremblay, S., & Chtourou, M. S. (2011). Is banner blindness genuine? Eye tracking internet text advertising. *Applied cognitive psychology, 25*(5), 708–716.

Hilbig, B. E., Zettler, I., & Heydasch, T. (2012). Personality, punishment and public goods: strategic shifts towards cooperation as a matter of dispositional honesty–humility. *European journal of personality, 26*(3), 245–254.

Hine, T. (1995). *The total packaging: the secret history and hidden meanings of boxes, bottles, cans and other persuasive containers.* Little Brown.

Hoyer, W. D., Chandy, R., Dorotic, M., Krafft, M., & Singh, S. S. (2010). Consumer cocreation in new product development. *Journal of service research, 13*(3), 283–296.

Hunter, B. T. (1995). The sales appeal of scents (using synthetic food scents to increase sales). *Consumer research magazine, 78*(10), 8–10.

Jedetski, J., Adelman, L., & Yeo, C. (2002). How web site decision technology affects consumers. *IEEE Internet Computing, 6*(2), 72–79.

Johansson, P., Hall, L., Sikström, S., & Olsson, A. (2005). Failure to detect mismatches between intention and outcome in a simple decision task. *Science, 310*(5745), 116–119.

Kahn, B. E., & Schmittlein, D. C. (1989). Shopping trip behavior: an empirical investigation. *Marketing letters, 1*(1), 55–69.

Kahneman, D., & Tversky, A. (1979). On the interpretation of intuitive probability: a reply to Jonathan Cohen. *Cognition, 7*(4), 409–411.

Kahneman, D., & Tversky, A. (2013). Prospect theory: an analysis of decision under risk. In *Handbook of the fundamentals of financial decision making: Part I,* edited by L. C. McClean and W. T. Ziemba, 99–127. World Scientific.

Knowles, E. S., & Bassett, R. L. (1976). Groups and crowds as social entities: effects of activity, size, and member similarity on nonmembers. *Journal of personality and social psychology, 34*(5), 837.

Kohli, C., Leuthesser, L., & Suri, R. (2007). Got slogan? Guidelines for creating effective slogans. *Business horizons, 50*(5), 415–422.

Kruglanski, A. W., & Webster, D. M. (1996). Motivated closing of the mind: 'seizing' and 'freezing'. *Psychological review, 103*(2), 263.

Lauterborn, B. (1990). New marketing litany: four Ps passé: C-words take over. *Advertising Age, 61*(41), 26.

Lazarus, R. S. (1991). *Emotion and adaptation.* Oxford University Press.

Lindstädt, N., & Budzinski, O. (2011). Newspaper vs. online advertising–is there a niche for newspapers in modern advertising markets? *SSRN electronic journal,* http://dx.doi.org/10.2139/ssrn.1948487.

Lockyer, T. (2006). Would a restaurant menu item by any other name taste as sweet? *Hospitality review, 24*(1), 3.

Lohse, G. L. (1997). Consumer eye movement patterns on yellow pages advertising. *Journal of advertising, 26*(1), 61–73.

Lumpkin, J. R., & Robert, E. H. (1985). Retailers' offerings and elderly consumers' needs: do retailers understand the elderly? *Journal of business research, 16*(4), 313–326.

Machleit, K. A., Eroglu, S. A. & Mantel, S. P. (2000) Perceived retail crowding and shopping satisfaction: what modifies this relationship?. *Journal of consumer psychology, 9*(1), 29–42.

McGeoch, J. A. (1932). Forgetting and the law of disuse. *Psychological review, 39*(4), 352.

McGuire, W. J. (1996). The Yale communication and attitude-change program in the 1950s. *American communication research: the remembered history*, 39–59.

McKinney, F. (1935). Retroactive inhibition and recognition memory. *Journal of experimental psychology, 18*(5), 585.

Mehrabian, A., & Russell, J. A. (1974). *An approach to environmental psychology.* MIT Press.

North, A. C., & Hargreaves, D. J. (1998). The effect of music on atmosphere and purchase intentions in a cafeteria 1. *Journal of applied social psychology, 28*(24), 2254–2273.

Pavesic, D. (2005) The psychology of menu design: reinvent your 'silent salesperson' to increase check averages and guest loyalty. *Hospitality faculty publications,* paper 5, Georgia State University.

Payne, J. W., Payne, J. W., Bettman, J. R., & Johnson, E. J. (1993). *The adaptive decision maker.* Cambridge University Press.

Porublev, E., Brace-Govan, J., Minahan, S., & Dubelaar, C. (2009). To wrap or not to wrap? What is expected? Some initial findings from a study of gift wrapping. In *ANZMAC 2009: Sustainable management and marketing conference, January, 2009*, 1–8. Monash University.

Richarme, M. (2005). Consumer decision-making models, strategies, and theories, oh my! *Decision analyst, 604.*

Roediger, H. L., & Crowder, R. G. (1976). A serial position effect in recall of United States presidents. *Bulletin of the Psychonomic Society, 8*(4), 275–278.

Schachtman, T. R., Walker, J., & Fowler, S. (2011). Effects of conditioning in advertising. In *Associative learning and conditioning theory: human and non-human applications*, edited by T. R. Schachtman and S. Reilly, 481–506. New York: Oxford University Press.

Schifferstein, H. N., & Spence, C. (2008). Multisensory product experience. *Product experience* (pp. 133–161). Elsevier.

Scott, S. G., & Bruce, R. A. (1995). Decision-making style: The development and assessment of a new measure. *Educational and psychological measurement, 55*(5), 818–831.

Sheets, V. L., & Manzer, C. D. (1991). Affect, cognition, and urban vegetation: some effects of adding trees along city streets. *Environment and behavior, 23*(3), 285–304.

Shleifer, A. (2012). Psychologists at the gate: a review of Daniel Kahneman's thinking, fast and slow. *Journal of economic literature, 50*(4), 1080–1091.

Simon, H. A. (1956). Rational choice and the structure of the environment. *Psychological review, 63*(2), 129.

Sinha, P. K., Banerjee, A., & Uniyal, D. P. (2002). Deciding where to buy: store choice behaviour of Indian shoppers. *Vikalpa, 27*(2), 13–28.

Snyder, M., & Monson, T. C. (1975). Persons, situations, and the control of social behavior. *Journal of personality and social psychology, 32*(4), 637.

Snyder, M., & Swann, W. B. (1976). When actions reflect attitudes: the politics of impression management. *Journal of personality and social psychology, 34*(5), 1034.

Sommer, R. (1969). *Personal space*. Englewood Cliffs, NJ: Prentice Hall.

Spangenberg, E. R., Crowley, A. E., & Henderson, P. W. (1996). Improving the store environment: do olfactory cues affect evaluations and behaviors? *Journal of marketing, 60*, 67–80.

Stokols, D. (1972). On the distinction between density and crowding: some implications for future research. *Psychological review, 79*(3), 275.

Teichert, M., & Bolz, J. (2018). How senses work together: cross-modal interactions between primary sensory cortices. *Neural plasticity, 2018*, 5380921.

Von Neumann, J., & Morgenstern, O. (2007). *Theory of games and economic behavior*. Princeton University Press.

Vrechopoulos, A. P., O'Keefe, R. M., Doukidis, G. I. & Siomkos, G. J. (2004). Virtual store layout: an experimental comparison in the context of grocery retail. *Journal of retailing, 80(1)*, 13–22.

Wansink, B., Van Ittersum, K., & Painter, J. E. (2004) How descriptive food names bias sensory perceptions in restaurants. *Food quality and preference, 16*(5), 393–400.

Weisman, J. (1981). Evaluating architectural legibility: way-finding in the built environment. *Environment and behavior, 13*(2), 189–204.

Wesson, D.W., & Wilson, D.A. (2010). Smelling sounds: olfactory–auditory sensory convergence in the olfactory tubercle. *Journal of neuroscience, 30*(8), 3013–3021.

Woods, A. T., Poliakoff, E., Lloyd, D. M., Kuenzel, J, Hodson, R, Gonda, H., Batchelor, J., Dijksterhuis, G. B. & Thomas, A. (2010). Effect of background noise on food perception. *Food quality and preference, 22*(1), 42–47.

Yalch, R., & Bryce, W. (1981). Effects of a reactance-reduction technique on reciprocation in personal selling. In *The changing marketing environment: new theories and applications*, edited by K. Bernhardt et al., 128–134. American Marketing Association.

Yalch, R. F. (1981). Memory in a jingle jungle: music as a mnemonic device in communicating advertising slogans. *Journal of applied psychology, 76*(April), 268–275.

Zampini, M., & Spence, C. (2004). The role of auditory cues in modulating the perceived crispness and staleness of potato chips. *Journal of sensory studies, 19*(5), 347–363.

Zielske, H. A., & Henry, W. A. (1980). Remembering and forgetting television ads. *Journal of advertising research, 20*(2), 7–13.

> ## Chapter 8
> # Health psychology

Introduction

In this chapter you will learn about several fascinating aspects of health psychology. You will learn about different components of the relationship between the patient and the practitioner, in terms of verbal and non-verbal communication and communication style. You will also learn about how health services can be misused; from delaying seeking treatment to an interesting condition called Munchausen syndrome. You will cover types of and explanations for non-adherence to treatment, along with ways of measuring non-adherence, before moving on to look at how adherence can be improved. You will also develop a better understanding of pain in terms of different types of pain and explanations of pain, followed by different ways of measuring and managing pain. There will be a similar approach to understanding stress by looking at sources of stress, measures of stress and ways of managing stress. Finally, you will learn about health

promotion, by covering strategies for promoting health, health in the school and workplace, and factors that can result in changes in health beliefs.

As you learn about health psychology in this chapter you will also revisit research methods and you will see how the psychological issues and debates apply to these topics. To help illustrate topics we will look at many relevant studies. Example studies are included to demonstrate and help explain the theories and ideas that are covered. You will also learn about five key studies, which you will learn in more detail, starting with the context and background to the study, then looking in detail at the design and then the findings, results and conclusions. You will consider the methodological evaluation of each key study, as well as how it can be applied to everyday life. By the end of the chapter, you will have a good knowledge and understanding about many aspects of health psychology.

GETTING STARTED

Health psychology is an area of psychology that focuses on how different factors affect attitudes and behaviours in response to health and illness. We will all have had some sort of interaction with health services at some point in our lives. How did you feel when visiting the doctor? Did you like them? Did you trust them? Did you follow their advice on a treatment plan? Many aspects of the social approach will come into play here; consider general concepts surrounding interactions with others and how we respond to different people. Furthermore, a doctor is an authority figure so there are factors that may influence how likely you are to obey them.

The biological approach will be relevant when we consider the pain and stress sections of this topic. You will learn about the body's response and how hormone levels and neurological activity change in response to both pain and stress. Think about a time when you have been in pain. Why did the

pain occur? What was your experience of it? And, importantly, how did you manage it? Think about a time when you have been stressed. How did it make you feel, and how did you cope with it? The cognitive approach relates to pain and stress as well because they are not just physical experiences, but both are experienced through our thoughts and processing of information as well.

Finally, health promotion is a bit more abstract to think about: you may have been part of an intervention programme but you may not have realised it. You may still be living a better life as a result. The learning approach is important when considering health promotions, for example we will look at how a token economy (using reinforcement) can improve health and safety in a workplace, and how children's diets can be improved by using modelling and reinforcement.

8.1 The patient–practitioner relationship

This section will explore different aspects of the relationship between the patient and the practitioner, and the implications of this relationship. A practitioner can refer to any medical professional, such as a doctor, nurse or pharmacist. Mainly we are referring to a doctor, and this could either be a general practitioner (GP), who sees patients at a doctor's surgery for relatively minor conditions, or a doctor at a hospital who may specialise in a particular area. We will consider the different ways that doctors and patients may communicate with each other, and the diagnostic style a doctor uses. We will also look at the effects of these different relationships, as well as the reasons why patients may delay seeking treatment.

Practitioner and patient interpersonal skills

Non-verbal communications

Would you expect your doctor to wear a formal suit and tie? Or a white coat? Would you be happy if your doctor was wearing jeans and a t-shirt? And, most importantly, does it matter? Research into **non-verbal communication** from doctors has suggested that what clothes your doctor wears will affect how you view them (Colt et al., 1989).

> **KEY WORD**
>
> **non-verbal communication:** any interactions that take place other than talking, for example body language and clothing

Example study

McKinstry and Wang (1991) aimed to investigate whether patients think the way their doctor dresses is important, what their preference is and whether patients think the way the doctor dresses influences their effectiveness as a doctor. The researchers were also interested to find out if there were demographic differences in the beliefs of the patients. Participants across five general practices (doctor's surgeries) in Scotland (475 participants in total) were asked to complete an interview after they had visited the doctor's surgery. Participants were shown eight photographs; five photos of the same man dressed differently, and three photos of the same woman dressed differently (see Figure 8.1). The male doctor was dressed in white coat over formal suit; formal suit; tweed jacket and informal shirt and tie; cardigan, sports shirt and casual trousers; and jeans and a t-shirt. The female doctor was dressed in white coat over skirt and jumper; skirt, blouse and woollen jumper; and pink trousers, jumper and gold earrings. There were fewer variations for the female doctor as it was felt there were less distinct styles used by women in general practice. The models posed in the same way for each photo. Patients were asked 'which doctor would you feel happiest about seeing for the first time?' and were asked to give a score from 0 to 5 for each photo. They were also asked about their confidence in the ability of the doctors in the photos, whether they would be unhappy about consulting with any of them, and which one looked most like their own doctor. Finally, patients were asked a set of closed questions about doctors' dress in general, and their attitudes to different items of dress.

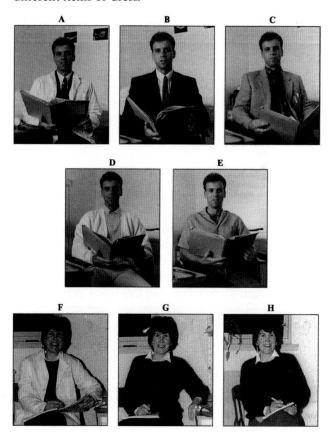

Figure 8.1: McKinstry and Wang (1991) investigated the effect of doctors' clothes

Results showed that the doctor in the smart suit was the most popular of the male doctors, followed by tweed jacket and tie, and white coat over suit (which were almost identical in their rankings). The doctor in the jeans scored the lowest by far. Similarly, the female doctor in the more traditional clothing was most popular (jumper and skirt), followed by the one in the white coat. Overall, the scores for the woman were higher than the scores for the man. Age had a significant effect on ratings, with older patients more likely to give high scores to both the male and the female doctor wearing the white coat. Those in social classes 1 and 2 (professional and managerial positions) were more likely to give high scores to a traditionally dressed doctor; with the male doctor in the white coat the most popular for social class 1 patients. The strongest association was with which general practice the participant attends, where preferences varied significantly across almost all categories of dress. When asked whether the patient would feel more confident in the ability of any of the doctors 41% answered 'yes'. These patients were most likely to be confident in the male doctor in the suit, followed by the white coat, and in the female doctor in the white coat, followed by the skirt and jumper. When asked whether the patient would be unhappy consulting with any of the doctors, 28% said 'yes', with the male doctor wearing jeans being the most selected photo. General attitudes to doctors' dress showed that 64% of patients thought that the way their doctor dressed was very important or quite important. Table 8.1 shows patients' responses to particular items of doctors' dress. There were differences in responses to specific dress in terms of age, sex and social class.

Verbal communications

There can be difficulties in communication between practitioner and patient, particularly when it comes to understanding medical terminology. The focus of research into this communication difficulty tends to focus on the patient's limitations and holds them, rather than the practitioner, responsible for any difficulties. Samora et al. (1961) report a long list of what they called 'patient deficiencies' including: unwillingness to receive unpleasant information, problems with memory recall, differences based on status, age or ethnicity and differences in the ability to understand medical terms. It could be argued instead that the practitioner should take responsibility for ensuring the patient understands any medical terms that are used.

Example study

McKinlay (1975) aimed to investigate the perceived and actual comprehension of medical terms by a sample of lower working-class families in Scotland. For one

	Percentage of respondents (n = 475)
Believe male doctors should usually wear a:	
White coat	15
Suit	44
Tie	67
Would object to male doctor:	
Wearing jeans	59
Wearing an earring	55
Having long hair	46
Believe female doctors should usually wear:	
White coat	34
Skirt (rather than trousers)	57
Would object to female doctor:	
Wearing jeans	63
Wearing lots of jewellery	60

Table 8.1: Patients' responses to particular items of doctors dress: McKinstry and Wang (1991). *n* = total number of respondents

month, the researcher joined doctors on their rounds in the obstetrics and gynaecology wards (hospital wards for anything relating to pregnancy and childbirth) at a hospital, in order to gather a list of 57 words that were used regularly by a range of doctors or in the literature that was distributed to mothers at clinics (see Figure 8.2). The list was then sent out to doctors who regularly served the maternity hospital, and they were asked to cross off any terms they wouldn't generally use. This resulted in a list of 13 words, which was presented in an interview to the respondents. The words were first sounded out and then used in the context of a sentence, and the respondent was asked to explain their understanding of the term. The responses were recorded and then two doctors scored each response independently in terms of accuracy. A group of 18 other doctors were given the list of 13 medical terms and were asked, for each word, to say whether they would expect the average lower working-class mother to: not understand at all and say so; get the meaning quite wrong; have an incomplete or vague understanding; or understand pretty well.

Figure 8.2: Women visiting the maternity clinic were tested for their understanding of medical terms

Results showed that, for most words, the two doctor's scores were closely matched. The researchers compared the comprehension level of under-utilisers (who did not attend antenatal care regularly) and utilisers (who attended antenatal care as expected) and found that, for 11 out of the 13 words, utilisers had a better understanding than under-utilisers. Furthermore, utilisers for whom this was not their first baby also showed a better understanding of medical terms than those who were pregnant for the first time. Both findings appear to show that experience seems to increase understanding levels. When comparing scores for comprehension of the mothers with expectation of the doctors, results showed that, for the most part, doctors greatly underestimated the mothers' understanding. For example, the term 'breech' (related to the position of the baby in the womb) was understood adequately by 84% of under-utilisers and by 100% of utilisers, but doctors predicted that understanding of this term would be adequate in only 22% of respondents. There were three (rather technical) terms, however, that doctors anticipated a much higher level of understanding than was actually found. Although there were not enough data for proper analysis, it appeared that more senior doctors had a greater expectation of patient understanding than did junior doctors. A final finding shows that there is a negative correlation between the number of words from the list of medical terms that a doctor claims to use regularly, and their expected patient understanding level. In other words, there is a clear tendency among doctors to use words without any expectation of patients to understand their meaning.

RESEARCH METHODS

The use of *self-report* methods such as *questionnaires* and interviews in research into practitioner and patient interpersonal skills has both strengths and weaknesses. The strengths of McKinstry and Wang's use of questionnaires are that it allows patients to express their thoughts and feelings rather than just observing their behaviour. Furthermore, the questions used were closed questions using Likert-type scales, allowing *quantitative data* to be gathered, which can be compared and analysed to understand trends and patterns. The problems of using a questionnaire like this is that it may be subject to *social desirability* or there may be *demand characteristics*. The patients may either give answers that they think will make them look good or may work out what the research is about and then change their responses, accordingly, reducing the *validity* of the study. The closed questionnaires do not allow for *qualitative data* to be collected so we cannot gather a detailed understanding of the patients' thoughts and feelings. Using the same two sets of photos with the same models is important as it is standardised and ensures *reliability*. Finally, the use of 475 participants across a wide range of ages and from five different surgeries is important as it makes the results *generalisable* to the wider *population*. However, the sample is limited in that all patients were from the same area, there were significantly more women than men and there was not a balanced proportion of social class.

McKinlay's use of interviews to get an understanding of patients' comprehension of medical terms was important as it enabled the terms to be sounded out and used in the context of a sentence. If the terms had been presented by questionnaire it wouldn't be possible to know whether an inaccurate response was actually due to difficulty reading the term rather than an actual lack of comprehension. McKinlay ensured high levels of reliability by having two doctors blindly and independently rate the mothers' responses and found a high level of agreement. In addition, 18 doctors were asked to anonymously rate their expectation of patient understanding of the terms, again increasing reliability.

ISSUES AND DEBATES

Application to real life is relevant for research in this section because it is investigating the effect of doctors' verbal and non-verbal communication on patients' perceptions. It will be really important for doctors' surgeries to learn from this research and implement the findings to encourage their patients' confidence and satisfaction in their doctors. To understand that, for example, the clothing a doctor wears can affect how confident a patient is in the doctor, and therefore how likely they are to follow advice, could have huge implications. It would be very simple to change a policy relating to what doctors should wear and this could lead to significant changes in the confidence and satisfaction of patients. It is, however, important to consider that there will be cultural differences in patient preference, as well as changes in patients' views since the study was carried out. Furthermore, research that shows a doctor's tendency to underestimate their patients' understanding is of great importance in everyday life; the more doctors and patients can understand each other the more effective and successful the relationship will be.

Patient and practitioner diagnosis and style

Practitioner diagnosis

There are three main parts of a practitioner diagnosis: making a diagnosis, presenting a diagnosis and coping with diagnosis.

Making a diagnosis requires **disclosure of information** from the patient, and this can sometimes be a difficult process. Some patients may struggle to communicate effectively for various reasons, and this can lead to errors in diagnosis. Sarafino (2006) described how patients may find it difficult to disclose information accurately when they:

- become angry or critical of the doctor
- ignore what the doctor is asking
- insist on medication or tests that are not necessary
- want to be given a certificate for an illness they do not have
- make inappropriate remarks towards the doctor.

Robinson and West (1992) investigated how much information was disclosed by 69 patients at a clinic via a computerised interview compared to a paper questionnaire that was passed to a doctor or nurse. Results showed that patients gave more information in the computerised interview than the questionnaire, and both methods gathered more information than the doctor gained when speaking to patients to treat them. This suggests that patients may not give full and accurate information to doctors, particularly if it is of a sensitive or potentially embarrassing nature.

Depending on the information that the doctor receives they will hopefully make an accurate diagnosis, which leads to successful treatment. However, sometimes doctors can make errors in diagnosis, and this is more likely to happen if the patient is not completely honest, minimises or exaggerates some of their symptoms or other details of their condition. The two types of misdiagnoses are:

- A **false positive diagnosis**: this is also referred to as a type 1 error. It occurs when the patient is healthy, but the doctor misdiagnoses them as being unwell.
- A **false negative diagnosis**: this is also referred to as a type 2 error. It occurs when the patient is unwell and does have a condition or illness but the doctor misdiagnoses them as being healthy.

Both types of misdiagnoses can be dangerous and damaging. If a patient is unwell but the doctor misses it and tells them they are healthy, they will not be given any treatment they require and their symptoms will persist, or potentially worsen. This could lead to a more severe illness, the possibility of hospitalisation or more invasive treatment, and could potentially be fatal. If a patient is healthy but a doctor misdiagnoses them with something, this will not have quite the same potential

KEY WORDS

disclosure of information: when the patient tells the doctor information about their symptoms and their experience for the doctor to make a diagnosis

false positive diagnosis: occurs when the patient is healthy, but the doctor diagnoses them with an illness or a condition incorrectly

false negative diagnosis: occurs when the patient is unwell, but the doctor misdiagnoses them as being healthy

serious repercussions but there could still be damaging consequences. A patient may be given medication that they do not need, which may lead to side effects or other consequences, such as change in lifestyle. Furthermore, if a patient realises that either of these types of misdiagnosis have been made it could make them less confident in the doctor. That may lead to them not seeking medical help in the future when needed or may make them less likely to adhere to medical advice in the future.

Once a diagnosis has been made, the practitioner needs to present the diagnosis to the patient. The traditional method of presenting a diagnosis is face to face, but there is a range of evidence that suggests this may not be the best, or only, method.

Cooke and Colver (2016) carried out research where they asked 77 patients with suspected skin cancer how they would prefer to be informed of their diagnosis, following a biopsy. Patients could choose to either be informed face to face, by telephone or in a letter.

The patients were given an information leaflet explaining the pros and cons of each option.

One month after receiving the biopsy result, patients were sent a questionnaire asking various closed questions about how they received their diagnosis, whether they had been given the information leaflet and if they were satisfied with the method at the time and in hindsight. Of the 77 patients, 48% chose to receive their diagnosis by letter, 37% by phone, 11% face to face and 5% a combination of two methods. 89% received their diagnosis in the chosen manner (seven could not be contacted by phone so a letter was sent). 94% of patients were happy with the way they received their diagnosis and, when asked if they would have changed the method they chose in hindsight, 80% remained happy with their original choice. Only 11% said they wished they had made a different choice, and only 5% would have chosen face to face retrospectively. There was no evidence for age difference in the method that was chosen. See Table 8.2 for pros and cons of the three different methods.

Method	Pros	Cons
Letter	• It can be re-read at any time to help process. • Avoids having to go to hospital for an appointment. • Has contact number for specialist nurse.	• It takes longer to be typed and posted. • Impersonal. • Can't ask questions straight away.
Telephone	• Quickest method. • Avoids having to go to hospital for an appointment. • Can be in your own home.	• You may find it difficult to have the conversation over the phone. • You may be out when you receive the call. • If contact can't be made, a letter will be sent instead.
Face to face	• More personal. • Opportunity for questions. • A relative can be with you.	• Have to attend hospital. • After a call from a secretary asking you to come in for an appointment there will be a wait where you won't have access to information.

Table 8.2: Pros and cons of methods of receiving a diagnosis, as found by Cooke and Colver (2016)

Research by Karri et al. (2009) found that 52% of patients diagnosed with skin cancer preferred to receive the diagnosis by letter rather than face to face. Despite these findings, 25 specialist nurses reported that most skin care centres do not believe it is necessary to offer alternative methods to the traditional face-to-face approach.

The way in which a patient copes with a diagnosis, and whether that is affected by the way the diagnosis is presented to them, has been investigated by Schofield et al. (2003). Schofield et al. sent out a questionnaire to patients four months after they received a diagnosis of skin cancer, to find out the relationship between the communication from doctors and the patients' satisfaction, anxiety and depression levels. Results showed that 32% of the 131 patients received their diagnosis by telephone rather than face to face. There were no significant differences in satisfaction, anxiety or depression levels between patients who received their diagnosis by phone or face to face.

However, Schofield et al. did find several factors surrounding the communication they received that *did* influence their satisfaction (whether by telephone or face to face). Satisfaction was higher when patients felt they had been prepared for the diagnosis, when the word 'cancer' had been used, when the patient felt that they had 'been told everything' (including about the severity of the cancer and their life expectancy), and when they felt information had been presented clearly. Anxiety levels were lower for patients who were prepared for the diagnosis, who could discuss their questions on the same day as the diagnosis, those who felt the level of information given matched their needs, and for those who felt their emotional needs were met (through reassurance and willingness to discuss the patients' emotions). For depression, the main factor linked to lower depression was matching the information to the individual's needs.

The evidence seems to show that there are individual differences in how a patient would prefer to receive a diagnosis and that most remain happy with their choice at a later date. The way a patient copes with a diagnosis seems to be more to do with clarity of the information presented and the way individual needs were met, rather than by the method that is used.

Key study: Savage and Armstrong (1990)

Savage, R., & Armstrong, D. (1990). Effect of a general practitioner's consulting style on patients' satisfaction: a controlled study. *British medical journal, 301(6758), 968–970.*

Context

There are two styles that can be adopted by the practitioner during a consultation: **doctor-centred style** and **patient-centred style**. As the name suggests, the doctor-centred (directed) style is led by the doctor, with the patient being passive during the consultation. The doctor will be focused on the first symptoms that they are given and will often ignore any new symptoms explained by the patient. The doctor-centred style involves the doctor asking closed questions, which require short replies and does not encourage any discussion. The atmosphere is impersonal, and the focus is on finding a medical explanation for the symptoms. In contrast, however, a patient-centred (sharing) style is much less controlled by the doctor, and the patient is a much more active part of the consultation. The doctor asks *open questions*, which encourages the patient to share information and their thoughts and feelings on the matter. The atmosphere is much more personal, medical jargon is avoided, and the patient is involved in decision-making.

KEY WORDS

doctor-centred style: a consultation style where the doctor leads, asks closed questions and does not encourage discussion with the patient

patient-centred style: a consultation style where the patient is an active part of the consultation and discussion is encouraged, leading to a joint decision being made

---

Main theories and explanations

Doctors can use different styles when consulting with a patient and making a diagnosis. These different styles can have an effect on the outcome for the patient, both in terms of how accurate the diagnosis is and how satisfied they feel about their experience. The style a doctor uses may suit some patients more than others, so it is important for research to be carried out to find out more about which styles work best for which sorts of patients. Much research has shown the effect of different styles of consultation used by practitioners. Katon and Kleinman (1980) find the benefits of adopting a **sharing style** during consultations. When the patient feels more a part of the decision-making process, the doctor can have a clearer understanding of the patient's problem and patient is more likely to follow any advice they are given. In contrast, Inglefinger (1980) suggests that, for effective medicine, a doctor should adopt a **directing style** and show authoritarianism and domination to make the patient feel better and more reassured.

KEY WORDS

sharing style: this is when a doctor discusses with the patient what they think might be wrong and the doctor and patient agree on a course of action together

directing style: this is when a doctor is authoritative and dominating and tells the patient what is wrong and what they should do next

---

Aims

The aim of this research was to compare the effectiveness of directing and sharing styles of consultation by a general practitioner on patients' satisfaction with the consultation.

Design

The research was carried out by one general practitioner during his surgery over a four-month period. A random number generator was used to select four patients for the study during each of the doctor's surgeries. Patients aged 16 to 75 years, presenting with any symptom, were eligible, and patients were excluded only if they presented with life-threatening conditions, or for administrative or preventative measures. In total, 200 patients completed all parts of the study so were included in the results. Patients gave written consent to the use of an audio recording of their consultation for a research study.

A set of cards was produced to randomly allocate either a directing or shared style. These cards contained prompts covering the five main parts of the consultation, to ensure a uniform approach (see Table 8.3). The cards were face down on the doctor's desk and turned over at the appropriate time, following an initial greeting and patient description of their problem. At the end of the consultation the patient was asked to complete a questionnaire about their satisfaction and were asked to complete a further questionnaire one week later. The time of the consultation was recorded, along with the demographics and other data relating to the patient.

To ensure the styles were carried out effectively, an independent observer analysed 40 random tape recordings of consultations and confirmed that all aspects were covered in every consultation. The intended style was identified correctly in 39 out of the 40 recordings.

Results, findings and conclusions

Results showed that there were no significant differences in the mean length of consultations between the two styles.

Overall, patients reported a high level of satisfaction for their consultation, with only three giving neutral or negative responses. Results showed that the patients who

Part of consultation	Style of consultation	
	Directing	Sharing
Judgement on the consultation	'This is a serious problem'	'Why do you think this has happened now?'
Diagnosis	'You are suffering from...'	'What do you think is wrong?'
Treatment	'It is essential that you take this medication'	'Would you like a prescription?'
Prognosis	'You should be better in...days'	'What do these symptoms or problems mean to you?'
Follow-up and closure	'Come and see me in...days'	'When would you like to come and see me again?'

Table 8.3: Examples of directing and sharing styles of consultation in the study by Savage and Armstrong (1990)

received a directing style were more likely to feel that the doctor completely understood their problem, and that the explanation they received was excellent. This was the case immediately following the consultation and one week later, although the ratings had all declined in the follow-up questionnaire. Furthermore, those who received a directing style were more likely to feel that they had been greatly helped (their illness or condition had greatly improved) one week later.

After one week, for patients who rarely attended surgery, had a physical problem, were not investigated or received a prescription, the directing style led to a greater feeling that the doctor understood them. Factors that did not lead to a significant difference in satisfaction between the two styles were: consultations longer than 9 minutes, those where the main treatment was advice, those who were experiencing a chronic problem and those for conditions that the patient thought had a psychological basis.

It can be concluded that a directing style leads to higher patient satisfaction in terms of perception of the doctor's understanding of the problem, the quality of the doctor's explanation, and the subjective improvement one week later. This contradicts the general view held by researchers and doctors alike, who tend to feel that a shared style is a better way forward. It appears that for simple physical illnesses that require a traditional biomedical approach to diagnosis and treatment, the directing approach is most effective. However, for other problems, such as chronic or psychological illnesses, the benefit of the directing approach is removed. Further investigation could be carried out to get a better understanding of these different factors.

Evaluation

Savage and Armstrong's research was a field experiment where patients were visiting the doctor with a complaint in the same way they would do normally: they did not know they were involved in a study into doctor consultation styles. This is an important strength as it increases the validity of the study; the patients' responses to the questionnaire would be accurate and honest appraisals. In terms of the questionnaires, the use of closed questions gathered quantitative data that allow for comparisons and analysis to be carried out. However, there was a lack of open questions leading to qualitative data, so we have not been able to gather detailed insight into the patients' thoughts and feelings. The use of a questionnaire immediately after the consultation as well as one a week

later increases the validity of the research as it allows us to see how the patients' views changed over time, and to measure how much they thought the consultation helped. The research was carried out in a standardised way. The same doctor carried out all the trials so there would not be any differences in terms of other characteristics of the doctor: only the different style that he used. The research was also standardised because the doctor was given prompts to use to make sure he properly portrayed the selected style across all parts of the consultation. The use of a standardised approach increases the reliability of the results. Finally, the sample is limited in that all patients were from the same surgery over a four-month period, but there were patients of both sexes and a range of ages.

Application to everyday life is relevant to Savage and Armstrong's study because it shows important findings in relation to doctors' consultation style. Any information about consultation styles is useful for surgeries to know so that they can advise their doctors to consider the consultation style they use in order to lead to increased confidence and satisfaction of their patients. The findings of this study are particularly important though, because they contradict the general view that a sharing approach is more appealing to patients. Instead, this research suggests that a directing style leads to higher levels of confidence and satisfaction in patients, particularly for those with simple physical conditions.

RESEARCH METHODS

Research such as that by Robinson and West is useful because it is carried out in a real-life setting, such as a clinic. This means the study has high *ecological validity* and the results can be generalised beyond the research setting. However, the research was only carried out in one clinic, with a small sample so caution should be used when generalising the results to other patients or to those in other settings. Research by Cooke and Colver and Schofield et al. used self-report methods to gather information from patients. The use of questionnaires was beneficial because it meant the patients could complete them in their own time, and the questionnaires provided quantitative data, allowing analyses to be made. However, the downsides of using these questionnaires with closed questions is the lack of qualitative data, meaning there has not been detailed information gathered about each patient's experience. How might qualitative data have been collected?

Individual versus situational explanations is particularly relevant when considering research into practitioner diagnosis and style. A situational explanation would suggest that there is a particular style that is most appropriate to be used in a medical setting. If the situation can best explain which style is most effective we would expect research to show that either sharing or directing style is best. This is not the case, instead research shows that there are strengths and weaknesses to both styles and that some patients are more satisfied with a directing style and others are more satisfied with a sharing style. This suggests that individual explanations are more accurate and that individual differences between patients will affect which style would be preferable.

When considering research into patient and practitioner diagnosis and style it is important to consider cultural differences. Most research carried out in this area has been conducted in the USA, with some research conducted in the UK and other parts of Europe. There is not very much research available into patient and practitioner diagnosis and style in non-Western cultures. This means that it is important to look at research into this area with caution, and to be aware that we cannot necessarily generalise the results to all cultures. Although there are likely to be cultural differences in relation to the majority of the research we cover in this section, the topic of diagnosis and style is going to be particularly subject to cultural difference. To overcome this issue, it would be beneficial for research to be carried out across different cultures so we are able to get a more valid view of the similarities and differences between cultures.

ACTIVITY 8.1

Use what you have learned about practitioner and patient interactions to describe an 'ideal' doctor. Consider what they might look like and how they might interact with a patient.

Misusing health services

Delay in seeking treatment

For many patients there is a delay between noticing a symptom and seeking treatment, and this can have serious implications. There are several factors that have been found to influence the delay in seeking medical care, relating to emotional factors, behavioural factors, beliefs about the symptom, type of symptom and **sociodemographic factors**.

Example study

Safer et al. (1979) investigated the reasons for delaying seeking medical care as well as the factors that influence this. Safer et al. began by proposing that, instead of looking at the time between developing a symptom and getting medical care as one period of time, it is more accurate to break it down into three stages (see Figure 8.3).

According to Safer et al., the three stages that can account for the delay in seeking treatment are:

- **Appraisal delay**: the time the patient takes to appraise (or judge) a symptom as a sign of illness. This involves deciding whether or not there is something wrong, i.e. that they are 'ill'.

- **Illness delay**: the time between when the patient decides they are ill and when they decide to seek medical care.

- **Utilisation delay**: the time from the decision to seek care until they actually access services. This can include the consideration of whether the costs of care (time, effort, money) are worth it.

KEY WORDS

sociodemographic factors: characteristics of a person, such as age, sex, education and ethnicity

appraisal delay: the time the patient takes to appraise a symptom as a sign of illness. This involves deciding whether or not there is something wrong, i.e. that they are 'ill'

illness delay: the time between when the patient decides they are ill and when they decide to seek medical care

utilisation delay: the time from the decision to seek care until they actually access services. This can include the consideration of whether the costs of care (time, effort, money) are worth it

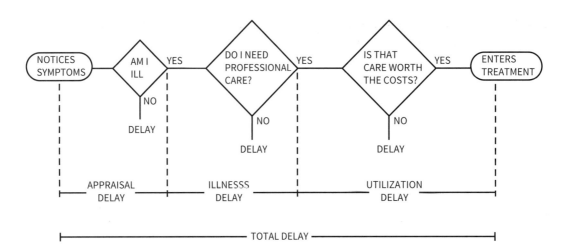

Figure 8.3: Safer et al. (1979) identifies three stages in the delay in seeking treatment

Safer et al. investigated the effect of the following predicting factors on each of the stages of delay:

- Sensory or perceptual experience of the symptom, e.g. pain or bleeding.

- Self-appraisal processes, e.g. observing the symptom for signs of change.

- Coping response to symptoms, e.g. home remedies.

- Emotional reactions to the health threat, e.g. fear and distress.

- The imagined consequences of the symptoms, e.g. imagining that surgery is required.

- The situational barriers to receiving care, e.g. cost of services.

The first three factors were considered to be the most probable predictors of appraisal delay; emotional factors (including conceptual beliefs about illness and medical services) and imagined consequences were considered to be the most probable predictors of illness delay and situational (and sociodemographic) factors were considered to be most probable predictors of utilisation delay.

Patients attending one of four clinics for the first time for a particular illness were invited to complete a 45-minute questionnaire and interview. In total, 93 patients completed the interview, with a wide range of age and ethnicity and slightly more females than males. The interview was designed to measure both the types of delay (appraisal delay, illness delay and utilisation delay) and total delay time from first noticing the symptom to deciding to see a doctor, as well as the predictors of

delay. There was a mix of open questions and closed questions using Likert-type scales.

Results showed that there was no significant correlation between the length of each of the three stages of delay. The mean total delay was 57 days, but this was greatly affected by a few extremes; the median total delay was only eight days. Six variables correlated significantly with total delay:

- The variable that was most significantly correlated with total delay was a recent, competing problem or change in life that was unrelated to the medical condition (such as marriage or divorce). Patients not reporting other problems delayed on average 7.2 days, whereas those reporting one or more problems delayed 23.8 days.

- The second most significantly correlated variable to total delay was whether the patient had a painful symptom: those with pain delayed 8.6 days, compared to 23.3 days for those without pain.

- Third, was whether the patient read about their symptom: if they did not read about it, they delayed 11.5 days, if they read a bit, they delayed 26.4 days and if they read a lot about their symptom, they delayed 50.2 days.

- Age was also significantly correlated with total delay: patients under 45 years delayed 9.1 days, compared to patients over 45, who delayed 23.5 days.

- The final two variables that correlated were only borderline significant: those who waited to see if their symptom went away or changed delayed 8.9 days, compared to those who did not wait, who delayed 23 days. Last, was a conceptual belief:

those who felt their symptom could be cured delayed only 9.4 days, whereas those who felt their symptom could not be cured delayed 15.2 days.

In terms of the three stages of delay, the results are summarised:

- The average length of appraisal delay was 4.2 days. Two sensory factors and one appraisal strategy were found to be significant predictors of appraisal delay. The presence of a painful symptom or of bleeding (sensory factors) was associated with decreased appraisal delay, while reading about the symptom (appraisal strategy) was associated with increased appraisal delay.

- The average length of illness delay was 3.1 days. There was one sensory factor and one imagery factor that were significant correlates of length of illness delay. If a patient experienced solely a new symptom (sensory factor), their illness delay was significantly shorter than if they experienced new and old, or old, frequently experienced symptoms. If a patient imagined negative consequences of being unwell, such as imagining themselves on an operating table (imagery factor), this was associated with a longer illness delay than those with little or no negative imagery.

- The average length of utilisation delay was 2.5 days. A situational factor, a sensory factor and a conceptual factor were significantly correlated with length of utilisation delay. Those who were concerned about cost delayed longer than those who were not concerned about cost (situational factor). Those who experienced pain (sensory factor) waited less time than those who did not experience pain. Finally, patients who felt that their symptom could be cured had a shorter utilisation delay than those who felt that their symptom could not be cured, but there was not a significant difference in length of delay in the other two stages of delay.

In summary, Safer et al. found that situational factors, sensory factors, conceptual beliefs, sociodemographic factors and appraisal strategies were all significantly correlated with total delay. The most useful information, however, comes from the analysis of the factors in relation to each of the stages of delay. Appraisal delay was predicted by sensory factors and appraisal strategies; illness delay was predicted by sensory and imagery factors; utilisation delay was predicted by sensory, conceptual and situational factors.

Alternative explanations for delay

There are, however, alternative explanations for delay, for example the Health Belief Model. The Health Belief Model can be used to explain a range of health-related behaviours, including delay in seeking treatment. The Health Belief Model was proposed in the 1950s by the US Public Health Service, and updated in the 1980s, and is still widely used today. The model states that people's decisions about health-related behaviour, such as delaying seeking treatment, are due to their health perceptions and can be broken down into the following factors:

- Perceived severity: the likelihood of a person changing their health behaviours depends on how serious they think the consequences may be. For example, somebody would be more likely to delay seeking treatment for a minor illness rather than something more serious.

- Perceived susceptibility: a person is more likely to change their health behaviour if they feel that they are particularly at risk. For example, somebody is more likely to delay seeking treatment if they don't think they are likely to be at risk of something serious.

- Perceived benefits: people are less likely to change a behaviour if they don't think the change will benefit them. For example, someone is more likely to delay seeking treatment if they don't feel confident the treatment will work.

- Perceived barriers: there are many reasons that people think changing health behaviour will be hard, and this can stop them from making the changes. Perceived barriers include expense, effort, discomfort and inconvenience. People are more likely to delay seeking treatment if they perceive any of these barriers to be in place.

- Cues to action: an external event is often required to act as a trigger to make somebody take action. They may want to make a positive health change but until something external triggers them, they may not behave accordingly. For example, someone may be concerned about a symptom but delay seeking treatment until they see a poster or an advert advising people to get symptoms checked by a doctor, or they hear that a friend has just received a diagnosis.

- Self-efficacy: this factor was added to the model in 1988. It considers a person's belief in their ability to make a health-related change. If you believe you are capable of doing something you are more likely to do it. For example, someone is more likely to delay seeking treatment if they are not confident that they can go through the diagnosis or treatment process.

Munchausen syndrome versus malingering

Munchausen syndrome is a serious mental disorder where someone pretends to be unwell, deliberately makes themselves unwell, or hurts themselves. Usually, a pre-existing disorder is present, but this is deliberately aggravated, or new symptoms made up. Munchausen syndrome is distinct from **malingering**, which occurs when somebody deliberately makes themselves unwell or pretends to be unwell for an obvious incentive such as avoiding criminal prosecution, receiving compensation or gaining disability allowance. With Munchausen syndrome these incentives are not involved; the person pretends they are unwell or makes themselves unwell purely for the psychological benefit of assuming the sick role, with no external incentives for the behaviour.

> ### KEY WORDS
>
> **munchausen syndrome:** a serious mental disorder where someone pretends to be unwell, deliberately makes themselves unwell, or hurts themselves in order to get attention
>
> **malingering:** this occurs when somebody deliberately makes themselves unwell or pretends to be unwell for an obvious incentive such as avoiding criminal prosecution, receiving compensation or gaining disability allowance

Munchausen syndrome is a type of factitious (artificially created) disorder. It is a diagnosable condition, according to both the **ICD** and **DSM**.

> ### KEY WORDS
>
> **ICD:** International Statistical Classification of Diseases and related health problems. It is the global standard for making diagnoses and collecting data
>
> **DSM:** the *Diagnostic and Statistical Manual of Mental Disorders* is produced by the American Psychiatric Association and is used to make diagnoses of mental disorders

The diagnostic features of Munchausen syndrome are as follows:

Essential features:

- **Pathologic** lying
- **Peregrination** (travelling or wandering)
- Recurrent, feigned or simulated illness

Supporting features:

- Borderline and/or antisocial personality traits
- Deprivation in childhood
- **Equanimity** for diagnostic procedures
- Equanimity for treatments or operations
- Evidence of self-induced physical signs
- Knowledge or experience of a medical field
- Most likely to be male
- Multiple hospitalisations
- Multiple scars (mostly abdominal)
- Police record
- Unusual or dramatic presentation

> ### KEY WORDS
>
> **pathologic:** behaviour that is compulsive, it happens frequently and is very difficult to stop
>
> **peregrination:** wandering off or travelling in a meandering way
>
> **equanimity:** a sense of calm and composure in a difficult situation
>
> **prevalence:** how common something is across the population

If any of these features are present in a patient, particularly the essential features, it is important for doctors to pay close attention as Munchausen syndrome is very difficult to diagnose and even more difficult to treat. The main reason it is difficult to treat Munchausen syndrome is because patients tend to disappear very early on. There is limited information on the **prevalence** of Munchausen syndrome, but it is thought to be very rare. It could be that cases have been overreported because patients change their identities and move around presenting to different hospitals and doctors so often.

Example study

Aleem and Ajarim (1995) reported on a case of a 22-year-old female university student who attended hospital and was initially suspected to be suffering from immune deficiency (a condition where the immune system does not work properly). The patient had initially been seen at age 17, suffering from amenorrhea (lack of menstrual cycle) and was prescribed medication. Over the following months the patient developed recurring deep vein thrombosis (DVT; a dangerous condition when a blood clot forms in the vein) and was hospitalised and given anti-coagulants (blood thinners). Soon after, the patient went to hospital again complaining of painful swellings on both sides of the groin, along with weakness in the legs. This led to several investigative methods as well as a change in medication and surgery. In the latest hospital admission, the patient complained of a painful swelling above her right breast and reported having several similar swellings in her abdomen over recent months. These previous swellings required hospitalisations and surgeries on approximately 20 occasions. A range of tests were carried out and eventually surgical drainage was required as signs of an abscess developed. Four days later, a similar lump appeared in the opposite breast, which also had to be surgically drained. The lumps could not be explained, and further tests showed a range of organisms in the lumps, which also could not be explained. This led to suspicion of Munchausen syndrome and a psychiatric consultation was made where it was suggested the patient undergo long-term psychotherapy. The patient was very defensive and extremely rationalising in her answers and appeared to be under a great deal of stress. Finally, a nurse found evidence suggesting that the patient was causing the abscesses herself. When the patient was told about this by another patient, she became very angry and left the hospital against medical advice and was lost to follow-up. The diagnosis of Munchausen syndrome was confirmed.

ACTIVITY 8.2

Re-read the case study by Aleem and Ajarim (1995) and write down the key parts of the case study, including:

- what may have triggered Munchausen syndrome
- the first signs of the syndrome
- when and why medical staff became suspicious and
- how the medical staff finally confirmed the diagnosis.

REFLECTION

When you have completed Activity 8.2 stop to consider *how* you carried out the task.

Consider:

- How did you start the task? Were you confident with the process or did you have to think twice before starting?
- Did you work through the case study methodically or did you deal with each point as it came to you?
- Did you scan the case study for the information you required? Or did you read every part in detail? How did your method work?
- What have you learned from the activity?
- Could you use the skills from this activity in future tasks?

RESEARCH METHODS

Safer et al. used interviews to gather their data about patients' experiences. The key strength of this is that it allows us to gain an insight into patients' thoughts and feelings, and to gather retrospective data about their experience since their symptom first appeared. The interview used open and closed questions so it collected qualitative and quantitative data, allowing for detailed information as well as data that can be analysed. A further strength is that Safer et al. decided to turn the questionnaire into an interview, where the questions were read out because a *pilot study* showed that some patients struggled to read or understand some of the items. This is important as it increases the validity of the research; we know that patients will understand the questions or could ask for clarity if they were unsure. The problems of using an interview to gather information like this is that it relies on the patients' subjective interpretation, for example relating to how severe their pain is, or their reasons for delay. Furthermore, patients may be less willing to give sensitive information in an interview, rather than a questionnaire because it would be easier to write the information down than speak it aloud to an interview in person. Lastly, because the questions are asking about a potentially long stretch of time, the responses may not be accurate. Patients may misremember when symptoms were first noticed or how long it took them to make a decision, for example.

Aleem and Ajarim's research into Munchausen syndrome was a *case study*. This is useful as it provides lots of detail into the individual, in terms of her current presentation as well as a full case history. This increases the validity of the research as we are able to get a good, accurate understanding of the individual over a period of time, rather than just a snapshot. The problem with using a case study, however, is that it is based just on one individual, so the results cannot be generalised. We can learn a lot about this individual, but the study cannot be *replicated* and cannot be tested for reliability as the set of circumstances are unique to this case.

ISSUES AND DEBATES

Both Safer et al. and Aleem and Ajarim took a holistic approach to their research. In trying to gather a detailed and accurate understanding of their patients, both sets of researchers consider the patients in a holistic manner. Safer et al. conducted a detailed interview designed to find out about a whole range of aspects relating to the patients, in terms of sociodemographic factors, social situations, experience of the current symptom, overall thoughts and feelings about illness and medical care, and much more. This allowed for complex analysis to be carried out to get a broad understanding of the patients. Similarly, Aleem and Ajarim considered a range of information about their patient, including her medical history, family background and upbringing, and psychological well-being. A holistic approach is beneficial as it looks at the individual as a whole, and this gives a full and accurate picture. However, the downside to a holistic approach may be that it is difficult to get a clear answer as there are so many different factors that interact and make for a complex set of data. A reductionist approach, however, might look at a patient and try to explain their symptoms or behaviour from purely a biological perspective. This attempt at explaining complex human behaviour by looking just at biological factors such as blood test results or scans could result in misdiagnosis or a lack of a full understanding of the individual and their experience.

Questions

1   McKinlay (1975) used interviews with patients. Why was it important they used interviews rather than any other technique?

2   Disclosure of information is an essential step toward an accurate diagnosis. What can a doctor do to encourage full and accurate disclosure of information from the patient?

3   How do we distinguish between someone with Munchausen syndrome and a malingerer? And why is it so important to make the distinction?

8.2 Adherence to medical advice

Types of non-adherence and reasons why patients don't adhere

Adherence has been defined by the **World Health Organization (WHO)** as: 'the degree to which the person's behaviour corresponds with the agreed recommendations from a health care provider'. There are two main types of **non-adherence**: failure to follow treatments and failure to attend appointments. There are serious consequences to both types of non-adherence, both for the individual themselves and wider.

> ### KEY WORDS
>
> **adherence:** how much a person's behaviour follows what their healthcare provider recommends and is agreed on
>
> **World Health Organization (WHO):** an organisation within the United Nations, to direct international health advice and lead global health responses
>
> **non-adherence:** failure to follow treatments and failure to attend appointments

Failure to follow treatment can be broken down into three different types:

- Primary non-adherence: this occurs when a doctor writes a prescription, but the medication is never collected; in other words, the patient does not hand in the prescription to get the medication they have been prescribed.

- Non-persistence: this occurs when the patient starts to take the medication but stops, without being advised to do so by a medical professional. This is usually unintentional and often happens due to a miscommunication between the patient and the medical professional, or due to the patient's difficulty in following treatment due to issues such as cost, difficulty accessing medication, forgetting to take the medication, etc. Intentional non-

adherence is less likely, but tends to take place due to patients' beliefs, attitudes and motivation.

- Non-conforming: this involves ways in which medication is not taken as prescribed. This could include missing doses, taking medication at incorrect times or in incorrect doses.

The rate of non-adherence varies widely between studies and has been recorded at anywhere between 10% and 92%. WHO carried out a review in 2003 and found that non-adherence to medication in developed countries was approximately 50%. Approximately half of this non-adherence is considered to be intentional, and non-adherence is more likely with chronic (long-term) rather than acute (short-term) conditions.

Failure to attend appointments is another problem, with non-attendance rates at primary care (general practitioners) in the UK being reported at between 2.9% and 11.7%, and in the USA between 5% and 55%.

Problems caused by non-adherence include the following:

- Waste of medication: if medication is received but not taken it is wasted, which has huge economic consequences, as well potential issues relating to supply and demand.

- Time lost due to missed appointments: research by the Doctor Patient Partnership and Institute of Healthcare Management in the UK found that 17 million GP appointments and 5.5 million practice nurse appointments were missed in 2000, at an estimated cost of £150 million.

- Progression of illness: if medication is not taken the illness will most likely progress, leading to possible hospitalisation or stronger or more invasive treatments being required in the long-term.

- Increased use of medical resources: related to the progression of illness, if untreated, a condition may worsen to the point where the patient may require hospital visits, hospital admissions and admission to nursing homes.

- Reduced functional abilities: if a disease or condition is left untreated it can affect the patients' ability to function properly and may leave them unable to work, etc.

- Lower quality of life: when left untreated, as well as the symptoms worsening, so will the quality of life of the patient, this will likely continue to decline until or unless treatment is adhered to.

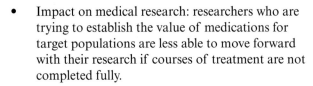

- Impact on medical research: researchers who are trying to establish the value of medications for target populations are less able to move forward with their research if courses of treatment are not completed fully.

As we can see, the negative implications are serious and wide-reaching, not just affecting the individual themselves but also having financial implications for medical services.

Explanations of why people do not adhere

One explanation for why patients do not adhere to medication is called rational non-adherence. This means that some people do not adhere because of a deliberate decision to adjust medication. There can be many reasons for this, including side effects, perception of the effectiveness of the medication and cost. Laba et al. (2012) investigated rational non-adherence.

Example study

Laba et al. (2012) carried out research to find out which factors contribute the most to rational non-adherence, and to investigate whether factors relating to specific medicines and patient background contribute to non-adherence. An online sampling system was used to collect a representative sample of 161 Australian participants, in terms of age and gender, and included a range of education level and income.

An online survey was used, which had three sections: section one asked questions about current medication use and attitudes towards medication and section three asked for background information about the participant. Section two was the Discrete Choice Experiment (DCE), where ten hypothetical situations were presented, and the participant was asked to choose from one of two alternatives. Participants were asked to imagine they are currently taking two medications for different long-term conditions, and were asked which of the two medications they would be happiest to continue taking. For each medication the participant would be given information regarding the following factors:

- Symptom severity

- Symptom frequency while on the medication

- The chance of early death from the illness while on the medication

- The severity of the medication side effects

- The change of future unwanted medication side effects

- How the medication is taken

- Alcohol restrictions

- The monthly cost to you of the medications

This was designed to find out which of the factors are the most important in determining non-adherence to medication. In total 32 choice sets were designed, and these were split into four versions of the surveys, along with a repeated choice set to check for consistency and rationality behind the decision-making.

Results showed that six out of the eight factors listed above had a significant effect on the decision to continue with a medication. Symptom severity and alcohol restrictions did not have a significant effect on adherence. Participant background characteristics did not make a significant difference to the effect of the factors, and neither did it matter if participants were currently taking medication or not. The monthly cost of the medication was found to be a significant factor in non-adherence only for those who do not have private medical insurance (and therefore have to pay for medication themselves), but not for those with insurance (where the insurance company pays for the medication). Further analysis of the data shows how participants were willing to trade between levels of factors. For example, participants would be significantly more willing to continue with a treatment if it only needed to be taken once a day, compared to four times a day. However, they would prefer to continue with the task of taking the medication four times a day if it reduced their risk of unwanted side effects in the future by 20%. Analysis also showed that most participants (58%) considered harms to be of greater importance than benefits when making decisions about adherence. Finally, the risk of current side effects was considered to be more important than future side effects, however, the medication's ability to reduce the risk of death was seen to be more important than the reduction in symptom frequency.

The Health Belief Model

The Health Belief Model is another explanation for why people do not adhere. See the text on 'Alternative explanations for delay' in Section 8.1 for a full description of the Health Belief Model. The factors described in the Health Belief Model can be applied to non-adherence:

- Perceived severity: somebody would be less likely to adhere to medication for a minor illness than for a more serious one.

- Perceived susceptibility: somebody would be less likely to adhere to medication if they don't think they are at risk of illness.

- Perceived benefits: someone is less likely to adhere to medication if they don't feel confident the treatment will work.

- Perceived barriers: people are less likely to adhere if they perceive barriers to be in place, such as inconvenience, cost, discomfort.

- Cues to action: a person is more likely to adhere to medication if they have been exposed to a trigger, such as a loved one dying from a similar condition.

- Self-efficacy: someone is more likely to adhere to medication if they have confidence that they can see it through and keep up with the treatment plan.

Measuring non-adherence

Patients' non-adherence can be measured in a range of different ways, including subjective measures such as interview, objective measures such as pill counting and medication dispensers, and biological measures such as blood and urine samples.

Subjective measures

A subjective measure of non-adherence is a clinical interview, where the patient is interviewed and asked a range of questions to gather an understanding of their adherence to their medication. The **Medical Adherence Measure (MAM)** is one example of a semi-structured clinical interview designed to collect data about patients' adherence. The items in the interview assess patients in terms of their knowledge of the prescribed treatment regimen, self-reported adherence, any systems used to manage the regimen (such as medical dispensers or reminders) and any perceived barriers to adherence. Interviews such as the MAM emphasise a supporting patient–practitioner relationship, where advice and support can be offered to increase adherence and improve patient care. Strengths of the interview are that it allows an insight into the patients' thoughts and feelings about their treatment, rather than the objective measures that just count or track quantitative

data. The obvious weakness of the interview is that patients may not tell the truth, either due to feelings of embarrassment or guilt, or feeling that they may get in trouble. If patients don't tell the truth the clinical interview is largely useless, but if it is carried out in a supportive and collaborative way so that the patient is encouraged to be honest it can be a successful and beneficial measure of non-adherence.

Example study

Riekert and Drotar (1999) wanted to investigate the effects of non-participation in studies of treatment adherence in adolescents with chronic health conditions. It was expected that those who refused to participate in a study about treatment adherence would show less treatment adherence. Adolescents (aged 11–18 years) who attended a clinic for type 1 diabetes and who lived with at least one family member were approached and asked to take part in the study. In total the sample consisted of 94 families, categorised into three groups: 52 participants (who completed the whole study), 28 nonreturners (who agreed to take part in the study but failed to return their questionnaires) and 14 nonconsenters (who completed the initial adherence interview and demographic information sheet but refused to continue with further questionnaires).

The adolescent completed the initial adherence interview, which was a semi-structured interview asking a range of questions about different aspects of behaviour to manage their diabetes, resulting in an overall adherence score. Parents filled out the demographic information sheet, which asked questions about the adolescent's age, gender, ethnicity, number of hospitalisations and disease severity, as well as questions about the parents' marital status, number of children and level of education. Further questionnaires were given for adolescents and their parents to complete and send back in a prepaid envelope. It was estimated that the parents' questionnaires would take approximately half an hour to complete, and asked about the relationship with their child. It was estimated that the adolescents' questionnaires would take about one hour to complete, and asked about their relationship with their parents. All participants had a medical chart review, which gathered information on their treatment adherence, such as number of blood sugar tests per day and most recent level of metabolic control (a measure of how well the diabetes was being managed).

Comparison of demographic information between the three groups (participants, nonreturners and nonconsenters) did not differ significantly, except for

> **KEY WORD**
>
> **Medical Adherence Measure (MAM):** a semi-structured clinical interview designed to collect data about patients' adherence

father's education, which was higher for the participant group than for nonreturner group. However, two of the health-related variables did differ significantly between groups. Those who failed to return their questionnaires completed significantly fewer blood sugar checks per day than those who did return their questionnaires, or those who did not consent. Those who failed to return their questionnaires also scored significantly lower on the adherence interview than those who did return their questionnaires. As the adherence score included questions about blood sugar testing, these values were removed to see if the differences between adherence were due solely to differences in blood sugar testing. Results showed that, even with the answers about blood sugar testing removed, there were still significant differences in adherence score between those in the participant group and those in the nonreturner group. Overall, this study shows that adolescents from families who returned their questionnaires had significantly higher adherence scores and tested their blood sugar significantly more frequently than those from families who failed to return their questionnaires. It has been suggested that a possible explanation for these differences between the groups is because adherence and returning the questionnaires both require organisation and planning abilities so those with better organisation skills may be more likely to adhere and to return the questionnaires. It could also be that those who did not return the questionnaires lacked incentive or did not want to discuss issues around diabetes or the relationships within their families.

Objective measures

Simple **medical dispensers**, such as seen in Figure 8.4, can help measure adherence as they allow for the correct tablets to be placed in certain containers for each day of the week. Therefore, at the end of the week a carer or medical professional can easily see if there are any tablets left in the dispenser as a simple measure of non-adherence.

Similarly, **pill counting** is a straightforward way of measuring the *amount* of medication that has been taken: by asking patients to bring all medication at each medical review and counting how many pills remain at the end of a certain time period, you can easily calculate what percentage of prescribed medication a patient has taken. However, there are problems; first, it relies on the patient bringing all their medication with them to each appointment. Second, you cannot know they

Figure 8.4: A medical dispenser can help measure adherence

actually took the medication, just that it is no longer in the bottle, so it is easy for somebody to conceal the fact that they have not taken the medication. A third problem is that you are not able to track the pattern in which the medication was taken. This is where electronic measuring devices, such as the TrackCap (see Figure 8.5) described by Chung and Naya next, come into play. They track when and how often a bottle of medication is opened, allowing you, in theory, to track whether medication is being taken at the correct times of day or at correct intervals, rather than just how many tablets are taken. The problem, however, is that electronic measuring devices do not provide evidence that the medication is actually being taken, just that the container is opened at certain times. A final problem with electronic measuring devices is that they are expensive so they cannot be used on a large scale.

KEY WORDS

medical dispensers: products that allow for the correct tablets to be placed in certain containers for each day of the week

pill counting: by asking patients to bring all medication at each medical review and counting how many pills remain at the end of a certain time period you can easily calculate what percentage of prescribed medication a patient has taken

---

Figure 8.5: The TrackCap is a medical adherence measure

Example study

Chung and Naya (2000) wished to investigate the effectiveness of electronically measuring adherence and **compliance** to medication in asthma patients. In a 12-week trial, 57 asthma patients were given three weeks' worth of zafirlukast, an oral medication that treats asthma. After each three-week period, the patient attended a clinic for a physical assessment and to return any unused tablets and have the bottle replaced with a new set of three weeks' worth of tablets. Patients were instructed to take one tablet in the morning and one in the evening, approximately 12 hours apart. The patients were told that compliance was being measured as part of the study but were not told how this would take place. The bottles of medication were fitted with a TrackCap **medication event monitoring system (MEMS) device**, that recorded the time and date every time the cap was removed and replaced. Days were classified as:

- Insufficient interval adherence: days with two events less than eight hours apart

- Undercompliance: days with only one event

- No compliance: days with no events

- Over-compliance: days with more than two events

Before looking at the results it is important to distinguish between the terms adherence and compliance. The terms are often used interchangeably but there is a slight distinction. Compliance refers to a passive following of medical orders, so in this study compliance is measured by percentage of days where the correct amount of medication is taken. Adherence refers to more of a collaboration between doctor and patient and relates to the patient fully understanding medical

advice and following it completely accurately, even adjusting lifestyle to meet requirements. In this study, adherence is measured by the percentage of days that both tablets are taken at approximately 12 hours apart, as instructed.

Results from the TrackCap show that median adherence was 71%, and median compliance was 89%. Results show that 66% of patients had good compliance (they took over 80% of prescribed doses), and on days when two tablets were taken, the mean time between tablets was 12 hours 34 minutes (though with a large range). Patients had one TrackCap event on a median of 19% of days, insufficient interval adherence on a median of 2% of days, patients took no tablets on 1% of days, and were over-compliant on a median of 2% of days. As a measure of how accurate TrackCap is, compliance was also measured by a tablet count (how many tablets were left over at the end of the trial period). Based on a tablet count, median compliance was 92%, so slightly higher than the TrackCap measure. For 83% of patients the difference between the two measures was marginal, suggesting patients took more than one tablet out at a time on occasion. For a minority of patients, however, it appears that they removed more medication than prescribed regularly, and one patient took up to a week's supply out of the bottle at each opening. Two patients recorded multiple events before clinic visits, suggesting they suspected tablet counting so they removed tablets to try to conceal their non-compliance. Overall, the study showed that compliance was consistently high throughout the 12 weeks of treatment, and adherence, although slightly lower than compliance, was still good. The study also showed that, although compliance was measured higher by use of a tablet count than by the TrackCap, there was only a slight difference, so it can be concluded that the TrackCap is an accurate measure of compliance and adherence to medication.

KEY WORDS

compliance: passive following of medical orders, for example the percentage of days where the correct amount of medication is taken

medication event monitoring system (MEMS) device: a device that records the time and date of every time the cap of a medicine container was removed and replaced. TrackCap is the brand used in this study

Biological measures

Biological measures of non-adherence, such as blood and urine samples, are the most accurate and objective measures. These are fairly routine tests that can be carried out when a patient visits a clinic. Blood and urine samples provide accurate readings of the levels of certain drugs in the patient's system, which can be used to measure the patient's adherence to their prescribed treatment. This method of measuring non-adherence is not subjective and does not rely on a patient's honesty; it is a highly valid and reliable measure. However, the main disadvantage of this measure, compared to the others we have discussed, is that it is expensive and takes time to do so it would not be appropriate to use on a large scale.

RESEARCH METHODS

Riekert and Drotar used more than one measure of adherence score from the adherence interview, as well as number of blood sugar checks. This increases the reliability of the findings as the researchers were able to test for consistency between the two measures. By carrying out an interview and giving participants a score, as well as recording the number of blood sugar checks, Riekert and Drotar were able to gather quantitative data, allowing for analysis and comparison between participants. However, a problem with the research is that it relies on self-report, so participants might not give accurate answers, either because they want to deliberately hide the truth about their adherence, or because they may not remember accurately.

Chung and Naya followed 57 patients in a clinical trial, so this was a relatively small sample. However, the trial was 12 weeks long, so this allowed a reasonable length of time to measure the patients' compliance and adherence, increasing the validity of the results. An important aspect of the trial was that the patients knew that compliance would be measured as part of the research to comply with *ethical guidelines*. However, the patients did not know that the TrackCap was used to take the measurements. This was important because it ensured the patients didn't change their behaviour as a result, but instead behaved how they naturally would, so this increased the validity of the results. Finally, as a way of measuring the accuracy of the TrackCap, compliance was also measured using pill counting, and the results were compared.

ISSUES AND DEBATES

The majority of the research into the different methods used to measure non-adherence take a nomothetic approach. Large amounts of data are collected in clinical trials, and these data are used to make generalisations about the wider population. One strength of a nomothetic approach is that it is based on large amounts of quantitative data, based on objective, scientific measures. A further strength of a nomothetic approach is that it allows for predictions to be made, and decisions can be made to try to make improvements, for example finding ways to help increase adherence. However, the main weakness of a nomothetic approach, as opposed to an idiographic approach, is that it does not allow for people to be considered as individuals. Furthermore, due to the lack of qualitative data and lack of focus on individuals, the nomothetic approach can't apply to everyone in full and accurate detail, as the idiographic approach would.

Improving adherence

As we have seen, non-adherence can have serious negative consequences, so it is really important to find ways to improve adherence. This could be through individual behavioural techniques, such as personalised prompts, contracts and customising treatment, or through community interventions, such as the use of lotteries or generic prompts.

Contracts can be implemented, whereby patients and medical practitioners have a discussion to clarify the requirements of taking the medication. A contract is then drawn up and the patient signs it (or it can be verbal), to agree that they will adhere to medication. Bosch-Capblanch et al. (2007) carried out a review of previous studies and found that the use of contracts generally increased adherence to medication in patients with a range of illnesses, but that there was little evidence of long-term improvements to adherence.

Prompts can be used to improve adherence, such as through reminder phone calls, text messages or medication boxes. The use of prompts can help improve adherence in instances where the main cause of non-adherence is forgetting to take medication or to take the prescription to a pharmacist. There has been mixed evidence for the success of prompts but research by Strandbygaard et al. (2010) found that adherence to medication in asthma sufferers increased significantly if they received one text message a day to remind them.

Customising treatment can improve adherence as it involves adjusting the treatment regime to better fit the patient's lifestyle or to make it easier or more convenient for them to adhere. Evidence from Shi (2007) found that customising treatment by simplifying dosage frequency can improve adherence to treatment, and evidence from Schroeder (2004) found that reducing twice-daily to once-daily dosing improved adherence. Another way of customising treatment is by changing the treatment to reduce side effects. There is conflicting evidence on the effect of minimising side effects on adherence, but research shows that this can improve adherence to treatment.

Example study

Chaney et al. (2004) investigated improving adherence in children suffering from asthma. Asthma can be a dangerous condition, but luckily it can be treated effectively, especially in children, through the use of an inhaler. Research has shown that children often do not adhere to treatment and use their inhalers as they should, and this is partly due to lack of adherence by the children and partly due to lack of adherence by the parents because of the stress it causes to try to make children use their inhaler. Standard treatment for children with asthma involves inhaling the medication from an inhaler with the use of a spacer, to hold the medicine in place so it can be breathed in more easily (see Figure 8.6).

Figure 8.6: A standard spacer used to help inhale asthma medicine

The study aimed to compare the adherence of children with asthma using the Funhaler (see Figure 8.7), to those using the traditional spacer. The Funhaler is designed to act effectively as a spacer and to connect to an inhaler in the same way as a standard spacer but is made to be fun

by adding a whistle and a toy element. When the child uses deep breathing the toy spins at an optimum level and the whistle will sound; the idea being that using the Funhaler is fun, and correct use is encouraged.

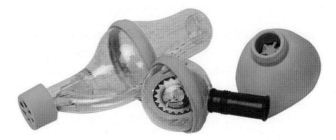

Figure 8.7: The Funhaler is designed to improve adherence to asthma treatment (Chaney et al. 2004)

A total of 32 children aged 1.5 to 6 years, with asthma who used an inhaler and a standard spacer, were recruited to take part in the two-week study. Parents were contacted and asked to complete a questionnaire asking a set of closed questions about attitudes and adherence to the recommended treatment and frequency of medication. Participants were then invited to use the Funhaler for two weeks and were given the same questionnaire to complete after the two weeks were completed. Parents were contacted by phone on an ad hoc basis while using their standard treatment and the Funhaler, to be asked if their child had taken their treatment on the previous day.

Results from the random questioning of parents showed that 59% of children on their standard treatment had been medicated the previous day, compared to 81% when using the Funhaler. Furthermore, when using their standard treatment children only achieved the recommended four or more breath cycles per treatment 50% of the time, but they achieved this 80% of the time using the Funhaler. When using the standard spacer, only 10% of parents reported being always successful with treatment, but this increased to 73% when using the Funhaler. There were far fewer problems such as screaming when faced with the spacer, or unwillingness to breathe through the device, with the Funhaler than with the standard spacer. Finally, the attitudes of children and parents changed dramatically when responding to the Funhaler compared to the standard spacer. Fear was a typical response to the standard spacers, with only 10% of children showing pleasure. However, there were no reports of fear in response to the Funhaler and in fact 70% displayed pleasure as a response. Only 10% of parents reported their approach to the standard treatment as being 'completely happy'; however, 60% reported a 'completely happy' approach to the Funhaler and no parents indicated strong concern or dislike. The Funhaler has clearly been a very effective device in increasing adherence and improving the attitudes and experiences of children with asthma, and their parents.

ACTIVITY 8.3

Chaney et al. investigated improving adherence in children with asthma by making the spacer fun. How could you use a similar approach to improve adherence in children suffering from eczema (a skin condition) that requires them to put cream on two times a day?

Key study: Yokley and Glenwick (1984)

Yokley, J. M., & Glenwick, D. S. (1984). Increasing the immunization of preschool children; an evaluation of applied community interventions. *Journal of applied behavior analysis, 17*(3), 313–325.

Context

In the 1970s and 1980s there was a significant increase in the use of a range of methods to try to tackle socially significant community problems, such as reducing pollution and conserving energy. This approach was also applied to promote healthy behaviours, such as improving dental care, promoting the importance of good nutrition and to encourage the use of seat belts. Up to this point, these attempts had not been applied to immunisations, although figures in the lead up to this study have shown that uptake of childhood immunisations can be very low in some areas. This can have serious repercussions, not only because children are left vulnerable to serious childhood illnesses, but also some children's education would suffer as some schools banned children who were not fully immunised. Research has shown that the later children started to receive their immunisations, the greater their risk of not completing the immunisation programme before school entry age, and therefore risking a ban from school.

Main theories and explanations

Research has shown that **community interventions**, such as multiple prompts and lotteries, can have a positive effect on the number of children being immunised against potentially fatal childhood illnesses. Byrne et al. (1970)

measured the effect of multiple prompts to encourage immunisations. He sent out a computer-generated motivational prompt to half of parents with two-month-old babies (immunisation age) in Rhode Island. If there was no response after 30 days, a second 'more emotional' prompt was sent out, and if there was still no response, a telephone or house call was made. Results showed that for lower and upper classes there was a significant 10% increase in immunisations, compared to those who received no prompts, and a 5% (non-significant) increase for middle class participants. White (1976) carried out an informal field study where radio DJs encouraged to parents to get their school-aged children immunised. Prizes were offered, including a lottery for a week's holiday in the Bahamas, where every signed immunisation permission slip was added to the draw, and one was drawn at random. This led to 92.6% of permission slips being returned.

Aims

The aim of this study was to evaluate the effectiveness of four different conditions for motivating parents of preschool children to get their children immunised. The conditions were:

- A mailed general prompt

- A mailed specific prompt

- A mailed specific prompt and expanded clinic hours to increase access and convenience

- A mailed specific prompt and a monetary incentive, in the form of a cash lottery

It was expected that the greatest impact would be the specific prompt with the monetary incentive, followed by the specific prompt and increased access, then the specific prompt alone, and last, the general prompt alone.

Design

The study was carried out on the entire population of **immunisation-deficient** preschool clients (aged five and under) at a public health clinic in an American city.

KEY WORDS

community interventions: any attempts to encourage a certain behaviour in a town or city, using methods such as leafleting, letters and lotteries

immunisation-deficient: children who were found to be in need of at least one immunisation

Of the 2,101 pre-schoolers, 1,133 (53.9%) were found to be in need of at least one immunisation. There was an even number of boys and girls: 64% were Caucasian and the mean number of immunisations needed was 5.2.

The families in the 'general prompt' group were mailed a prompt with general immunisation information, urging parents to get their children's immunisations up to date, but without any specific or personal information. Families in the 'specific prompt' group were mailed a prompt that named the target child, as well as the specific immunisations they required, and giving the clinic's location and hours. Those in the 'increased access' group received the specific prompt, as well as information about extra out-of-hours sessions at the clinic, where childcare facilities were present, and parents were told they could leave their children at the free childcare for the full session if they wished. The 'monetary incentive' group received the specific prompt, as well as information about a cash lottery that offered three cash prize draws, requiring a ticket to be handed in when the child was taken for their immunisation. There were two control groups: the contact control group received a telephone contact (but no mailing), requesting information about immunisations and demographics but not giving any prompts, and the no-contact control group, who were not contacted at all during the study. The researchers were interested in three dependent measures: the number of target children receiving one or more immunisations, the number of target children attending the clinic for any reason, and the total number of immunisations received by target children. The immediate effect of all conditions was measured after two weeks (the time during which the monetary incentive and the increased clinic access were relevant), and a follow-up measure was also taken at two and three months later. Checks were put in place to ensure the accuracy of the specific prompts that were written, the names and addresses, and that the correct immunisations were given at the clinic. A random sample of 10% of specific prompts were checked and 93% were found to be completely accurate, for the sample of name and mailing addresses there was 100% accuracy, and reliability of immunisations given by clinic staff was 80%.

Results, findings and conclusions

Results showed that there were significant differences between groups in terms of the number of children immunised, the frequency of children attending the clinic, and total immunisations given. As expected, the monetary incentive group had the biggest impact,

followed, in descending order, by increased access group, specific prompt group, general prompt group and control groups. These findings remained significant at both the two-month and three-month follow-ups, as seen in Figure 8.8. The specific prompt and monetary incentive method produced a 29% increase in the number of immunisations given.

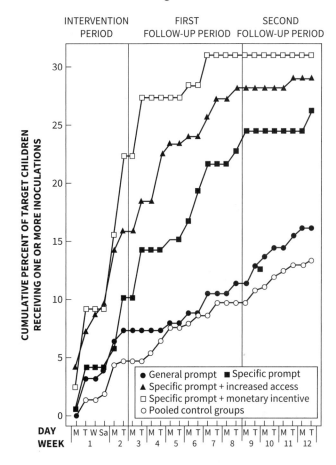

Figure 8.8: The results of Yokley and Glenwick's intervention remained significant at a two-month and three-month follow-up

As well as measuring the effectiveness of each method, the researchers also wanted to find out which was the most cost-effective method. Results showed that the specific prompt was the most cost-effective intervention, with the specific prompt and monetary incentive being the least cost-effective in the long run. The increased access was considered to be the least cost-effective initially but as the impact continued at both the follow-ups, it became slightly more cost-effective in the long run than the monetary incentive. However, when considering the extent of the impact of each intervention immediately, and at both follow-ups, the specific prompt and monetary incentive was found to be the most cost-effective significant intervention in the long run. These results have implications for national departments of health and other healthcare providers, in terms of having a better understanding of how best to use community intervention programmes effectively.

Evaluation

Yokley and Glenwick carried out a large-scale study on a huge target population of immune-deficient children, providing large amounts of data. These data were representative of the entire target population, so the data have high population validity. The research was also longitudinal in that there was the immediate two-week measure, as well as a follow-up measure two and three months later. This increases the validity of the research as it shows the long-term impact of each intervention, rather than just the immediate benefits. The researchers' use of checks to make sure the accuracy of the specific prompts, the mailing addresses, and the provision of correct immunisations are all important controls. This ensures the validity and reliability of the study as we can be confident in the accuracy and consistency of the findings.

The research by Yokley and Glenwick has great importance in terms of application to everyday life as the implications could influence approaches used by departments of health and other healthcare providers. An understanding that general prompts are not very effective, but that specific prompts, with or without monetary incentives, are significantly more effective could make a huge difference in immunisation uptake, as well as a range of other important health-related campaigns. The use of a monetary incentive may not be appropriate in all cases, however, it could be used in isolated cases where a particular immune-deficient population needs to be targeted, as a relatively quick, easy and cost-effective way of increasing numbers of immunisations.

RESEARCH METHODS

The study by Chaney et al. was a field experiment, which gives it high ecological validity, as we can see the change in adherence to treatment in real life for patients who used the Funhaler compared to the standard spacer. The study used *repeated measures*, which increases the validity as it allows us to see the difference in attitude and adherence for the same people before and after using the Funhaler, so we know any differences in results cannot be due to *participant variables*.

RESEARCH METHODS

How could *matched pairs* have been used instead of repeated measures? One weakness, however, is that the study relies on self-report from the parents about their attitudes as well as their level of adherence, so there is a real risk that the results are not valid. Parents may well not tell the full truth about their level of adherence, for example, as they know they should make their children take the treatment everyday so their answers may be swayed by social desirability. A further weakness is the small sample and short time period that was used, so not a lot of data were gathered. Further research would be needed, with a larger and more varied sample, and over a longer period of time to collect more valid data on the usefulness of the Funhaler. This is particularly important as children are likely to be interested by the Funhaler initially because it is new and exciting, but it is only a successful method if the change lasts once the initial excitement has passed.

ISSUES AND DEBATES

Research into improving adherence, such as the study carried out by Chaney et al., can be applied to everyday life. Non-adherence to treatment can have serious consequences so anything that can be done to improve adherence to treatment will be useful and beneficial. Understanding the effectiveness of individual or community interventions is a really important part of improving adherence to treatment and maximising the effectiveness of the treatments for a wide range of illnesses. Most of the methods of improving adherence are relatively cost- and time-effective so they are easy to implement, and the benefits can be significant and far-reaching.

Questions

4   Non-adherence has negative implications for the individual but there are wider implications too. What are some wider implications of non-adherence and why are they important?

5   Chung and Naya (2000) used a Trackcap to measure adherence. They told their participants that they would be measuring their adherence but not that they were using the Trackcap. Why were the participants given some but not all of the information?

6 Chaney et al. (2004) used repeated measures in their study. Why was this? And why didn't they use a control group?

8.3 Pain

Types and theories of pain

Types of pain

Pain is not just an unpleasant experience; it also has a really important function. It acts as a signal to let us know that whatever we are doing is potentially damaging and we should stop. Pain also works by making us less likely to repeat the damaging behaviour again.

There are two broad types of pain: **acute pain** and **chronic pain**. Acute pain can be severe but comes on quickly and lasts a relatively short period of time. Acute pain is usually in a very specific location and has an identifiable source, for example injury or illness. It is usually easy to treat with pain medication, changes to environment or behaviour, or some form of therapy such as physiotherapy. Chronic pain, on the other hand, is pain that lasts for a relatively long period of time, usually for at least one month, and is resistant to treatment. Chronic pain is likely to be the result of long-term behavioural factors such as physical exertion, or due to chronic illnesses such as cancer. Chronic pain can be difficult to treat and can have a significant impact on quality of life, relationships and mental health. Acute pain can develop into chronic pain if it is not treated effectively. Chronic pain is more common in females and in the elderly, and the most common type of chronic pain is **muscoskeletal**, especially joint and back pain.

One particular type of pain is **phantom limb pain (PLP)**, which can be a common problem for people who lose a limb. Even though the arm or leg is no longer there, PLP occurs when the individual still experiences pain as coming from that area. PLP is very difficult to treat successfully and many people who suffer from it will experience pain for the rest of their life. There has been some success treating PLP with **mirror treatment** (see Figure 8.9). Ramachandran and Rogers-Ramachandran (1996) successfully treated patients with PLP following upper limb (arm) amputations. Mirror treatment works by placing the remaining arm into a box, with a mirror down the middle so that when it is viewed at a slight angle it looks to the patient as if they have two intact arms. Patients then take part in a range of arm movement exercises, eventually leading to some people experiencing a reduction in phantom pain (although some experienced little or no improvement).

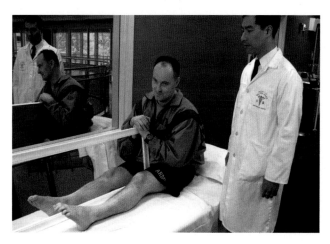

Figure 8.9: Mirror treatment can successfully treat phantom limb pain

---

KEY WORDS

acute pain: can be severe but comes on quickly and lasts of a relatively short period of time. Acute pain is usually in a very specific location and has an identifiable source

chronic pain: pain that lasts for a relatively long period of time and is resistant to treatment. Chronic pain is likely to be the result of long-term behavioural factors such as physical exertion, or due to chronic illnesses such as cancer

muscoskeletal: referring to the muscles, bones, ligaments and tendons in the body

---

KEY WORDS

phantom limb pain (PLP): a common problem for people who lose a limb. Even though the arm or leg is no longer there, PLP occurs when the individual still experiences pain as coming from that area. PLP is very difficult to treat

mirror treatment: a treatment for PLP that works by placing the remaining arm into a box, with a mirror down the middle so that when it is viewed at a slight angle it looks to the patient as if the patient has two intact arms. Patients then take part in a range of arm movement exercises, eventually leading to some people experiencing a reduction in phantom pain

Example study

MacLachlan et al. (2004) reported on the first case study that reported on the use of mirror treatment on a person with lower limb (leg) PLP. The individual studied was a 32-year-old man named Alan, who had to have life-saving surgery to remove his leg at the hip. He was extremely unwell for several weeks afterward so only become fully aware of the amputation five weeks later. Within two days of Alan becoming fully conscious, he began to experience phantom limb pain, as well as pain at the point of amputation. At the beginning of the day, the pain was mild and initially he felt as if two of his toes were crossed, and experienced 'pins and needles' in his toes. As the day went on the pain worse, and by late afternoon the pain was severe. Alan experienced a full phantom leg and felt as though the leg was shorter than his other leg, felt that it was in a cast and that the leg was stretching backward with the toes pointing downwards. Alan had tried pain medication and a course of transcutaneous electrical nerve stimulation (**TENS**) treatment (see the section on Managing and controlling pain for more detail on TENS) with little effect, so he decided to give mirror treatment a try, on the understanding that it had not been used successfully to treat lower limb PLP before.

Alan followed the procedure of mirror treatment as described before, with ten repetitions each of ten different exercises including: straightening and bending the leg, pointing the foot up and down, clenching and unclenching toes and moving the foot in circles. At first, the exercises were carried out twice a day, initially with a physiotherapist present. After a few days Alan could carry out the exercises alone, and eventually without the mirror; at this stage the exercises were carried out up to four times a day. In total, the programme lasted three weeks.

Alan found some exercises more difficult than others, and it took four sessions before he began to feel as if he had any control over the phantom leg, although he felt emotional at seeing the reflected leg for the first time. Over the second week, the feeling of crossed toes decreased and by the end of the third week there was no sensation of crossed toes, and phantom pain was minimal. Alan was also asked to rate the level of phantom pain and stump pain (1 = none at all, 10 = excruciating), control over his phantom leg (0% = none at all, 100% = full control), and to indicate the position of his phantom leg. At the start, Alan reported phantom pain in the range of 5–9 and stump pain in the range of 0–2. At the end of the third week Alan rated his phantom pain as 0 and stump pain as 1. Furthermore, Alan's sense of control of his phantom

leg increased from 0–3% initially, to 25–30% after three weeks. The phantom leg remained feeling shorter than the intact leg, but, with effort, it could be 'straightened out'. In summary, this study showed mirror treatment to be an effective treatment for PLP in lower limbs, in much the same way as it is for upper limb pain.

KEY WORD

TENS treatment: a small electric current is passed through electrodes to the painful area, and this reduces pain by reducing the pain signals that go to the brain and spinal cord and by stimulating the production of endorphins

---

Theories of pain

Two theories of pain are **specificity theory** and **gate control theory**.

Specificity theory (Von Frey, 1895) proposes that there is a separate sensory system for processing pain, in the same way as there are for the senses such as hearing and vision. Specialised pain receptors respond to stimuli and, via nerve impulses, send signals to the brain. The brain then processes the signal as the sensation of pain, and quickly responds with a motor response to try to stop the pain. For example, if you touch something hot, the nerve impulses from pain receptors in your hand travel up to your brain, to be processed as a pain sensation, so your brain sends a message back to the muscles in your hand, telling them to move your hand away from the source of the pain. This happens automatically and almost instantaneously.

KEY WORDS

specificity theory: proposes that specialised pain receptors respond to stmuli and, via nerve impulses, send signals to the brain. The brain then processes the signal as the sensation of pain, and quickly responds with a motor response to try to stop the pain

gate control theory: proposes that the spinal cord contains a 'gate' that either prevents pain signals from entering the brain or allows them to continue. This theory can explain why our emotional state or our expectations affect how much something hurts

---

Gate control theory (Melzack & Wall, 1965) proposes that the spinal cord contains a 'gate' that either prevents pain signals from entering the brain or allows them to continue. This theory can explain why our emotional state, or our expectations affect how much something hurts. The gating mechanism occurs in the **dorsal horn** of the spinal cord, where both small nerve fibres (pain fibres) and large nerve fibres (fibres for touch, pressure and other skin sensations) carry information to. When there is more large fibre activity compared to small fibre activity people experience less pain (the pain gates are closed). When there is more small fibre activity, pain signals can be sent to the brain so that pain can be perceived (the pain gates are open). This explains why we rub injuries after they happen, for example if you bang your elbow on a table you will rub where it hurts for a few moments. The increase in normal touch sensation (large fibres) inhibits the activity of the pain fibres (small fibres) so pain perception is reduced (see Figure 8.10).

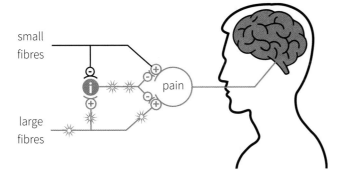

Figure 8.10: Gate control theory explains how pain may or may not be experienced

---

KEY WORD

dorsal horn: the area of the spinal cord where the gating mechanism occurs, which receives information from small nerve fibres (pain) and large nerve fibres (touch) and sends this information to the brain

RESEARCH METHODS

MacLachlan et al.'s research is a case study, allowing them to gather information about one individual. One key strength of the case study is that lots of detailed information can be collected, allowing an accurate insight into the specific case. A weakness, however, is that the results of the case study cannot be generalised to the wider population and the study cannot be replicated to check for reliability. Qualitative and quantitative information was gathered. Qualitative data allow for a good understanding about the individual's thoughts and feelings and allowed for a detailed case history to be taken. Quantitative data, in the form of Likert-type scales, allowed for statistical analysis to be carried out, to provide a measure of the change in symptoms throughout the treatment. The problem with using these Likert-type scales to assess factors such as pain and sense of control is that they are subjective; they only tell us what rating this individual gives, and there isn't another more objective measure used as comparison.

ISSUES AND DEBATES

Application to everyday life is important here because pain can be debilitating and can have a huge impact on a person's quality of life, so it is essential for us to understand it as much as possible. Understanding the function of pain may help someone come to terms with their experience of pain and understanding the differences between types if pain is important when considering treatments. Furthermore, understanding different theories of pain can also help our understanding of how pain is processed and experienced, which can also help with development of treatments.

The case study by MacLachlan et al. is particularly important in terms of application to everyday life as it was the first reported case of successfully using mirror treatment to treat PLP, so this research can be beneficial for others. How could the individual versus situational explanation be applied to explanations of pain?

Measuring pain

For pain to be treated effectively, it first needs to be understood as well as possible, in terms of the quality and intensity of the pain. There are several methods used to measure pain, including subjective measures (such as clinical interview and psychometric measures) and behavioural/observational measures.

Subjective measures

When a patient first presents with pain (usually chronic), the doctor will gather a medical history and carry out a medical examination, and they will also carry out a **clinical interview**. This involves asking the patient a range of open questions and will focus on getting an understanding of the patient's experience of their pain. The clinical interview will also include evaluating a range of factors (such as behavioural and psychological) that influence the patient's experience and reporting of the pain. The acronym 'ACT-UP' (Activities, Coping, Think, Upset, People) can be used as a guide for an initial clinical interview as follows:

- Activities: how does the pain affect your life in terms of eating, sleeping, physical activities, relationships, etc.?

- Coping: how do you deal/cope with your pain? What makes it better or worse?

- Think: do you think your pain will ever get better?

- Upset: have you been feeling anxious or depressed?

- People: how do people respond when you have pain?

As well as gathering factual information during the interview, the doctor will observe the patient's behaviour as well as their (and their family members') thoughts and feelings about their pain, their adherence to treatment and their expectations and goals.

A key strength of a clinical interview is that it allows the clinician to get a good understanding of the patient and their experience of their pain. The only way to know how someone thinks or feels is to ask them, and pain is a very subjective experience. A further strength of a clinical interview is that it collects qualitative data with lots of rich detail to get a deep and thorough understanding. A weakness of a clinical interview is that it relies solely on the patient giving their opinion and interpretation of things, which may not be accurate. Some people may downplay their symptoms in order not to make a fuss, or because they fear the possible outcome if they say the full extent of their pain. Others may, however, exaggerate their pain in order to get attention or to be taken seriously, or to be given stronger pain medication.

Psychometric measures and visual rating scales

Other methods of measuring pain are psychometric measures and visual rating scales. The **McGill pain questionnaire (MPQ)** is designed to assess the quality and intensity of subjective pain and can be used with patients with a range of conditions, such as cancer and muscular pain. The MPQ is composed of 78 words, of which the patient chooses the words that best describe their pain. These words are assigned a value based on their severity and the patient is then given a total score from 0 (no pain) to 78 (severe pain). The MPQ covers several categories:

- Pain descriptors: including words such as flickering, sharp, searing, tender, tugging.

- Affective: including words such as tiring, sickening, terrifying, wretched.

- Evaluation of pain: including words such as annoying, troublesome, intense, unbearable.

- Miscellaneous: including words such as spreading, numb, squeezing.

The MPQ also asks which, out of a list of items, increase or decrease the pain, such as:

- Eating
- Heat
- Cold
- Weather changes
- Movement

KEY WORDS

clinical interview: involves asking the patient a range of open questions and will focus on getting an understanding of the patient's experience of their pain as well as evaluating a range of factors (such as behavioural and psychological) that influence the patient's experience and reporting of the pain

McGill pain questionnaire (MPQ): is designed to assess pain, and is composed of 78 words, of which the patient chooses the words that best describe their pain. These words are assigned a value based on their severity and the patient is then given a total score from 0 (no pain) to 78 (severe pain)

- Rest

- Mild exercise

Finally, the MPQ asks a range of questions to measure the strength of the pain, including how the pain is best described now, when it is at its worst, and when it is least painful, with the following responses:

- Mild

- Discomforting

- Distressing

- Horrible

- Excruciating

A strength of the MPQ is that it can be used to assess changes in pain over time and to assess the effectiveness of pain management and treatment. The MPQ gathers quantitative data, which allow for statistical analysis to be carried out and for comparisons to be easily made. The MPQ is relatively quick and easy to administer. A weakness of the MPQ and other psychometric tests is that it involves closed questions, which may force a patient to choose an answer that doesn't fully represent how they feel. The lack of open questions means no qualitative data can be collected, so it isn't possible to get full detailed information about the patient and their experience.

A **Visual Analogue Scale (VAS)** is an instrument used to measure pain (or other symptoms) on a continuum from no pain to an extreme amount of pain, rather than trying to assign pain into discrete categories such as mild, moderate and severe. VAS can be presented in many ways, but the simplest is a horizontal line (usually 100 mm long), with the ends defined in the extreme limits (such as no pain to most extreme pain: see Figure 8.11). The patient marks where along the line they feel best represents their current pain and this is then transferred to a numerical value by measuring the distance (in mm) from the end point (no pain) to the patient's mark, giving a score between 0 and 100. The following cut-off points have been recommended:

- No pain: 0–4 mm

- Mild pain: 5–44 mm

> **KEY WORD**
>
> **Visual Analogue Scale (VAS):** an instrument to measure pain by asking a patient to mark on a line where best represents their pain from no pain to extreme pain. The position of the mark is then transferred into a numerical value

- Moderate pain: 45–74 mm

- Severe pain: 75–100 mm

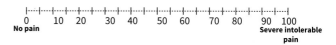

Figure 8.11: A Visual Analogue Scale is an instrument used to measure pain

A VAS is beneficial because it is extremely quick and easy to administer. It is an effective method of detecting change in pain over time and is more sensitive to small changes than using descriptive categories such as mild, moderate, severe. The collection of quantitative data means that analysis can be carried out and comparisons can be made. However, VAS does not collect detailed qualitative data and does not gather a range of items such as the McGill pain questionnaire, so it is relatively limited.

Key study: Brudvik et al. (2016)

Brudvik, C., Moutte, S. D., Baste, V., & Morken, T. (2016). A comparison of pain assessment by physicians, parents and children in an outpatient setting. *Emergency medicine journal, 34*(3), 138–144.

Context

Research has shown that children are often not given appropriate pain management across all aspects of healthcare, but particularly in outpatient settings, such as emergency departments (Grant 2006).

Grant (2006) also adds that analgesia (pain medication) is not used frequently enough, that there is often a delay in administration and that the dosage is often too low. For anybody to experience an illness or injury that requires a visit to the emergency department is a scary and unpleasant experience, but for a child it is important not to underestimate the possible repercussions, especially when their pain isn't managed properly. Inadequate pain management can not only have short-term problems such as slower healing but can also lead to longer-term problems such as anxiety and fear of medical care. There have been many reasons suggested for the lack of pain management in emergency departments, such as time constraints, fear of reduced productivity, and reluctance to give children pain medication due to possible side effects (Fein et al. 2012; Brown et al. 2003).

Main theories and explanations

We have already considered the different ways of measuring pain and the difficulty in gathering accurate measures of pain. Research (and life experience) shows us that someone's experience of pain is subjective and that there are individual differences in a person's pain threshold (how much pain they can manage). Research also shows that many measures of pain we use are not applicable to children because a child will not be able to understand or respond appropriately. However, there are pain scales designed specifically for use with children so we should be able to assess a child's pain level appropriately.

However, research by Singer et al. (2009) has found that pain assessments by parents and practitioners are generally lower than the pain assessments made by the child patient themselves. Morrow et al. (2012) investigated the experience of children with chronic illnesses and found that the reports of quality of life made by the children differed from reports made by doctors and parents.

Aims

The aims of this research were:

- To investigate the level of agreement of pain intensity when measured by the children, parents and physicians.

- To estimate the influence of children's age, medical condition, and severity of pain on the difference in pain assessment given by children, parents and physicians.

- To see how the pain assessments affected the physicians' administration of pain relief.

Design

The sample consisted of 243 children aged 3–15 years (53% boys) who attended a Norwegian emergency department over a 17-day period. The patients, their parents, and the physician who treated them all completed a questionnaire. There were 51 different physicians, 57% were men and 51% had children of their own. Half of the physicians had over five years of medical experience and 30% had a speciality in family medicine but none of them specialised in paediatrics.

Different measures were used to assess pain, in order to ensure the measures were age appropriate. Children aged 3–8 years filled out the **Faces Pain Rating Scale-Revised (FPS-R)**, which had six faces showing increasing levels

of pain (see Figure 8.12). Children aged 9–15 years used the Visual Analogue Scale (VAS) and **Coloured Analogue Scale (CAS)** where they marked on a line where their pain was from no pain (green) through to the worst thinkable pain (red) (see Figure 8.13). Parents and physicians completed the **Numeric Rating Scale (NRS)** to estimate the child's level of pain from 0 to 10. Parents completed their score before the child completed theirs, but they were not completely blind to each other's ratings, however parents and children were instructed not to tell the physician of their ratings. As well as pain assessments, the parent's questionnaires gathered demographic information. Physician's questionnaires gathered information about their medical experience, speciality and if they had their own children. The child's diagnosis was classified as either: infections, fractures, wound injuries/soft tissue or ligament/muscle injuries. Most children had soft tissues, ligament or muscle injuries (51%), followed by fractures, infections and wound injuries.

KEY WORDS

Faces Pain Rating Scale-Revised (FPS-R): a pain rating scale suitable for children aged 3–8 years, showing six faces showing increasing levels of pain

Coloured Analogue Scale (CAS): a pain rating scale suitable for children aged 9–15 years, where respondents marked on a line where their pain was from no pain (green) through to worst thinkable pain (red)

Numeric Rating Scale (NRS): a scale from 0 to 10 where respondents give the numerical value that best represents their pain

Pain measurement scale

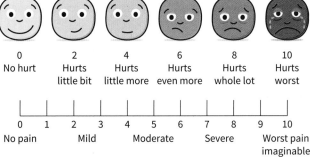

Figure 8.12: The Faces Pain Rating Scale-Revised can be used to measure pain in young children

Figure 8.13: A coloured analogue scale can be used to measure pain in older children

Results, findings and conclusions

The doctors assessed the child's mean pain to be NRS = 3.2. The parents' assessment was higher (NRS = 4.8), and children's own evaluation was highest (NRS = 5.5). On average, physicians assessed pain level to be NRS = 2.3 lower than the child's assessment and NRS = 1.6 lower than the parents' assessment. Parents and doctors assessed the mean pain intensity rating to be lower for younger children, although there was very little difference in ratings for children at different ages (meaning that for younger children compared to older children there was a greater difference between the child's assessment and that of the parent and physician). There was very little agreement in pain assessments between parents and physicians (15% agreement), and between children and physicians (14.6% agreement). Agreement between ratings by parents and their children was higher at 40.1% agreement. The difference in pain assessment by physician and children decreased with pain severity. The mean difference in NRS was 3.2 in children with mild pain, 1.2 in children with moderate pain and –0.6 in children with severe pain (sometimes physician's estimates of pain were higher than the child's assessment for severe pain).

Physicians were asked whether they felt the child's pain reaction was in concordance (as expected) with the medical condition. When the physician felt that the child's response was as expected for their condition, the mean difference between physician's assessment and child's assessment was significantly lower than when concordance was low (NRS = 2.0 compared to NRS = 3.1).

Differences in pain assessment were not associated with mean waiting time for the children, child's gender, physician's gender or experience, or whether the physician had their own children. Physicians gave painkillers to 8.6% of children, and these children had a mean NRS = 4.9 according to physician's assessment. Painkillers were given to 4.1% of children with mild

pain, 9% of children with moderate pain and 42% of children with severe pain, according to physician's assessment. However, when looking at the children's rating of pain only 14.3% of children with severe pain received painkillers.

In conclusion, the research showed that emergency department physicians significantly underestimate pain compared to parents and children. This is the case across all conditions and ages but is less likely to occur with fractures and less likely to occur with children aged eight and over.

ACTIVITY 8.4

Design three scales to measure pain: one suitable for a child aged 3–8 years, one for a child aged 9–16 years, and one for an adult.

Evaluation

Brudvik et al.'s study had a relatively large sample of children, and physicians' data were gathered from children with a wide range of ages and conditions, and from doctors with a range of experience and backgrounds, increasing the validity of the results. The study was carried out in a real-life setting so it has high ecological validity and we can assume the findings would be applicable beyond the research setting. However, the study did use self-report measures, so it is possible that these don't give a true representation of what the participants really think or feel. This may be particularly the case for the doctors who may feel that they should adjust their assessments because they know they are involved in a study.

Application to real life is relevant for the study by Brudvik et al. because it is investigating the differences in pain assessments between children, parents and physicians. This will have real-life implications because the findings can be used to educate doctors about this issue, and this could help doctors give a more accurate assessment of a child's pain. This could then potentially increase the likelihood of a child being given painkillers which would not only reduce their pain at the time but also make the child less likely to be scared or anxious about hospitals and doctors in the future. Another important message to take away from this study and apply to real life is the finding that parents' assessments of the child's pain is a much closer match to the child's own assessment than the doctor's is (although still lower on average than the child's assessment). If doctors are aware of this it could encourage them to rely on the judgements of the parents when making assessments of pain, either when it is not possible to get an assessment directly from the child, or as another measure.

Behavioural/observational measures

Finally, there are behavioural/observational measures of pain, such as the **UAB (University of Alabama) pain behaviour scale**. This is a scale consisting of ten target behaviours, and the person observing the patient (someone who lives with the patient) records detail about each of the target behaviours over a period of time. For each of the target behaviours the observer reports on the severity, frequency or intensity of each behaviour every day. Each behaviour is assigned either 0, ½ or 1 mark and a total score is calculated out of a total of 10, with a high score reflecting a more marked pain associated behaviour and a greater level of impairment.

Some of the target behaviours and response options can be seen in Table 8.4.

The UAB pain behaviour scale is a useful tool as it gathers information about outward signs of pain, which can be observed by someone else. However, there are problems because this relies on the interpretation of the person completing the scale. The observer may not witness the true extent of the behaviours that are being expressed, or they may not interpret the behaviours accurately. A further problem is that scores on the UAB pain behaviour scale do not correlate well with the McGill pain questionnaire, suggesting that outward displays of pain-related behaviours are not closely related to subjective experience of pain. It could be that someone displaying a large amount of pain behaviour is not necessarily in large amounts of pain, they may have been conditioned or reinforced for acting this way. Or it could be that someone is experiencing large amounts of pain but has learned not to express this pain outwardly as a way of coping better, or of protecting those around them.

> ### KEY WORD
>
> UAB (University of Alabama) pain behaviour scale: a scale consisting of ten target behaviours. An observer completes the scale, recording detail about each of the target behaviours over a period of time

Parameter	Finding	Points
Verbal complaints	None	0
	Occasional	0.5
	Frequent	1
Down time (time spent lying down between 8 am and 8 pm)	None	0
	0 to 60 minutes	0.5
	>60 minutes	1
Mobility	No visible impairment	0
	Mild limp and/mildly impaired walking	0.5
	Marked limp and/or laboured walking	1
Facial grimaces	None	0
	Mild and/or infrequent	0.5
	Severe and/or frequent	1

Table 8.4: Some examples of the behaviours and ratings included in the UAB pain behaviour scale

The idiographic versus nomothetic debate is relevant to the different ways of measuring pain we have considered. The clinical interview takes an idiographic approach as it considers the patient as an individual and the aim is to gather lots of detailed qualitative data to really understand the patient's unique experience. The psychometric measures, visual rating measures and behavioural/observational measures, however, all take a nomothetic approach. These measures aim to gather quantitative data in large amounts and are intended to be used for a wide range of people. They do not allow for lots of detailed information to be gathered about each person's unique experience, but instead offer a way of measuring pain that will generally work well for most people. What considerations should there be for research involving children?

Managing and controlling pain

Biological treatments

There are many different biological treatments for pain. One biochemical treatment for pain is a group of drugs called **analgesics**. Analgesics are medicines used to relieve pain and are often referred to as painkillers. Analgesics differ in terms of how they work and their potency (strength). There are two main groups of analgesics that work differently to each other: **nonsteroidal anti-inflammatory drugs (NSAIDs)** and **opioids**.

> ### KEY WORDS
>
> **analgesics:** medicines used to relieve pain, are often referred to as painkillers
>
> **nonsteroidal anti-inflammatory drugs (NSAIDs):** a type of analgesic that reduce pain by reducing the production of the hormone-like substances that cause pain, prostaglandins
>
> **opioids:** a type of analgesic which works by attaching to opioid receptors in the brain. These cells then release signals that reduce perception of pain and increase feelings of pleasure

NSAIDs reduce pain by reducing the production of the hormone-like substances that cause pain, **prostaglandins**. NSAIDs can be bought over the counter or are available

> ### KEY WORD
>
> **prostaglandins:** hormone-like substances that cause pain

in stronger forms by prescription. NSAIDs can have side effects such as indigestion, headaches and drowsiness.

Opioids work by entering your blood stream and attaching to opioid receptors in your brain. These cells then release signals that reduce your perception of pain and increase your feelings of pleasure. Opioids tend to be used for acute pain, and are very effective, but there is a risk of side effects such as drowsiness, slowed heart rate and addiction (due to the positive mood boost they provide).

Psychological treatments

Cognitive strategies can be an effective alternative to biological treatments for pain or can be used alongside biological treatments. Cognitive strategies are more likely to be effective in reducing acute pain, such as pain following surgery.

One cognitive strategy is **attention diversion**. This strategy involves finding ways to shift your attention away from the pain and onto something else instead. Attention diversion doesn't remove the pain but helps stop it from being the main focus of your attention, which can make the pain easier to manage. Attention diversion works because it involves competition for attention between the pain and a consciously directed focus on some form of information processing activity. Activities used in attention diversion can include:

- Puzzles
- Massage
- Stress ball
- Crafting
- Audio books or music
- Counting
- Deep breathing

> ### KEY WORD
>
> **attention diversion:** a cognitive pain management strategy that involves the person finding ways to shift their attention away from the pain and onto something else instead

The distraction techniques will need to be practised as it is not easy to distract attention during peaks of severe pain so the skill will need to be built up over time. There will be some trial and error to find the right technique for each individual as some techniques work better than others depending on the individual and their circumstances (see Figure 8.14). Attention diversion tends to be more effective in managing mild or moderate pain, rather than severe pain.

Figure 8.14: A stress ball may help individuals manage pain

Another cognitive strategy for managing pain is **non-pain imagery**. This strategy involves the person thinking about a calm and relaxing situation or scene and focusing on this rather than the pain (see Figure 8.15). As a result, the individual is likely to be able to slow their breathing, reduce their heart rate and lower their blood pressure. These components all help to feel a sense of calm and relaxation, which in turn helps to manage the pain. Non-pain imagery can be achieved through the use of an auditory recording, to talk the individual through the relaxing scene and how to focus on different aspects of the imagery. Practice is required to achieve a full sense of relaxation and calm, and to engage all of the senses. As with attention diversion, non-pain imagery is more likely to be effective in managing mild or moderate pain, and less effective for severe pain.

> KEY WORD
>
> **non-pain imagery:** a cognitive pain management strategy that involves the person thinking about a calm and relaxing situation or scene and focusing on this rather than the pain

Figure 8.15: Imagining a calm and relaxing scene can be a successful cognitive strategy for managing stress

A third cognitive strategy for managing pain is **cognitive redefinition**. Cognitive redefinition involves the patient replacing threatening or negative thoughts about the pain with more rational or positive thoughts. The pain doesn't go away but this strategy allows the patient to manage the pain better as a result of changing the way they think about the pain. There are two types of self-statement for managing pain:

- Coping statements: these emphasise the person's ability to tolerate the pain. For example, 'it hurts but you are in control'.

- Reinterpretative statements: these help to remove the negative associations with pain. For example, 'it's not the worst thing that could happen'.

Cognitive redefinition is the cognitive strategy that is most likely to be effective in managing severe pain.

Key strengths of all three cognitive strategies are that they do not have any negative side effects, and they can be learned relatively easily and then practised and used without professional help.

> ACTIVITY 8.5
>
> A friend is having surgery and is worried about the pain they may experience afterwards. As well as the pain medication given to them by the hospital, they also want to find a psychological way to manage their pain. What would you recommend to them, and why?

> KEY WORD
>
> **cognitive redefinition:** a cognitive pain management strategy that involves the person replacing threatening or negative thoughts about the pain with more rational or positive thoughts

Alternative treatments

As well as the more traditional methods of pain management, such as biological methods, there is also a range of alternative treatments that can be used to help manage pain.

Acupuncture is an ancient Asian method for treating many conditions and managing pain, which is now used widely across Western cultures. Acupuncture can be used to treat a wide range of pains including headaches, back pain and nerve pain. Acupuncture involves the insertion of very fine needles in the skin at specific points. An acupuncturist typically inserts between four and ten needles and leaves them in place for 10 to 30 minutes, and usually a course of several sessions is recommended. It is believed that acupuncture works by releasing **endorphins**, and by increasing the levels of serotonin in the brain.

There is mixed evidence about the effectiveness of acupuncture in relieving pain and it is difficult to tell whether any positive effects are just a placebo effect or whether the acupuncture is actually having an effect. However, side effects and complications are extremely rare so it could be argued that, whether any positive outcome is placebo or not, there is little harm in considering acupuncture as a pain management strategy.

A second alternative treatment is stimulation therapy/ TENS (transcutaneous electrical nerve stimulation). A TENS machine is a small device that uses electrodes to deliver a mild electrical current to the painful area. The electrical current is experienced as a tingling sensation on the skin (see Figure 8.16). The electrical impulses work by reducing the pain signals that go to the brain and spinal cord, helping to relieve pain and relax muscles. The electrical impulses may also stimulate the production of endorphins. TENS machines can be used to reduce pain associated with a range of conditions including arthritis and sports injuries and are also used as pain relief during childbirth. Much like acupuncture, there is limited evidence showing that TENS is a reliable method of pain relief, but it does seem to work well for some people and some conditions. TENS only offers temporary relief,

while it is in use, but it is very safe to use so could offer a good alternative method of pain management.

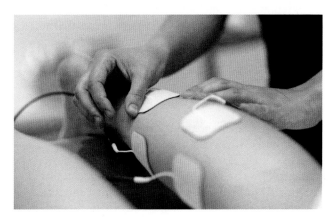

Figure 8.16: Stimulation therapy/TENS uses electrodes to deliver a mild electrical current to help manage pain

ISSUES AND DEBATES

The different treatments we have looked at for managing pain highlight cultural differences. Biological treatments are most commonly used in Western cultures such as the USA. These treatments are certainly effective, and usually work quickly, but they do often have side effects. However, acupuncture is an ancient Asian approach to management of pain and is not subject to the risk of side effects or addiction that are associated with biological treatments. These cultural differences in approaching management of pain used to be significant: traditionally those in Western cultures would not have considered acupuncture as a viable option. However, in more recent years acupuncture has become more and more popular as an alternative treatment in Western cultures, and it is now seen as a respectable and effective method of pain management either instead of, or most likely in addition to, biological treatments.

KEY WORDS

acupuncture: an ancient Asian method of pain management that involves the insertion of very fine needles in the skin at specific points

endorphins: the body's natural pain-killing chemicals

Questions

7 MacLachlan et al. (2004) investigated mirror treatment for PLP by carrying out a case study. Why do you think they chose a case study? How else could they have investigated mirror treatment for PLP?

8 Brudvik et al. (2016) found that doctors tend to significantly underestimate the pain experienced

by children in emergency departments. Give three reasons why this could be a problem.

9 Acupuncture and stimulation therapy/TENS are two alternative therapies for pain. What are the strengths of acupuncture and stimulation therapy/TENS, compared to using painkillers?

8.4 Stress

Most people experience stress to some degree on a regular basis. Stress can be considered in terms of the physiological response of the body to an external stimulus or it can be thought of more as an emotional reaction to something. Selye (1976) defined stress as 'the nonspecific response of the body to any demand'. This is a very broad definition, because stress can be experienced in many different ways, depending on the individual and the circumstances. Stress also has many different sources, ranging from an environmental threat, workplace, life events or personality type.

Sources of stress

Physiology of stress

General adaptation syndrome (GAS) is the three-stage process that describes the biological changes the body goes through when it is under stress. GAS can occur with any type of stress and in modern society we are exposed to a range of long-term stressors related to work, finances or family difficulties. Selye (1936) proposed GAS after observing lab rats undergoing physiological changes when they were exposed to stress. The three stages of stress are identified as alarm, resistance and exhaustion (see Figure 8.17).

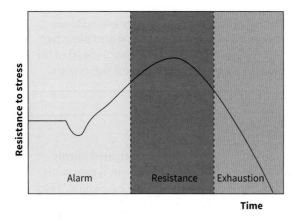

Figure 8.17: The general adaptation syndrome describes the three stages of stress as alarm, resistance and exhaustion

- Alarm reaction stage: the initial symptoms the body experiences when faced with a stressful situation. The **fight or flight response**, where cortisol (a stress hormone) is released, as well as a release of adrenaline to give you increased energy. There are also several changes to your body such as increased heart rate and faster breathing, to enable more oxygen to be pumped around your body. These changes are your body's natural response to a stressor to prepare you to either flee (flight) or defend yourself (fight).

- Resistance stage: after the initial shock of a stressor has passed, your body starts to return to normal and to repair itself, although it remains on high alert for a while. If the stressor has passed, your body continues to repair and recover, your heart rate and blood pressure return to normal and there is no lasting damage. However, if the stressful event is ongoing, your body remains on high alert and adapts to live with this higher stress level. The stress hormone cortisol will continue to be secreted and your blood pressure will remain at a higher level. You will often be unaware of the physiological changes going on in your body during this stage, but there may be outward signs such as irritability, frustration and poor concentration. If the resistance stage continues for too long this can lead to the exhaustion stage.

- Exhaustion stage: if you are exposed to prolonged or chronic stress this can drain you of emotional, mental and physical resources and your body will no longer be able to fight the stress effectively. Signs of exhaustion include fatigue, depression, anxiety and a decreased tolerance for stress. There are also serious physical effects of the exhaustion stage of stress, as described in the next section (see Figure 8.18).

KEY WORDS

general adaptation syndrome (GAS): a three-stage process that describes the biological changes the body goes through when it is under stress. The three stages are alarm, resistance and exhaustion

fight or flight response: the body's natural initial response to a stressor, which leads to physiological changes in the body, so you are prepared to either flee or to defend yourself

There are many effects of stress on health, including relatively minor problems such as:

- Headaches
- Insomnia
- Changes in appetite
- Nausea
- Heartburn
- Muscle aches and pains

However, chronic stress can also lead to very serious health problems such as:

- Type 2 diabetes
- Alcohol or substance abuse
- High blood pressure leading to an increased risk of stroke or heart attack
- A weakened immune system: if the immune system cannot work as well as it should you are more susceptible to viruses such as colds and flu as well as other infections. A weakened immune system

also means you are likely to take longer to recover from an illness or injury.

Causes of stress

Holmes and Rahe (1967) proposed that **life events** are a main cause of stress. Life events are any major changes in your life and can be either positive (such as marriage or having a baby) or negative (such as serious illness or death of a loved one). The key aspect of a life event is that it requires some aspect of transition in your life. Holmes and Rahe suggest that any change requires mental energy and leads to stress.

In order to measure the effect of life events on health Holmes and Rahe constructed the **Social Readjustment Rating Scale (SRRS)**. See the section on Measures of stress for details on this measure.

Rahe (1970) gave the SRRS to 2500 male American sailors to assess how many life events they had experienced in the previous six months. During the following six months, while the sailors were on a tour of duty, their health status was recorded. Results showed that there was a significant (but small) positive correlation between life

HOW STRESS AFFECTS THE BODY

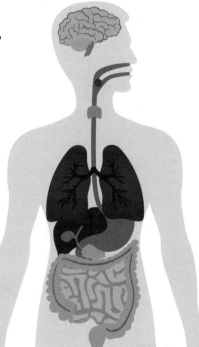

Brain
Difficulty concentrating, anxiety, depression, irritability, mood, mind fog

Cardiovascular
Higher cholesterol, high blood pressure, increased risk of heart attack and stroke

Joints and muscles
increased inflammation, tension, aches and pains, muscle tightness

Skin
hair loss, dull/brittle hair, brittle nails, dry skin, acne, delayed tissue repair

Immune system
decreased immune function, lowered immune defences, increased risk of becoming ill, increase in recovery time

Gut
nutrient absorption, diarrhoea, constipation, indigestion, bloating, pain and discomfort

Figure 8.18: Chronic stress can have serious negative effects to many aspects of health

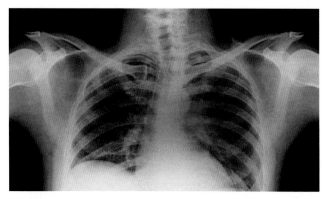

Figure 8.19: Coronary heart disease can be fatal

change score and illness score, meaning that as life change score increased, so did the frequency of illness.

Work is another cause of stress. There are many aspects of the work that can be responsible for causing stress, such as the physical environment, interpersonal relationships and the pressure of meeting targets. Coronary heart disease (CHD) is one of many stress-related illnesses and is the main subject of research by Chandola et al. (2008).

Example study

Chandola et al. (2008) investigated the link between workplace stress and CHD (see Figure 8.19). This was a longitudinal study that followed just over 10,000 male and female civil servants in London, UK, from 1985 to 2004. There were seven phases over this time period, which involved postal questionnaires as well as alternate phases including a clinical examination as well. Work stress was assessed using the job-strain questionnaire. When participants report job demands as high and job control as low this is recorded as job strain. Similarly, iso-strain is recorded when job strain is reported alongside social isolation at work (without supportive co-workers or supervisors). A total work stress score was assigned to each participant based on the total number of reported incidents of work strain or iso-strain in phases 1 and 2.

For those aged 37–49 at phase 2 there was a significant association between greater reports of work stress and higher risk of CHD events. There was little association between work stress and CHD incidents for those aged 50 and over. For the younger age group, greater work stress was associated with poorer health behaviours (which increase the risk of CHD events) including eating less fruit and vegetables, drinking more alcohol and being less physically active. Adjusting for the effect of these health behaviours only slightly reduced the association between work stress and CHD events. This means that approximately 32% of the effect of work stress on CHD can be explained by the effect of work stress on unhealthy behaviours. In conclusion, the study shows that work stress is a significant indicator of CHD events in those under the age of 50, partly due to the increase in unhealthy behaviours, but partly due to physiological changes (such as increased cortisol and higher blood pressure) as a direct result of work stress.

A third cause of stress is personality type. Friedman and Roseman (1978) identified two personality types: type A and type B. **Type A personality** describes somebody who has three key traits (see Figure 8.20):

- Competitiveness: people with type A tend to be very competitive and strive towards goals, without feeling a sense of joy in the challenge or in their achievements. Type A personalities are self-critical and have a significant life imbalance, meaning their work life significantly outweighs their home life.

- Time urgency: type A personalities have a constant sense of time urgency and become impatient with delays or 'wasted' time very quickly. People with a type A personality keep very tight schedules and often try to do more than one thing at a time.

- Hostility: type A individuals are prone to anger and hostility and tend to see the worst in others, display envy and have a lack compassion for others. The anger and hostility may be expressed outwardly in terms of aggression or bullying of others, or it may be kept inside. Hostility is the greatest predictor of type A personality and is the greatest predictor of heart disease.

Figure 8.20: Time urgency is one of three key traits of someone with type A personality

In comparison, a type B personality is more relaxed, patient and easy-going. Those with type B personality do not become over focused on work but work towards goals steadily and enjoy achievements. Type B personalities are more tolerant of others, experience lower anxiety and are more creative than type A personalities. See the section on Measures of stress for detail on the personality test used by Friedman and Rosenman to measure personality types.

Friedman and Rosenman conducted a longitudinal study to test their hypothesis that type A personality could predict heart disease. They gave questionnaires to 3,000 men aged between 39 and 59 and, based on their responses, classified the men as either type A or type B (approximately half were type A and half were type B). The men were then followed for eight and a half years, and the findings showed that more than twice as many type A men as type B men developed CHD. In total, after eight years, 257 of the participants had developed CHD and 70% of those were type A. When results were adjusted to account for smoking and other lifestyle factors the results still showed that those with type A were almost twice as likely to develop CHD than those with type B.

RESEARCH METHODS

All three studies used to investigate causes of stress (Rahe, Chandola et al. and Friedman & Rosenman) have used large samples, with Chandola et al. having over 10,000 participants. This is a really important strength of all the research as it allows for large amounts of data to be collected and analysed. The samples of each, however, are limited to an extent in that they are all the same sort of people and from the same area. All the studies are also longitudinal, with Chandola et al. observing participants for 19 years and Freidman and Rosenman observing their participants for over eight years. This is really important as it increases the validity of the research; we can see the long-term effects of work stress or personality type, which is much more accurate and useful than a short-term snapshot study that would not gather complete data. What are downsides of longitudinal research using large samples?

ISSUES AND DEBATES

The freewill versus determinism debate is particularly relevant when considering the causes of stress. When considering that stress is caused by life events (Holmes & Rahe), work stress (Chandola et al.), or personality type (Friedman & Rosenman) these are all very deterministic theories. Each explanation is saying that you are stressed, and therefore at increased risk of stress-related illness, because of circumstances that have happened to you or because of your personality. This is useful to an extent as it suggests that human behaviour is predictable so we can get a better understanding of the risk factors for people and use this to help people. However, all three causes of stress ignore free will, which is the view that everyone has the ability to make decisions for themselves and they are, to some extent, responsible for their own lives because of the decisions that they make. It may be that someone has experienced many life events, has a stressful time at work or has certain personality traits, but they may use their free will to overcome these risk factors and choose to make healthy decisions. These healthy choices could relate to lifestyle, such as exercising and eating healthily, or they could be related to the causes of stress, for example changing career or number of hours spent working.

Measures of stress

There are both biological and psychological measures of stress, both of which have strengths and weaknesses. We will consider two biological measures and two psychological measures.

Biological

Biological measures of stress include recording devices and sample tests.

Recording devices for heart rate and brain function

One recording device that can be used to measure stress is fMRI (functional magnetic resonance imaging) (see Figure 8.21). FMRI is a scanning technique used to measure activity in the brain by tracking the changes in flow of oxygenated blood. When a part of the brain is active it requires more oxygen so there will be increased cerebral blood flow (CBF) to that area. The fMRI therefore allows us to see how different parts of the brain respond to different stimuli or activity, which gives a scientific and objective illustration of what is happening in the brain. To measure the brain's response to stress participants will usually be asked to complete certain stress-inducing tasks while in the scanner, and then images will be compared to rest periods to identify areas of the brain active during different sorts of stressors. Brain areas shown by fMRIs to be most active in response to stress include the amygdala, hippocampus and the hypothalamus.

> ### ACTIVITY 8.6
>
> A neighbour is going to have an fMRI scan and they say they only know that it 'shows what the brain is doing'. How could you explain it to her in more detail, in a way that would help her understand?

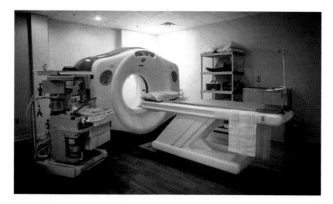

Figure 8.21: An fMRI scanner can be used to measure stress

> ### KEY WORDS
>
> **cerebral blood flow (CBF):** the increase in blood flow to parts of the brain that are active is measured by an MRI scanner
>
> **pulse oximeter:** a small clip that is placed on the finger and can be used to measure oxygen saturation and heart rate

Another recording device used to measure stress is a **pulse oximeter** (see Figure 8.22), which can be used to measure heart rate. It is a small clip that is placed on the finger, and passes small beams of light through the finger to measure the amount of oxygen in the blood. The process is non-invasive and painless. The pulse oximeter then tells you your oxygen saturation and your heart rate. Although stress can lead to an increase in heart rate, it is important to remember that high heart rate could be a result of many different reasons. Furthermore, for some people, stress does not necessarily increase heart rate so there is no direct link between increased heart rate and stress.

Figure 8.22: A pulse oximeter is a device used to measure heart rate

Example study

Wang et al. (2005) aimed to use fMRI to measure cerebral blood flow (CBF) changes in response to mild to moderate stress as a result of a maths task. Thirty American participants took part in the study, with 23 (average age 24 years, 11 female) participating in the stress experiment and seven (average age 23 years, four female) in the control experiment. Participants were given four MRI scans (8 minutes each); the first and last were baselines, the second was during a low-stress task and the third was during a high-stress task. The low-stress task involved the participant counting aloud backwards from 1,000, this was designed to control for activation of auditory and verbal centres. The high-stress task required the participant to subtract 13 from a four-digit number, answering aloud and receiving prompts to speed up, as well as having to start again if an error is made. Self-report stress and anxiety (on a scale of 1–9), and saliva samples to test for cortisol were collected straight after entering the scanner and after each scan. Participants also reported their level of effort, frustration and task difficulty (on a scale of 1–9) following the low- and high-stress tasks. Heart rate was recorded throughout the study, using a pulse oximeter. The control group were not required to complete any tasks but self-report, heart rate and saliva tests were collected in the same way as the control group to check for any stress caused by the MRI scanning. All participants took part between 3 and 5 pm to control for any fluctuations in cortisol levels throughout the day.

Results showed that the stress tasks had the expected response: self-reported stress and anxiety, heart rate and cortisol levels all increased with the high-stress task then reduced again during the second baseline period (cortisol level lagged by approximately 10 minutes as expected). The ventral **right prefrontal cortex (RPFC)** is a part of the brain previously shown to be associated with negative emotions such as sadness and fear, as well as increased vigilance to threat-related cues. As expected, a positive correlation was found between the change in CBF in the RPFC and subjective ratings of stress (see Figure 8.23). This means that the more stressful the participant found the task, the more activity there would be in the RPFC part of their brain, showing us that brain activity correlates with self assessment of stress. Similarly, CBF in the RPFC was greater in those who had higher salivary cortisol levels and those with higher reported anxiety levels. This shows that RPFC CBF changes in relation to both subjective and objective measures of stress. The activity in the RPFC remained higher even after the stressful activity ended,

suggesting that psychological stress leads to a prolonged state of heightened vigilance and emotional arousal. Difficulty and effort were not associated with RPFC changes, so the research concludes that it is not just increased cognitive demand, but stress specifically that is responsible for the changes in the RPFC.

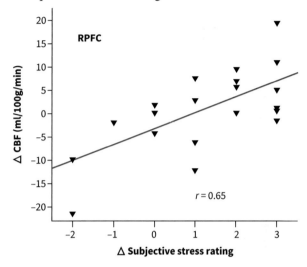

Figure 8.23: Wang et al. (2005) found a correlation between change in CBF in the RPFC and subjective ratings of stress

Sample tests for salivary cortisol

Sample tests for salivary cortisol can also be used as a measure of stress. Cortisol is a stress hormone, so stress can be assessed by measuring the level of cortisol in your saliva.

Example study

Evans and Wener (2007) used salivary cortisol tests as one of several measures of stress in commuters who were faced with crowding on the train. The research aimed to investigate the effect that overall crowding of the train, and crowding in the immediate space surrounding the participant, had on stress levels. The sample consisted of 139 adult commuters who travelled from New Jersey into Manhattan, New York City, for work every day.

A saliva sample was collected from each participant at the end of their morning trip to work, and at the same time at home on the following weekend. The difference in salivary cortisol levels in different situations has been found to be a reliable and valid marker of stress. Motivation was measured near the end of the commute by persistence in a proofreading task (measured by the number of errors detected). Mood was assessed during the commute by the completion of two five-point scales (carefree–burdened and contented–frustrated). Crowding was assessed at the

---

KEY WORD

right prefrontal cortex (RPFC): a part of the brain previously shown to be associated with negative emotions such as sadness and fear, as well as increased vigilance to threat-related cues

distal level (the density of crowding across the whole train carriage) and at the proximal level (the number of people who were sitting on the same row as the participant).

Results showed that distal crowding (crowding in the whole carriage) did not have a significant effect on any of the measures of stress. However, proximal crowding (in the immediate area) had a significant effect on stress, according to all three measures: cortisol level, proofreading and mood. The researchers therefore conclude that it is only really crowding in the area immediately around your seat that has a significant effect on stress, not the number of people in the carriage as a whole.

Psychological

Two self-report questionnaires relating to the causes of stress were covered previously: Friedman and Rosenman's personality test and Holmes and Rahe's life events questionnaire.

Friedman and Rosenman constructed a personality test to measure type A and type B personality (see the section on Sources of stress for more detail on the personality types). A series of questions were devised in order to classify a respondent as being either type A or type B personality. Answers that show a tendency toward competitiveness, time urgency and hostility would lead to a classification of type A personality. Some of the questions from Frideman and Rosenman's personality test included:

- Do you feel guilty if you use spare time to relax?

- Do you need to win to derive enjoyment from games and sports?

- Do you generally move, walk and eat rapidly?

- Do you often try to do more than one thing at a time?

Holmes and Rahe constructed the Social Readjustment Rating Scale (SRRS) to measure life events (see the section on Sources of stress for more detail on Holmes and Rahe's life events). Holmes and Rahe examined over 5,000 medical records to determine whether stressful life events caused illness. As a result of their examination, Holmes and Rahe compiled a list of 43 life events that had occurred prior to the patients' illnesses. The SRRS is compiled of these 43 life events, which are ranked according to the amount of change they cause, and each life event is given a score in terms of life change units (LCUs). See Table 8.5 for some examples of life events and their LCUs. For example, death of a spouse (husband or wife) is 100 LCUs whereas a holiday is 13 LCUs. The respondent must identify any of the events they have experienced during a period of time (usually

in the last year). The respondent then gets a total score of LCUs, and this total is intended to predict how likely the person is to suffer a stress-related health breakdown.

Rank	Life event	Life change units (LCUs)
1	Death of a spouse	100
2	Divorce	73
7	Marriage	50
10	Retirement	45
12	Pregnancy	40
23	Son or daughter leaving home	29
43	Minor violations of the law	11

Table 8.5: Examples of some of the life events, with their rank and LCUs, from Holmes and Rahe's Social Readjustment Rating Scale

RESEARCH METHODS

The use of biological measures, particularly the fMRI, is scientific and objective and not subject to interpretation. This means the results are valid and reliable and are easy to replicate. Quantitative data are easy to collate and use carry out statistical analysis to allow us to get a good understanding of the effect of stress on the body. The fMRI, pulse oximeter and sample tests are also all non-invasive; nothing is placed into the body, and they are all harmless, which is important because it means they can all ethically be used to measure the effects of stress in a medical setting as well as for research into stress.

The use of self-report by Friedman and Rosenman and Holmes and Rahe has both strengths and weaknesses. A key strength is that this is the best way to gather information about people's experiences and thoughts and feelings. However, a weakness could be that the information reported is subjective and it is down to the participant how they interpret the questions and what answers they give. This could reduce validity as people may not give honest accounts because of social desirability or because of how they see a situation (e.g., in Friedman and Rosenman's research people may not wish to admit to being hostile or may not realise that they are).

Managing stress

There are many different methods of managing stress, including biological therapies such as anti-anxiety drugs and psychological therapies such as **biofeedback** and imagery. We will focus on psychological therapies.

KEY WORD

biofeedback: a technique that uses electrical sensors to allow you to receive information about different functions of your body, by changes on a monitor or a beeping sound. Receiving this feedback allows you to make changes, such as relaxing muscles or slowing down your breathing

Psychological therapies

Biofeedback is one psychological therapy that can be used to manage stress. Biofeedback is a technique that allows you to learn how to control some of your body's functions, such as your heart rate or muscle tension. Electrical sensors are used to allow you to receive information about different functions of your body, by changes on a monitor or a beeping sound (see Figure 8.24). Receiving this feedback allows you to make changes, such as relaxing muscles or slowing down your breathing. Biofeedback requires training from an expert initially, with the intention of learning how to do it yourself at home. These changes can have health benefits in terms of reducing pain, high blood pressure and anxiety or stress.

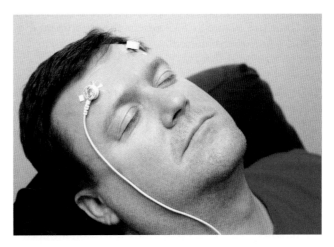

Figure 8.24: Biofeedback is one way of managing stress

Example study

Budzynski et al. (1969) carried out a study using an analogue monitor to measure muscle tension on the forehead. The forehead is a difficult muscle to relax deeply so the suggestion was that if biofeedback could work effectively for this it would be successful in other muscle relaxation too. The study involved 15 participants who were asked to lie quietly with their eyes closed and to concentrate on deeply relaxing their forehead muscle. This took place over 20 one-minute trials, with trials between one and three days apart, and at the same time each day. The participants were randomly assigned to one of three experimental conditions, and were all told to relax deeply, especially the forehead muscle:

- Feedback group: the monitor would sound a different pitched tone to indicate muscle relaxation (low tone represented muscle relaxation) so the participant knew they were doing the right thing and would be able to repeat that behaviour to master the muscle relaxation.

- Irrelevant feedback group: the monitor would give a constant low tone (irrelevant feedback) and the participants were told the constant low tone would help them to relax.

- No feedback group: no tone (no feedback) was given, and the participants were told to relax in silence.

Results showed that there were clear differences between the three groups in terms of reduction of muscle tension over time (see Figure 8.25). Those in the experimental group who received biofeedback showed less muscle tension than the other two groups, starting from the first feedback session, and this pattern continued throughout the trials. The percentage decline in muscle tension for each group was particularly striking. The feedback group showed a mean decrease of 50%, the no feedback group showed a mean decrease of 24% and the irrelevant feedback group showed a mean *increase* of 28%. Further evidence for the effectiveness of biofeedback came from studying the participant from the irrelevant feedback group that had the least reduction in muscle tension. However, when he was given biofeedback sessions, his muscle tension dropped significantly, and after just three feedback sessions, his muscle tension was 60% less than it had been originally. This study shows that, compared to the two other conditions, feedback does significantly reduce the amount of muscle tension in the forehead, both initially and throughout the programme.

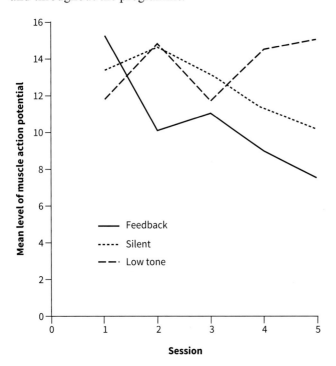

Figure 8.25: Budzynski et al. (1969) found clear differences between the three groups in terms of reduction in muscle tension over time

Another psychological therapy for managing stress is use of imagery. This has been studied by Bridge et al. (1988).

Key study: Bridge et al. (1988)

Bridge, L. R., Benson, P., Pietroni, P. C., & Priest, R. G. (1988). Relaxation and imagery in the treatment of breast cancer. *British medical journal*, *297*, 1169–1172.

Context

Receiving a diagnosis of cancer, along with the required treatments and uncertainty about the future causes stress. People receiving a cancer diagnosis will likely experience stress due to the fear and anxiety around the symptoms they will experience, the difficult treatments they will need to endure, as well as the fear that they may lose 'their health, their role and their life'. (Maguire 1981).

The treatment of the cancer itself is a big enough challenge for the patient and their family, so if the associated stress that is likely to be experienced can be alleviated this will be hugely beneficial. If stress can be relieved it can give the patient a more positive outlook and more emotional resources available to them to deal with the cancer and associated difficulties. Research in the area has shown that relaxation imagery can be successful in managing stress in those with a range of illnesses, such as hypertension, as well as patients with cancer (Simonton and Simonton 1975).

Main theories and explanations

Relaxation techniques reduce stress by allowing the person to focus on muscle relaxation and deep breathing. This slows breathing rate and leads to a calmer state and reduces tension which, in turn, reduces stress (McLean 1986). Relaxation techniques require the individual to focus their senses on particular groups of muscles. The individual may be asked to tighten those muscles and hold for a few sessions, while paying attention to the tension. They would then relax the muscles slowly, and pay attention to the feeling of relaxation that occurs as a result. Deep and slow breathing is also important in relaxation because if you breathe too quickly it can make you feel dizzy and anxious. The individual would be encouraged to take a slow breath in, followed by a slow breath out.

Use of imagery is another technique to reduce stress as it involves imagining a peaceful scene, which leads to a sense of calm and relaxation (Lyles et al. 1982). The individual would be encouraged to create in their mind a place they can relax, whether that is real or imaginary, but where you feel safe, calm and happy. It is important to imagine the calm place in as much detail as possible, including all your senses, then to close your eyes and imagine being there. This, combined with the muscle relaxation and breathing techniques, should encourage feelings of calm and reduce stress levels.

Aims

The researchers aimed to find out the effect of relaxation and imagery on the stress experienced by cancer patients. They hypothesised that relaxation and imagery would both lead to a reduction in stress compared to patients who did not undergo either treatment. They also hypothesised that the women who underwent relaxation and imagery would have more of a positive effect than those who only had relaxation.

Design

The sample consisted of 139 women who were outpatients undergoing a six-week course of radiotherapy, following a diagnosis of early breast cancer. The women were all under the age of 70 and all attended a hospital in London, UK. The women were informed that they would be randomly assigned to one of three conditions, and they would be asked to fill in questionnaires assessing their mood at the start of the programme (after undergoing one radiotherapy session) and after the six-week programme.

The three conditions were: control group (no treatment given), relaxation, and relaxation plus imagery. Those in the two treatment groups were taught a relaxation technique involving directing sensory awareness on certain muscle groups, as well instructions for deep breathing. Those in the relaxation plus imagery group were also taught to imagine a peaceful scene as a way of enhancing relaxation. The women were given a tape to be listened to for 15 minutes every day, which repeated the instructions they had been given. Women in all three groups were seen by a researcher for half an hour once a week for the six weeks, during which those in the treatment groups practised their exercises and those in the control group were encouraged to talk about themselves and their interests.

Two questionnaires were used: the **profile of mood states questionnaire** and the **Leeds general scale** for the self-assessment of depression and anxiety. The profile of mood states questionnaire used 65 items to give scores across several aspects such as tension, fatigue, anger and confusion, resulting in a total mood disturbance score. The Leeds general scale measures the severity of anxiety and depressive symptoms for those who are not formally diagnosed with a mental health condition. The scale contains six items each for anxiety and depression, each rated on a four-point scale.

KEY WORDS

profile of mood states questionnaire: a self-report questionnaire that uses 65 items to give scores across several aspects such as tension, fatigue, anger and confusion, resulting in a total mood disturbance score

Leeds general scale: a self-report questionnaire that measures the severity of anxiety and depressive symptoms for those who are not formally diagnosed. The scale contains six items each for anxiety and depression, each rated on a four-point scale

Results, findings and conclusions

Results showed that the change in total mood disturbance score differed significantly between the three groups (but this was not the case for the Leeds general scale). Changes in mood state were as expected for patients in the relaxation group and relaxation and imagery group. Mood state for women in the relaxation group and in the relaxation and imagery group improved after the six weeks, with the greatest improvement shown for the relaxation and imagery group. In comparison, however, the mood state of women in the control group actually worsened after the six weeks. Further analysis showed that both relaxation and imagery were more effective in reducing total mood disturbance in women aged 55, compared to younger patients. This seemed to be due to the effect of relaxation and imagery particularly on reducing the older women's depression and tension scores. Women who scored particularly high in anger in the initial assessments did not respond as well to relaxation or relaxation and imagery compared to those with lower anger levels. This could be because, due to high levels of anger, these women were unable to gain any benefits from the relaxation techniques. In conclusion, the results show that relaxation, and particularly relaxation and imagery, do have a positive effect on mood state.

Evaluation

The study by Bridge et al. had a reasonable sized sample of patients, however all patients were women, and all were attending the same hospital for the same cancer. On the one hand, the fact that the sample had all been diagnosed with the same cancer at the same stage was a strength because it meant that illness or stage would not be a *confounding variable* affecting the results. However, this also means that the sample is not representative of the general population so the results cannot be generalised to people with other conditions, or to men. The participants were *randomly allocated* to one of the three conditions, which increases validity and reduces the effect of participant bias. It is also a strength that the study used a control group of women who did not undergo any relaxation treatment, as this enabled a comparison to be made, again increasing the validity. The use of self-report questionnaires was a strength because it meant these methods were fairly quick and easy for the patients to complete, rather than a lengthy interview or other measure that might be too much of a commitment for women already undergoing radiotherapy for cancer. Further strengths of the use of the questionnaires are that they used closed questions with Likert-type scales so quantitative data were gathered, allowing for statistical analysis to be carried out and comparisons to be made between groups and pre- and post-treatment. A weakness of these measures is that they did not gather qualitative data, so there was not an opportunity to collect detailed feelings and experiences from the women.

Application to everyday life is particularly relevant to the study by Bridge et al. because investigating the effects of relaxation techniques on stress can benefit other patients experiencing similar circumstances. The results showed that, overall, relaxation techniques had a positive effect on the women's mood after six weeks of treatment. This information can be used to help advise other women suffering from cancer that relaxation techniques might help them too. Reducing the stress experienced by women undergoing treatment for cancer is beneficial not just because the patients will feel better, but it would also mean that they have more emotional and mental energy available to cope with treatments

and other changes they will need to manage. Although this research specifically focused on women with breast cancer, there is no reason that the same wouldn't be found for women with other conditions or men with a range of conditions. How could the idiographic versus nomothetic approach be applied to research such as Bridge et al.?

Preventing stress

One way of preventing stress is through **stress inoculation training (SIT)**, which is a type of cognitive-behavioural therapy, designed by Meichenbaum, specifically to help people cope with stress. The idea behind SIT is that, by exposing people to increasing levels of perceived stress, they can practise coping skills and develop an increased tolerance for stress. SIT will be different for everyone but will tend to include several weekly sessions for anywhere between 8 and 40 sessions.

> **KEY WORD**
>
> **stress inoculation training (SIT):** a type of cognitive-behavioural therapy designed to expose people to increasing levels of stress to develop coping skills. There are three phases: conceptualisation, skills acquisition and rehearsal, and application and follow-through

There are three phases of SIT:

- Conceptualisation: in this stage, the client and therapist work together to get an understanding of the client's sources of stress. The client talks through their experiences and current method of dealing with stress. The therapist then shows the client how to reframe a stressor as a problem that can be solved. It is important at this stage that the client understands that there are some parts of a stressor that can be changed and some parts that cannot.

- Skills acquisition and rehearsal: clients learn new coping skills, which are designed to suit their unique set of circumstances. Initially the coping skills are practised in the therapy setting before being gradually applied in the real world. A range of cognitive and behavioural coping skills are taught, including problem-solving skills, relaxation techniques, mindfulness training and diversion techniques.

- Application and follow-through: this is the time for clients to apply what they have learned in the real world, with increasingly more stressful situations. To build up to this, techniques may be used, such as visualising a stressful situation or role-playing.

SIT can be a very effective way of dealing with stress because it is tailored to meet the specific needs of the individual, and several coping strategies are taught. This puts the individual in a position where they are able to deal with a range of different stressors in a way that best suits them, and these skills can be used for a lifetime. A downside is that it requires a significant time commitment as it does take a while for the coping skills to be learned and practised. Furthermore, SIT does not work for everyone, as it relies on the individual being willing or able to change the way they think about and deal with things.

RESEARCH METHODS

Budzynski et al. had a small sample of only 15 participants so this only allowed for small amounts of data to be collected and analysed. However, the use of three conditions increased the validity of the study as it allowed for comparisons to be made between those receiving feedback and those not receiving feedback. Participants were randomly assigned to one of the three conditions, so this removes researcher bias and participant variables. The measure of muscle tension is a biological measure, meaning it is scientific and objective, which increases the validity and reliability of the results. The research is also easy to replicate, allowing it to be checked for reliability. Why is it important to check for reliability?

ISSUES AND DEBATES

The three methods of managing stress that have been covered in this section (biofeedback, relaxation and imagery, and SIT) are all psychological therapies. This means that they all fall on the nurture side of the nature versus nurture debate. The therapies all consider psychological

CONTINUED

or behavioural changes as a way of managing stress. This approach has strengths in that they are non-invasive and do not have side effects. However, they ignore the nature side of the debate, which suggests that stress can be managed from a biological approach, for example with the use of anti-anxiety tablets. Anti-anxiety medication is one of the most widely used treatments of stress worldwide and works much more quickly and easily than any of the psychological therapies we have considered. There are strengths and weaknesses to both psychological and biological methods of managing stress, but perhaps an interactionist approach might be the best way forward: a combination of drug treatment and psychological therapies.

Research into managing stress is a good place to consider *ethical issues*. To investigate the effectiveness of different methods of stress management it is important to use experiments where participants in one condition undergo the stress management and participants in another condition do not, so that we are able to compare the participants' stress levels afterwards. However, the ethics of experiments such as this should be considered. For example, some patients with cancer in the study by Bridge et al. were not given the relaxation or imagery stress management and their mood state declined, whereas those who used the stress management techniques had an improved mood state. A cost–benefit analysis is important to consider here: do the costs to the participants who did not receive the stress management techniques weigh up against the benefits gained from the findings of the research? As a result of this research it can be concluded that relaxation and imagery can be effective and beneficial methods of stress management for cancer patients, and likely for a range of patients with other conditions too.

Questions

10 Holmes and Rahe propose life events as a main cause of stress. Why are some of some of the life events positive and some negative?

11 Wang et al. (2005) used several methods of measuring stress in their study. Why was this important?

12 Budzynski et al. (1969) measured the effectiveness of biofeedback on muscle tension. Describe the three groups they used and why they had three groups.

8.5 Health promotion

Strategies for promoting health

Understanding what behaviours and decisions are important for our good health is important. However, what is also really important is making people aware of this and encouraging them to carry out these healthy behaviours and decisions. Strategies for promoting health can come in many forms, and we will cover two: fear arousal (scaring people into improving their health) and providing information (giving information so that people know how to improve their health).

Fear arousal

Example study

Janis and Feshbach (1953) aimed to investigate the effects of using fear appeals in communications that are presented in an impersonal group situation. Furthermore, the research aimed to explore the possible adverse effects that might arise from defensive reactions. The study used three different levels of fear appeal in communication to 200 high school students about dental hygiene. Questionnaires were used to gather students' emotional responses to the communication as well as to find out about changes in dental hygiene beliefs, attitudes and practices. Each group was presented with a recorded lecture and accompanying slides, all were approximately the same length, provided by the same speaker in a similar manner, and contained the same information about causes of tooth decay and the same recommendations for oral hygiene. The three groups only differed in the amount of fear-arousing material presented:

- Form 1 contained a strong fear appeal, focusing on the painful consequences of tooth decay, diseased gums and other dangers resulting from poor dental hygiene. Personalised threat references were used, where the audience was directly referred to, for example, statements that suggest 'this could happen to you'. The slides used included 11 very graphic and realistic photos showing tooth decay and mouth infections.

- Form 2 contained moderate fear appeal, where the dangers were still described, but in a milder and more factual manner, using impersonal language. The slides used included nine photos, with milder examples than were shown in form 1.

- Form 3 presented a minimal appeal where there was hardly any mention of the negative consequences of poor dental hygiene (focus on tooth decay in the other two presentations was replaced with information about tooth growth and function). There were no realistic photos, only use of X-rays and diagrams.

In addition to these three groups described, there was also a control group, who were given a similar lecture on a completely different subject. The four groups were approximately equal in terms of age, sex, education level and IQ.

Questionnaires were given out to all students one week before the lectures, as part of a broader questionnaire about several aspects of health (with questions of interest relating to dental hygiene being dispersed amongst other questions). Immediately following the lectures, students were given a questionnaire to measure the immediate effects of the communication, then a follow-up questionnaire was given one week later, to measure the carry-on effects of the communication.

Results showed that emotional reactions immediately after the lectures varied significantly between those in the strong fear form and those in the minimal fear form. For example, when asked whether the person 'felt worried a few times or many times about their own mouth condition' during the lecture, the percentages who answered 'yes' were 74% for strong group, 60% for moderate group, and 48% for minimal group. Based on their responses to the questionnaire following the talk, students were given an overall score for level of concern. Results showed that those in the strong group were significantly more concerned than those in the other two groups, and that those in the moderate group were more concerned than those in the minimal group (mean scores out of 10 were 7.8 for strong, 6.6 for moderate and 5.9 for minimal).

The research also investigated change in behaviour as a result of the talks. One week before the talks, all students answered five questions about how they cleaned their teeth, and were given the same questions two weeks later, after being informed on the correct procedure for teeth cleaning in the talks. Contrary to the idea of fear arousal encouraging healthy behaviours, the results showed that those in the minimal group showed significantly more improvement in teeth cleaning, and that those in the strong group showed the least improvement. Furthermore, those in the minimal group were more likely to visit the dentist in the week following the talk than those in the moderate or strong group (18% of the minimal group, 14% of the moderate group, and 10% of the strong group). It is important to state that this only shows us that students in the minimal group were more likely to *say* that they followed the toothbrushing advice and went to the dentist, we cannot prove that they actually did carry out these behaviours.

Finally, results showed that those in the minimal group were more resistance to contradictory propaganda following their talk. The talk spoke about the importance of the right toothbrush, then in the questionnaire one week later there was a paragraph explaining how a group of dentists claimed it didn't matter what sort of toothbrush you used. Students were then asked how important they felt it was to use the right sort of toothbrush. Results showed students in all three experimental groups showed some resistance to propaganda and were more likely to say that it did matter what toothbrush you used (compared to the control group), but that those in the minimal group were significantly more likely to resist propaganda than the other two groups.

Overall, the study showed that the minimal appeal was the most effective communication because it led to more resistance to contradictory propaganda and led to a higher incidence of adherence to advice (at least as measured by self-reports). There were not any positive effects of the strong or moderate groups that would make them worth using instead of the minimal group. A strong fear arousal does not increase the likelihood of the audience taking information and guidance on board, and in fact seems to have the opposite effect.

Providing information
Example study

Lewin et al. (1992) aimed to investigate the effect of giving information to help people improve their own health. The study involved 190 participants who had been admitted to hospital after experiencing a confirmed myocardial infarction (MI; a heart attack, a serious medical emergency where the blood supply to the heart

is suddenly blocked). Three days after the MI, patients were assigned to either the control or the experimental group. This was carried out in a stratified way to ensure each group had an equal proportion of age, social class and initial level of psychological distress. The person who held the list was blind to the purpose of the study and the medical staff treating the patients were blind to the group the participants were in.

On discharge from hospital, those in the experimental group were given a copy of *the manual*, which consisted of six weekly sections including education, home-based exercise programme and a recorded relaxation and stress management programme. The manual also contained specific self-help treatments for intrusive and distressing thoughts, anxiety, depression and other psychological problems common with patients following an MI. The patient, and their partner where possible, was introduced to the manual by the facilitator, who explained the components and how to use them. Patients in the control group were also given time with the facilitator, and were given a range of leaflets from different sources that gave them information about recovery from an MI. After one, three and six weeks, all patients were contacted by the facilitator, usually by a brief phone call or during a clinic visit. Those in the experimental group had a check on their progress with the programme and were encouraged to stick to the exercises. Those in the control group were given general encouragement and support and had questions answered. Anxiety, depression and general psychological health were assessed by questionnaires after six weeks, six months and one year, and the patients' doctor surgeries were asked to report the number of contacts they had had after six months and after one year.

Results showed that anxiety levels had dropped significantly more for participants in the experimental group compared to the control group, at both six weeks and one year. Depression scores only differed significantly at six weeks. The number of patients showing poor general psychological health (referred to as 'caseness') was significantly lower for those in the experimental group than those in the control group, at six weeks, six months and one year. Results also showed that, for patients who were identified as particularly distressed at the time of the MI, anxiety and depression levels were significantly higher for those in the control group at each follow-up. Visits to the doctor and readmission to hospital were higher for those in the control group than those in the experimental group for both the first six months and the following six months. Lewin et al. concluded that providing patients with information, and with a self-help programme, can significantly improve their recovery after an MI, and can significantly improve their psychological health during recovery.

RESEARCH METHODS

One strength of Janis and Feshbach's research is that they compared three experimental groups with a control group. The use of a control group increased the validity of the study as it shows that any changes in behaviour are more likely to be due to the changes that are being made. All groups were approximately equal in terms of age, sex, education level and IQ, which also increases the validity as we can be fairly sure that any differences between the groups are not due to any of these characteristics.

A strength of Lewin et al.'s research is that it has high ecological validity because it involved patients who had suffered an MI and needed to recover, so the educational programme used was embedded in a real-life situation. This means that the results can be applied beyond the research setting and it can be assumed similar results would be found for others in a similar situation. The study is limited in that it only included people suffering an MI so we cannot confidently apply the results to people with other medical conditions, although similar programmes could be designed for other situations.

ISSUES AND DEBATES

Application to real life has particular relevance for research into strategies for promoting health, such as that by Janis and Feshbach and by Lewin et al. Encouraging healthy behaviours is really important for society, both on an individual level to enable to people to live healthier lives, and also on a wider level in terms of cutting costs for healthcare and support needed for those who live less healthy lifestyles. Research that investigates effective ways to promote healthy behaviours is absolutely key because it can be a difficult task. Understanding the success (or lack of success) of different approaches, as well as looking at different circumstances in which these approaches are more likely to work are incredibly important.

Health promotion in schools and worksites

Schools with a focus on healthy eating

Healthy eating is a really important aspect of health in general, because it reduces the risk of so many health conditions such as diabetes, heart disease and cancer. It is important to start healthy eating habits from a young age so that the behaviour is integrated into people's lives and will hopefully continue into adulthood. Krebs-Smith et al. (1995) found that one of the strongest predictors of adults eating fruit and vegetables is the extent to which they ate them during childhood. Schools are one of the best places to promote healthy eating as it can be part of their education programme as well as part of normal school life, such as offering healthy school dinners and having guidance on healthy lunchboxes.

Example study

Tapper et al. (2003) report some of the key findings of a survey by the UK Department of Health (2000), which found that four- to six-year-olds eat an average of only two portions of fruit and vegetables per day and less than 4% eat the recommended five or more portions per day. Previous attempts at encouraging children to eat more fruit and vegetables have involved health education campaigns, where children and their parents are informed what they should be eating with the hope that they will follow this advice, however, evidence shows that this has limited success (Contento et al., 1992). The Bangor Food Research Unit (BFRU) has attempted to take a different approach, using three main techniques to try to change children's eating habits: taste exposure, modelling and rewards.

- Taste exposure: the more you taste a new food, the more likely you are to like it. There are probably examples of things you didn't like to eat as a child, but you now enjoy. So, encouraging a child to keep trying a new food may result in them learning to like it.

- Modelling: there are certain factors that make modelling (where a child observes and imitates a behaviour) more likely. A child is more likely to imitate someone that they like or admire; that is the same age or slightly older and that has their behaviour rewarded. Observing more than one model is also shown to be more effective than observing just one model. Research shows that modelling affects a child's food preference and eating patterns (Birch, 1980).

- Rewards: there is mixed evidence for the role of rewards. Much research shows that rewards can encourage particular behaviours (Cameron et al., 2001), but other research suggests that rewarding behaviour reduces the intrinsic motivation for the behaviour (Deci et al., 1999). Rewards are most effective when they are highly desirable, achievable, a consequence of performance, and when it is clear that they are for behaviour that is enjoyable and high status (e.g., a certificate for hard work). This factor can be confusing when it comes to food because if you tell a child that they can only have pudding if they eat their vegetables, this is suggesting to the child that pudding is better than vegetables (and that vegetables are bad). In this situation, children may also feel that their behaviour is being managed: they may eat the vegetables this time, but they will be unlikely to repeat the behaviour in the absence of pudding.

The study was carried out at home with five- to six-year-old 'fussy eaters' who rarely ate fruit and vegetables. Four different procedures were used (first for fruit and then for vegetables): presentation only, rewarded taste exposure, peer modelling, and rewarded taste exposure combined with peer modelling. Peer modelling involved a video of some slightly older children (the 'Food Dudes') who gain superpowers from eating fruit and vegetables, and battle against the 'Junk Punks' who want to destroy all fruit and vegetables and take over the planet (see Figure 8.26). The reward aspect involved items such as Food Dude stickers and pens for eating target amounts of fruit and vegetables. Results showed that the combination of peer modelling and rewards was very effective at increasing children's consumption of fruit and vegetables. Initially, children ate on average only 4% of the fruit and 1% of vegetables presented to them at home by their parents. Following the modelling and rewards, this increased to 100% of fruit and 83% of vegetables. Six months later, even though the rewards and modelling had stopped, children were still eating 100% of fruit presented to them and 83% of vegetables, and were also trying other fruits and vegetables. In contrast, the presentation of fruit and vegetables alone had no effect on consumption and peer modelling without rewards had minimal effects. There were some positive effects with rewards only (especially with fruit) but these were nowhere near the levels achieved when combined with peer modelling.

Figure 8.26: The Food Dudes acted as peer models to encourage the eating of fruit and vegetables

The real test of the effectiveness of the programme was to see if it could have a significant impact on the consumption of large groups of children so the researchers set up a programme to be trialled at a nursery. In this study, there were rewards and video-modelling using two cartoon characters tailored to the age of the nursery children (aged two to four years). The intervention was introduced at mid-morning snack time, first with fruit and then with vegetables. Levels of fruit and vegetables consumed during lunchtimes were also recorded to see if any effect of the intervention was seen at lunchtime as well. The results showed that following the intervention, fruit consumption increased from 30% to 71%. This followed a maintenance phase where there were no videos, and the rewards were intermittent. At a 15-month follow-up, consumption levels were at 79%, with lunchtime consumption also increasing, from 17% baseline to 79% at the follow-up. Consumption of vegetables rose from 34% to 87% at snack time after the intervention, and at a nine-month follow-up it remained at 86%. Three years later, with very intermittent maintenance procedures, the children at the nursery consumed an average of 80% of the fruit and vegetables presented to them at snack time and lunchtime.

The intervention programme was then expanded to schools where fruit and vegetables were offered alongside other snacks such as crisps and chocolate. Results showed that even when faced with the choice of other snacks, fruit consumption more than doubled (28% to 59%) and vegetable consumption increased from 8% to 32% at the six-month follow-up. There was a subset of children who took part in a home-based study at the same time and similarly positive results were found with these children at home as well. A 'whole school' programme was designed to target children from aged 4–11 years old, including a Food Dude video, Food Dude rewards and a home pack and letters from the Food Dudes, as well as information for staff on how to run the intervention. The main intervention phase lasted 16 days, followed by a maintenance phase where there were no videos, and the letters and rewards became more intermittent. The intervention was initially carried out in three schools, and results showed that there were large, statistically significant increases in fruit and vegetable consumptions across all schools, all age groups and in both boys and girls. A subset of parents also reported an increase in fruit and vegetable consumption at home.

The researchers summarise the three main reasons they think the intervention works:

- The intervention gets children to try fruit and vegetables repeatedly, which leads to them eventually liking them for the taste and choosing to eat them even when there are no longer rewards.

- The intervention changes the culture within the school, so the consumption of fruit and vegetables becomes socially reinforced by their peers.

- The children come to see themselves as 'fruit and vegetable eaters' so they are guided by this self-concept: they see a piece of fruit and think to themselves 'I always eat my fruit' and this guides their behaviour.

The UK Food Standards Agency and Department of Health commissioned the programme, or modified versions of the programme to be rolled out to hundreds of schools across the UK.

> ### ACTIVITY 8.7
>
> How could you promote good dental hygiene in young children? Use the research by Tapper et al. (2003) to help you.

Worksites with a focus on health and safety

Health and safety are essential considerations in any workplace, and some workplaces have more potential risks than others. Even in more dangerous workplaces, staff do not always put health and safety first. There are ways of trying to encourage health and safety in the workplace, such as using a reward system, called a **token economy**, as illustrated in the study by Fox et al. (1987). This study is also discussed in Chapter 9.

> ### KEY WORD
>
> **token economy:** a reward system used, where tokens are given for specific desirable behaviour and these tokens can then be exchanged for goods.

Example study

Fox et al. (1987) investigated how a token economy could be used to encourage a focus on health and safety of workers in open-pit mines. Mining is a dangerous line of work, with hundreds of deaths and thousands of injuries each year in the USA. Not only is this a concern due to the risk to individuals, but also to the time (and therefore money) lost due to injuries. This study took place at two open-pit mines, both of which used similar methods for mining, including heavy machinery, and both of which had significantly higher than average injury rates in the five years before the study. The participants were employees in all areas of the two mines, including management and clerical staff, as well as mining equipment operators. During the several years of the study the number of employees at the two mines ranged from between approximately 650 and 11,000. Before the study, there were standard health and safety procedures in place including training for new employees, ongoing refresher training for all employees, and frequent inspections.

Workers at the mines were split into four groups, based on the number of lost-time injuries (injuries that led to time off work) reported previously.

- Group 1: workers in the least hazardous jobs, who spent at least 75% of their work time in an office.

- Group 2: included foremen, supervisors, technicians and surveyors.

- Group 3: included mechanics, labourers and machinery operators.

- Group 4: workers in the most hazardous jobs, including electricians, scraper operators and fuel workers.

The researchers introduced a token economy, where miners were given a certain number of trading stamps ('tokens') at the end of each month, along with their pay, for every month that they didn't suffer a lost-time injury or compensation injury. The number of trading stamps was greatest for those in group 4 and lowest for those in the least risky jobs in group 1.

Employees were given extra stamps if everyone under a particular supervisor was injury-free during the month. Additionally, there were further stamps awarded for safety suggestions that were adopted by the mine, as well as any acts that prevented serious injury to others, or prevented damage to the equipment. An employee who suffered a lost-time injury missed out on stamps for between one and six months depending on the number of days they missed, and for between one and six months for any damage caused to equipment. The trading stamps acted as **secondary reinforcers**, meaning that they do not have any value in themselves, but they are valuable because they can then be exchanged for **primary reinforcers** (items with intrinsic value). In this case, the trading stamps could be exchanged at redemption stores or via a catalogue for any number of household items, ranging from spice racks to microwaves and gas barbecues.

KEY WORDS

secondary reinforcers: something that does not have any value itself, it only has value because of what it can be exchanged for

primary reinforcers: anything that has intrinsic value, that gives pleasure and acts as a reward

To measure the effectiveness of the token economy, data were collected on the number of job-related injuries that lead to the worker being absent from work for one or more days (frequency rate), as well as the total number of hours missed (severity rate). Data were also collected on the cost incurred as a result of any damage to equipment, compensation to staff or medical care provided. A **cost–benefit analysis** was calculated to weigh up the cost of money spent on the trading stamps, compared to the money saved as a result of the token economy.

Results showed that, during the token economy, the number of days lost due to injury fell to 11% and 2% of the baseline for each of the mines. The number of lost-time injuries during the token economy also fell significantly to between 15% and 32% of the baseline rates (see Figure 8.27). Costs of accidents and injuries at both mines decreased by approximately 90% during the token economy. The cost–benefit analysis of dollars spent on the trading stamps, compared to money saved on accidents and injuries was very positive. For one mine between 18.1 and 27.8 dollars was saved for every dollar spent and for the other mine between 12.9 and

20.7 dollars was saved for every dollar spent. Overall, the researchers are pleased to report that the token economy benefited all those involved. Both mines had a significant reduction in lost-time injuries and in number of days lost from work, and the employees also benefited from exchanging the stamps for goods. In the last 10 years of the token economy, the number of days lost from work due to injuries had fallen to a quarter of the national average at one of the mines, and one-twelfth of the national average at the other mine. The results provide strong evidence of the effectiveness of behavioural programmes such as this, and that they can be maintained for long periods of time.

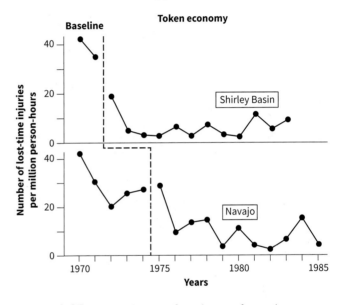

Figure 8.27: Fox et al. (1987) found a significant drop in lost-time injuries following the introduction of a token economy

ACTIVITY 8.8

You are employed by a building site manager to improve health and safety at the workplace after a series of accidents has taken place. Use Fox et al.'s study to help you devise a plan.

KEY WORD

cost–benefit analysis: a process to calculate the benefits of a situation (such as money made) minus the costs (money or time spent) to calculate whether the decision was successful

The studies by Tapper et al. (2003) and Fox et al. (1987) are both field experiments, meaning they are carried out in natural settings. This means that the studies have high ecological validity, and the results can confidently be generalised beyond the research setting. This is particularly important for research into healthy eating and health and safety so that the results can be used in other settings and benefit other people. The studies are both longitudinal, with Fox et al. being carried out over several years. This is an important strength as it increases the validity of the research because it allows us to see long-term effects rather than just a snapshot. Both of the studies gathered quantitative data that are objective and allow for analysis and comparisons to be made, so that trends and changes can be seen over time.

ISSUES AND DEBATES

The study by Tapper et al. (2003) uses children, first in their home environment, then in a nursery setting, followed by classes in schools and whole school programmes. When using children in psychological research the ethical considerations are particularly important to consider. It is essential to get fully *informed consent* from both the children and their parents before the research takes place, and to fully debrief parents and children afterwards. It is also important to be particularly careful to *protect the participants from harm* when working with children. In the case of the study by Tapper et al., the children would not be subject to any harm, but healthy eating could be considered to be a sensitive issue, for example, children may feel bad about themselves if they don't eat as much fruit and vegetables as they learn they are supposed to. How could individual versus situational explanations be applied to research into health promotions in school and worksites?

Individual factors in changing health beliefs

Unrealistic optimism

Unrealistic optimism refers to an error in judgement where people have a tendency to expect that bad things will happen to other people but not to themselves. This is an interesting phenomenon because it is very difficult to disprove: without knowing every detail of a person's life it is impossible to know whether they are in fact less at risk of something terrible happening to them than the average person. For example, someone may think that they are less likely than the average person to die of a heart attack. This could be unrealistic optimism or it could be true because perhaps they exercise regularly, have a healthy diet and live a relatively stress-free life. However, if you look at a group of people who all believe that they are less likely than the average person to experience something terrible, it becomes clear that there is an error, demonstrating unrealistic optimism. Research shows that people have a tendency to show unrealistic optimism when asked about their risk for things such as car accidents, illness or crime (Robertson, 1977, Harris & Guten, 1979 and Weinstein, 1980). Unrealistic optimism can be a reason for disregarding positive health advice. If you believe that bad things are less likely to happen to you, this is a way of justifying to yourself why you don't need to listen to positive health advice. For example, you may read health advice about reducing salt in your diet because it can lead to an increased risk of high blood pressure and heart attack. However, unrealistic optimism may make you believe that this is not likely to apply to you, so you may be inclined to ignore the advice.

KEY WORD

unrealistic optimism: an error in judgement where people have a tendency to expect that bad things will happen to other people but not themselves

Example study

Weinstein (1980) wished to investigate the hypothesis that people believe negative events are less likely to happen to them than others, and that positive events are more likely to happen to them than others. They also aimed to investigate a range of factors that might influence this, such as:

- The intensity of the positive or negative outcome.
- The perceived probability of the event occurring.
- Personal experience of the event.
- Perceived controllability of the event.
- Perceived stereotype about the type of person who is likely to be affected.

Study 1: a group of diverse college students were asked to judge the likelihood of 18 positive and 24 negative life events taking place in their life compared to other students at the same college and of the same sex as them. Positive events included owning your own home, living past 80, marrying someone wealthy and having a mentally gifted child. Negative events included being fired from your job, having a heart attack before age 40, being injured in a car accident or being sued by someone. For each event students were asked: 'compared to other Cook students – same sex as you – what do you think are the chances that the following events will happen to you?' The choices ranged from '100% less (no chance)', through 80% less, 60% less and so on then up to 80% more, 100% more, and ending with three times average and five times average. For each event, a different group of students were asked to say what percentage of students they think would experience it, how controllable the event was, and how desirable the event was. Finally, students were asked to rate their personal experience of each event (whether it has happened to them, their friends or acquaintances) and to rate the salience of a high chance group (the extent to which they can imagine a particular person this event is more likely to happen to).

Results showed that the main hypothesis was strongly supported: the average **comparative judgement** for all positive events was 15.4% above zero (zero being the actual likelihood of the event occurring) and for all negative events was 20.4% less than zero. This shows that students do show unrealistic optimism: they think there is a greater chance of a positive event happening to them than to others and a lesser chance of a negative event happening to them than to others. The results also show that all of the factors investigated showed correlations in the directions predicted:

- Comparative judgements were higher for a more desirable event, and lower for a less desirable event.
- Comparative judgements were higher for events with a higher perceived probability.
- Comparative judgements were higher for events with previous personal experience.

- Comparative judgements were lower for a negative event with high controllability, and comparative judgements were higher for a positive event with high controllability.
- Comparative judgements were lower for a negative event with a stereotype attached.

Perceived probability and degree of desirability were significantly correlated with positive events and stereotype salience, perceived controllability and personal experience were significantly correlated with negative events.

> ### KEY WORD
>
> **comparative judgement:** a judgement made about how likely you feel you are to experience a particular event compared to the average (of people similar to you)

Study 2: the researchers were interested to investigate the suggestion that unrealistic optimism occurs because people's image of others is inaccurate or incomplete. To test this, the researchers used the participants from Study 1 who had rated the likelihood of each event occurring (not those who made the comparative judgements). Before this group (120 females) were asked to make comparative judgements, they were asked to list the factors that increase or decrease the likelihood of the event happening to them. Some participants were then given copies of lists made by other students and asked to consider this when making their comparative judgements. It was predicted that this would decrease or eliminate the unrealistic optimism. The researchers also wanted to make sure that the results in Study 1 were not because of students getting confused and making ratings of overall likelihood of an event happening with judgements of the event happening to them compared to others. To test this, half of the participants were given very clear and explicit instructions not to confuse the comparative judgements with judgements of the event occurring in the population. Participants were randomly assigned to one of the three conditions when they arrived. All participants made comparative judgements for the pre-treatment first ten events (positive and negative). The experimental group were then asked to list factors that influence their judgements and were given a set of five lists of others' factors, then asked to make comparative judgements on the remaining events: treatment events and post-treatment events. Control group 1 listed their own reasons but did not receive lists from other people. Control group 2 did not make lists of their own reasons or receive lists from others while making comparative judgements, but they were asked to make their own lists after the judgements had been made. Half of the participants in each group were given a cover sheet with the clear and explicit instructions not to confuse comparative judgements with overall probability ratings.

Results showed that the extra warning not to confuse comparative judgements did not have a significant effect on results, so this shows that participants were clear about the task and had not been confused. Participants in the experimental group (who saw other people's listed factors) were significantly less optimistic with negative events than either of the control groups. For positive events, the experimental group and control group 1 (who listed their own reasons but did not see others' lists) were both significantly less optimistic than control group 2 (who did not make their own lists or see others' lists). The results relating to negative events indicate that unrealistic optimism comes from an inaccurate view of other people, as expected. The results relating to positive events suggests that just listing our own factors leads to a decrease in optimism, suggesting that our initial thoughts about the future are optimistic but that our later, more reflective thoughts are more realistic. However, although writing the list of factors and reading others' factors reduced optimism, it did not eliminate optimistic biases completely; comparative judgements were still unrealistically optimistic for positive and negative events.

Further analysis into the factors provided by participants showed that there were more favourable reasons given for both positive and negative events that produced the greatest optimism than for the events that produced the least optimism. This was the case whether the participants wrote the lists at the time of making the judgement (experimental group and control group 1) or whether they made their lists at a later stage (control group 2). The strong correlation between the degree of optimism reported (comparative judgement) and the number of favourable and unfavourable reasons given, for all groups, supports the theory that making mental lists similar to this is an important stage in making comparative judgements.

Positive psychology

Psychology has been primarily focused on suffering. From research into criminality, violence and trauma to developing an understanding of psychological disorders and, as a result, discovering treatments. However, this has overshadowed any efforts to enhance states that make life worth living. This is where positive psychology comes in.

Example study

Seligman (2004) reports on *positive psychology*, which he describes as 'the scientific study of the three different happy lives: the **Pleasant Life**, the **Good Life** and the **Meaningful Life**.'

- The Pleasant Life is about positive emotions.

- The Good Life is about positive traits, primarily strengths and values but also talents.

- The Meaningful Life is about positive institutions such as a strong family and democracy.

> **KEY WORDS**
>
> **positive psychology:** the scientific study of the three different happy lives: the Pleasant Life, the Good Life and the Meaningful Life
>
> **Pleasant Life:** is about positive emotions
>
> **Good Life:** is about positive traits, primarily strengths and values but also talents
>
> **Meaningful Life:** is about positive institutions such as a strong family and democracy

Seligman wished to find out whether a science of positive psychology can lead us to happiness. He did this by teaching an annual seminar to students at the University of Pennsylvania, USA. The course began with detailed personal introductions, where students were encouraged to use listening skills to find underlying positive strengths and virtues in their classmates. The following four sessions were spent learning about what has been scientifically documented about positive emotion: about the past (contentment, satisfaction, serenity), about the future (optimism, hope, trust, faith) and about the present (joy, comfort, pleasure). Research covered topics such as:

- depressive realism (happy people may be less accurate than miserable people)

- wealth and life satisfaction (the richest people are no happier than average people)

- set ranges for positive emotion (lottery winners and paraplegics revert to their pre-existing level of happiness or misery within a year because the capacity for pleasure is thought to be about 50% inherited, so is resistant to change).

The class discussed techniques for increasing positive emotions. For example, students discovered how to dispute unrealistic catastrophic thoughts to increase optimism, or how to practise gratitude.

The focus then turns to happiness in the present, focusing on pleasures and how to enhance them. Students took part in homework tasks where they practice skills of savouring (sharing experiences with others and collecting mementos) and mindfulness (looking at experiences from new angles and slowing down). Experiencing pleasures and having skills, such as savouring and mindfulness, is what Seligman refers to as the Pleasant Life.

To consider the Good Life, it is important to distinguish between pleasures and gratifications. Pleasure is described as a felt, conscious positive feeling, which disappears soon afterwards; something you might experience when eating good food or having a hot shower. Gratification tends to lead to longer-lasting good feeling, but one that is elusive and hard to explain, such as how you might feel if you volunteer at a homeless shelter or go rock-climbing. This is explained as being due to total immersion, with a lack of consciousness, so feelings can only take place retrospectively (thinking 'wow that was amazing!' after finishing the climb). Pleasures are associated with the Pleasant Life, but gratifications are associated with the Good Life. Gratifications require us to identify our greatest strengths and virtues and use them as often as possible to meet challenges (in work, love, play and parenting) and obtain gratification. Students took the VIA (Values-in-action Institute of the Mayerson Foundation) questionnaire to identify their five main strengths and virtues from a list including kindness, perseverance, love of learning and spirituality. After identifying their top five strengths and virtues, all students said they did not get to use these strengths every day, so a homework task encouraged them to find a way to incorporate their strengths into everyday tasks.

KEY WORD

VIA (Values-in-action Institute of the Mayerson Foundation) questionnaire: a questionnaire designed to identify a person's top strengths and virtues from a list

The final part of the course studies the third happy life, the Meaningful Life. Positive psychology describes meaning as belonging to something larger. The Meaningful Life is similar to the Good Life, in that it requires you to identify and use your highest strengths and virtues, but in this case, you must use these to serve something larger than you are. These larger things are Positive Institutions, such as your family, college or workplace. Students were encouraged to create family trees of the strengths of their parents, siblings and grandparents, or to imagine a positive human future and their role in it. As part of the course, students read *Aging Well* by George Vaillant, which compares the lives of the top Harvard graduates with those who were uneducated and came from a lower socioeconomic status. A 60-year study of the men showed that the higher education made little or no difference in 'success in life'. Aside from having a higher income, the Harvard graduates were no better off than the other men on a range of measures such as life satisfaction, marital happiness, maturity, freedom from depression and alcoholism or longevity. Seligman and his students concluded that spending thousands of dollars on education might be more likely to lead to success in life if it taught material covered in this course. Seligman sums up his work on positive psychology by saying: 'In the end, I believe that we learn more when lighting candles than when cursing the darkness.'

Key study: Shoshani and Steinmetz (2014)

Shoshani, A., & Steinmetz, S. (2014). Positive psychology at school: a school-based intervention to promote adolescents' mental health and well-being. *Journal of happiness studies, 15*(6), 1289–1311.

Context

Costello et al. (2004) report that there has been a dramatic rise in reported mental health disorders in children and adolescents since the late 1990s. The World Health Organization (WHO, 2005) found rates of mental health disorders in those under the age of 18 to range between 8% and 20%. Furthermore, Huebner et al. (2000) found that 25% of American students reported an 'unhappy' or 'terrible' existence, or high levels of negative school or family experiences. During this time, positive psychology has progressed in terms of understanding these trends and beginning to make interventions to build toward positive outcomes.

There has also been a change in the culture of education in this same time period. The focus is much more on academic achievement, with assessments and curriculum goals a priority, with less of a focus on the social and emotional components of education (Hargreaves, 2003).

Main theories and explanations

Recent research has begun to consider a dual factor model when considering the relationship between well-being and ill-being. For example, Greenspoon and Saklofske (2001) defined mental health as two distinct but related dimensions of mental illness and positive mental health. The suggestion is that mental illness and positive mental health are not opposite ends of the same scale; it is possible experience high levels of distress alongside high levels of subjective well-being. Subjective well-being is defined as consisting of a cognitive component (life satisfaction) and an affective component (the presence of positive feeling and absence of negative emotional experiences). Subjective well-being is particularly relevant in studies in schools as subjective well-being is associated with good academic achievement, social competence, physical health, and engagement at school (Antaramian et al., 2010), as well as better relationships with parents, teachers and peers (Gilman & Huebner, 2006). There are two main approaches to explaining well-being: the hedonic approach and the eudaimonic approach (Ryan & Deci, 2000). The hedonic approach for well-being focuses on maximising pleasure and minimising pain so it involves ideas such as positive emotions, life satisfaction and happiness. The eudaimonic approach for well-being focuses more on realising your potential, with an emphasis on meaning, autonomy and purpose in life.

Aims

The aim of the research was to see whether participation in an intervention programme would increase participants' self-efficacy, optimism, life satisfaction and self-esteem, and decrease levels of psychological distress and mental health problems. The research also aimed to discover if there were demographic differences in the effectiveness of the intervention programme, for

example gender, level of family income or single versus two-parent households.

Design

The sample was 1,167 students, aged 11–14 years, at two large middle schools in the centre of Israel. A total of 35 middle schools in the area were selected for the initial pool, and the principals of eight of these schools showed an interest in the positive psychology intervention programme. Of these eight schools, one was randomly allocated to the intervention programme and another, matched for demographics, acted as a control group, and would participate in the intervention programme after completion of the study. Almost all the participants were Jewish (with differing levels of religious observance), there was a mix of socioeconomic status, and 64% lived in a two-parent family and 36% lived in a single-parent family.

The **Brief Symptom Inventory (BSI)** was used to measure the adolescents' mental health. The BSI was designed for use with adolescents and reports norms for that age range. The BSI contained 53 self-report items rated on a four-point Likert scale, measuring 10 subscales including depression, anxiety, paranoid ideation, hostility and interpersonal sensitivity. Other scales were used alongside the BSI: the Rosenberg self-esteem scale (RSE), the general self-efficacy scale, satisfaction with life scale (SWLS) and the life orientation test-revised (LOT-R) to measure optimism.

The intervention programme involved two aspects that ran alongside each other over the course of a school year. Teachers attended 15 two-hour long training workshops, run by clinical psychologists, to train them in group dynamics and positive psychology. Alongside this, teachers administered an age-appropriate similar programme to their students, using a textbook and materials provided by the researchers. The classroom programme included activities, discussions, video clips to watch and talk about and poems and stories to read: all dealing with the key aspects of positive psychology. For example, to address gratitude, students were asked to list five or more things they were grateful for that week and share their reflections with the group. The control group continued with their usual studies and did not take part in any positive psychology activities. Questionnaires were given out to all participants before the programme began, in September 2010, at the end of the academic year, when the programme ended, in June 2011, as well as follow-ups in December 2011 and June 2012.

Findings, results and conclusions

At the start of the study, there were significant differences in the mental health of students according to particular variables. Students from a lower income, or from a single-parent household, were more likely to report signs of poor mental health, such as anxiety and depression, and were likely to have lower self-esteem, optimism and life satisfaction. Boys were more likely to show anxiety, lower self-efficacy, optimism and life satisfaction than girls, but girls were more likely to show other signs of poor mental health and lower self-esteem. Involvement in the intervention was associated with fewer mental health symptoms over time, compared to those in the control group, who showed an increase in mental health symptoms. Students in the intervention programme showed significant decreases from the beginning to the end of the study in general distress (see Figure 8.28), depression symptoms, anxiety symptoms and interpersonal sensitivity. Those in the intervention programme reported significant increases in self-esteem, self-efficacy and optimism, while those in the control group reported a decrease in self-esteem and self-efficacy, and only a slight increase in optimism over time. Unexpectedly, there was no significant difference between the intervention group and the control group in changes over time for life satisfaction. High risk students (low income or single-parent household) showed less of an improvement in mental health symptoms as a result of the intervention programme than low risk students, however, they did still show improvements.

This study clearly shows a successful application of positive psychology. The results show quite clearly that the intervention programme was associated with an improvement in mental health symptoms for those involved, compared to those in the control group. Some students responded less well to the intervention programme than others, but an improvement was reported for these students, nonetheless. The intervention programme had a positive impact on the culture of the entire school, placing an emphasis on the quality of the relationships between staff and students, which should have a positive effect on the whole school community in the long-term.

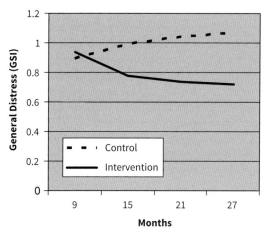

Figure 8.28: Shoshani and Steinmetz (2014) found that students in the intervention programme showed a significant decrease in levels of distress

Evaluation

The sample was limited, in that the intervention programme was only carried out in one school, so caution must be used when generalising the results to the wider population. A strength, however, is that the study used another school as a control, which was matched as closely as possible on demographics. This increased the validity of the study as it enabled the results of the intervention programme to be compared directly to similar participants who were not undergoing the intervention programme. A further increase in the validity came from the longitudinal nature of the study, which allowed the researchers to see the effect of the intervention programme, and the changes in the control group over time, rather than just during or immediately after the programme. The intervention programme was carried out in a school environment and was administered to students by staff so this increases the ecological validity; the results can be generalised beyond the research setting and the intervention programme can be administered to future year groups of students as well. One weakness of the study was the reliance solely on self-report measures. This could lead to a decrease in validity due to students being subject to social desirability and therefore not giving accurate reports, or due to demand characteristics where students may be inclined to give more positive reports following the intervention because they realise that is what the researchers expect. How else could the researchers have collected data?

Application to everyday life is relevant to the study by Shoshani and Steinmetz because they have trialled an application of positive psychology through an intervention in a school and seen the positive effects on the mental health of the students over a two-year period. These results can be applied to everyday life because other schools can learn from this and could carry out the intervention programme, or something similar in their own schools and hopefully see similar improvements in their children. Not only was the intervention programme effective for the students directly involved, but it also improved the culture of the entire school and all staff involved. This will have positive effects for children and staff at the school for years to come, and other schools can also learn from this and take a similar approach. Adolescent mental health has become increasingly concerning over the last couple of decades so any intervention that can help combat this issue is a really important contribution.

RESEARCH METHODS

Weinstein (1980) relied on *self-report* to measure unrealistic optimism, and the students may give inaccurate answers due to demand characteristics, where they may realise what the study is about and change their answers accordingly. Furthermore, students may not give accurate answers because they don't want to look silly, or they may not have understood the task, or any of the scenarios properly. However, Weinstein did address this concern in study 2, by giving very clear instructions of the task, and how not to get confused, to half of the participants and there were no significant differences with this group, suggesting confusion wasn't a problem. The second study also increased the validity of the research by addressing potential issues or uncertainties in the first study; this is really important in gathering accurate data and getting a better understanding of what is being shown. One weakness of the study is that the participants were all college students from the same place, so the results cannot be generalised to the wider population, particularly as it could be argued that younger people may have a different level of unrealistic optimism than older adults.

ISSUES AND DEBATES

The research into *positive psychology* can be applied to everyday life, in order to benefit the wider population. As we discussed previously, most of psychology is focused on when things go wrong and how to help those with mental health disorders, but it is also so important to focus on the positives and how to enhance positive experiences and traits. Seligman's programme of study, for example, could be not only studied by many more college students, but an adapted version could be accessible to the wider population. If people are able to understand positive psychology and the science behind important aspects like gratitude and gratification, they may be able to live a more fulfilling and meaningful life, benefiting not only themselves but also others. In what ways should cultural differences be considered in research into positive psychology?

Questions

13 Janis and Feshbach (1953) found that a strong fear appeal was not a successful way of promoting healthy behaviour, and in fact low fear appeal was much more effective. Why was this?

14 Fox et al. (1987) investigated the effectiveness of token economy on improving health and safety in the workplace. How did this token economy benefit the workers and the owners of the mine?

15 Weinstein (1980) carried out two studies as part of the investigation into unrealistic optimism. Why did Weinstein carry out the second study?

SELF-EVALUATION CHECKLIST

After studying this chapter, copy and complete a table like this:

I can	Needs more work	Almost there	Ready to move on	Coursebook	Workbook
describe, evaluate, compare and apply research into practitioner and patient interpersonal skills					
describe, evaluate, compare and apply research into practitioner diagnosis and style					
describe, evaluate, compare and apply research into misusing health services					
describe, evaluate, compare and apply research into types of non-adherence and reasons why patients don't adhere					
describe, evaluate, compare and apply research into measuring non-adherence					
describe, evaluate, compare and apply research into improving adherence					
describe, evaluate, compare and apply research into types and theories of pain					
describe, evaluate, compare and apply research into measuring pain					
describe, evaluate, compare and apply research into managing and controlling pain					
describe, evaluate, compare and apply research into sources of stress					
describe, evaluate, compare and apply research into measuring stress					
describe, evaluate, compare and apply research into managing stress					
describe, evaluate, compare and apply research into strategies for promoting health					
describe, evaluate, compare and apply research into health promotion in schools and worksites					
describe, evaluate, compare and apply research into individual factors in changing health beliefs.					

PROJECT

You are a support worker for an elderly patient who suffers from a condition that gives them chronic pain. The pain relies on several different medications to be taken correctly every day to keep it under control. The patient also needs to go for regular appointments for tests and check-ups. The patient's symptoms have got worse recently because he isn't taking his medication and keeps missing his appointments. He is now finding the pain very difficult to manage and it is making him very stressed.

Your task is to consider the possible reasons for the difficulties the patient is having, and to devise a plan of action to help him.

You can work on your own or in pairs.

You should consider the following aspects of the patient's experience, and how to make improvements for him:

- Why he might be missing appointments?
- Why isn't he taking his medication as prescribed?
- What sort of pain is he experiencing? How can it be measured?
- What could he do to improve his pain? Are there psychological therapies he could try? Alternative treatments?
- What could be done to measure his stress levels? What could he do to help manage his stress?

Your project should presented in a clear format, perhaps using a table or bullet points, where each possible issue is described, and a solution is presented alongside it. You should refer to relevant research where appropriate.

Peer assessment

When you have completed your project, join up with someone else and discuss and compare your plans. Did you both take a similar approach? Did you focus on different issues? Could you use ideas from each other to improve your action plan? Spend time adding to or amending your plan of action to improve it, based on what you have seen.

EXAM-STYLE QUESTIONS

1 **Outline** the findings of **one** study into the effect of non-verbal communication onto practitioner–patient relationships. [3]

2 a **Describe** the sample used by Savage and Armstrong (1990). [2]

  b Describe the conclusion of Savage and Armstrong (1990). [2]

  c **Give one** strength and **one** limitation of the study by Savage and Armstrong (1990). [4]

3 a Laba et al. (2012) gave participants hypothetical situations relating to eight factors. Name **three** of the factors. [3]

  b Describe the results of the study by Laba et al. (2012). Explain at least **two** findings in your answer. [4]

4 a What were the **four** different conditions in the study by Yokley and Glenwick (1984)? [2]

  b What results did Yokley and Glenwick expect to find in relation to these conditions? [2]

COMMAND WORDS

outline: set out main points

describe: state the points of a topic / give characteristics and main features

give: produce an answer from a given source or recall / memory

EXAM-STYLE QUESTIONS

5 **a** Describe specificity theory of pain. **[4]**

  b Describe gate control theory of pain. **[4]**

6 **a** Describe the McGill pain questionnaire and give **one** strength and one limitation of it. **[6]**

  b Describe the UAB pain behaviour scale and give **one** strength and one limitation of it. **[6]**

7 **a** Briefly describe life events as a cause of stress. **[3]**

  b Briefly describe type A personality as a cause of stress. **[3]**

  c **Compare** life events and type A personality as causes of stress. **[6]**

8 **a** Briefly describe the procedure and findings of the study by Bridge et al. (1988). **[4]**

  b **Evaluate** the study by Bridge et al. (1988) **[10]**

9 How might application to everyday life be relevant to research, such as Tapper et al. (2003), into promoting healthy eating in schools? **[4]**

10 **a** Describe what is meant by unrealistic optimism. **[3]**

  b Describe what is meant by The Pleasant Life, The Good Life, and The Meaningful Life, according to Seligman. **[6]**

[Total: 81]

COMMAND WORDS

compare: identify/comment on similarities and/or differences

evaluate: judge or calculate the quality, importance, amount, or value of something

Additional references

Antaramian, S. P., Scott Huebner, E., Hills, K. J., & Valois, R. F. (2010). A dual-factor model of mental health: toward a more comprehensive understanding of youth functioning. *The American journal of orthopsychiatry*, 80(4), 462–472.

Aleem, A., & Ajarim, D. S. (1995). Munchausen syndrome – presenting as immunodeficiency: a case report and review of literature. *Annals of Saudi medicine*, 15(4) [online], 404–406.

Birch, L. L. (1980). Effects of peer models' food choices and eating behaviors on preschoolers' food preferences. *Child development*, 489–496.

Bosch-Capblanch, X., Abba, K., Prictor, M., & Garner, P. (2007). Contracts between patients and healthcare practitioners for improving patients' adherence to treatment, prevention and health promotion activities. *Cochrane database of systematic reviews*, (2).

Brown, J. C., Klein, E. J., Lewis, C. W., et al. (2003). Emergency department analgesia for fracture pain. *Annals of emergency medicine*, 42, 197–205.

Budzynski, T. H., & Stoyva, J. M. (1969) An instrument for producing deep muscle relaxation by means of analog information feedback. *Journal of applied behavior analysis*, 2(4), 231–237.

Byrne, E., Schaffer, W., Dini, E., & Case, G. (1970). Infant immunization surveillance: cost vs. effect. *Journal of the American Medical Association*, 212, 770–773.

Cameron, J. (2001). Negative effects of reward on intrinsic motivation–a limited phenomenon: comment on Deci, Koestner, and Ryan (2001). *Review of educational research*, 71(1), 29–42.

Chandola, T., Britton, A., Brunner, E., Hemingway, H., Malik, M., Kumari, M., Bradrick, E., Kivimaki, M., & Marmot, M. (2008). Work stress and coronary heart disease: what are the mechanisms? *European heart journal*, *29*(5), [online], 640–648.

Chaney, G., Clements, B., Landau, L., Bulsara, M., & Watt, P. (2004). A new asthma spacer device to improve compliance in children: a pilot study. *Respirology*, *9*(4), 499–506.

Chung, K. F., & Naya, I. (2000). Compliance with an oral asthma medication: a pilot study using an electronic monitoring device. *Respiratory medicine*, *94*(9) [online], 852–858.

Colt, H. G., & Solot, J. A. (1989). Attitudes of patients and physicians regarding physician dress and demeanor in the emergency department. *Annals of emergency medicine*, *18*(2), 145–151.

Contento, I. R., Manning, A. D., & Shannon, B. (1992). Research perspective on school-based nutrition education. *Journal of nutrition education*, *24*(5), 247–260.

Cooke, N., & Colver, G. B. (2016). How to convey a diagnosis of skin cancer: patient preferences. *British journal of dermatology*, *2*(175), 398–400.

Costello, E. J., Mustillo, S., Keller, G., & Angold, A. (2004). Prevalence of psychiatric disorders in childhood and adolescence. In *Mental health services: a public health perspective* edited by B. L. Levin, J. Petrila, and K. D. Hennessy, 111–128. Oxford University Press.

Deci, E. L., Koestner, R., & Ryan, R. M. (1999). The undermining effect is a reality after all–extrinsic rewards, task interest, and self-determination: reply to Eisenberger, Pierce, and Cameron (1999) and Lepper, Henderlong, and Gingras (1999). *Psychological bulletin*, *125*(6), 692–700.

Department of Health (2000). The NHS pan: a plan for investment, a plan for reform. London:The Stationery Office.

Evans, G. W., & Wener, R. E. (2007). Crowding and personal space invasion on the train: please don't make me sit in the middle. *Journal of environmental psychology*, *27*(1), [online] 90–94.

Fein, J. A., Zempsky, W. T., & Cravero, J. P. (2012). Committee on Pediatric Emergency Medicine and Section on Anesthesiology and Pain Medicine; American Academy of Pediatrics. Relief of pain and anxiety in pediatric patients in emergency medical systems. *Pediatrics*, *130*, e1391–1405

Fox, D. K., Hopkins, B. L., & Anger, W. K. (1987). The long-term effects of a token economy in safety performance in open pit mining. *Journal of applied behavior analysis*, *20*(3) [online], 215–224.

Friedman, M., & Rosenman, R. H. (1971). Type A behavior pattern: its association with coronary heart disease. *Annals of clinical research*, *3*(6), 300–312.

Gilman, R., & Huebner, E. S. (2006). Characteristics of adolescents who report very high life satisfaction. *Journal of youth and adolescence*, *35*(3), 293–301.

Grant, P. S. (2006). Analgesia delivery in the ED. *American journal of emergency medicine*, *24*, 806–809.

Greenspoon, P. J., & Saklofske, D. H. (2001). Toward an integration of subjective wellbeing and psychopathology. *Social indicators research*, *54*, 81–108.

Hargreaves, A. (2003). *Teaching in the knowledge society: education in the age of insecurity*. Teachers College Press.

Harris, D. M., & Guten, S. (1979). Health protective behavior: an exploratory study. *Journal of health and social behavior*, *20*, 17–29.

Holmes, T. H., & Rahe, R. H. (1967). The Social Readjustment Rating Scale. *Journal of psychosomatic research*. *11*(2), 213–218.

Huebner, E. S., Drane, W., & Valois, R. F. (2000). Levels and demographic correlates of adolescent life satisfaction reports. *School psychology international*, *21*(3), 281–292.

Inglefinger, F. J. (1980). Arrogance. *New England journal of medicine*, *303*, 1507–1511.

Janis, I. L., & Feshbach, S. (1953). Effects of fear-arousing communications. *The journal of abnormal and social psychology*, *48*(1) [online], 78–92.

Karri, V., Bragg, T. W. H., Jones, A., Soldin, M., & Misch, K. (2009). Patient satisfaction with receiving skin cancer diagnosis by letter: comparison with face-to-face consultation. *Journal of plastic, reconstructive & aesthetic surgery*, *62*(8), 1059–1062.

Katon, W., & Kleinman, A. (1980). Doctor–patient negotiation and other social science strategies in patient care. In *The relevance of social science for medicine*, edited by L. Eisenberg & A. Kleinman, 253–283. Reidel.

Krebs-Smith, S. M., Heimendinger, J., Patterson, B. H., Subar, A. F., Kessler, R., & Pivonka, E. (1995). Psychosocial factors associated with fruit and vegetable consumption. *American journal of health promotion*, *10*(2), 98–104.

Laba, T. L., Brien, J. A., & Jan, S. (2012). Understanding rational non-adherence to medications. A discrete choice experiment in a community sample in Australia. *BMC family practice*, 13(1), 1–10.

Lewin, R. J. P., Furze, G., Robinson, J., Griffith, K., Wiseman, S., Pye, M., & Boyle, R. (2002). A randomised controlled trial of a self-management plan for patients with newly diagnosed angina. *British journal of general practice*, *52* [online], 194–201.

Lyles, J. N., Burish, T. G., Krozely, M. G., & Oldham, R. K. (1982). Efficacy of relaxation training and guided imagery in reducing the aversiveness of cancer chemotherapy. *Journal of consulting and clinical psychology*, *50*, 509–524.

MacLachlan, M., McDonald, D., & Waloch, J. (2004). Mirror treatment of lower limb phantom pain: a case study. *Disability and rehabilitation*, *26*(14/15), 901–904.

Maguire, P. (1981). Psychological and social consequences of cancer. In *Recent advances in clinical oncology*, edited by C. J. Williams & J. W. A. Whitehouse, p. 376. London: Churchill Livingstone.

McKinlay, J. B. (1975). Who is really ignorant – physician or patient? *Journal of health and social behavior*, *16*(1) [online], 3–11.

McKinstry, B., & Wang, J. X. (1991). Putting on the style: what patients think of the way their doctor dresses. *British journal of general practice*, 41(348) [online], 270, 275–278.

McLean, J. (1986). The use of relaxation techniques in general practice. *Practitioner*, *230*, 1079–1084.

Melzack, R., & Wall, P. D. (1965). Pain mechanisms: a new theory. *Science*, *150*(3699), 971–979.

Morrow, A. M., Hayen, A., Quine, S., et al. (2012). A comparison of doctors', parents' and children's reports of health states and health-related quality of life in children with chronic conditions. *Child: care, health and development, 38*, 186–195.

Rahe, R. H., Mahan, J. L., & Arthur, R. J. (1970). Prediction of near-future health change from subjects' preceding life changes. *Journal of psychosomatic research, 14*(4), 401–406.

Ramachandran, V. S., & Rogers-Ramachandran, D. (1996). Synaesthesia in phantom limbs induced with mirrors. *Proceedings of the Royal Society of London. Series B: biological sciences, 263*(1369), 377–386.

Riekart, K. A., & Drotar, D. (1999). Who participates in research on adherence to treatment in insulin-dependent diabetes mellitus? Implications and Recommendations for Research. *Journal of pediatric psychology, 24*(3) [online], 253–258.

Robertson, L. S. (1977). Car crashes: perceived vulnerability and willingness to pay for crash protection. *Journal of community health, 3*, 136–141.

Robinson, R., & West, R. (1992). A comparison of computer and questionnaire methods of history-taking in a genito-urinary clinic. *Psychology and health, 6*(1–2), 77–84.

Ryan, R. M., & Deci, E. L. (2000). Self determination theory and the facilitation of intrinsic motivation, social development, and well-being. *American psychologist, 55*, 68–78.

Safer, M. A., Tharps, Q. J., Jackson, T. C., & Leventhal, H. (1979). Determinants of three stages of delay in seeking care at a medical clinic. *Medical care, 17*(1), [online], 11–29.

Samora, J., Saunders, L., & Larson, R. F. (1961). Medical vocabulary knowledge among hospital patients. *Journal of health and human behavior*, 83–92.

Sarafino, E. P. (2006). *Health psychology: biopsychosocial interactions*. John Wiley.

Schofield, P. E., Butow, P. N., Thompson, J. F., Tattersall, M. H. N., Beeney, L. J., & Dunn, S. M. (2003). Psychological responses of patients receiving a diagnosis of cancer. *Annals of oncology, 14*(1), 48–56.

Schroeder, K., Fahey, T., & Ebrahim, S. (2004). Interventions for improving adherence to treatment in patients with high blood pressure in ambulatory settings. *Cochrane Database of systematic reviews*, (3).

Seligman, M. E. (2004). Can happiness be taught? *Daedalus, 133*(2), 80–87.

Selye, H. (1936). *Stress without distress*. New York: Lippincott.

Shi, S., Wu, J., Chen, H., Chen, H., Wu, J., & Zeng, F. (2007). Single-and multiple-dose pharmacokinetics of pirfenidone, an antifibrotic agent, in healthy Chinese volunteers. *The journal of clinical pharmacology, 47*(10), 1268–1276.

Simonton, O. C., & Simonton, S. S. (1975). Belief systems and management of the emotional aspects of malignancy. *Transpersonal psychology, 7*, 29–47.

Singer, A. J., Gulla, J., & Thode, H. C. Jr (2002). Parents and practitioners are poor judges of young children's pain severity. *Academic emergency medicine, 9*, 609–612.

Strandbygaard, U., Thomsen, S. F., & Backer, V. (2010). A daily SMS reminder increases adherence to asthma treatment: a three-month follow-up study. *Respiratory medicine, 104*(2), 166–171.

Tapper, K., Horne, P. J., & Lowe, C. F. (2003). The Food Dudes to the rescue. *Psychologist*, *16*(1) [online], 18–21.

Weinstein, N. D. (1980). Unrealistic optimism about future life events. *Journal of personality and social psychology*, *39*(5), 806.

White, J. (1976). Because we care. *American education*, *12*, 26–28.

World Health Organization (WHO) (2005). *Atlas: child and adolescent mental health resources*. Geneva: World Health Organization.

Chapter 9

Organisational psychology

LEARNING INTENTIONS

In this chapter you will learn how to:

- describe, evaluate and compare theory and research into motivation to work in terms of needs theories, cognitive theories and motivators at work

- describe, evaluate and compare theory and research into leadership and management in terms of traditional and modern theories of leadership, leadership styles, leaders and followers

- describe, evaluate and compare theory and research into group behaviour in organisations in terms of group development and decision-making, individual and group performance and conflict at work

- describe, evaluate and compare theory and research into organisational work conditions in terms of physical work conditions, temporal conditions and health and safety

- describe, evaluate and compare theory and research into satisfaction at work in terms of theories of job satisfaction, measuring job satisfaction and attitudes to work.

Introduction

In this chapter, you will explore five key topics from within organisational psychology. First, you will consider motivation to work; including need theories of motivation, cognitive theories of motivation and motivators at work. You will explore issues of leadership and management, including ways of measuring leadership, leadership styles and followership. Next, you will look at group behaviour in organisations. This topic explores group behaviours and team roles, group decision-making, and the causes and management of conflict and bullying at work. You will also learn about different organisational work conditions including physical work conditions and the famous Hawthorne effect, the effects of shift work and identifying, monitoring and reducing healthy and safety risks in the workplace. Finally, you will explore the topic of satisfaction at work, including theories and measurement of workplace satisfaction and the quality of working life, employee sabotage, absenteeism and workplace commitment.

GETTING STARTED

Organisations take many different forms; they can include profit-making businesses as well as voluntary or public institutions. Organisational psychology brings together theories and research from across psychology and applies this to the study of organisations. This chapter will consider the world of work, and how individuals and groups within an organisation function and influence each other and have an effect on the organisation itself.

KEY WORDS

organisation: a group of people who come together for a particular purpose, for example a company, department or institution

organisational psychology: the applied study of the ways in which people think, feel and behave within organisations

You will be considering psychometric approaches within this chapter. These are attempts to measure personality and cognitive functioning in order to ensure that people and their organisational roles are well suited. You may also be able to think of some applications already based on the psychology you learned in your AS course. For example, the Social Approach to psychology may be relevant when considering issues such as leadership and followership, motivation, quality of working life, employee sabotage and group processes. Aspects of the cognitive approach such as memory and attention, and also theoretical models of decision-making and other cognitive processes are also crucial in understanding how individuals make sense of their roles within organisations. What decision-making do you think happens within organisations? You might want to think about the different decisions employers and employees of organisations might have to make and the factors that influence decisions in the workplace.

Likewise, aspects such as working conditions that affect people's mind and bodies are of interest to organisational psychologists. How might working different shift patterns be a challenge for employees? Which shift patterns are likely to be most difficult for the body to cope with? Can you judge which of the AS approaches this topic is most closely linked to?

Some techniques and models from the Learning Approach are also relevant to organisational psychology. For example, consider how employees are rewarded for their work. Organisational psychology explores ways in which operant conditioning can be used to motivate positive employee behaviour and increase productivity.

You may wish to review your notes on these AS topics before you begin this chapter. This will also help remind you of some of the strengths and weaknesses of each approach which will be relevant to evaluating topics in organisational psychology.

KEY WORD

psychometrics: the theory of or methods used to test and measure psychological phenomena, for example intelligence or personality testing

9.1 Motivation to work

Psychologists are interested in what motivates people to work. Apart from perhaps the obvious answer (they need money), it is useful to understand how work can fulfil people's needs, how goals can motivate employees and internal and external motivation to work.

Need theories

Maslow's hierarchy of needs

Maslow's original hierarchy of needs (Maslow, 1943) is one of the best-known theories of motivation. It proposes that we need to satisfy our basic human **needs** before we can begin to satisfy higher needs. Maslow claimed that all needs of humans could be arranged in a **hierarchy**. A person moves through the hierarchy by fulfilling each level, so that they need to meet the basic physiological needs before moving trying to meet needs that are higher up the hierarchy such as safety or social needs. Some people may never move through the entire hierarchy.

> **KEY WORDS**
>
> **needs:** in psychology, these are things that are required or wanted by a person
>
> **hierarchy:** a way of arranging items (e.g. needs) to show that some items are above, equal to or below others in terms of importance or status

Maslow's original hierarchy lists five levels of needs (as shown in Figure 9.1).

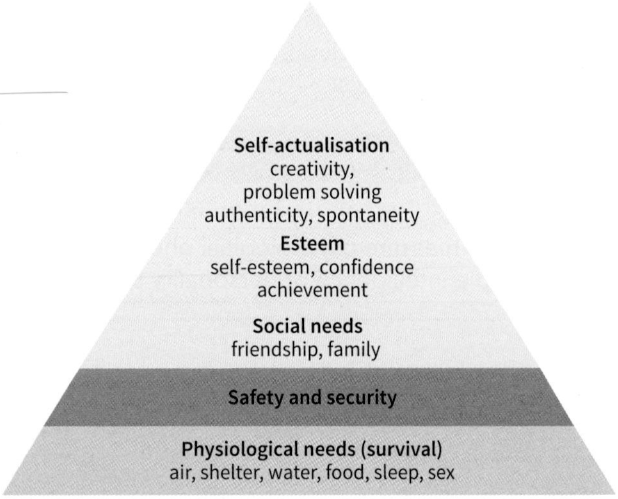

Figure 9.1: Maslow's original hierarchy of needs

1 Biological and physiological needs: this stage focuses on our basic survival needs.

2 Safety needs: this stage covers a range of safety and security needs including those provided by a stable society with appropriate legal and justice systems. If a country is in the middle of a civil war, or people are living as refugees, they are unable to meet their safety and security needs.

3 Love and belongingness needs: also known as 'social needs' the focus is primarily on friendship and family.

4 Esteem needs: this level refers to achievements; skills, status, independence, and so on. These esteem needs could be met very differently in different people. Some may feel a great sense of esteem through their family roles, through their well-paid jobs, through voluntary work that helps others or through the creation of something that receives public praise.

5 Transcendence needs: this refers to our ability to help others to also achieve self-actualisation.

There have been some attempts to put Maslow's theory of needs into practice. For example, Saeednia (2011) tested Maslow's theory using a scale measuring basic-needs-satisfaction. 300 participants were assessed on a scale based on physiological, safety, love, esteem and cognitive needs. The scale was found to be a valid and reliable measure.

Most organisations allow employees to satisfy the basic needs, for example providing break times for them to have meals and rest. Clear rules and responsibilities at work can provide security, and self-esteem needs can be met through recognising employees' achievement and making them feel like part of a team. Once these lower order needs have been met, the organisation may have encouraged enough self-motivation for employees to strive for higher order needs such as self-actualisation.

McClelland's Theory of Achievement Motivation

McClelland's Theory of Achievement Motivation dates back to 1965 but the concept of achievement motivation is still often referred to in the workplace context. This theory proposes that there are different needs that motivate people and that these differences are measurable. There are three types of need identified in this theory:

• Need for *achievement*: the need to get things done, to accomplish things, to be a success. People who have a high need for achievement (N-Ach) will be driven to succeed and are highly motivated by challenges and appraisals.

- Need for *affiliation*: the need to be liked by others, to be accepted as part of a group, to put effort into developing and maintaining social relationships. People who have a high need for affiliation will tend to prefer working with others to working alone and will be motivated by cooperative tasks.

- Need for *power*: the need to have influence and control over others. People with a high need for power will be motivated by the chance to gain status or prestige or to be looked up to by others.

This theory is often applied within organisational settings as these are measurable qualities of a person; one person may have a higher need for power than another. It is likely that someone who will make a good manager will have a need for power but not a need for affiliation. We will be looking at leadership later in this chapter.

Need for achievement (N-Ach) can be measured with the use of the Thematic Apperception Test or TAT. These are a series of ambiguous images which the individual is asked to interpret. For example, they might be given the picture in Figure 9.2 and asked to consider what is happening, what has just happened, what is going to happen next and what the person in the picture is thinking.

Figure 9.2: What story is this picture telling you?

social needs through the provision of social clubs or events. They might also provide education and training, rewards and bonus schemes to meet self-esteem needs. Similarly, McClelland's theory can be applied in the workplace to help understand personal characteristics and to ensure that people are given roles that suit their particular need for achievement.

Self-actualisation for Maslow refers to the desire for self-fulfilment, which can be met in many different ways. The ways to meet this need are specific to the individual rather than the situation; for example, some individuals may self-actualise through becoming a parent and others through becoming a successful athlete. However, McClelland's theory applies equally to people, regardless of individual differences such as race, gender or age.

There may also be cultural differences between different populations in relation to which needs are most important, and the ways in which they can be satisfied. For example, in less wealthy nations, life satisfaction is more likely to be associated with having safety needs met than with the satisfaction of self-esteem needs (Oishi et al., 1999). In contrast, McClelland's approach does not consider that culture (or any other individual differences) can influence our motivation needs.

ISSUES AND DEBATES

Freewill is the idea that we have choices about how we behave. However, according to need theories, motivation is based on pre-determined set of needs that influence our behaviours.

Cognitive theories

Cognitive theories differ from need theories in that they examine the thinking processes involved in motivation.

Locke and Latham's goal-setting theory

Goal-setting theory opposes McClelland's idea that internal motives were largely unconscious and measurable only by projective tests. Locke and Latham

based their work on the assumption that human behaviour is affected by conscious planning and intention.

KEY WORD

goal: the desired result of a person's work or effort

Locke (1981) suggested that goal setting was a key motivator in getting people to work hard and improve their performance. Locke and Latham (1984) suggest that setting specific goals produces higher levels of performance than setting vague goals. For example, stating as a goal 'I want to earn more money' is too vague and is less likely to affect the way a person behaves. In contrast, someone who states 'I want to earn $50 more each week' will be more likely to achieve this. Specific goals are often harder to achieve and present a greater challenge; goal-setting theory claims that this will make the individual try harder. This idea sound counter-intuitive but Locke and Latham (1984) provide evidence from many studies that support this claim.

Goal-setting theory provides guidance on how to set goals, based on five key principles which are referred to as 4C F standing for Clarity, Challenge, Complexity, Commitment and Feedback.

- *Clarity*: goals should be clear, specific, unambiguous and measurable.
- *Challenge*: goals should be relevant, make the goal setter feel they are being stretched so that achieving the goals is a genuine reward.
- *Complexity*: goals must be achievable so it is best to break down complex goals into separate tasks to be achieved within a specific time period.
- *Commitment*: goals must be understood and accepted by the goal setter in order to be effective. Goals set by other people are less likely to be accepted/committed to by the person trying to achieve them.
- *Feedback*: goal setting must involve feedback on task progress and achievement.

The importance of feedback in this model is crucial. If the only assessment was whether the goal had been reached or not, it is possible that many weaknesses in performance may be missed. There may be easier, quicker or even more effective ways of achieving the same goal. Feedback needs to be positive and constructive and focus on the strategies used. This process should also allow for reflection by the individual rather than simply feedback from a superior.

The SMART method of goal setting developed from these five principles. SMART targets are targets or goals that are Specific, Measurable, Attainable, Relevant and have a Timescale. For example, a SMART target in business would look like this:

Specific: I want to set up a business selling jewellery I have made myself.

Measurable: I will aim to sell five items on eBay to begin with.

Attainable: I will start with an eBay store and then research other options.

Relevant: I will be turning my hobby into a money-making enterprise.

Timescale: I will aim to list five items on eBay within one week and 20 items within two weeks.

ACTIVITY 9.1

SMART targets are used in many schools. For example, teachers might use SMART targets to help define specific ways for students to improve their knowledge or skills.

1 Write three SMART targets for your A Level Psychology course.

2 Explain whether you think this method of goal-setting a useful strategy.

Vroom's VIE (expectancy) theory

Like the cognitive theory of goal setting, expectancy theory (Vroom, 1964) proposes that workers are rational beings whose decision-making is guided by logical thought processes. However, the emphasis of this theory is that potential costs and rewards play a significant role in motivation to work. Vroom recognised that a worker's performance would be influenced by a wide range of factors, including knowledge, skills and experience as well as individual characteristics such as personality and different ambitions and goals. Despite this, he claims that all workers can be motivated if the following conditions are met:

- there is a clear relationship between effort and performance
- the favourable performance is rewarded
- the reward satisfies a need
- the desire to satisfy the need is strong enough to make the effort worthwhile

Vroom proposes an equation, which states that:

$$\text{motivation} = \text{expectancy} \times \text{instrumentality} \times \text{valence}$$

KEY WORD

expectancy: a state of hopefulness that an event or experience will happen

Expectancy is the perception of how much effort relates to performance as well as a worker's confidence in what they are capable of doing. Expectancy can be modified by the provision of additional resources or by training and supervision (see Figure 9.3)

Instrumentality is the perception of how much effort will be rewarded and whether workers actually believe that they will be given the reward that has been offered. Instrumentality will be positively affected if the management makes sure that rewards are always given as promised. Valence is the perception of the strength or the size of the reward as well as the extent to which this reward is needed or wanted. It is likely that a small reward will produce low motivation regardless of the values of expectancy and instrumentality, and similarly if the value of any one of the three is low, then overall motivation is likely to be low.

Figure 9.3: Offering employees opportunities for training and development can change their expectancy

In this section, we have been examining motivation from the cognitive approach. Both goal-setting and expectancy theory focus on how an individual perceives the situation that they are in, rather than the situation itself.

As with the previous section, much of this work is theoretical although clearly these ideas have been tested in real-life situations. While this will give the research high *ecological validity*, it is likely to be difficult to *generalise* to other different organisations due to the huge number of variables involved. In other words, it will never be possible to conduct highly controlled research when dealing with real organisations and their employees and so conclusions need to be considered carefully.

ISSUES AND DEBATES

As with the previous section, both theories can be usefully and effectively *applied to the workplace*. For example, in goal-setting when goals are specific, measurable and achievable they are shown to be more effective. Roberts (1994) points out that a manager cannot simply say 'do your best' and expect this to motivate employees. It is therefore crucial that we understand exactly what types of goal and what type of feedback will be most useful. Expectancy theory can also be applied in similar ways such as involving workers in the goal-setting process and ensuring that rewards are appropriate and will be valued by workers.

In contrast with needs theories, cognitive theories of motivation might be considered more *holistic*. Although Maslow's hierarchy of needs in particular is often described as holistic, the theory does not explain the thinking processes behind an individual's motivation. Both goal-setting and expectancy theory consider in detail a wide range of factors including how a person's perception of effort and their estimation of reward and time influence their motivation to achieve.

Motivators at work

Intrinsic and extrinsic motivation

ACTIVITY 9.2

Do you have a job or would you like one? If so, why? Write down all the reasons you can think of before reading any further.

Now think about the job that you would like to have when you have finished your education. Write down all the reasons why you would like to have this job.

KEY WORDS

intrinsic: something that comes from within; internal

extrinsic: something that comes from the outside; external

Motivation can be internal or external. Internal (or **intrinsic**) motivators come from within and include factors such as enjoyment or a sense of satisfaction or achievement. This means that motivation comes from the actual performance of the task rather than from the potential consequences of completing the tasks. In contrast the potential rewards are called external motivators. External (or **extrinsic**) motivators create a sense of motivation because of an external reward such as money, promotion and bonuses.

Different types of organisation might offer different types of motivator. For example, someone who works in finance may experience high levels of external motivators such as the amount they can earn and the potential for additional bonuses. In contrast someone who chooses to work in some aspect of health and social care is unlikely to experience the same level of financial reward but may be rewarded and motivated by as a sense of helping others and making a difference.

ACTIVITY 9.3

Look back at the list you made in the Activity 9.2 regarding a job you would like to have in the future. Identify which reasons are internal motivators and which are external motivators. Was there a difference between the job you have now and the job that you would like to have in the future?

Extrinsic motivators: types of reward system

Reward systems vary from organisation to organisation and can include pay, bonuses, profit sharing and performance-related pay. Pay may be linked to performance so the harder or quicker someone works, the more money they can earn. Bonuses are sometimes offered in addition to a salary and can be significant sums of money in sectors such as finance. Profit sharing by an organisation means that a percentage of the company profit is shared among all the workers. This gives workers a stronger sense of belonging to the organisation and can lead to increased motivation. These systems might not be available in all organisations as not all organisations are set up to make a profit. Most health and education organisations, for example, do not have profit as their primary aim.

It is uncertain whether monetary rewards are successful in improving **productivity** because evidence exists on both side of this debate. A paper by de Waal and Jansen (2011) summarises a number of research findings in this area. They cite studies demonstrating that over half the growth in productivity in Chinese State industries could be attributed to the use of bonuses (Yao, 1997, cited in de Wall & Jansen) and studies demonstrating the positive effects of performance-related pay (Belfield & Marsden, 2005). Hollowell (2005, cited in de Wall & Jansen) claimed that those organisations paying their senior executives on high performance-related pay scales maintained strong stock markets presences.

However, de Waal and Jansen also offer contradictory evidence. They cite studies that demonstrate that in organisations with very high inequalities (the difference between the highest paid and the lowest paid member of the organisation) there is also very high turnover of staff. This would suggest that any gains in productivity shown by the high performers are outweighed by the costs to the low performers. Finally, research conducted in a number of organisations in the UK (Fattorusso et al., 2007) and Holland (Duffhues & Kabir, 2008) found no relationship between the size of bonus payments and performance.

KEY WORD

productivity: how much work is completed over a certain period of time or with a certain amount of effort

Intrinsic motivators: non-monetary rewards

Non-monetary rewards include praise, respect, recognition, empowerment and a sense of belonging. In an organisational context, monetary rewards are usually promised from the start. For most employees, there will be a clear understanding of how much they will be paid, for example. This may affect your extrinsic motivation: you go to work to earn a salary.

Praise, respect and recognition, however, can also be extremely motivating and act as positive reinforcement. Think about how you feel when you are praised for an achievement in the classroom. This is not an external reward like money: instead, it is a reward that makes you feel good about yourself. Achievement of a difficult task or even simply the completion of a task can lead to a feeling of empowerment. Empowerment makes you feel as though you can achieve anything! Unlike extrinsic monetary rewards, recognition is not promised from the start and only happens when a worker is recognised for their contributions or achievements. Not everyone is motivated by money all of the time and not all organisations are designed to make a profit.

Praise and recognition in organisational settings can take many forms: as simple as an employer thanking an employee for completing a project. Recognition can be made more formal by the employee receiving a formal letter of thanks from their manager or someone more senior. Public forms of recognition include award ceremonies or 'employee of the month' schemes (see Figure 9.4). Employees can also be empowered at work through receiving additional responsibility, such as controlling a particular aspect of their job or working environment.

Figure 9.4: Employee of the month schemes offer recognition to staff and act as a form of intrinsic motivator

Evidence also suggests that **staff turnover** can also be reduced by non-monetary rewards. Building positive affective relationships between managers and workers and making sure that workers know that they are appreciated and that their efforts are valued makes people more likely to stay and increases their satisfaction ratings (Brown & Armstrong, 1999). This type of intrinsic motivator develops an employee's sense of belonging.

> **KEY WORD**
>
> **staff turnover:** the number of employees who leave an organisation during a certain period of time

Rose (1998) estimates that around 75% of organisations in the UK had some form of non-monetary recognition scheme. Reed (a large UK based recruitment company) found that recognition was rated as the most important factor in achieving job satisfaction, whereas salary was rated sixth. The issues of staff turnover, absenteeism and job satisfaction will be explored later in this chapter.

Self-determination theory

Self-determination is a theory of motivation and personality that is based on the assumption that human behaviour is motivated by an innate need for growth and improvement. Deci and Ryan (1985) first used the term 'self-determination' in their 1985 book *Self-Determination and Intrinsic Motivation in Human Behavior*. Self-determination theory focuses on intrinsic motivation rather than extrinsic motivation as the primary method by which individuals improve themselves. Self-determined behaviours are likely to be intrinsically driven and targeted at feeling good about oneself, or feelings of enjoying the behaviour.

> **KEY WORD**
>
> **self-determination theory:** a theory of motivation concerned with intrinsic needs and personal growth

Deci and Ryan identify the following innate psychological needs that are essential to self-determination and well-being:

- *Competence*: this is the need to effectively deal with our surroundings. Competence is possessed by a person who has sufficient knowledge or skills to complete a task, interact effectively within their environment, and achieve their goals. Positive feedback, e.g. recognition, can enhance competence, but negative feedback or undertaking a task that is too challenging can undermine feelings of competence.

- *Relatedness*: the need to belong to a group or be close to others. This is possessed by a person who feels a sense of belonging or closeness to other people. Relatedness helps the person access support to achieve goals and is enhanced when the person feels wanted in a group. Conflict with or exclusion from groups can reduce relatedness.

- *Autonomy*: the ability to feel independent and in control of one's choices. Autonomy is possessed by a person who feels in control of their choices and their future. Being given freedom to monitor and manage their own behaviour enhances autonomy; being controlled or coerced reduces autonomy.

Deci and Ryan argue that self-determination can directly affect motivation to work. For example, if a person holds the belief that they can manage their own planning and behaviour, they can also find the motivation to complete their goals. Extrinsic rewards can undermine self-determination. Offering external rewards for behaviour that is already intrinsically motivated reduces feelings of autonomy that can make the behaviour dependent on external forces. For example, a teacher who goes into school during the holidays to tidy up their classroom is acting autonomously; they want their classroom to look clean and be functional for them and their students. If they were offered extra pay to do this task, this reward takes the place of self-determination (e.g. 'love of the job') and may make the teacher's motivation increasingly dependent on monetary reward.

RESEARCH METHODS

This section can be considered to take a behaviourist approach to the topic of motivation as it considers the effect of certain outcomes (reinforcements) on behaviour rather than focusing on the cognitive aspects. As a result, it can be challenging to conduct research testing observable motivation in the workplace. This is because one's motivation is a cognitive aspect that cannot be directly observed; studying motivation in this way will rely on self-report, which can introduce bias. Employees may not even be fully aware of their motivations or able to convey these to researchers.

Studies that use self-report methods to assess the importance of extrinsic and intrinsic needs might be subject to *social desirability bias*. For example, participants may prefer to indicate their motivation is more intrinsic than extrinsic as they do not want to appear to be greedy or that they do not enjoy their jobs. This bias impacts on the *validity* of the research relating to theories of motivation.

ISSUES AND DEBATES

Studying the different factors that act as motivators in work can be *applied to the real world*. It is useful for managers of teams and organisations when considering what motivates their workers. For example, a monetary reward is not always possible and recognising that non-monetary rewards such as praise and recognition can be equally effective (in some organisations at least) may ensure that managers recognise the value of these rewards to ensure the motivation of their workers. Analysing sources of motivation is also useful for individuals when they are deciding the jobs or sectors to work in.

However, we can also consider individual differences here; what motivates one person may not motivate another. The *individual–situational* debate is also relevant as the situation may well interact with the individual in determining the most effective motivators. Someone working in a highly creative environment is likely to be motivated by praise and recognition for their creativity whereas non-monetary rewards may not be as effective in the competitive business world.

ACTIVITY 9.4

Design a laboratory-based study to test whether praise or money would be a more effective motivator for the completion of a boring, repetitive task. Include the following:

1   A testable hypothesis you could use

2   The independent and dependent variables you would be manipulating and measuring

3   The sample you would select

4   Brief details of a procedure

5   One strength and one weakness of your proposed study

Key study: Landry et al. (2019)

Landry, A.T., Zhang, Y. Papachristopoulos, K., & Forest, J. (2019). Applying self-determination theory to understand the motivational impact of cash rewards: new evidence from lab experiments. *International journal of Psychology, 55*(3), 487–498.

Context

Monetary rewards are used by many organisations as a way of encouraging productivity and ensuring staff retention. Such rewards are usually presented as a form of extrinsic motivation. However, they are high cost to the employer, and the research is mixed about the relationship between extrinsic motivation and employee performance.

The researchers in this study were interested to test whether the way in which a reward was presented (as either supporting or controlling a psychological need) could influence a person's performance.

Main theories and explanations

As we have seen in earlier in this topic, financial incentives can have a motivational impact on employees and are used by many organisations. However, self-determination theory (Deci & Ryan, 1985) argues that motivation is primarily intrinsic and that rewards should be meaningful and support psychological needs of competence, relatedness and autonomy.

Each of the three psychological needs identified within self-determination theory can be either supported or controlled (i.e. threatened) either by the nature or the meaning of the reward itself. In other words, the same reward presented in two different ways can have different effects on employee motivation and performance.

Aims

This study investigated the effect on individuals' motivation and performance when a reward was presented as either supporting or controlling the individual's psychological needs.

The hypotheses tested in this study were:

Hypothesis 1: Presenting rewards in an autonomy-supportive way would lead to better performance than presenting rewards in an autonomy-controlling way.

Hypothesis 2: The effect of supporting rewards on performance is to support psychological needs and increase intrinsic motivation, whereas the effect of controlling rewards on performance is to frustrate psychological needs and increase extrinsic motivation.

Design

Participants in Study 1 of this study were 123 French-speaking students from a Canadian university, 60% of whom were female. The students had a mean age of 23 years and were a volunteer sample who gave their informed consent to participate. They were randomly assigned to one of two conditions, making this an independent groups design.

The independent variable of reward was operationalised as either 'autonomy-threatening' or 'autonomy-supported'. Participants were asked to read a paragraph of instructions about the task they had to perform. In the autonomy-supportive condition, a reward for participation was offered 'as a token of appreciation for their contribution'. In the autonomy-controlling condition, the reward was mentioned 'to reinforce the performance standards for the task at hand'.

Participants completed a shortened version of a self-report known as the Basic Psychological Needs Satisfaction Scale in which they rated the extent to which they felt their psychological needs were fulfilled or frustrated. Participants also reported their intrinsic and extrinsic motivation using the Situational Motivation Scale.

The task participants had to complete in Study 1 was to work out a short series of anagrams. To control for confounding variables, participants were asked to rate the value of the reward they had been offered to control for individual differences in perception of value. Another control measure was that participants completed an affect (emotion) scale in order to control for individual differences in their mood after reading the instruction paragraph.

Results, findings and conclusions

The self-report measures showed that psychological need satisfaction (autonomy-supported) was positively related to intrinsic motivation and performance. Psychological need satisfaction was also negatively related to extrinsic motivation. Psychological need frustration (autonomy-controlled) was negatively related to intrinsic motivation and performance, and positively related to extrinsic motivation.

This means that presenting a reward in a way that supports autonomy leads to better performance on the anagram task than presenting the reward in a way that controls or threatens autonomy. This is because supporting needs involves intrinsic, rather than extrinsic, motivation.

The conclusion was that using rewards that support psychological needs can increase intrinsic motivation and overall employee performance more effectively than rewards that undermine psychological needs.

Evaluation

The sample for Study 1 consisted of volunteers from one university, which is an unrepresentative sample. The students were all volunteers undertaking an educational course on organisational behaviour. However, the study was replicated on a larger more diverse sample in Study 2 and achieved the same results, indicating the *generalisability* of the findings were good.

This was a laboratory experiment with high levels of control and therefore *validity*. For example, individual differences in mood and perceived value of reward were taken into account. This means the researchers can be more confident that manipulating the independent variable of reward (as either autonomy-controlled or autonomy-supported) had an effect on the dependent variable of performance.

However, as a laboratory experiment, the environment was artificial and unlike a workplace. The task of anagram-solving also lacked mundane realism as it is not reflective of a typical task a person would encounter in their workplace. This means the *ecological validity* of the study was low. Using this research method meant that the study was also high in *reliability* as the instruction, task, timings and scales used were all standardised.

The findings of this study are *applicable to* real-life. Employers can use intrinsic motivation, e.g. rewards that support autonomy relatedness and competence, to improve the motivation and performance of their employees. This may also reduce staff turnover and boost productivity. One way to increase autonomy could be to give leadership roles to employees, for example by taking the lead on a presentation or responsibility for part of a project. This application can be extended to other psychological needs such as competence, which can be supported in the workplace through constructive feedback. This can help individuals understand how to improve their work and can make them feel valued.

The debate over *freewill and determinism* is also relevant to the study by Landry et al. Determinists argue that the cause of human behaviour exists outside the individual. As this research shows, a person's motivation and performance are determined by how their psychological need is fulfilled or threatened by the external environment (i.e. the meaning given to the reward). However, self-determination theory does view external factors as intertwined with internal desire for growth and improvement that allow us to have freewill and pursue autonomy.

Questions

1   a   Define what is meant by 'self-actualisation' in Maslow's hierarchy of needs.

    b   Why might self-actualisation not be possible for all employees?

2   Explain one way in which Vroom's expectancy theory can be used within a real organisation.

3   Compare internal and external motivation.

9.2 Leadership and management

Traditional and modern theories of leadership

ACTIVITY 9.5

This section is about leadership and management. Research the meanings of leadership and management. Make a chart illustrating the similarities and differences between the terms.

Universalist theories

Universalist theories of leadership all look at the personal qualities or characteristics that are shared, i.e. universal to all great leaders.

One of the best known of these theories is the 'Great Man Theory' first proposed by philosopher Thomas Carlyle in 1840 and now referred to as the 'Great Person Theory'. This theory argues that great leaders are born with certain traits that enable them to rise to power and lead using their instincts. According to this theory leaders are born and not made – in other words this can be understood as part of the nature–nurture debate and will be considered in the issues and debates feature.

A second universalist theory is that of a charismatic leader: someone with the **charisma** and the interpersonal skills to inspire and lead others. Such people tend to have excellent public speaking skills and high levels of confidence. They are sometimes described as 'visionaries' and are often unconventional in their approach and may even display unstable behaviours. Charismatic leaders often challenge legitimate authority and may act illegally.

A third universalist theory of leaders is **transformational** leadership. A transformational leader like Martin Luther King Jr is an inspiration to their followers, enabling them to achieve big or unexpected change (Figure 9.5). Transformational leaders support followers to think for themselves to mobilise change. They care about their followers, encourage them and uphold moral values.

Figure 9.5: Martin Luther King Jr can be considered a transformational leader for inspiring his followers to challenge social injustice in 1960s USA

KEY WORDS

charisma: the quality of being charming or appealing to others in a way that inspires devotion

transformational: the ability to produce a significant change in a situation

Behaviourist theories

Behavioural theories of leadership look at the specific behaviours shown by leaders rather than the personal qualities of leaders.

Researchers at Ohio State University (Stogdill & Coons, 1957) have collated data from numerous studies of leaders and their workers and have identified over 100 different behaviours shown by leaders. Through further analysis these behaviours were shown to fall into two distinct categories. The categories are independent of each other, and every leader could be classified as 'high' or 'low' in the types of behaviour they show:

- *Initiating structure*: this includes allocating tasks to people, creating groups and defining their goals, setting deadlines and ensuring that they are met and making sure that workers are working to a set standard.

- *Consideration*: this is the category of behaviours shown by leaders who express a genuine concern for the feelings of workers. These leaders will establish a rapport with workers and show trust and respect. They will listen to workers more often than the other category of leader and will try to improve performance by boosting self-confidence.

A similar set of studies were conducted at the University of Michigan and this also produced two main types of behaviour shown by leaders. These types are very similar to the ones identified by Stogdill and Coons, but were referred to as:

- *Task-oriented behaviours:* not surprisingly, this refers to behaviours that focus specifically on the task to be completed. Leaders focus on the structure (as in the 'initiating structure' leadership behaviour category described previously) and will set targets and standards, supervise and monitor workers and progress.

- *Relationship-oriented behaviours:* these leaders have a focus on the well-being of the workforce. Leaders would spend time examining and understanding the interpersonal relationships between workers and those between workers and managers. This type of behaviour overlaps with the 'consideration' leadership behaviour described previously.

Adaptive challenges

As organisations grow ever larger and more complex, it could be argued that traditional forms of leadership are no longer suitable. If these traditional methods are not working, then there is a need to change or a need for adaptation. Working practices and organisational norms and values that made an organisation successful in the past may now be irrelevant and the organisation must confront the need for change.

Heifetz (2009) and Heifetz et al. (1997) define leadership as the 'art of mobilising people (in organisations and communities) to tackle tough issues, adapt and thrive' (2009). The argument is that leadership itself has to change. Rather than leading by providing solutions, the leader must lead by shifting the responsibility for change to the workforce.

This may be distressing for some people as employees may have to take on new roles, learn new skills, align with new values or even accept that there is no longer a place for them within the organisation. Employees are used to management solving problems for them and this will also have to change. The role of the adaptive leader is no longer to maintain and protect the organisational norms and values but to allow disorientation, conflict and challenge to create a new organisation that can survive. The differences between traditional leadership and adaptive leadership are summarised in Table 9.1.

Heifetz et al. (2009) offer six key principles of adaptive leadership and these are as follows:

1 'Get on the balcony'. An adaptive leader needs to see the whole picture and to view the organisation and the way it works as if they were observing from above.

2 Identify the adaptive change. An adaptive leader needs to not only identify the need for change

but be able to determine the nature and extent of the change required, be that to organisational structure, values, working practices or working relationships.

3 Regulate distress. Adaptive change will both stress and distress those who are experiencing it. This cannot be avoided but it can be managed. The pressure needs to be enough to motivate people to change but not so much that it overwhelms them. The adaptive leader needs to be able to tolerate the uncertainty and frustration and to communicate confidence.

4 Maintain disciplined attention. An adaptive leader must be open to contrasting points of view. Rather than avoiding or covering up issues that are difficult or disturbing, they must confront the issues directly.

5 Give the work back to the people. An adaptive leader must recognise that everyone in the organisation has special access to information that comes only from their experiences in their particular role. Adaptive leaders must step back from the traditional role of telling people what to do and, by allowing them to use their special knowledge, recognise that they are best placed to identify the solutions to the problems.

6 Protect voices of leadership from below. Heifetz et al. argue that 'giving a voice to all people is the foundation of an organisation that is willing to experiment and learn'. In many organisations, those who speak up are silenced. An adaptive leader needs to listen to these voices to learn of impending challenges. Ignoring them can be fatal for the organisation.

As an example of leadership styles, Heifetz and Linsky, in their book *Leadership on the Line* (2002), refer to Henry Fonda's character in the film *12 Angry Men* (see Figure 9.6) as an example of the adaptive leader in action.

Leader's responsibilities	Type of organisational work	
	Technical / routine	Adaptive
Direction	Define problems and solutions	Identify challenges and ask questions
Orientation	Establish clear responsibilities for staff	Question current roles and responsibilities
Protection	Protect organisations from threats	Allow organisation to be exposed to some pressure
Managing conflict	Resolve disputes and keep order	Let conflict and problems emerge
Shaping norms	Maintain existing norms	Identify and question norms

Table 9.1: Leadership responsibilities in technical/routine and adaptive work situations (adapted from Heifetz, 2001)

Fonda plays the only jury member who initially votes 'not guilty' in a murder trial. Through the film, his behaviour encourages the other jurors to explore their own prejudices and biases and to look at the evidence from different perspectives. Heifetz and Linksy claim that Fonda's character is a powerful example of adaptive leadership.

Figure 9.6: Henry Fonda's character in the film *12 Angry Men* is an example of adaptive leadership

RESEARCH METHODS

The work conducted by Ohio State University and by the University of Michigan brings together huge amounts of data collected from a wide range of organisations and individuals. This gives their findings a great deal of support, and conclusions drawn from these findings can be *generalised* easily.

In contrast, Heifetz adaptive model of leadership has not been investigated thoroughly through empirical research studies. This means there is a lack of evidence to suggest whether the theory can be applied to organisations in the real world, so it is difficult to judge whether the principles and claims of the theory are *valid*.

ISSUES AND DEBATES

Theories of leadership raise a number of crucial evaluation issues. To begin with, we will consider the *nature versus nurture debate*. Are leaders born

CONTINUED

or made? The Great Person Theory described previously would certainly be on the nature side of this debate while the other theories may leave room for some development of leadership skills. For example, the behaviourist theories of leadership argue that leadership presence can be developed. The arguments proposed by Heifetz et al. also suggest that leadership needs to able to adapt and change and that leadership skills can be learned.

The theory of adaptive leadership also allows us to consider the *individual–situational debate*. Heifetz et al. argue strongly for the need for adaptive leadership where the more traditional styles of leadership have failed or when the situation is highly uncertain. This might occur in an organisation that has just been taken over by another, or when the organisation is in financial difficulty. As with the earlier theories of leadership, we can also consider whether some individuals may be better able to provide adaptive leadership than others.

Finally, it is important to consider the issue of *usefulness or application to everyday life*. Traditional, modern, behaviourist and adaptive theories of leadership theories have been applied within organisations all over the world. Understanding the type of leadership exhibited by a leader can make a significant contribution to the success or otherwise of a wide variety of organisations.

Leadership style

Styles of leader behaviour

There have been many attempts to explain different styles of leader behaviour and we will examine one of these explanations by Muczyk and Reimann in this section. Research prior to this explanation had focused on benefits of the **democratic** style of leadership. A democratic style of leader is a person who maintains the ideal of social equality and values the input of followers in making decisions within an organisation. The contrasting style of **autocratic** leadership is one in which leaders control the decision-making and keep a rigid distinction between them and their followers.

democratic leadership: behaviour style in which the leader shares decision-making with group members

autocratic leadership: behaviour style in which the leader controls all the decisions with little to no input from group members

Muczyk and Reimann (1987) argue that democraic leadership may not always be the most effective and that it may be harmful in some situations. They argue that 'leadership is a two-way street, so a democratic style will be effective only if followers are both willing and able to participate actively in the decision-making process. If they are not, the leader cannot be democratic without also being 'directive' and following up very closely to see that directives are being carried out properly' (page 301).

In this quote, Muczyk and Riemann are emphasising the difference between 'participation' and 'direction'. They view direction as a separate dimension of leadership and one that could work in conjunction with participation.

Combining direction with participation produces four styles of leadership and may help us understand the question of which style of leadership is best in which situation, as shown in Table 9.2.

This means that as well as the democratic/autocratic distinction, there are two further leadership factors that need to be considered:

- *Participation*: low participation would be an autocratic leader and high participation would be a democratic or participative leader.

- *Direction*: low direction would be **permissive** with little or only general supervision and high would be directive, with close supervision and constant follow-up.

KEY WORDS

directive: behaviour style with a high amount of leader direction

permissive: behaviour style with a low amount of leader direction

		Degree of employee participation in decision-making	
		Low	High
Amount of leader direction	High	*Directive autocrat:* Makes unilateral decisions. Supervises workers closely. Useful when there is a need for quick decisions and supervision of new staff or poor managers	*Directive democrat:* Invites full participation in decisions. Monitors closely. Useful when there is a need for complex decisions involving many experts, needing an overall direction
	Low	*Permissive autocrat:* Leader makes decisions themselves. Allows staff to choose how to implement these decisions. Useful where tasks are relatively simple or where staff are highly skilled and need little supervision	*Permissive democrat:* Seen as 'ideal' leader in (primarily American) literature. Invites high degree of participation in decisions. Allows for autonomy of implementation. Good for highly skilled, trusted employees

Table 9.2: Muczyk and Reimann (1987)'s four styles of leader behaviours

The directive behaviour refers to how the leader deals with what happens after the decision has been made. A non-directive leader (permissive) will leave their followers to decide how to reach the goal and will offer very little direction or guidance. A directive leader, however, will specify how tasks are to be completed and will follow up progress throughout the implementation stage.

One of the key problems in previous research is that researchers have tended to see decision-making and the execution of this decision to be the same thing. This is a crucial point as clearly the process of making a decision is quite separate from the process of ensuring that this decision is carried through. Deciding that something should happen is not the same as ensuring that it does happen.

ACTIVITY 9.6

1   Select a leader of an organisation of your choice (e.g. a politician, headteacher/principal or the leader of a business).

2   Research the leadership behaviours of this individual: you may want to use news articles about the leader, their online profile or personal experience.

3   Write a short article analysing their leader behaviours: how do their behaviours fit the four styles presented by Muczyk and Reimann?

Levels of leadership

As well as different styles of leader behaviour, there are different levels of leadership that exist for any style of leader. The idea of three levels of leadership was introduced by James Scouller in a book published in 2011. Scouller explains how leadership presence can be developed and this theory is sometimes referred to as the 3P model of leadership due to the three key elements. The model is usually presented in diagram form as three circles and four outwardly directed arrows, with personal leadership in the centre (Figure 9.7):

- Public leadership: these are the behaviours required to influence groups of people. One example would be holding a meeting in which the individual hopes to influence the opinions of others. The public level

is an 'outer' level of leadership, which is externally facing and visible to others; it deals with group building and trust.

- Private leadership: these are the behaviours involved in influencing individuals. This can involve getting to know individuals within a team and agreeing individual goals that contribute towards group aims. This is also an 'outer' level of leadership as it deals with coaching, managing and even removing individual members from a group.

- Personal leadership: these are the leadership qualities shown by the individual. It relates to the psychological and ethical development of a leader, as well as their technical ability. It includes the skills and beliefs of a leader: their emotions, subconscious behaviours and their 'presence'. Scouller argued that leaders need to 'grow their leadership presence, know-how and skill' through developing their technical know-how and skill, demonstrating the right attitude towards other people and working on psychological self-mastery. This final aspect is the most crucial aspect of developing a leadership presence.

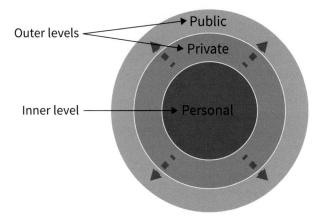

Figure 9.7: Scouller's three levels of leadership model

Scouller argues that personal leadership is the most powerful of the three levels because it impacts on the private and public leadership behaviours of an individual. He compared the effect of personal leadership to the effect to dropping a pebble in a pond and seeing the ripples spreading out from the centre (Figure 9.8), hence the four red arrows pointing outward in Figure 9.7.

Figure 9.8: Personal leadership spreads like ripples

RESEARCH METHODS

In this section, we have considered two theoretical models. It is possible to test these models in real-life situations. The concepts of participative and directive leader behaviours have been tested in diverse organisational settings from hospitals to schools and businesses. These studies are typically based on self-report measures of leader behaviours from leaders and their followers. Using a standardised questionnaire or interview to survey participants can increase the reliability of such studies. However, the research method relies on how accurately leaders and followers can assess their own or other's behaviours, and may also be influenced by *social desirability bias*. Both of these factors can lower the *validity* of research into the influence of leader behaviours.

However, as a theoretical model, Scouller's three levels of leadership model is not as easy to test. The model does not define leadership 'presence' in terms of common personality characteristics. This makes it quite different from other models that typically use psychometric testing to quantify the characteristics of leader. Without a clear basis for *quantitative* measurement, the concept of the 3Ps could be considered vague and unscientific.

ISSUES AND DEBATES

The most obvious evaluation issue to begin with is the *individual–situational* debate. Muczyk and Reimann's four types of leader behaviour consider the relationship between the individual (leader) and the situation directly (the type and needs of an organisation and employees) and makes the point that different leadership styles will be effective in different situations. Likewise, the 3P model of levels of leadership clearly shows that different skills will be required for different situations. For example, it can help us understand why trying to persuade an individual is different to trying to persuade a group.

Additionally, the 3P model is a theory of *nurture* rather than *nature*. It says that 'leadership presence' cannot be defined by common pre-determined qualities or behaviours. Scouller argues that leaders should let their presence develop according to their individual personality and enhance their presence through self-mastery.

The contribution to the area of leadership styles made by Muczyk and Reimann has been significant. Highlighting the difference between making a decision and ensuring that that decision is implemented (followed through to its completion) is extremely valuable and will allow organisations to recognise that as with leadership in general, there are many styles and these styles suit different situations and groups. Ensuring that the right leader is in charge will ensure the successful completion of the task. This explanation is highly applicable to real life.

Leadership style and gender

Gender is a further area of influence on leadership. Researchers in this area are interested in differences between males' and females' leadership styles and the effects of those styles.

Key study: Cuadrado et al. (2008)

Cuadrado, I., Morales, J. F., & Recio, P. (2008). **Women's access to managerial positions: an experimental study of leadership styles and gender.** *The Spanish journal of psychology*, 11(1), 55–65.

KEY WORDS

relationship-oriented: leaders who are focused on supporting and motivating their teams using communication and positive interactions

task-oriented: leaders who are focused on completing the necessary steps or tasks to reach a goal using structure and planning

Context

Women are generally under-represented in positions of power within organisations, in contrast with their male counterparts. One example is the UK National Health Service (NHS), where women constitute three-quarters of the workforce, yet occupy relatively few senior leadership roles. Current data indicate that only 37% of NHS trust directors are women (Taylor & Hartley, 2021).

Researchers have sought to understand the reasons why women experience a 'glass ceiling effect' in management, especially when they hold equal qualifications and experience to men. The glass ceiling is a metaphor for the invisible barrier that prevents a certain group of people (in this case, women) from progressing beyond a certain level in a hierarchy.

Main theories and explanations

One explanation for the under-representation of women in managerial positions is that women are likely to be less popular if they use male-stereotypical leadership behaviours or styles. Because women are stereotyped as being cooperative, gentle and even passive this means that behaviours that do not fit people's expectations may be a barrier to career progression. In other words, organisations are less likely to promote women to positions of power and authority because many of the qualities that we have seen in the successful leader behaviours in this topic are incongruent with how society expects women to behave, i.e. in a democratic, **relationship-oriented** style.

The effect of this gender difference is that either women choose to use leadership styles that are less effective, or if they do use stereotypically male styles, they face prejudice from their organisations in terms of earning a promotion. In this study, the researchers consider the explanation that females receive less favourable evaluations of their work when they use autocratic and **task-oriented** styles that are considered stereotypically male.

Aims

The study first aimed to investigate the effect of female and male leaders using stereotypical or non-stereotypical leadership styles on their work evaluations. The second aim was to test whether the sex of the evaluator would have an impact on how well female or male leaders were evaluated on their work performance. Cuadrado et al. tested four different hypotheses.

Hypothesis 1: Female leaders will receive less favourable evaluations than male leaders when using stereotypically masculine leadership behaviours.

Hypothesis 2: Male leaders will not receive less favourable evaluations than female leaders when they use stereotypically feminine leadership behaviours.

Hypothesis 3: Female leaders will receive less favourable evaluations from male evaluators than from female evaluators.

Hypothesis 4: Male leaders will receive similar evaluations from both male and female evaluators.

Design

The sample was made up of 136 psychology students from the National Open University of Spain, 53% women (mean age 27 years) and 47% men (mean age 29 years). The participants were told they were taking part in a study on decision-making and were randomly allocated to each experimental condition. This meant the study was a laboratory experiment using an independent groups design.

The independent variables were the sex of the leader (female or male), the sex of the evaluator (female or male) and leadership style (female-stereotypical or male-stereotypical).

The dependent variables were adjective list, **leadership capacity** and **leadership efficacy**.

leadership efficacy: the ability of a leader to produce a desired outcome

leadership capacity: the attitude and knowledge required for effective leadership

Participants were asked to evaluate a supervisor (male or female, depending on which experimental condition they were allocated to) of an emergency medical service. The supervisor was stated to have been occupying their leadership position for a trial period. Participants read a description of the supervisor's behaviour and were asked to complete an anonymous questionnaire to help make an evaluation about the supervisor's work.

Four different versions of the description were written, with the only changes being to the leader's sex (male 'Carlos' or female 'Lucia') and their leadership style (stereotypically masculine / autocratic or stereotypically feminine / democratic). The narrative was a description of the supervisor's behaviour.

The questionnaires that were used to measure the dependent variables all used a seven-point Likert scale (1 = never applicable to the leader, 7 = always applicable to the leader) and were:

1 A list of seven positive and seven negative adjectives that the participants had to rate to help judge the image the participants had formed of the leader. Positive adjectives included intelligent, honest and clever, while negative adjectives included forgetful, bossy or discouraging.

2 A measure of four items of leadership capacity, again with a seven-point Likert scale of agreement. This included items such as 'X is a competent supervisor'.

3 A measure of leadership effectiveness with five items with a scale of agreement. This included statements such as 'X does not perform his/her works as a supervisor well enough'.

Results, findings and conclusions

It had been expected that using a stereotypically feminine style of leadership would disadvantage supervisors and that participants would rate this style worse than the stereotypically masculine style (Hypotheses 1 and 2). However, the graph of results shown in Figure 9.9 indicate that the democratic, feminine style was favoured in both female and male leaders. The description of the supervisors who adopted this style were scored most highly across the measures of adjective list, leadership capacity and performance efficacy. This finding was true of both male and female evaluators.

There were no statistically significant differences between the sex of the evaluator and the ratings, meaning that male and female evaluators were very similar overall. The same was true of the sex of the leader; the evaluator's sex had no influence on how they rated male or female supervisors (Hypotheses 3 and 4).

The conclusion of the study was that autocratic, stereotypically masculine leadership is evaluated less favourably than democratic, stereotypically feminine leadership in both female and male leaders. The researchers suggest that the growth in popularity of democratic leadership styles within organisations over recent years may be the reason for the results.

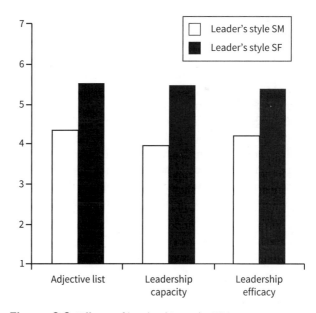

Figure 9.9: Effects of leadership style (SM = stereotypically masculine; SF = stereotypically feminine) on the three dependent variables (adjective list, leadership capacity and leadership efficacy)

Evaluation

The sample consisted of student volunteers of a similar age, which could be considered an *unrepresentative* sample. It is possible that if the study was conducted with a wider range of ages and occupations, the results may be different. This is because stereotypical beliefs may be more or less prevalent in other populations.

This was a laboratory experiment with high levels of *reliability* and *validity*. For example, the descriptive narrative used in the experimental conditions was kept the same apart from the manipulation of leadership style and the sex of the supervisor. This is an example of standardisation of procedure. In contrast, one control in the study was that the participants were randomly allocated to conditions. These aspects of design mean the researchers can be more confident about the relationship between the IVs and DVs.

However, as a laboratory experiment that used a number of self-report scales, the study lacks *ecological validity*. Employers in real organisations are unlikely to use such measures as the only method for evaluating leadership effectiveness; and they rely on more than a description of a leader's work. However, the use of self-reports meant that *quantitative data* were captured for each measurement. This enhances the objectivity and comparability of the findings.

In terms of *applicability to real life*, the findings of this study suggest that organisations should take into account the contributions and the value of feminine styles. Instead of acting as barriers to success in traditionally masculine settings, democratic styles can be advantageous. This means for example that employers could consider the importance of the feminine styles when training individuals for managerial positions. Increasing access for women to leadership positions has great social value in changing harmful gender stereotypes through recognising the value of democratic forms of leadership.

Leaders and followers

Leadership Practices Inventory

Kouzes and Posner (1987) argue that leadership is a 'measurable, learnable and teachable set of behaviours'. They developed the Leadership Practices Inventory (LPI) to measure the extent to which an individual engages in each of the five practices of exemplary leadership that they established through their research with successful leaders. These include modelling desired behaviours, inspiring others, challenging the accepted practices, enabling others and encouraging and rewarding others. The LPI consists of six behavioural statements for each of these practices and examples of these statements are shown in Table 9.3.

Five leadership practices	Examples of behavioural statements
1 Model the way	• 'sets a personal example of what he/she expects of others' • 'is clear about his/her personal philosophy of leadership'
2 Inspire a shared vision	• 'describes a compelling image of what our future could be like' • 'appeals to others to share an exciting dream of the future'
3 Challenge the process	• 'experiments and takes risks even when there is a chance of failure' • 'challenges people to try out new and innovative ways to do their work'
4 Enable others to act	• 'Treats others with dignity and respect' • 'Supports the decisions that people make on their own'
5 Encourage the heart	• 'Praises people for a job well done'. • 'Makes it a point to let people know about his/her confidence in their abilities'

Table 9.3: LPI with examples of behavioural statements

The LPI consists of the individual's self-ratings of the frequency with which they demonstrate these behaviours as well as a number of observer ratings. These are combined on the final profile. Kouzes and Posner strongly believe that leadership is learned rather than something one is born with. This means that the profile that is produced after completion of the LPI does not simply provide a picture of the behaviours that someone exhibits but can be used to identify areas for personal development. They claim that there are many different ways in which different types of people (e.g., introverts versus extroverts) can be developed into successful leaders.

Followership

In this section we have so far focused on leaders. We will consider now the concept of 'followership', because without followers, there could not be leaders. Followership refers to a role held by certain individuals in an organisation, team or group. Specifically, it is the way in which an individual actively follows a leader. It is important to recognise that the role of leader can only be understood by also examining the reciprocal role of follower: Kelley (1988) claims that the study of 'followership' will lead to a better understanding of leadership. The success or failure of a group may not be solely down to the ability of a leader but may also be dependent on how well the followers can follow.

Kelley identified two dimensions that help explain followership. The first of these is independent critical thinking in which individuals are more or less considerate and questioning about what is going on around them. The second dimension is whether the individual is active or passive. Passive behaviour is where followers step back and wait for others to act whereas active followers are motivated to act to meet organisational goals if they see the opportunity.

This gives us five styles of followers (see Figure 9.10), described as follows:

1   The *sheep*: these individuals are passive, lack commitment and require external motivation and constant supervision from the leader. Sheep perform a task they have been given and then stop; they do not use initiative or critical thinking.

2   The *yes-people*: these individuals are committed to the leader and the goal (or task) of the organisation (or group/team). These conformist individuals do not question the decisions or actions of the leader. Further, yes-people will defend their leader when faced with opposition from others.

3   The *survivors*: these individuals are not trail-blazers; they will not stand behind controversial or unique ideas until most people in the group

have expressed their support. These individuals go with the flow and survive changes within the organisation well.

4   The *alienated followers*: these individuals are negative and critical as they question the decisions and actions of the leader. However, they do not often voice such criticism and are fairly passive in carrying out their role.

5   The *effective followers*: these exemplary individuals are positive, active and independent thinkers. Effective followers will not unquestioningly accept the decisions or actions of a leader until they have evaluated them completely. Furthermore, these types of follower can succeed without the presence of a leader.

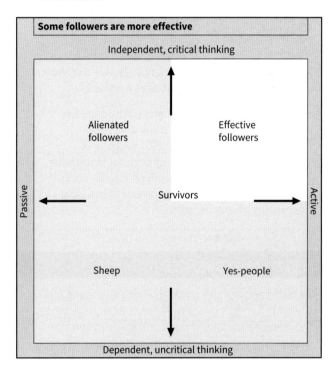

Figure 9.10: Kelley's named types of followers

Kelley also described four main qualities of effective followers:

1   *Self-management*: the ability to think critically, work independently and control one's actions. Followers must be able to manage themselves well for leaders to delegate tasks to these individuals.

2   *Commitment*: an individual's dedication to the goal, vision or cause of a group or organisation. This quality helps keep the follower's morale and energy levels high.

3   *Competence*: possessing the skills and aptitudes necessary to complete the goal or task for the group or organisation. Individuals with this quality often hold skills higher than their average co-worker and pursue knowledge by upgrading their skills (e.g. through further education or training).

4   *Courage*: maintaining one's beliefs and upholding ethical standards, even in the face of dishonest or corrupt leaders. These individuals are loyal, honest and open with their leaders.

RESEARCH METHODS

As with previous sections, the focus of Muczyk and Reimann's and Kelley's work is on theoretical models rather than empirical research such as Cuadrado et al. (2008). A criticism of the LPI model is one that could be made about any *psychometric* test. As we have seen, individuals are prone to *social desirability bias* and may not report their leadership practices accurately.

However, tests like the LPI scale are relatively easy to administer and to mark and produce *quantitative data*, such as self-ratings and observer ratings of each behavioural statement. This type of data can be analysed easily and offer an objective, *reliable* ways of measuring personality characteristics.

ISSUES AND DEBATES

As with many of the other theories that we have examined in this chapter, Kelley's work highlights the importance of the relationship between the leader and the situation; in this case the type of followers that the leader must lead. Increasing our understanding of these relationships is clearly useful for organisations and can be *applied to real-life* in a variety of ways. For example, less effective followers expect training and development to come to them and will not seek it out willingly. According to Kelley, a leader will need to give these employees care and attention in order to get them to undertake training for their roles.

In the context of the *nature versus nurture debate*, Kouzes and Posner argue that leadership is something that can be learned rather than something that we are born with. By exploring the

CONTINUED

personality characteristics of an individual, they can suggest different ways in which different types of people can be developed into successful leaders.

Considering also the *individual–situational debate*, it could also be argued that it should be possible to develop someone into the most successful type of leader based not only on their existing personality type and attitudes but also on the situation (group) that they are going to lead.

Kelley shifts the focus from leaders to followers although does not directly address the question of whether followership qualities are born or made. We might assume that Kelley suggests that the follower types are based on innate qualities of an individual, but it is likely that the follower qualities discussed before the follower types are qualities that could be developed.

Finally, it should be noted that is difficult to construct fair (unbiased) tests of leadership practices. This is a recurring challenge with psychometric testing and is due to cultural differences between the designers of tests and the diverse populations on which they are used. In other words, such tests may reveal more about the assumptions of the test-maker than anything accurate about the behaviours of leaders.

ACTIVITY 9.7

In a pair or small group try a short role play of each of Kelley's five styles of followers. One person can take the role of the leader giving direction, and the other can respond with key behaviours from one of the styles: sheep, yes-people, survivors, alienated or effective followers. See if your partner can guess the type of followers you are role-playing.

Questions

4   Compare the behaviour of a 'task-oriented' leader and a relationship-oriented leader.

5   In Scouller's 'three levels of leadership model', which level did he suggest was the most important and why?

6   Identify the four qualities of effective followers according to Kelley.

9.3 Group behaviour in organisations

Organisations can consist of several people, or even several thousand people. Whatever their size, group behaviour within organisations is a fascinating area of theory and research, partly because of the different ways we think and behave in groups.

Group development and decision-making

Stages of group development

ACTIVITY 9.8

Think about some of the groups that you belong to and consider the following questions:

1 How did this group or groups form?
2 How has the group changed over time?
3 Were there any notable stages of change in the group?

An organisation can be thought of as one large group of individuals. However, there are often many groups within various organisations, and these groups can be of different sizes. For example, these might include operational teams, employees across a company working at the same level or people engaged on a specific project.

Psychologists have been interested in how groups form, establish roles and make decisions. Tuckman's theory of group development has been applied to countless groups since its original proposal in 1965. He proposes that all groups go through the same five stages during their formation: *forming – storming – norming – performing – adjourning*. Each of these stages is explained in Figure 9.11.

Example study

Tuckman and Jensen (2010) reviewed existing research to see whether this model of group development had been tested on participants to investigate any new models in light of Tuckman's hypothesis. One study by Runkel et al. (1971) tested this model on groups of college students who were assigned a written report. Observers watched and recorded the group's behaviour, which was found to support Tuckman's four stage model. This methodology could have been biased, however, as the observers were looking for the group behaviour that would fit the existing model. Tuckman

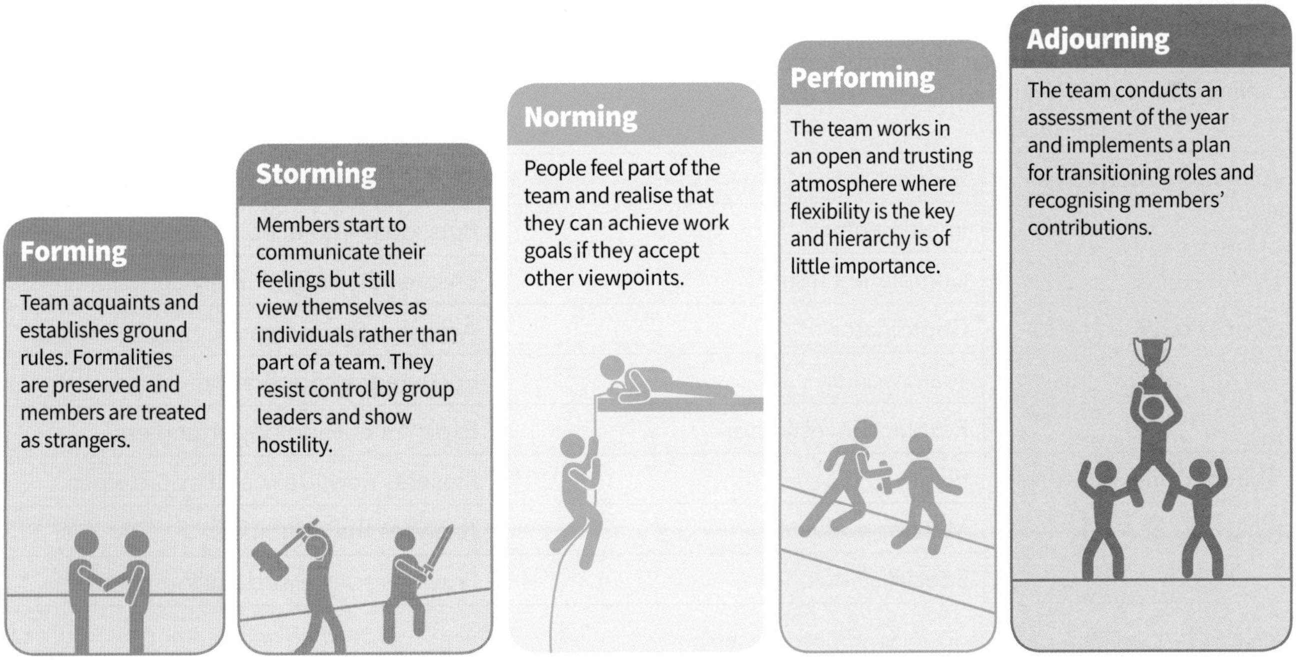
Forming
Team acquaints and establishes ground rules. Formalities are preserved and members are treated as strangers.
Storming
Members start to communicate their feelings but still view themselves as individuals rather than part of a team. They resist control by group leaders and show hostility.
Norming
People feel part of the team and realise that they can achieve work goals if they accept other viewpoints.
Performing
The team works in an open and trusting atmosphere where flexibility is the key and hierarchy is of little importance.
Adjourning
The team conducts an assessment of the year and implements a plan for transitioning roles and recognising members' contributions.

Figure 9.11: Tuckman's stages of group development

and Jensen's review concludes that there remains a lack of research into the model, as well as proposing that the original model be adapted to account for a final stage of group development 'adjourning', in which the group ends its involvement.

Team roles

Belbin's Theory of Team Roles (1981) takes a slightly different approach to understanding group behaviour. Belbin proposes that an ideal team contains people who are prepared to take on different roles. Each of these roles is outlined in Table 9.4.

Action-oriented roles include 'shapers'; people who challenge the team to improve. They are dynamic and usually extroverted people who enjoy stimulating others, questioning established views and finding the best approaches for solving problems. Shapers tend to see obstacles as exciting challenges, although they may also be argumentative and upset colleagues. Next are implementers; the people who get things done. They turn the team's ideas and concepts into practical actions and plans. They tend to be people who work systematically and efficiently and are very well organised. However, they can be inflexible and resistant to change. The third type of action-oriented role is the completer-finisher. These people ensure that projects are completed thoroughly without mistakes with close attention to the smallest of details. Completer-finishers are concerned with deadlines and will push the team to make sure the job is completed on time. They are described as perfectionists and may worry unnecessarily and find it hard to delegate.

People-oriented roles include coordinators; those individuals who take on the traditional team-leader role and guide the team to the objectives. They are often excellent listeners, recognising the value of each team member. They are calm and good-natured, and delegate tasks very effectively. Coordinators, however, may delegate too much personal responsibility, and can be manipulative. In contrast, team workers are the people who provide support and make sure that people within the team are working together effectively. These people are negotiators and are flexible, diplomatic and perceptive. These tend to be popular people who prioritise team cohesion and help people get along but can also be indecisive and struggle to commit. Last, resource investigators are innovative and curious. They explore the available options, develop contacts and negotiate for resources on behalf of the team. They are enthusiastic team members, who identify and work with external stakeholders to help the team accomplish its objective. Resource investigators are outgoing and people are generally positive towards them. However, they may lose enthusiasm quickly.

Of the thought-oriented roles, the plant is the creative person who comes up with new ideas. They thrive on praise but struggle to take criticism. Plants are often introverted and prefer to work on their own; their ideas can sometimes be impractical and they may also be poor communicators. Monitor-evaluators on the other hand are good at analysing and evaluating the ideas that other people propose. They are smart, objective and strategic and weigh the pros and cons of different options before coming to a decision, but can be seen as detached or

Action-oriented roles	Shaper	Challenges the team to improve
	Implementer	Puts ideas into action
	Completer-finisher	Ensures thorough, timely completion
People-oriented roles	Coordinator	Acts as a chairperson
	Team worker	Encourages cooperation
	Resource investigator	Explores outside opportunities
Thought-oriented roles	Plant	Presents new ideas and approaches
	Monitor-evaluator	Analyses the options
	Specialist	Provides specialised skills

Table 9.4: A summary of the team roles proposed by Belbin

unemotional. Last, specialists are people who have specialised knowledge that is needed to get the job done. They pride themselves on their skills and expertise but may sometimes focus on technicalities at the expense of the bigger picture.

Faulty decision-making

Psychologists are interested in studying decision-making within groups, particularly in instances where a group has experienced a poor outcome. The reasoning that underlies such decisions can be described as 'faulty'. One example of faulty group decision-making is groupthink.

Groupthink

Groupthink is defined as a psychological phenomenon that occurs within a group of people, in which the desire for harmony or conformity in the group results in an irrational or dysfunctional decision-making outcome. In other words, the group creates a situation in which a decision is made that would not have been made by individuals.

KEY WORD

conformity: showing behaviour or beliefs that match those of the rest of a group

---

ACTIVITY 9.9

A notorious example of groupthink in the business sector was the collapse of the airline 'Swissair' in 2001.

1 Research the failure of this airline.

2 Apply the principles of groupthink to show the faulty decision-making that occurred.

3 Use your research to script and record a short podcast on this example.

Janis (1971) identified eight different features or symptoms that indicate groupthink and these are:

1 Illusions of invulnerability. This means that members of the group believe that they can do no wrong and can never be in any sort of trouble. This can lead to overly optimistic thinking about likely outcomes and encourages risky decision-making.

2 Unquestioned beliefs. A lack of questioning, particularly from a legal or moral standpoint, can prevent group members from considering all the possible consequences of their decisions.

3 Rationalising. This is where group members ignore warning signs and assume that everything will be alright.

4 Stereotyping. Group decision-making can involve stereotypical views of those who raise issues or point out problems. This can mean that they are ignored or labelled as members of an 'out-group'.

5 Self-censorship. In a group situation we are less likely to listen to our own doubts or misgivings as it appears to us that no one else has any doubts or misgivings. This is a little like the 'diffusion of responsibility' seen in bystanders to an accident when they assume that, since no one else is responding, that there is no real emergency (see Section 5.2 on the study by Piliavin et al.). In this way, everyone is convinced that there is nothing to worry about.

6 Mind guards. Janis described these as 'self-appointed censors to hide problematic information from the group'. We don't want the rest of the group to see that we are worried and so we hide this. Unfortunately, if everyone is feeling the same way and hiding their feelings, this can lead to some very risky decisions.

7 Illusions of unanimity. Groups behaving in the ways that we have just considered will produce the illusion of being unanimous or agreement.

8 Direct pressure to conform. Groups can place dissenters (those who disagree) or those who question under a great deal of pressure, in some cases making them appear as though they are being disloyal or traitorous by asking questions.

KEY WORDS

out-group: a group to which an individual does not belong, in contrast with an in-group which is a group the person feels they belong to

unanimity: the act of being in agreement with all people involved

---

Groupthink can lead to extremely poor decision-making. However, groupthink can also have benefits. Especially when working with a large number of people, it often allows the group to make decisions, complete tasks and finish projects efficiently.

Groupthink is caused by a number of factors. It occurs more in situations where group members are very similar to one another and is more likely to take place if there is an extremely charismatic leader. High levels of stress or situations that are morally challenging also seem to increase the chances of groupthink occurring.

To reduce the risk of groupthink, leaders need to give group members the opportunity to express their own ideas or argue against ideas that have already been proposed. Breaking up members into smaller independent teams can also be helpful. The leader should avoid stating their views too forcefully, especially at the start of the discussion, to ensure that people are able to develop their own views first. If someone is instructed to deliberately present the opposing view regardless of their own personal viewpoints, this can also reduce the likelihood of groupthink occurring and encourage the group members to take a critical perspective.

Cognitive limitations and errors

Individuals in a group decision-making setting are often functioning under substantial cognitive demands. As a result, cognitive and motivational biases can often affect group decision-making adversely. Forsyth (2006) suggests that there are three types of potential bias that may affect group decision-making. He describes each of these as 'sins', meaning a mistake in a non-religious sense.

KEY WORDS

bias: systematic errors in thinking that happen when people are interpreting information. Cognitive bias affects the decisions and judgements that all of us make

fundamental attribution error: a bias in which people pay less attention to situational explanations for behaviour and over-emphasise dispositional explanations

---

The first is called 'Sins of Commission' and refers to the misuse of information in the decision-making process. There are a number of different sub-types of the Sin of Commission. For example, it may involve the use of information in the decision-making process that has already been shown to be inaccurate (belief perseverance). Alternatively, it may be shown by group members remaining committed to a plan because some investment of time or money has already been made even though this plan may now be obviously flawed (known as sunken cost bias). If a group chooses to use information despite having been told to ignore it then they are guilty of 'extra-evidentiary' bias and, finally, falsely overestimating the importance of past knowledge or experience is termed 'hindsight' bias.

The second type of bias is 'Sins of Omission' and this is overlooking key information. One sub-type is the base rate bias: unintentionally ignoring very basic relevant information. Another sub-type is the fundamental attribution error is made when members of a group make decisions based on inaccurate appraisals of an individual's behaviour.

The third category is 'Sins of Imprecision' and this involves relying too heavily on biases and heuristics that over-simplify complex decisions. Sub-types include the availability heuristic (over-reliance on the information that is most easily and readily available), the conjunctive bias (failing to consider relationships between events) and the representativeness heuristic (where group members rely too heavily on decision-making factors that may appear meaningful but are actually just misleading).

RESEARCH METHODS

Tuckman's model was originally proposed as an explanation of small groups and may not be *generalised* to understand the development of larger groups. Tuckman also does not provide guidance on timescales for moving from one stage to another and neither does he recognise that group formation is often cyclical rather than linear.

One practical problem with studying Belbin's team roles is that many groups may be smaller than nine. Belbin recognised this himself and, in practice, group members in small groups will often take on more than one role. Unfortunately, much of the research into Belbin's team roles suggests that many management teams have too many implementers and shapers and not enough plants and team workers. This is likely to mean that plans are formulated and given detail fairly quickly, but that they may lack creativity and may alienate some members (Arnold et al., 2005).

ISSUES AND DEBATES

Tuckman's model of group formation is extremely *applicable to real life* in providing guidance on how groups form and in allowing organisations to see that these stages are part of the normal developmental processes. His work has been extremely influential in understanding the stages that groups pass through.

In contrast, Belbin takes into account differing team roles that group members might have to use, meaning both Belbin and Tuckman's theories together offer a more *holistic* explanation of group development and roles. An important application of Belbin's work (and an important part of the development of a group) is to assess the preferred roles of each team member and to encourage all members to appreciate the characteristics and the strengths of the others. Belbin must be also be given credit for his focus on the need for diversity within teams and the value of different characteristics and skills.

Janis's exploration of groupthink is also useful and can be applied in organisations to ensure that the negative outcomes of groupthink are avoided. The strategies outlined here for remaining aware of groupthink is good practice for any organisation where decision-making occurs regularly. Forsyth

examines cognitive limitations and errors in even more detail and knowledge of these biases would be valuable information within an organisation that takes decisions frequently. Acknowledging and recognising the possibility of these errors will allow an organisation to take steps to reduce them.

Janis's discussion of the risks, benefits and ways of challenging groupthink is linked to the *individual–situational* debate in psychology. Rather than focusing on flaws in an individual's personality, Janis explains faulty decision-making behaviour as being caused by environmental factors. For Janis these include the pressure to conform to group thinking and the effect of in-group/out-group behaviours that lead to group members failing to question unwise decisions.

Janis' symptoms of groupthink originated from his case study examination of the Bay of Pigs disaster. This is an example of *idiographic* rather than *nomothetic* research. This is because he analysed qualitative data, investigating the specific groups of individuals and personalities involved in decision-making in a detailed way. For Janis this was very useful as his results acted as a source of ideas to develop his theory, which has since been used to explain other instances of groupthink.

KEY WORD

in-group: any social group to which a person identifies with as a member

out-group: any group to which a person does not belong or identify with

Individual and group performance

Theories of individual and group performance

In this section we will consider influences on the effort or performance of teams and individuals. Much of this

topic based on the two assumptions from the social approach, which as a reminder are:

1 Our behaviour, cognitions and emotions can be influenced by the actual, implied or imagined presence of others.

2 All of our behaviour, cognitions and emotions can be influenced by social contexts and social environments.

Social facilitation

Norman Triplett observed in 1898 that cyclists performed better (i.e. raced faster) when they were training in a group rather than alone. The term for this phenomenon of improved performance in the presence of others was later labelled **social facilitation** by Allport (1920).

> KEY WORD
>
> **social facilitation:** when people show increased performance or effort in the real or imagined presences of others

There are two types of social facilitation: co-action effects and audience effect. Co-action effect occurs when a person is doing the same task alongside others and demonstrates an improved performance. One example might be a runner who has a personal best time achieved during solo training, and is able to beat that time when they train with other runners (see Figure 9.12). Likewise, increased working from home during the Covid-19 pandemic has led to the rising popularity of 'virtual co-working'. Using webcams, workers can each say hello and set out their task objectives at the start, then sit quietly working at their computers for the duration of a 1-hour session. The intention of this is to encourage accountability and focus through the presence of another person who is also working.

Figure 9.12: Athletes often train alongside others to facilitate improvement to their performance times

These two examples produce what is known as 'co-actor effects' in social facilitation; the other person is also engaged on a similar task. But facilitation can also occur when there are passive observers (people who are not undertaking a similar task) to an individual's performance. This is known as the 'audience effect'.

In addition, the type of task people undertake can affect their performance. This means that the presence of others does not always lead to facilitation. When people are attempting new or difficult tasks, their performance may be worsened by the presence of others. You may be familiar with this feeling of not wanting to be watched doing something for the first time! This is known as social inhibition. In contrast, social facilitation is most readily observed when individuals are performing a task with which they are familiar or find easy.

Three factors are thought to be involved in social facilitation:

Cognitive factors

The real or implied presence of others during a task can create a conflict in which the individual is torn between giving attention to the audience and giving attention to the task. The conflict motivates a person to pay more attention to their task and therefore increases performance.

Affective factors

When others are present, this may cause a person to worry or be anxious about what the audience thinks of them. Will the audience approve or disapprove of the person's behaviour? This influence can improve performance and is known as **evaluation apprehension**.

Physiological factors

As social facilitation theory explains, performance of easy or instinctive behaviours are improved in the presence of others and performance of new or difficult behaviours are often worsened. Zajonc (1966) explains this relationship through '**drive theory**' in which people are aroused by the challenge of a task and presence of the audience and feel compelled to complete the task. According to Zajonc, people rely on their dominant responses to perform tasks and choose behaviours that will most effectively reduce their arousal. On a routine, easy task the dominant response will usually be a straightforward and correct choice. On a challenging task, drive theory suggests that the arousal produced by the audience is stressful and drives us to choose dominant responses that are not always well matched to the task.

KEY WORDS

drive theory: when a person experiences increased internal motivation to reach a goal. These drivers can be primary (i.e. for survival) or secondary (i.e. learned)

evaluation apprehension: when a person experiences arousal from having an audience who they believe may evaluate (show approval or disapproval of) their performance

social loafing: when people perform worse on a task in the presence of others than they would do alone

Social loafing

Social loafing occurs when people do not work as hard in the presence of others as they do alone. This is more prevalent when people feel that their behaviour is not being closely watched. A French engineer called Max Ringelmann (1913) studied agricultural workers and found that although groups outperform individuals, groups usually do not perform as well as they could if each individual was working at maximum capacity independently. In other words, the whole is less than the sum of its parts. Ringelmann believed that some output was lost through workers not coordinating work well together as well as reduced motivation overall.

The cause of social loafing can be explained through social impact theory (Latané, 1981), which proposes that individuals can be both a source and a target of social influence. This means they can either exert social pressure over others or be subject to social pressure themselves. Latané treats this theory as a kind of social law that has three rules of social impact. These are shown in Table 9.5 alongside mathematical equations Latané believes can be used to quantify the amount of social pressure in any given situation.

Social impact theory therefore suggests that when individuals work together, social influence can be diffused across all the group members in the team. If there is insufficient supervision from a manager, the strength, immediacy and number of influencing people is reduced. This means pressure to perform well is significantly reduced, which can cause social loafing.

Rule and equation	Description	Example
Social Force $i = f(SIN)$ 'i' is for impact 'f' is a multiplicative function applied to the bracketed (SIN)	Level of pressure for people to change their behaviour: 1 Strength (S): the power of the influencing person 2 Immediacy (I): how close and recent the influence is 3 Numbers (N): the amount of influencing people	In Milgram's study (obedience) the experimenter (N) was dressed in authoritative clothes (S) and stood in the same room as participants (I)
Psycho-social Law	The first source of influence has the biggest effect on people, but subsequent courses are less effective	Being watched by two people is not twice as bad as being watched by one person
Divisions of Impact $i = f(1/SIN)$	Social force is diffused across all the people it is directed at. If directed at one individual, the pressure is very high, but could be divided if there were more targets	If one learner refuses to obey the request of a teacher, they face much more pressure than if their entire class also refuses

Table 9.5: The rules of social impact theory

The role of culture in group performance

Research studies of social loafing have been conducted across different cultural contexts. Cultures can be categorised as either 'individualistic' or 'collectivistic' cultures in terms of their values around work, family and society as a whole. Research suggests that different types of culture can be more or less prone to social loafing.

> ### KEY WORDS
>
> **individualistic:** a culture in which personal goals are seen as more important than group goals
>
> **collectivistic:** a culture in which group goals are seen as more important than individual wants or needs

An individualistic culture is one characterised by emphasis on personal achievement and competition, even at the expense of group goals. Reliance on others is often discouraged. Social loafing may occur more readily in individualistic cultures within in-groups if a person thinks their contributions are not recognised by the group.

A collectivistic culture is one in which people see themselves as part of a very small number of in-groups and are motivated to work hard within group contexts. People from collectivistic cultures tend to view out-group members with greater distrust in comparison to people from individualistic cultures, meaning that when they compete with out-groups, collectivists may be more competitive. Those from collectivistic cultures are motivated more by the collective outcomes and thus are less likely to exhibit social loafing in their in-groups.

Example study

Earley (1993) used an experiment to investigate the influence of culture, group membership and efficacy (work performance) in relation to social loafing. A volunteer sample of 60 Chinese, 45 Israeli and 60 American managers took part in a task in which they had to sort and complete items in a work inbox (e.g. filling out forms, rating job applications). China and Israel were chosen as examples of collectivistic cultures, while the USA is considered an individualistic culture.

Participants were randomly assigned to one of three group conditions:

1   In-group: participants were told they were part of a group of ten people whose collective performance would be assessed at the end of the task.

Participants were told that they had been grouped together because each had lots of interests in common, were from the same region of the country and were likely to be friends if they got to know one another.

2   Out-group: participants were told they were part of a group of ten people whose collective performance would be assessed at the end of the task. Participants were told as they had been grouped together because they all had very different interests and were from different regions of the country.

3   Individual: participants were told they would be working alone and to work as hard as they could at the task. Participants were asked to write their name at the top of each task in the inbox.

The researchers measured work performance as the number of correctly completed inbox items completed by each participant over 1 hour. Individualism–collectivism, self-efficacy, group efficacy and anticipated outcome were all measured on self-report scales for each participant. Efficacy in this context means the ability a person or group has to produce an intended outcome.

The results showed that participants who self-reported highly for collectivisms do socially loaf when working in an out-group context, either in a group or individual condition. Participation in either an in-group or out-group resulted in worse performance and rating of efficacy for those who scored as individualists within the individual condition. However, collectivists performed best and rated highest for efficacy in the in-group condition. Collectivism was shown to be higher in the Chinese and Israeli managers than in the managers from the USA. This study concludes that collectivists view their individual work as an important contribution to their group's goals more so than individualists.

Performance monitoring

Performance monitoring of employees occurs when employers use surveillance methods to observe employee behaviours. There are a number of reasons why organisations may use performance monitoring including to measure and track employee performance. As well as physical human observation, organisations might choose to use software and email monitoring and telephone or video recording. Some of these methods can also be used to check compliance with health, safety and security measures and to check whether employees are performing their roles correctly and productively.

Tomczak et al. (2018) states that nearly 80% of organisations in the USA use some form of **electronic performance monitoring (EPM)** for the purposes of performance appraisal, safety and logistical tracking. They argue, however, that such systems can have a negative effect on employees and are in some cases associated with lowered worker satisfaction, commitment and perception of fairness. To manage such adverse reaction to employee monitoring, Tomczak et al. recommend that monitoring is open, transparent and restricted to work-related contexts only, that it is used primarily for training and development and not for punishment purposes.

KEY WORD

electronic performance monitoring (EPM): the use of electronic systems to monitor and evaluate performance

RESEARCH METHODS

In the cross-cultural study of social loafing by Earley (1993), the experimental task of inbox sorting was designed to be fairly realistic, which may have increased the *validity* of the study as it simulated a real-life work task with which the participants would be familiar. The sample was fairly large and chosen to represent a range of ages and occupations, which makes the findings more *generalisable* to a wider population. The researchers also used a range of measurements including self-reports and an objective count of tasks competed. These measures collected *quantitative data* that allowed easy comparison of results; they could establish objectively that collectivistic participants performed better in the in-group condition than the individual or out-group conditions, for example.

ISSUES AND DEBATES

Application to real life can be seen in the theory of social facilitation. Understanding that people will work more effectively when in the presence of others has led to increased employee

CONTINUED

performance monitoring. This type of monitoring has been shown to work effectively when carried out electronically, which is more efficient and adaptable for use in different organisations.

Cultural difference is an important issue in relation to the study of social loafing. Cultures can be classified as collectivistic or individualistic and it is important to recognise that each holds different values in relation to the importance of group goals. For example, strategies for encouraging improvements in employee performance in collectivistic cultures (such as encouraging in-group identity in the workplace) may be less effective in individualistic cultures where workers may be more motivated by personal rewards.

Key study: Claypoole and Szalma (2019)

Claypoole, V. L., & Szalma, J. L. (2019). Electronic performance monitoring and sustained attention: social facilitation for modern applications. *Computers in human behavior,* **94, 25–34.**

Context

As we have seen, performance monitoring of employees is one method for measuring and potentially enhancing the performance of employees. Sustained attention, otherwise known as **vigilance**, is often an essential part of many work-related tasks, such as driving, medical testing or security screening. Workers performing such tasks have to stay focused and attentive for extended periods of time (see Figure 9.13). Previous research has shown that vigilance 'drops off' over time which can have serious consequences, for example in missing a security threat or losing concentration while driving a lorry.

KEY WORD

vigilance: sustained concentration over a period of time, including watching for hazards

Figure 9.13: Security monitoring at airports is challenging as it requires sustained concentration

Main theories and explanations

As we saw in an earlier section, social facilitation has two main effects when a worker is in the presence of another person. First, the worker's performance improves if their task is routine or easy and second, the worker's performance worsens if the task is complex or unfamiliar. Previous research on social facilitation supports this relationship between performance and task difficulty.

The theory of social facilitation can be extended to electronic monitoring, i.e. a camera or other device recording workers can act as a social presence. Research into electronic performance monitoring (EPM) suggests it can improve employee productivity and performance on tasks that last only a short time. This study extends the investigation of EPM to examine its effects on longer-duration sustained attention tasks, such as vigilance.

Aim

The aim of this study was to investigate the effects of EPM on sustained attention and to test whether video-based monitoring is an effective form of EPM.

It was predicted in Experiment 1 that using electronic presence on a sustained attention (vigilance) task would lead to improved performance. Experiment 2 was carried out to determine whether different forms of video-based EPM would replicate the results of Experiment 1.

Design

A sample of 106 student participants (65 female, 41 male) with a mean age of 20.57 from a university in the USA volunteered to take part in this laboratory experiment. Participants gave their informed consent to take part, their details were anonymised, they received course credits for participation and were debriefed at the end of the study.

There were two conditions of the independent variable of monitoring: electronic presence and the control group. The control group contained no form of performance monitoring. In the electronic presence condition, participants were monitored by a webcam placed on top of the computer screen ('to monitor performance and engagement while they completed the task') and video recorder placed 1 metre behind participants, which they were told would record their performance for later evaluation. No participants chose to withdraw from the study after receiving this information.

After being randomly assigned to a condition of the experiment, participants completed a short demographics questionnaire. The participants had to complete a sustained attention task in which they had to press the space bar in response to a critical signal appearing on the computer screen over a period of 24 minutes. The critical signal was defined as any two-digit number resulting in a difference of 1 or 0. The critical signals were programmed to appear randomly five times within each 6-minute block of the task.

The dependent variable being measured was the performance on the sustained attention test. This was measured as proportion of correctly detected critical signals, false alarms (mistakes) and response time.

Results, findings and conclusions

As expected, it was found that vigilance decreased over the course of the 24-minute experiment as fewer correct detections of the critical signal were found towards the end of the task. The number of false alarms decreased over time and the median response time increased over time in both conditions, supporting the findings of previous research into sustained attention.

Participants in the experimental condition of EPM were found to have a greater proportion of correct detections of the critical signal (mean = 0.69) compared to those in the control condition who completed the task without monitoring (mean = 0.60). The proportion of false alarms was also recorded and those in the EPM condition made fewer false alarms than those in the control group. Finally, median response times were shown to be faster in the EPM condition (767 ms) than in the control condition (802 ms).

The researchers concluded from Experiment 1 that electronic monitoring can produce effects that are similar to the social presence of a human, in other words, vigilance task performance was facilitated. The findings of Experiment 2 support this conclusion and suggested that using two forms of electronic presence at the same time could enhance performance effects even more than a singular form of electronic presence.

Evaluation

This study lacks *ecological validity* as it took place in an artificial environment. If participants had been in their own places of work performing realistic tasks the detection rate or response time results might have been different; they might have felt more compelled to perform the experimental task more accurately and efficiently, for example. How do you think the results of this study might be different if it was carried out in a real workplace? You might want to consider the challenges researchers would experience in this instance.

The findings may be difficult to *generalise* because of the sample used; university students. The results may not be applicable to older people as there may be differences in attention and who may be affected by performance monitoring in different ways.

However, the study was highly *reliable* due to using a standardised procedure with set timings for the display of stimuli such as the critical signals, the positioning of the EPM equipment and the information provided to the participants. This meant that the results of the study are likely to be similar if repeated.

This study has high *applicability to real life*. Most existing research has indicated that EPM is useful for monitoring basic, clerical work. However, the focus of this study was vigilance, meaning EPM can be used for critical tasks requiring extended focus to enhance performance and reduce the likelihood of errors. Some of this theory has already been applied through the development of on-board driver monitoring systems that check the safety and performance of long-distance drivers.

Conflict at work

Group conflict

Conflict at work can distract employees from their jobs, reduce overall productivity and waste time, resources and money. Goals can become distorted as people become more focused on the conflict than on their jobs. Conflict can have significant effects on the physical and psychological health of the people involved, increasing absenteeism and turnover and reducing staff satisfaction. Conflict that constitutes bullying or harassment can have negative effects for the individuals involved, the way in which the company functions, and even affect public perception of the company.

> ### KEY WORDS
>
> absenteeism: regular non-attendance at work without good reason
>
> intra-group: members of the same social group
>
> inter-group: members of different social groups
>
> interpersonal: communication or relationships between people

There are several types of conflict that can occur in organisational contexts. These include:

- Intra-individual conflict: an internal conflict in which the person struggles to make a decision, due to conflicting thoughts or values.

- Inter-individual conflict: conflict between two or more individuals within a group.

- Intra-group conflict: when multiple people within the same group are in conflict.

- Inter-group conflict: conflict between two groups within the same organisation.

All forms of conflict can interfere with the achievement of a goal and all organisations will attempt to keep conflicts to a minimum. Although there can be numerous causes of conflict within a group, these may be divided into two broad categories: organisational factors and interpersonal factors.

Organisational factors are issues that are specific to the context of an organisation (e.g. school, workplace, voluntary group). These could be conflict over status or salary, or disagreements over how to achieve a goal. A lack of resources or space can also create conflict.

Interpersonal factors may be as simple as a personality clash between two people or that they do not work well together for some reason. If the interpersonal conflict is between leaders of different groups, then this can produce increased conflict very easily. We will consider ways of handling such conflict in the next section.

Conflict handling

Thomas and Kilmann (1974) suggest five modes that can be used to manage group conflict:

- Competition: individuals may persist in conflict until someone wins and someone loses. At this point, the conflict is over.

- Accommodation: here, one individual will need to make a sacrifice to reduce the conflict. This can be extremely effective in reducing conflict and preventing further damage to the relationship.

- Compromise: each group or individual under conflict must make some compromise and give up something to reduce the conflict. This will be effective only if both sides lose comparable things.

- Collaboration: the group has to work together to overcome the conflict.

- Avoidance: avoidance involves suppressing the conflict or withdrawing from the conflict completely. This does not resolve the conflict, which is still there and has not been addressed. This can be effective in creating a cooling-off period.

The Thomas–Kilmann Conflict Mode Instrument (TKI) is a test which can be used to assess an individual's behaviour in conflict situations. It is composed of 30 statements that the participant has to choose from, and produces a 'profile' of that person's 'most used' to 'least used' conflict style.

The effectiveness of any of the five conflict-handling modes is dependent on the requirements of the specific situation, and also the ability of an individual to effectively use that mode. Using the TKI can help people identify that they rely on some modes more or less than necessary. The overuse or underuse of each mode carries its own risks. For example, collaborating can help a person creatively combine ideas from people with different perspectives on a problem, but it can also mean work is often delayed due to numerous conversations about the same issue. Overuse of the competing mode can lead other team members being reluctant to speak up about issues that are important to them, but it is a good mode to use when trying to manage a crisis.

ACTIVITY 9.10

You are part of a group that has been given responsibility for organising an event for students leaving the school at the end of the year.

1 Make a list of all the possible causes of conflict.

2 How would you classify these causes: as organisational or interpersonal?

3 Choose two modes from Thomas–Kilmann's five conflict-handling modes and apply them to your conflicts.

Bullying at work

A key issue in considering group behaviour in organisations is bullying. The term 'bullying' can refer to a wide range of behaviours.

Example study

A review article by **Einarsen (1999)** defines bullying as 'hostile and aggressive behaviour, either physical or non-physical, directed at one or more colleagues or subordinates'. Bullying causes humiliation, offence and distress and may also affect an individual's work performance and create a negative working environment.

Zapf (cited in Einarsen, 1999) suggests that there are five types of bullying behaviour: work-related, physical violence, personal attacks, verbal threats and social isolation. These are explained in Figure 9.14.

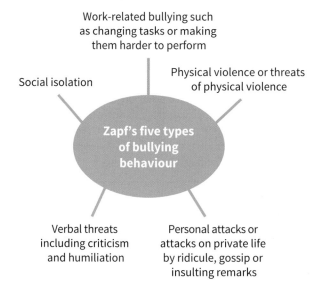

Figure 9.14: Zapf's five types of bullying behaviour

One of the key factors in workplace bullying is power. Einarsen claims that managers and supervisors are perceived as the bullies in most cases and that bullying by a superior creates more psychological distress than bullying by a peer. Bullying tends to develop gradually. Four phases of bullying are suggested by Einarsen:

- aggressive behaviour
- bullying
- **stigmatisation**
- severe trauma

Causes of bullying can be divided into two broad areas: individual or personality factors of the victim and of the bully and psycho-social or situational factors. One study reported on by Einarsen (Bjorkqvist et al., 1994) surveyed employees at a Finnish university and identified three main perceived reasons for bullying. These were competition concerning status and job position, envy and the aggressor being uncertain about their own abilities. A surprisingly high proportion felt that the personality of the victim was also a significant factor. Many other studies reported by Einarsen support these findings.

KEY WORDS

bullying: pattern of behaviour in which one or more people harm and/or embarrass others

stigmatisation: regarding a person as worthy of disapproval

There is some evidence to support the notion that victims of bullying are different from their non-bullied colleagues. Studies have found that victims are more sensitive, suspicious and angry, tend to have lower self-esteem and be more anxious in social settings.

However, these conclusions need to be considered carefully and are not intended to blame the victim rather than the bully. It is highly likely that the personality differences identified are as result of the bullying, but this can only be established through longitudinal research that has not been conducted.

Other research has focused on the situational factors that may promote (or at least allow) bullying to take place. These include:

- deficiencies in work design
- deficiencies in leadership behaviour
- socially exposed position of the victim
- low morale in the department.

Finally, Einarsen concludes by discussing the need to identify different types of bullying. He argues that we need to move away from treating all bullying as one phenomenon and that we need to develop an understanding of the very many different types. Predatory bullying is where the victim has done nothing to trigger the bullying behaviour, but is 'accidentally' in a situation where a predator is demonstrating power over others. This would be what might be termed 'institutional harassment' where a culture of bullying and aggression is ingrained throughout the organisation. The victim may be a member of a certain group (the first woman in that role for example) and this may produce bullying behaviour against the individual as a representative of that group. Bullying may also occur when people are highly stressed or frustrated, and are looking for someone to vent their frustration on. This is called **scapegoating** and has also been used as an explanation of prejudice. In many cases, the organisation effectively tolerates the bullying by not responding appropriately to it or by failing to have the correct policies and procedures in place.

RESEARCH METHODS

One strength of the TKI tool is that it was designed to reduce *social desirability bias*, which is so often a problem for self-reports. All of the 30 statements contained in the assessment of conflict handling are intentionally worded to appear equally desirable to the test-taker. This can increase the validity of the assessment as no one style appears to be better than another.

The research by Einarsen (1999) is a review article of a large number of studies into bullying. The paper presents the findings of a variety of research on the topic, meaning it overcomes issues such as the *generalisability* of findings of individual studies. However, the field of research into workplace bullying would benefit from longitudinal research. By studying participants over a longer period of time, rather than the cross-sectional studies reviewed by Einarsen, psychologists could explore the effects of interventions to prevent or manage bullying.

ISSUES AND DEBATES

The management of conflict and bullying is extremely important for all organisations. Einarsen (1999) offers a starting point in identifying that conflict may have *individual or situational* causes. Situational causes will be something to do with the organisation, for example low morale or poor leadership. However, conflict may also be a result of personality factors such as low self-esteem and anger issues. Understanding the causes of conflict and bullying are important as each may require very different strategies to manage and reduce.

CONTINUED

Having a range of strategies for managing conflict is obviously important for all organisations. Explanations and research in this area are highly *applicable to everyday life*. An organisation must consider when is it appropriate to allow the individuals concerned to continue to fight until one of them wins and when it is appropriate to step in and offer some sort of compromise solution. This is important for organisations and for organisational psychologists to recognise so that they can strive for the most effective and harmonious working environments in which bullying is challenged and prevented.

Questions

7 a Name Tuckman's stages of group formation.

   b Explain what happens in the 'norming' stage.

8 Define what is meant by the term 'groupthink'.

9 Suggest two ways in which group conflict might be managed.

9.4 Organisational work conditions

The physical work conditions such as lighting, space, layout and ventilation are factors psychologists are interested in when investigating worker well-being and productivity. Employees' health can also be influenced by the hours and patterns of work they undertake. This section also looks at the causes for accidents at work and how these can be monitored and reduced.

Physical work conditions

The Hawthorne studies

The original Hawthorne studies were conducted between 1924 and 1927 at the Hawthorne Works in Cicero, Illinois, USA (see Figure 9.15). The managers of the Hawthorne Works, along with Massachusetts Institute of Technology (MIT) and Harvard University, examined the effects on productivity of lighting changes and work structure changes such as working hours and break times. At the time, the Works employed round 29,000 people.

The workers' productivity was reported to have increased with almost any change in the lighting. This surprising finding was later termed the **Hawthorne effect**. The Hawthorne effect is a concept that refers to the phenomena of behaviour changing simply because it is being investigated, rather than as a result of any of the variables that were being manipulated. This term was first used by Henry Landsberger in 1958 to describe the phenomenon.

> **KEY WORD**
>
> **Hawthorne effect:** when those being observed change their behaviour purely as a response to their awareness of being observed

Example study

The original **Hawthorne** studies (Mayo, 1933), which are said to demonstrate the effect, however, have been reconsidered by researchers over time. Kompier (2006) reviewed the method and findings used in the original studies and argued that the studies lacked methodological controls, meaning the reported findings lacked validity.

In the first study, the effect of lighting on productivity was examined. An experimental group was exposed to decreasing levels of light while a control group received a constant level of light. Interestingly, both groups steadily increased their performance on their tasks (introducing the idea of the Hawthorne effect). It was not until the light was only as bright as moonlight that the experimental group showed any decrease in productivity, which seemed to reduce the likelihood that physical work conditions mattered. The researchers concluded that lighting level did not significantly affect productivity so long as it was sufficient for the job to be done. However, Kompier notes from the original research, lighting was not only factor that influenced employee output: the results could have been influenced by a number of other variables.

A series of further experiments were conducted that explored the effect of these other variables. In each of these studies, the original researchers were forced to conclude that the variable under examination was not responsible for the increased productivity and some other variable must be responsible. Indeed, Kompier notes that reanalysis of the original data shows no clear increase in worker output across the various trials. In other words, there was no clear evidence of a Hawthorne effect.

In the original studies, it was reported that the improved relationships between the workers and the management was important to productivity. However, in a 'relay study' in which workers assembled relay switches for telephones, a preferred wage incentive system was introduced and worker output rose. After the preferred

Figure 9.15: The Hawthorne effect was the name given to the explanation for changes to worker output in an electrical factory, such as this one

incentive system was taken away, output dropped. Data from interviews with the Hawthorne workers showed that from a list of the 15 most important work issues, 'payment' was ranked first, whereas 'supervision' ranked fourth. For this reason, Kompier describes the study's original conclusion that social factors are more important than pay as a myth.

Kompier is critical of the Hawthorne studies for their lack of scientific rigour, lack of control groups, changes of participants and failure to record worker output in a reliable way. He explains that the Hawthorne effect has effectively achieved the status of an 'urban legend'; the idea that workers could become more productive without better pay or conditions was too good a story to be untrue! While Kompier agrees there is a role for social factors in influencing employee performance, he argues that giving more weight to these factors shows a bias towards subjective, relational explanations at the expense of valid and objective physical influences. Kompier concludes that using the Hawthorne effect to explain the results of intervention studies is likely to add more confusion than clarity.

Design of the workplace environment

Organisational psychologists are interested in how the design of the workplace environment influences employees' motivation and satisfaction. One key change in many office-based organisations is the move to open-plan offices.

Example study

Oldham and Brass (1979) have conducted a field study that shows that employee satisfaction ratings fell dramatically after the working environment was changed to an open plan one.

This research was conducted in a large newspaper office in the USA. At the start of the research, all the employees worked in a conventional 'multi-cellular' office (Figure 9.16). Each department was in a separate office and within each office desks or workstations were separated from each other by internal walls, or by filing cabinets and partitions. This meant that employees had their own space and that to interact with anyone, it was necessary to travel down corridors and around partitions.

The management had been considering a change of office location for a number of reasons. First, the current office space was nowhere near a railway and this meant that papers had to be moved from the offices to the railway station by truck, creating additional

Figure 9.16: Multi-cellular office

expense as well as using up valuable time. Second, the current office had many practical problems; it lacked air conditioning, was difficult to heat and there was limited storage space. Finally, the management believed that an open-plan office would improve communication between individuals and departments and create a more positive working environment. All of these reasons meant that a move to new office premises was necessary.

The new office was purpose built and was located next to a railway line. It was constructed as a typical open-plan design. There were no internal walls and no cabinets or partitions more than 3 feet (1 metre) high. There were no private offices anywhere in the building although two meeting rooms were available. All members of a department were still grouped together as they had been in the old building and the amount of space was roughly equivalent in both old and new buildings. The only exception to this was staff working in the pressroom, who kept their working space as it had been. This was useful as these staff formed a type of naturally occurring *control group*.

Staff were fully informed at all stages of this process and data was collected at the beginning of the research which revealed that most staff were in agreement that the old building was no longer 'fit for purpose'. It is also important to note that the change in office was the only change: the move did not produce any other changes to people's working conditions, contracts, salaries or duties. Data were all collected at the offices. The first set of data was collected approximately eight weeks before the move to the open-plan office. The authors used the abbreviation T1 (time 1) for this. Data were then collected nine weeks after the move (T2) and then again 18 weeks after the move (T3).

Participants were told that the study was designed to assess employees' reactions to their new office and to their work. Data were collected using a questionnaire that was given out to groups ranging from two to 12 people. Participants were asked to put their names on the questionnaires so that their responses could be followed through the different stages of the study. However, they were assured that their responses would be confidential. Management and staff were also questioned more informally to gather additional feedback about the move to the new office.

All the full-time employees were invited to participate. This was a total of 140 people of whom 128 participated in some way. A total of 76 participated in all three stages of the study and most of the results presented by the authors are based on these 76 participants. Five members of the pressroom formed the control group. Although they completed the questionnaires at all three time periods, the fact that their working environment remained unchanged meant that little if any change over time was predicted for this group.

Briefly, the questionnaire measured the following:

- work satisfaction
- interpersonal satisfaction
- internal work motivation.

The experimenters predicted that there would be an increase in supervisor and co-worker feedback, friendship opportunities, intra-departmental and inter-departmental interaction.

Findings were that employees' internal motivation and satisfaction with work and colleagues actually decreased sharply after the move to the open-plan office. The control group showed no such changes. The interview data revealed that workers felt that they were in a 'fishbowl', that it was difficult to concentrate and complete a task. It was also difficult to develop friendships and impossible to do something like invite someone for a drink after work without the whole office hearing. A supervisor also commented that it was difficult to provide feedback to a worker without moving to a private meeting room. These findings suggest that the physical space rather than any other factors is responsible for the changes experienced by the employees.

RESEARCH METHODS

The Hawthorne studies discussed by Kompier and the study into open-plan offices by Oldham and Brass were both experimental studies. The Hawthorne studies can be described as a *field experiment* as the experimenters manipulated the variables that they were interested in but did this in a real working environment as opposed to a laboratory environment. This gives the research high levels of *ecological validity*, which means that the results can easily be applied to the real world. However, conducting research in this way also produces very low levels of control. As we saw earlier, there are a number of other variables that were not considered at the time of the research that might actually offer a better explanation of the findings than the explanations that were offered at the time.

In a similar way, the study by Oldham and Brass also has high levels of ecological validity but low levels of control. This can be described as a *natural experiment*; the experimenters did not move the workers from one office environment to the other for the purposes of the research but took advantage of this naturally occurring change (*independent variable*) to investigate the effects. Unfortunately, in this kind of study it is going to be almost impossible to control for every possible variable and this does mean there are weaknesses with the way that this study was conducted. The *control group* only contained five individuals, which makes comparisons difficult. The researchers were only able to collect data on worker motivation and worker satisfaction and it is possible that scores on productivity or efficiency, for example, may have shown significant benefits of moving to the open-plan office. Finally, it is also possible that the negative ratings would have been temporary and continuing to monitor the employees over a longer time period would have shown more positive results later.

ISSUES AND DEBATES

One of the main themes in this section is the effect of working conditions (the situation in which a person is working), and so the *individual–situational* debate is relevant. Both the Hawthorne

CONTINUED

studies and Oldham and Brass's study of open-plan designs demonstrate that situation (change and/or layout of space) can have significant effects on the individuals who work in these situations.

It is important for organisations and for organisational psychologists to recognise that the conclusions from these studies have *application to real-life* so that they can strive for the most effective and harmonious working environments. For example, the Hawthorne studies showed that while social factors can be important in influencing employee productivity, they are not the only factor and pay and conditions are likely to remain a primary concern for employees.

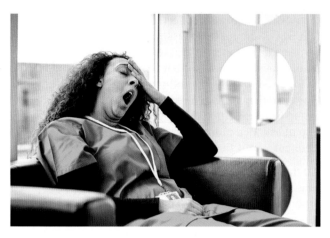

Figure 9.17: Healthcare workers often engage in shift work

Temporal conditions of work environments

Design of work

Temporal conditions refer to the time conditions under which people work. Many people work at night in a variety of organisations; manufacturing sometimes continues for 24 hours; healthcare needs to be available 24 hours a day and leisure and retail services are becoming increasingly available 24 hours a day (see Figure 9.17). This means that increasing numbers of people work 'shifts', a term used to describe any working pattern that does not involve the same work pattern every week. To maintain 24-hour service many organisations run a rotation of three shifts a day. A day shift is typically 6 a.m. till 2 p.m., an afternoon (or twilight) shift would be 2 p.m. to 10 p.m. and a night shift 10 p.m. to 6 a.m.

KEY WORD

temporal conditions: relating to time and how working patterns are arranged

It is important to manage shifts so that any negative effects can be reduced. Pheasant (1991) identifies two main approaches to the organisation of shift working and these are rapid rotation theory and slow rotation theory.

- Rapid rotation shifts are frequent shift changes that workers have to follow. Metropolitan rotas are where workers work two day shifts, then two afternoon shifts and then two night shifts. They then have two days off before the shift pattern starts all over again. Note that this is a total of eight days per rotation so that the weekly pattern shifts a day ahead each week. A continental rota is where workers complete two day shifts, two twilight shifts, three night shifts, then two days off work, two day shifts, three twilight shifts, two night shifts and then three days off work. After this the cycle begins again.

- Slow rotation shift changes are infrequent changes; for example, working day shifts for several weeks and then night shifts for several weeks. It is suggested that this kind of slow rotation can allow *circadian rhythms* to adapt to one shift without being forced to change too rapidly and cause health problems.

On-call working refers to those employees who are on stand-by to begin work, often at short notice. These employees are expected to be available for work outside of their regular hours, and so may be at home while on call. Workers in sectors such as health or social care may be on call for overnight periods, for example in a care home where they are unlikely to be needed overnight. This is also known as 'sleep-in' working and the employee may be permitted to rest and sleep unless needed during the night.

Flexible working is a term given to a type of pattern of work that is different from traditional or regular hours, e.g. 9 a.m.–5 p.m. 5 days a week. Flexible working is offered by some organisations to help their employees achieve a balance between their work and the rest of their lives. Often, it is provided within the constraints of still meeting the organisation's needs (e.g. employees may have a start time 'window' to be available to customers), and often employees may need to apply for a flexible working arrangement which must be agreed by the organisations.

Examples of flexible working include:

- Change to working hours that fit in with education commitments or care arrangements

- Working compressed hours: full-time hours are fulfilled over fewer, but longer working days (e.g. 10 hours per day, 4 days a week, instead of 8 hours per day, 5 days a week)

- Flexitime: working hours are arranged around agreed core times, e.g. 10 a.m.–6 p.m. instead of 9 a.m.–5 p.m.

- Working from home or remotely for all or part of contracted hours

The effects of shift work

In Knutsson's (2003) review of the effects of shift work, he brings together evidence on the relationship between working at night or on a shift work pattern and specific serious medical disorders. He begins by noting that there is no specific evidence that suggests that shift work actually affects longevity (the lifespan of a person). Two studies are mentioned that have directly compared mortality rates between day workers and shift workers, one conducted in the UK and one conducted in Denmark. The UK study reported no significant difference and the Danish study reported a very tiny increase in relative death risk for shift workers. Knutsson then moves on to examine specific disorders and conditions:

- *Gastrointestinal disease*: this is significantly more common in shift workers than in day workers, with more symptoms (most commonly constipation and diarrhoea) experienced when working night shifts. There is also some evidence that peptic ulcers are more common in those who regularly work shifts, including taxi and truck drivers, factory workers, printers and night security guards The risk of ulcers of the small intestine is also reported to be doubled in shift workers.

- **Cardiovascular** *disease*: it is well known that working conditions can contribute to the risk of cardiovascular disease. This includes physical factors such as chemicals, noise and vibrations as well as psycho-social factors such as stress and the organisation of work schedules. Studies conducted in a range of different countries also support the relationship between shift work and cardiovascular disease.

- *Cancer*: there has been some interest in this area and some research has revealed an increased risk of breast cancer in women who work night shifts. These studies have been conducted with nurses, flight attendants and radio and telegraph operators. However, increased exposure to other carcinogens in these occupations could not be controlled for. There has been some discussion about the role of low levels of melatonin (a hormone which helps regulate the sleep–wake cycle) but there is no conclusive evidence for the risk of cancer being increased by shift work.

- *Diabetes and other metabolic disturbances*: concentrations of certain substances in the body, including potassium, uric acid, glucose and cholesterol, are higher during night work, which may be related to increased metabolic disturbances. Studies of weight and body mass index (BMI) have tended to be inconclusive, although some have shown higher BMIs in those working shift work. However, there is evidence to support the increased chances of developing diabetes if you work shifts.

- *Pregnancy*: studies show relationships between shift work and low birth weight as well as shift work and premature birth. One paper has reported an increased risk of miscarriage among shift workers. Knutsson argues that this evidence is strong and that pregnant women would be well advised to avoid shift work.

- *Exacerbation of existing disorders*: many normal biological processes follow a circadian rhythm and this can be interrupted or interfered with by shift work. This means that taking medicines is more complex when working shifts. Even taking the same dose at the same time can cause different effects due to the differences in the internal body clock. Sleep

KEY WORD

cardiovascular: the system that includes the heart and blood vessels

deprivation can also affect existing disorders such as the frequency of epileptic seizures and asthma attacks.

ACTIVITY 9.11

Shift work is associated with a number of specific disorders and conditions which affect different parts of the human body.

1   Draw an outline of a human body.

2   Identify each relevant area of the body mentioned in the research from this section: you may need to research locations!

3   Include a brief summary of the link between shift work and each part of the body you have identified.

As well as considering the overall health effects, shift work has been studied as a factor that affects the likelihood or accidents or **near-misses**.

KEY WORD

near-miss: an event with the potential to result in, but that does not actually cause, damage or injury

Example study

Gold et al. (1992) conducted a survey of Massachusetts nurses that asked about shift work, sleep and accidents. This study used a self-administered questionnaire and was handed out to 878 registered nurses between June and September 1986. They were asked whether they worked variable shifts or whether they always worked the same shift. The nurse was asked to give information relating to the current week, the previous two weeks and the following week on the number of day, evening or night shifts worked. They were also asked to record their sleep and wake times for all shifts and for days off.

The questionnaire also asked about:

- quality of sleep
- use of alcohol
- use of prescription or non-prescription medication
- sleeping aids

- times they had 'nodded off' (fallen asleep) at work (in the past week)
- times they had 'nodded off' while driving to and from work (in the past year)
- accidents, errors and 'near-miss' accidents in the past year: this included driving accidents, medication errors, job procedural errors and work-related personal injuries that could be attributed to sleepiness.

They were divided into groups dependent on their work practices. Day and evening shift work was grouped together as the shift from day to evening work has not been shown to disrupt circadian rhythms. The other groups were those who worked night shifts only and 'rotators'; those who changed shift patterns frequently. Of the 878 questionnaires given out, 687 were returned. The mean age of the sample was 33.9 years.

Results showed that rotators and night shift workers reported fewer hours of sleep than day/evening workers. The researchers used a concept of 'anchor sleep' (defined as having four or more hours sleep during the same clock hours every night).

The results showed that 92% of the day / evening nurses obtained regular anchor sleep but only 6.3% of the night nurses and none of the rotators obtained anchor sleep regularly throughout the month. Anchor sleep disruption was experienced by 49% of the day/evening workers, 94% of the rotators and 2.9% of the night nurses.

Night nurses were 1.8 times more likely to report poor quality sleep than the day/evening workers and rotators were 2.8 times more likely to report poor quality sleep than the day/evening workers. Night nurses and rotators were twice as likely to use medications to help them sleep.

Nodding off on the night shift occurred at least once a week in 35% of rotators, 32% of night nurses and 20% of day/evening workers who worked the occasional night shift. In contrast, only 2.7% of day/evening nurses and 2.8% of rotators reported any incidences of nodding off on day or evening shifts.

When compared to day/evening nurses, rotators were 3.9 times as likely and night nurses 3.6 times as likely to nod off while driving to and from work in the previous year.

Although length of time working at the hospital, age and use of alcohol were factors that contributed to errors, even when these factors were taken into account, rotators reported twice as many accidents as day/evening nurses.

The results are consistent with laboratory demonstrations of the effects of sleep deprivation and the disruption of circadian rhythms, particularly in the sense of increased cognitive errors. The researchers conclude that the application of circadian principles to the design of work schedules may produce improved health and safety for nurses and patients.

RESEARCH METHODS

A *correlation* shows a relationship between two things; for example, a relationship between working shifts and an increased chance of gastrointestinal disorders. However, it does not show that working shifts causes an increase in gastrointestinal disorders even though it might seem to make sense to interpret the results in this way. In order to show a causal relationship, researchers must conduct experiments. An experimental group would need to work changing shifts for a period of time while the control group would work normal day shifts. Any significant differences in the incidence of gastrointestinal disorders then could lead to the conclusion that working shifts causes gastrointestinal disorders. However, this type of research would raise many ethical issues and would be unlikely to be conducted.

It is also difficult to draw causal conclusions from the research by Gold, although this can be described as *quasi-experimental* as he was able to compare two naturally occurring groups, thus creating an *independent variable*. However, he was not able to randomly allocate participants to these different groups meaning that there may be many differences between them that might explain the results he found. However, the research findings are supported by laboratory experiments into short-term sleep deprivation and cognitive errors. Finally, there may be reporting biases in this study and a *longitudinal study* to track accidents and errors and to correlate these with shift work patterns might be more effective.

ISSUES AND DEBATES

It is possible to consider the material in this section in relation to the *nature versus nurture debate*. Shift work may interfere with the natural functioning of the body and this is likely to explain

CONTINUED

the many negative effects. We have a natural circadian rhythm and working constantly changing shifts (nurture) may disrupt this.

All of the research considered in this section has useful *real-world applications*. By identifying the risks that shift working may pose, not only are individuals able to make informed decisions about their own working practices, but employers are able to establish procedures designed to minimise these risks.

Health and safety

Accidents at work

Traditionally a person-centred explanation of error has been used to explain why accidents at work occur. This human error theory assumes that errors are caused by human failings and also that some individuals are more likely than others to make mistakes. Errors can then theoretically be reduced by identifying and targeting interventions at those individuals who make the most errors. Some critics describe human error theory as a blame-oriented approach. The problem with such an explanation is that it can create fear amongst employees who anticipate punishment at work. While the approach does hold individuals accountable for their work and mistakes, it may be unfair to always blame the individual for an accident at work. It has been suggested that blaming individuals may be more emotionally satisfying than blaming institutions and is potentially more convenient than trying to address the wider system.

Technology has led to the development of machinery that largely replaces many of the tasks previously done by human workers. This leaves the human as the 'operator' of the machine and the interaction between the machine and its operator is sometimes extremely complex and the consequences of 'human error' can be catastrophic (Nagel, 1988). An operator-machine systems theory has been proposed in contrast to the human error theory. The systems model suggests that errors are caused by systems in which humans play a small part. Rather than arguing that some individuals are more prone to error than others, this model argues that the most errors tend to be made by those carrying out tasks that are more difficult or where mistakes are most noticeable (i.e. they result in most damage or injury at work).

A famous example of systems error with near catastrophic consequences occurred at the Three Mile Island nuclear power plant in the USA in 1979, as shown in Figure 9.18. An employee shut down an alternate feedwater pipe and went off duty without turning this back on again. The reactor started to overheat and warning sirens began to sound but no one at the power plant knew what the problem was. It took 2 hours and 18 minutes to find the fault. Further delay could have led to an explosion and large-scale release of radioactive material. It is not appropriate to simply blame the operator for his error. Nothing in the system had been designed to tell anyone that the pipe had been turned off and when a relief valve also failed to open, no warning system was in place. Later examination of the processes required to identify the fault revealed that the operators looking for the fault had to scan over 1,600 gauges. For some reason, colours had been used differently in different systems and in some places a colour represented safety whereas in another part of the system it represented danger. It was clear that while there had been human errors there were also significant failings in the design of the systems as well as the safety procedures.

Figure 9.18: Three Mile Island: the site of a serious incident relating to operator–machine systems error

Analysis of the causes of errors leading to accidents have been categorised by psychologists. In the example of the Three Mile Island incident, an error of commission was committed; this means doing something that should not have been done: shutting off the feedwater pipe. In contrast, an error of omission

is a mistake in which an individual does not do something which should have been done. There are other types of human error that can lead to accidents at work, such as an error of sequence (when actions are carried out in the wrong order, skipped or repeated) or error of timing (when an action is performed too late or too early).

Since the incident we have seen the development of 'human factors' experts, who ensure that the design of machine controls and displays reflect our knowledge and understanding not only of human cognition, but of the limitations of human cognition. This might involve making sure that display systems are clear and easy to interpret, that operators are not expected to maintain vigilance for too long without a break (such as the tasks performed by air traffic controllers) and that there are tried and tested emergency procedures.

Reducing accidents at work

The following study by Fox et al. (1987) demonstrates one way in which workers' behaviours can be changed in order to help prevent accidents like the ones described in the previous section. This study uses a token economy, which is a type of operant conditioning. This study is also discussed in Chapter 8.

Example study

A study by **Fox et al. (1987)** investigated the use of a token economy to reward workers for not having accidents or injuries for a specified amount of time. The study was conducted at two open pit mines (see Figure 9.19) and their associated product processing plants. Both mines were in the USA. Before the study, the number of days lost from work due to injuries on the job in one of the mines was over eight times the national average for all mines and three times the national average at the other mine. In the five years preceding this study, two people had been killed and a third person had suffered a permanent disability.

The two settings were similar in many ways. They used the same mining procedures and were of similar sizes. Injuries had occurred in all areas of both mines but were particularly associated with the use and maintenance of heavy equipment.

Figure 9.19: The study by Fox et al. (1987) took place at two open pit mines, such as this one

The participants in this study were the employees at the two mines, including office and clerical workers, engineers, managers, and custodial, maintenance and production workers. The number of employees in the first mine was 197 when data collection began in 1970, rose to a high of 606 by 1979 and then decreased to 214 by 1983 due to the declining value of the uranium ore mined there. The second mine employed 450 staff in 1970 which had increased to 501 in 1983 and remained relatively stable from there. Table 9.6 shows how workers were divided into four groups based on the numbers of working days lost due to injury.

The token economy systems began in 1972 in the first mine and in 1975 in the second. Workers were given a specified number of 'trading stamps' with their pay envelope if they had not suffered a lost time injury or injury that required a doctor's attention during the month. The amount of trading stamps varied by the risk factors of each group, for example in the first mine, Group 1 received 300 stamps, Group 2 received 400 stamps, Group 3 received 500 stamps and Group 4 received 700 stamps. In addition to these 'rewards' all workers managed by a common supervisor were given further stamps if the whole group of workers under that supervisor had avoided

Group number	Types of employee
1	Workers in the least hazardous jobs, mainly office workers
2	Foremen, shift supervisors, technicians, engineers and surveyors
3	Mechanics, labourers, maintenance workers and operators of bulldozers, front end loaders, shovels, draglines and trucks
4	Workers in the most hazardous jobs, including electricians, scraper operators and fuel and lube workers

Table 9.6: Workers at the pit mines and processing plants in the study by Fox et al. (1987)

lost time or medically treated injuries. Further still, any safety suggestions that were subsequently adopted by the miner, any acts that prevented injury to others or damage to property could be rewarded with amounts ranging from 500 to 25,000 stamps.

ACTIVITY 9.12

A token economy is an application of the behaviourist approach. It involves rewarding people for desirable behaviour such as remaining in the presence of a phobic object.

Draw a storyboard that demonstrates how a token economy could be used to encourage someone who needs to overcome their fear of public speaking in order to try for a promotion in work.

However, a worker who missed one or two days of work due to injury would receive no stamps for one month. If three or four days of work were lost, they would receive no stamps for two months and if five or six days were lost there would be no reward for three months, increasing like this up to a maximum of six months with no reward if more than ten days were lost. No one in the group would receive any of the group award if any time had been lost and anyone responsible for an accident that damaged equipment would lose their individual stamp award for one month for every $2000 of damage up to a maximum of six months. All members of that worker's group would lose their group award for as many months as the individual lost his individual awards. Anyone failing to report an accident or injury would lose all of their individual awards for one month and their group would lose their group award for the same length of time.

Six weeks before this scheme was started, workers were given information about how this would work. One month before the start of the scheme, any worker who had not had an equipment-damaging accident or a lost time injury was given 1,000 stamps.

Stamps could be 'spent' at local stores and could be exchanged for anything from a huge range of merchandise. In 1972, 3,000 stamps would buy a spice rack, 7,600 would buy a comforter for a full-size bed and 20,400 stamps would buy a gas-fired barbecue. No restrictions were placed on how the stamps could be spent and the authors report that casual conversations around the mines revealed a range of products being purchased including microwave ovens and cuckoo clocks!

The miners had to keep careful safety data including the number of accidents (referred to as frequency rate) and the total numbers of days lost (severity). In addition, direct costs of these injuries and accidents were recorded under the headings of compensation insurance, medical care and repairing damaged equipment. The mines also kept data on the cost of the trading stamps. This allowed a benefit-to-cost ratio to be calculated to see if the dollars saved as a result of operating the token economy exceeded the cost of the token economy.

The results showed that there were significant decreases in number of days lost in both mines in the first years that the token economy was operating. Costs of accidents and injuries in the first mine declined from a baseline average of $294,000 to an average of $29,000 for the years that the token economy was in effect. A similar decline was seen in the second mine, from a baseline average of $367,696 to an average of $38 972. Both declines were approximately 90%. The costs of the token economy scheme in the first mine never rose above $13,850 and the costs in the second mine was $21,940 in the first year but between $11,000 and $13,000 in subsequent years.

These findings indicate that the use of a token economy benefitted all both employees and employers. Days lost from work decreased, accidents and injuries decreased and no deaths or permanent disabilities occurred at either mine during the time that the token economy was in operation. Towards the end of the scheme, the number of days lost was around a quarter of the national average in the first mine and one-twelfth the national average in the second mine. In addition to the much-lowered risk of accident, workers also benefitted from the goods they were able to buy with their trading stamps. Although no direct measure of this was taken, anecdotal evidence suggests that these stamps were appreciated by all workers even though they were doubtful to begin with. In fact, one of the unions even requested that the programme be written into contracts and when stamps were left out of a small number of workers' pay envelopes the spouse of one called the mine to complain and the spouse of another drove 50 miles (80 km) to collect them!

Monitoring accidents

Accidents at work can occur even when plans are in place to prevent them. For this reason, it can be useful (and sometimes a legal requirement) to monitor and report accidents. Organisations usually have policies and procedures in place to prevent, manage and review accidents as part of their risk management strategy.

Sometimes, accidents or near-misses act as useful sources of information about what works and does not work in terms of health and safety procedures. Monitoring and reviewing measures designed to prevent accidents and understanding the nature and cause of an accident can help improve the processes, identify areas for training and prevent further accidents. For example, investigations can uncover breaches in health and safety procedures or identify that extra safety measures are needed. As well finding out the cause of workplace accidents, monitoring can help employees feel as though their well-being is a priority.

Dekker (2015) identifies the following four reasons for engaging in accident investigation and monitoring:

- **Epistemological**: establishing what happened to give understanding to the individuals and groups involved

- Preventive: identifying ways to avoid similar accidents in future

- Moral: understanding the errors or breaches that took place to reinforce correct practice and establish accountability

- **Existential**: finding an explanation for any injury or loss of life

KEY WORDS

epistemological: relating to knowledge

existential: relating to being alive or existing

However, Dekker argues that accident monitoring may be more art than science in the sense that different investigators may reach different conclusions, even with the same facts. An insurer with a financial interest in the outcome of an investigation might interpret or look for different information than the organisation itself. Dekker supports this with the example of two official investigations into an aeroplane crash, one by an aviation authority and the other by the airline itself. The aviation authority concluded that contributing factors to the crash included the pilot acting in haste and losing awareness of the situation. However, the airline's report found that the air traffic controller was inattentive and radar coverage of the area was poor.

RESEARCH METHODS

Some critics of the behaviourist approach argue that using token economies as in the study by Fox et al. is controlling and, in some cases, can be *unethical*. However, in this instance the use of rewards proved highly effective and was not used instead of safety training but in addition to the safety training. Many organisations offer similar schemes where workers are rewarded in this way and there is little evidence to suggest it causes harm to participants.

Additionally, the study was carried out in the workers' natural environment: the pit mines and processing plants. This means that the study had high *ecological validity*. The researchers could be fairly sure that using a similar token economy to reduce accidents at other sites would produce a similar benefit-to-cost ratio because these workers are likely to behave in a similar way.

ISSUES AND DEBATES

The study by Fox et al. demonstrates the effectiveness of the application of psychological principles to the workplace. The *application* of a token economy is a simple behaviourist technique that offers consistent and predictable rewards to desired behaviours. The usefulness of the token economy in this instance is obvious. The number of accidents was reduced significantly and worker safety was increased. Likewise, accident monitoring and investigation is used widely within organisations to improve health and safety practice. However, its effectiveness depends on the detail, accuracy and objectiveness of information collected regarding accidents at work.

However, behaviourist techniques are often criticised for being overly *deterministic*. The study by Fox et al. shows that the way the working environment (situation) is constructed can have significant effects on the way that individuals behave. The results showed that workers' behaviour can be controlled through use of a token economy. However, this ignores the role of freewill and personality factors which may also influence a person's approach to health and safety.

Key study: Swat (1997)

Swat, K. (1997). Monitoring of accidents and risk events in industrial plants. *Journal of occupational health*, 39(2), 100–104.

Context

The researchers of this study wanted to investigate effective accident monitoring in Poland. At the time of the research, the methods used to document accidents were generally considered infective. Rather than using facts and systematic reasoning from accident monitoring to inform safety management, these had typically been solved intuitively. In other words, informal measures were put in place to resolve the immediate problem without formal discussion or analysis.

In addition, there was little evidence retained by organisations of the losses that resulted from accidents. This made it difficult to quantify the severity and frequency of injuries to workers or the loss of productivity from stopping work due to accidents. The overall lack of standardisation of the approach to investigating and recording accidents at work presented an opportunity to improve accident monitoring.

Main theories and explanations

As we have seen in this section, information such as the number of reported injuries offers an important source of information on accident risk. Looking at the severity, frequency and causes of accidents is helpful in targeting resources correctly at improving safety systems, procedures and training for workers who may be at risk. Effective monitoring of accidents can go beyond a simple theory of human error and instead use a system-focused approach to understand the causes and complexities of accidents at work.

Aim

The aim of this study was to develop a method that could be used by organisations to record risk events to help in finding the causes of accidents and prevent them in future.

Design

In the first stage of this study, a range of industrial plants located in the city of Lodz were selected for review: foundry (metalwork), machinery, meat processing and furniture. The four sites employed around 3,000 workers in total.

Eighty-three accidents were reviewed from the year 1993. For the purposes of this research, an accident was defined as a formally reported case of a sudden undesired event at work with a negative effect on the health of one or more workers leading to sick days or death. Accident frequency was determined as the number of accidents producing injury/injuries which required sick leave days per 100 employees in a year. Accident severity rate was counted as the number of sick leave days taken per accident. The researchers reviewed accident reports provided by safety supervisors, investigated individual accident protocols, and interviewed safety supervisors and line managers.

In an earlier review (1994) that was also reported on in this paper, Swat looked at minor accidents or 'incidents' at the meat plant which included all first-aid cases reported in the plant and assessed the total number of incidents, including results of the interviews with employees.

Results, findings and conclusions

The accident frequency was shown to be highest in the foundry plant and the severity rate was highest in the machinery plant. The following types of accident were noted:

- falls and slips
- accidents connected with manual work
- accidents connected with contact with working parts of machinery
- accidents connected with contact with sources of energy
- other.

The frequency of each type of accident varied across plants, however. For example, the frequency rate for fall and slip accidents (per 100 employees) was 0.7 on average for all plants. However, the frequency rate was 1.2 for the meat processing plant compared with 0.3 for the furniture plant.

Swat distinguished four different faults that resulted in these accidents:

1. Insufficient supervision (e.g. when a manager fails to ensure a worker has followed safe procedures)
2. Poor workplace organisation (e.g. inadequate personal protective equipment or trying to work too quickly)
3. Technical factors (e.g. when objects or equipment are faulty)

4   Worker error (e.g. an individual, unexpected mistake made by the employee)

The first cause, insufficient supervision, was found in 89% of accidents studied. Poor workplace organisation was part of or the entire cause of 40% of accidents. Worker error was involved in 14% of accidents but technical factors were responsible for only 11 % of the cases studied. The cause of nine accidents could not clearly be explained.

Overall, poor **housekeeping** was the overarching reason for the faults listed before and was involved in 46% of all accidents. In other words, the four faults identified by Swat could in many cases be linked to poor housekeeping (e.g. workers neglecting to report faulty equipment = 'technical factors' fault). This is an important finding because housekeeping is relatively easy to control as part of safety management. The frequency and types of accident depend on housekeeping, for example in relation to trips and falls which had causes such as broken staircases and wet or slippery floors without warning signage as in Figure 9.20.

KEY WORD

housekeeping: in an organisational context this refers to managing and maintaining the processes, property and equipment of an organisation

---

Findings of the second study revealed 254 injuries that required first aid or medical treatment. Only 23 of these days were counted as official accidents as they necessitated sick leave. Data from interviews with the employees involved in incidents in the meat processing plant suggest this figure was actually as high as 520. This means that 95% of all incidents were not reported.

In conclusion, Swat recommends the following improvement to accident monitoring:

1   Accidents should be recorded by type and circumstance to allow for comparison with similar types of accident to better understand the safety context for future.

2   Minor accidents or incidents, e.g. those requiring first aid, should be reported as they offer better statistical data about the nature of frequent accidents.

3   Poor housekeeping is a frequent source of accidents and major risk factor for accidents and should be a priority in safety monitoring systems.

Figure 9.20: Accidents at work can be prevented by following housekeeping rules

Evaluation

This study reviewed a large number of industrial accidents. Because this was carried out in retrospect, it was an *ethical* way of studying accidents and accident prevention. This is a challenging area to research because of the need to protect participants from harm. The findings reported here were part of a three-year *longitudinal study* on accident monitoring. Although time-consuming, the strength of this type of research is that is can show change over a period of time using the same participants or setting.

As the accidents had already taken place within an organisational context, the study can be said to have high *ecological validity*. The behaviour recorded within the study can be applied to real life and is likely to reflect what would be found regarding accident monitoring in other industrial settings.

It is difficult to judge the *reliability* of this study. It gathered interview data from personnel across different plants. These individuals might not have given accurate or consistent accounts of what happened during an accident or incident due to forgetting or pressure from the researchers, making this data *subjective*. However, the frequency and severity of accidents was recorded as *quantitative data* in the form of the number of days of sick leave which is a consistent and *objective* measure.

This key study by Swat (1997) is an example of *nomothetic* research. The study extracts statistical data from a large number of separate accidents on the frequency and severity of accidents to classify them by type and cause. In other words, the researchers are looking for similarities between each of the accidents or incidents studied to generate a theory that can be applied to all accident monitoring.

The findings of this study are useful in real life in that they highlight the importance of systematically recording accidents, incidents and even near-misses. Major accidents are statistically rarer, meaning they offer less meaningful insights into the cause and management of more frequent accidents at work. Organisations would benefit from going beyond minimum legal requirements for accident reporting in order to establish monitoring and investigation systems that reduce risk and prevent harm to employees.

Questions

10 Outline two effects of shift work on health.

11 How did Fox et al. measure the effectiveness of their token economy?

12 Describe one conclusion that can be drawn from the study by Swat (1997).

9.5 Satisfaction at work

Organisational psychologists have attempted to measure employee satisfaction as well as studying and predicting reasons for employee dissatisfaction and destructive behaviour. These aspects of organisations are important because they affect the well-being of people as well as the success of organisations.

Theories of job satisfaction

Two-factor theory

The two-factor theory proposed by Frederick Herzberg (1959) states that job satisfaction and job dissatisfaction are separate to each other. Herzberg proposes that there are certain factors that cause satisfaction, and there are other factors that cause dissatisfaction.

He states that workers are not satisfied with jobs which only meet their lower order needs (i.e. physiological and safety needs according to Maslow's hierarchy, which are usually met by getting paid to work and therefore being able to afford food and shelter). Instead, individuals also look for the gratification of higher-level needs such as

relatedness or self-esteem needs that are likely to be met by the nature of the work itself.

Herzberg suggests that one group of job characteristics leads to worker satisfaction while another, completely separate group of job characteristics leads to worker dissatisfaction. This contradicts the logical assumption that satisfaction and dissatisfaction are on a continuum, from satisfied to dissatisfied, rather than being unrelated.

Herzberg conducted over 200 interviews with engineers and accountants in the Pittsburgh area and asked them to describe periods in their lives when they were 'exceedingly happy' and 'exceedingly unhappy' with their jobs. Interviewees were asked to give as much information as they could, with specific focus on the changes that took place.

Herzberg found that factors related to the job itself could make people feel a sense of achievement and thus a sense of satisfaction; he called these **motivational factors**. However, if the job lacked these gratifying characteristics this did not lead to dissatisfaction. Dissatisfaction actually comes from very different factors, such as working conditions, technical problems and salary levels that Herzberg termed '**hygiene factors**'. This means that these two factors need to be considered separately – increasing satisfaction is not the same thing as decreasing dissatisfaction.

> ## KEY WORDS
>
> **motivational factors:** also known as satisfiers, these are intrinsic elements of the work including recognition, possibility of personal growth and the pleasure of the work itself
>
> **hygiene factors:** also known as dissatisfiers, these are extrinsic elements of the work environment, e.g. company policies, pay and conditions

The two-factor theory produces four possible combinations of these two factors:

- High hygiene + high motivation = the ideal situation, where employees are highly motivated and have few complaints.

- High hygiene + low motivation = employees have few complaints but are not highly motivated. The job is viewed mostly as a way to get paid.

- Low hygiene + high motivation = employees are motivated but have a lot of complaints. For example, a situation where the job is exciting and challenging but salaries and work conditions are insufficient.

- Low hygiene + low motivation = this is the worst situation, where employees are not motivated and have many complaints.

ACTIVITY 9.13

An employer of a large organisation has noticed that staff turnover has increased significantly in the past year. Can you explain how the employer can identify the causes of satisfaction and dissatisfaction amongst employees? What solutions would you suggest to enhance both hygiene and motivational factors?

Job characteristics

Job Characteristics Theory (Hackman 1976) acts as a framework for analysing how job characteristics affects job satisfaction and other work outcomes. It is a theory that can be used to create jobs that appeal to workers and keep them motivated. Five key dimensions, described in the model as core 'job characteristics' are identified by Hackman and Oldham:

- *Skill variety*: a job should require different skills and allow workers to use a range of the skills.

- *Task identity*: a job should require a worker to complete a whole piece of work rather than a single task in isolation.

- *Task significance*: the job should have a worthwhile impact on others, whether inside or outside of the organisation.

- *Autonomy*: the job should allow the worker some freedom in planning, scheduling and carrying out their work.

- *Feedback*: the job itself (rather than other people) should provide information on how well the worker is performing the job, i.e. it is clear that the task has been completed well by looking at the outcome.

These job characteristics are responsible for producing three critical **psychological states**: experienced meaningfulness, experienced responsibility and knowledge of results. Meaningfulness is the extent to which the employee experiences the work as having a purpose that allows the employee to demonstrate their value to others. Responsibility is the degree to which the employee feels accountable for their work performance and outcomes. Last, knowledge of results is the extent to which the jobholder is aware of how well they are performing their job.

The psychological states mediate the relationship between job characteristics and work-related outcomes such as motivation, satisfaction and work performance, as shown in Figure 9.21. If an employee is experiencing the three psychological states, it allows them to have positive feelings about themselves when they perform well. Feeling good about work then also helps employees to keep performing well.

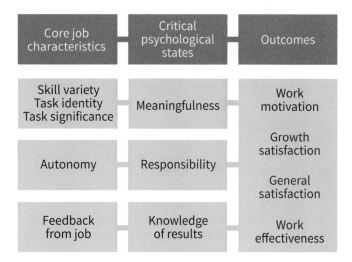

Figure 9.21: Hackman and Oldham's job characteristics model

KEY WORDS

job characteristic: the feature of a particular job, task or role which can be viewed as a dimension, e.g. high or low skill variety

psychological state: the experience of a set of particular thoughts and feelings

Techniques of job design

This subsection on the techniques of job design brings the two theories of job satisfaction together as they demonstrate the very many ways in which jobs can be redesigned and the effects that this can have. Once a job has begun, there are further techniques of job design that can increase satisfaction and motivation in workers.

Example study

A literature review by **Belias and Skikas (2013)** found that effective job design can stimulate employees' interest to work and to increase their job satisfaction, leading to high levels of employee performance and productivity. This review is linked to Herzberg's theory of job satisfaction in that it considers how each technique of job design can motivate workers.

In their review of studies into job design, Belias and Skikas define job enrichment as involving workers in a wider variety of tasks to perform to help increase their level of skill and responsibility. They suggest that variety, the belief that the task is important, the use of abilities and feedback is essential to enrich a job. Job enrichment can help workers feel greater interest and control over their work, increasing motivation and satisfaction.

Belias and Skikas view job rotation as the practice of regularly changing workers' tasks within their normal role in a pre-determined way. For example, in a kitchen, workers could rotate around all the different preparation areas; in a large supermarket, workers could rotate between departments and between tasks within these departments. The review suggests that job rotation can also introduce variety and prevent workers from becoming bored by completing just one task. An additional benefit is that the increased skills and experience of the worker means that they can undertake different functions within their organisation, dependent on need.

Last, job enlargement is defined by Belias and Skikas as increasing the quantity or type of tasks. Horizontal job enlargement involves giving workers more tasks to do but at the same level of challenge to increase variety. Vertical job enlargement involves the addition of further decision-making responsibilities and/or higher-level, more challenging tasks (Arnold et al., 2005). This increases variety within a job and the workers' abilities and sense of empowerment and status. For example, although someone is not given a formal promotion, they

are given more freedom to do their job in the way that they think is best. Allowing teams to manage themselves is another example of vertical job enlargement.

RESEARCH METHODS

Herzberg's is a theoretical model based on interviews with over 200 participants, which means it is a large enough sample to *generalise* from and there is enough data to support the predictions made in the model.

Likewise, Job Characteristics Theory has also generated empirical research. It provides precise, testable hypotheses and there have been several studies that demonstrate the core characteristics do *correlate* with motivation and satisfaction. However, Arnold et al. note that it is surprising that there have been very few attempts to experimentally manipulate jobs so that they have more of the core job characteristics. Of those that have been done, findings suggest that changes to job characteristics have an impact on satisfaction and motivation rather than work performance.

The techniques of job design technique have been implemented in real-life situations and their effects measured. The review by Belias and Skikas, includes *field experiments*, meaning that the researchers need to take great care in interpreting their findings (see the Hawthorne effect, discussed in Section 9.4) as it can be challenging to control for extraneous variables in a complex, natural environment such as a workplace.

ISSUES AND DEBATES

The practical *applications* of Herzberg's models are that those in charge of organisations would be advised to focus on increasing characteristics which produce worker satisfaction (motivational factors), while decreasing factors that produce worker dissatisfaction (hygiene factors). To increase satisfaction, managers can consider enhancing opportunities for gaining responsibility or working autonomously. If workers are dissatisfied, then the manager should focus on improving supervision and general working conditions.

CONTINUED

Hackman and Oldham's Job Characteristics Theory also has many useful *applications*. By identifying the core job characteristics that produce critical psychological states, which in turn affect motivation, satisfaction and work performance, organisations can design jobs around these characteristics. This theory also fits within an *individual–situational debate*. Hackman and Oldham make clear that even relatively small changes to the job characteristics (situation) can impact on the employee (individual) and their attitudes.

Measuring job satisfaction

Job Descriptive Index

Job satisfaction is typically measured through self-report measures which include questionnaires and rating scales. The Job Descriptive Index (Smith et al., 1969) is one of the best known and most widely used measures of job satisfaction. It measures five aspects of job satisfaction:

1 experience of the work
2 salary
3 promotion prospects
4 experience of supervision
5 experience of co-workers.

It is a basic scale to which workers answer either *yes*, *no* or *can't decide* in response to a series of statements about their job (see Table 9.7 for an example item).

This is an interesting example of a scale to study as the results are compared with standardised norms based on data from a large sample of people which is regularly updated. Any individual's score can be compared with normative scores in respect of age, gender, job level, education and 'community prosperity'. This means that rather than simply measuring the satisfaction of an individual, their satisfaction can be compared with these norms to see whether the individual is more or less satisfied with their job than other similar individuals. Some of the advantages of the Job Descriptive Index identified by Smith et al. include that it measures specific, objective areas of job satisfaction rather than satisfaction in general terms. It is relatively easy to read and does not use any complex language, which makes it suitable to use with a large variety of people.

ISSUES AND DEBATES

The Job Descriptive Index (JDI) is an example of *nomothetic* research that collects quantitative data. The questionnaire respondents are each seen as examples of a whole population and their thoughts and beliefs about work. *Idiographic* research is usually qualitative and would focus more deeply on the experience of the individual

Jobs in general
Think of your job in general. All in all, what is it like most of the time? In the space beside each word or phrase, write
Y for 'yes' if it describes your job
N for 'no' if it does not describe it
? for '?' if you cannot decide
Pleasant
Bad
Great
Waste of time
Good
Undesirable
Worthwhile
Worse than most
Acceptable
Superior
Better than most
Disagreeable
Makes me content
Inadequate
Excellent
Rotten
Enjoyable
Poor

Table 9.7: Extract from the Job Descriptive Index

Walton's Quality of Working Life

Quality of working life (QWL) is a term used commonly in organisational psychology, but is often described in different ways. Heskett et al. (1997) propose that QWL is the feelings that employees have towards their jobs, colleagues and companies and that these feelings would affect an organisation's growth and profitability. Others see QWL as a process by which an organisation responds to employee needs. For the purposes of this discussion, we will consider the QWL in its broadest sense: a range of factors such as job security, reward systems, pay levels and opportunity for growth which determine an employee's feelings about their working life.

Walton (1974) developed a typology which can be used to assess QWL and this consists of eight key conditions:

- Fair and adequate payment: to measure this, the researcher could ask questions to determine whether the pay received by the worker is enough to live on or whether it is equivalent to the pay that other workers are receiving. They might also ask participants to rate their agreement with statements such as 'I am satisfied with the amount of money I earn'.

- Safe and healthy working conditions: Walton's typology can be used to assess a range of health and safety issues which may contribute to QWL. For example, appropriate clothing and safety procedures may be in place as a result of employer concern, union action or legislation and while this may vary from culture to culture it is evident that this is required for QWL.

- Providing opportunities to use and develop skills: people will rate their QWL higher if they are given autonomy and independence to do their jobs and if there is scope to develop their skills.

- Opportunity for career growth and security: relates to the chance an employee has to develop their work role as well as the sense of security felt in that job. For example, there has been a move away from permanent employment to fixed term or 'zero-hours' contracts (without guaranteed weekly hours) in some cultures recently. This lack of security can reduce perceived QWL.

- Positive social relationships/integration within the workplace: QWL is affected by the social context. Positive relationships at work are beneficial to increasing productivity and satisfaction as well as lowering stress, absenteeism and staff turnover.

- The total life space: sometimes referred to as 'work–life balance'. Any assessment of QWL would need to measure the extent to which employees were able to maintain this balance. For example, allowing someone an afternoon off to watch their child take part in a school performance will improve an employee's ratings of their QWL.

- Constitutionalism (policies and procedures) in the workplace: relates to whether the workplace has appropriate policies in place, for example for dealing with bullying. QWL is impacted by the extent to which employees feel the organisational culture is valuable and supportive.

- Social relevance: finally, QWL is enhanced when people can evaluate the importance of what they do (or what the organisation does) for other people in a positive way.

Within each key condition, Walton elaborated on five sub-criteria to form his QWL questionnaire. This 35 item self-report consisted of questions such as:

How satisfied are you with your remuneration?

How satisfied are you with your salubrity conditions in your workplace?

Respondents answered on a scale of (1–5) with 5 being very satisfied and 1 being very dissatisfied. Walton's QWL questionnaire is still influential today. However, it has undergone a number of modifications by other researchers who note the use of confusing technical language, e.g. *salubrity* (work conditions) and *remuneration* (salary). These terms might not be familiar to many people, so by updating and adapting the questionnaire, the QWL has retained its value as a tool for highlighting the gap between human values (life) and technological and economic growth (work).

RESEARCH METHODS

Both of the areas discussed in this section involve some type of *psychometric* testing. We have considered the strengths and weaknesses of psychometric tests earlier in this chapter. It is important to realise that although such tests can be relatively easy to administer and score, they are prone to *demand characteristics* and *social desirability bias*, and flaws in their construction can have serious effects on the outcomes.

The Job Description Index has many strengths in comparison with other similar tests. It is one of the most thoroughly tested and carefully validated tests and is based on standardised norms, which means that each individual's score can be compared to a bank of scores taken from a huge sample of participants in many different occupations. It is therefore possible to identify whether the individual is more or less satisfied than others of the same age, sex, occupation and so on. This means it is high in both *reliability* and *validity*.

ISSUES AND DEBATES

Psychometric testing in the form of the JDI and QWL is popular in some organisational settings. The results gained from using the JDI can be *applied in real life* to improving aspects of the working environment. This can advantage organisations by making their workers more satisfied and hence more motivated and productive.

Finally, we examined quality of working life. This is a very useful, although very broad, concept whose application has generated a range of initiatives in many organisations from the development of workable policies for dealing with bullying, allowing for compassionate leave or the ability to work flexibly through to the provision of social activities designed to improve employees' quality of working life (see Figure 9.22). In what way does this topic contribute to the reductionism versus holism debate? You might want to consider how research in this area looks at a whole range of personal, social and emotional factors.

Figure 9.22 Employees can struggle to balance their work and life commitments

Attitudes to work

Workplace sabotage

Workplace **sabotage** describes behaviours that are designed to break laws or organisational rules and deliberately try to stop work from taking place. These behaviours are most commonly the result of dissatisfaction and powerlessness. Sabotage has professional and legal consequences for both the saboteur and the organisation, resulting in employee termination, legal action and loss of capital.

Dubois (1980) identifies three methods of workplace sabotage by employees:

1 Destruction of machinery or goods: this method of sabotage includes arson, deliberately breaking machinery and sabotaging the product of the work (see Figure 9.23).

2 Stopping production: some ways to stop production include limiting or halting the supply or raw materials of components, strike action or preventing the final product being delivered to customers.

3 Slowing down production: this can be achieved by working slowly, working strictly according to rules, working unenthusiastically, absenteeism, labour turnover and refusing to work.

The following study by Giacalone and Rosenfeld (1987) explores a number of reasons for workplace sabotage, including **restoration equity** and **retaliation**. Restoration equity occurs when employees feel that the level of their contributions is not equal to their reward. Sabotage is one method employees may choose to use to restore a fair balance. However, employee retaliation is behaviour intended to disrupt or avenge organisational injustice and is more closely related to aggressive behaviours.

KEY WORDS

sabotage: in the workplace this includes any employee behaviour designed to cause a production or profit loss to the organisation

restoration equity: to return a situation to one of balance or fairness

retaliation: an act of counter-attack or revenge

Key study: Giacalone and Rosenfeld (1987)

Giacalone, R. A., & Rosenfeld, P. (1987). Reasons for employee sabotage in the workplace. Journal of *business and psychology*, 1(4), 367–378.

Context

Figure 9.23: Destruction of machinery or goods is one form of workplace sabotage

Workplace sabotage is a challenging area to study, as it is often associated with criminal activity and therefore covert. Because it may have legal implications, employers may prefer not to discuss acts of sabotage with those outside of the organisation. Likewise, employees may not wish to report their own acts of sabotage or implicate others as they fear the repercussions (job loss or the threat of legal action). At the time in which this study was conducted, the cost of employee sabotage was believed to be increasing, meaning it was of interest to organisational psychologists.

For this reason, research in this area is important but challenging. Evidence suggests that research data are often more reliable when conducted in a way that maintains the anonymity of the participants, for example via questionnaires. Similarly, conducting the research away from the workplace may produce more valid responses as participants are less concerned about revealing sensitive information.

Main theories and explanations

Giacalone and Rosenfeld define workplace sabotage as any employee behaviour that intends to effect production or profit loss for a particular organisation. They view sabotage essentially as an act of aggression and a chance for the employee to display a public image that they feel is in their best interests, for example to appear tough. When there is conflict between management and the employee, this can make the employee look weak or incompetent, so sabotage becomes a form of counter-attack to regain the identity of appearing strong, competent and back in control.

Reasons or explanations for sabotage are important to the saboteur as they minimise the severity of the act of sabotage, showing a justifiable motive for the act. Making the act of sabotage seem legitimate can help relieve any sense of guilt or responsibility allowing the saboteur to maintain self-respect. Some individuals think that the reasons for sabotage are justified or acceptable whereas other people do not. These individual differences in the number and type of reasons that particular persons will accept as justifiable might make it more likely it is that an individual would engage in sabotage.

Aim

The study by Giacalone and Rosenfeld aimed to explore the reasons used to justify sabotage by employees within an organisation. Specifically, the researchers chose to consider the justifiability of four general methods of sabotage (slowdowns, destructiveness, dishonesty and causing chaos) to see how these linked to the level of justification employees gave for sabotage.

The hypothesis of this study predicted that participants who accepted more reasons for sabotage were more likely to justify sabotage than those who did not accept many reasons, regardless of the sabotage type.

Design

The participants of this study were 38 unionised labourers working in an electrical factory. A 'Sabotage Methods Questionnaire' was constructed with the help of an ex-employee (with five years' service) who listed all the ways that were used by the employees to sabotage the company. This produced a total of 29 general sabotage methods (e.g. losing paperwork, pulling the fire alarm, or leaving graffiti on bathroom walls) that could be grouped into four general categories:

- Work slowdowns
- Destruction of machinery, premises or products
- Dishonesty
- Causing chaos

A further list was created of ten reasons for sabotage:

1 Self defence
2 Revenge
3 An eye for an eye
4 Protect oneself from boss / company
5 To protect friends or family from boss / company
6 To protect one's job
7 The foreman / company deserved it
8 The foreman / company hurt me previously
9 No one was hurt by the action
10 Release of frustrations
11 Just for fun

Each participant was given the list of four sabotage methods and the list of 11 sabotage reasons and asked to rate them individually on a scale of 1 (not at all justifiable) to 7 (totally justifiable). A median split was performed on the potential reasons for sabotage creating two groups: high-reason acceptors (those who accepted a wide variety of reasons for sabotage) and low-reason acceptors (those who accepted few if any reasons for sabotage).

> **KEY WORD**
>
> median split: where a group is split into two using the mid-point as the division. Using a median split turns a continuous variable into a categorical one

Results, findings and conclusions

Results included the following differences: high-reason acceptors justified production slowdowns more than low-reason acceptors. High-reason acceptors also justified destruction of machinery, premises or products more than low-reason acceptors. Unexpectedly, high-reason acceptors did not justify dishonesty more than low-reason acceptors but high-reason acceptors did justify causing chaos more than low-reason accepters.

The researchers concluded that while acceptance seems to affect justification of sabotage in many forms,

this is not the case for dishonesty. This is possibly seen as different from the other forms of sabotage. Work slowdowns, destruction and causing chaos may be aimed at hurting the company, but they do not represent potential monetary gains for the employee. This may make dishonesty a qualitatively different form of sabotage (justified for very different reasons such as poor salaries) and potentially interpreted in very different ways by employers or bosses. If this type of sabotage was simply interpreted as self-serving, then it has not served the desired demonstrative function. It may also be that dishonesty threatens self-esteem in a way that the other forms of sabotage do not.

Evaluation

The researchers in this study conducted a survey on sabotage. The advantage of this is that a large amount of *quantitative data* could be collected about employee attitudes towards sabotage and this could be easily compared and replicated, meaning the results are likely to be *reliable*. However, surveys suffer from the same weaknesses as all self-report methods and probably the most important one here is *social desirability bias*. It may be that respondents were concerned about who would see their answers and this may have had an impact on what they were prepared to say.

On the other hand, the questionnaire was *anonymised* and so the identity of the participants was protected. This means they may have given more *valid* responses. It is also a more *ethical* way of investigating a sensitive area of organisational psychology, as respondents to the survey were protected from negative consequences of engaging with the research.

The study was also able to use a quasi-experimental approach when comparing the high-reason acceptors with the low-reason acceptors and this has provided results that can be *applied to real life*. In particular, the finding that both groups saw 'dishonesty' as qualitatively different from all other forms of sabotage is a useful one. This could allow employers to respond to dishonesty in a different way from how they might respond to other acts of sabotage.

This study clearly shows how the workplace environment (*situation*) can impact on the individual's behaviour. The researchers place particular importance on organisational management recognising and deterring individual saboteurs as opposed to trying to resolve the reasons for sabotage.

Absenteeism and organisational commitment

Absenteeism is one of the main costs to employers. In the UK, the Confederation of Business and Industry found that workplace stress was one of the major causes of absenteeism. Absenteeism can be voluntary or involuntary. Involuntary absenteeism is when the worker has no choice but to be absent, usually due to illness. Organisations will expect some illnesses and should have policies in place to deal with this (e.g., a school may have a regular 'supply teacher' to cover for absences). Voluntary absenteeism is where the worker has chosen not to attend work without such a reason. This type of absenteeism can be due to dissatisfaction, but is a difficult factor to measure.

The paper by Blau and Boal (1987) combine the concepts of job involvement and **organisational commitment** as a way of predicting turnover and absenteeism with their organisational commitment model. Job involvement is the extent to which a person psychologically identifies with their job. Job involvement can be high or low, and organisational commitment can also be high or low. This produces four possible categories of commitment:

- High job involvement and high organisational commitment
- High job involvement and low organisational commitment
- Low job involvement and high organisational commitment
- Low job involvement and low organisational commitment

Each of these situations is predicted to have a different impact on turnover and absenteeism. The first group, high job involvement and high organisational commitment, describes individuals for whom work is important to their self-esteem. These individuals will exert a great deal of time and effort in their jobs. In addition, because they identify strongly with the organisation, it is predicted that they will also become highly involved with group activities that help to

maintain the organisation. They can be seen to represent the most valued members of the organisation and are likely to get promoted. It is expected that this group will show the lowest level of turnover and absenteeism, although if members of this group were to be absent or leave this would have a greater impact on the organisation, because they are harder to replace.

The second group contains individuals who show a high level of job involvement and a low level of organisational commitment. Although their work is important to them, they do not identify with the organisation or its goals. They are likely to show high levels of effort for individual tasks but a low level of effort for group tasks. If the first groups are the 'stars' of the organisation, then this group are the 'lone wolves'. Such people are highly sensitive to factors such as working conditions and pay. If better opportunities were to arise elsewhere these people would leave. The effect of turnover here would be different from the first group. Despite their high levels of individual effort, they do not integrate themselves within the organisation. This can breed resentment if others then need to pick up their group work tasks and perceived inequities can damage the cohesiveness of the group. Blau and Boal also argue that absenteeism among this group is likely to reflect them taking career enhancing opportunities: and being more willing to violate absenteeism policies if there is a conflict between a work goal and a personal goal.

The third group includes people who show a low level of job involvement but a high level of organisational commitment. Their work is not personally important to them but they do identify with the organisation and its goals. They may exert little effort on individual tasks but a great deal on group maintenance tasks. Blau and Boal describe these people as the corporate citizens of the organisation. Their absence can have a significant impact on others.

Finally, the fourth group is those individuals who exhibit low levels of both job involvement and organisational commitment. Work is not viewed as being important to their self-image and so they do not put a great deal of effort into individual tasks and as the organisation is not strongly identified with, they do not contribute to group maintenance. These are the least valuable members of an organisation and are described as 'apathetic employees'.

KEY WORD

organisational commitment: the mental and emotional bond an individual employee has to an organisation

Choose one of the four combinations of job involvement and organisational commitment proposed by Blau and Boal. Write a short scenario describing an employee from the combination you have chosen. Swap scenarios with another student. Can you identify which situation is described in their scenario?

REFLECTION

Consider the activity you have just completed. What approach did you take to designing your scenario? How did you embed the elements of job involvement and organisational commitment? Try to evaluate whether this was the right approach for the task or whether you would try things differently next time.

RESEARCH METHODS

As we saw in the evaluation of Giacalone and Rosenfeld's study, researching workplace sabotage can be difficult. This is because it is a sensitive area of human behaviour that has far-reaching consequences for individuals and the organisations for which they work. There can be *ethical issues* to consider around maintaining the *anonymity* of participants, and trying to collect *reliable* and *valid* data as participants may be reluctant to reveal information that appears to be undesirable or anti-social.

Blau and Boal's model of absenteeism and commitment has been investigated in various pieces of empirical research. The challenges of measuring such factors through self-report is that the individual reports how committed they are. In one way this is a highly *valid* method because that employee is in the best position to know how they feel about the organisation for which they work. However, employees can be biased (or responding to *demand characteristics*). Can you think of an alternative way researchers could study organisational commitment? What would be the benefits and limitations of such a method in comparison with self-report?

ISSUES AND DEBATES

Blau and Boal's model is *applicable to real life* as it brings together the concepts of job involvement and organisational commitment. This idea is useful in allowing organisations to be able to predict potential staff turnover, for example. The organisations can plan for staff leaving or being absent and/or put measures in place to reduce the risk to work output. Prediction of employee retention and output, even if not 100% correct, is essential to effectively running large organisations. Likewise, understanding the methods and reasons for workplace sabotage are important for organisations who should seek to minimise criminal activity, destruction of property and financial loss.

Walton's typology has been used to develop a variety of techniques to measure QWL in a variety of organisations and cultures. However different these organisations and cultures are these same eight components of QWL will be valid, meaning *cultural differences* are accepted as a feature of this model.

Questions

13 From Herzberg's two-factor theory of job satisfaction, give examples of the following:
   a factors that affect job satisfaction
   b factors that affect job dissatisfaction.
14 Define what is meant by 'job rotation'.
15 There have been several examples of psychometric tests in this section.
   a State one strength of psychometric tests.
   b State one weakness of psychometric tests.

SELF-EVALUATION CHECKLIST

After studying this chapter, copy and complete a table like this:

I can	Fully confident	Fairly confident	Need to revisit	Coursebook	Workbook
describe, evaluate, compare and apply needs theories of motivation at work					
describe, evaluate, compare and apply cognitive theories of motivation at work					
describe, evaluate, compare and apply theory and research into motivators at work					
describe, evaluate, compare and apply traditional and modern theories of leadership					
describe, evaluate, compare and apply theory and research into leadership styles					
describe, evaluate, compare and apply theory and research into leaders and followers					
describe, evaluate, compare and apply theory and research into group development and decision-making					
describe, evaluate, compare and apply theory and research into individual and group performance					
describe, evaluate, compare and apply theory and research into conflict at work					
describe, evaluate, compare and apply theory and research into physical work conditions					
describe, evaluate, compare and apply theory and research into temporal conditions					
describe, evaluate, compare and apply theory and research into health and safety					
describe, evaluate, compare and apply theories of job satisfaction					
describe, evaluate, compare and apply research into measuring job satisfaction					
describe, evaluate, compare and apply theory and research into attitudes to work.					

PROJECT

One example of a transformational leader is Nobel Peace Prize winner, Nelson Mandela:

'Nelson Mandela joined the African National Congress in 1944 and was engaged in resistance against the ruling National Party's apartheid policies after 1948. He was widely accepted as the most significant black leader in South Africa and became a potent symbol of resistance as the anti-apartheid movement gathered strength. He consistently refused to compromise his political position to obtain his freedom.' (adapted from www.nobelprize.org/prizes/peace/1993/mandela/biographical/ 30th March 2021)

Working on your own or with a partner, you will produce a poster on a transformational leader of your choice. To complete the project, follow these steps:

1   Use the internet, other media or your own knowledge to identify a transformational leader.

This person can lead any type of organisation e.g. political, voluntary, educational.

2   Using the information in this chapter on universalist theories of leadership (in the subsection 'Universalist theories'), your class notes and any other relevant resources, consider:

* The circumstances in which the individual rose to their position as leader

* The wider social, political or organisational context in which the leader was trying to enact change

* The qualities demonstrated by the leader which could qualify them as 'transformational'

3   Create your poster including the information from your research, supported with suitable images or diagrams.

Peer assessment

Once you have completed your poster, share it with the rest of your class as part of a peer assessment. You should aim to give feedback on another learner's poster in the following areas.

1   Breadth of research: is there evidence that the learner has used one or more sources in their research, or does the work seem to be anecdotal or lacking facts?

2   How well does the finished poster explain what is meant by transformational leadership? You could rate this using a smiley face system.

3   Is there any detail that the poster is missing or isn't explained clearly? Make a comment on what worked well and what could be made clearer.

EXAM-STYLE QUESTIONS

1   **Outline one** application of Latham and Locke's goal-setting theory.   [3]

2   **Discuss** the freewill and determinism debate in the context of the key study by Landry et al. (2019).   [6]

3   Heifetz outlines six principles in meeting adaptive challenges.

    a   **Describe three** of these principles.   [6]

    b   **Analyse** the responsibilities of an adaptive leader.   [4]

COMMAND WORD

outline: set out main points

describe: state the points of a topic / give characteristics and main features

analyse: examine in detail to show meaning, identify elements and the relationship between them

CONTINUED

4   Groupthink is one example of faulty decision-making.
    Suggest a procedure for a study to investigate groupthink.   [5]

5   Shift work is one design of work that is often used in organisations
    that operate 24 hours a day, 7 days a week.

    a   Define what is meant by 'shift work'.   [2]

    b   Describe **one** study that has investigated the effects of shift work.   [4]

    c   Discuss **one** strength and **one** weakness of the study you described
        in part **b**.   [6]

6   Describe what psychologists have found out about the effect of
    open-plan offices.   [6]

7   Describe features of the sample used in the study by Giacalone
    and Rosenfeld (1987).   [3]

8   **Define** what is meant by 'organisational commitment'.   [3]

9   Outline the differences between voluntary and involuntary absenteeism.   [4]

[Total: 50]

COMMAND WORD

suggest: apply knowledge and understanding to situations where there are a range of valid responses in order to make proposals / put forward considerations

define: give the precise meaning of a term or concept' for greater differentiation

Additional references

Allport, F. H. (1920). The influence of the group upon association and thought. *Journal of experimental psychology, 3*(3), 159.

Arnold, J., Silvester, J., Cooper, C. L., Robertson, I. T., & Patterson, F. M. (2005). *Work psychology: understanding human behaviour in the workplace.* London: Pearson Education.

Belbin, R. M. (2010). *Management teams.* London: Routledge.

Björkqvist, K., Österman, K., & Hjelt-Bäck, M. (1994). Aggression among university employees. *Aggressive behavior, 20*(3), 173–184.

Blau, G. J., & Boal, K. B. (1987). Conceptualizing how job involvement and organizational commitment affect turnover and absenteeism. *Academy of management review, 12*(2), 288–300.

Brown, D., & Armstrong, M. (1999). *Paying for contribution: real performance-related pay strategies.* Kogan Page Publishers.

Cuadrado, I., Morales, J. F., & Reeio, P. (2008). Women's access to managerial positions: an experimental study of leadership styles and gender. *Spanish journal of psychology, 11*(1), 55.

de Waal, A., & Jansen, P. (2013, April). The bonus as hygiene factor: the role of reward systems in the high performance organization. Evidence-Based HRM: A Global Forum for Empirical Scholarship. Emerald Group Publishing.

Deci, E. L., & Ryan, R. M. (1985). *Self-determination and intrinsic motivation in human behavior.* New York: Springer.

Dekker, S. W. (2015). The psychology of accident investigation: epistemological, preventive, moral and existential meaning-making. *Theoretical issues in ergonomics science, 16*(3), 202–213.

Dubois, P. (1980). *Sabotage in industry.* Harmondsworth, UK: Penguin.

Earley, P. C. (1993). East meets West meets Mideast: further explorations of collectivistic and individualistic work groups. *Academy of management journal, 36*(2), 319–348.

Forsyth, D. R. (2006). Decision making. In Forsyth, D. R. (2009). *Group dynamics*, 5th edition (317–349). Belmont, CA: Wadsworth Publishing.

Fattorusso, J., Skovoroda, R., Buck, T., & Bruce, A. (2007). UK executive bonuses and transparency - a research note. *British journal of industrial relations, 45*(3), 518 -536.

Giacalone, R. A., & Rosenfeld, P. (1987). Reasons for employee sabotage in the workplace. *Journal of business and psychology, 1*(4), 367–378.

Gold, D. R., Rogacz, S., Bock, N., Tosteson, T. D., Baum, T. M., Speizer, F. E., & Czeisler, C. A. (1992). Rotating shift work, sleep, and accidents related to sleepiness in hospital nurses. *American journal of public health, 82*(7), 1011–1014.

Hackman, J. R., & Oldham, G. R. (1976). Motivation through the design of work: test of a theory. *Organizational behavior and human performance, 16*(2), 250–279.

Heifetz, R. A., & Laurie, D. L. (1997). The work of leadership. *Harvard business review, 75*, 124–134.

Heifetz, R. A., Heifetz, R., Grashow, A., & Linsky, M. (2009). *The practice of adaptive leadership: tools and tactics for changing your organization and the world.* Boston: Harvard Business Press.

Herzberg. F., Mausner, B., & Snyderman, B. (1959). *The motivation to work.* New York: Wiley.

Heskett, J., Sasser, W. E., & Schlesinger, L. A. (1997). *The service profit chain: how leading companies link profit and growth to loyalty, satisfaction, and value.* New York: Free Press.

Janis, I. (1971). *Groupthink. Psychology today, 5*(6), 44–76.

Kelley, R. E. (1988). In praise of followers. *Harvard business review, 66*, 142–148.

Knutsson, A. (2003). Health disorders of shift workers. *Occupational medicine, 53*(2), 103–108.

Kompier, M. A. (2006). The `Hawthorne effect' is a myth, but what keeps the story going? *Scandinavian journal of work, environment & health, 32*, 402–412.

Kouzes, J. & Posner, B. (1987). Leadership practices inventory: LPI. Available from www.leadershipchallenge.com/lpileadershippracticesinventory.

Landry, A.T., Zhang, Y., Papachristopoulos, K., & Forest, J. (2019). Applying self-determination theory to understand the motivational impact of cash rewards: new evidence from lab experiments. *International journal of psychology, 55*.

Latané, B. (1981). The psychology of social impact. *American psychologist, 36*(4), 343.
Locke, E. A., & Latham, G. P. (1984). *Goal setting: a motivational technique that works!* Englewood Cliffs, NJ: Prentice Hall.

Maslow, A. H. (1943). A theory of human motivation. *Psychological review, 50*(4), 370.

Mayo, E. (1933). *The human problems of an industrial civilization.* New York: Macmillan.

Muczyk, J. P., & Reimann, B. C. (1987). The case for directive leadership. *Academy of management perspectives, 1*(4), 301–311.

Nagel, D. C. (1988). Human error in aviation operations. In E. L. Wiener & D. C. Nagel (Eds), *Human factors in aviation* (263–303). Academic Press.

Oishi, S., Diener, E., Suh, E., & Lucas, R. E. (1999). Value as a moderator in subjective well-being. *Journal of personality, 67*(1), 157–184.

Pheasant, S. (1991). *Ergonomics, work and health.* Basingstoke: Macmillan International Higher Education.

Ringelmann, M. (1913). Appareils de cultur mecanique avec treuils et cables (resultats d'essais) [Mechanical tilling equipment with winches and cables (results of tests)]. *Annales de l'Institut National Agronomique, 2e série, 12,* 299–343.

Roberts, G. E. (1994). Maximizing performance appraisal system acceptance: perspectives from municipal government personnel administrators. *Public personnel management, 23*(4), 525–549.

Rose, M. (1998). Performance related pay in schools: an assessment of the Green papers. London: NUT.

Saeednia, Y. (2011). Generating a scale measuring hierarchy of basic needs. *Procediasocial and behavioral sciences, 15,* 3084–3094.

Scouller, J. (2011). *The three levels of leadership: how to develop your leadership presence, knowhow, and skill.* Cirencester: Management Books.

Smith, P. C., Kendall, L. M., & Hulin, C. L. (1969) *The measurement of satisfaction in work and retirement: a strategy for the study of attitudes.* Chicago: Rand McNally.

Stogdill, R. M. & Coons, A. E. (Eds) (1957). *Leader behavior: its description and measurement.* Columbus: The Ohio State University, Bureau of Business Research.

Taylor, J., & Hartley, N. (2021) The King's Fund, available at www.kingsfund.org.uk/blog/2013/07/why-aren%E2%80%99t-there-more-women-leaders-nhs (accessed 7 April 2021).

Thomas, K. W., & Kilmann, R. H. (1974). Thomas -Kilmann conflict mode instrument. Tuxedo, NY: Xicom.

Tomczak, D. L., Lanzo, L. A., & Aguinis, H. (2018). Evidence-based recommendations for employee performance monitoring. *Business horizons, 61*(2), 251–259.

Triplett, N. (1898). The dymogenic factors in pacemaking and competition. *American journal of psychology, 9,* 507–533.

Tuckman, B. W., & Jensen, M. A. (2010). Stages of small-group development revisited. *Group facilitation: a research & application journal, 10.*

Vroom, V. H. (1964). *Work and motivation.* New York: Wiley.

Walton, R.E. (1974). QWL indicators: prospects and problems. In Portugal, A. H. (Ed.), *Measuring*

Zajonc, R. B., & Markus, H. (1984). Affect and cognition: the hard interface. *Emotions, cognition, and behavior,* 73–102.

> Glossary

Command words

Below are the syllabus definitions for command words which may be used in exams.

The information in this section is taken from the Cambridge Assessment International Education syllabus (9990) for examination from 2024. You should always refer to the appropriate syllabus document for the year of your examination to confirm the details and for more information. The syllabus document is available on the Cambridge Assessment International Education website www.cambridgeinternational.org.

analyse: examine in detail to show meaning, identify elements and the relationship between them

compare: identify/comment on similarities and/or differences

define: give precise meaning

describe: state the points of a topic / give characteristics and main features

evaluate: judge or calculate the quality, importance, amount, or value of something

explain: set out purposes or reasons / make the relationships between things clear / say why and/or how and support with relevant evidence

give: produce an answer from a given source or recall / memory

identify: name / select / recognise

outline: set out main points

state: express in clear terms

suggest: apply knowledge and understanding to situations where there are a range of valid responses in order to make proposals / put forward considerations

Key words

absenteeism: regular non-attendance at work without good reason

acupuncture: an ancient Asian method of pain management that involves the insertion of very fine needles in the skin at specific points

acute episode: a period of time during which a person is suffering with psychotic symptoms, such as hallucinations or delusions

acute pain: can be severe but comes on quickly and lasts of a relatively short period of time. Acute pain is usually in a very specific location and has an identifiable source

adherence: how much a person's behaviour follows what their healthcare provider recommends and is agreed on

adoption study: a type of study looking at the similarities between adopted individuals and their biological parents as a way of investigating the differing influences of biology and environment

aggression: behaviour that is aimed at harming others either physically or psychologically

aim: the intention of the study, the idea being tested or the purpose of the research, such as to investigate a question or solve a problem

alternative hypothesis: the testable statement predicting a difference between levels of the independent variable in an experiment (or a relationship between variables in a correlation)

ambience: the atmosphere or 'feel' of a place, often affected by sound, scent and sight

amplitude: the 'height' of waves, e.g. on an EEG (indicating voltage)

analgesics: medicines used to relieve pain, are often referred to as painkillers

anti-psychotics: a type of medication that is used to treat psychotic disorders, such as schizophrenia, by affecting levels of neurotransmitters in the brain

appraisal delay: the time the patient takes to appraise a symptom as a sign of illness. This involves deciding whether or not there is something wrong, i.e. that they are 'ill'

arousal: the extent to which we are alert, for example responsive to external sensory stimuli. It has physiological and psychological components and is mediated by the nervous system and hormones

attention diversion: a cognitive pain management strategy that involves the person finding ways to shift their attention away from the pain and onto something else instead

attention: the concentration of mental effort on a particular stimulus. It may be focused or divided

attribution: the cognitive process by which individuals explain the causes of behaviour and events. Our attributions may be faulty or biased: tending to always look to specific causes for behaviour on the basis of our previous life experience

authority: a person or organisation in a position of power who can give orders and requires obedience

autism spectrum disorder (ASD): a diagnostic category (previously including autism and Asperger's syndrome). Symptoms, appearing in childhood, present a range of difficulties with social interaction and communication and restricted, repetitive, or inflexible behaviours or interests

Autism Spectrum Quotient Test (AQ): a self-report questionnaire with scores ranging from 0 to 50. A higher score suggests that the person completing it has more autistic traits

autocratic leadership: behaviour style in which the leader controls all the decisions with little to no input from group members

banner blindness: the tendency to avoid looking at banners containing adverts, when viewing websites

bar chart: a graph used for data in discrete categories and total or average scores. There are gaps between each bar that is plotted on the graph because the columns are not related in a linear way

basic emotions: feelings such as happy, sad, angry, afraid and disgust. They are understood worldwide, and by very young children, and can be recognised without the need to attribute a belief to the person

behaviour chaining: a process that allows separately trained behaviours to be performed in sequence in response to cues

behavioural categories: the activities recorded in an observation. They should be operationalised (clearly defined) and should break a continuous stream of activity into discrete recordable events. They must be observable actions rather than inferred states

bias: systematic errors in thinking that happen when people are interpreting information. Cognitive bias affects the decisions and judgements that all of us make

biofeedback: a technique that uses electrical sensors to allow you to receive information about different functions of your body, by changes on a monitor or a beeping sound. Receiving this feedback allows you to make changes, such as relaxing muscles or slowing down your breathing

blank slate: The idea that all individuals are born without any mental content, and that all knowledge must come from experience

Blood Injection Phobia Inventory (BIPI): a self-report measure of blood-injection phobia

brand awareness: the extent to which consumers are familiar with a brand

brand name: the name used by a company to distinguish its products or services from other companies' products or services. It is the company's key identity and cannot be easily changed

brand recognition: the ability for consumers to recognise a brand from visual or auditory cues such as logos or slogans

Brief Symptom Inventory (BSI): a 53-item self-report measure designed to assess nine symptom dimensions (such as hostility, anxiety and depression) over the last seven days

Brief Symptom Inventory (BSI): a scale designed to measure adolescents' mental health. It contains 53 self-report items rated on a four-point Likert scale, measuring ten subscales including depression, anxiety, paranoid ideation, hostility and interpersonal sensitivity

building configuration: the overall size and shape of a building, and the way the building is laid out

bullying: pattern of behaviour in which one or more people harm and/or embarrass others

bureaucratic hierarchy: decisions are made based on who pays the most money; so, the businesses that pay the most money will get the best spaces

bystander: a person who is present but not directly involved in a situation

bystander apathy: when a bystander does not show concern for a person in need

captive animal welfare: Psychologists working with animals that are confined or outside of their normal environment must ensure the health and well-being of the animals. As part of this captive management, an animal's natural needs for accommodation, environment, freedom of movement, food, water and care should be appropriately met

cardiovascular: the system that includes the heart and blood vessels

case study: a research method in which a single instance, e.g. one person, family or institution, is studied in detail

causal relationship: a link between two variables such that a change in one variable is responsible for (i.e. causes) the change in the other variable, such as in an experiment

ceiling effect: this occurs when a test is too easy and all participants in a condition achieve a very high score. This is problematic as it does not allow the researcher to differentiate between results

central gaze cascade: the tendency to focus more and more attention on the central option immediately before the decision is made

cerebral blood flow (CBF): the increase in blood flow to parts of the brain that are active is measured by an MRI scanner

cerebral cortex: the outermost layer of the brain, responsible for different functions, such as thought, perception, and memory

charisma: the quality of being charming or appealing to others in a way that inspires devotion

choice blindness: refers to a person's inability to notice mismatches between intention and outcome in a decision

chronic pain: pain that lasts for a relatively long period of time and is resistant to treatment. Chronic pain is likely to be the result of long-term behavioural factors such as physical exertion, or due to chronic illnesses such as cancer

circadian rhythm: a cycle that repeats daily, i.e. approximately every 24 hours, such as the sleep/ wake cycle

classical conditioning: learning through association, studied in both humans and animals

clinical interview: involves asking the patient a range of open questions and will focus on getting an understanding of the patient's experience of their pain as well as evaluating a range of factors (such as behavioural and psychological) that influence the patient's experience and reporting of the pain

closed questions: a question format in questionnaires, interviews or test items that produces quantitative data. They have only a few, stated alternative responses and no opportunity to expand on answers

cognitive dissonance: the feeling of discomfort that comes from holding two conflicting beliefs, or when there is a conflict between beliefs and behaviours

cognitive redefinition: a cognitive pain management strategy that involves the person replacing threatening or negative thoughts about the pain with more rational or positive thoughts

cognitive-behaviour therapy (CBT): a treatment that incorporates aspects of cognitive and behavioural approaches to treating psychological disorders, such as schizophrenia

cohort: a group of participants selected at the same age or stage

collectivistic: a culture in which group goals are seen as more important than individual wants or needs

Coloured Analogue Scale (CAS): a pain rating scale suitable for children aged 9–15 years, where respondents marked on a line where their pain was from no pain (green) through to worst thinkable pain (red)

community interventions: any attempts to encourage a certain behaviour in a town or city, using methods such as leafleting, letters and lotteries

comparative judgement: a judgement made about how likely you feel you are to experience a particular event compared to the average (of people similar to you)

compensatory strategies: a strategy where the value of one attribute can be allowed to compensate for another

competitor-focused sales techniques: the seller focuses on how they compare to their competitors

complex emotions: require an understanding of someone else's cognitive state, that is the attribution of a belief or intention to the person. They are therefore harder to identify

compliance: passive following of medical orders, for example the percentage of days where the correct amount of medication is taken

concordance: the presence of a particular observable trait or disorder in both individuals between family members and within a set of twins; for example, the likelihood that one twin will have schizophrenia if the other twin has schizophrenia

concurrent task: an additional activity with a cognitive demand that we can perform at the same time as a main (primary) task

concurrent validity: a way to judge validity by comparing measures of the same phenomenon in different ways at the same time to show that they produce similar results in the same circumstances

confederate: someone who is involved in the study but acts as if they are not

confidentiality: participants' results and personal information should be kept safely and not released to anyone outside the study

conformity: showing behaviour or beliefs that match those of the rest of a group

confounding variable: an uncontrolled variable that acts systematically on one level of the IV so could hide or exaggerate differences between levels and therefore 'confound' or confuse the results making it difficult to understand the effect of the IV on the DV

content analysis: is a research tool used to measure and analyse the presence of certain words or terms in qualitative data, such as verbal discussions or text

contrast effect: a cognitive bias where our perception is altered because we compare two things to each other, rather than assessing each individually

control condition: a level of the IV in an experiment from which the IV itself is absent. It is compared to one or more experimental conditions

control group: a group of participants often used in an experiment, who do not receive the manipulation of the independent variable and can be used for comparison with the experimental group or groups

controlled observation: a study conducted by watching the participants' behaviour in a situation in which the social or physical environment has been manipulated by the researchers. It can be conducted in either the participants' normal environment or in an artificial situation

controls: ways to keep potential confounding variables constant, for example between levels of the IV, to ensure measured differences in the DV are likely to be due to the IV, raising validity

coronary heart disease (CHD): a condition that is a major cause of death worldwide. It occurs when the arteries become blocked so the heart cannot pump enough oxygenated blood around the body

correlation coefficient: a number between –1 and 1 that shows the strength of a relationship between two variables with a coefficient of –1 meaning there is a perfect negative correlation and a coefficient of 1 meaning there is a perfect positive correlation

correlation: a research method that looks for a relationship between two measured variables. A change in one variable is related to a change in the other (although these changes cannot be assumed to be causal)

cost–benefit analysis: a process to calculate the benefits of a situation (such as money made) minus the costs (money or time spent) to calculate whether the decision was successful

cost–benefit model: involves a decision-making process in which a person weighs up both the advantages and disadvantages of helping. If it seems beneficial to help, then the person is more likely to do so; if the risks are too great, they may not help

counterbalancing: a way to overcome order effects in a repeated measures design. Each possible order of levels of the IV is performed by a different sub-group of participants. This can be described as an ABBA design, as half the participants do condition A then B, and half do B then A

counterconditioning: replacing a conditioned response, such as fear, with another response, such as a feeling of calm

co-variables: the two measured variables in a correlation.

covert observer: the role of the observer is not obvious, e.g. because they are hidden or disguised

cross-sectional study: compares people at different ages or stages by comparing different groups of participants at one point in time

customer-focused sales technique: the seller looks at potential customers and considers their wants and needs

daydreaming: a mildly altered state of consciousness in which we experience a sense of being 'lost in our thoughts', typically positive ones, and a detachment from our environment

debriefing: giving participants a full explanation of the aims and potential consequences of the study at the end of a study so that they leave in at least as positive a condition as they arrived

deception: participants should not be deliberately misinformed (lied to) about the aim or procedure of the study. If this is unavoidable, the study should be planned to minimise the risk of distress, and participants should be thoroughly debriefed. It may be done to reduce the effects of demand characteristics but should be avoided

delusion of reference: a strongly held belief that events in the environment are related to you, for example the belief that a television programme is talking about you

demand characteristics: features of the experimental situation which give away the aims. They can cause participants to try to change their behaviour, for example to match their beliefs about what is supposed to happen, which reduces the validity of the study

democratic leadership: behaviour style in which the leader shares decision-making with group members

depressive episode: a period of at least two weeks, which involves depressed mood or lack of interest in usual activities for most of the day, nearly every day

desensitisation: to reduce and extinguish a response (e.g. fear) to stimuli (e.g. a syringe)

destructive obedience: obedience that has potential to cause psychological or physical harm or injury to another

Diagnostic and Statistical Manual (DSM): published by the American Psychiatric Association, it is used as a classification and diagnostic tool by doctors, psychiatrists and psychologists across the globe

differential effect: when one or more individuals experience a difference in outcome when exposed to the same stimuli

diffusion of responsibility: when there are other people available to help in an emergency, an individual may be less likely to take action because they feel a reduced sense of personal responsibility

directing style: this is when a doctor is authoritative and dominating and tells the patient what is wrong and what they should do next

directional (one-tailed) hypothesis: a statement predicting the direction of a relationship between variables, for example in an experiment whether the levels of the IV will produce an increase or a decrease in the DV (or in a correlation whether an increase in one variable will be linked to an increase or a decrease in another variable)

directive: behaviour style with a high amount of leader direction

disclosure of information: when the patient tells the doctor information about their symptoms and their experience for the doctor to make a diagnosis

disrupt-then-reframe' (DTR) technique: a technique intended to confuse consumers with a disruptive message and then reduce this confusion (or ambiguity) by reframing the message

distractor task: a task given to participants between learning and recall in a memory task, to distract them from consciously rehearsing the learned information

divided attention: the ability to split mental effort between two or more simultaneous tasks (called 'dual tasks'), for example driving a car and talking to a passenger

dizygotic (DZ) twins: non-identical twins, who share approximately 50% of their DNA with one another

doctor-centred style: a consultation style where the doctor leads, asks closed questions and does not encourage discussion with the patient

dorsal horn: the area of the spinal cord where the gating mechanism occurs, which receives information from small nerve fibres (pain) and large nerve fibres (touch) and sends this information to the brain

double-blind placebo controlled: neither the patient, nor the psychologists directly involved with the patient, know who has been given the real drug and who has been given the placebo

dream: a vivid, visual sequence of imagery that occurs at regular intervals during sleep and is associated with rapid eye movements

drive theory: when a person experiences increased internal motivation to reach a goal. These drivers can be primary (i.e. for survival) or secondary (i.e. learned)

drug trial: research studies where different drugs or medications are given to groups of people and their responses or outcomes are compared

DSM: the *Diagnostic and Statistical Manual of Mental Disorders* is produced by the American Psychiatric Association and is used to make diagnoses of mental disorders

early-onset: when a disorder starts at a significantly younger age than average. Schizophrenia typically starts during early adulthood so any development during childhood would be classed as early-onset

ecological validity: the extent to which the findings of research in one situation would generalise to other situations. This is influenced by whether the situation (e.g. a laboratory) represents the real world effectively and whether the task is relevant to real life (has mundane realism)

electroencephalograph (EEG): a machine used to detect and record electrical activity in nerve and muscle cells when many are active at the same time. It uses macroelectrodes, which are large electrodes stuck to the skin or scalp

electronic performance monitoring (EPM): the use of electronic systems to monitor and evaluate performance

empathy: how people respond to the observed experiences of others, seeing or imagining experiences from the other person's point of view and feeling concerned or upset for them

endorphins: the body's natural pain-killing chemicals

episodic mood disorder: a condition characterised by episodes of time where mood is either very low or very high

epistemological: relating to knowledge

equanimity: a sense of calm and composure in a difficult situation

ethical guidelines: pieces of advice that guide psychologists to consider the welfare of participants and wider society

ethical issues: problems in research that raise concerns about the welfare of participants (or have the potential for a wider negative impact on society)

evaluation apprehension: when a person experiences arousal from having an audience who they believe may evaluate (show approval or disapproval of) their performance

evaluative learning: a form of classical conditioning wherein attitudes towards stimuli are considered to be the product of complex thought processes and emotions, which lead an individual to perceive or evaluate a previously neutral stimulus negatively. Attitudes acquired through evaluative learning may be harder to change than more superficial associations

evolution: the consequence of the process of natural selection, such that offspring that have inherited beneficial characteristics are more likely to survive

existential: relating to being alive or existing

expectancy: a state of hopefulness that an event or experience will happen

experiment: an investigation that allows researchers to look for a causal relationship; an independent variable is manipulated and is expected to be responsible for changes in the dependent variable

experimental condition: one or more of the situations in an experiment that represent different levels of the IV and are compared (or compared to a control condition)

experimental design: the way in which participants are allocated to levels of the IV

extraneous variable: this either acts randomly, affecting the DV in all levels of the IV or systematically, i.e. on one level of the IV (called a confounding variable) so can obscure the effect of the IV, making the results difficult to interpret

extrinsic: something that comes from the outside; external

eye fixations: recordings of where participants focused on the screen

eye magnets: anything that interrupts eye-movement patterns and draws attention to a particular item

eye tracking: a method using a computer to record the pattern of eye movement of a participant

eye-movement patterns: the pattern that most people tend to follow when looking at, for example, a menu. This can be helpful in designing menus

eyewitness testimony: evidence provided by an individual who has seen (or heard) a crime being committed. This information is used by the legal system

Faces Pain Rating Scale-Revised (FPS-R): a pain rating scale suitable for children aged 3–8 years, showing six faces showing increasing levels of pain

false memory: a piece of stored information an individual believes to be an accurate memory but which is the consequence of later additional and untrue information, such as in a question about an event seen by an eyewitness

false negative diagnosis: occurs when the patient is unwell, but the doctor misdiagnoses them as being healthy

false positive diagnosis: occurs when the patient is healthy, but the doctor diagnoses them with an illness or a condition incorrectly

false positive response: giving an affirmative (positive) but incorrect answer to a question. For example, mistakenly picking out a person in a line-up when the real culprit is not there

family study: a type of study investigating whether biological relatives of those with a disorder are more likely than non-biological relatives to be similarly affected

fatigue effect: a situation where participants' performance declines because they experience the experimental task more than once, e.g. due to physical tiredness or boredom with the task

field experiment: an investigation looking for a causal relationship in which an independent variable is manipulated and is expected to be responsible for changes in the dependent variable. It is conducted in the normal environment for the participants for the behaviour being investigated and some control of variables is possible

fight or flight response: the body's natural initial response to a stressor, which leads to physiological changes in the body, so you are prepared to either flee or to defend yourself

filler questions: items put into a questionnaire, interview or test to disguise the aim of the study by hiding the important questions among irrelevant ones so that participants are less likely to work out the aims and then alter their behaviour

fixation time: in an eye-tracking study, the amount of time the participant focuses attention on the stimulus

flattened affect: the absence or reduction of an outward expression of feelings or emotions, such as a facial expression

fMRI (functional magnetic resonance imaging): a scanning technique used to measure activity in the brain by tracking the changes in flow of oxygenated blood. When a part of the brain is active it requires more oxygen so there will be an increased blood flow to that area

focused attention: the picking out of a particular input from a mass of information, such as many items presented together, or a rapid succession of individual items, for example concentrating on your teacher's voice even when there is building work outside and the learner next to you is whispering

foil: a 'foil' is something that is used as a contrast to something else. In Baron-Cohen et al.'s study the 'foil words' were the (incorrect) alternative words participants could choose to describe the eyes

follower: a person who supports and takes direction from a leader

followership: the ability and behaviour of followers to interact with and respond to their leaders

framing: the use of borders or boxes to group certain items together and draw a customer's eye to them

frequency: the number of events per fixed period of time, e.g. the number of eye movements per minute (approximately 60 per minute in REM sleep) or the number of brain waves (cycles) per second, or Hertz (Hz), e.g. 13–30 Hz for beta waves

fundamental attribution error: a bias in which people pay less attention to situational explanations for behaviour and over-emphasise dispositional explanations

gambling disorder: a disorder involving a pattern of persistent or recurring gambling behaviour either online or offline

gate control theory: proposes that the spinal cord contains a 'gate' that either prevents pain signals from entering the brain or allows them to continue. This theory can explain why our emotional state or our expectations affect how much something hurts

gender stereotype: a bias exhibited in society, which may be held by people and represented, for example, in books or toys that assign particular traits, behaviours, emotions, occupations, etc. to males and females

general adaptation syndrome (GAS): a three-stage process that describes the biological changes the body goes through when it is under stress. The three stages are alarm, resistance and exhaustion

generalisability: how widely findings apply, e.g. to other settings and populations

generalise: to apply the findings of a study more widely, e.g. to other settings and populations

genes: units of heredity, which carry instructions coded in DNA from one generation to the next to control development and influence, for example, personality and intelligence

goal: the desired result of a person's work or effort

Good Life: is about positive traits, primarily strengths and values but also talents

Good Samaritan: this term originates from the New Testament in the Bible. It refers to a story of a Samaritan (person originating from ancient Samaria) who stops to offer help to an injured stranger. The term now refers to someone who offers help to others experiencing difficulty

grandiose delusion: a strongly held belief that you are someone with special abilities or special powers, for example the belief that you are a superhero

habituated: when a person becomes accustomed to something. When someone is frequently exposed to a certain stimulus then over time, they become used to it

hard-sell approach: the product quality is central to the marketing approach

Hawthorne effect: when those being observed change their behaviour purely as a response to their awareness of being observed

heritability: the extent to which the presence of a disorder (or a trait) is due to the genetic variance in the population, i.e. the extent to which it is inherited

heuristics: mental shortcuts that can help us when making decisions but can lead to errors in judgement

hierarchy: a way of arranging items (e.g. needs) to show that some items are above, equal to or below others in terms of importance or status

high self-monitoring: an individual who strives to be the type of person required for any social situation, so they adjust their behaviour from situation to situation

histogram: a graph used to illustrate continuous data, e.g. to show the distribution of a set of scores. It has a bar for each score value, or group of scores, along the x-axis. The y-axis has frequency of each category

hormones: chemicals that are released from glands and travel around the body in the blood to communicate between organs

housekeeping: in an organisational context this refers to managing and maintaining the processes, property and equipment of an organisation

human crowding: a person's demand for space is not met due to the high number of people in a space

hygiene factors: also known as dissatisfiers, these are extrinsic elements of the work environment, e.g. company policies, pay and conditions

hypomanic episode: a less extreme version of a manic episode, which involves several days of persistent elevated mood or increased irritability

hypothesis (plural hypotheses): a testable statement based on the aims of an investigation

ICD: International Statistical Classification of Diseases and related health problems. It is the global standard for making diagnoses and collecting data

ICD-11: the 11th edition of the International Classification of Diseases. This is the global standard for coding health information and includes both physical and mental health disorders. It was developed and is updated by the World Health Organization (WHO)

idiographic: attempts to describe the nature of the individual

illness delay: the time between when the patient decides they are ill and when they decide to seek medical care

imagery exposure therapy: therapy in which the person is asked to vividly imagine their feared object, situation or activity

immunisation-deficient: children who were found to be in need of at least one immunisation

in vitro: instances where exposure to the phobic stimulus is imagined, such as through a visualisation exercise

in vivo: instances when the individual is directly exposed to the stimulus in real life

independent measures design: an experimental design in which a different group of participants is used for each level of the IV (condition)

independent variable (IV): the factor under investigation in an experiment that is manipulated to create two or more conditions (levels) and is expected to be responsible for changes in the dependent variable

individual differences: stable and enduring ways in which people vary in terms of emotion behaviour or cognition. These can result in differences such as in personality, abilities or mental health. They may be the consequence of the environment or genetics (or both)

individualistic: a culture in which personal goals are seen as more important than group goals

individual-situational explanations: this is the debate about the relative influence or interaction of a person's unique physiology or personality (individual) and factors in the environment (situational) on thinking and behaviour.

information processing objective: the reason for looking at the advert; whether the participant is looking at the advert to decide on a purchase or to just rate advert on interest

informed consent: knowing enough about a study to decide whether you want to agree to participate

in-group: any social group to which a person identifies with as a member

inhibit: to hinder or prevent. In neuropsychology, inhibition occurs when a chemical or chemical process is reduced or stopped

input: how we take incoming information in, for example eyes (detecting light, colour and movement), ears (detecting sound), skin (detecting pressure)

intelligence quotient (IQ): a measure of general reasoning and problem solving ability

interaction effect: the effect of two or more independent variables (e.g. OT x empathy x condition) on at least one dependent variable (e.g. personal space preference) in which the combined effect of the IVs is greater or less than each variable on their own

inter-group: members of different social groups

International Classification of Disorders (ICD): published by the World Health Organization (WHO) and although similar to the DSM, it has a wider scope and covers all health-related conditions, not only mental health and psychological conditions

inter-observer reliability: the consistency between two researchers watching the same event, i.e. whether they will produce the same records

interpersonal sensitivity: a tendency to focus on feelings of personal inadequacy or inferiority, and a feeling of marked discomfort during interpersonal interactions

interpersonal: communication or relationships between people

interpersonal distance (personal space): the area of space around a person in which they prefer not to have others enter. It is like a bubble that moves with the person. This bubble may be larger or smaller depending on the social situation the person is in

inter-rater reliability: the extent to which two researchers interpreting qualitative responses in a questionnaire (or interview) will produce the same records from the same raw data

interview: a research method using verbal questions asked directly, using techniques such as face to face or telephone

intra-group: members of the same social group

intrinsic: something that comes from within; internal

IQ (Intelligence Quotient): a measure of intelligence that produces a score representing a person's mental ability. The average range of IQ is between 85 and 115

job characteristic: the feature of a particular job, task or role which can be viewed as a dimension, e.g. high or low skill variety

kleptomania: a disorder characterised by a powerful impulse to steal. This impulse is very hard to resist and the person will often steal things as a result

laboratory experiment: a research method in which there is an IV, a DV and strict controls. It looks for a causal relationship and is conducted in a setting that is not in the usual environment for the participants with regard to the behaviour they are performing

leadership capacity: the attitude and knowledge required for effective leadership

leadership efficacy: the ability of a leader to produce a desired outcome

Leeds general scale: a self-report questionnaire that measures the severity of anxiety and depressive symptoms for those who are not formally diagnosed. The scale contains six items each for anxiety and depression, each rated on a four-point scale

legitimacy: the extent to which an authority figure (or organisation) is perceived as being worthy of obedience. For example, a police officer may appear to be more legitimate if they are wearing a badge and uniform

life events: any major changes in your life (either positive or negative). The key aspect of a life event is that it requires some aspect of transition in your life

line-up: a source of evidence used by the legal system. A witness is shown a line of people or array of photographs of faces and is asked to attempt to identify the perpetrator of the crime (although they may not be present)

localisation of function: refers to the way that particular brain areas are responsible for different activities

logo: a symbol used by a company to act as a visual cue to allow faster processing and universal brand recognition across languages and cultures

longitudinal design: an experimental design where the same participants are tested on two or more occasions over a long time, e.g. before and after a six-month intervention

longitudinal study: a research method that follows a group of participants over time, weeks to decades, looking at changes in variables to explore development or changes due to experiences, such as interventions, drugs or therapies

low self-monitoring: an individual who does not amend their behaviour to fit into different social situations; instead they are guided by their own attitudes and feelings

malingering: this occurs when somebody deliberately makes themselves unwell or pretends to be unwell for an obvious incentive such as avoiding criminal prosecution, receiving compensation or gaining disability allowance

manic episode: a period of at least week where mood is extremely high

matched pairs design: an experimental design in which participants are arranged into pairs. Each pair is similar in ways that are important to the study and one member of each pair performs in a different level of the IV

McGill pain questionnaire (MPQ): is designed to assess pain, and is composed of 78 words, of which the patient chooses the words that best describe their pain. These words are assigned a value based on their severity and the patient is then given a total score from 0 (no pain) to 78 (severe pain)

mean: the measure of central tendency calculated by adding up the values of all the scores and dividing by the number of scores in the data set

Meaningful Life: is about positive institutions such as a strong family and democracy

measure of central tendency: a mathematical way to find the typical or average score from a data set, using the mode, median or mean

measure of spread: a mathematical way to describe the variation or dispersion within a data set

median split: where a group is split into two using the mid-point as the division. Using a median split turns a continuous variable into a categorical one

median: the measure of central tendency that identifies the middle score of a data set, which is in rank order (smallest to largest). If there are two numbers in the middle, they are added together and divided by two

mediating factors: any variable or process that affects the relationship between the stimulus and the response

Medical Adherence Measure (MAM): a semi-structured clinical interview designed to collect data about patients' adherence

medical dispensers: products that allow for the correct tablets to be placed in certain containers for each day of the week

medication event monitoring system (MEMS) device: a device that records the time and date of every time the cap of a medicine container was removed and replaced. TrackCap is the brand used in this study

meta-analysis: data from a range of studies into the same subject is combined and analysed to get an overall understanding of the trends

mindfulness: is a state achieved through meditation that aims to increase awareness of the present-moment experience and enable a person to look at themselves in a compassionate, non-judgemental way

mirror treatment: a treatment for PLP that works by placing the remaining arm into a box, with a mirror down the middle so that when it is viewed at a slight angle it looks to the patient as if the patient has two intact arms. Patients then take part in a range of arm movement exercises, eventually leading to some people experiencing a reduction in phantom pain

mixed episode: a period of two weeks where there is a mixture of manic and depressive states

mode: the measure of central tendency that identifies the most frequent score(s) in a data set

model: a person who inspires or encourages others to imitate positive or negative behaviours

modelling: when we watch a person (model) perform the desired behaviour, e.g. helping behaviour

monozygotic (MZ) twins: identical twins, who share 100% of their DNA with one another

motivational factors: also known as satisfiers, these are intrinsic elements of the work including recognition, possibility of personal growth and the pleasure of the work itself

multiple unit prices: a promotion where a reduced price is offered if you buy several of an item

Munchausen syndrome: a serious mental disorder where someone pretends to be unwell, deliberately makes themselves unwell, or hurts themselves in order to get attention

muscle relaxation: used in therapies to relieve tension from within the body and mind. It can be induced using medication, visualisation exercises or repetition of calming phrases

muscoskeletal: referring to the muscles, bones, ligaments and tendons in the body

naturalistic observation: a study conducted by watching the participants' behaviour in their normal environment without interference from the researchers in either the social or physical environment

nature: innate, genetic factors which influence behaviour

near-miss: an event with the potential to result in, but that does not actually cause, damage or injury

need for cognitive closure (NFCC): the extent to which the customer has a dislike of ambiguity and a desire for a firm answer to a question

needs: in psychology, these are things that are required or wanted by a person

negative correlation: a relationship between two variables in which an increase in one accompanies a decrease in the other, i.e. higher scores on one variable correspond with lower scores on the other

negative reinforcement: an increased likelihood of repeating the behaviour, due to the removal of something negative or unpleasant

negative symptom: this occurs when level of functioning or experience falls below normal levels

nervous system: the brain, spinal cord and 'body' neurons, which detect and process incoming sensory messages, make decisions, and send messages out to organs and tissues, such as glands and muscles, to coordinate the body

neurons: cells of the nervous system that are specialised for communication. They have a cell body, dendrites and an axon

neurotransmitter: a chemical messenger that enables communication between the neurons in the brain

nomothetic: attempts to establish general laws of human behaviour

non-adherence to medication: this occurs when a patient goes against a physician's instructions for drug dosage, for instance by stopping taking their medication

non-adherence: failure to follow treatments and failure to attend appointments

non-compensatory strategies: a strategy where each attribute is evaluated individually

non-directional (two-tailed) hypothesis: a statement predicting only that one variable will be related to another, for example that there will be a difference in the DV between levels of the IV in an experiment (or that there will be a relationship between the measured variables in a correlation)

non-pain imagery: a cognitive pain management strategy that involves the person thinking about a calm and relaxing situation or scene and focusing on this rather than the pain

non-participant observer: a researcher who does not become involved in the situation being studied

non-rapid eye movement (nREM) sleep: the stages of sleep (1–4) in which our eyes are still. It is also called quiescent (quiet) sleep. It is not associated with dreaming

nonsteroidal anti-inflammatory drugs (NSAIDs): a type of analgesic that reduce pain by reducing the production of the hormone-like substances that cause pain, prostaglandins

non-verbal communication: any interactions that take place other than talking, for example, body language and clothing

null hypothesis: a testable statement saying that any difference or correlation in the results is due to chance, that is, that no pattern in the results has arisen because of the variables being studied

Numeric Rating Scale (NRS): a scale from 0 to 10 where respondents give the numerical value that best represents their pain

nurture: environmental influences on behaviour

obedience: following a direct order from a person or people in authority

objectivity: the impact of an unbiased external viewpoint on, for example, how data is interpreted. Interpretation is not affected by an individual's feelings, beliefs or experiences, so should be consistent between different researchers

oestrogen: a hormone released mainly by the ovaries, so is considered to be a 'female' hormone

olfactory tubercle: a processing centre in the olfactory cortex, with many functions including processing of odour and taste

operant conditioning: learning through the consequences of our actions

open questions: a question format in questionnaires, interviews or test items that produces qualitative data. Participants give full and detailed answers in their own words, that is, no categories or choices are given

operational: the clear description of a variable such that it can be accurately manipulated, measured or quantified, and the study can be replicated. This includes the way that the IV and DV in experiments and the co-variables in correlations are described

operationalisation: the clear definition or description of a variable so that it can be accurately manipulated,

measured or quantified, and the study can be replicated. This includes the independent variable and dependent variable in experiments and the co-variables in correlations

opiate antagonists: a group of drugs that have traditionally been used to treat substance abuse. They work by blocking the reward centres in the brain that are activated by drug or alcohol use

opioids: a type of analgesic which works by attaching to opioid receptors in the brain. These cells then release signals that reduce perception of pain and increase feelings of pleasure

opportunity sample: participants are chosen because they are available, for example university students are selected because they are present at the university where the research is taking place

order effects: practice and fatigue effects are the consequences of participating in a study more than once, for example in a repeated measures design. They cause changes in performance between conditions that are not due to the IV, so can obscure the effect on the DV

organisation: a group of people who come together for a particular purpose, for example a company, department or institution

organisational commitment: the mental and emotional bond an individual employee has to an organisation

organisational psychology: the applied study of the ways in which people think, feel and behave within organisations

out-group: a group to which an individual does not belong, in contrast with an in-group which is a group the person feels they belong to

output: how we send information out, for example voice, body (such as hands for writing, drawing, moving)

overt observer: the role of the observer is obvious to the participants

oxytocin: a social hormone found in humans that heightens the importance of social cues and is linked to positive social behaviours such as helping others

PAD model: a model designed to demonstrate how physical environments influence people through emotional impact: pleasure, arousal and dominance

partially compensatory strategies: a strategy where items are considered in relation to one another in terms of important attributes

participant observer: a researcher who watches from the perspective of being part of the social setting

participant variables: individual differences between participants (such as age, personality and intelligence) that could affect their behaviour in a study that would hide or exaggerate differences between levels of the IV

pathologic: behaviour that is compulsive, it happens frequently and is very difficult to stop

patient-centred style: a consultation style where the patient is an active part of the consultation and discussion is encouraged, leading to a joint decision being made

peregrination: wandering off or travelling in a meandering way

permissive: behaviour style with a low amount of leader direction

persecutory delusion: a strongly held belief that you are in danger, that you are being conspired against and that others are pursuing you to try to do you harm

persecutory ideations: the belief that people want to hurt you, despite there being no evidence to back this up

phantom limb pain (PLP): a common problem for people who lose a limb. Even though the arm or leg is no longer there, PLP occurs when the individual still experiences pain as coming from that area. PLP is very difficult to treat

phlebotomy: the process of taking a sample of blood

phobia: the irrational, persistent fear of an object or event (stimulus) that poses little real danger but creates anxiety and avoidance in the sufferer

pictographs: a way of providing information using images only

pill counting: by asking patients to bring all medication at each medical review and counting how many pills remain at the end of a certain time period you can easily calculate what percentage of prescribed medication a patient has taken

pilot study: a small-scale test of the procedure of a study before the main study is conducted. It aims to ensure that the procedure and materials are valid and reliable, so that they can be adapted if not

placebo: a pill or procedure given to a patient who believes it to be a real treatment that in fact has no active 'ingredient', i.e. no active drug in the case of a pill or no therapeutic value in the case of an intervention

planogram: a diagram that shows how and where specific retail products should be placed on retail shelves or displays in order to increase customer purchases

play: behaviour typical of childhood, that appears to be done for fun rather than any useful purpose. It may be solitary or social and may or may not involve interaction with an object. Objects designed for the purpose of play are called 'toys'

Pleasant Life: is about positive emotions

polymorphism: a variation in a gene or genes

population: the group, sharing one or more characteristics, from which a sample is drawn

positive correlation: a relationship between two variables in which an increase in one accompanies an increase in the other, i.e. the two variables increase together

positive psychology: the scientific study of the three different happy lives: the Pleasant Life, the Good Life and the Meaningful Life

positive reinforcement: when a behaviour results in a reward, such as money or attention, that behaviour is likely to be repeated again

positive reinforcer: a reward for behaviour that fulfils a biological need is known as a primary positive reinforcer. A stimulus that is associated with primary reinforcers can also be learned and is known as a secondary reinforcer

positive symptom: an experience that is 'in addition to' or 'a distortion of' normal experience

positron emission tomography (PET) scanning: a technique that uses gamma cameras to detect radioactive tracers, such as glucose that is injected into the blood. The tracer accumulates in areas of high activity during the scan, allowing them to become visible for analysis

post-mortem studies: the examination of a person's brain after they have died, to investigate abnormalities that could explain symptoms or conditions they experienced when they were alive

practice effect: a situation where participants' performance improves because they experience the experimental task more than once, for example due to familiarity or learning the task

presumptive consent: this can be obtained when informed consent cannot be obtained from actual participants. A similar group of people to the anticipated sample are given full details of the proposed study and asked if they would find the study acceptable or not. If they would be happy to be involved, the study can continue

prevalence: how common something is across the population

primacy effect: an effect found in memory research, which shows that, when recalling a list of words, you are more likely to recall words from the start of the list than those from the middle

primary reinforcers: anything that has intrinsic value, that gives pleasure and acts as a reward

primary task: the activity we are supposed to be concentrating on, even though we may be doing something else as well, such as doodling

primed: you are 'ready' or 'prepared' to act in a certain way in a particular scenario

privacy: participants' emotions and physical space should not be invaded, for example they should not be observed in situations or places where they would not expect to be seen

proactive interference: this is the process that occurs when information is hard to recall because of previous learning that has taken place

processing: how information is dealt with, for example thinking and decision-making in the brain, brain functions such as short-term and long-term memory

product placement: when a branded product is given a prominent position within a scene in a television programme or film

product-focused sales techniques: the focus is primarily on the quality of the product

productivity: how much work is completed over a certain period of time or with a certain amount of effort

projective test: a personality test that uses ambiguous stimuli such an ink blots or Thematic Apperception Test images. The response given to the stimuli is thought to reveal hidden emotions and conflicts that the individual projects onto the image

propaganda: when information is spread in support of a cause; it is often seen in a negative light, where false claims are made, and incorrect information is spread

prospect theory: this model proposes that people consider that an item is more precious when they own it, and that gains and losses are considered differently

prostaglandins: hormone-like substances that cause pain

protection from harm: participants should not be exposed to any greater physical or psychological risk than they would expect in their day-to-day life

psychiatrist: a doctor with specialised medical training to deal with the diagnosis and treatment of disorders (most psychologists are not medical doctors)

psychological state: the experience of a set of particular thoughts and feelings

psychometric testing: a method of measuring personality traits, emotional states or other experiences by using sets of questions and numerical scales

psychometrics: the theory of or methods used to test and measure psychological phenomena, for example intelligence or personality testing

pyromania: a disorder characterised by a powerful impulse to set fires. This impulse is very hard to resist, which leads to the person persistently setting fires

qualitative data: descriptive, in-depth results indicating the *quality* of a psychological characteristic, such as responses to open questions in self-reports or case studies and detailed observations

quantitative data: numerical results about the amount or *quantity* of a psychological measure, such as pulse rate or a score on an intelligence test

quasi-experiment: quasi means 'almost', and refers to the fact that these experiments often have lots of control over the procedure, but not over how participants are allocated to conditions

questionnaire: a self-report research method that uses written questions through a 'paper and pencil' or online technique

radius: a straight line from any point on the circumference of a circle to the centre of the circle

random allocation: a way to reduce the effect of confounding variables such as individual differences. Participants are put in each level of the IV such that each person has an equal chance of being in any condition

random sampling: all members of the population (i.e. possible participants) are allocated numbers and a fixed amount of these are selected in an unbiased way, for example by taking numbers from a hat

randomisation: a way to overcome order effects in a repeated measures design. Each participant is allocated to perform in the different levels of the IV in a way that ensures they have an equal chance of participating in the different levels in any order

randomised control trial (RCT): a study where the participants are randomly assigned to either the treatment condition or a control condition

range: the difference between the biggest and smallest values in the data set plus one (a measure of spread)

rapid eye movement (REM) sleep: a stage of sleep in which our eyes move rapidly under the lids, which is associated with vivid, visual dreams

ratio: the proportionate number of one item compared to another item

recency effect: an effect found in memory research, which shows that, when recalling a list of words, you are more likely to recall words from the end of the list (the most 'recent') than those from the middle

relationship-oriented: leaders who are focused on supporting and motivating their teams using communication and positive interactions

reliability: the extent to which a procedure, task or measure is consistent, for example, that it would produce the same results with the same people on each occasion

repeated measures design: an experimental design in which each participant performs in every level of the IV

replicability: the extent to which the procedure of a study can be kept the same whenever the research is repeated. This is especially important when a study is repeated, either by the same or different researchers to verify results. It also enables researchers conducting other studies to follow exactly the same procedure to test different aspects of a problem, different participant groups, etc.

replication: keeping the procedure and materials exactly the same between studies when attempting, for example, to verify results or to enable other studies to use exactly the same techniques to answer related questions

restoration equity: to return a situation to one of balance or fairness

retaliation: an act of counter-attack or revenge

retrieval failure: when forgetting occurs due to either retroactive or proactive interference

retroactive interference: this is the process that occurs when information is hard to recall because of new information that is learned

right prefrontal cortex (RPFC): a part of the brain previously shown to be associated with negative emotions such as sadness and fear, as well as increased vigilance to threat-related cues

right to withdraw: a participant should know they can remove themselves, and their data, from a study at any time

sabotage: in the workplace this includes any employee behaviour designed to cause a production or profit loss to the organisation

sample attrition: the loss of participants from a sample over time. This may be due to many reasons, such as losing contact, the desire to discontinue, for example though boredom, being unavailable or death

sample: the group of people selected to represent the population in a study

sampling technique: the method used to obtain the participants for a study from the population

satisficing: the theory that a decision is made based on finding an option that is 'good enough' and then stopping

scapegoating: blaming a person (often inaccurately) for mistakes or wrong-doing

scatter graph: a way to display data from a correlational study. Each point on the graph represents the point where one participant's score on each scale for the co-variables cross

schemas: units of knowledge about the world. As we grow and learn, information from our senses is arranged meaningfully in our minds; it helps us to categorise new experiences and details. Our individual systems of schema underlie virtually all cognition, such as reasoning, memory and perception

secondary positive reinforcement (SPR) training: training in which a secondary reinforcer such as a sound marker is used and then followed with administration of a primary positive reinforcer (typically food)

secondary reinforcers: something that does not have any value itself, it only has value because of what it can be exchanged for

self-control: a form of cognitive-behaviour therapy. It involves using 'self-talk'; the individual is taught to recognise difficult situations, acknowledge troubling thoughts and consider alternative, positive thoughts

self-determination theory: a theory of motivation concerned with intrinsic needs and personal growth

self-report: a research method, such as a questionnaire or interview, which obtains data by asking participants to provide information about themselves

semi-structured interview: an interview format using a fixed list of open and closed questions. The interviewer can add more questions if necessary

sensory cortices: the different parts of the cortex that are responsible for processing information from each of the senses

sex-typed behaviour: actions that are typically performed by one particular sex and are seen in society as more appropriate for that sex. For example, aggression is seen as masculine-type behaviour and was more commonly imitated by boys in the study

sexually dimorphic: any differences between males and females of any species that are not just differences in organs. These differences are caused by inheriting either male or female patterns of genetic material

sharing style: this is when a doctor discusses with the patient what they think might be wrong and the doctor and patient agree on a course of action together

side effects: any consequences of taking a medication, other than the intended one. These can range from mild to severe and can affect physical, emotional or cognitive functioning

situational variable: a confounding variable caused by an aspect of the environment, for example the amount of light or noise

sleep: a state of reduced conscious awareness and reduced movement, which occurs on a daily cycle

slogan: a short memorable phrase used in advertising a product

social cues: these are facial expressions or body language which people use to send messages to one another, for example a smile to indicate happiness

social desirability bias: trying to present oneself in the best light by determining what a task requires

social facilitation: when people show increased performance or effort in the real or imagined presences of others

social learning: the learning of a new behaviour that is observed in a role model and imitated later in the absence of that model

social loafing: when people perform worse on a task in the presence of others than they would do alone

social pressure: the influence of a person or group on another person or group

Social Readjustment Rating Scale (SRRS): a scale consisting of 43 life events; the respondent must identify any of the events they have experienced during a period of time. Each life event is given a score in terms of life change units (LCUs) and a total score is used to predict likelihood of stress-related illness

social roles: these are the ways in which we behave as members of a social group. A person can have a number of different roles as they adapt their behaviour to meet expectations

social salience: the importance or attention someone gives to cues from other people, e.g. body language, interpersonal distance and expressions

social structure: a system where there are certain rules and expectations that people are expected to follow when they are part of this system

socialisation: the process of learning to behave in socially acceptable ways. This may differ somewhat for the two genders and in different cultures

sociodemographic factors: characteristics of a person, such as age, sex, education and ethnicity

soft-sell approach: the product image is central to the marketing approach

spatial crowding: a person's demand for space is not met due to the high number of physical objects in a space

specificity theory: proposes that specialised pain receptors respond to stimuli and, via nerve impulses, send signals to the brain. The brain then processes the signal as the sensation of pain, and quickly responds with a motor response to try to stop the pain

staff turnover: the number of employees who leave an organisation during a certain period of time

standard deviation: a calculation of the average difference between each score in the data set and the mean. Bigger values indicate greater variation (a measure of spread)

standardisation: keeping the procedure for each participant in a study (e.g. an experiment or interview) exactly the same to ensure that any differences between participants or conditions are due to the variables under investigation rather than differences in the way they were treated

standardised instructions: the written or verbal information given to participants at the beginning and sometimes during a study that ensures the experience of all participants, regardless of level of the IV, is as similar as possible

stigmatisation: regarding a person as worthy of disapproval

stimulus: an event or object which leads to a behavioural response

stimulus-organism-response (S-O-R model): a model that can be applied to explain consumer behaviours. Stimuli, such as physical environment, affects consumer's attitude, which further affects behaviour

stoicism: a philosophy where one of the principles is that the individual is not directly affected by external things but by their own *perception* of external things

stooge or confederate: someone who is playing a role in a piece of research and has been instructed as to how to behave by the researcher

structured interview: an interview format using questions in a fixed order that may be scripted. Consistency might also be required for the interviewer's posture, voice, etc. so they are standardised

structured observation: a study in which the observer records only a limited range of behaviours

subjective well-being: consists of a cognitive component (life satisfaction) and an affective component (the presence of positive feeling and absence of negative emotional experiences)

subjectivity: the effect of an individual's personal viewpoint on, for example, how they interpret data. Interpretation can differ between individual researchers as a viewpoint may be biased by one's feelings, beliefs or experiences, so is not independent of the situation

suggestive selling: an attempt to encourage sales by 'suggesting' something to the customer, e.g. earrings that match a necklace

synapse: the region of communication between neurons that is specialised to send and receive chemical messages

System 1 thinking: 'thinking fast', involving automatic, unconscious thinking, which is non-statistical and uses associations

System 2 thinking: 'thinking slow', involving conscious controlled thinking, which is deliberate and costly to use

task-oriented: leaders who are focused on completing the necessary steps or tasks to reach a goal using structure and planning

temporal conditions: relating to time and how working patterns are arranged

TENS treatment: a small electric current is passed through electrodes to the painful area, and this reduces pain by reducing the pain signals that go to the brain and spinal cord and by stimulating the production of endorphins

testosterone: a hormone released mainly by the testes, so is considered to be a 'male' hormone. It is an example of an androgen

test–retest: a way to measure the consistency of a test or task. The test is used twice and if the participants' two sets of scores are similar, i.e. correlate well, it has good reliability

theory of mind: a cognitive ability that enables one person to comprehend that other people have separate feelings, beliefs, knowledge and desires that can be different from their own. It enables one person to detect the emotional state of another person

token economy: a reward system used, where tokens are given for specific desirable behaviour and these tokens can then be exchanged for goods

tolerance: after a long period of time, the body's response to a particular drug may reduce, so the medication is no longer as effective

transformational: the ability to produce a significant change in a situation

triangulation: is when different techniques, e.g. observations, interviews and tests, are used to study the same phenomenon. If they produce similar results, this suggests the findings are valid

twin study: a type of study that compares sets of twins to analyse similarities and differences. This may include concordance for intelligence or mental disorders. Both monozygotic (MZ) and dizygotic (DZ) twins are studied, and their concordance rate is compared

type A personality: somebody who is prone to competitiveness, time urgency and hostility and, as a result, is more at risk of stress-related illnesses such as CHD

UAB (University of Alabama) pain behaviour scale: a scale consisting of ten target behaviours. An observer completes the scale, recording detail about each of the target behaviours over a period of time

ultradian rhythm: a cycle hat repeats more often than daily, e.g. the occurrence of periods of dreaming every 90 minutes during sleep

unanimity: the act of being in agreement with all people involved

uncontrolled variable: a variable that either acts randomly, affecting the DV in all levels of the IV, or systematically, i.e. on one level of the IV (called a confounding variable) so can obscure the effect of the IV, making the results difficult to interpret, the effects of which have not or cannot be limited or eliminated

unrealistic optimism: an error in judgement where people have a tendency to expect that bad things will happen to other people but not themselves

unstructured interview: an interview format in which most questions (after the first one) depend on the respondent's answers. A list of topics may be given to the interviewer

unstructured observation: a study in which the observer records the whole range of possible behaviours, which is usually confined to a pilot stage at the beginning of a study to refine the behavioural categories to be observed

utilisation delay: the time from the decision to seek care until they actually access services. This can include the consideration of whether the costs of care (time, effort, money) are worth it

utility theory: the theory that a decision is made rationally and that a person makes a decision based on optimising the likely outcomes of their actions

validity: the extent to which the researcher is testing what they claim to be testing

VIA (Values-in-action Institute of the Mayerson Foundation) questionnaire: a questionnaire designed to identify a person's top strengths and virtues from a list

vigilance: sustained concentration over a period of time, including watching for hazards

virtual reality (VR): a computer-generated simulation where a person uses special goggles and a screen or gloves to interact with a three-dimensional environment

Visual Analogue Scale (VAS): an instrument to measure pain by asking a patient to mark on a line where best represents their pain from no pain to extreme pain. The position of the mark is then transferred into a numerical value

volunteer (self-selected) sample: participants are invited to participate, for example through advertisements via email or notices. Those who reply become the sample

wayfinding: refers to our ability to know where we are and to plan a route to where we are going. Certain tools can help us with wayfinding, for example to find our way around a shopping mall, we may rely on maps and signs

white collar workers: are individuals who work in professional occupations, as compared to 'blue collar' workers which refers to those who perform manual work

withdrawal: the physical or mental negative effects on a person when they stop taking or reduce some medications. Symptoms can be relatively mild or can be severe

World Health Organization (WHO): an organisation within the United Nations, to direct international health advice and lead global health responses

Yale-Brown Obsessive Compulsive Scale Modified for Pathological Gambling (PG-YBOCS): a clinician-administered scale to assess gambling severity by assessing symptoms over the previous seven days, in terms of both gambling urges/thoughts and gambling behaviour

> Index

suggestive selling 264
survivors 393
Swat, K. 420
synapses 65
system 1/system 2 thinking 267–8
Szalma, J. L. 403

take-the-best heuristics 263
Tapper, K. 354, 358
target-absent rejection 115, 116
target-present identification 115, 116
Tärning, B. 267
task-oriented behaviours 384
task-oriented styles 390
Taylor, S. 226
temporal conditions 412–15
TENS treatment *see* transcutaneous electrical nerve
    stimulation (TENS) treatment
testosterone 65
test–retest procedure 54
theory of mind 104
Thomas, K. W. 406
Thomas–Kilmann Conflict Mode Instrument (TKI) 406
token economy 356
tolerance 221
transcutaneous electrical nerve stimulation (TENS)
    treatment 330
transformational leadership 384
transmission of aggression 125–32
triangulation 22
Tuckman, B. W. 395, 398, 399
Tuckman's stages of group development 395
Tversky, A. 260, 266, 267
twin studies 187
two-factor theory 422–3
type A personality 342
typical antipsychotics 190–1

UAB (University of Alabama) pain behaviour scale 336
ultradian rhythms 67
unanimity 397
uncontrolled variables 6, 73, 102
universalist theories 383
unrealistic optimism 358
unstructured interview 20
unstructured observation 25
utility theory 260

valid consent 49
validity 11, 55, 102, 137, 143, 157, 170, 179
Vangel, M. 81

van Rompay, T. J. 272
variables
    application of knowledge 35
    controlling of 34
    definition 33
    manipulation/measurement 33
    standardisation 34
verbal communications 306–7
Verheyen, G. R. 196
VIA (Values-in-action Institute of the Mayerson
    Foundation) questionnaire 361
vigilance 403
Vinayagamoorthy, V. 184
virtual reality (VR) 184
    design 185
    evaluation 186
    findings and conclusions 186
Visual Analogue Scale (VAS) 333
visual rating scales of pain 332
volunteer (self-selected) sampling 37, 154
Von Neumann, J. 260
Vrechopoulos, A. P. 240, 241
Vroom's VIE (expectancy) theory 377

Wallen, K. 75
Walton's quality of working life 426
Wang, J. X. 305–7, 344, 345
Wansink, B. 264, 266
Watson, J. B. 214, 215, 217
wayfinding 246–7
Weinstein, N. D. 358–9, 364
Wener, R. E. 345
West, R. 308
Wheelwright, S. 104
white collar workers 154
withdrawal 200
Wolpe, J. 218
Woods, A. T. 242, 244
Woods, P. J. 202
workplace environment
    design of 410
    disorders 413–14
    health and safety 415–22
    physical conditions 408–11
    shift work effects 413
    temporal conditions of 412–15
    see also organisations
work satisfaction 422
    attitudes to work 427
    characteristics of job 423
    employee sabotage in workplace 428–30